W0006068

The Abortion Act 1967

The Abortion Act 1967 may be the most contested law in UK history as it sits on a fault line between the shifting tectonic plates of a rapidly transforming society. While it has survived repeated calls for its reform, with its text barely altered for over five decades, women's experiences of accessing abortion services under it have evolved considerably. Drawing on extensive archival research and interviews, this book explores how the Abortion Act was given meaning by a diverse cast of actors including women seeking access to services, doctors and service providers, campaigners, judges, lawyers and policymakers. By adopting an innovative biographical approach to the law, this book shows that the Abortion Act is a 'living law'. Using this historically grounded sociolegal approach, this enlightening book demonstrates how the Abortion Act both shaped and was shaped by a constantly changing society.

Sally Sheldon is a professor of law at the University of Bristol and University of Technology Sydney, a Fellow of the Academy of Social Sciences, an editor of the journal *Social & Legal Studies* and Cambridge University Press's Law in Context series, and a former trustee of the Abortion Support Network and the British Pregnancy Advisory Service. She has published extensively in health-care law and ethics. She was formerly a professor in Kent Law School, where she worked on the research for this book.

Gayle Davis is a senior lecturer in the history of medicine at the University of Edinburgh. She has published widely on the history of medicine and reproductive health, including the recent co-edited volumes *Abortion across Borders: Transnational Travel and Access to Abortion Services* (2019) and *The Palgrave Handbook of Infertility in History* (2017).

Jane O'Neill is a social historian whose research interests include twentieth-century youth, gender and sexual behaviour. She has published on the history of courtship, contraception and abortion in journals such as *History* and in edited volumes including *Students in Twentieth-Century Britain and Ireland* (2017).

Clare Parker is a historian who has worked at universities in the UK and Australia. She has published on the history of medicine and the politics of abortion and sexuality. She is also a consultant archivist currently working with the State Library of South Australia.

The U.S. reversal of constitutional abortion rights renders this book both timely and authoritative. The four authors' superlative erudition and insightful arguments highlight the "biography" of UK abortion law since the 1960s, a specific, turbulent historical context. This is an instant classic, its subject unlikely to generate consensus any time soon, making it a landmark achievement by its formidably talented authors.

– Judith A. Allen, *Distinguished Professor and Walter Professor of History*
Indiana University

This ever so readable book brings conceptual clarity and fascinating historical detail to understanding the dynamic nature of an abortion law. The book will be an invaluable guide in post-decriminalisation jurisdictions, like Australia, as health laws replace criminal laws on abortion, also becoming living texts open to contest and interpretation.

– Barbara Baird, *Associate Professor in Women's & Gender Studies, Flinders University and Co-Convenor South Australian Abortion Action Coalition.*

Built on impressive historiographical and socio-legal foundations, *The Abortion Act* brings together an astounding range of materials to document and explain the resilience, evolution, and contestation of this one, decades-old statute. Written with sensitivity, rigour, and elegance, it is essential reading on abortion regulation, legal and political innovation, and the everyday politics of reproductive rights in the UK.

– Professor Fiona de Londras, *Chair of Global Legal Studies, University of Birmingham.*

This is an exemplary account of struggles to fix the meaning of Britain's most controversial law. It is eye-opening to see how, over a half-century, pitched battles and quiet reforms revolutionized the practice of abortion in ways no one foresaw in 1967 – while hardly altering the statute itself.

– Nick Hopwood, *Professor of History of Science and Medicine, University of Cambridge*

This fascinating book is essential reading for anyone who seeks to understand UK abortion law, but it is of much wider significance. It shows how legal meanings are created through the complex interplay of theory and practice. Everyone who cares about the processes of law reform should study it closely.

– Professor Sir Jonathan *Montgomery FMedSci, LLM, Hon FRPCH, Faculty of Laws, University College London.*

This important and impressive book chronicles the coming into force of what can be labelled the most contested Act of Parliament in English legal history. It dives deep into an impressive range of archives and is bolstered by an informative set of oral history interviews. This is a must read for theorists of social movements, feminists, socio-legal and critical legal scholars, as well as historians of the twenty-first century.

– Professor Linda Mulcahy FAcSS, *Chair of Socio-Legal Studies and Director of the Centre for Socio-Legal Studies, University of Oxford.*

Qualifying in medicine in 1969 in Aberdeen, and inspired by Dugald Baird's *Fifth Freedom*, I grew up with the implications of the 1967 Abortion Act. And so it was fascinating to read and understand the legal and social history, the twists and turns, of where we are now. Thoroughly researched and well presented, this book is a must for all who care about Women's Health.

– Professor Allan Templeton CBE FMedSci, *Former President of the RCOG, and Emeritus Professor of Obstetrics and Gynaecology, University of Aberdeen*

Law in Context

Series editors
Professor Kenneth Armstrong
University of Cambridge
Professor Maksymilian Del Mar
Queen Mary, University of London
Professor Sally Sheldon
University of Bristol and University of Technology Sydney

Editorial advisory board
Professor Bronwen Morgan
University of New South Wales
Emeritus Professor William Twining
University College London

Since 1970, the Law in Context series has been at the forefront of a movement to broaden the study of law. The series is a vehicle for the publication of innovative monographs and texts that treat law and legal phenomena critically in their cultural, social, political, technological, environmental and economic contexts. A contextual approach involves treating legal subjects broadly, using materials from other humanities and social sciences, and from any other discipline that helps to explain the operation in practice of the particular legal field or legal phenomena under investigation. It is intended that this orientation is at once more stimulating and more revealing than the bare exposition of legal rules. The series includes original research monographs, coursebooks and textbooks that foreground contextual approaches and methods. The series includes and welcomes books on the study of law in all its contexts, including domestic legal systems, European and international law, transnational and global legal processes, and comparative law.

Books in the Series
Acosta: *The National versus the Foreigner in South America: 200 Years of Migration and Citizenship Law*
Ali: *Modern Challenges to Islamic Law*
Alyagon Darr: *Plausible Crime Stories: The Legal History of Sexual Offences in Mandate Palestine*
Anderson, Schum & Twining: *Analysis of Evidence, 2ⁿᵈ Edition*
Ashworth: *Sentencing and Criminal Justice, 6ᵗʰ Edition*
Barton & Douglas: *Law and Parenthood*
Baxi, McCrudden & Paliwala: *Law's Ethical, Global and Theoretical Contexts: Essays in Honour of William Twining*
Beecher-Monas: *Evaluating Scientific Evidence: An Interdisciplinary Framework for Intellectual Due Process*
Bell: *French Legal Cultures*

Seppänen: *Ideological Conflict and the Rule of Law in Contemporary China: Useful Paradoxes*

Siems: *Comparative Law, 3rd Edition*

Stapleton: *Product Liability*

Stewart: *Gender, Law and Justice in a Global Market*

Tamanaha: *Law as a Means to an End: Threat to the Rule of Law*

Tuori: *Properties of Law: Modern Law and After*

Turpin & Tomkins: *British Government and the Constitution: Text and Materials, 7th Edition*

Twining: *General Jurisprudence: Understanding Law from a Global Perspective*

Twining: *Globalisation and Legal Theory*

Twining: *Human Rights, Southern Voices: Francis Deng, Abdullahi An-Na'im, Yash Ghai and Upendra Baxi*

Twining: *Jurist in Context: A Memoir*

Twining: *Karl Llewellyn and the Realist Movement, 2nd Edition*

Twining: *Rethinking Evidence: Exploratory Essays, 2nd Edition*

Twining & Miers: *How to Do Things with Rules, 5th Edition*

Wan: *Film and Constitutional Controversy*

Ward: *A Critical Introduction to European Law, 3rd Edition*

Ward: *Law, Text, Terror*

Ward: *Shakespeare and Legal Imagination*

Wells & Quick: *Lacey, Wells and Quick: Reconstructing Criminal Law: Text and Materials, 4th Edition*

Zander: *Cases and Materials on the English Legal System, 10th Edition*

Zander: *The Law-Making Process, 6th Edition*

International Journal of Law in Context: A Global Forum for Interdisciplinary Legal Studies

The *International Journal of Law in Context* is the companion journal to the Law in Context book series and provides a forum for interdisciplinary legal studies and offers intellectual space for ground-breaking critical research. It publishes contextual work about law and its relationship with other disciplines including but not limited to science, literature, humanities, philosophy, sociology, psychology, ethics, history and geography. More information about the journal and how to submit an article can be found at http://journals.cambridge.org/ijc

The Abortion Act 1967

A Biography of a UK Law

SALLY SHELDON
University of Bristol and University of Technology Sydney

GAYLE DAVIS
University of Edinburgh

JANE O'NEILL
University of Edinburgh

CLARE PARKER
University of Adelaide

Shaftesbury Road, Cambridge CB2 8EA, United Kingdom

One Liberty Plaza, 20th Floor, New York, NY 10006, USA

477 Williamstown Road, Port Melbourne, VIC 3207, Australia

314–321, 3rd Floor, Plot 3, Splendor Forum, Jasola District Centre, New Delhi – 110025, India

103 Penang Road, #05–06/07, Visioncrest Commercial, Singapore 238467

Cambridge University Press is part of Cambridge University Press & Assessment, a department of the University of Cambridge.

We share the University's mission to contribute to society through the pursuit of education, learning and research at the highest international levels of excellence.

www.cambridge.org
Information on this title: www.cambridge.org/9781108733656

DOI: 10.1017/9781108677295

© Sally Sheldon, Gayle Davis, Jane O'Neill and Clare Parker 2023

This publication is in copyright. Subject to statutory exception and to the provisions of relevant collective licensing agreements, no reproduction of any part may take place without the written permission of Cambridge University Press & Assessment.

First published 2023
First paperback edition 2023

A catalogue record for this publication is available from the British Library

ISBN   978-1-108-49638-4   Hardback
ISBN   978-1-108-73365-6   Paperback

Cambridge University Press & Assessment has no responsibility for the persistence or accuracy of URLs for external or third-party internet websites referred to in this publication and does not guarantee that any content on such websites is, or will remain, accurate or appropriate.

Contents

Acknowledgements

Our biography of the Abortion Act has been many years in the making and has benefitted greatly from the support and constructive engagement of a considerable number of people.

This book is drawn from a project funded by the Arts and Humanities Research Council (AH/N00213X/1). We are very grateful to the Arts and Humanities Research Council for their understanding as we needed to request two no-cost extensions when our work was delayed by a series of unforeseen events including three babies, bereavements, assorted health problems and, ultimately, a global pandemic. We are also grateful to our editors: Professor Kenneth Armstrong encouraged us to submit a book proposal for the Law in Context series and subsequently invited one of us to join him and Professor Maks del Mar as a series editor. Finola O'Sullivan and Marianne Nield at Cambridge University Press were constructive and supportive editors. The book has also benefitted greatly from the careful hand of our copy editor, John Marr.

We further benefitted from the collective wisdom, support and encouragement of the colleagues who sat on our Advisory Board: Dr Jennie Bristow, Ms Libby Brooks, Professor Bernard M. Dickens, Dr Lesley Hall, Professor Billie Hunter, Professor Linda Mulchay, Ms Eleanor Payne, Professor Bill Rolston, Professor Simon Szreter and Professor Allan Templeton. We also enjoyed excellent support from professional services colleagues and occasional research assistance offered by postgraduate students and postdoctoral researchers at both Kent and Edinburgh: Aastha Aggarwal, Jessica Campbell, Stephen Crawford, Zahra Jaffer, Ellie Mathioudaki, Toluwani Mokuolu, Alison Nuttall and Philemon Omede. We are further indebted to the archivists and librarians who shared their expertise, supported our research and offered access to wonderfully rich resources (a full list of archives visited is included in the Bibliography).

We are also particularly grateful to those who gave generously of their time to share their memories of and insights into the operation of the Abortion Act (a full list of interviewees is provided in Appendix 3). They helped shape and improve our understanding of events in a way that went far beyond the necessarily limited direct quotations from our conversations with them in the pages to follow. With their kind permission, transcripts and recordings of these interviews are to be lodged in the Wellcome Archive, where we hope that they will offer a valuable record for future researchers.

We also gratefully acknowledge the support, insight and robust feedback of the many academic colleagues in law, history and other disciplines who have helped shape this work through feedback on the proposal for the research project that gave rise to this book, through critical comments on conference and seminar papers and draft journal articles drawing on the research and through discussions of emerging ideas in less formal settings. It is impossible to name all of those who have helped us over the past five years, but we count ourselves fortunate to be part of such supportive and insightful academic communities.

Last but not least, we are grateful to the friends, partners and families who have sustained and supported us as we completed this project.

Needless to say, any errors remain our own.

Significant parts of Chapter 6 have been published as S. Sheldon, J. O'Neill, C. Parker and G. Davis, '"Too Much, Too Indigestible, Too Fast"? The Decades of Struggle for Abortion Law Reform in Northern Ireland', *Modern Law Review*, 83:4 (2020), 761–796.

Table of Cases

Table of Legislation

UK Legislation

Irish Legislation

Statutory Instruments

1

Introduction

I have had numerous women, young ladies, say to me, words along the line of thank you for what you did. I haven't had an abortion, I hope I need never need one, but I know that it is there should I need it. And this has given me the courage, the drive, to go on and have a career to do what I wanted to do, in the knowledge that it wouldn't all be brought to a stop by an unplanned pregnancy.[1]

The 50 years of the Act has really, in our view, corrupted morals. It's corrupted the medical profession. It's destroyed nine million lives of the actual babies who have lost their lives. But then there is a huge number of women out there who are suffering through abortion.[2]

In 2017, two laws that had profoundly shaped the UK each reached their fiftieth anniversaries. The Sexual Offences Act 1967 had partially decriminalised same-sex male sexual acts in England and Wales. It was widely celebrated as an important milestone towards sweeping away the discriminatory attitudes of the past. Amongst the many major events organised to mark its passage were a BBC season of programming, 'Gay Britannia',[3] the Tate's exhibition on Queer British Art[4] and the British Museum's exhibition 'Desire, Love, Identity'.[5] The traditionally conservative broadsheet newspaper, *The Telegraph*, issued a guide to the best LGBTQ events.[6]

In partially decriminalising abortion in Britain, the Abortion Act 1967 has had an impact on modern UK history that was equally profound. Part of the

---

[1] Diane Munday (formerly Abortion Law Reform Association and Birmingham (later British) Pregnancy Advisory Service) interviewed by Jane O'Neill, 10 November 2017.

[2] John Deighan (Society for the Protection of Unborn Children) interviewed by Jane O'Neill, 29 January 2018.

[3] BBC, 'Gay Britannia'.

[4] Tate Britain, 'Queer British Art 1861–1967'.

[5] British Museum, 'Desire, Love, Identity: Exploring LGBTQ Histories'.

[6] 'Sexual Offences Act Turns 50: The Best LGBTQ Culture Events on in Britain this July', *Telegraph*, 30 June 2017. Other events were held at The National Archives and the National and the Old Vic theatres: The National Archives, '1967 Sexual Offences Act: 50 Years On'; Liverpool's Walker Gallery: Liverpool Museums, 'Coming Out'.

same permissive wave of reforms introduced under Harold Wilson's Labour Government, the Act has been described as 'one of the finest, most humane and far-sighted pieces of legislation in the twentieth century',[7] and a 'landmark of social legislation' that ended 'the sordid injustice of well-to-do women paying for abortions on demand in private clinics and less fortunate souls risking life and limb in the hands of back-street abortionists'.[8] However, its anniversary was marked by little celebration beyond a few conferences and exhibitions organised by campaigners. A small number of BBC programmes were broadcast, placing a heavy focus on ethical debate.[9] All in all, the tone was muted and equivocal, suggesting 'an occasion for sombre reflection, not celebration'.[10] Indeed, some went further. In a speech outside the House of Commons to mark the anniversary, the Abortion Act's greatest parliamentary critic, Lord Alton, suggested that, with over eight million pregnancies by then ended under it, '[a]bortion has caused more human destruction in the UK than Nazi Germany ... only the Black Death has extinguished a greater proportion of our nation'.[11] While the UK public has moved to accept liberal abortion laws and Lord Alton's view is today firmly in the minority,[12] it is difficult to think of another law that has remained on the statute books despite being the subject of such fierce and sustained contestation over so long a period. Another Liberal, David Steel, piloted the Abortion Act through Parliament. He reports still receiving 'fan letters and hate letters, every week. Fifty years on.'[13]

In this book, we offer a biography of this fiercely contested law. The events that led to its conception have already been well documented and, as such, our account of them will be brief.[14] Our story rather begins in earnest in April 1968, when the Abortion Act came into force. The battles that had preceded its introduction would be nothing to those that followed thereafter: these would involve some of the largest mass protests and most intense and prolonged political lobbying ever seen in the UK and repeated attempts at further reform in Parliament. Further, long after it passed onto the statute books, the Act

---

[7] 'Let the Act Act', *Medical News Tribune*, 13 February 1970.

[8] Boothroyd, *Betty Boothroyd: The Autobiography*, 196.

[9] E.g. *Abortion on Trial*, which asked 'if the law is fit for purpose in 2017', and a special episode of *The Moral Maze*. BBC2, 'Abortion on Trial'; BBC Radio 4, 'The Moral Maze: 50 Years of the Abortion Act'.

[10] '50 Years After the Abortion Act, Why Can't We Still Have a Proper Debate on the Issue?', *Spectator*, 21 October 2017.

[11] Alton, 'Truth Should Speak to Power'.

[12] See National Centre for Social Research, *British Social Attitudes*, no. 34, and discussion in Chapter 4, pp. 113–14.

[13] David Steel interviewed by Jane O'Neill, 5 February 2018.

[14] The most detailed account is that of Hindell and Simms, *Abortion Law Reformed*. See also Keown, *Abortion, Doctors and the Law*; Sheldon, *Beyond Control*; Farmer, *By Their Fruits*.

would continue to acquire legal meaning through a complex process of ongoing struggle and negotiation between women, doctors, service providers, officials and campaigners, conducted under the harsh spotlight of media attention; occasionally these disputes would reach the ultimate arbiters of legal meaning: the law courts. And all of this would take place against the backdrop of a rapidly evolving Britain, with the Act itself playing an important role in driving changes and the stories told about it changing apace. A study of the Abortion Act is necessarily also a study of changing gender and familial norms and the growth of a visible disability rights movement. It is a study of the declining authority of the church in framing moral debates and a corresponding rise in belief in science as a way of ordering our world. It is a study of changes within that science – including new treatment methods and diagnostic and *in utero* visualisation technologies – and shifting medical relationships and clinical practices within evolving institutional settings. Finally, it is a study of changing political ideologies, including ideas of nationhood, and the disputed constitutional settlement between England, Wales, Scotland and Northern Ireland.

In short, a biography of the Abortion Act is also the story of the modern UK.

The Run Up to Reform

It is sometimes assumed that the Abortion Act was the result of feminist campaigns. This is not true. In later years, the demand for safe, legal abortion would indeed become a key plank in the demands of the second-wave feminist movement. In the 1960s, however, the case for reform was primarily rooted in concerns with public health and social justice and, to a lesser extent, eugenics.[15] Attempts to reform abortion law had begun in earnest in the 1930s with the formation of the Abortion Law Reform Association (ALRA), but these were interrupted by World War Two.[16] It thus took until the early 1950s before reform was first discussed in Westminster and until the mid-1960s before the 'first grand debate on abortion'.[17] By this time, ALRA had been reinvigorated by a younger generation of activists, including three – Madeleine Simms, Diane Munday and Dilys Cossey – who would go on to work indefatigably on the issue for decades to come. Simms would also co-author *Abortion*

---

[15] See generally Hindell and Simms, *Abortion Law Reformed*; Brookes, *Abortion in England 1900–1967*. For an impressively detailed exploration of the links between the abortion law reform and eugenics movements, albeit systematically overplaying the significance of this factor at the expense of others, see Farmer, *By Their Fruits*.

[16] Hindell and Simms, *Abortion Law Reformed*, chapter 2.

[17] Ibid., 136.

Law Reformed, which remains the definitive account of the passage of the Abortion Act.[18]

This new generation of campaigners worked hard to build public support for reform. Munday recalls going to Downing Street to lobby Harold Wilson, then newly appointed as Prime Minister. He told them, 'this is a petty, middle-class Hampstead-type reform. Go away and tell me that it's something people want and we might look at it.'[19] They set to. Simms became '*the* champion letter writer':

> She would write to the *Guardian*. The *Guardian* published the letter. And then, Madeleine wanted the correspondence to continue. She would then write another letter, pretending it was from a retired Major in a county town, right-wing person, and put the opposite point of view. And then that gave her the ability to write in a second time, keeping up the argument![20]

Munday was likewise 'a writer of memos and looker at facts, not a marcher and flag-waver'.[21] She took on the bulk of public speaking, addressing hundreds of meetings at a time when even the word 'abortion' remained taboo,[22] and always dressing for her audience, sporting what her husband called her 'speaking hat'.[23] The meetings were a revelation, with her willingness to talk about her own abortion opening 'floodgates'. At her first meeting, at Hatfield Townswomen's Guild,

> one after another of them, thirty of them at least, of the fifty or so that were there, came up to me in the interval and said something like, 'you know dear, I had an abortion, it was back in the 30s, my husband had lost his job and we already had five children. We couldn't afford any more'. That was the common picture . . . Everybody you spoke to, if they hadn't had one themselves, or a daughter, they knew somebody who had. And many of them said, I looked after a friend, or my sister or somebody, when it went wrong.[24]

While a later cartoon would picture a young Liberal MP, David Steel, riding in on a white charger to deliver abortion law reform,[25] the ground was thus laid for him. Indeed, when Steel entered Parliament, in a by-election in 1965,

---

[18] Ibid.
[19] Munday interviewed by O'Neill.
[20] Caroline Woodroffe interviewed by Jane O'Neill, 26 October 2017.
[21] Munday interviewed by O'Neill.
[22] Ibid.
[23] Ibid.
[24] Ibid.
[25] BPAS Archives, cartoon of David Steel in Birth Control Trust, *Abortion: Ten Years On*, May 1978, 3.

Knight of Steel

he knew little about abortion but nonetheless 'ticked the box' on an ALRA leaflet sent to all parliamentary candidates.[26] When he won third place in the Private Members' ballot, guaranteeing him the necessary parliamentary time to introduce a Bill of his own choosing, Steel deemed the opportunity too precious to waste on 'a minor cause or tilting at gigantic windmills', determining to 'take up one of the great social reforms'. Capital punishment and divorce law reform had been addressed already, and opinion in his constituency was against reform of the law criminalising sex between men. Thus, by 'a process of elimination', he decided to tackle abortion.[27] Two works had also exerted a powerful influence on his thinking. *Abortion: An Ethical Discussion*, produced by the Church of England, had admitted the moral permissibility of abortion in some limited circumstances;[28] and Alice Jenkins' *Law for the Rich* had described the 'plight of desperate women who are faced with the prospect of an unwanted birth', while 'safe surgical termination remained the prerogative of the rich'.[29] With his Bill, Steel thus aimed to 'stamp out from this country the scourge of criminal abortion', with all the public health benefits that would entail.[30]

While Steel was young and inexperienced, he quickly established himself as an astute politician, later going on to lead the Liberal Party for many years. He also had other attributes that made him an ideal sponsor for an abortion bill: he was a good-looking, Christian son of the Manse, who – in the midst of the campaign – became a father for the first time.[31] Steel was also blessed with good luck: his Bill fell within an unusually long parliamentary session, and key members of the Wilson Government were sympathetic.[32] Further, public and parliamentary opinion were ready for reform. A previous Bill introduced by Lord Silkin had succeeded in the House of Lords, demonstrating the existence of cross-party support for reform. A recent German measles epidemic and the thalidomide scandal had each led to well-publicised cases of children born with serious levels of impairment and were still fresh in people's minds.[33] At a time before a recognisable disability rights movement, the birth of a disabled child was widely seen as a tragedy for all concerned, with abortion offering a 'respectable' solution to a public health problem.[34] Opinion was also shaped

---

[26] Steel interviewed by O'Neill.
[27] Steel, *Against Goliath*, 60.
[28] Church of England Board for Social Responsibility, *Abortion: An Ethical Discussion*.
[29] Jenkins, *Law for the Rich*, 21, 29. See Steel, *Against Goliath*, 60–61, for the influence on his thinking.
[30] *Hansard*, House of Commons (HC), 7 February 1975, vol. 885, cols 1764–67.
[31] Hindell and Simms, *Abortion Law Reformed*, 156–57.
[32] Steel interviewed by O'Neill; Steel, *Against Goliath*; Hindell and Simms, *Abortion Law Reformed*.
[33] Following reports of British thalidomide cases, a national opinion poll revealed that almost 80% of people were in favour of abortion where a child might be born 'seriously deformed': Hindell and Simms, *Abortion Law Reformed*, 87.
[34] Reagan, *Dangerous Pregnancies*, 104; Simms, 'Britain', 34.

by a growing concern with the 'population question', with fears that overpopulation might '[engulf] mankind in the foreseeable future'.[35] Fertility control was seen as an essential means to address poverty, giving people the possibility 'of restricting the size of their families in proportion to their personal resources'.[36]

At the time that Steel was considering his options, abortion was subject to onerous criminal prohibitions in the common law in Scotland[37] and the Offences Against the Person Act 1861 in the rest of the UK. The 1861 Act provides a maximum sentence of life imprisonment for any pregnant woman or third party who, with the intention of procuring a miscarriage, 'shall unlawfully administer ... any poison or other noxious thing, or shall unlawfully use any instrument or other means whatsoever with the like intent'. A lesser penalty (up to five years imprisonment) applies to the unlawful supply or procurement of the means to commit such an offence.[38] No distinction is drawn between abortion earlier and later in pregnancy, nor between a woman who ends her own pregnancy and a third-party abortionist. Nor was any explicit statutory exception provided for cases where abortion was necessary to save a woman's life or health, with a fragile and ambiguous sphere of legality for doctors who chose to end a pregnancy in such a case carved out by the common law.[39] While this exception permitted wealthier women to have 'Harley Street legal' abortions in conditions of safety, those who could not afford the fees were left to seek out the services of local backstreet abortionists, who might attempt to dislodge a pregnancy using a rubber tube, sharp implement or injection of soapy water. It was generally these medically unqualified abortionists, sought out by poorer women, who were prosecuted for illegal abortion.[40]

It is impossible to know how many illegal abortions took place before the passage of the 1967 Act, with estimates ranging from 10,000 to 250,000 per year.[41] Likewise, we cannot know how many women died or were permanently injured as a result of procedures that went wrong: official sources record 35–40 deaths each year; others have suggested far higher numbers, with death

---

[35] Brudenell, 'Foreword', ix–xi. See generally Ehrlich, *The Population Bomb*.

[36] Jenkins, *Law for the Rich*, 82; Hindell and Simms, *Abortion Law Reformed*, 225.

[37] See generally Davis and Davidson, '"The Fifth Freedom" or "Hideous Atheistic Expediency"'.

[38] Offences Against the Person Act 1861, sections 58 and 59.

[39] Under *R v Bourne* [1938] 3 All ER 615, 'procurement of miscarriage' was deemed lawful where a doctor ended a pregnancy in good faith to preserve a woman's life, including where necessary to prevent her from becoming a 'mental or physical wreck'. See Bourne, *A Doctor's Creed*, chapter 5. In Scotland, a doctor who acted in good faith would be seen as lacking the relevant criminal intention that might render them liable to prosecution: see Gordon, *The Criminal Law of Scotland*; Davis and Davidson, '"The Fifth Freedom" or "Hideous Atheistic Expediency"'.

[40] See generally Potts et al., *Abortion*, chapter 7; Dickens, *Abortion and the Law*; Ferris, *The Nameless*, chapter 3; Hindell and Simms, *Abortion Law Reformed*, 14.

[41] Dickens, *Abortion and the Law*, 73; *Report of the Committee on the Working of the Abortion Act (Lane Report)*, vol. 1, 506. See Potts et al., *Abortion*, 83–87 and Farmer, *By Their Fruits*, chapter 2, for contrasting considerations of the evidence.

certificates written in such a way as to preserve the good name of the family.[42] However, dealing with the consequences of illegal abortion are vivid memories for those who worked on gynaecology wards before the introduction of the Abortion Act.[43] For this study, we interviewed a retired doctor, David Baird, who remembers that the hospital where he worked in the early 1960s had a ward reserved for the treatment of septic abortion. Having spent time overseas, he returned after 1967 to find it repurposed for infertility treatment services.[44]

These factors contributed to a broad consensus in favour of the need for clarification of abortion law and, perhaps, some limited further liberalisation. Beyond that, however, the consensus fell away. First, medical opinion was deeply divided as to the shape that any reform should take.[45] Second, while the Church of England admitted the acceptability of abortion in some limited circumstances, the Catholic Church was implacably opposed.[46] These twin influences – medicine and religion – would remain key forces in disputes regarding the Abortion Act throughout the years to follow, themselves being subject to change in ways that would have a profound influence on the Act's development.

The Medical Termination of Pregnancy Bill 1966

Steel's Medical Termination of Pregnancy Bill was drafted by 'Britain's foremost scholar of criminal law', Professor Glanville Williams.[47] The president of ALRA and a vice president of the Voluntary Euthanasia Society, Williams was a deeply utilitarian thinker, humanitarian and 'radical outsider'.[48] While Williams believed in abortion on request, the consensus within ALRA was that that would be attempting to go 'a bit too far'.[49] The Bill that he drafted for Steel thus provided that abortion would be lawful only under conditions of strict medical control: where it was performed by a doctor on NHS or other approved premises and where two doctors believed in good faith that abortion was necessary to avoid serious risk to life or of grave injury to a woman's health; that there was substantial risk of physical or mental impairment in a

---

[42] Ferris, *The Nameless*, 73–75; Dickens, *Abortion and the Law*, 113, puts the number of deaths from criminal abortions in excess of 200 per year; Glanville Williams, *The Sanctity of Life and the Criminal Law*, 194, hints at a still higher figure.

[43] For a moving set of interviews with women and doctors, see *Kind to Women*, 2018.

[44] David Baird interviewed by Gayle Davis, 13 November 2017. See also David Steel on the health impacts of the Abortion Act, *Hansard*, HC, 7 February 1975, vol. 885, cols 1764–67.

[45] See Keown, *Abortion, Doctors and the Law*; McGuinness and Thomson, 'Medicine and Abortion Law'; Amery, 'Social Questions, Medical Answers'.

[46] Pope Paul VI, *Humanae Vitae*, 1968.

[47] 'Glanville Williams, 86, Teacher and Authority on Criminal Law', *New York Times*, 21 April 1997.

[48] 'Obituary: Professor Glanville Williams', *Independent*, 17 April 1997.

[49] Dilys Cossey interviewed by Jane O'Neill, 4 October 2017.

child; that a woman's 'capacity as a mother would be severely overstrained by the care of a child'; or that she was a 'defective' or had become pregnant under the age of 16 or as a result of rape.[50] The reform was intended to move abortion 'into the hands of the medical profession', where it would be openly performed in safe and hygienic conditions, eliminating the scourge of unsafe backstreet provision and offering relief in limited, deserving cases.[51]

Introducing the Bill, Steel emphasised that he was not legislating for abortion on request. Rather, he aimed to stamp out backstreet abortion, eliminate the uncertainty and unfairness of existing law, and provide relief for women struggling with the demands of repeated motherhood.[52] How to draw a satisfactory line between those cases deemed deserving of relief and those that were not would prove the thorniest problem facing him and a particular bone of contention in the debates to follow. His Bill offered the House of Commons its first opportunity for a full-length debate of abortion, and it would be subject to amendment as it progressed through its various legislative stages: Diane Munday remembers that '[e]ach time it went in, it came out a different Bill'.[53]

The major grounds for opposition to the Bill were neatly encapsulated in the first speech made against it. In what would become a pervasive feature of speeches opposing permissive abortion laws over the years to follow, the accomplished barrister William Wells MP (Lab) began by dismissing the relevance of his Catholic faith. He emphasised that those who opposed the Bill were 'not only upholding the common tradition of Christianity, but [were] protecting principles which stand at the very root of an ordered society'.[54] While accepting the need to address the issue of backstreet abortions, Wells made three key points that would be repeated time and again in the months and years to follow.

First, Wells argued that the Bill threatened the independence of the medical profession, placing any doctor who opposed abortion in an invidious position. Still worse was the position of nurses, with the risk that Catholic girls from Ireland would in future be told, 'Do not go and nurse in England because you will have to do things which are against your conscience.'[55] These comments foreshadowed a range of other concerns regarding the role of doctors expressed in the debates to follow. Most importantly, while the Steel Bill provided that abortion would need to be certified by two 'registered medical practitioners', it imposed no further requirement regarding their specialty,

---

[50] Medical Termination of Pregnancy Bill 1966; see Hindell and Simms, *Abortion Law Reformed*, appendix 1.

[51] *Hansard*, HC, 13 July 1967, vol. 750, col. 1348.

[52] *Hansard*, HC, 22 July 1966, vol. 732, col. 1075.

[53] Munday interviewed by O'Neill.

[54] *Hansard*, HC, 22 July 1966, vol. 732, col. 1081. See also St John-Stevas in HC, 22 July 1966, vol. 732, col. 1153.

[55] *Hansard*, HC, 22 July 1966, vol. 732, col. 1084.

length of service or NHS affiliation. The desirability of imposing such restrictions as a safeguard against abuse was narrowly rejected in each House but would remain a lively point of dispute in the years to come.[56]

Second, implicitly acknowledging the acceptability of abortion for reason of fetal anomaly, Wells worried that the Bill would result in the 'destruction of potentially healthy babies'.[57] Most of those who spoke against the inclusion of a fetal anomaly ground likewise opposed it on the basis that, given the inaccuracy of then-available screening and testing techniques, there was a risk of 'the slaughter of thousands of potentially healthy children to avoid the birth of a few deformed ones'.[58] Giving his maiden speech, Edward Lyons MP (Lab) was almost certainly the first MP to share a personal experience of abortion within Parliament, and indeed he would remain the only one to do so for another 50 years. His willingness to speak on this subject reflects widespread acceptance of the permissibility of abortion for fetal anomaly.[59] Having decided on termination following his wife's exposure to rubella, Lyons reported that they had then encountered 'diverse, contradictory and evasive reasons for refusal', before finally finding a doctor prepared to operate. He attacked a law 'that seeks to force the production of blind and twisted babies and drives members of a high and proud profession in fear to shifts and evasions'.[60]

Finally, Wells argued that the Bill undermined respect for the sanctity of human life.[61] While a principled moral concern with the sanctity of life has remained a major driver of opposition to abortion (as we will see), this reason would be only rarely explicitly stated within Parliament in later years.[62] For now, it was contested by one of Steel's key medical supporters in Parliament, Dr John Dunwoody MP (Lab), who replied that there is 'more to life than merely survival', and that 'far from undermining respect for the sanctity of human life this Bill could enhance respect for human life in the fullest sense of the phrase'.[63]

All of these points were closely contested. However, in a period when 'family planning' remained controversial,[64] the most fiercely disputed aspect

---

[56] See generally Hindell and Simms, *Abortion Law Reformed*.

[57] *Hansard*, HC, 22 July 1966, vol. 732, col. 1084.

[58] St John-Stevas in *Hansard*, HC, 29 June 1967, vol. 749, col. 1050.

[59] It was 2018 before another MP broke this silence; see Chapter 7, p. 251.

[60] Lyons in *Hansard*, HC, 22 July 1966, vol. 732, col. 1090.

[61] *Hansard*, HC, 22 July 1966, vol. 732, col. 1080.

[62] See generally Chapters 3 and 7.

[63] *Hansard*, HC, 22 July 1966, vol. 732, cols 1096–97.

[64] It was only with The National Health Service (Family Planning) Act 1967 that local health authorities in England and Wales were empowered to give birth control advice regardless of marital status and on social as well as medical grounds. Given the discretionary nature of the legislation, wide disparities remained between local authorities. The Health Services and Public Health Act 1968 made the same provisions for Scotland, with provision in Northern Ireland not following until 1972. See Cook, *The Long Sexual Revolution*, especially chapter 14; Davidson and Davis, *The Sexual State*, chapter 6; McCormick, 'The Scarlet Woman in Person'.

of the Steel Bill was inevitably that it permitted abortion for non-medical reasons. Then newly elected, Jill Knight MP (Con) would become a leading opponent of the Abortion Act and a powerful parliamentary advocate for 'family values', being best remembered today as the architect of the notorious 'Clause 28' prohibiting promotion of 'the teaching of the acceptability of homosexuality as a pretended family relationship'.[65] Knight was keen to emphasise that she was not a Catholic and, moreover, that she supported abortion in some circumstances.[66] Indeed, she would probably have abstained in any vote on abortion law had she not been persuaded to take an interest by the consultant gynaecologist and psychiatrist at her local hospital.[67] Thus persuaded, however, she would become and remain active on the issue for another five decades.[68] In an intervention for which she would later be 'pulled up' by the Speaker of the House of Commons for being 'too emotional',[69] Knight argued that the Bill was 'so wide and so loose that any woman who felt that her coming baby would be an inconvenience would be able to get rid of it':

> There is something very wrong indeed about this. Babies are not like bad teeth to be jerked out just because they cause suffering. An unborn baby is a baby nevertheless. Would the sponsors of the Bill think it right to kill a baby they can see? Of course they would not. Why then do they think it right to kill one they cannot see?[70]

Concerns with abortions on what would come to be called 'the social ground' were raised repeatedly. Some of those who opposed reform worried, like Knight, that it would permit selfish, irresponsible and promiscuous women to end pregnancies for reasons of mere convenience.[71] Its supporters emphasised, rather, the need to help women in serious and extreme circumstances, such as the 'distracted multi-child mother, often the wife of a drunken husband'.[72] Moreover, they noted the potential consequences not just for the women themselves but also for the family unit and for society of refusing them relief.[73] Renée Short, Barbara Castle and Jo Richardson were 'three galvanic redheads' whose 'fiery brand of well-informed socialism' enlivened the Labour

---

[65] Local Government Act 1988, Section 28. See generally Baroness Knight of Collingtree interviewed by Mike Greenwood, 9 May 2012.

[66] *Hansard*, HC, 22 July 1966, vol. 732, col. 1100.

[67] Knight represented Birmingham Edgbaston, making it likely that the two doctors involved were the gynaecologist Hugh McLaren and the psychiatrist Myre Sim, each of whom practised in Birmingham and figure in Chapter 2. Knight interviewed by Greenwood.

[68] Knight remained an MP until 1997, when she was appointed to the House of Lords, retiring only in 2016.

[69] Knight interviewed by Greenwood.

[70] *Hansard*, HC, 22 July 1966, vol. 732, cols 1100, 1107.

[71] Sheldon, 'Who is the Mother to Make the Judgment?'.

[72] Lyons in *Hansard*, HC, 22 July 1966, vol. 732, col. 1089. See generally Sheldon, 'Who is the Mother to Make the Judgment?'.

[73] See generally Sheldon, 'Who is the Mother to Make the Judgment?', 3–22.

Party in the 1970s[74] and represented a central pillar in defence of the Abortion Act.[75] Short painted a vivid picture of 'unfortunate unwanted children born into inadequate homes, disabled children [and] mentally defective children' who 'pass through multiple foster homes' before emerging 'more difficult and more disturbed . . . delinquent adolescents' who would become 'the parents of more unwanted delinquent adolescent children in the next generation, generating another cycle of cruelty and neglect'.[76]

Campaigning around the Bill was intense, requiring 'superb organisation'. Diane Munday recalls making use of a small flat in Petit France, almost opposite to the House of Commons, with MPs stocking it with 'mattresses, sleeping bags, the lot':

> We had a rota of supporting MPs sleeping in there. And people on schedules. Peter Jackson was our whip, he was an MP, telling them the next shift could . . . five of them could go out because there were five on their way over. So we always got people who were wide enough awake to speak. I was speech writing . . . It wasn't the done thing to behave like that but I knew then that we wouldn't have got the Act without it – we fought for every clause which would have got whittled away, whittled away.[77]

Over the years to come, attempts to reform and defend the Abortion Act would offer a textbook case in parliamentary strategizing and procedural creativity.[78] For now, the reformers' efforts paid off. At the end of the second reading debate, MPs voted for the Bill to go forward by a majority of almost eight to one, with Enoch Powell MP (Con) querying the small number passing through the 'no' lobby by asking, 'Where are the Romans?'[79] This sizeable majority had two major consequences. First, the Bill's opponents 'were jerked out of their lethargy'.[80] While David Steel moved into 'endless meetings with all manner of bodies for and against the bill', his opponents also organised.[81] The Society for the Protection of Unborn Children (SPUC) was established in January 1967. It emphasised that it was 'non-Catholic', initially going so far as to bar Catholics from sitting on its Committee, and that its membership included 'humanists, agnostics, and some Christians and Church of England people' united by their strong opposition to 'taking human life'.[82] There were

---

[74] 'Renee Short: Fiery Labour MP for Wolverhampton', *Independent*, 20 January 2003.

[75] Albeit with Castle's role remaining behind the scenes; see Chapter 2.

[76] Short in *Hansard*, HC, 22 July 1966, vol. 732, col 1162. See generally Farmer, *By Their Fruits*, on the eugenic aspects of the case for reform.

[77] Munday interviewed by O'Neill.

[78] See Chapters 3 and 7, especially p. 107.

[79] Quoted in St John-Stevas, *The Two Cities*, 30.

[80] Hindell and Simms, *Abortion Law Reformed*, 165.

[81] Steel, *Against Goliath*, 64.

[82] SPUC founder, Elspeth Rhys Williams, quoted in *Guardian*, 14 February 1967. See further Marsh and Chambers, *Abortion Politics*, 57; Lovenduski, 'Parliament, Pressure Groups, Networks and the Women's Movement', 58.

also seven senior gynaecologists on the Committee, including Aleck Bourne, who had played an important earlier role in clarifying abortion law, and Hugh McLaren and Ian Donald, who would play an active and influential role in debates for years to come.[83] SPUC did not oppose the Bill outright. Rather, it aimed to amend it so as not to 'open the floodgates to abortion on demand', to amplify the voices of doctors who opposed a liberal law, and to educate the public about the 'unpalatable realities' of abortion.[84]

A second important consequence of the large numbers who voted in favour of the Steel Bill at its second reading was to give Steel a large majority of supporters on the House of Commons Committee that would now scrutinise it clause by clause.[85] Steel – a careful and strategic politician – responded by filling his 22 seats on the Committee with constituency neighbours, as many doctors as possible and two 'senior women', Renée Short (Lab) and Joan Vickers (Con).[86] While opponents of the Bill on the Committee were consequently few in number, they included four MPs who would take particularly prominent roles in later debates: Norman St John-Stevas, Jill Knight and Bernard Braine (all Con) and Leo Abse (Lab). This meant that just three seats on the Committee were occupied by women, reflecting the small number (26) of female MPs at that time. With abortion not yet generally accepted as an issue of special concern to women or one on which they had particular authority to speak, this was not raised as a matter of concern. This would change.[87]

Norman St John-Stevas would emerge as the most articulate opponent of the Steel Bill and, later, a powerful critic of the Abortion Act, attacking it both within Parliament and in a regular column in the *Catholic Herald*.[88] A colourful politician with 'outstanding intellectual gifts'[89] and 'the flamboyant mannerisms of an Edwardian aesthete',[90] St John-Stevas had two important loyalties: Catholicism and Conservativism.[91] Working with SPUC, he enlisted the help of Catholic societies to collect an impressive 530,000 signatures opposing the Bill, with the resulting petition needing to be delivered by shopping trolley.[92] While Steel's solid majority on the Committee ensured that the Bill emerged just as he had intended it, St John-Stevas did persuade him to accept the addition of a conscience clause, allowing those who objected to

[83]   *Guardian*, 14 February 1967. On Bourne's earlier role, see footnote 39.
[84]   *Guardian*, 14 February 1967.
[85]   Committee membership reflects the division at the second reading, resulting in 22 people who had supported the Bill (selected by Steel), three who had opposed it and five who had abstained. See Hindell and Simms, *Abortion Law Reformed*, 180–81.
[86]   Steel, *Against Goliath*, 63.
[87]   See Chapter 3.
[88]   Steel, *Against Goliath*, 64.
[89]   'Lord St John of Fawsley – Obituary', *Guardian*, 5 March 2012.
[90]   'Lord St John of Fawsley', *Telegraph*, 5 March 2012.
[91]   St John-Stevas, *The Two Cities*, 13, 22.
[92]   Hindell and Simms, *Abortion Law Reformed*, 96–97.

abortion to opt out of participation in treatment.[93] 'Somewhat to the irritation' of ALRA, Steel also accepted one other significant amendment at this stage on the advice of the eminent doctor and Regius Professor of Midwifery at the University of Aberdeen, Sir Dugald Baird.[94] Baird had witnessed first-hand 'the tyranny of excessive fertility', with high maternal mortality resulting from repeated childbearing, lack of advice on family planning and lack of access to safe abortion during the Depression of the 1930s.[95] Convinced that social and medical considerations were inseparable, he persuaded Steel of the merits of amending the Bill to replace three of the more specifically worded grounds for abortion in favour of a ground containing just 'a general phrase about the wellbeing of the woman'.[96] As it reached its final stages in the House of Commons, the Bill thus contained just two grounds for abortion: one permitting it on the basis of substantial risk of serious fetal anomaly and one where abortion posed a risk to a woman's 'well-being', with the doctor permitted to take into account her 'total environment actual or reasonably foreseeable'. ALRA felt so badly betrayed by Steel's action in deleting the other two clauses without prior consultation that it considered withdrawing its support from the Bill.[97]

At this point, the Bill's progress could also easily have stalled for another reason: a Private Member's Bill is easily blocked by its opponents unless the Government creates additional space for it in the tight parliamentary schedule. Now Steel's good fortune in having supportive individuals in key Government roles became crucial. He met with Richard Crossman, the Leader of the House. In the service of the cause, he determinedly downed a 'revolting mixture' of whisky that Crossman had absent-mindedly topped up with brandy and left assured of the extra time that he needed.[98]

The Bill secured a comfortable two-to-one majority at its third reading. It then proceeded to the House of Lords, where it was piloted by Lord Silkin, whose own abortion law reform Bill had successfully completed its passage there two years before. By now, its opponents were better organised, with

---

[93] Steel also notes the significance of 'very intense arguments' with members of a leading Catholic seminary in his constituency; Steel interviewed by O'Neill. See also *Hansard*, House of Lords (HL), 23 March 2018, vol. 790, col 576. Such a provision had also appeared in an earlier Bill drafted by Williams, a conscientious objector during World War Two: Glazebrook, 'Glanville Llewelyn Williams 1911–1997', 411–35. Steel, *Against Goliath*, 64; Hindell and Simms, *Abortion Law Reformed*, 186.

[94] Steel interviewed by O'Neill. See further Steel, *Against Goliath*, 64. Sir Dugald was the father of David Baird, whose memories of the impact of the Abortion Act were noted earlier in this chapter.

[95] Baird, 'A Fifth Freedom?', 1141; Davis and Davidson, '"The Fifth Freedom" or "Hideous Atheistic Expediency"'.

[96] Steel interviewed by O'Neill. This catch-all provision replaced the grounds permitting abortion on the basis of a woman's physical and mental health, the overstraining of her 'capacity as a mother' and where the woman was a 'defective' or where pregnancy resulted from rape.

[97] Hindell and Simms, *Abortion Law Reformed*, 178–79.

[98] Steel, *Against Goliath*, 65.

lobbying so intense that it overwhelmed the antiquated House of Lords mail system.[99] Opposition was led by Sir Reginald Manningham-Buller, Lord Dilhorne, a Conservative peer and senior lawyer.[100] Famously nicknamed 'Sir Reginald Bullying-Manner',[101] he was a formidable opponent. An eminent colleague on the bench recalled that his 'disagreeableness was so pervasive, his persistence so interminable, the obstructions he manned so far flung, his objectives apparently so insignificant, that sooner or later you would be tempted to ask yourself whether the game was worth the candle' and 'if you asked yourself that, you were finished'.[102] Lord Dilhorne brought all of these skills to bear against the Steel Bill, reviving many of the concerns that had exercised the Commons.[103] He achieved one concession. With it being unclear what degree of risk might be sufficient to justify an abortion on the basis of a woman's 'well-being', the Lord Chief Justice proposed a clarifying amendment: that abortion should be legal only where the risk to life or health of continuing a pregnancy would be greater than that of ending it. Lord Silkin accepted the change, the amendment was moved by Lord Dilhorne and it passed without a vote.

When the Bill returned to the House of Commons, the astute St John-Stevas immediately grasped the implications of this last-minute amendment intended to tighten its restrictions: if abortion were as safe as the reformers claimed – or became so in the future – then this seemingly modest amendment was anything but. Rather, abortion would be legally justified in all cases, risking turning the Bill into one that permitted abortion on demand.[104] While ALRA had considered withdrawing support from the 'emaciated' Bill that emerged from Committee, they now believed that this amendment had 'saved the day'.[105]

At this final stage, Steel's Medical Termination of Pregnancy Bill was renamed, becoming the Abortion Act. For St John-Stevas, it was 'as well to call a spade a spade'.[106] For Steel, the new title was 'technically correct' in that the legislation made no provision for termination of a viable fetus, with professional practice being to refer to 'abortion' only until viability (whereas 'termination' included any stage of pregnancy).[107] Under this new title, the Bill passed onto the statute books on 27 October 1967. While this was a victory for

---

[99] Hindell and Simms, *Abortion Law Reformed*, 210, noting that ALRA sent circulars to private addresses.

[100] Former Attorney General and Lord Chancellor, thereafter becoming a Law Lord.

[101] By Bernard Levin, the 'father of the modern sketch'. See 'A homage to Levin, father of the modern sketch', *Guardian*, 22 October 2004.

[102] Lord Devlin cited in Sackar, *Lord Devlin*, 228.

[103] *Hansard*, HL, 23 October 1967, vol. 285, cols 1397–509.

[104] St John-Stevas in *Hansard*, HC, 25 October 1967, vol. 751, cols 1742–43.

[105] Cossey interviewed by O'Neill.

[106] St John-Stevas in *Hansard*, HC, 25 October 1967, vol. 751, col. 1781.

[107] Steel in *Hansard*, HC, 25 October 1967, vol. 751, col. 1781.

ALRA, campaigners were painfully aware of the enormous compromises that had been made. Munday recalls:

> I was conscious throughout the negotiations . . . that it was absolutely iniquitous to have that two doctor clause in. How could, or should, somebody who's probably never seen the woman before, and is never going to see her afterwards, make such an important decision for that woman's life and future? We had to accept it. It was also appalling to exclude Northern Irish women. But if we hadn't done it, we wouldn't have got anything at all. It was by the skin of its teeth getting that through.[108]

The Abortion Act 1967

While it had changed during its passage through Parliament, the legislative vision of Glanville Williams remains clearly apparent in the text of the Abortion Act. The Act did not repeal or amend existing criminal prohibitions against abortion but sat alongside them, carving out an exemption where three conditions are met. First, the pregnancy must be 'terminated by a registered medical practitioner'. Second, any treatment for the termination of pregnancy must be carried out in an NHS hospital or in another specially approved place. Third, two registered medical practitioners must be of the good faith opinion:

(a) that the continuance of the pregnancy would involve risk to the life of the pregnant woman, or of injury to the physical or mental health of the pregnant woman or any existing children of her family, greater than if the pregnancy were terminated; or
(b) that there is a substantial risk that if the child were born it would suffer from such physical or mental abnormalities as to be seriously handicapped.[109]

In deciding whether the first ground was met, doctors might take account of 'the pregnant woman's actual or reasonably foreseeable environment'.[110] For Steel, this foregrounding of the need for 'socio-medical care' was the Act's key achievement.[111] The Act also permitted the close monitoring of legal abortion by way of notification requirements, which underpin the annual publication of volumes of statistics.[112] In line with the compromise agreed with St John-Stevas, health professionals were given a statutorily enshrined right of conscientious objection, permitting them to refuse to participate in any treatment authorised by the Act.[113]

---

[108] Munday interviewed by O'Neill.
[109] Abortion Act 1967, Section 1(1).
[110] Section 1(2).
[111] Steel, 'Foreword' in Hindell and Simms, *Abortion Law Reformed*, 7.
[112] Section 2(1).
[113] Section 4.

The Abortion Act also has two other important features that provoked no significant debate during its legislative passage but would become enormously important in subsequent years. First, it was taken as a given that it would not apply to Northern Ireland,[114] with such exclusion deemed normal with regard to legislation on an issue of sexual morality.[115] Moreover, as a Scottish MP, Steel was particularly keenly aware of the significance of the fact that health was a devolved matter;[116] ALRA was primarily London based, and the reformers had understood that any attempt to include Northern Ireland within the Bill would have doomed it to failure. This did not prevent Northern Irish MPs from participating in voting on it, even though this meant remaining in London well into the weekend.[117] They would continue to take a keen interest in the Abortion Act, and in turn the Abortion Act would come to play a hugely significant role in the region, notwithstanding its formal exclusion from the Act's purview.[118]

A second, vitally significant feature of the Abortion Act that just 'wasn't on the radar' in 1967 was the issue of time limits.[119] First, no consideration was given to when a line might be drawn between contraception and 'procurement of miscarriage', determining when the legality of an intervention became contingent on compliance with the Abortion Act. Many years later, this would become a matter of significant dispute.[120] Second, equally little attention was given to the upper time limit for abortion. We have seen that Steel intended the Act to apply only prior to viability, with nothing within it 'affect[ing] the provisions of the Infant Life (Preservation) Act 1929 (protecting the life of the viable fetus)'.[121] However, it is a striking omission to modern eyes that the long and furious parliamentary debates that preceded the Act's introduction contained only the most perfunctory of passing references to this issue.[122] A later House of Lords Select Committee can be forgiven for wrongly concluding that an upper time limit had been read into the Act entirely 'inadvertently' (apparently missing Steel's statement in the Commons regarding the renaming of the Abortion Act)[123] and finding it 'quite extraordinary that [an upper time limit] was not spelt out in unambiguous terms in the 1967 Act'.[124] A concern

---

[114] Section 7(3).

[115] See generally Sheldon et al., 'Too Much, Too Indigestible, Too Fast?'.

[116] Steel interviewed by O'Neill. See further Chapter 6, and Sheldon et al., 'Too Much, Too Indigestible, Too Fast?', 761–96.

[117] Audrey Simpson interviewed by Jane O'Neill, 27 September 2017.

[118] See Chapter 6.

[119] Munday interviewed by O'Neill.

[120] See Chapter 5, pp. 158–60.

[121] Section 5(1).

[122] Knight in *Hansard*, HC, 22 July 1966, vol. 732, col. 1102.

[123] HL, *Report of the Select Committee on the Infant Life (Preservation) Bill [H.L.]*, 1987–88, HL 50, para. 17. See further Chapter 3.

[124] HL, *Report of the Select Committee on the Infant Life (Preservation) Bill [H.L.]*, 1987–88, HL 50, para. 17.

with the upper time limit for abortion would soon emerge as a – and for many years *the* – dominant focus of dispute regarding the Abortion Act.[125]

A 'Biography' of the Abortion Act

With the Abortion Act passed, Vera Houghton, the ALRA Chair, concluded that the group might now be disbanded. Munday disagreed:

> At the end of the campaign, I was out three or four nights a week on platforms with [SPUC]. I said . . . 'in my view, they will never give up. They are going to attack this ink before the Queen's signature is dry on the bit of paper'. 'No, no' – and she actually said to me, it still hurts – 'you've attended too many SPUC meetings for your own good, you can't see the wood for the trees'. And that was the only time Vera was ever, ever wrong. I said, 'Well at least let us keep ALRA going, and give it a new brief to oversee, for a year, the way the Act is working out. You go over to your new organisation and I will stay behind and run this one', which I did as General Secretary. And within six months we had another Bill.[126]

History would prove Munday right. Between the Abortion Act coming into effect and this book going to press, *Hansard* would record more than 60 instances where proposals were made to amend abortion law, a large majority of them suggesting restrictive measures.[127] Moreover, campaigners would find themselves fighting on a range of other fronts: equally important to these attempts at further legal reform would be sustained contestation regarding the proper interpretation and implementation of the Abortion Act.

These ongoing struggles would be a defining feature of what we frame as the Abortion Act's 'biography'. While our use of that term in the study of a law is novel,[128] biography offers a useful shorthand to denote a historical, contextual study of a subject that is simultaneously attentive to both continuity and change within it over an extended period. Biography emphasises that a law cannot be fully understood at just one moment in its existence; rather, it must be examined as a continuing and changing subject that is rooted in evolving social and cultural landscapes and always in the process of accumulating meaning.[129] In this sense, we follow others who have been inspired to move beyond human subjects to offer 'biographies' of archaeological artefacts, diseases and cities.[130]

---

[125] Chapter 2, pp. 50–56; Chapter 3, pp. 93–108; Chapter 5, pp. 153–58; Chapter 7, pp. 234–36.

[126] Munday interviewed by O'Neill.

[127] See Appendix 2.

[128] Legal biography is evolving in interesting ways but has thus far focused on human subjects. Mulcahy and Sugarman, 'Introduction', 1–6; Sugarman, 'From Legal Biography to Legal Life Writing', 7, 32.

[129] Kopytoff, 'The Cultural Biography of Things'.

[130] E.g. Gosden and Marshall, 'The Cultural Biography of Objects', 169; Mukherjee, *The Emperor of All Maladies*; Ackroyd, *London: The Biography*.

When applied to a statute, this approach has three major implications, which mark a biography of the Abortion Act as different from an explanation of the factors that led to its introduction[131] or from accounts of specific episodes in its life.[132] First, biography foregrounds a basic sociolegal insight: that law is a living and evolving thing that needs to be studied as it is interpreted and takes effect in practice rather than as it exists on the statute books.[133] Even where a statute's text remains unchanged, its acquisition of legal meaning is an ongoing process that involves interpretative work, development and consolidation of received understandings, evolving practices and moments of challenge, rupture and revision. Such evolution inevitably both reflects and influences the shifting broader social and institutional contexts within which a law is read, understood and applied.[134] Second, a statute – and particularly one characterised by considerable controversy – also acquires a broader social and symbolic meaning, which stands in no necessary relationship to the intention of its drafters nor to its doctrinal meaning as developed by lawyers.[135] The stories told about a law – and what that law represents in broader cultural terms – can and will evolve, whilst at times revealing roots that go deep into its history. Finally, the subject of a biography can offer a window through which to glimpse aspects of the world evolving around it.[136] As Virginia Woolf put it, biography must offer the story of the stream as well as that of the fish.[137]

When we began work on our biography of the Abortion Act, we had no intention on relying on military metaphors to tell its story. However, the language of war, battles, struggles and contestation is frequently used by campaigners and eventually also forced itself onto our narrative. The story that emerges overwhelmingly from a close reading of the sources is one of sustained and bitterly contested battles over the social and cultural meaning of abortion, the correct legal interpretation of the Act, and whether and how it should be reformed. In the pages that follow, we trace the contours of this war. As we will see, while struggle has remained at the heart of the Abortion Act's biography, the nature of the battles fought regarding it has changed markedly over time.

---

[131] Hindell and Simms, *Abortion Law Reformed*, on the Abortion Act. For other important studies of the emergence of legislation, see Carson, 'Symbolic and Instrumental Dimensions of Early Factory Legislation'; Nelken, *The Limits of the Legal Process*.

[132] E.g. Marsh and Chambers, *Abortion Politics*, offering detailed explorations of a specific reform attempt.

[133] For the significance of focusing on 'technical law' as part of this project, see Cowan and Wincott, 'Exploring the Legal'.

[134] Cotterell, *The Sociology of Law*.

[135] Nelken, *The Limits of the Legal Process*.

[136] Gillings and Pollard, 'Non-Portable Stone Artifacts and Contexts of Meaning', 179.

[137] Woolf, 'Sketch of the Past', 90.

In this first chapter, we have described how the Abortion Act had 'a difficult birth, but good midwifery',[138] with its opponents ultimately defeated in their hope that it would 'be stillborn'.[139] In the next, we trace its very early, formative years. The Act's meaning would be negotiated as women arrived in doctors' surgeries seeking services that they now believed to be lawful. Doctors would work hard to understand the new law and how best to conduct their own clinical practice within it, and professional meetings would witness fierce dispute regarding its proper interpretation. Over time, different under-standings coexisted, became established or fell out of use. Dominant practices settled into received understandings and became consolidated in professional codes, internal policy and procedure documents, official guidance and medical curricula. The chapter ends in 1974 with the publication of the highly influen-tial Lane Report, which offered an authoritative and detailed review of the Act's operation in these early years.

The deliberations of the Lane Committee operated as a buffer against any immediate attempts to reform the Abortion Act. After 1974, however, came a series of major parliamentary attacks that were deeply enmeshed with wider disputes regarding changing gender and familial norms. These restrictive Bills, which will be considered in Chapter 3, were led by men, most of them Tories, and were framed in terms of defending family values, personal responsibility and moral standards. While the Abortion Act was not a product of the women's movement, the movement would now claim and defend it, itself being importantly shaped in the process. Within Parliament, its defence would be led by female Labour MPs, who would bond together as such for the first time, speaking a language of social justice and women's rights. Over the course of two decades, the centre ground for debate would gradually shift. At the end of the 1980s, a final Ballot Bill attempting restrictive reform would be pro-posed by the Catholic Liberal Democrat MP David Alton, who eschewed the language of family values conservativism and the earlier focus on restricting abortion to 'deserving' categories of women. Rather, Alton focused exclusively on restricting the upper time limit for abortion, framing his case in a language of social justice, civil liberties and scientific advance. The chapter ends when, after more than two decades of repeated attacks, in 1990, Parliament would finally be given the opportunity for a meaningful vote on the Abortion Act, using it to endorse its broad framework. Moreover, an important tipping point had now been reached: for the first time, liberalising amendments were discussed alongside restrictive ones.

In the meantime, outside Parliament, the Abortion Act had become embed-ded in daily life. Abortion for non-medical reasons became gradually more widely accepted, services were embedded and streamlined and abortion tech-nologies became safer and less technically demanding. In Chapter 4, we

---

[138] Cossey interviewed by O'Neill.
[139] McLaren, 'The Abortion Bill', 565–66.

consider how dispute would come increasingly to turn on the 'normalisation' of abortion. Those on one side of the debate would fight for services under the Act to be mainstreamed, destigmatised and made available as a necessary, routine part of women's healthcare. Those on the other side saw rather the trivialisation of a procedure that should only ever be an exceptional measure of last resort, driven by a profit-motivated 'abortion industry'. While these disputes would find focus in contestation regarding the meaning of the Abortion Act, they were always also about far more, lying along a fault line between competing visions of gender, family, religion, science and society. Each new technical innovation or service development offered the site for a new battle, ostensibly narrowly focused on the acceptability or safety of abortion, the quality of services or the welfare of women, but always also reflecting divergent empirical beliefs and broader visions of the good.

As we see in Chapter 5, some of these battles would find their way into the courts, as broader struggles over the meaning of the Act became framed as narrow, technical questions of statutory interpretation. Considering these cases together, it is striking how little of the modern meaning of the Abortion Act would have been apparent even to the best informed and most farsighted commentator in 1967. Almost all key provisions of the Abortion Act and the wider statutory framework within which it operated would be litigated. Most challenges would be brought or supported by anti-abortion campaigners seeking to establish a more restrictive reading of its terms and to publicise perceived abuses of them; in later years, a much smaller number would be brought by those seeking a more liberal reading. Over time, the focus and framing of these disputes would change in line with the shifting centre of the moral debate, with legal argumentation reflecting rhetorical strategies likely to be persuasive to concrete audiences within specific historical, cultural and political contexts.[140] The moral beliefs of individual judges would sometimes be glimpsed in their rulings. However, the courts would encounter statutory text that was already saturated with the meanings acquired in clinical practice, and this would exert a powerful influence on their reasoning.

In Chapter 6, we turn to consider that part of the UK that was omitted from the Abortion Act: Northern Ireland. Notwithstanding this formal exclusion, the Abortion Act has played an important role in the region such that a biography of the Abortion Act necessarily offers the story of not just a British law but, rather, of a UK one. Over the past five decades, Northern Irish women have travelled in large numbers to access legal abortions in Britain, with the Act offering a 'release valve' that would limit the numbers of dangerous backstreet abortions and the mortality and morbidity that have driven reform elsewhere. Further, the Abortion Act would form a key focus of campaigns for and against abortion law reform within Northern Ireland, and

---

[140] Harrington, Series and Ruck-Keene, 'Law and Rhetoric', 302–27.

when reform eventually came the Act would play a role in shaping it. Moreover, as we will see, this new Northern Irish law would come in turn to be used as a powerful lever to argue for reform of the Abortion Act.

In Chapter 7, we return to Westminster, where, following a brief hiatus after 1990, attacks on the Abortion Act would again intensify. Those bringing them would follow in the footsteps of David Alton, with politicians who placed particular emphasis on their Christian faith in driving their parliamentary work making the case for narrowly focused reform measures in a language of clinical advance, female empowerment and civil liberties. One marked change was nonetheless apparent: these attacks would now be led by Tory women. In the meantime, pro-choice MPs would move off the defensive and argue for further liberalisation of the law. Reflecting a significant shift in the centre ground of the debate, each side would now claim to be defending the interests of women, and each would claim to be supported by clinical science and medical opinion, with the gulf between them more than ever presented not as a moral but an empirical one. Above all, each would claim to be offering necessary modernisation of an outdated Abortion Act, whilst offering radically different visions of what such modernisation required.

A Note on Sources, Methods and Objectivity

This book draws upon hundreds of days' research conducted in 17 archives, including official government and parliamentary archives across the UK, the archives of professional medical bodies, collections held by university libraries, the Women's Libraries in Glasgow and London and the Wellcome Collection, which holds an enormous body of material relating to the history of science and medicine.[141] Through some of these archives, we have been able to consult the papers of individuals, campaign groups, trade unions and community organisations. These offer a vital supplement to the government papers in national archives and the records of professional bodies. We benefitted especially from the extensive resources donated to the Wellcome Collection by the National Abortion Campaign and ALRA, the latter very significantly due to the sustained hoarding instincts of Diane Munday. Having been active in ALRA, Munday went on to work as the Public Relations Officer at the Birmingham (later British) Pregnancy Advisory Service (BPAS), where she was also key to creating the BPAS archive. We were particularly fortunate in being permitted access to this before it was donated to Wellcome, which has

---

[141] Only where we have made reference to material found within a specific archive within this book is the archive listed in the Bibliography. A full list of all archives consulted can be found on the project's website: Sheldon et al., 'Sources', https://research.kent.ac.uk/abortion-act/sources/.

imposed its own cataloguing system on it and restricted public access to some of the files we consulted.[142]

One notable omission in the archives is a major collection of resources collated by a Pro-Life organisation. With the exception of the British Library's collection of SPUC newsletters, the significant quantity of anti-abortion material consulted has been found primarily in the collections of Pro-Choice individuals or groups. While there is no reason to doubt its authenticity, this collection method clearly influences what is available: this is generally published material rather than the private letters, memoranda or minutes that might cast light on 'behind-the-scenes' discussions (as are abundantly available for Pro-Choice groups). It is to be hoped that future researchers may benefit from such material being lodged in public archives, thus adding important further context to the resources currently available.

Our major sources for the period prior to the 1990s were found in these physical archives. From that point on, some records are unavailable because of the 30 year rule applied to many government files or because of archives' own restrictions on material deemed sensitive. Further, more recent material is less likely to be found in archives, either because of sensitivities about the documents becoming public or because those who hold them are still active and have not yet wished to donate their collections. It is also likely that there are fewer filing cabinets in attics and spare rooms slowly filling up with carefully preserved pieces of paper as records become digital. Newsletters and campaign materials are likewise increasingly circulated online. For this reason, much of our recent source material has been obtained directly from websites. Other online sources date to a period before the advent of the Internet but are now most conveniently accessed in digitised form: notably, we have made extensive use of *Hansard*, published parliamentary reports, editions of medical journals and digitised newspapers.

Our study of paper and digital resources was supplemented by oral history interviews with 18 people who could claim extensive experience of the Abortion Act, generally counted in decades, relating either to involvement in services related to abortion or in campaigns regarding the Act.[143] As well as offering invaluable personal recollections and insights, these individuals were able to speak to gaps or discrepancies in the published sources. Their accounts were gathered in semi-structured interviews, lasting between one and three hours, conducted at a time and place of the interviewee's choosing and drawing on a general list of topics and questions adapted to take account of the nature of the individual's involvement with the Abortion Act. Interviews

---

[142] A list of the main archives and major collections consulted is included in the Bibliography.

[143] A list of our interviewees, together with brief biographies, is included in Appendix 3. Ethical approval for this component of the study was obtained from the School of History, Classics and Archaeology, University of Edinburgh (16 March 2015), with an amendment, agreed in June 2017, permitting interviewees to be asked to consent to transcripts being shared with other researchers.

were generally conducted by O'Neill, with interviewees given the opportunity to review a full transcript and to make any desired redactions.[144] All interviewees consented to the transcripts being made publicly available in the Wellcome Collection.[145] Recordings are likewise available where no substantial redactions of the transcript were requested.

In seeking to offer a detailed account of the five decades of the Abortion Act's operation, the current work differs in scope from a number of earlier accounts that described its introduction, considered specific attempts to amend it or – in the case of parliamentarians' memoires – focused on their own involvement.[146] These accounts have invariably been written by individuals with strongly held views on abortion and a history of advocacy on the issue.[147] The most detailed account of the introduction of the Act, on which we relied extensively above, was co-authored by Madeleine Simms (ALRA) and the journalist Keith Hindell, who was later to become a director of the Pregnancy Advisory Service.[148] Ann Farmer, who offers a sharply contrasting account that foregrounds the influence of eugenic beliefs on the framing and defence of the Abortion Act, was an active member of the Labour Life Group.[149] John Keown, Professor of Christian Ethics at the Kennedy Institute and author of a rigorous and highly regarded account of the development of abortion law from 1803 to 1982, is a member of the Pontifical Academy for Life and has advised Pro-Life campaigners inside and outside Parliament.[150] A study of the White Bill (1975) was written by authors who 'stand uncompromisingly for the fight of women to control their own fertility'.[151] A book on the subsequent Corrie Bill (1979) was co-authored by a leading member of the coalition that had mobilised opposition to it.[152] Much more recently, a wide-ranging book published to coincide with the fiftieth anniversary of the Abortion Act was written by an executive member of Abortion Rights.[153]

The current work is no exception. While three of its authors have no history of advocacy on this issue, one author is a former trustee of BPAS and the

---

[144] With the exception of David Baird and Anna Glasier, who were interviewed by Davis.

[145] The transfer of files to Wellcome is underway at the time of going to press.

[146] Most notably, see Alton with Holmes, *Whose Choice Anyway?* Many politicians include brief discussions of abortion within their own biographies; in Steel's case, this amounts to just seven pages of a 367 page biography.

[147] A recent book by Amery, *Beyond Pro-Life and Pro-Choice*, is an apparent exception. While Amery argues for an approach grounded in reproductive justice, she declares no affiliation with any campaign group and appears not to have been involved in any advocacy work.

[148] Hindell and Simms, *Abortion Law Reformed*; Hindell, *A Gilded Vagabond*.

[149] See Farmer, *By Their Fruits*, appendix A, for a detailed discussion of the influences on her opposition to abortion.

[150] See discussion of *R (Smeaton)* v *Secretary of State for Health* (2002) in Chapter 5.

[151] Greenwood and Young, *Abortion in Demand*.

[152] Joanna Chambers was the co-ordinator of Co-ord (the Co-ordinating Committee in Defence of the 1967 Act); Marsh and Chambers, *Abortion Politics*, x.

[153] Orr, *Abortion Wars*.

Abortion Support Network and has advocated for further liberalisation of abortion law.[154] Notwithstanding this fact, like previous authors, we found that protagonists on both sides of the debate were generous in agreeing to speak with us.[155] While we have worked hard to avoid bias in our work, our own reading of the above literature found that the extent to which previous authors have achieved this goal varies greatly. The extent to which the current work succeeds is a matter for the reader's own judgement.

It is necessary to pause on one challenge that we faced in this regard: the absence of a morally neutral terminology that will satisfy all readers. Our reading of five decades of debates about abortion suggests that, over that time, usage of key terms has hardened into a series of shibboleths that reveals a speaker's ideological stance before any argument is made: 'fetus' is met with 'baby', 'child' or 'infant'; 'pregnant woman' (or much more recently 'pregnant person') with 'mother'; 'pro-choice' with 'pro-abortion'; 'anti-abortion' with 'pro-life'; 'service providers' or 'health professionals' with 'abortion industry'. Here, we follow the language used within the Abortion Act in referring to 'pregnant women' and reserving the term 'mothers' for those involved in the social activity of caring for a born child. We avoid as inappropriate for a historical study the term 'pregnant persons', which reflects an important but very recent recognition that transgender men and non-binary people may also be affected by abortion laws. The choice of terminology regarding the 'fetus' or 'unborn baby' is still more difficult. The latter term appears to accept the unborn 'as already an infant, already a person'.[156] The former will appear loaded to some precisely in refusing the latter for this reason, with the term 'fetus' appearing too 'cosy': Jack Scarisbrick, co-founder of Life, asks, 'Why Latinism, when there is a perfectly good bit of Anglo Saxon?'[157] We have nonetheless opted to use the medical term 'fetus', using it interchangeably with 'the unborn' to refer to the period from implantation until birth. A further set of problems emerge around the language of handicap, impairment, disability and anomaly. Here, we use 'anomaly' to describe an abnormality in a fetus, 'impairment' to describe a physical or mental abnormality in a living person and 'disability' and 'disabled people' to recognise that the disadvantage suffered as a result reflects the interaction between an impairment and a wider environmental and social context.[158]

---

[154] Sheldon was a trustee of BPAS from 2009 to 2018 and a trustee of Abortion Support Network from 2018 to 2022, and she offered advice on Diana Johnson MP's two abortion Bills; see Chapter 7, pp. 250–51. See generally Sheldon, 'The Decriminalisation of Abortion', 334–65.

[155] We had only one direct refusal from someone unwilling to speak with us: email from David Alton to Jane O'Neill, 12 April 2018, on file with the authors. See Hindell and Simms, *Abortion Law Reformed*, acknowledgments, and March and Chambers, *Abortion Politics*, ix–x, recording thanks to interviewees who were campaigners and parliamentarians on each side of the debate.

[156] Lupton, *The Social Worlds of the Unborn*, 6. See further Han, 'Pregnant with Ideas', 59–60.

[157] Jack Scarisbrick interviewed by Jane O'Neill, 7 November 2017.

[158] Shakespeare, *Disability Rights and Wrongs Revisited*, 2.

Finally, the terms 'Pro-Life' and 'Pro-Choice' are widely used today but were not commonly used by early campaigners, and this terminology is likewise fiercely contested. Contemporary Pro-Life campaigners frequently refer to their opponents as 'pro-abortion', eliciting the response that Pro-Choice campaigners are no more pro-abortion than they are pro-birth but, rather, that they support women being permitted to make their own choices.[159] Pro-Choice advocates have likewise contested the right of their opponents to claim a monopoly on being 'pro-life',[160] instead describing them as 'anti-choice'.[161] On occasion, each side describes the other in more colourful terms.[162] In the pages to follow, we use interchangeably the terminology that seems to us most accurately to capture the groups' positions – anti-abortion and pro-choice – along with the terms widely used by the campaigners themselves – Pro-Life and Pro-Choice – with capital letters to remind the reader that these are proper nouns. While it was some time before the groups consistently adopted this terminology themselves and conventions regarding its use hardened,[163] for convenience we use these terms throughout discussion of the entire period considered in this book. Individual actors within these movements inevitably have more complex positions than this binary division might suggest,[164] with important disputes taking place within, as well as between, the two sides of the debate.[165] Nonetheless, as will become clear in the pages to follow, there have been two clearly recognisable 'sides' to the abortion debate that run consistently throughout the biography of the Abortion Act 'on tram lines that never converge'.[166]

Our biography covers the period from April 1968, when the Abortion Act came into force, until September 2021, when we completed this manuscript. Towards the end of this period, the Labour MP Diana Johnson introduced two Ten Minute Rule Bills calling for the decriminalisation of abortion. In each speech, she thanked Sheldon for her legal advice.[167] This provoked an article

---

[159] Simpson interviewed by O'Neill: 'I'm not pro-abortion ... abortion is not the right answer for a lot of women. But I think they have to have the right to make that choice.'

[160] Steel in *Hansard*, HL, 21 June 1990, vol. 174, col. 1184.

[161] As Simpson puts it, 'they are not pro-life, because they are certainly not pro the life of the woman. They are anti-choice.' Simpson interviewed by O'Neill.

[162] Anti-abortion advocates frequently characterise their opponents as a profit-hungry 'abortion industry'; for examples see Chapter 4. Early Pro-Choice literature frequently references Pro-Life groups as 'the Compulsory Pregnancy Lobby'; Steel notes that SPUC was 'irreverently' called the 'Society for the Production of Unwanted Children'. Steel, *Against Goliath*, 66.

[163] SPUC's election material in the early 1970s, for example, repeatedly refers to the need to elect 'anti-abortion' candidates; e.g. Wellcome Library, SA/BCC/C34, Letter from Phyllis Bowman (SPUC) to Supporters, c. 1973, and SPUC, 'General Election'; SPUC advertisement in *Catholic Herald*, 25 January 1974. Similarly, it is possible to find many early examples where campaigners self-identify as 'pro-abortion'; e.g. see Marsh and Chambers, *Abortion Politics*, which was co-authored by Jo Chambers, chair of Co-ord.

[164] This is the central claim of Amery, *Beyond Pro-Life and Pro-Choice*.

[165] E.g. see Chapter 3, pp. 85–7, 90, and Chapter 4, pp. 121–22.

[166] Alton, *What Kind of Country?*, 170.

[167] *Hansard*, HC, 13 March 2017, vol. 623, col. 27.

in the *Daily Mail* that quoted two Pro-Life MPs attacking the awarding of the grant that supported the research for this book and citing concerns with potential bias.[168] The article drew particular attention to the fact that just over £3,000 had been awarded to support another planned output: a teaching resource. Reports of the story rippled out across Pro-Life and Christian websites, with one subsequent headline going as far as to claim that the 'UK is paying an abortion activist $600K+ to write a book about abortion for children'.[169] Beyond offering a minor illustration of how swiftly facts in this area become distorted – a leitmotif within the book to follow – this incident was also an interesting one for four researchers seeking to craft a biography of the Abortion Act. While our own professional biographies have each been shaped to greater or lesser degrees by the Act, we had now also become a very minor footnote in the story to follow.

[168] 'Fury as Pro-Choice Activist is Handed £500,000 of Taxpayers' Cash to Write a Book on Abortion', *Daily Mail*, 9 April 2017.

[169] Hodges, 'UK is Paying an Abortion Activist $600K+ to Write a Book about Abortion for Children'.

2

The Early Years

> All in all, we [in the Royal College of Obstetricians and Gynaecologists] did not expect a very great change in practice from that obtaining before the Act. We thought there would be a slightly more liberal attitude to the problem, for that, after all, was the purpose of the new law. How wrong we were.[1]

The Abortion Act came into effect on 27 April 1968. As women seeking access to abortion services began to arrive in their doctors' surgeries in rapidly increasing numbers, David Steel welcomed the fact that they could now 'come openly through their family doctors instead of risking a back-street operation'.[2] Glasgow gynaecologist and SPUC founding member Ian Donald took a dimmer view, complaining that women appeared to perceive the Act 'as indicating the right to abortion on demand'.[3] Doctors listened to women's stories and considered their requests. There was enormous variation in their interpretations of the new law and, consequently, in women's success in accessing abortion within the NHS. A rapidly expanding non-NHS sector developed to meet demand. Campaigners would also play an important role in shaping understandings and implementation of the new Act.

The major lines of controversy surrounding the Abortion Act became clear in these early years. The first came as no surprise: the question of 'social' abortions and the proper exercise of a doctor's role as a gatekeeper to them had been bitterly contested in Parliament. Now dispute continued outside it, fuelled by allegations that the Act was being abused by a profit-driven 'abortion industry', with some doctors permitting abortion 'on demand'. The second major focus of concern was on an issue that had passed largely unremarked upon during the passage of the Abortion Act: the upper gestational limit for abortion. Controversy would be driven by shocking media reports of live aborted babies being abandoned to die or, worse, sold for use in research. These twin concerns quickly gathered momentum, coming to a head in 1974 with the publication of two very different reports into the operation of

---

[1] Lewis, 'The Abortion Act', 241.

[2] Wellcome Library, Papers of the Abortion Law Reform Association, SA/ALR/G69, D. Steel, Speech to the Annual General Meeting of the Abortion Law Reform Association, 'Abortion Act Vindicates 16 years of Effort', 19 October 1968.

[3] Donald, 'Naught for Your Comfort', 286.

the Act: a sensationalist and mendacious media exposé and a sober and extensive judge-led review.

Over these first six years, the meaning of the Abortion Act was analysed, negotiated and bitterly disputed, with understandings of its terms emerging and gradually settling and embedding into received interpretations and practices. Simultaneously, the major battle lines of dispute regarding the Act's meaning were being laid for the decades to follow.

The 'Social Clause' and the Doctors' Gatekeeper Role

Medical Decision-Making

The introduction of the Abortion Act had a seismic effect within NHS gynaecology services. There had probably been fewer than 10,000 legal abortions in England and Wales in 1967.[4] By 1973, there would be over 167,000.[5] In Scotland, numbers quadrupled over the first three years of the Act's operation, rising even in Aberdeen where the development of an NHS service under Sir Dugald Baird had predated its introduction.[6] With no additional resources made available to meet demand and abortion requiring on average one week's recuperation in hospital, the strain on existing facilities was intense.[7] One gynaecologist explained,

> It is difficult to assess a patient, sent up with a request for termination, whom one has never seen before, with a completely impartial mind, uninfluenced by the number of similar requests the same day, the number of patients still waiting to be seen, the number of beds available, and the number of patients on the waiting list. It is difficult to think of her case impartially other than as a burden on the gynaecologist, instead of one of interest and pleasure in diagnosis and treatment. It is also very difficult not to be influenced by the dislike of the actual operation which can be difficult and dangerous.[8]

The disruption was often particularly resented by nursing staff, who were divorced from the decision-making process around abortion yet closely involved in women's care.[9] The matron of Bellshill Maternity Hospital complained:

---

[4] 9,100; see *Report of the Committee on the Working of the Abortion Act* (hereafter *Lane Report*), vol. 1, 11.

[5] 167,149; see *Registrar General's Statistical Review of England and Wales, Supplement on Abortion.*

[6] *Lane Report*, vol. 2, 2. See further Baird, 'The Abortion Act 1967', 293; Davis and Davidson, '"The Fifth Freedom" or "Hideous Atheistic Expediency"', 29–48.

[7] In 1968, the average length of hospital stay was 7.8 days, falling to 5.3 days in 1971. *Lane Report*, vol. 2, para. 165.

[8] Boutwood, 'The Effect of the Act on Gynaecological Practice', 49–56, 57.

[9] See *Lane Report*, vol. 2, para. 371. Tensions would eventually come to a head in the Royal College of Nursing case (see Chapter 5).

[T]his problem has been foisted upon us without the necessary resources of space, theatre time and personnel to deal with it. . . . [O]ur commitments to our ordinary patients are barely met, standards of nursing care are falling, and yet we have to spread our professional skills still further to cope with this additional category of patient.[10]

It fell to two doctors to determine whether an abortion was justified for an individual patient. As we saw in Chapter 1, Parliament devoted considerable time and attention to the precise wording of the circumstances in which they should do so. In statutory language agreed after many hours of debate, the Abortion Act provided that abortion would be lawful where

two registered medical practitioners are of the opinion, formed in good faith . . . that the continuance of the pregnancy would involve risk to the life of the pregnant woman, or of injury to the physical or mental health of the pregnant woman or any existing children of her family, greater than if the pregnancy were terminated . . . account may be taken of the pregnant woman's actual or reasonably foreseeable environment.[11]

The Act also provided that abortion might be authorised on the basis of 'substantial risk' of serious fetal anomaly, with this provision causing little controversy in these early years.

Doctors were sharply divided on how best to interpret this broadly worded first ground for abortion (and, indeed, on the merits of the Abortion Act more generally). However, there was widespread agreement (if not complete consensus) on two points. First, if an abortion was to be considered, the final decision as to whether it was appropriate was a medical one: women's views were important but not determinative. A study of 16 general practitioners (GPs) who met regularly to discuss case studies of patients requesting abortion noted that it was felt by many, particularly the female GPs,

that the patient should have some say over what should happen to her body, i.e. that she should have some liberty in her choice. However, it was considered by the majority that this freedom could not be accepted absolutely, because there were doubts in the doctors' minds as to whether a woman in such a predicament would know what was in her best interests. In other words, she might get what she wanted, but not what she needed.[12]

Second, it was generally agreed that significant investigative work and deliberation were required before a doctor could reach a decision, with the GPs in this study able to report an extraordinary level of detail regarding their patients' lives. Where a GP did not have close, first-hand knowledge of their patient's situation, they might interview her husband and use social workers,

---

[10] Wellcome Library, SA/ALR/C22, Board of Management for Coatbridge, Airdrie and District Hospitals, 1972, Submission to the Lane Committee on the Working of the Abortion Act (CWAA). See also Wellcome Library, SA/ALR/C41, Lothian and Peebles Executive Council, Edinburgh, 2 November 1971, Submission to the Lane CWAA. See further Hordern, *Legal Abortion*, 105.

[11] Section 1.

[12] Tunnadine and Green, *Unwanted Pregnancy*, 4.

health visitors or probation officers to find out more.[13] In these early years, a psychiatric evaluation was often sought, with psychiatrists likewise expecting to conduct wide-ranging interviews and investigations that might address a woman's relationships since childhood, her dreams and unrehearsed behaviour, and even her history of bed-wetting as a child.[14]

In these early years, the question of how doctors should interpret the Abortion Act and carry out their responsibilities under it was widely discussed in the pages of medical journals and at medical symposia. Medical opinion was initially sharply divided, with many doctors feeling ill-prepared to adjudicate abortion requests, which 'typically [do] not require them to diagnose and treat a morbid condition, but rather to consider the wishes, wonders and worries of normal people in normal health'.[15] One in 10 consultant gynaecologists instantly took a very liberal interpretation of the Act, around 6 per cent asserted their conscientious objection to abortion in all circumstances, and the rest settled uneasily along the spectrum between these two poles.[16] Family doctors and psychiatrists, who were closer to the situation of the pregnant woman and further removed from the actual operation, tended towards more liberal interpretations.[17] In each case, around a third supported abortion on request, subject to the investigations described above and the ultimate approval of the doctor.[18] Sir John Peel, Surgeon-Gynaecologist to the Queen and immediate past President of the Royal College of Obstetricians and Gynaecologists (RCOG), summarised that the Act had introduced a 'chaotic muddle', with its meaning 'largely depend[ent] on what you want it to mean'.[19] It is difficult to disagree.

As doctors struggled to interpret and apply the Act, they developed a range of strategies to cope with their responsibilities under it. Glasgow psychiatrist I. M. Ingram identified a 'variety of games' in these responses.[20] First, with some believing that too many patients requested an abortion 'for reasons of mere inconvenience' or that abortion removed 'a natural barrier to promiscuity',[21] GPs might discourage the pregnant woman from seeking an abortion, refuse to refer her to a specialist, or refer her with a neutral letter

---

[13] Dudley-Brown, 'The Duties of the GP under the Abortion Act'.

[14] See e.g. Hordern, *Legal Abortion*; Tunnadine and Green, *Unwanted Pregnancy*; report of a visit to Dr Bloom in Litchfield and Kentish, *Babies for Burning*, 80–89.

[15] Lafitte, *The Abortion Hurdle Race*, 8.

[16] Lewis, 'The Abortion Act (1967)', 529–35.

[17] Constable, in Medical Protection Society, *The Abortion Act 1967 Proceedings of a Symposium* (hereafter MPS, *Symposium*), 30, noted 'most of those in favour of abortion on demand or easier abortion are those most remote from the performance of the task'.

[18] Waite, 'Consultant Psychiatrists and Abortion', 76; provided the termination was requested before the tenth week and the woman had seriously considered the alternatives.

[19] MPS, *Symposium*, 31–32. For a brief overview of Peel's life, see 'Sir John Peel', *Telegraph*, 2 January 2006.

[20] Ingram, 'Abortion Games', 969; for a critical response, see Baird, 'Abortion Games', 1145. Ingram drew on Berne, *Games People Play*.

[21] National Records of Scotland (NRS), HH102/1232, Submissions to the Lane Committee, Evidence of Argyll and Clyde Area Health Board's Area Medical Committee, September 1974; Wellcome Library, SA/ALR/C25, Evidence of Royal College of Physicians, Edinburgh to the Lane CWAA, 1972.

committing themselves to no decision.[22] This, in Ingram's view, amounted to playing 'Pontius Pilate' and evading medical responsibilities under the Act. Second, with most doctors more willing to agree to a termination in early pregnancy when the procedure was more straightforward, some gynaecologists and psychiatrists reached informal agreements not to recommend termination after 12 weeks 'except for compelling reasons'.[23] This allowed some GPs to play the game of 'Waiting List', causing delay as a means to block access to services.[24] Alternatively, with a 'Bounced Cheque', they might avoid confrontation by referring a woman to a specialist antagonistic to abortion, with it quickly becoming known which units would readily carry out abortions and which were 'likely to prove sticky'.[25] With his position on abortion widely known, most referrals to the eminent Glasgow gynaecologist Ian Donald came from doctors seeking support for their view that a request for termination should be refused.[26]

Senior gynaecologists developed their own strategies. Ingram described how senior hospital doctors operated as 'Big White Chiefs' able to impose a policy prejudging all individual cases, with 'covert ethical, religious, and personal motives' often to be inferred behind an ostensible medical rationale.[27] Donald was one such doctor, with the recollections of those who worked with him giving a sense of the authority wielded by a senior hospital doctor in those years: he is remembered as 'a visionary', worshipped by his patients, 'intimidating ... because he was totally brilliant' and 'a clinical chief of the old school, a full-blooded figure, larger than life to many people'.[28] It is unsurprising that such a figure would influence 'the whole generation of people around him'.[29] In areas where senior gynaecologists opposed to abor-

---

[22] A committee of interested doctors and social workers initiated by the Scottish Council for the Unmarried Mother and Her Child and the Brook Advisory Service 'to consider how the Abortion Act can be more effectively and humanely administered' found that, when faced with young women in particular, many GPs were unwilling to discuss abortion on non-medical grounds, would not refer the patient and did not let her know that she had a right to a second opinion or how she might obtain one. Glasgow Caledonian University (GCU) Archive Centre, One Parent Families Scotland, Box 69, 2, Scottish Council for the Unmarried Mother and Her Child Consideration of Abortion and Counselling Provision, Letter dated 14 September 1971, Reports of Consultation and Advisory Service Pilot, Edinburgh 1970–72.

[23] Hamill and Ingram, 'Psychiatric and Social Factors', 230. While official statistics do not record the numbers of women refused terminations, numerous examples of refusals by gynaecologists after 12 weeks are evident in case studies recorded in the archives. See e.g. GCU Archive Centre, One Parent Families Scotland, Box 69, 2, Appendices, Report on Pilot Study, 1971.

[24] Williams and Hindell, *Abortion and Contraception*, 18–19; *Lane Report*, vol. 3, 47, 76.

[25] Donald, 'Naught for Your Comfort', 286.

[26] Ibid.; *Scottish Daily Record*, 16 May 1973.

[27] Ingram, 'Abortion Games', 969.

[28] Contributions of Professor John MacVicar at 47, Professor Stuart Campbell at 61 and Dr James Willocks at 47, all in Tansey and Christie (eds), *Looking at the Unborn*.

[29] David Baird interviewed by Gayle Davis, 13 November 2017.

tion like Donald held sway, provision of NHS services was consequently limited.[30] Diane Munday recalls:

> [R]ight from the start, before the Act was passed, it was absolutely clear that there was at least one area of the country, Birmingham, that would not provide abortion . . .. There was also the gynaecologist in Glasgow and, I think, one . . . in Leeds. And they were the three founders of SPUC. And each of them had said that they would not murder little babies in their area. Birmingham was the centre of the opposition, because of [Hugh] McLaren.[31]

A letter sent from one Birmingham consultant – possibly McLaren – to a married woman who had requested an abortion illustrates how a 'Chief's' views could translate into hospital policy:

> Regretfully I have to inform you that we do not do abortions unless there is a medical or psychological reason. In your case it appears that it is just inconvenient, and being a maternity hospital, where we try to preserve the lives of our babies and not deliberately destroy them, I must decline.[32]

Birmingham and Glasgow would, for many years, remain amongst the most difficult places in Britain in which to obtain NHS abortion services, as senior doctors appointed more junior colleagues in their own image and influenced those they trained. The *Scottish Daily Record* reported battles between 'diehard pro and anti-abortion forces' in Glasgow, whilst in Edinburgh abortions 'seem[ed] to be left pretty much to the consciences of individual doctors', and in Dundee they were carried out 'almost for the asking'.[33] Over two-thirds of the Scottish women who came to BPAS in the 1970s originated from within a 20-mile radius of Glasgow.[34]

Senior gynaecologists sympathetic to abortion also had a powerful impact, with a similarly enduring influence in driving what Ingram called the 'Woman's Lib' interpretation of the Abortion Act.[35] A young David Paintin was initially opposed to abortion but, having trained under Sir Dugald Baird in Aberdeen, emerged as a leading advocate for liberal abortion laws. Baird's son, David (who would later become a distinguished doctor and medical researcher in his own right), recalls that his father told Paintin, 'well, that's alright, we've got enough staff here, you don't have to do it but you will have to see the women [facing] unwanted pregnancy', explaining that 'within a year, because he systematically would listen to what they had to say, Paintin was

---

[30] Paintin, *Abortion Law Reform in Britain*, 66; Hindell and Simms, *Abortion Law Reformed*, chapter 10.

[31] Diane Munday interviewed by Jane O'Neill, 10 November 2017. The three gynaecologists were McLaren, Donald and Professor J. S. Scott in Leeds; see Hindell and Simms, *Abortion Law Reformed*, 95–96.

[32] Quoted in Lafitte, *The Abortion Hurdle Race*, 6.

[33] *Scottish Daily Record*, 16 May 1973.

[34] BPAS Archives, 'BPAS Consolidates Success in Glasgow with Open Evening', BPAS press release, 15 May 1978.

[35] Davis and Davidson, '"The Fifth Freedom" or "Hideous Atheistic Expediency"', 29–48.

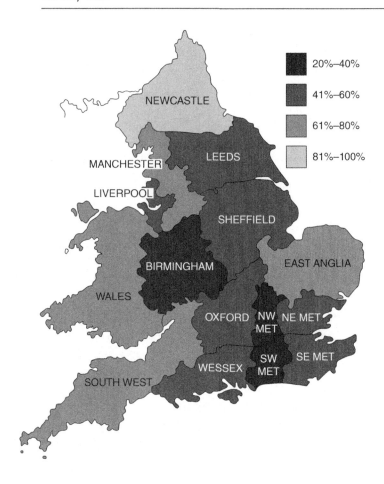

Proportion of resident abortion patients in each region who obtained abortion under the NHS in their home region in 1971. From the *Report of the Committee on the Working of the Abortion Act* (the 'Lane Report'), reproduced under Open Government Licence (www.nationalarchives.gov.uk/doc/open-government-licence/version/2/).

converted'.[36] Just south of the border, Dorothea Kerslake, a consultant gynaecologist and advocate of liberal abortion laws, likewise oversaw the development of services in Newcastle General Hospital, initially accommodating almost all legal terminations in the city.[37] In 1973, 98 per cent of abortions in Newcastle were performed within the NHS compared to just 19 per cent of those in Birmingham.[38]

[36] Baird interviewed by Davis.

[37] Lawson et al., 'Management of the Abortion Problem', 1288. The authors describe how Kerslake's retirement in 1970 'made drastic action inevitable', with Newcastle hospitals then persuaded to band together to continue her work.

[38] Or 33% of those performed on Birmingham residents, with the disparity reflecting the establishment of the BPAS in Birmingham leading women from other regions to travel there to

This marked regional disparity exacerbated local pressures, with higher numbers of women requesting abortion services in areas neighbouring those under the control of a senior gynaecologist hostile to abortion. Some doctors reacted by playing 'Catchment Area' to manage demand,[39] a response criticised as constituting 'a selective discrimination in medical matters against human dignity'.[40] Kerslake queried how such restrictions might be deemed appropriate for abortion services but not for a 'chest operation or even plastic surgery'.[41] Alternatively, a doctor might implement an informal rationing policy of refusing cases that they considered less meritorious (e.g. single girls) when other areas of their workload appeared more pressing. For some, 'if a choice ha[d] to be made between more terminations and a reduction in the gynaecological waiting list they would unreservedly choose the latter'.[42]

Other doctors sought to limit future demand on services with the game of 'Sterilisation' as a precondition for agreeing to perform an abortion. The eminent obstetrician and gynaecologist Aleck Bourne, who had famously tested the law in the 1930s to confirm the legality of therapeutic abortion, explained to a medical symposium that he was in favour of abortion only in limited circumstances.[43] Moreover:

> I think most of you probably agree that most abortions, if they are necessary at all, need sterilization too; not all of them of course, but a large number do. The grand multipara, who is sagging everywhere – breasts, abdomen, her spirits, her emotions, everything sags – she is miserable, depressed: she is the one I have aborted perhaps more than any other.[44]

In these very early years, sterilisation accompanied NHS abortion in a sizeable proportion of cases, with rates highest in areas where access to services was most tightly restricted: in 1971, around 40 per cent of NHS abortions in Birmingham were accompanied by sterilisation, compared to less than 1 per cent in the non-NHS sector, where a self-funding patient had greater control over her treatment.[45] In some cases, at least, sterilisation was used in a coercive

---

access services. Office of Population Censuses and Surveys (OPCS), *Registrar General's Statistical Review of England and Wales for the Year 1973*.

[39] Baird, 'The Abortion Act 1967', 294.

[40] Wellcome Library, SA/ALR/C113, W. Weinberg, MD, London, 10 November 1971, Submission to the Lane CWAA.

[41] Wellcome Library, SA/ALR/C75, Miss Dorothea Kerslake, FRCOG, 26 January 1972, Submission to the Lane CWAA.

[42] Wellcome Library, SA/ALR/C27, A. Smith, Scottish Association of Executive Councils, 20 December 1971, Submission to the Lane CWAA.

[43] On *R v Bourne*, see Chapter 1, p. 7.

[44] MPS, *Symposium*, Discussion, 84. A 'multipara' is a woman who has carried more than one pregnancy resulting in viable offspring. While Bourne had established the legality of abortion in some circumstances, he had emerged as a vocal advocate against further liberalisation of the law, later joining SPUC. See Bourne in 'Don't Alter the Abortion Law', *Daily Mail*, 9 August 1962.

[45] OPCS, *Statistical Review* 1971; for discussion see *Lane Report*, vol. 2, para. 74.

and punitive way.[46] However, with the quality of clinical data regarding abortion improving dramatically as a result of reporting procedures under the Abortion Act, it rapidly became clear that simultaneous sterilisation increased the risk of maternal mortality from abortion significantly and its use fell into abeyance.[47]

Ingram was also critical of doctors who, far from imposing their own views, refused to take decisions. The game of 'Plumber' described the gynaecologist who claimed to be merely 'an honest, simple craftsman whose abilities [were] bounded by the female pelvis', leaving consideration of social or psychiatric issues to the GP, social worker or psychiatrist.[48] Psychiatric expertise was heavily relied upon in these very early years, with it taking time for gynaecologists to grow more confident in making their own judgements in reliance on a letter from a GP.[49] However, this was a fine line: Ingram was equally critical of gynaecologists who enthusiastically played the game of 'Amateur Psychiatrist' or 'Young Dr Kildare', turning to psychosocial diagnosis, moral judgements and assessments of social deprivation that lay beyond their medical expertise.[50]

Psychiatrists developed their own strategies. 'Sim's Position' – named for a prominent anti-abortion psychiatrist Myre Sim – held that no psychiatric indications for abortion existed, given that suicide was rare during pregnancy and major psychoses were not believed to be worsened by it.[51] Controversially, this reading of the Abortion Act interpreted its reference to mental health as meaning the absence of psychotic illness and nothing more. At the other extreme, Ingram's game of 'Woman's Lib' reflected another controversial view: that any abortion might be justified under the Act, since the continuance of a pregnancy always involves greater risk to a woman than if it were

---

[46] Birth Control Trust, 'The Failure of the NHS', 3–8. See further this chapter, p. 42.

[47] *Lane Report*, vol. 1, para. 119, referring to the increased risk of maternal mortality in abortions performed by dilatation and curettage where accompanied by sterilisation. See abortion statistics in annual volumes, published variously as *Registrar General's Statistical Review of England and Wales, Supplement on Abortion* (1968–1973); Office of Population Censuses and Surveys, *Abortion Statistics* (1974–2001); and Department of Health, *Abortion Statistics, England and Wales* (2002–2020).

[48] Ingram, 'Abortion Games', 969.

[49] Hordern, *Legal Abortion*, 115. By 1974, the number of patients referred for a psychiatric opinion thus 'dwindled sharply' in most areas, NRS, HH102/1232, Letter from G. C. Timbury, Honorary Divisional Secretary of the Royal College of Psychiatrists, Glasgow, to A. Laurie, Scottish Home and Health Department, 20 November 1974. This was generally welcomed by psychiatrists, who had complained that they 'should not be required to "fill a gap"' where other doctors would not make a decision, with their involvement necessary only 'when there [was] definite evidence of some abnormal mental state'. See Wellcome Library, SA/ALR/C33, Royal College of Physicians and Surgeons of Glasgow, January 1972, Submission to Lane CWAA. See further Priest, 'The Impact of the Abortion Act', 293; Todd, 'Psychiatric Experience of the Abortion Act (1967)', 489–95.

[50] See further Horobin, *Experience with Abortion*; Lafitte, *The Abortion Hurdle Race*.

[51] See Sim, 'Abortion and the Psychiatrist', 148. 'Sim's Position' is also an examination position in gynaecology.

terminated[52] or because the mental health of a woman forced to bear an unwanted child must automatically suffer.[53] One distinguished psychiatrist recommended that 'we as doctors should revert to being advisers and not judges' as a woman's knowledge 'that it is *her* final decision and not the doctor's may well make many a woman more responsible than she is now'. He recognised that this view would be shocking to many, and particularly to men.[54]

Ingram's final game – 'Cash Before Delivery' – was played by doctors who took an equally permissive interpretation of the Abortion Act but for less respectable reasons, for 'while the 1967 Act cast out some devils in the form of backstreet abortionists, it also allowed in a few medically qualified goblins'.[55] While private abortion practice predated the Abortion Act, a large 'grey market' in services now expanded rapidly. While the 'goblins' were probably relatively few in number,[56] a lack of robust enforcement under the Act allowed them to flourish.[57] The eminent pathologist and pioneer of forensic medicine Professor Keith Simpson described the 'disgraceful' way in which they operated with 'comparative immunity':

> Telephone numbers that require passwords, a call from 'Marguerite' in order to achieve a response, contacts that refer patients to particular practitioners in certain areas, deposit moneys that bring only a certification of suitability under one of the three or four permissive headings and cash-down operations at chosen addresses . . . [58]

With the 'good faith' of such doctors clearly at issue, Simpson concluded that '[i]f such practices are rife – and in my view it is quite clear that they are – criminal abortion is far from being a dying art. The new Act has legitimized the practice for those who can afford it.'[59]

The 'Cash Before Delivery' doctors provoked particularly grave alarm within Parliament, and calls to eliminate their operation began almost before the ink had dried on the Abortion Act. Starting with a Ten Minute Rule Bill

---

[52] See further 'The Royal College of Psychiatrists' Memorandum on the Abortion Act in Practice', 449; Tooley, in MPS, *Symposium*; Peel, in MPS, *Symposium*.

[53] See Priest, 'The Impact of the Abortion Act', 294, noting that psychiatric diagnosis was 'reputed to be soft, flexible and accommodating'.

[54] Tredgold, in MPS, *Symposium*, 27, emphasis in original. See further Hamill and Ingram, 'Psychiatric and Social Factors', 231.

[55] Potts et al., *Abortion*, 300.

[56] *Lane Report*, vol. 1, para. 443, suggested that this may have been as few as about 20 or 30 members of the medical profession and those associated with them.

[57] Howe, in MPS, *Symposium*, Discussion, 91, noted that local authority inspection processes were limited given the 'immense range of inspectorial duties' imposed on them; see further Keown, *Abortion, Doctors and the Law*, 130–36.

[58] Simpson, 'Criminal Abortion', in MPS, *Symposium*, 58–59.

[59] Ibid., 60.

put forward in summer 1969 by Norman St John-Stevas,[60] a total of five Bills were proposed in as many years by male Conservative MPs demanding additional restrictions on the doctors who authorised or performed abortions or those who offered advice regarding or referred into abortion services.[61] The breadth of support for action to curb this 'nasty trade' was demonstrated by the fact that two of these Bills were co-sponsored by David Steel.[62] However, divisions between those seeking restriction of the Abortion Act were already emerging. Michael Grylls (Con) proposed a prohibition on charging a fee for advice or information about abortion other than by medical practitioners or other approved persons.[63] His Bill fell after four members, including Jill Knight, a SPUC committee member, walked out believing that it did not go far enough to curb abuses of the Act.[64] Such divisions would widen, going on to cause significant problems for the advocates of restrictive reform over the years to follow.

ALRA rejected such measures on the basis that they would offer 'not a safeguard but a bottleneck'.[65] The Government likewise opposed them on the basis that the Abortion Act must be allowed to bed in before further amendment was considered. However, it acceded to MPs' calls for an independent review of the operation of the Abortion Act.[66] In June 1971, it announced the appointment of a committee chaired by Dame Elizabeth Lane, who had been the first female English County Court and High Court judge.[67] Highly unusually, a majority of committee members were women, with 'two eminent consultant gynaecologists, a professor of psychiatry, two general practitioners, other members of the medical and nursing professions, the headmistress of a girls' school, a social worker ... [and] a Scottish Q.C.'.[68] Discreet steps were reportedly taken to exclude Catholics, with one member – Juliet Cheetham – believing that she had been appointed in ignorance of her faith, which she then carefully concealed for fear of being pigeonholed as an anti-abortion fanatic.[69]

[60] *Hansard*, House of Commons (HC), 15 July 1969, vol. 787, col. 412.

[61] St John-Stevas, A Bill to Improve the Law Governing Abortion and the Status and Rights of the Medical Profession 1969; Irvine, Abortion Law (Reform) Bill 1969; Hunt, Medical Services (Referral) Bill 1971; Grylls, Abortion (Amendment) Bill 1973; Grylls, Abortion (Amendment) Bill 1974.

[62] Medical Services (Referral) Bill 1971 and Abortion (Amendment) Bill 1974.

[63] Abortion (Amendment) Bill 1974.

[64] 'How a Thwarted Pressure Group Reacts', *Sunday Times*, 11 August 1974; The National Archives (TNA), MH 156/352, Letter from Baroness Falkender to Dr P. Norris (SPUC), 24 October 1974; 'MPs Halt Abortion Reform', *Guardian*, 25 July 1974.

[65] Commenting specifically on the St John-Stevas Bill, see Hindell and Simms, *Abortion Law Reformed*, 207.

[66] 'Abortion Inquiry Demanded by 250 MPs', *Times*, 24 July 1970.

[67] Lane, *Hear the Other Side*, 150. See further NRS, HH61/1315, Draft Memo by the Secretary of State for Social Services, 1970.

[68] Lane, *Hear the Other Side*, 150. See Wivel, 'Abortion Policy and Politics on the Lane Committee'.

[69] See Wivel, 'Abortion Policy and on the Lane Committee', 30–31, also noting that Denis Pereira Gray recalled that he was asked whether he was Catholic during the selection process.

The Committee's terms of reference were confined to the 'operation' of the Abortion Act, assuming that the grounds for legal abortion would remain unaltered.[70]

Women's Experience of Accessing Abortion Services

While Ingram's 'abortion games' offered a deliberately light-hearted exercise in caricature, the ideal types that he described were firmly grounded in reality and had a very real impact on women facing unwanted pregnancies, with patterns established in these early years continuing to be reported throughout the 1980s and into the 1990s.[71] In the words of Francois Lafitte, first chair of BPAS, women would be forced to run a 'hurdle race' to access legal abortion services.[72] Their chances of success would depend on both luck – in terms of which of Ingram's 'games' their doctors would play – and ability, with the most vulnerable women often the least adept hurdlers.

The first hurdle faced by women was to obtain adequate information about available services, with Lafitte deploring the fact that

> the NHS should issue no official information leaflets on abortion rights, pro-
> cedures and facilities or available counselling services; that the network of family
> planning consultation centres which the NHS is creating should cover all forms
> of fertility regulation *except* abortion; that there should be a publicly accessible
> local C list of doctors willing to advise on contraception, but no A list for
> abortion; that the public should be confused by the welter of commercially
> motivated 'pregnancy advice' and 'pregnancy testing' agencies that are tolerated,
> while restrictions are imposed on advertising by reputable voluntary social
> services.[73]

The problem of inadequate information was compounded by the fact that GPs were often reluctant to raise the possibility of abortion, leaving women to broach the subject.[74]

With the option of abortion raised, women faced a second hurdle: the need to convince their GPs to refer them for NHS services. Their success here would depend on a range of factors including – as we have seen – geography, their doctors' personal views on abortion, and how advanced their pregnancies were. Women in rural areas might face particular problems, with concerns regarding confidentiality acute in places where the 'whole community' knows if someone visits a GP.[75] Scottish campaigners were sufficiently concerned to

---

[70] *Lane Report*, vol. 1, para. 1.
[71] See generally O'Neill, 'Abortion Games'. In this section, we draw *inter alia* on women's accounts of accessing services that were published across the 1970s–1990s. These accounts do not generally include an indication of exactly when the reported experience took place.
[72] Lafitte, *The Abortion Hurdle Race*.
[73] Ibid, emphasis in original.
[74] See Macintyre, *Single and Pregnant*, 73–77; *Lane Report*, vol. 3, 76.
[75] Ann Henderson interviewed by Jane O'Neill, 25 July 2017.

set up a 'support group for ... women in more remote areas who actually wanted to bypass their own doctor'.[76] Some women put off approaching their GP, fearing disapproval or – for younger women – that their parents might be informed, with doctors' reluctance to recommend abortion likely to be compounded by any such delay.[77] The circumstances that led to a woman's pregnancy were also important.[78] Young, unmarried women were likely to provoke 'the most moralistic response', particularly if they were believed to have slept with a casual acquaintance.[79] Separated, widowed and divorced women were the most likely to obtain abortions within the NHS and least likely to encounter delay.[80] Class and education were each also potentially significant, with middle-class and better educated women often more knowledgeable about the law, better able to put their case across convincingly and more likely to have the means to pay for a private procedure if unable to access NHS services.[81] Women in the semi-skilled and unskilled classes were more likely to face delays in receiving attention and treatment, with the effect being more severe 'the lower their social class and the poorer their education'.[82] They might also be deemed better able to cope with an unwanted pregnancy, for – as one psychiatrist asserted – a woman 'in a responsible professional job ... being higher in the social scale, has farther to fall'.[83] The relevance of a woman's race or ethnicity is less frequently discussed in these accounts than in the corresponding US literature, yet it undoubtedly played a role.[84] One black woman noted that she was the only woman at a pro-choice meeting 'to say she had got an abortion easily', the reason being that 'she was black and her doctor was racist' and 'never granted white women abortions, or even the pill'.[85] Racialised stereotypes regarding black women's perceived promiscuity and hyperfertility might influence white doctors to favour birth control methods

[76] Eileen Cook interviewed by Jane O'Neill, 11 September 2017.

[77] Todd, 'Psychiatric Experience of the Abortion Act', 492. See generally Lafitte, *Abortion Hurdle Race*. See further the Cartwright and Lucas study in *Lane Report*, vol. 3, 8: 19% did not approach their own doctor or any doctor of that practice.

[78] Hordern, *Legal Abortion*, 86–90.

[79] Hamill and Ingram, 'Psychiatric and Social Factors in the Abortion Decision', 231, noting that those recommended for abortion had a mean age of 31 years, while for those refused it was 24. See further Williams and Hindell, *Abortion and Contraception*, 19; *Lane Report*, vol. 3, 77; Macintyre, *Single and Pregnant*, 74–75, 85; Briggs and Mack, 'Termination of Pregnancy in the Unmarried', 398–400.

[80] *Lane Report*, vol. 3, 34–35; See further Diggory, 'Some Experiences of Therapeutic Abortion', 873.

[81] Lafitte, *Abortion Hurdle Race*; Macintyre, *Single and Pregnant*, 22.

[82] Lafitte, *Abortion Hurdle Race*.

[83] Hordern, *Legal Abortion*, 87.

[84] On the USA, see e.g. Roberts, *Killing the Black Body*, chapter 2. For a comparative discussion of the American and British situations, see Jones, 'Human Weeds, Not Fit to Breed?'.

[85] 'Gail from London', cited in McGrane and Nicholls, 'Tribunal on Abortion Rights', 26–27. See further Bryan, Dadzie and Scafe, *The Heart of the Race*, 105.

for these patients that would 'remove their contraceptive agency',[86] with there being reports of black women forced to agree to sterilisations as well as unwanted terminations.[87]

Those women who secured a GP referral would face the further significant hurdle of convincing their gynaecologists. In the meantime, with doctors less likely to agree to terminate a more advanced pregnancy, the clock was ticking, with some women being painfully affected by GPs' games of 'Bounced Cheque' or 'Waiting List'. Some reported that doctors had lied about the options available to them: one was told by her gynaecologist 'not that she was morally wrong to have an abortion, but that because she was 14 weeks pregnant it was illegal'.[88] Delay was exacerbated by the pressures on the NHS, as hospitals struggled to meet demand for services. In 1972, one study found that three-quarters of women approached their GP before 10 weeks but only one in five were seen by a hospital consultant within a week of referral; almost a third waited for more than two weeks; and some waited more than four. Women then risked being refused treatment by the consultant (including because their pregnancy was now too far advanced) or, if accepted for treatment, they might wait anything up to another five weeks for an abortion.[89]

In negotiating these encounters, women required a clear and convincing explanation of their reasons for wishing to end their pregnancies. For those who could not claim the grounds seen as most compelling – risk to their own physical health or of fetal anomaly – contraceptive failure was generally seen as the most respectable justification. However, even here sympathy could not be assumed, with the use of contraception itself still controversial in the late 1960s and early 1970s and doctors who had heard repeated stories of contraceptive failure becoming sceptical regarding their veracity.[90] Those requesting a second abortion would particularly struggle to fit within the narrative of the respectable woman who had simply made an unfortunate mistake,[91] with repeated unplanned pregnancies seen by doctors as 'a character trait of a particular type of personality',[92] 'not uncommon in the impulsive, the psychopathic and the unintelligent'.[93] Women who had had abortions were often similarly critical of those who faced multiple unplanned pregnancies or appeared to lack a 'good reason' for abortion: one explained that if women

---

[86] Jones, 'Human Weeds, Not Fit to Breed?', 53, 55; Bryan, Dadzie and Scafe, *The Heart of the Race*.

[87] Bryan, Dadzie and Scafe, *The Heart of the Race*, 103.

[88] S. McLennan proposing motion 'Abortion', Scottish Trades Union Congress, *Annual Report 1980*, 489.

[89] Chalmers and Anderson, 'Factors Affecting Gestational Age at Therapeutic Abortion', 1324.

[90] One family planning specialist reported having sometimes been told by other doctors that if a woman had chosen to go to a birth control clinic, she deserved to get pregnant. Howard, in MPS, *Symposium*, 64, 67. See further below on doctors' scepticism.

[91] Macintyre, *Single and Pregnant*, 74–75.

[92] Tunnadine and Green, *Unwanted Pregnancy*, 47–48.

[93] Hordern, *Legal Abortion*, 90.

were 'in for the first time and had been using contraception, well, it's a shame. But if they are in for a second time they are absolute sluts.'[94]

Women might also find themselves under pressure to accept intrusive forms of contraception as a precondition for abortion. Marge Berer would go on to become a leading advocate for liberal abortion laws. She reports her experience of abortion in the mid-1970s:

> [T]he doctor came around the ward, the whole ward full of women like me having an abortion … and he said, 'I am just going to pop an IUD [intrauterine device] in after I do this.' Everybody said, 'oh, okay,' and I said, 'no, not okay. I am not having an IUD. I've already had an IUD once and it didn't suit me and I am not going to have another one.' I had to actually fight with him over that, briefly. He didn't put it in in the end. But that was the kind of, you know, you have had an abortion, you've been irresponsible with your contraception, so we are going to help you by giving you a method that you can't and don't have to control.[95]

Others were less fortunate, finding it impossible to resist a doctor playing Ingram's game of 'Sterilisation'. One reported:

> I was sent by my GP to a consultant who twice refused to give me a termination … when he did eventually agree, he told me I would have to be sterilized at the same time. I didn't want this as I really hoped to have a baby at another time, when circumstances would be better. But he went on delaying until I agreed, and then the abortion was done at four and a half months … since then I have never been able to have a child and I have lived with terrible sadness. It was blackmail.[96]

Pressure to agree to sterilisation appeared to be a particularly prominent issue affecting black and working-class women. Eileen Cook explains that there was 'this very condescending attitude to women, that women somehow can't … be trusted to make their own decision about whether they want children or not. And that the less educated you are, or the poorer you are, however you want to put it, the more likely that needs to be the case.'[97] This concern was sufficiently prevalent for the Women's Abortion and Contraception Campaign to include within its mission statement the aim of ensuring that women should never be pressured to accept sterilisation as a precondition for abortion.[98]

Some medical accounts suggest that women welcomed the detailed investigation that preceded an abortion referral as a means of ensuring that this was

[94] Williams and Hindell, *Abortion and Contraception*, 19–23. See further Macintyre, *Single and Pregnant*, 123–25.

[95] Marge Berer interviewed by Jane O'Neill, 8 November 2017.

[96] Neustatter and Newson, *Mixed Feelings*, 79. See also *Lane Report*, vol. 3, 67.

[97] Cook interviewed by O'Neill. For the significant racialised dimension, see e.g. Bryan, Dadzie and Scafe, *The Heart of the Race*, 103–04.

[98] Bazlington and Cowen, *The Guardian Directory of Pressure Groups and Representative Organisations*, 166–67.

'a considered decision, taken by two independent medical practitioners in light of the total situation'.[99] However, it is also apparent that many resented and resisted it, with this feeling gradually strengthening over time as women began to approach the medical interview process in an increasingly functional way.[100] Moreover, women became aware of what was expected in these medical interviews, developing their own strategies in response, including what Ingram described as playing the 'psychiatric case'.[101] In addition to the 'humiliating and degrading' 'charade' of needing to 'exaggerate her distress',[102] this strategy also carried real dangers: one woman was told that an abortion referral would be considered only on her admission to a mental hospital.[103] The narrative of a 'nice girl who made a mistake' might be successful, particularly where the woman demonstrated 'a demeanour of shame and regret in the consultation'.[104] However, this also carried risks: if in a relationship that was deemed sufficiently stable, a GP might attempt to persuade her against abortion and in favour of marriage.[105] Others responded with stories of desertion by a boyfriend[106] or played upon doctors' biases with stories of interracial relationships as 'a manipulatory tactic' to persuade them to authorise the termination of the resulting pregnancies.[107] In later years, Pro-Choice groups would start to publish information for women, emphasising the variability of doctors' views and practice, explaining what reasons were likely to prove convincing and advising women to be proactive in pushing for referrals and appointments, including changing doctors if necessary.[108] For their part, doctors became keenly aware of attempts to manipulate them, with some growing increasingly sceptical about 'claims of accidental or occasional intercourse'[109] and suspecting that contraceptive failure 'was a far less common occurrence than many of the women would have the doctor believe'.[110]

Given the power of Ingram's 'Big White Chiefs', women also experienced enormous regional disparities in NHS provision. In those regions where NHS

[99] Hordern, *Legal Abortion*, 90; see also Williams and Hindell, *Abortion and Contraception*, 22.

[100] See Allen, *Family Planning, Sterilisation and Abortion Services*; O'Neill, 'Abortion Games', 187–88. Howard, in MPS, *Symposium*, 69, complained that women 'do not ask to be understood' but come in saying 'I know what I want: I want an abortion and I want you to arrange this: I don't want to talk to you about myself.' See also Macintyre, *Single and Pregnant*, 81; Anna Glasier interviewed by Gayle Davis, 13 November 2017.

[101] See also Williams and Hindell, *Abortion and Contraception*, 11–13.

[102] Gynaecologist Peter Diggory in *Guardian*, 6 February 1975.

[103] 'Others faced ridicule and opposition from the doctors they approached for help.' Glasgow Women's Library, Papers of the Scottish Abortion Campaign, SAC 5.6, 'Speaking Out for Choice', *Women's Choice: A Magazine of Reproductive Rights*, vol. 2 no. 1 (1994), 10–12.

[104] Macintyre, *Single and Pregnant*, 85; Williams and Hindell, *Abortion and Contraception*, 23.

[105] Macintyre, *Single and Pregnant*, 75; O'Neill, 'Abortion Games', 176–77.

[106] Williams and Hindell, *Abortion and Contraception*, 11–13.

[107] Macintyre, *Single and Pregnant*, 82.

[108] *Harpies and Quines: The Abortion Issue*, August/September 1993, 18.

[109] Macintyre, *Single and Pregnant*, 81.

[110] Clark et al., 'Sequels of Unwanted Pregnancy', 501; Tunnadine and Green, *Unwanted Pregnancy*, 32, 106.

abortion rates were low, only 'the more deserving cases' would be treated within the NHS,[111] and over the course of later years this would become entrenched in a system of informal means testing, with GPs increasingly steering women towards the private sector as a way to preserve limited resources or where they believed women had no chance of getting an NHS abortion.[112] One woman who had been raped by her estranged husband reported that her GP had told her that she could 'try the NHS, but it's not an illness and people should pay for it'.[113] Young unmarried girls or women who had already been seen on a previous occasion were particularly unlikely to be accepted for NHS services,[114] with doctors wary of condoning reliance on abortion as a means of birth control. In one case, a 17-year-old with learning disabilities living in an overcrowded home was reportedly rejected for the abortion recommended by her GP because she had terminated a pregnancy in the previous year. The consultant had advised that 'abortion should not be used as a means of contraception' and that, given her irresponsible behaviour, she did not 'deserve' one.[115] In the private sector, women's chances of being accepted for treatment were radically different: in 1972, just 1 per cent of referrals to non-NHS providers were refused compared to 20 per cent of referrals into the NHS.[116] This disparity is all the more marked given that GPs would be likely to avoid referrals to gynaecologists known to be unsympathetic to abortion unless deliberately offering a 'Bounced Cheque'.

With Britain at the vanguard of liberalising abortion law reform, many of the women seeking abortions in the early years came from overseas. In 1968, around one in 20 abortions were performed on non-resident women; by 1973, the proportion was more than one in three. In that year, over 56,000 women travelled to end pregnancies in England and Wales, coming mainly from France and West Germany.[117] Overseas women were particularly vulnerable to the worst excesses of the 'Cash Before Delivery' doctors, who operated within what the media swiftly dubbed a profit-hungry 'abortion industry', with London proclaimed to be the 'abortion capital of the world'.[118] Many arrived ill-prepared and sought advice from train station or airport staff, with a

---

[111] Williams and Hindell, *Abortion and Contraception*, 1, 18–19.

[112] Ashton et al., 'Wessex Abortion Studies', 141; Allen, *Counselling Services*, 143–45; Abortion Law Reform Association, *A Report on NHS Abortion Services*. For examples see Pipes, *Understanding Abortion*, 60; Neustatter and Newson, *Mixed Feelings*, 59.

[113] Allen, *Counselling Services*, 143.

[114] Allen, *Counselling Services*, 164, 167, 176–77, noting that young women were particularly vulnerable to being persuaded or 'overpowered' by doctors.

[115] *Glasgow Herald*, 10 August 1982. See generally Pipes, *Understanding Abortion*, 139–40.

[116] Peel, *Unplanned Pregnancy*, 35. The report concluded that the Abortion Act was generally very strictly interpreted within the NHS but that abortion was available 'on demand' in many private clinics.

[117] OPCS, *Registrar General's Statistical Review of England and Wales for the Year 1973*. See further Sethna, 'From Heathrow Airport to Harley Street'.

[118] See e.g. 'Foreign Girls come to London', *Times*, 30 December 1968.

lucrative business of 'taxi touts' developing outside major travel hubs in search of unwitting women who might be delivered to private clinics on commission.[119] The result was

> a procession of unhappy women who after a short visit leave these shores without the foetus which entered unnoticed through the immigration barrier and minus the requisite number of Deutschmarks, Swiss francs, and American dollars. Only time will be able to assess the gravity of this complication in terms of its effect on international regard for British medicine and British ethics. Deterioration has already begun and has widespread implications which as a profession many of us deplore.[120]

In the event, this 'procession of unhappy women' dwindled swiftly as other countries' abortion laws were liberalised: the numbers travelling from France fell by over 30,000 in the course of the two years following the liberalisation of French abortion law in early 1975.[121] However, travel from the island of Ireland would remain a significant aspect of the biography of the Abortion Act: around 1,000 women from Northern Ireland and 1,500 from the Irish Republic were reported to have terminated pregnancies in England in 1973, with numbers continuing to grow over the decades to follow. The Act would remain the basis for legal abortions for women from the island of Ireland for another five decades. Travel would also persist from certain areas of Scotland into England.

Women's experience of accessing NHS services under the Abortion Act thus depended on their age, marital situation, race, class and geography. Some women received excellent care and were grateful for the time that their doctors took in exploring options with them. Others were exploited by 'Cash Before Delivery' doctors, subject to 'Bounced Cheques', resentful of their doctors' intrusive questioning and moralising judgement and, at the extreme, victims of coerced sterilisation. However, women were not passive in this process. While accorded no formal right to treatment by the Abortion Act, women exerted a powerful persuasive influence on their doctors, helping to shape their interpretations of the Abortion Act. David Baird reflects that, prior to 1968, many doctors 'probably hadn't thought about [abortion] because they said it is illegal. Unless they had some personal experience themselves, it probably wouldn't have occurred to them ... It wasn't a problem that filled their waiting rooms.'[122] Most were thus far from entrenched in absolutist

---

[119] See Sethna, 'From Heathrow Airport to Harley Street'.

[120] Stallworthy, in MPS, *Symposium*, 41–48.

[121] Law 75-17 was introduced in January 1975. Some 36,443 French women had been treated in England and Wales in 1974, falling to 4,568 in 1976. Abortion statistics have been collated from multiple volumes, published as Office of Population Censuses and Surveys, *Abortion Statistics*.

[122] Baird interviewed by Davis.

positions that saw abortion as always or never justified.[123] The Abortion Act brought the experiences of women seeking terminations into sight for a larger number and broader range of medical professionals, with their views developing and solidifying in the years after 1968. Their daily acts of interpretation, which would give meaning to the Abortion Act, were far from an exercise in abstract moral reasoning: they would rather be considered, negotiated and honed during conversations with real women describing real problems, anxieties and aspirations. In some instances – as where doctors came to resent women's perceived attempts to manipulate them through invented stories – this may have resulted in a hardening of opposition to abortion. However, the more marked effect is likely to have been that seen in the young David Paintin, with women's stories tending to engender empathy and persuade doctors towards a liberal interpretation of the Act.[124] While it was doctors who gave meaning to the 'social clause' of the Abortion Act through these quotidian acts of interpretation, women thus also played a pivotal role.

The Role of the Charitable Sector

Campaigners on both sides of the issue would also play a formative role in shaping understandings and giving meaning to the Abortion Act in these early years. Most significantly, concerns that women would struggle to access NHS abortion services within areas controlled by anti-abortion senior doctors led ALRA members to create BPAS in 1968 and the London Pregnancy Advisory Service (PAS) in 1969.[125] The first chair of the BPAS board of trustees was Francois Lafitte, the adopted son of the sexologist Havelock Ellis, a member of ALRA and the Council of the Eugenics Society and Professor of Social Policy at Birmingham University. It was initially intended that the organisation should be called Abortions Aid. However, the name was changed on the advice of the Charity Commission, which – ironically given what was to follow – believed that there would not be enough women wanting an abortion to justify awarding charitable status on so narrow a focus.[126]

BPAS initially planned to establish a 'disinterested service able to advise, and share the troubles of, couples and single women' and to put them in touch with GPs who would charge a modest fee, 'listen without hostility' and then refer them into the NHS.[127] However, this plan was swiftly revised when just 64 of more than 2,000 women thus referred were accepted for NHS treatment.

---

[123] Lewis, 'The Abortion Act (1967)'; Waite, 'Consultant Psychiatrists and Abortion'; Constable, in MPS, *Symposium*.

[124] See O'Neill, 'Abortion Games', 182–84.

[125] See Paintin, *Abortion Law Reform in Britain*, 66–72. Marie Stopes International followed in 1976.

[126] Munday interviewed by O'Neill; Paintin, *Abortion Law Reform in Britain*, 66.

[127] BPAS Archives, Francois Lafitte, witness statement in *Lafitte and ors* v *Serpentine Press and ors*, QBD, unreported (26 January 1978), 3; Munday interviewed by O'Neill.

The remainder were redirected to private London doctors where they were charged hefty fees, leaving BPAS to fear that it might become 'a machine for the enrichment of commercial abortion interests'.[128] The organisation thus needed to adapt. Diane Munday recalls:

> [E]very time there was an unmet need, we tried to close that gap and provide the service ... There were a couple of financiers who offered to put the money up for a clinic ... They put the money up, they took any profit that was made but BPAS ran it. . . . Then Nan [Smith, the first Director of BPAS] got the idea – she was a great entrepreneur – that if they could borrow money, these venture capitalists, and do it, why couldn't BPAS borrow money and do their own? Why should anybody make some profit out of it, why couldn't it be totally non-profit making? ... So slowly, as gaps in provision for women or substandard services for women emerge, BPAS says, 'this isn't acceptable. What needs doing? Okay, we will do it' ... as abuses arose, or bad practices became uncovered, we introduced something new to guard against it.[129]

The impact was significant. In 1968, two-thirds of Birmingham women seeking abortion needed to travel to another NHS region; within three years, this number had fallen to just one-fifth, as those refused access to abortion within the NHS were accepted by BPAS.[130] At a time when private clinics charged £150–£600 for an abortion,[131] BPAS charged up to £65 (prices that were 'probably the lowest in the country'), while still managing to waive charges in the neediest cases.[132] It went on to establish clinics in Brighton and London and, as a result, in 1972 changed its name to the *British Pregnancy Advisory Service*.[133] Over the decades to follow, it would continue to expand whilst remaining committed to plugging gaps in NHS provision. It also became a powerful force in driving a liberal reading of the Abortion Act.

Overseas women also began to find their way to the abortion charities. They were not always particularly welcome given 'language difficulties' and their lack of a family doctor.[134] However, in 1972, on the request of airport staff, PAS set up a Traveller Help Unit at Heathrow Airport.[135] By 1974, overseas

---

[128] BPAS Archives, Francois Lafitte, witness statement, with figures taken from Statement Regarding Surplus of Charity, 13 May 1977, both submitted in *Lafitte and ors* v *Serpentine Press and ors*, QBD, unreported (26 January 1978), 3.

[129] Munday interviewed by O'Neill.

[130] See *Registrar General's Quarterly Returns for England and Wales*, 1968; OPCS *Statistical Review*, 1971.

[131] Paintin, *Abortion Law Reform in Britain*, 67.

[132] BPAS Archives, Francois Lafitte, witness statement, submitted in *Lafitte and ors* v *Serpentine Press and ors*, QBD, unreported (26 January 1978), 3. A total of £139,959 in grants had been awarded to patients by 1976, with more money set aside to facilitate loans. See BPAS Archives, Francois Lafitte, witness statement, with figures taken from Statement Regarding Surplus of Charity, 13 May 1977.

[133] Lafitte witness statement, ibid., 4. See further Paintin, *Abortion Law Reform in Britain*, chapter 5.

[134] Paintin, *Abortion Law Reform in Britain*, 69.

[135] Ibid.

women, generally referred by doctors in France, formed around 40 per cent of the clients seen at the BPAS clinic in Brighton, where they could see a French-speaking counsellor but would be accepted for treatment only if capacity remained once those 'of the British Isles' had been accommodated.[136]

The founders of BPAS and PAS saw these organisations as a necessary but temporary solution during the Abortion Act's 'settling down' period, which should last only until the NHS was ready to take over all services.[137] Munday nonetheless reports a struggle with her conscience:

> I can remember discussing it with my husband and saying, 'On the one hand, I think I don't want anything to do with setting up an alternative private medicine system. On the other, who am I to salve my conscience by leaving women at the mercy of an unsympathetic NHS when we could do something to help them?' . . . [But] if we took that pressure off, we were letting them off the hook and leaving the private bit to run alongside. And, of course, this was exactly what had happened.[138]

By 1972, almost 60 per cent of abortions performed in England and Wales were performed outside the NHS, with a rapidly increasing proportion of them offered by the abortion charities.[139] The same development was not seen in Scotland, where no charitable sector emerged and legal abortion remained largely within the NHS.[140] Partly for this reason, Scottish abortion services would not excite the same level of controversy as seen elsewhere in Britain, where particular attention has focused on non-NHS providers. However, many women refused access to NHS services in Scotland would be forced to travel south,[141] with the Glasgow–Liverpool train becoming nicknamed 'the Abortion Express'.[142]

In 1974, Diane Munday left ALRA and moved to BPAS, where she would remain for another 16 years, deliberately retaining her self-employed status so that she 'wouldn't get the charity into hot water campaigning politically'.[143] In just one month of part-time work in the mid-1970s, she reports working on an important libel action, undertaking six public speaking engagements, writing a

---

[136] BPAS Archives, Babies for Burning Evidence 4, Francois Lafitte, draft witness statement submitted in the case of *Lafitte and ors* v *Serpentine Press and ors*, QBD, unreported (26 January 1978).

[137] Munday interviewed by O'Neill.

[138] Ibid.

[139] See Chapter 4, Figure 1, p. 117.

[140] Just 2% of terminations performed in Scotland were provided outside the NHS in 1972. See NRS, HH61/1315, Hector Monro, Scottish Office, to Tam Dalyell, House of Commons, 18 April 1972.

[141] In 1972, 7,600 abortions were carried out in Scotland, Scottish Home and Health Department (SHHD), *Health Bulletin*, vol. 31 (1973); and 835 women travelled to access services in England, OPCS, *Registrar General's Statistical Review of England and Wales for the Year 1972. Supplement on Abortion*.

[142] *Scottish Daily Record*, 16 May 1973, 3.

[143] Munday interviewed by O'Neill.

number of press releases, taking three groups of journalists on organised clinic visits (resulting in five feature articles), and writing around 30 letters to newspapers, with at least 12 of them published.[144] With an active battle for public opinion now underway, writing to challenge misleading media claims about BPAS's work would become a significant part of Munday's job, with many of her letters threatening defamation suits.[145]

Pro-Life campaigners also moved into service provision. In 1970, a second major charity, Life, was formed by breakaway SPUC members.[146] It was more absolutist in its opposition to abortion and focused on public education and practical support rather than parliamentary lobbying. Jack Scarisbrick, who co-founded the group with his wife, Nuala, explains:

> I joined SPUC but was always nervous about that because, in the early days, it was not absolutist. It seemed to me that if you allow one abortion, you allow all. And so, eventually, it was decided, with Nuala playing a major part in this, that we wanted to start something which would say no to all abortion. As much abortion as there is infanticide, you can't distinguish between the two. And, secondly, since we had known what it was like being pregnant, and not necessarily always welcome, we knew that it was impossible to say 'thou shalt not', without helping people not to. There had to be a care service for the crisis pregnancy alongside the anti-abortion talk and action. Unless there was compassion and realising the reality of the crisis pregnancy and the urgency, your anti-abortion words would sound sanctimonious, and hollow.[147]

While the Scarisbricks are Catholic, Life was established as 'a non-denominational and non-party-political association' that avoided 'preaching'[148] and would not 'express any public views on any matters pertaining to contraception or sterilisation'.[149] Over the 1970s, it began to circulate pamphlets and advertisements offering graphic descriptions of abortion procedures and describing associated risks including 'difficulty keeping your next pregnancy going' and 'permanent sterility'.[150] It also developed a network of support services including counselling during pregnancy and after abortion, referral to adoption services, temporary housing, support for women with

---

[144] BPAS Archives, Report to Trustees, 22 April 1976. The libel action concerned *Babies for Burning*, see below.

[145] Many dozens of such letters are retained in the archives. See e.g. correspondence in BPAS Archives; Lafitte Archives at the University of Birmingham, Cadbury Research Library, box 10.

[146] 'Second thoughts on life', *Daily Mirror*, 16 December 1970; BPAS Archives, Life Documents, Life constitution, no date. See generally Marsh and Chambers, *Abortion Politics*.

[147] Jack Scarisbrick interviewed by Jane O'Neill, 7 November 2017.

[148] Wellcome Library, SA/ALR/G17, Life Groups leaflet, no date; BPAS Archives, Life Documents, 'Guide to Running a LIFE Caring Service', no date, 1. See also 'Second Thoughts on Life', *Daily Mirror*, 16 December 1970.

[149] BPAS Archives, Life Documents, Life Constitution, no date.

[150] Wellcome Library, SA/ALR/G17, 'Pregnant? LIFE Will Help You', no date.

infant or disabled children, and outreach to schools, colleges and community groups.[151]

Life's services were initially informal, with members offering accommodation in their homes.[152] Josephine Quintavalle became involved when she moved to London in the 1970s. She recalls 'a great sense of voluntary work, that you should do something, and often you did it through your churches':

> There was a very strong middle-class contingency, where families didn't need two salaries, and so you had this wonderful free workforce which was the wife. They maybe had an au pair or they certainly had the chance to have somebody look after the kids periodically, so there was a strong, usually well-educated, useful number of women who could be called upon to do voluntary work in the community.[153]

Over time, Life formalised and professionalised its services, acquiring its first house in 1973 through the gift of a generous Catholic priest.[154] Services rolled out across Britain and, later, Northern Ireland. When local authorities acquired a statutory duty to house homeless pregnant women, they would frequently turn to Life for help in discharging it.[155] By the late 1970s, the charity had opened 40 houses, with another 60 in various stages of negotiation.[156] Alongside this focus on practical support, Life would also come to play a powerful role in shaping perceptions of the Abortion Act, publicising what it saw as abuses of the Act and the corresponding harms caused to women, challenging the claim that access to abortion should be made easier, and promoting their own services as a preferable, practical alternative.

The 'Living Abortus'

The nature of doctors' gatekeeper role and how it should be exercised with regard to abortions sought on 'social' grounds had been the most controversial aspect of the Abortion Act as it progressed through Parliament, and it should have surprised no one when it continued to provoke attention following the Act's introduction. However, a second controversial aspect of the Act now emerged that had passed largely unnoticed in Parliament: the upper time limit for abortion.

Public concern regarding this issue was initially raised by an abortion performed at Stobhill General Hospital, Glasgow. Dating a pregnancy was a far from exact science, then relying on physical examination and information

---

[151] BPAS Archives, Life Documents, Life Information Pack, c. late 1970s; Life Care and Housing Trust, 'Guidelines for the Management of LIFE Offices and Houses', September 1979.

[152] Scarisbrick, *Let There Be Life*, 9.

[153] Josephine Quintavalle interviewed by Jane O'Neill, 6 October 2017.

[154] Scarisbrick interviewed by O'Neill.

[155] Housing (Homeless Persons) Act 1977; Scarisbrick, *Let There Be Life*, 9–10.

[156] Marsh and Chambers, *Abortion Politics*, 60–61.

provided by the woman regarding the date of her last menstrual period. Here, believing a woman to be around 26 weeks pregnant, a gynaecologist performed a termination by hysterotomy (where the fetus is removed through a surgical incision in the uterus). A baby boy was delivered pale, limp and with no pulse. Believed to be dead, his body was placed in two paper bags and left outside the hospital boiler room on top of some bags of rubbish while the attendant had lunch and the incinerator heated up.[157] On his return, the attendant heard the baby 'whimper'. Subsequent efforts to save his life failed.[158]

The hospital's procedure for the disposal of fetal remains went curiously unremarked in subsequent reports of the case, with it being some years before there would be any serious discussion of the need for 'sensitive disposal' of fetal remains.[159] However, there was widespread shock and revulsion that a termination had been performed at what was later determined to have been around 32 weeks' gestation, with a baby then left to die. The resulting investigation recommended the prohibition of abortion when the fetus was approaching viability and the routine availability of the means of resuscitation where abortions were to be performed later in pregnancy.[160] Having taken legal advice, the Government concluded that no further action was necessary as, where a clinician had real reason to believe that a fetus was viable, there was already a legal obligation to take all reasonable steps to preserve its life irrespective of the duration of the pregnancy.[161] While legally correct, this did little to quell concerns.

A second scandal followed shortly after. While clinical research on fetal tissue predated the Abortion Act,[162] the rapid rise in the number of abortions performed openly under it had led to a corresponding increase in the tissue available, with researchers keen to make use of it.[163] In 1970, it was reported that a London clinic had sold fetuses to a researcher who planned to keep

[157] NRS, AD63/1246, Lord Advocate's Department (internal memo) 'Death of Baby at Stobhill Hospital on 20 January 1969', para. 6.

[158] 'Death of a Baby: Inquiry in Glasgow', *British Medical Journal*, 704–05; NRS, AD63/1246, Lord Advocate's Department (internal memo) 'Death of Baby at Stobhill Hospital on 20 January 1969'.

[159] See Dubow, *Ourselves Unborn*, 41, for a discussion of the marked evolution in attitudes towards the disposal of fetal remains in the USA, with 'fetal bodies ... transformed from curiosities and specimens inspiring wonder and awe into "babies" and "human bodies" deserving sympathy and burial'.

[160] 'Death of a Baby: Inquiry in Glasgow', *British Medical Journal*, 704–05; NRS, AD63/1246; Lord Advocate's Department (internal memo) 'Death of Baby at Stobhill Hospital on 20 January 1969'.

[161] *Hansard*, HC, 24 July 1969, vol. 787, cols 484–85. For the legal advice, see NRS, AD63/1246, Lord Advocate's Department (internal memo) 'Death of Baby at Stobhill Hospital on 20 January 1969'.

[162] The Royal Marsden Hospital had been financed by the Medical Research Council to run a fetal tissue bank for 12 years. Simms, 'The Great Foetus Mystery'.

[163] TNA, MH 156/151, Sir John Peel Advisory Group: use of fetuses and fetal material for research, 'Memo by the Chairman on the Written Evidence'.

them alive on a heart–lung machine until 40 weeks of development for experimentation.[164] In a macabre twist, one fetus was said to have been linked to the circulation of a dog in pursuit of immunology research.[165] Concerns were fed by broader anxieties regarding the poorly regulated activities of the 'Cash Before Delivery' doctors. The clinic was said to have been paid for the tissue,[166] leading Hugh McLaren to complain that this practice 'smack[ed] of a fish market' in human fetuses.[167]

The fact that abortions were occurring in conditions of greater transparency under the Abortion Act permitted greater scrutiny of the actions, motivations and moral sensibilities of those involved, bringing conflicting views regarding the moral status of the unborn into sharp relief. While for some fetal remains were the corpse of a tiny 'potential person' requiring 'reverential handling',[168] others saw only the 'shapeless jelly'[169] of medical waste, which offered 'a perfectly legitimate and valuable' research resource.[170] One Cambridge researcher told *The Sun* that, as a fetus is incapable of feeling pain until its brain was sufficiently formed, it was 'merely a pulsating "vegetable"'. Suggesting that this sensibility was not exclusive to medical researchers, the *Sun* journalist appeared to find nothing shocking in it, concluding that 'if a foetus can be of use in helping doctors find a way to preserving life, who really wants to stop them?'.[171]

The scandal tracked broader fault lines in opinion regarding the Abortion Act, with the Act's opponents directly attributing worrying research practices to its poor framing.[172] With the use of fetal tissue subject to no specific regulation, one reporter concluded that these reports offered the 'strongest ammunition yet for amending the Act'.[173] For his part, St John-Stevas felt strongly vindicated, having 'warned ceaselessly about undermining of respect for human life which would inevitably follow' the Act, with the implications

---

[164] 'Abortion Trade in Unborn Babies', *Daily Express*, 16 May 1970.

[165] Ibid.; St John-Stevas, 'The Scandal of the Foetuses'.

[166] The doctor concerned initially told the Department of Health and Social Security that he had bought the tissue but later claimed that no money had changed hands. TNA, BN 13/225, Use of human fetuses for research, 'Experimental Use of Foetal Material: Allegations by Mr St John-Stevas, MP'.

[167] TNA, MH 156/151, Sir John Peel Advisory Group: use of fetuses and fetal material for research, Hugh McLaren, Use of Fetuses, Memo, 15 September 1970.

[168] TNA, MH 156/151, Sir John Peel Advisory Group: use of fetuses and fetal material for research, Board for Social Responsibility (BSR), Memo to the Committee on the use of fetuses and fetal materials for research, January 1971. The BSR is part of the General Synod of the Church of England.

[169] Ibid.

[170] See generally Morgan, 'Properly Disposed of', 247–74, noting similar attitudes amongst Baltimore embryologists in the early twentieth century, 249.

[171] 'Unborn Babies: Let's Keep Cool', *Sun*, 20 May 1970.

[172] TNA, MH 156/151, Sir John Peel Advisory Group: use of fetuses and fetal material for research, Submission by the SPUC to the Peel Committee.

[173] 'Clinics Deny Foetus Sales', *Observer*, 17 May 1970.

'seen by the few, hav[ing] now been brought home to the many'.[174] *The Telegraph* summarised:

> [The view of the opponents of the Act] that an unborn child is a sacred entity, not to be destroyed except for the gravest reasons, will now be seen as reflecting a much deeper human instinct than our legislators imagined. The philosophy that regards a foetus as expendable whenever its survival is unwelcome on 'social' grounds must equally allow it to be used for the eminently social purpose of medical progress. If it is sacrilege to make practical use of a discarded foetus, what term must be applied to the fate that befell it in its mother's womb?[175]

Now the Government acted. First, it advised all licensed nursing homes that the supply of fetal material for research was 'no part of their functions' and that the imminent renewal of their licences would depend on their compliance.[176] This provoked fury amongst some doctors, with one complaining:

> I am on the obstetrics list and have been sending the foetuses to hospitals for 30 years. This is common practice among London doctors and I for one don't intend to stop doing it because of the Minister's ban. Hospitals need foetal material for research purposes and for the Minister to interfere with this perfectly legitimate and scientifically valuable routine is to my mind quite indefensible.[177]

The Telegraph also queried the fact that this restriction applied only to non-NHS services for 'what is morally wrong under a system of free enterprise cannot be morally right under socialism'.[178] However, anxieties regarding the activities of the non-NHS sector in this area were becoming firmly entrenched, with the need for an additional level of regulation to guard against the greater dangers of abusive practice in the latter taking firm hold.

Second, the Government established two reviews. The first – conducted by the Department of Health and Social Security – examined the specific claims made by St John-Stevas. It found that no 'live fetus' had been sought by the doctor at the heart of the allegations, with his use of the word 'live' rather intended to mean 'fresh', 'living cells in isolated tissue'.[179] Notwithstanding inconsistencies in the doctor's account, it was accepted that there had probably been no payment to the nursing home. His unlikely sounding explanation for the story that a fetus would be linked to a dog's circulation – that he had invented it to test the discretion of the nurse who had acted as a

---

[174] St John-Stevas, 'The Scandal of the Foetuses'.
[175] 'Anatomy Lesson', *Sunday Telegraph*, 17 May 1970.
[176] 'Crossman Foetus Ban Sparks New Row', *Evening Standard*, 19 May 1970. Richard Crossman was then Secretary of State for Social Services.
[177] Ibid.
[178] 'Anatomy Lesson', *Sunday Telegraph*, 17 May 1970.
[179] TNA, BN 13/225, Use of human fetuses for research, 'Experimental Use of Foetal Material: Allegations by Mr St John Stevas, MP'.

whistle-blower – was also believed.[180] The sympathetic framing of the report and conclusion that the matter be dropped gives some credence to St John-Stevas' suspicion of bias in the investigation, perhaps because the doctor was acquainted with the investigator:

> No harm has been done to the public except from the undesirable publicity that has already occurred . . . [The doctor] is a rather juvenile personality who can do and say recklessly silly things but he is not fundamentally ill-intentioned or ungenerous and he is a devoted and useful worker. There is no point in damaging him unnecessarily.[181]

Madeleine Simms complained that, on the contrary, the Department's findings had been 'hushed up' to protect St John-Stevas from public embarrassment.[182] Whatever the truth of the matter, the investigation's conclusions received far less coverage than had the initial reports: devoid of 'scandal', noted Simms, it was no longer news.[183] This pattern of widespread, sensationalist coverage of a shocking story, with the results of the subsequent investigation far less widely reported and disbelieved or attacked as a cover-up, would recur repeatedly over the subsequent decades.[184]

The Government also established a Committee to investigate the broader 'ethical, medical, social and legal implications of using fetuses and fetal material for research'.[185] The Chair was former RCOG President Sir John Peel, who had been praised for his diplomatic skills and negotiation of deep divisions within the RCOG in chairing the committee that advised the Government as the Abortion Act progressed through Parliament.[186] There was thus much to recommend him as the person to 'take the steam out of the public debate'[187] and produce 'a formula to satisfy public anxiety without inhibiting research'.[188] Peel found that research using fetal material was of such public health benefit that it should continue. However, with private abortion clinics controlled by those who 'are not always the most attractive

[180] TNA, MH 156/151, Sir John Peel Advisory Group: use of fetuses and fetal material for research, Mr Wendt, Report by RHL Cohen, 17 July 1970.

[181] Ibid.

[182] Simms, 'The Great Foetus Mystery', 592.

[183] Ibid.

[184] See Chapter 4.

[185] Department of Health and Social Security, *The Use of Fetuses and Fetal Material for Research: Report of the Advisory Group* (*Peel Report*), 1. See 'Foetus work inquiry pledge', *Guardian*, 19 May 1970.

[186] Members of Council had included Hugh McLaren, as well as several Roman Catholics who objected to abortion on religious grounds. 'Sir John Peel' Obituary, *Telegraph*, 2 January 2006.

[187] TNA, BN 13/225, Use of human fetuses for research, Letter from Baroness Serota to Harold Wilson PM, 19 May 1970.

[188] TNA, MH 156/151, Sir John Peel Advisory Group: use of fetuses and fetal material for research, Minutes of 1st Meeting of AG, 30 July 1970.

or scrupulous members of the medical profession',[189] robust safe[
needed. Approval should be sought from a hospital ethics comn......
any fetal material was used; no payment should be made for such material;
researchers should enjoy a right of conscientious objection; no experiments
should be conducted upon a viable fetus that were inconsistent with treatment
necessary to promote its life; and tissue should only be used where there was
'no known objection' from a 'parent'.[190] The relatively modest weight
accorded to women's wishes reflected the concern that to ask for explicit
consent 'could be an unnecessary source of distress to parents'.[191] The
Committee also made a further recommendation, which clearly went beyond
its terms of reference: that for 'ethical, medical and social reasons', gestation of
20 weeks should be regarded as *prima facie* proof of viability, with all relevant
legislation amended accordingly.[192]

The Peel Code was swiftly implemented in its near entirety and was
followed until the late 1980s, when further scientific developments forced
its review.[193] The aim of producing a formula to satisfy public anxiety
without inhibiting research was largely met: certainly, the UK avoided the
pitched controversy seen in the USA, where four Boston doctors who had
transferred fetuses from pathology to research laboratories were shortly to be
charged with 'violation of sepulture'.[194] However, the Committee's recommendation regarding the upper time limit was seen as beyond its remit in
'seeking to protect the fetus against unwarranted abortion rather than
against unjustifiable research'.[195] The Government deferred consideration
of this issue pending publication of the findings of the Lane Committee.[196]
Before that time, however, the most horrifying and wide-ranging attack of all
on the Abortion Act would be published. Diane Munday recalls that the
book, *Babies for Burning*, 'would have destroyed the Act, I am in no doubt at
all, unless we had done something'.[197]

[189] TNA, MH 156/151, Judge E. B. McLellan (Peel Committee member), 'Provisional Statement of
      the Law Concerning Experiments on Fetuses and Fetal Material' (October 1970), 2.
[190] Peel Code of Practice, Recommendation 3, in *Peel Report*, 12.
[191] *Peel Report*, 9. Woods and Taylor, 'Ethical and Governance Challenges in Human Fetal Tissue
      Research', 17, described this as 'well-meaning but paternalistic'.
[192] *Peel Report*, 6–7. Peel himself emphasised that the Committee's remit was research not
      abortion, TNA, MH 156/151, Sir John Peel Advisory Group: use of foetuses and foetal material
      for research, Minutes of 1st Meeting of AG, 30 July 1970.
[193] *Review of the Guidance on the Research Use of Fetuses and Fetal Material* (Polkinghorne
      Report).
[194] Dubow, *Ourselves Unborn*, chapter 3.
[195] TNA, MH 156/151, Sir John Peel Advisory Group: use of fetuses and fetal material for
      research, Report on the Peel AG on the Use of Fetuses for Research, 4 October 1971, signed BR
      Rayner pp DM Jackson.
[196] Ibid.
[197] Munday interviewed by O'Neill.

Babies for Burning

Babies for Burning resulted from an investigation conducted by two freelance journalists who – in their words – had compiled a 'disturbing dossier that should make even the most hardened pro-abortionists re-examine their dogma'.[198] Michael Litchfield and Susan Kentish had posed as a couple facing an unwanted pregnancy and visited non-NHS pregnancy testing services, doctors' surgeries and abortion clinics. They were armed with a concealed tape recorder, allowing them to claim that '[e]very fact we state, we can prove'.[199] Shortly before Lane was due to report, in March 1974, their stories were emblazoned across the front pages of successive editions of the most widely read Sunday paper, the *News of the World*, under the banner of 'Phantom Babies'.[200] In December, the stories were repeated and expanded in the book.[201]

Babies for Burning offered an important salvo in the battle over the meaning of the Abortion Act. First, it claimed to have proved 'beyond all doubt that a state of abortion on demand exists in Britain'.[202] Equipped with a 'shallow cover story' of 'a childless, utterly selfish' married couple with 'no possible reason in the world for qualifying for an abortion under the Act',[203] Kentish was repeatedly accepted for treatment. One service provider told her that while she could obtain an abortion in a private clinic, she would not stand 'an earthly chance' within the NHS for, after all, 'what good reason have you got to say you don't want this child?'.[204] Another emphasised that two gynaecologists would make a final decision but advised that 'if you did not want to have a child at all – that's good enough for them'.[205] A third reassured her that, while she would need to see two doctors, she would find them 'very sympathetic'; all that mattered were the couple's 'private reasons' and that it was 'nothing to do with anybody else'.[206] Defending herself in a subsequent libel action, Kentish explained that they had found that the Abortion Act was being 'abused and treated with contempt'.[207]

---

[198] Litchfield and Kentish, *Babies for Burning*, back cover.

[199] Litchfield and Kentish, *Babies for Burning*, 11–12.

[200] The reports appeared over three weeks from 24 February 1974 at a time when the newspaper reported a circulation of 5.5 million. See BPAS Archives, *Bloom v Litchfield, Kentish and others*, QBD (7–8 March 1977), transcript, 7.

[201] Litchfield and Kentish, *Babies for Burning*.

[202] Ibid., 76.

[203] Ibid.

[204] Litchfield and Kentish, 'Abortions with a Chauffeur Service', *News of the World*, 17 March 1974.

[205] Litchfield and Kentish, 'If you Don't Want a Child, That's Good Enough', *News of the World*, 17 March 1974.

[206] Litchfield and Kentish, *Babies for Burning*, 113.

[207] BPAS Archives, *Bloom v Litchfield, Kentish and others*, QBD (7–8 March 1977), transcript, 28. See Chapter 5.

Thus far, *Babies for Burning* contained an important 'core of truth'.[208] However, its allegations ranged far beyond the claim that abortion was available on demand, painting a horrifying picture of the excesses of a barely regulated, profit-driven 'abortion industry'. Amongst the litany of appalling abuses alleged, three stood out. First, it was claimed that women were being routinely, deliberately and wrongly diagnosed as pregnant in order that they could be sold unnecessary abortions: these were the 'phantom babies' of the newspaper headlines. In one of the most striking allegations of the investigation – published under the banner 'Dear Sir, We Regret you are Pregnant' – Michael Litchfield described how positive pregnancy diagnoses were returned by all seven of the pregnancy advisory services to which he had sent his own urine for testing.[209]

Second, the journalists reported 'harrowing and macabre' tales of 'butchery and carnage' in the USA, suggesting that these offered a cautionary tale of 'what racketeering and profiteering can besiege a country without stringent legislation'. American gynaecologists 'who specialise in abortion rather than life-preservation' were claimed to bribe pregnant women to have abortions, with one Dr Malcolm Ridley claiming to have been 'dropping [the] child into an incinerator', even as expectant husbands 'have been clutching a bunch of flowers and wiping away the nervous sweat'. Dr Ridley also described deliberately performing later abortions in such a way as to produce live babies, who might be sold for medical experimentation, 'some of them living for more than a year without being officially born'.[210]

Third, it was claimed that British fetuses were being 'sold to cosmetic factories to be churned into soap'.[211] Potently combining concerns regarding later abortions with a deep suspicion of the motivation of abortion doctors in the private sector, the journalists claimed that a doctor who admired the 'very progressive ideas and philosophies' of Adolf Hitler had told Litchfield:

> You see, I get some very big babies. It's such a shame to toss them in the incinerator, when they could be put to so much better use. We do a lot of late terminations. We specialise in them. I do ones that other people won't touch. I do them at seven months without hesitation. The law says twenty-eight weeks is the legal limit, but it is impossible to determine at what stage a termination was performed after the baby is burned, so it does not matter when one does it, really. If the mother is prepared to take the risk, then I'm game.
>
> Now, many of the babies I get are fully-formed and are living for quite a time before they are disposed of. One morning, I had four of them lined up crying their heads off. I hadn't the time to kill them there and then because we were so

---

[208] 'Abortion Horror Tales Revealed as Fantasies', *Sunday Times*, 30 March 1975.
[209] *Daily Express*, 2 October 1974.
[210] Litchfield and Kentish, *Babies for Burning*, 171–73.
[211] Litchfield and Kentish, *Babies for Burning*, back cover.

busy. I was so loathe to drop them in the incinerator because there was so much animal fat that could have been used commercially.[212]

These more shocking allegations would eventually be emphatically disproven or, at best, left uncorroborated due to conveniently mislaid audio cassettes. However, *Babies for Burning* remains a fascinating artefact of the cultural struggles regarding the meaning of a highly controversial law then in its early infancy. The stories fell upon fertile ground, finding a readership already horrified by what it had heard regarding the operation of the Abortion Act and prepared to believe the worst of those who worked within abortion services. Many important commentators – including MPs and at least two prominent *Times* journalists – repeated its claims uncritically,[213] with *Babies for Burning* becoming 'the most influential medical book of the 1970s, simply because so many people believed its fantastic allegations'.[214] It was republished in at least four languages, quickly becoming established as the 'bible of the pro-life movement'.[215] Diane Munday recalls attending a 'very big meeting', with anti-abortion supporters bussed in:

> The Catholic Church organised them. The priest and a couple of nuns would be on the coach. They would not be charged, they'd get a day out and all for free. Brownie points for the effort! So who would not go? . . . [*Babies for Burning* is] black, size of a Penguin, with little red writing. Very striking. I just looked and I just saw a sea of these books. The authors sent a copy to every MP. They all had copies. And they were just standing up waving it, shouting, 'murderer, murderer, murderer!'[216]

With the journalists' original audio recordings and full transcripts still available, *Babies for Burning* also offers a fascinating insight into early service provision under the Abortion Act.[217] It confirms the widespread existence of abortion on request in the non-NHS sector, the lengthy and detailed interviews that preceded the authorisation of an abortion and – while this features nowhere in the journalists' published reports – numerous instances of the sympathetic care offered to women.

Diane Munday led the fight against *Babies for Burning*, foreshadowing the central advocacy role that BPAS would come to play in shaping

---

[212] Litchfield and Kentish, *Babies for Burning*, 148.

[213] R. Butt, 'This Awful Silence Hanging over Abortion on Demand', *Times*, 23 January 1975; Leo Abse, 'Leo Abse MP on the Murder Trade of the London Abortion Clinics', *Spectator*, 18 January 1975; Malcolm Muggeridge, 'What the Abortion Argument is About', *Sunday Times*, 2 February 1975; BPAS Archives, transcript of interview with Sue Kentish on *The Jimmy Young Show*, BBC Radio 2, 27 December 1974.

[214] Devlin, 'Book for Burning?'.

[215] BPAS Archives, Evidence 4, Francois Lafitte, affidavit in *Lafitte and ors*.

[216] Munday interviewed by O'Neill.

[217] We consulted the files while they were still held at BPAS. All paper files have since been donated to the Wellcome Collection. No attempt was made to listen to the cassette recordings given their age and likely fragility.

understandings of the Abortion Act. First, she persuaded *The Sunday Times* to investigate, working with journalists to demonstrate that many purported 'facts' presented in the book were inventions.[218] Litchfield had not, as he had claimed, been awarded a Pulitzer Prize. Dr Ridley did not exist. Far from being an admirer of Hitler, the 'babies for soap' doctor turned out to be an elderly, rather deaf, Jewish survivor of the concentration camps who had lost his wife and son in Auschwitz (he told *The Times* that he had offered to supply fetal material for research, without charge and subject to proper approvals).[219] The journalists claimed that recordings of this most shocking and damning interview had been lost somewhere at the *News of the World*.[220] A subsequent police investigation found that only those with a strong vested interest in confirming the story would testify to having heard it, and that Litchfield himself was a 'thoroughly unreliable witness'.[221] While the investigating officer was also suspicious of the doctor involved – concluding that he may well either have engaged in the practices described in the book or, at least, turned a blind eye to them[222] – medical commentators were unconvinced, emphasising that the story was medically implausible given the lack of sub-cutaneous fat in a fetus.[223] The full extent of the intricate deceit that had underpinned the headline, 'Dear Sir, We Regret you are Pregnant', would be revealed only many years later in a successful libel action brought by one of the pregnancy testing services named in the reports.[224]

The abortion charities had also been roundly attacked in the book, with a chapter devoted to an elaborate set of allegations regarding the exploitation of overseas women in BPAS's Brighton clinic.[225] BPAS was well acquainted with the law of libel, having been the subject of regular attacks in local newspapers (a press cuttings agency sent a 'great fat envelope every morning' with 'two or three hundred' items to read).[226] Having found some 'friendly lawyers', Munday persuaded the BPAS trustees that they needed to sue, notwithstanding the costs, explaining, 'we can't let it go; it will destroy the Abortion Act'.[227] After a protracted struggle, on the day before the trial was due to start, the charity won an apology and full retraction of all allegations against it, which Munday ensured was well publicised, with a well-attended press conference

---

[218] Munday interviewed by O'Neill.

[219] 'Abortion Horror Tales Revealed as Fantasies', *Sunday Times*, 30 March 1975.

[220] House of Commons, *Special Reports and Minutes of Evidence of the Select Committee on the Abortion (Amendment) Bill*, evidence given by Michael Litchfield and Susan Kentish, paras 1282–94, 1301, 7 July 1975.

[221] TNA, DPP 2/5536, Special Officer's Report Re 'Babies for Burning', 6 February 1975.

[222] 'One suspects also that [the doctor] has either engaged in disposal of foetuses for soap or turned a blind eye to the practice.' TNA, DPP 2/5536, document signed DGW, 18 July 1975.

[223] E.g. Devlin, 'Book for Burning?'.

[224] BPAS Archives, *Pond v News Group Newspapers* QBD, 11 July 1980, unreported.

[225] Litchfield and Kentish, *Babies for Burning*, Section 3: The Charities.

[226] Munday interviewed by O'Neill.

[227] Ibid.

held at a pub in Fleet Street offering free drinks for the press ('that brings them in!').[228] Two of the other parties named in the book also sued, with the owner of the pregnancy testing service winning very significant damages.[229] The publisher of *Babies for Burning* was liquidated;[230] Litchfield and Kentish were bankrupted.[231]

While roundly discredited, *Babies for Burning* nonetheless had an important ongoing impact. Most immediately, for those directly involved, it was a 'horrible', 'awful' experience, with Caroline Woodroffe (then Director of the Brook Advisory Service) recalling one 'wonderful' doctor who never fully recovered from the 'terrible breach of trust'.[232] The wider chilling effect on those working within abortion services or considering whether to enter them is impossible to quantify but easy to imagine.[233] Second, Dilys Cossey suggests that the 'mega publicity' thus generated had 'fixed in the psyche of Parliament that there were lots of abuses going on', with the findings of the Lane Committee 'knocked ... off the agenda'.[234] Yet with so many of its sensationalist stories subsequently disproven, the book had also damaged the credibility of those arguing for restrictive reform.[235] In interview, Jack Scarisbrick reflected that the book 'didn't do us any good, I think'.[236]

The Lane Committee

Between publication of the *News of the World* 'phantom babies' stories and *Babies for Burning*, the long-awaited findings of the Lane Committee finally appeared. The Committee's work had been 'most harmonious and happy' if greatly protracted by being conducted in members' spare time alongside other professional commitments: Mrs Justice Lane wrote the whole of the first volume herself, except for the historical notes, which were contributed partly by a Committee member and partly by her husband.[237] The full Committee and its subcommittees met on dozens of occasions; made over 20 visits to hospitals and private clinics; surveyed hospitals, clinics, patients and social workers; considered 'numerous' published works; and took oral and written

---

[228] Ibid.

[229] BPAS Archives, *Lafitte and ors* v *Serpentine Press and ors*, QBD, apology read in open court, 26 January 1978; *Pond* v *News Group Newspapers* QBD, 11 July 1980, unreported; *Pond* v *Litchfield and Kentish* QBD, 8 December 1982, unreported; *Bloom* v *Litchfield, Kentish and others*, QBD, 7–8 March 1977, unreported. See further Chapter 5.

[230] BPAS Archives, various papers relating to Serpentine's liquidation.

[231] BPAS Archives, Summary of Debtor's Statement of Affairs for Kentish, 4 August 1981 and Litchfield, 19 February 1982.

[232] Caroline Woodroffe interviewed by Jane O'Neill, 26 October 2017.

[233] See further Chapter 8, p. 270.

[234] Dilys Cossey interviewed by Jane O'Neill, 4 October 2017.

[235] See Chapter 3, p. 73.

[236] Scarisbrick interviewed by O'Neill.

[237] Lane, *Hear the Other Side*, 153–54.

evidence from hundreds of individuals and organisations.[238] Th
hard to reach a unanimous position that would avoid diluting the
their findings, with such consensus achievable only following maₙy ᴜays of
discussion and sifting of evidence.[239] Moreover, at least some members saw
benefits to allowing time for the Abortion Act to bed in and did not rush to
conclude their work.[240]

The evidence gathered by Lane was voluminous, varied and, inevitably,
often conflicting. However, certain themes were dominant, reflecting the early
problems in the implementation of the Act described above. Many witnesses
spoke to the pressures upon hospital resources and personnel, the geographical variations in the implementation of the Act and resulting inequalities in
services, the activities of the private sector, the large numbers of foreign
women accessing services, the interpretation of the 'social clause' and difficulties in asserting conscientious objection rights.[241] Some of these issues were
seen as less of a concern by the Scottish witnesses, who believed it necessary
for Scotland to be included in the review only for the sake of 'uniformity in the
law rather than any current clamant problem in Scotland'.[242]

Nonetheless, numerous submissions received from witnesses on both sides
of the border requested the reduction of the upper time limit for abortion.
Such requests fell into two broad categories: first, some proposed a much
lower limit (most frequently 12 weeks), sometimes coupled with the suggestion that abortion should be more easily available within that period; and
second, 'many responsible medical, nursing and other organisations and
individuals' recommended a limit that might better reflect viability (typically
suggesting 20–26 weeks).[243] Many doctors favoured the suggestion that the
time limit should be reduced to 24 weeks, in light of the availability of 'modern
support systems'.[244] Nursing organisations tended to be more conservative,
voicing strong support for the upper limit of 20 weeks recommended by

[238] *Lane Report*, vol. 1, paras 4–10, noting that 33 plenary meetings were held over 54 days, with
the four subcommittees chalking up a further 31 meetings between them (Medical and Social;
Procedural; the National Health Service; and the Private Sector).

[239] Wivel, 'Abortion Policy and Politics on the Lane Committee'; Pereira Gray, 'The Lane
Committee', presentation at *Abortion Act 1967 Conference: A Promise Fulfilled?* Royal College
of Obstetricians and Gynaecologists, London, 24–25 October 2017.

[240] Cheetham, 'The Lane Committee', comments made at *Abortion Act 1967 Conference:
A Promise Fulfilled?*, Royal College of Obstetricians and Gynaecologists, London, 24–25
October 2017.

[241] See generally *Lane Report*, vols 1 and 2. See further Donald, 'Naught for Your Comfort', 279,
on discrimination in appointments processes.

[242] NRS, HH61/1315, W. Miller to R. Bell, 4 November 1970; W. Miller, SHHD, to R. Hughes,
Department of Health and Social Security, 16 November 1970.

[243] Lane Report, vol. 1, paras 276–77.

[244] NRS, HH60/665, R. P. Fraser to G. N. Monro, 8 December 1973.

Peel,[245] or favouring 12 weeks, after which time morbidity rates rose and greater distress was caused to patients and staff.[246]

Several churches and religious groups submitted evidence. Unsurprisingly, the Catholic Church offered the harshest criticism of the Act, claiming that it provided 'abortion on demand', that overseas women were 'actively facilitated' in seeking abortions, that in 'many instances' abortions had 'adverse effects', and that Catholic gynaecologists were subject to discrimination in appointment processes. It also noted considerable support amongst Catholics for a 12 week upper time limit on abortion.[247] The Church of England was less trenchant in its criticisms but cautioned that abortion should not be used to replace contraception, emphasising the importance of high-quality counselling services and lamenting geographical variation in access to abortion. It nonetheless refrained from advocating for restrictive amendment of the Abortion Act.[248]

Large numbers of women also gave evidence, reporting both positive and negative experiences of seeking to access abortion services, with many emphasising the difficulty of obtaining a prompt referral or the impact of being turned away by a trusted practitioner with a conscientious objection to abortion. The final report emphasised 'the great importance of [the woman's] wishes' and called for medical practitioners to ensure that each woman's case was 'carefully considered' in light of them.[249] Elizabeth Lane would later describe how her position – which had initially been formed through trying criminal cases of illegal abortion – shifted during the course of the Committee's work. While she remained 'wholly unimpressed by those who, sometimes fiercely, advocated abortion on demand', she had gradually come firmly 'to believe in the rightness of the Act, despite the abuses of it which existed'.[250]

The Committee's findings were published in April 1974 in a detailed 200 page report, accompanied by appendices and supporting volumes of statistical evidence and patient surveys. Given the furore surrounding Litchfield and Kentish's reports in the *News of the World* and the scathing criticisms articulated by many witnesses, its strong and unanimous support for

---

[245] E.g. Scottish Association of Nurse Administrators, Royal College of Midwives (Scottish Council) and the Scottish District Nursing Association.

[246] NRS, HH102/1232, PLC, Submission of Royal College of Midwives (Scottish Council), 30 July 1974.

[247] Wellcome Library, SA/ALR/C25, Memorandum Prepared by a Representative Catholic Committee under the Chairmanship of the Bishop of Brentwood for submission to the Lane Committee, c. 1971.

[248] Wellcome Library, SA/ALR/C25, Church of England Board for Social Responsibility, Evidence Submitted to the Lane Committee on the Working of the Abortion Act 1967, December 1971; *Guardian*, 5 April 1974.

[249] Wivel, 'Abortion Policy and Politics on the Lane Committee', 125–26.

[250] Lane, *Hear the Other Side*, 151. See further Wivel, 'Abortion Policy and Politics on the Lane Committee'.

the Abortion Act took the Act's critics and defenders equally by sur report acknowledged significant problems with the Act's operation, ...g the 'considerable strain' imposed on the NHS, pronounced inequalities in services and instances of 'gross irresponsibility' and profiteering within the private sector.[251] Overall, however, problems with the implementation of the Abortion Act were judged to be greatly outweighed by its benefits in alleviating a 'vast amount of individual suffering'.[252] Abuses were 'confined to a small minority of doctors', with the non-NHS sector having 'enabled many patients to have treatment in the privacy and with the amenities they desire', compensating for deficiencies in NHS provision.[253]

Lane's recommendations thus tended towards emphasising the need for continuity, subject to some further regulation. Services should remain part of obstetrics and gynaecology rather than be dealt with through the establishment of separate abortion units within the NHS; private sector provision should remain without statutory restriction regarding the qualifications of the doctors involved or statutory control of fees; and non-resident women should continue to be permitted access to services. Further, abortion decisions should remain in the hands of doctors, not women, with those who played Ingram's game of 'Woman's Lib' condemned as 'not only failing to observe the criteria of the Act' but also 'failing to give [the woman] the care she needs'.[254]

Crucially, rather than recommending significant statutory reform, Lane thus made the case for more robust 'administrative and professional action' through licensing of services and better public education regarding contraception.[255] The Peel Code was welcomed,[256] and – having noted the 'revulsion and distress' caused to some NHS nurses and other ancillary staff charged with the disposal of fetal tissue – further arrangements for appropriate disposal were recommended, with operating doctors themselves advised to carry out as much of this work as possible.[257] The Committee's one suggestion for statutory reform concerned the upper time limit for abortion. Having given 'anxious consideration' to evidence that aborted fetuses had shown signs of life, the Committee found no case where a delivery at less than 24 weeks' gestation had resulted in a child surviving.[258] On this basis, Mrs Justice Lane was eventually persuaded to join other Committee members in making a unanimous recommendation that the appropriate limit was 24 weeks.[259]

---

[251] *Lane Report*, vol. 1, paras 601–03.
[252] *Lane Report*, vol. 1, para. 600.
[253] *Lane Report*, vol. 1, paras 603–04.
[254] For the full list of recommendations, see *Lane Report*, vol. 1, Section W.
[255] *Lane Report*, vol. 1, para. 605.
[256] *Lane Report*, vol. 1, paras 317–19.
[257] *Lane Report*, vol. 1, para. 319.
[258] *Lane Report*, vol. 1, para. 279.
[259] See Wivel, 'Abortion Policy and Politics on the Lane Committee', 122.

The Lane Report was generally well received. The *Daily Mail* found itself 'in sympathy with [its] central judgment' that while state-subsidised contraceptives and more abortions were 'sad and controversial causes to champion . . . sadder, far sadder to our way of thinking, is the bringing into this world of unwanted babies, many of whom grow up as deprived children'.[260] The RCOG also welcomed it, albeit with a minority of Council members regretting that the Committee's terms of reference precluded it from taking a view on the appropriateness of the 'social grounds' for termination.[261] A joint response from the Church of England and the Methodist Church was likewise supportive.[262]

On the other hand, the Catholic press was highly critical of the report,[263] and SPUC was bitterly disappointed that none of the restrictive amendments it had suggested were included.[264] While SPUC had initially welcomed the formation of the Committee, and especially the appointment of Lane[265] – who, on her own account, had initially been far from a liberal on the issue – it now rejected the report on the basis that it had not reviewed the evidence 'in a spirit of independent enquiry', having been 'biased in favour of a liberal abortion policy from the start'.[266] In response, it organised a rally attended by an estimated 60,000 people, with speakers including the veteran journalist Malcolm Muggeridge, William Price MP, who called the report 'one of the greatest whitewashes in the history of government enquiries', and Michael Litchfield.[267]

Unsurprisingly, the report was received more positively by Pro-Choice campaigners. Madeleine Simms would later claim Mrs Justice Lane as 'an unsung heroine of the Women's movement' (recognising that 'she would hardly have welcomed the accolade').[268] The Director of BPAS, Nan Smith, praised it as 'splendidly done',[269] and Diane Munday was so pleased with its 'vindication of all we have fought for' that she arranged for a summary to be sent to every MP.[270] Her own personal copy of the Report is now dog-eared,

---

[260] *Daily Mail*, 4 April 1974.

[261] Archives of the Royal College of Obstetricians and Gynaecologists, RCOG A4/16/18, Comments on the Report of the CWAA, from meeting held 15 June 1974.

[262] Wellcome Library, SA/ALR/C25, Church of England Board for Social Responsibility, Evidence Submitted to the Lane Committee on the Working of the Abortion Act 1967, December 1971; *Guardian*, 5 April 1974.

[263] *Catholic Herald*, 11 April 1974; 26 April 1974; 3 May 1974; St John-Stevas in 'Little Enlightenment from Lane', *The Tablet*, 13/20 April 1974, 362, suggesting that the Government had loaded the Committee, appointing only those with a 'pro-abortion bias'.

[264] Wellcome Library, SA/ALR/C25, Memorandum from the Society for the Protection of Unborn Children to the Lane Committee on the working of the Abortion Act, December 1971.

[265] 'How a Thwarted Pressure Group Reacts', *Sunday Times*, 11 August 1974.

[266] SPUC Bulletin no. 7, cited in 'How a Thwarted Pressure Group Reacts', *Sunday Times*, 11 August 1974.

[267] *Times*, 29 April 1974; BPAS Archives, Babies for Burning, transcript of BBC, *The World This Weekend*, 28 April 1974. An appendix to *Babies for Burning* describes the Lane Report as a 'whitewash', Litchfield and Kentish, *Babies for Burning*, 186.

[268] Simms, 'Remembering Mrs. Lane', National Abortion Campaign Newsletter 4, May 1995, cited in Wivel, 'Abortion Policy and Politics on the Lane Committee', 135.

[269] *Guardian*, 4 April 1974.

[270] Diane Munday Papers (awaiting cataloguing in the Wellcome Library), Miscellaneous Press Cuttings, Copy of the covering memo signed by Diane Munday, June 1974.

heavily annotated and held together by tape and treasury tags, powerfully illustrating the extent to which it became a repeated point of reference over the years to come.[271] However, Pro-Choice campaigners were not unequivocal in their praise. With the language of women's liberation now starting to take hold, they too criticised the Report, citing its refusal to recognise that women are 'in the best position to judge for ourselves what we want'.[272]

It is difficult to overstate the importance of the Lane Report to the biography of the Abortion Act. With a Conservative Government in power from 1970 to 1974, regular media stories highlighting the activities of 'Cash Before Delivery' doctors and sustained Pro-Life campaigning, there would almost certainly have been a parliamentary majority in favour of restricting the Act. The Committee's ongoing work offered an important buffer against immediate legislative action. In the meantime, even as the negative press coverage continued and the total number of abortions rose, maternal mortality rates fell and the public and medical profession became more used to, and more inclined to accept, legal abortion.[273] Thereafter, the Committee's findings offered an important perspective and a robust evidence base against which the more hyperbolic claims of abuses under the Act might be judged, suggesting that – where true – these did not reflect endemic problems but were rather the work of a minority. Its recommendation for regulatory action rather than statutory reform would also prove extremely influential.

Nonetheless, the Report could not hope to end controversy regarding the Abortion Act. And, for now, the Government delayed in responding to its recommendations, allowing emotions to continue to run high. One prominent supporter of the Abortion Act later argued:

> All that was needed in November 1974 when Labour Member James White drew lucky in the Ballot for Private Members' Bills was for a match to be put to the fire and this was supplied by the shocking allegations made in the book *Babies for Burning*. The conclusions of the Lane Committee were swept aside in the emotional surge of horror and disgust.[274]

These early years had seen nothing more than the opening salvoes of the war to restrict the Abortion Act. With the emergence of the second wave of the women's movement now claiming abortion rights as an important plank of female liberation, decades of battles both inside and outside Parliament were still to come.

---

[271] Copy now in possession of the authors.

[272] Underwood, 'The Lane Abortion Report'; see also Temkin, 'The Lane Committee Report on the Abortion Act', 659–60.

[273] Potts et al., *Abortion*, 313; see further Wivel, 'Abortion Policy and Politics on the Lane Committee', 135.

[274] BPAS Archives, Sinclair, 'Abortion and Parliament 1953–1978' in Birth Control Trust, *Abortion: Ten Years On*, May 1978, 14.

3

The Parliamentary Battle for Restrictive Reform

[A]ttack after attack after attack kept coming.[1]

Winning a high place in the ballot to bring a Private Member's Bill is precious. Most MPs will never enjoy the opportunity of guaranteed time in the packed parliamentary schedule to attempt legal reform on an issue of their own choosing; none would willingly waste it on 'a minor cause or tilting at gigantic windmills'.[2] In the five years following the publication of the Lane Report, no fewer than three MPs – James White, William Benyon and John Corrie – were sufficiently convinced of the necessity and feasibility of wide-ranging restrictive reform of the Abortion Act to choose to devote their Ballot Bills to the issue; a decade later, David Alton and Ann Widdecombe would follow them. The most furious battles over the Abortion Act were fought during these next 15 years. The Ballot Bills were accompanied by a constant stream of presentation and Ten Minute Rule Bills, abortion amendments tabled to other bills and Early Day Motions. Millions signed petitions concerning abortion law reform; hundreds of thousands marched; tens of thousands lobbied their MPs; and many thousands, if not millions, of newspaper articles and media broadcasts discussed the issue.[3]

Outside Parliament, the Pro-Life movement was initially clearly in the ascendancy. However, a powerful mass Pro-Choice movement, grounded in the emerging women's liberation movement, would now emerge to rival it. It is often assumed that the Abortion Act was a result of the women's movement. The opposite is closer to the truth. First, the possibility of planning families and careers given by greater fertility control made it far easier for women to participate in public life, including in political campaigning. Second, attacks

---

[1] Diane Munday interviewed by Jane O'Neill, 10 November 2017.

[2] David Steel, describing his decision to focus on abortion; see Chapter 1, p. 6. At the start of each new parliamentary year, backbench MPs can enter a ballot and those who draw high places may present a Bill of their choosing. These Ballot Bills take priority over other Private Members' Bills when time is allocated for debates and so have a better chance of becoming law. In the House of Lords, a Private Member's Bill ballot takes place at the start of a session to determine the order of the first 25 Private Members' Bills to be introduced.

[3] On Pro-Life campaigning over this period, see Dee, *The Anti-Abortion Campaign in England*.

on the Abortion Act would be a powerful galvanising force for mass feminist mobilisation and the forging of important coalitions. Third, the movement would be profoundly shaped by these campaigns: while Pro-Life campaigners drew on the infrastructure offered by churches for grass-roots mobilisation, Pro-Choice campaigners turned to the Labour Movement. Further, within Parliament, the repeated attacks upon the Abortion Act – led mainly by Tories and primarily by men – would provoke the first occasion for female Labour MPs to bond together as such, provoked by the indifference of their male colleagues. They would claim the Abortion Act not just, as David Steel had done, to be a humane and necessary public health measure offering relief for women in desperate circumstances; they would defend it as a fundamental prerequisite for women's liberty and equality.

David Alton reflects that debates regarding abortion have been 'undoubtedly the nastiest' on any subject within the House of Commons, 'run[ning] on tram lines that never converge', with 'no shared premises or ground rules'.[4] They were so bitter because, while ostensibly about abortion, these debates were always also about other things: speakers would draw on deeply conflicting familial and gender norms, ideas regarding personal and state responsibility and assumptions about the respective roles of religion and science in ordering the world.[5] While the debate would indeed run on tram lines that would never converge, the course of those tram lines would nonetheless change markedly over these next 15 years, with the Corrie and Alton Bills separated by far more than the eight years that divided them. John Corrie would offer a reassertion of Conservative family values and personal responsibility against a perceived pervasive moral decline. Aiming to occupy a middle ground between warring factions, he proposed to confine the Abortion Act to what he saw as the limits originally intended by Parliament, accepting the need for abortion but foreseeing a range of measures designed to limit access to it to truly 'deserving' women. David Alton was cut from a different cloth. Motivated by a principled absolutist opposition to abortion grounded in his strong Catholic faith, he spoke a language of social justice, feminism, civil rights and science infused with morality. Rather than seeking to distinguish between 'deserving' and 'undeserving' women, he spoke to the popular intuition that later abortions were morally qualitatively different from earlier ones, proposing a narrow reform focused exclusively on reducing the upper time limit. In 1990, when – after years of filibustering and strategic exploitation of parliamentary procedures to block reform – an opportunity for a meaningful vote on abortion would finally arrive, the debate would be framed in terms that owed far more to David Alton than to John Corrie.

---

[4] Alton, *What Kind of Country?*, 170.

[5] For insightful similar accounts of the US context, see Sanger, *About Abortion*; Dubow, *Ourselves Unborn*.

The White Bill 1975

By convention, abortion law reform is treated as an issue of conscience, with MPs not whipped to vote according to a party line.[6] Nonetheless, most of the significant attempts to restrict the Abortion Act over its five-decade biography have been led by Conservative MPs. The most important exceptions to that rule are James White and, some years later, David Alton.

In spring 1974, passions were running high. Litchfield and Kentish's allegations in the *News of the World* were exciting a media storm and Lane had reported, removing an important buffer against reform. White was an otherwise 'low profile', 'mainstream' Scottish Labour trade unionist and industrialist who prided himself on being one of the few MPs to hold a heavy goods vehicle (HGV) licence. What would motivate a diligent constituency MP, who rarely spoke in Parliament,[7] to devote his valuable third place in the ballot for Private Members' Bills to such a divisive issue?[8] White was initially reluctant. However, the Stobhill baby case had occurred in a neighbouring constituency, exerting a powerful influence on local opinion, with SPUC working hard to 'make abortion an election issue'.[9] White held a marginal seat in a strongly Catholic constituency and, on Election Day 1970, he had seen a Glasgow newspaper report of a group of nuns with his Tory opponent attacking Labour's support of the Abortion Act as immoral.[10] Further, the Lane Report had laid bare problems with the implementation of the Abortion Act, and White had read *Babies for Burning* in proofs.[11] While he would later deny its influence on his thinking following the book's discrediting, he initially claimed that all he had needed to know for his Bill was found within its pages.[12] White explained that he himself would have voted for the Abortion Act in 1967, for – until such time as a 'new Jerusalem' arrived, with no bad housing, poverty or alcoholic husbands – abortion should be available for 'women with problems'; however, it should not be permitted 'on demand', and there was a need to clamp down on the abusive practices in the private sector.[13]

[6] See Pattie et al., 'Voting without Party?'.

[7] 'Obituary: James White', *Telegraph*, 26 February 2009.

[8] 'Obituary: James White: MP who Sponsored the 1975 Abortion Amendment Bill', *Independent*, 24 February 2009; Abortion (Amendment) Bill 1975.

[9] Wellcome Library, Papers of the Birth Control Campaign (BCC), SA/BCC/C34, Letter from Phyllis Bowman (SPUC) to Supporters, c. December 1973, and SPUC, 'General Election'; SPUC advert in *Catholic Herald*, 25 January 1974.

[10] See Potts et al., *Abortion*, 324.

[11] James White in *Hansard*, House of Commons (HC), 7 February 1975, vol. 885, col. 1760. See also, 'Obituary: James White', *Independent*, 24 February 2009.

[12] See *Scottish Daily Record*, 1 April 1975; *Scottish Daily Record*, 5 December 1975.

[13] 'Obituary: James White', *Independent*, 24 February 2009. See further Keown, *Abortion, Doctors and the Law*, 141–46.

White thus declared himself as no 'zealot' on abortion,[14] rather seeking a 'middle ground' between those 'with strong religious beliefs [who] want the Act repealed altogether' and the calls for abortion on demand expressed in the 'shrill voice of *The Guardian*'.[15] However, his lack of detailed knowledge inevitably rendered him dependent on the greater expertise of others who stood far from the centre ground he sought to occupy. His Bill was master-minded largely by SPUC and drafted by Leo Abse, a fellow Labour MP, solicitor, and powerful critic of the Abortion Act.[16] The result was an enor-mously ambitious, wide-ranging Bill that proposed a reduction in the upper time limit for most abortions to 20 weeks, a range of other measures to clamp down on commercial exploitation, and a prohibition on the treatment of overseas women 'lured into Britain' for abortion.[17] Combined, these measures sought to confine the Abortion Act to what White saw as its proper limits: the provision of 'safe, responsible abortion for really deserving persons':[18]

> There are some 200,000 abortions done in this country every year and we think it is too many. We think people are using abortion instead of birth control. We don't want to make it difficult for the following categories: women with larger families, single women, young girls or women with housing problems. But we certainly don't think a woman should be able to have an abortion just because she wants to.[19]

To his opponents, White was attempting 'to neutralise the original Act by the fine print of clauses and regulations'.[20] In response, they drew heavily on the public health and social justice concerns that had motivated Steel.[21] However, with a burgeoning women's movement outside Parliament now fighting for 'free contraception and abortion on demand',[22] a new line of defence was also emerging within it, as the newly elected 'dynamo' with 'flaming red hair', Jo Richardson, joined Renée Short and Lena Jeger on the Labour benches.[23] These three women are each frequently remembered as 'outspoken', emerging as powerful advocates for women's rights at a time when many mocked the

---

[14] 'Obituary: James White', *Guardian*, 26 February 2009.

[15] *Hansard*, HC, 7 February 1975, vol. 885, cols 1757–58.

[16] Jack Scarisbrick interviewed by Jane O'Neill, 7 November 2017; 'Obituary: James White', *Telegraph*, 26 February 2009; Leo Abse, *Private Member*.

[17] James White in *Hansard*, HC, 7 February 1975, vol. 885, col. 1758.

[18] Modern Records Centre, University of Warwick, Trades Union Congress Archives (hereafter TUC Warwick), MSS.292D/824/1, material accompanying undated letter/circular by James White addressed 'Dear Comrade'.

[19] *Guardian*, 6 February 1975.

[20] Potts et al., *Abortion*, 324.

[21] MacFarquhar in *Hansard*, HC, 7 February 1975, vol. 885, col. 1853.

[22] Championed by two further small campaign groups: the Women's Abortion and Contraception Campaign (founded in 1972) and Reason: A Campaign for Common Sense on Abortion (founded in 1973). *The Times*, 24 November 1973, 28 November 1973; Wellcome Library, SA/BCC/C33, Reason Press Release, 19 November 1973.

[23] 'Obituary: Jo Richardson', *Independent*, 2 February 1994.

very idea of them.[24] While continuing to emphasise stories of the most heart-wrenching and 'deserving' cases for legal abortion, these Labour MPs would begin also to carve out a very different defence of the Abortion Act: as involving an issue that affected all women, with access to safe, legal services a precondition for female emancipation.[25] White's proposal to prohibit the treatment of overseas women was robustly condemned as telling women: '[Y]ou are not our sisters, you do not belong to humanity. Keep your problem at home.'[26]

With feelings running high, MPs keen to investigate the claims made in *Babies for Burning*, and David Steel joining calls for 'a full debate',[27] the Government agreed to establish a Select Committee to consider the White Bill.[28] As with the Lane Committee, this move again served as a buffer against immediate reform of the Abortion Act: the White Bill's progress was halted, with attention refocused on possible administrative solutions to abusive practices. Having first obtained a clear undertaking that the Committee might be re-established in the next parliamentary session were it not to complete its work in the current one, White withdrew his Bill. However, it was first put to a vote, winning a sizeable majority that shocked and galvanised defenders of the Abortion Act.[29]

Campaigning was intense. Over the last six years, the Pro-Life movement had grown strong in membership, skilled in parliamentary lobbying, and sophisticated in its use of the mass media.[30] While carefully avoiding giving succour to the idea that they were Roman Catholic 'front' organisations (a view prevalent within Pro-Choice groups),[31] SPUC and Life nonetheless drew significant support from churches. Guidance on how to establish a local Life group in the 1970s emphasised that Life was 'non-denominational and non-political', before advising that each group should have a member charged with lobbying clergy to place Life publications in the book display rack of local churches.[32] At that time, the Catholic Church was judged in its own right to be the most effective pressure group in British politics, given its ability to mobilise

[24] See 'Renee Short', *Guardian*, 20 January 2003; 'Obituary: Lena Jeger, MP', *Camden New Journal*, 8 March 2007.

[25] Jeger in *Hansard*, HC, 7 February 1975, vol. 885, col. 1830. See also Short, col. 1813.

[26] Jeger in *Hansard*, HC, 7 February 1975, vol. 885, col. 1831. See also Price, col. 1834.

[27] Steel in *Hansard*, HC, 7 February 1975, vol. 885, col. 1763; BPAS Archives, George Sinclair, 'Abortion and Parliament 1953–1978' in Birth Control Trust, *Abortion: Ten Years On*, May 1978, 14; Marsh and Chambers, *Abortion Politics*, 24.

[28] Owen in *Hansard*, HC, 7 February 1975, vol. 885, cols 1793–94. See further The National Archives (TNA), CAB 128/56/7, Minutes of Cabinet Meeting, 6 February 1975, 1.

[29] Ayes 203; Noes 88. See generally Marsh and Chambers, *Abortion Politics*, 24.

[30] In 1976, SPUC had 17,000 individual members and 150 branches: Bazlinton and Cowen, *The Guardian Directory of Pressure Groups and Representative Organisations*, 191.

[31] Marsh and Chambers, *Abortion Politics*.

[32] Wellcome Library, Papers of the Abortion Law Reform Association (ALRA), SA/ALR/G17, 'LIFE Groups', c. 1970s. See generally Marsh and Chambers, *Abortion Politics*.

its priests and bishops to raise a mass response from congregations.[33] This support was thus very significant.

In the early 1970s, the Pro-Life movement was in the clear ascendancy. ALRA had never been a mass membership organisation and, having secured the passage of the Abortion Act, its numbers had further dwindled as activists moved onto other concerns. Now, faced with the White Bill, its executive committee retired to hand control over to a younger generation,[34] and ALRA was joined by a second organisation that would become the 'more radical edge of the abortion movement': the National Abortion Campaign (NAC).[35] ALRA had worked through quiet diplomacy, evidence-based lobbying, public lectures and letters to newspapers. NAC organised consciousness-raising sessions, 'speak outs' where women shared experiences of abortion, and mass demonstrations.[36] Its inaugural conference attracted 1,000 delegates; its first march was claimed as the biggest on a woman's issue since those of the suffragettes.[37] These activists generally came from what Eileen Cook – who was involved from NAC's very first meeting – states 'people might call the lucky generation, the ones that were just covered by the "67 Act"', who were determined to defend the 'new reality' it created.[38] Marge Berer joined NAC soon after and recalls 'we were mostly young, we were passionate', and that soon 'there were local groups all over the country', with staff, a national steering committee and monthly national meetings.[39]

With the Pro-Choice and Pro-Life movements now each capable of mobilising mass demonstrations, there were nonetheless marked contrasts of style. In a vivid contemporary account (that undoubtedly says as much about the sympathies of its authors as the composition of the marchers), the first was heralded as the 'most significant show of the women's movement' to date, mobilising 'a wide spectrum of women'; whereas the second was composed of 'Church youth clubs, nuns with banners, the embittered middle aged and the sexually repressed young', joining to fight 'this age of permissiveness'.[40]

While Pro-Life groups relied heavily on churches for their campaigns, NAC turned naturally to the Labour Movement. Whatever reticence was

[33] Barker and Rush, *The Member of Parliament and His Information*, 54.

[34] See generally Marsh and Chambers, *Abortion Politics*, 42–46.

[35] Marge Berer interviewed by Jane O'Neill, 6 October 2017 and 8 November 2017.

[36] Berer interviewed by O'Neill; Wellcome Library, Papers of the National Abortion Campaign (NAC), SA/NAC/D/1/1, *NAC News* (no. 1), 25 April 1975, 1. See correspondence in Wellcome Library, SA/NAC/B/2/5 and generally Marsh and Chambers, *Abortion Politics*, 47–48.

[37] Marsh and Chambers, *Abortion Politics*, 47; Wellcome Library, SA/NAC/D/1/1, *NAC News* (no. 1), 25 April 1975, 2; SA/ALR/B37, *Breaking Chains* no. 15, December/January 1979/1980, 9; and no. 17, April/May 1980, 1.

[38] 'So when in 1975 I heard that James White had introduced the Bill, my immediate reaction was, "oh no you don't!" ... like most people, I had just assumed that this new reality of the '67 Act would be it. And the idea that some people would want to go backwards was frightening.' Eileen Cook interviewed by Jane O'Neill, 11 September 2017.

[39] Berer interviewed by O'Neill.

[40] Greenwood and Young, *Abortion in Demand*, 13.

encountered amongst male-dominated union hierarchies, the unions' women's officers could generally be relied upon to get abortion resolutions passed by local branches and then taken to the national level.[41] As Ann Henderson reflects, while it took women to raise the issue, it would then be 'quite easy to win the argument that abortion is a trade union issue, and why it's a class issue, and women's rights and women's equality are a class issue as well'.[42] While James White, himself a trade unionist, had promised a Bill that would 'protect working class women',[43] he thus found it condemned by the Trades Union Congress (TUC) as reflecting an 'attitude to women which relegates them towards auxiliary and reserve workforces and to second class citizenship'.[44] The Labour Party likewise mobilised against the Bill, and NAC's socialist feminist framing of the issue quickly became so dominant within the Labour Movement that even those who opposed liberal abortion laws felt obliged to adopt it. One speaker at the 1975 Labour Party Conference prefaced his comments by noting, '[a]s you can see, I am not a woman, neither am I a doctor', but 'I come here very much at the urging of my wife'.[45]

The Pro-Life movement had always had women in prominent roles; however, this new feminist defence of the Act required a calibrated response.[46] A new women-led group, Women for Life, was formed in early 1975 as a non-affiliated 'radical organisation fighting for women's rights'.[47] While welcoming male members as having 'an equal right' to be part of the feminist movement,[48] abortion was denounced as 'an instrument of sexist

---

[41] See e.g. Wellcome Library, SA/NAC/B/2, SW London NAC internal paper May 1977, advising on how to progress motions on abortion; also see SA/NAC/B/1/6; SA/NAC/B/1/7.

[42] Ann Henderson interviewed by Jane O'Neill, 25 July 2017. See further Cook interviewed by O'Neill: '[T]here was in general very little problem, if you lobbied, getting positive motions through union branches and things like that. It's a matter of really somebody had to go in there and raise the issue, if necessary. But people tended to be receptive'; Joyce Gould interviewed by Jane O'Neill, 4 October 2017; Berer interviewed by O'Neill; and Brooke, *Sexual Politics*, 209.

[43] TUC Warwick, MSS.292D/824/1, Letter from James White to 'Comrade' and attached outline of argument, c. 1975.

[44] TUC Warwick, MSS.292D/824/2, Resolutions of the 1975 Trades Councils' Conference, published 8 October 1975. Trades Union Congress, *Annual Report 1975*, Discussion of motion on Abortion condemning White Bill, proposed by Mrs T. Marsland (Tobacco Worker's Union), 416.

[45] Labour Party, *Report of the 74th Annual Conference of the Labour Party*, 1975, 241–42, 239. Paul Burgess, Farnworth constituency Labour Party (CLP), responding to Ann Warm, Dulwich CLP, attacking the 'male-dominated' House of Commons.

[46] E.g. Wellcome Library, SA/NAC/E/4/1/1, SPUC Bulletin no. 17, c. late 1975, describing a woman-only petition against 'the indiscriminate killing of unborn children'.

[47] Wellcome Library, SA/ALR/G17, Women for Life (London), 'Women for Life Accuse ALRA of Misusing Statistics', c. February 1975; 'What is Women for Life?', undated. See also SA/NAC/E/4/3, 'Little Boxes', Women for Life flyer, undated.

[48] Wellcome Library, SA/NAC/E/4/3, Charles J. Smith 'The Role of Men in Women for Life – From a Male Point of View' pamphlet, c. 1983; Glasgow Women's Library (GWL), Papers of the Scottish Abortion Campaign (SAC), SAC 5/2, 'A Message to Men . . . From Women for Life' pamphlet, c. 1981, finding excluding men as 'absurd as trying to ban whites from fighting racism'.

oppression',[49] with 'A Woman's Right to Choose' meaning 'a man's right to use'.[50] The group produced literature for women facing unwanted pregnancies,[51] and campaigned on welfare, employment and the promotion of a society in which raising children was the responsibility of the wider community, rendering abortion unnecessary.[52] Government and doctors were attacked for pressurising women into 'working class genocide'.[53]

With battle lines drawn outside Parliament, the Committee convened to consider the White Bill within it began to take evidence. Reflecting the White Bill's sizeable majority at its Second Reading, it was weighted nine to six in favour of its supporters. Four members were women, offering a larger female presence than on the Committee that had considered the Steel Bill, where the issue of gender balance had provoked no comment. However, with abortion now claimed as a women's issue, Lena Jeger proposed an amendment to make the Committee all female, for 'not one hon. Gentleman in this House has ever had an abortion or has had to contemplate having one'.[54] Another (male) MP agreed that it was 'rather grotesque for 600 grown men – some of them very elderly, or at least getting on a bit – solemnly to pronounce on what women should do with their bodies'.[55] Others regretted the attempt at obstruction: Teddy Taylor (Con) did not wish to 'minimise the contribution that ladies can make to the political progress of Britain', but argued that 'minorities within this House' should not be able to 'impose their will on it'.[56] Another MP reminded the House that everyone had the right to an opinion regarding the sanctity of human life and that there were male as well as female fetuses.[57] The Committee's membership remained unchanged.

The Committee initially concentrated on those areas of concern where it might hope to find agreement on strengthening effective controls through administrative action.[58] It took extensive evidence, including from Litchfield and Kentish, who, by now, had been seriously discredited, with White 'furious' at the 'great weapon' this offered against his Bill.[59] Leo Abse encouraged the journalists to admit that they had 'embellished' their story, so as not to overshadow the real and 'damning evidence against a large number of people'

[49] Wellcome Library, SA/NAC/E/4/3, Women for Life membership form, undated.
[50] GWL, SAC 5/2, 'A Message to Men . . . From Women for Life' pamphlet, c. 1981.
[51] Wellcome Library, SA/NAC/E/4/3, 'If you are Pregnant (and Didn't Want to Be)', Women for Life pamphlet, undated.
[52] Wellcome Library, SA/NAC/E/4/3, Women for Life membership form, undated.
[53] GWL, SAC 5.2, 'What is Women for Life?', c. 1975; TUC Warwick, MSS.292D/824/2, Debby Sanders, Secretary of Women for Life, Letters to TUC 23 April 1976, 12 August 1979.
[54] *Hansard*, HC, 26 February 1975, vol. 887, col. 507.
[55] Price in *Hansard*, HC, 26 February 1975, vol. 887, col. 519.
[56] Taylor in *Hansard*, HC, 26 February 1975, vol. 887, col. 505.
[57] Cormack in *Hansard*, HC, 26 February 1975, vol. 887, cols 522–23.
[58] BPAS Archives, Sinclair, 'Abortion and Parliament 1953–1978', 12–16.
[59] 'Abortion Book Storm Flares', *Scottish Daily Record*, 1 April 1975.

offered by their tapes.[60] They chose instead to offer a spirited defence of all claims.[61] Medical bodies also gave evidence, demonstrating that the medical support in favour of restrictive reform had now dwindled: the Abortion Act was increasingly accepted as a 'reasonable compromise', with abuses better addressed through administrative action than restrictive reform.[62] Life also gave evidence. Notwithstanding the apparently favourable composition of the Committee (which, in NAC's view, was packed with 'anti-abortion men'), Jack Scarisbrick recalls 'feeling you were talking to a brick wall', with one MP sleeping throughout before waking to head off to the bar.[63]

The Committee went on to produce four short reports.[64] The most important, published in July 1975, made nine interim recommendations, which echoed Lane's suggestions for tighter regulation.[65] The Government had initially been so uncertain of its own powers under the Act that, when it used them, it had carefully avoided publicising the fact.[66] Now, however, it acted decisively. Barbara Castle, the Labour Secretary of State for Health, was 'untypically nervous' in dealing with abortion, believing the issue to have cost her Catholic votes. She thus charged her Health Minister, David Owen, with overseeing a response.[67] Owen was a strongly independently minded MP.[68] 'Terrified' at the possibility of reopening the possibility of statutory reform (and risking restrictive amendment of the grounds for abortion), he determined – against the advice of his civil servants – that he had sufficient powers to act within the current law, and, if challenged, he would be ready to go to court to defend his view.[69]

[60] Abse in HC, *Special Reports and Minutes of Evidence of the Select Committee on the Abortion (Amendment) Bill*, 1974–1975, HC 692-II, para. 1480.

[61] HC, *Special Reports and Minutes of Evidence of the Select Committee on the Abortion (Amendment) Bill*, 1974–1975, 240–74.

[62] Wilkes, 'Working of the Abortion Act', 337; Keown, *Abortion, Doctors and the Law*, 141–46.

[63] Scarisbrick interviewed by O'Neill; Wellcome Library, SA/NAC/B/1/6 and 7, NAC press statement, 20 June 1975.

[64] Published together as *The Abortion (Amendment) Bill Together with the Proceedings of the Committee*, 1974–1975, 10 November 1975.

[65] HC, *Special Reports and Minutes of Evidence of the Select Committee on the Abortion (Amendment) Bill*, 1974–1975, vi.

[66] Evidence of Mr Fogden, Department of Health and Social Security (DHSS), explaining that '[t]he Secretary of State's action may be open to challenge in the Courts . . . so it has never been the policy to state publicly why they [nursing homes] have been closed down'. *Special Reports and Minutes of Evidence of the Select Committee on the Abortion (Amendment) Bill*, 1974–1975, 18.

[67] Owen, *Time to Declare*, 229.

[68] David Steel recalls that he 'is and always will be an Owenite. I do not decry that . . . Parliament could do with a few more individualist MPs. Fitting them into a team is another matter.' Steel, *Against Goliath*, 357.

[69] Owen, *Time to Declare*, 229; TNA, MH 156/362, Memo on Abortion – James White Bill, 10 January 1975; see also Letter from Dr David Owen to Mr Hulme, 12 December 1974. See further Owen, *Personally Speaking to Kenneth Harris*.

Owen devised a wide-ranging raft of regulatory measures that would both restrict abusive practices under the Abortion Act and protect it against more substantial challenge. Assurances were sought from approved nursing homes regarding fees, financial arrangements with referral agencies, and their treatment of overseas patients. Guidance was offered regarding good practice in counselling. Terminations after the twentieth week of pregnancy would be carried out only where resuscitation equipment was available. All health authorities and private nursing homes were required to adopt Peel's recommendations regarding the use and disposal of fetal material. Finally, it was made easier to investigate serious professional misconduct, and doctors would henceforth be required to specify whether or not they had examined a woman in person before authorising her termination.[70]

With a more robust regulatory response commanding widespread support, disagreement now focused on whether the Select Committee should reconvene in the following Parliamentary session. When Owen argued that Parliament should now defer further discussion until it was clear whether the new regulations were effective, an estimated 80,000 people joined a SPUC rally to demand that the Committee resume its work,[71] and MPs voted against him.[72] However, all common ground was now exhausted. When it reconvened, those members who supported the Abortion Act resigned rather than continue on 'a committee designed by its very composition to undermine' it,[73] and the major Pro-Choice organisations boycotted it.[74] Its fourth and final report, published in July 1976, contained further recommendations for significant restrictive statutory reform that broadly reflected the provisions of the White Bill.[75] The Government took no further action in response.

While it failed to achieve statutory reform, the White Bill nonetheless left an important legacy. Firstly, via the Committee's work, it had resulted in an additional layer of regulation of non-NHS service providers enforced through licensing provisions. While initially welcomed by all sides, this regulation – which continues to shape abortion services to this day – would become an important source of frustration to service providers.[76] Secondly – and ironically given that the White Bill was the one restrictive Bill in the Abortion Act's long history to be introduced by a Labour MP and confirmed trade unionist to boot – it had played a vital role in cementing what would become a crucial

---

[70] See Barbara Castle's statement to the House of Commons setting out the measures to be taken in *Hansard*, HC, 21 October 1975, vol. 898, cols 244–55; TNA, MH 156/379, Letter from DHSS to Approved Nursing Homes, 13 August 1976; Abortion (Amendment) Regulations 1976 and Abortion (Scotland) Amendment Regulations 1976; and Chapter 2, pp. 54–55. on the Peel Code.

[71] *Guardian*, 20 October 1975.

[72] *Hansard*, HC, 9 February 1976, vol. 905, col. 147.

[73] BPAS Archives, Sinclair, 'Abortion and Parliament 1953–1978', 15. Paintin, *Abortion Law Reform in Britain*, 87–88.

[74] See correspondence in Wellcome Library, NAC/B/1/5.

[75] HC, *First Report from the Select Committee on Abortion*, 1975–1976, vol. 1: Report, HC 573-I.

[76] See Chapter 4.

'new alliance between the masculinist left and the new, autonomous feminism'.[77] Galvanised in part by the need for solidarity in light of the Select Committee boycott, the Co-ordinating Committee in Defence of the 1967 Abortion Act (Co-ord) was established in March 1976. Beginning with 16 members, it would rapidly grow into a strong and highly effective umbrella organisation bringing together Pro-Choice groups, trade unions, doctors, service providers and a range of others. By 1980, it would have 56 member organisations.[78]

The Benyon Bill 1977

When the next attacks on the Abortion Act came – and they came quickly – they were led by Conservative male MPs seeking to defend traditional family values against declining moral standards and abuses of the Act. In 1977, William Benyon MP – a Tory landowner, retired naval officer and SPUC member – used his high place in the Private Members' ballot for a Bill that largely replicated the measures proposed by White.[79] By now, however, the major medical organisations had lined up against statutory change and the Government opposed him with some confidence, arguing that 'what Mr Benyon wants to do by law we are already doing by administrative action'.[80] The Bill also faced a sophisticated, multipronged response from Pro-Choice campaigners. Diane Munday was now installed at BPAS, where her lobbying skills and BPAS's experience in service provision combined to potent effect. When SPUC deployed its lobbyists to Parliament in support of the Benyon Bill, they found MPs forewarned. Having somehow obtained a copy of SPUC's briefing note, BPAS wrote to each MP, apprising them of its content (specifically that the note had advised lobbyists to resist any attempts from MPs to 'bully' them) and offering a detailed rebuttal of its 'out-of-context quotations, half-truths and carefully selected references often from outdated publications'.[81]

In the meantime, the campaign to defend the Abortion Act had secured its footing within the Labour Party, where Joyce Gould was now installed as Chief Women's Officer. In 1977, she strategically tabled two resolutions in support of abortion at the Labour Party Conference:

[77] Jolly, 'The Feelings behind the Slogans', 102. For a longer history of such links see Brooke, *Sexual Politics*; Hoggart, 'Socialist Feminism, Reproductive Rights and Political Action'.
[78] Marsh and Chambers, *Abortion Politics*, 51–53.
[79] Abortion Amendment Bill 1977.
[80] TNA, MH 156/555, transcript of interview with Roland Moyle on *London Today*, 17 July 1977; TNA, CAB 128/61/21, Minutes of Cabinet Meeting 26 May 1977, 1; CAB 128/62/2, Minutes of Cabinet Meeting 7 July 1977, 1; CAB 128/62/3, Minutes of Cabinet Meeting 14 July 1977, 2; correspondence in TNA, MH 156/554, /555 and /558.
[81] Cadbury Research Library, University of Birmingham, Papers of Francois Lafitte (hereafter Lafitte Papers), US72, Box 10, Letter to MPs from Francois Lafitte BPAS, 13 May 1977.

[W]e put a very good Pro-Choice resolution in [and another] through the Socialist Medical Association. They actually called for a three-line whip in the Commons, which we knew would get defeated ... We lost heavily on the three-line whip, which made people feel happy ... they could vote for the principle but at the same time their conscience was saying to them, 'no, no, we mustn't actually make it absolutely compulsory, because we know we have got Catholic colleagues' ... whereas they might have used the Catholic colleagues argument on the Pro-Choice one. It took a lot of work and a lot of influencing and a lot of discussion. But it went through ... and it's never been changed.[82]

Gould's 'very good Pro-Choice resolution' passed by an overwhelming majority, ensuring that activists could no longer be dismissed as mere 'NAC radicals' when they sought to maintain pressure on Labour MPs.[83]

The Benyon Bill passed its Second Reading but with a far smaller majority than the White Bill.[84] Women now made up seven of 16 members of the Committee convened to consider it.[85] While ALRA continued to campaign through polite, evidence-based argument, the more radical wing of the Pro-Choice movement was also highly visible. One Committee meeting was disrupted when 'Feminists Against Benyon' wearing 'various feminist badges' stormed the room, hurling stink bombs and streamers, bursting balloons and shouting 'free abortion on demand' and 'our bodies, our lives, our right to decide'.[86] Female Labour MPs decried the Bill as a strategy of the 'maleocracy' of the House of Commons 'to make it clear to women that their bodies are definitely not their own',[87] and its further progress was disrupted by delaying tactics. When it fell with the end of the Parliamentary session,[88] NAC celebrated with a women-only torchlit procession.[89]

A Ten Minute Rule Bill, introduced in the following year by the Conservative MP Bernard Braine, envisaged broadly similar changes.[90] However, Parliament was now starting to tire of attacks upon the Abortion Act. Many MPs appeared convinced either that increased regulation of the non-NHS sector was sufficient to remedy abusive practices or, at least, that time should be allowed to assess its efficacy. The well-publicised discrediting of *Babies for Burning* had generated doubts regarding the veracity of other media accounts of abuses under the Act.[91] Further, the medical profession was

---

[82] Gould interviewed by O'Neill.
[83] Marsh and Chambers, *Abortion Politics*, 67; Brooke, *Sexual Politics*, 210.
[84] 170 votes to 132, compared to White's 203 votes to 88.
[85] House of Commons Standing Committee C, *Minutes of Proceedings on the Abortion (Amendment) Bill*, 13 July 1977, HC 494.
[86] 'Feminists Raise a Stink', *Guardian*, 13 July 1977.
[87] Colquhoun in *Hansard*, HC, 25 February 1977, vol. 926, col. 847.
[88] See *Guardian*, 11 July 1977, 9; Paintin, *Abortion Law Reform in Britain 1964-2003*, 88.
[89] A regular feature of NAC campaigns, Anonymous, 'A Brief and Partial History of the NAC', in NAC (ed.), *A Celebration of 25 Years of Safe, Legal Abortion 1967-1992* (October 1992).
[90] See *Hansard*, HC, 21 February 1978, vol. 944, cols 1213–24.
[91] See Chapter 2, pp. 59–60.

now speaking 'with an almost united voice' in defence of the Abortion Act, with several years of experience having 'convinced them that this measure relieves their patients' of much suffering'.[92] The British Medical Association (BMA) Council – which had initially been strongly against abortions on 'social grounds' – now passed a motion to confirm its belief in the Act as 'a practical and humane piece of legislation'.[93]

This combination of factors might well have signalled an end to these wide-ranging attacks on the Abortion Act were it not for one very important fact. Thus far, significant attempts at restrictive reform had come either during periods of Labour Government or during the buffer against reform offered by the lengthy deliberations of the Lane Committee, which had neatly coincided with the Conservative Government of Edward Heath. However, in May 1979, the Tories won a decisive victory under Margaret Thatcher, marking the beginning of almost two decades of Conservative rule. Given widespread Tory antipathy towards liberal abortion laws, a restrictive Bill might now be expected to encounter a more sympathetic reception from both MPs and Government. The stage was set for a Bill that would enjoy far greater prospects of success; onto it walked John Corrie.

The Corrie Bill 1979

With the notable exception of Norman St John-Stevas, there is little in the biographies of early sponsors of restrictive reform measures to suggest any specific interest in the abortion issue, and none were seen as natural champions within the Pro-Life movement.[94] White was a former HGV driver and Labour trade unionist, Benyon a Tory landowner, and Braine a leader of 'crusades' against a wide-ranging miscellany of issues alongside abortion (including 'alcoholism, video nasties, Maplin and Stansted airports, war criminals' and 'those who planted potentially explosive methane, oil refineries and chemical stores on Canvey Island').[95] 'Farmer John' Corrie was no exception.[96] Having studied agriculture, Corrie generally focused on matters relating to fishing, farming and – later – African affairs.[97] His decision to devote his valuable, first-ranked place in the Private Members' Bill ballot to abortion law reform reflected not any particular personal interest in the issue but, rather, pressure from constituents (with MPs then likely to receive two to three times as many letters on abortion compared to any other issue)[98] and a

[92] *Lancet*, 'Benyon's Progress', 16 July 1977, 120–21. See generally Keown, *Abortion, Doctors and the Law*, 146–51.
[93] Motion 267 in *BMA*, 'Agenda of Annual Representative Meeting', 1642.
[94] Scarisbrick interviewed by O'Neill.
[95] 'Obituary: Lord Braine of Wheatley', *Guardian*, 7 January 2000.
[96] 'Why Farmer John Fights for 20 Week Rule', *Glasgow Daily Record*, 10 July 1979.
[97] Who's Who, 'Corrie, John Alexander'.
[98] Marsh and Chambers, *Abortion Politics*, 40.

widespread simmering frustration that Parliament had been denied a mean-ingful vote on legislation perceived as inherently flawed: while abortion had been 'well debated ... no conclusion has ever been reached'.[99]

Like White and Benyon, Corrie eschewed the absolutist moral arguments of Pro-Life campaigners in favour of pragmatic concerns with abusive practices and a pronounced hostility towards declining moral standards. He deplored the feckless conduct of women who used abortion as birth control and strongly reasserted family values and personal responsibility, proclaiming the need to avoid the situation where 'the State is doing such a good job [in looking after the "unmarried girl"] that people don't feel that it's worth getting married any more'.[100] He was also concerned with the upper time limit for abortion but framed this within a broader understanding of deserving and undeserving cases,[101] explaining that a 'girl has to be very naive not to know by 16 weeks that she is pregnant. If she is having an abortion she should have it by then. After 16 weeks she should be MADE to have her baby.'[102] When a constituent requested his help after her doctor refused to refer her for a fifth abortion, Corrie 'gave her very short shift ... any girl who has got to that stage does not deserve that sort of help'.[103]

Corrie enjoyed particularly strong support on the issue of the upper time limit for abortion. Further heart-wrenching cases of babies left to die following botched late procedures had followed that of the Stobhill baby, typically coming to light as a result of Life's network of whistle-blowers amongst nursing staff (who the BMA dubbed Life's 'spies').[104] In the 1970s and 1980s, Life repeatedly passed details of such cases to the police and to the media.[105] When these resulted in no official investigation or one that found no evidence of wrongdoing, some felt vindicated that the accusations had always been spurious,[106] whilst others alleged a systematic cover-up. One SPUC flyer asked in furious capitals:

ASK YOURSELF WHAT KIND OF COUNTRY WE ARE LIVING IN WHEN PEOPLE ARE TOO FRIGHTENED OF OFFICIALDOM TO SPEAK OUT

---

[99] Corrie in *Hansard*, HC, 13 July 1979, vol. 970, cols 891–983.

[100] From 'The John Corrie Special', Radio Clyde, 15 July 1979, quoted in Wellcome Library SA/NAC/B/3/6, BPAS, *Corrie Bill Newsletter* vol. 5 no. 9, September 1979. See further Jolly, 'The Feelings behind the Slogans', 102.

[101] Marsh and Chambers, *Abortion Politics*, 105–06.

[102] *Glasgow Evening Times*, 12 June 1979, emphasis in original. See Wellcome Library SA/NAC/B/3/6, BPAS, *Corrie Bill Newsletter* vol. 5 no. 9, September 1979.

[103] 'The John Corrie Special', Radio Clyde, 15 July 1979, quoted in Wellcome Library SA/NAC/B/3/6, BPAS, *Corrie Bill Newsletter* vol. 5 no. 9, September 1979.

[104] See *Nursing Mirror*, 22 January 1981; 'BMA Condemns Nurses who Spy on Doctors after Abortions', *Sunday Times*, 10 July 1983.

[105] See Director of Public Prosecutions evidence to House of Lords, *Special Report with Evidence of the Select Committee on the Infant Life (Preservation) Bill [HL]*, 1986–1987, HL 153, 168–71; BPAS Archives, BPAS, *The Foetus Myth*, c. 1970s.

[106] E.g. BPAS Archives, *The Foetus Myth*.

AND TELL THE TRUTH. WHY ARE THE AUTHORITIES SO FRIGHTENED OF PUBLIC ENQUIRIES?[107]

Regardless of the truth of the matter, many MPs believed that there must be some basis to the reports,[108] which appear to have been deliberately released at 'politically auspicious' moments.[109] Two cases were reported in April 1979, in the run up to the general election, generating significant media coverage. In Whiston, a 22 week-old 'doomed baby' was reported to have 'lived for two hours after it was aborted', with an 'angry Roman Catholic priest' criticising the failure to provide full medical aid.[110] In Wanstead, a '"crying" foetus' born alive following a termination at 20 weeks was said to have 'cried out' after being aborted, with patients in a nearby infertility ward reportedly weeping at the sound.[111]

Outside Parliament, the Pro-Life and Pro-Choice movements had grown in strength over the course of earlier campaigns and were now at their peak: Co-ord had 56 member organisations; NAC had 350 affiliated groups.[112] Marge Berer recalls of Co-ord meetings

> sitting around this enormous long table, probably 30 people at least, and having these relatively difficult conversations about what we supported, what we didn't, what was going to happen on the demonstration and who was going to lead it and what the slogans were going to be, the whole thing. It was a real exercise in political negotiation that I have, I have to say, never participated in anything so lively again in my life! ... We had legal experts, parliamentarians, health professionals, trade unions, ... a very dedicated group of Conservative Party members who were very supportive of abortion rights, and who did make it an all-party issue in many ways. There were religious groups for choice too. So everybody brought their own issues to the table.[113]

The Pro-Life movement was also formidable. SPUC and Life now boasted a combined membership of almost 50,000 individuals and 500 local groups, with the National Pro-Life Committee offering an umbrella forum that also brought in a range of smaller organisations representing nurses, teachers and members with political party affiliations.[114] Members were far from unequivocal in their support for the Corrie Bill.[115] However, while seen as flawed, it was welcomed as a means to 'save the lives of thousands of unborn children a

---

[107] Wellcome Library, NAC/E/4/1, SPUC 'Kill the Lies', c. early 1980s. Capitals in original.

[108] Marsh and Chambers, *Abortion Politics*, 105–06.

[109] 'Horror Story', *Guardian*, 3 April 1979; see BPAS Archives, *The Foetus Myth*.

[110] 'Doomed Baby Shock: Alive for Two Hours after Abortion', *Daily Express*, 20 April 1979.

[111] '"Crying" Foetus "Had No Chance of Life"', *Guardian*, 21 April 1979.

[112] Marsh and Chambers, *Abortion Politics*, 49–51.

[113] Berer interviewed by O'Neill.

[114] See generally Marsh and Chambers, *Abortion Politics*, 53–64.

[115] Marsh and Chambers, *Abortion Politics*. See BPAS Archives, Letter from Nuala Scarisbrick (Life) to members, 13 February 1980.

year',[116] potentially reducing the number of abortions by two-thirds.[117] Campaign literature was distributed through churches, support was solicited through sermons and parish newsletters,[118] and lists of how every MP had voted on abortion were sent to churches along with tips for effective campaigning for parishioners.[119] Campaign material was designed to appeal to the widest possible audience, featuring prominent pictures either of the unborn slumbering peacefully in utero or distressing images of piles of discarded fetal remains.[120] Drawing on these networks, Life collected an impressive 500,000 signatures for a petition supporting the Corrie Bill.[121]

Under the direction of the indomitable Phyllis Bowman, a 'key foundation [stone] upon which the world pro-life movement was built',[122] SPUC had also become a highly effective pressure group. It coordinated the arrival of an estimated 18,000 people – some having travelled from as far as Orkney – to lobby their MPs,[123] creating 'almost unprecedented' scenes of 'hundreds of people milling around' Parliament.[124] Its powers of mobilisation are illustrated by the experience of one newly elected Scottish MP, who was a strong supporter of the 1967 Act. He met with a small SPUC delegation from his constituency, telling them that his position had been clear at the election, that he had no intention of supporting Corrie, and that he would be more impressed with their claim to speak 'for the majority in his constituency' if it were supported by letters from them. In the next month he received 1,000 such letters from constituents and another 1,000 from the surrounding area.[125] The movement gained strong support from the churches, with the Catholic bishops of England, Wales and Scotland joining together, reportedly for the first time, to support the Bill and condemn a 'massive and growing trivialization' of human life.[126]

The Pro-Life movement received little support from mainstream professional medical bodies, who tended strongly to oppose the Corrie Bill. The RCOG did not actively campaign against it but its opposition was noted in the

---

[116] BPAS Archives, Letter from Nuala Scarisbrick (Life) to members, 13 February 1980.

[117] Scarisbrick cited in *Guardian*, 11 July 1979.

[118] This was now a well-established strategy: see e.g. *Church Times*, 5 March 1971; 31 May 1974; 2 January 1976; 21 April 1978; 5 January 1979; Marsh and Chambers, *Abortion Politics*, 58.

[119] *Church Times*, 19 January 1979.

[120] E.g. Wellcome Library, SA/NAC/E/4/1/3, SPUC flyer, 'A Foetus is a Baby – Don't Forget,' c. 1970s.

[121] BPAS Archives, Letter from Nuala Scarisbrick (Life) to members, 13 February 1980.

[122] Chris Whitehouse cited in 'Phyllis Bowman, Campaigner who Led Struggle against Abortion and Euthanasia, Dies aged 85', *Catholic Herald*, 7 May 2012.

[123] *Times*, 31 January 1980.

[124] Marsh and Chambers, *Abortion Politics*, 41.

[125] Ibid.

[126] *Times*, 24 January 1980; *Guardian*, 24 January 1980. The Board for Social Responsibility of the General Synod of the Church of England published 'Abortion: A Great Moral Evil', acknowledging internal differences of opinion but arguing that abortion could only be acceptable when a woman's life or health was at serious risk, see *Church Times*, 1 February 1980; *Times*, 30 January 1980.

media,[127] known to MPs,[128] and communicated to the Government.[129] While supporting the introduction of a 24 week upper time limit for abortion, it opposed Corrie's suggested 20 week limit,[130] as did the BMA and the Royal College of General Practitioners (RCGP).[131] Specific medical lobby groups also formed to defend the Act, including Doctors for a Woman's Choice on Abortion (which had 600 members by 1980) and the Doctors and Overpopulation Group (which had 2,000 members, including two former Health Ministers).[132] The Royal College of Nursing took a more guarded position.[133]

The abortion charities were also active, with BPAS circulating its own detailed commentaries on successive Bills.[134] Working with a BPAS doctor, Diane Munday also coordinated a response to SPUC's mass lobby:

> We hired a flatbed truck and we set up a tableau on the back of it of a woman in a hospital bed with a drip up, pipes coming out and a lot of young, dishy doctors and nurses. We put great big banners around the edge: 'This patient is Corrie-bund.' . . . And we had it driven round and round and round Parliament Square for about an hour, and we got all the press. And not the 20,000 people queueing to see their MPs![135]

However, the largest Pro-Choice demonstrations would be organised by NAC, which had also grown rapidly in strength, organisation and confidence as it notched up the defeats of successive restrictive Bills: a poster of the time shows a smiling woman amending a poster that reads 'Smash the ~~White~~, ~~Benyon~~, Corrie Bill'.[136] While Pro-Life literature featured images of fetuses, NAC posters featured either images of women or – in one memorable case – a cartoon of a heavily pregnant John Corrie with the tagline '[i]f men could get pregnant, abortion would always be free, safe and legal'.[137]

---

[127] E.g. *Times*, 29 January 1980; *Guardian*, 27 January 1980, 30 January 1980.

[128] E.g. *Hansard*, HC, 15 February 1980, vol. 978, cols 1938, 1949, 1966, 2018; 29 February 1980, vol. 979, col. 1794.

[129] TNA, MH 156/343, Letter from E. A. J. Alment to J. S. Metters, DHSS, 11 January 1980.

[130] Archives of the Royal College of Obstetricians and Gynaecologists, RCOG/A16/21, Item 19 for Meeting of Council 28 July 1979, written 18 July 1979.

[131] 'Abortion (Amendment) Bill: BMA's comments', *British Medical Journal*, 1163; RCOG A16/21, BMA, 'Full implications of Abortion Amendment Bill not made clear by sponsors, says BMA', Press Release, 11 July 1979; RCGP, Comments on Mr John Corrie's Abortion (Amendment) Bill, 1979. See generally Marsh and Chambers, *Abortion Politics*, 141; Keown, *Abortion, Doctors and the Law*, 152–58.

[132] Gerard Vaughan and David Owen. Marsh and Chambers, *Abortion Politics*, 45. Doctors for a Woman's Choice on Abortion would much later become Doctors for Choice. See further doctors' letters in *Observer*, 27 January 1980 and *Lancet*, 2 February 1980, 260.

[133] Wellcome Library, SA/NAC/B/8/2/13, Royal College of Nursing Paper 'The RCN and Abortions', 29 August 1979, 2.

[134] See Lafitte Papers, US72, Box 10, Letter from Francois Lafitte, 12 July 1979.

[135] Munday interviewed by O'Neill.

[136] Wellcome Library SA/NAC/B/3/1/6, Flyer, c. 1979, reproduced on p. 83, with the kind permission of Abortion Rights.

[137] Wellcome Library, SA/NAC/B/3/1/6, NAC Flyer, 'THE NATIONAL ABORTION CAMPAIGN says NO to the Corrie Anti-abortion Bill'. See also 'Corrie's Dream – A Frightening True Life Story' in same file, reproduced on p. 84 with the kind permission of Abortion Rights.

THE NATIONAL ABORTION CAMPAIGN

says NO

to the Corrie Anti-abortion Bill

IF John Corrie M.P. was pregnant after his Bill became law ....

would he be able to convince two doctors that continuing with his pregnancy would involve grave, substantial and serious risk?

would he go to a backstreet abortionist, when he finds that there are no charitable clinics or NHS facilities in his area?

would he be able to get an abortion after 20 weeks when his colleagues in Parliament have agreed with him that 'he should be made to have his baby'.

OR WOULD HE JOIN WITH US IN SAYING ....

FREE ABORTION ON DEMAND
A WOMAN'S RIGHT TO CHOOSE!

The strength of NAC's links within the Labour Movement were now clear. An estimated 100,000 marched against the Corrie Bill in London, with record numbers also seen in Glasgow, notwithstanding blizzard conditions.[138] The TUC had now become the first trade union federation anywhere in the world to call a demonstration against restrictive abortion laws in its own name.[139] This decision was deeply controversial in some quarters. The Catholic Men's Society rejected the need to advance the ability of women 'to control their own lives' as 'a little out of place when you consider just how much freedom they do have'.[140] Other members impugned the TUC as the 'lackey' of extreme feminists, having 'set comrade against comrade'[141] and made a mockery of the 'basic socialist philosophy of compassion and equality' in its support for the killing of 'unborn comrades'.[142] Several small left-wing Pro-Life groups were established. However, they were heavily outnumbered and failed to gain traction within the Labour Movement.[143]

As it developed in strength and diversity, schisms were also emerging within the Pro-Choice movement.[144] While the need to defend the Abortion Act was a powerful cohesive force, any attempt to contemplate 'positive legislation' provoked divisions,[145] and there were marked differences of style as well as substance. Diane Munday recalls that while some called for 'abortion on demand', she avoided that phrase 'like the plague ... you don't demand an abortion, two doctors have to agree to do it. You ask. You request. Not demand.' Moreover:

---

[138] Anonymous, 'A Brief and Partial History of the National Abortion Campaign', Scottish Trades Union Congress (STUC), *Annual Report 1980*, 487.

[139] McLennan in STUC, *Annual Report 1980*, 487. See generally *Times*, 3 March 1977, 5; Marsh and Chambers, *Abortion Politics*, 70; Brooke, *Sexual Politics*, 211.

[140] TUC Warwick, MSS.292D/824/2, Letter to Len Murray TUC from Joseph Mundoon, 17 August 1979.

[141] TUC Warwick, MSS.292D/824/3, Letters from Mrs K. M. to Len Murray, 29 October 1979; Anne H. to Len Murray, c. December 1979; Mary B. to Len Murray, 29 October 1979; John W. to Len Murray 29 October 1979.

[142] Wellcome Library, SA/ALR/G17, *Equality*, The Conscience of the Labour Movement, no. 1, c. 1976; SA/NAC/E/4/4, flyer for Socialist Campaign Against Abortion event, c. 1979; Wellcome Library Ephemera Collection, EPH620A, SPUC Labour Division pamphlet, c. late 1970s.

[143] The Socialist Campaign Against Abortion, the SPUC Labour Division and Life Labour Group all date from this period. See Wellcome Library, SA/NAC/E/4/1/1, NALGO Equal Opportunity News, no. 2, January 1979; SPUC Bulletin, no. 17, c. late 1975; SPUC Bulletin, no. 18, c. early 1976; SA/NAC/F/2, general correspondence.

[144] Berer interviewed by O'Neill; Cook interviewed by O'Neill.

[145] Disagreement over the content of a Bill proposed by ALRA in 1977 had grown so heated that BPAS came close to leaving Co-ord. See Wellcome Library, SA/NAC/E/2/1, ALRA, 'Positive Legislation – ALRA's Model Abortion Bill', paper for the NAC conference, March 1977; SA/NAC/B/1/3, Elana Ehrlich, 'NAC – Where we Are ... and Where are we Going?', 12 March 1976; SA/BCC/C28, Statement of NAC to Co-ord Meeting, 2 November 1978 and correspondence; Wellcome Library, Papers of Wendy Savage, PPWDS/C/1, 'Why NAC Does Not Support ALRA's Bill', paper presented at NAC conference, March 1977.

I didn't think waving banners in Parliament Square was as effective a way of lobbying as circulating [MPs] with reasoned argument documents, and offering to write speeches for the ones who said they agreed with us. . . . [These] yelling hordes of feminists just weren't my scene. . . . [One lady] did an Oxford Union debate and went in dungarees. And I said to her, 'I wore an evening dress, went out and bought one specially. Oxford Union always dresses up, they all wear dinner jackets for their debates . . . you are throwing away the good you are doing. They won't listen to you, just because of how you look.' She said, 'I am myself and I will be myself,' which you couldn't argue with. But to me she was wasting her efforts. She actually lost a debate, and I never lost one.[146]

Bitter internal disputes also took place within NAC regarding the merits of working within a broadly 'male-dominated trade union movement' and the compromises this entailed, with divisions tracking broader disagreement as to whether 'abortion was a bottom line thing'.[147] Particular ire was provoked by NAC's two-pronged response to the Corrie Bill, with material published in its own name describing a 'fight for the right to control our bodies and our own lives', and a distinct, more cautious Campaign Against the Corrie Bill (CACB) aiming merely to 'Defend the 1967 Abortion Act'.[148] Bradford NAC argued:

Ironically, at the end of the day, the people NAC is trying to impress as to our respectability still regard us as an ugly rabble, while other women feel, rightly, that we have betrayed them. . . . [T]he right of women to control their own bodies is subversive, representing as it does a central attack on the family and woman's place in the home. It cannot be made 'respectable'.[149]

Moreover, while the TUC's role in the demonstration was broadly welcomed, some attacked it as 'obscenely inappropriate that a march on this issue which so vitally and personally concerns women, should be led by men' and 'insulting in the extreme' that by the time the women-only section 'eventually arrived in Trafalgar Square, the platform had packed up and gone'.[150] Moreover,

---

[146] Munday interviewed by O'Neill.

[147] Cook interviewed by O'Neill. This was a key focus of discussion at the first NAC conference, which Cook attended. See Wellcome Library, SA/NAC/B/14, NAC, '1975–1985: Ten Years of Fighting for Women's Abortion Rights'; SA/NAC/D/1/1, *NAC News* (no. 1), 25 April 1975; GWL, Edinburgh Women's Centre Archive, EWC 3.3, NAC, 'A Woman's Right to Choose', c. 1976. See further this chapter, pp. 90–91.

[148] Wellcome Library, SA/NAC/B/3/1/6, NAC Against Corrie Leaflet; see also the careful framing of TUC Warwick, MSS.292E/824.1/1, leaflet 'Abortion: Keep it legal, keep it safe', 1979. See further Hoggart, 'Socialist Feminism, Reproductive Rights and Political Action', 112–14.

[149] Emphasis in original. Wellcome Library, SA/NAC/B/3/1/2, Letter from Bradford NAC to NAC HQ, 13 February 1980. See further Charnock, 'This Haunting Sadness', 18.

[150] TUC Warwick, MSS.292E/824.1/1, Letter from Angela Phillips, NAC/Labour Abortion Rights Campaign (LARC) TU Liaison, 22 November 1979. See also letters from Women in Media (9 November 1979), Dinah Bisdee (30 October 1979), Abortion Action Group (undated), Bristol Trades Union Council (12 November 1979); Debbie de Lange, for Haringey NAC (15 November 1979). See also Jolly, 'The feelings behind the slogans'.

[y]our organiser on the PA system at Hyde Park was speaking of 'protecting our women' as if women were feeble brainless little things with no views on matters like abortion which concern them. Somewhat as if he was talking about cruelty to dumb animals … Banners beginning 'TUC says …' smack strongly of patronising male attitudes from the patriarchal system (and the TUC is still very much a male-dominated institution) telling poor, ignorant women what is good for them.[151]

Berer reflects that 'it was never very easy to be in the feminist movement, ever. It was never comfortable. There was always somebody who thought you should have done it some other way.'[152]

For his part, John Corrie sought to rise above the fray, presenting himself as a pragmatic moderate, who – like White and Benyon – sought nothing more than to contain abortion services within the limits that Parliament had originally intended. Acknowledging that the worst abuses were now addressed through regulation, he aimed to prevent abortion 'on demand' by tightening the grounds for abortion, to reduce the upper time limit, to strengthen provision for conscientious objection, and to protect women from the alleged negative mental and physical health consequences of abortion.[153] Recognising the now-powerful understanding of abortion as a woman's issue, he reported that women had told him that if only 'they had known what it all entailed, they would not have gone through with the abortion'.[154] He worried that almost all who consulted non-NHS providers were referred for abortion, whereas women might be better supported through 'counselling on how they can be helped out of the difficult situation into which they have got themselves'.[155] He also criticised the fact that the woman 'alone … can decide whether to keep the baby. The father has no say whatever.'[156]

Corrie provoked a robust response from Labour women MPs. Inspired by the need to defend the Abortion Act, they had now bonded together into a formidable force that belied their small numbers, with informal discussions in the Lady Members' sitting room permitting a cohesive front in public debate and the 'articulation of a new self-confidence' that would subsequently also be

---

[151] TUC Warwick, MSS.292E/824.1/1, Letter from Dinah Bisdee to TUC General Secretary, 30 October 1979. This perspective was certainly not shared by all NAC members: indeed, our Scottish activist interviewees tended to emphasise very close and largely uncontroversial links with unions. For Henderson, 'the simplistic analysis of a Trade Union Movement doesn't really do justice to the role that the movement plays in fighting for working women's rights, of which abortion is a fundamental one … it felt like a joint effort … I think that the Scottish story, if there is one, would maybe reflect that those movements were not so far apart from each other as people might imagine they were.' Henderson interviewed by O'Neill.

[152] Berer interviewed by O'Neill.

[153] *Hansard*, HC, 13 July 1979, vol. 970, cols 892–96, 903.

[154] Corrie in *Hansard*, HC, 13 July 1979, vol. 970, cols 896–97.

[155] Corrie in *Hansard*, HC, 13 July 1979, vol. 970, col. 898; see McDonald's response, HC, 13 July 1979, vol. 970, col. 917.

[156] Corrie in *Hansard*, HC, 13 July 1979, vol. 970, col. 896.

mobilised in other contexts.[157] One study of the female MPs who sat in the late 1970s concluded that no other subject had the same impact in concentrating 'women's aspirations and self-awareness on one issue – rather as the suffragettes did in earlier days':

> Both gave women a focus, something precise and specifiable and central to their developing self-consciousness. The claim to control their own bodies, to choose maternity or otherwise, was both more politically impressive and more psychologically satisfying than diffuse and vague claims for 'liberation'. And yet in the abortion issue was also symbolised the wider demand by women that their ideas and priorities should be taken as they were presented and neither defined by men, nor distorted by being presented as seen through the lenses of male opinion.[158]

There were now only 19 women in the House of Commons, 11 of them on the Labour benches. However, six women – four of them Labour – spoke in the Second Reading debate, to powerful effect.[159] A journalist for *The Sunday Times* described Renée Short, Joan Lestor and Jo Richardson MPs as a 'terrifying cabal of ginger perms vitriolically united' in defence of the Act,[160] capturing a powerful visual contrast between these fiery Labour women (with Short 'smart as Bette Davis in her violet frock') and the grey-suited, older, Conservative MPs sitting opposite, including the 'bravura, Gilbert and Sullivan figure' of Bernard Braine and the 'smiling mother-in-law' of Jill Knight.[161] Labour women's defence of the Abortion Act again focused not just on the most extreme cases but also on abortion as an issue for all women.[162] Corrie's concern with irresponsible 'girls' was rebutted with the claim that 'women who undergo abortions do so only after the deepest and most careful thought'.[163]

Moderate MPs had other concerns, finding the Bill poorly drafted, with its text agreed only on the day of its publication.[164] However, with Corrie declaring himself open to further amendments,[165] it comfortably passed its Second Reading,[166] giving him a sizeable majority of supporters on the

---

[157] Vallance, *Women in the House*, 75, 88, 96. Vallance's research drew on interviews with most of the female MPs who sat in the late 1970s.

[158] Vallance, *Women in the House*, 92–93.

[159] See Kelly, 'Women Members of Parliament'. Those intervening were Richardson, Dunwoody, McDonald and Boothroyd (all Lab, against Corrie) and Knight and Kellett-Bowman (both Con, in support).

[160] 'The Abortion Debate – Or is it Debacle?', *Sunday Times*, 10 February 1980.

[161] Ibid.

[162] E.g. Richardson in *Hansard*, HC, 13 July 1979, vol. 970, cols 919, 923.

[163] Richardson in *Hansard*, HC, 13 July 1979, vol. 970, col. 919.

[164] Wellcome Library, SA/NAC/B/3/6, Co-ord, *New Humanist* (August 1979), in BPAS, *Corrie Bill Newsletter* vol. 5 no. 9, September 1979.

[165] *Hansard*, HC, 13 July 1979, vol. 970, cols 894–95.

[166] By 242 to 98 votes.

Committee convened to consider it.[167] Now, however, his problems began to bite. While the five members who opposed the Bill worked effectively together 'night and day',[168] its 10 supporters were more fundamentalist than Corrie, far from united and often unwilling to compromise. The price that Corrie paid for their support was considerable pressure to include specific clauses.[169] His Bill emerged from the Committee larger than he had intended, redrafted to such an extent that it required lengthy further debate and including provisions unlikely to command support amongst moderate MPs.[170] These problems were ably exploited by his opponents, who tabled large numbers of amendments at the Report stage in order to talk out the Bill.[171] Joyce Gould recalls frenzied activity:

> [T]he campaigners, the people like NAC and ALRA and all of them, they all worked together under the Coordinating Committee ... they would sit in Jo [Richardson]'s office all night writing the stuff up ready for the next day, and it was just incredible. They would sit in the corridors and we had lawyers and all sorts of advisors and people. It was a real height of activity ... [and] a height of emotion too, because we had to get it right.[172]

While abortion votes are not whipped, Labour's Conference resolution in support of the Act nonetheless now became important. Gould took a seat in the spectator's box in the chamber, recalling that 'a party official had never ever been there before ... [and] having me sitting there as the MPs were going in to vote scared them so much that they all went in the right lobby!'.[173] Most devastatingly of all for Corrie, any hope that a Tory Government would be receptive to requests for extra parliamentary time were now dashed. Recognising the sensitivity of the issue, Margaret Thatcher resisted his entreaties both as a matter of principle and because the Bill was likely to create divisions amongst her supporters.[174]

---

[167] Just two (Richardson and McDonald) of the five Committee members opposing the Bill were women, reflecting a strategic choice to prefer MPs who were knowledgeable regarding parliamentary procedures, see Marsh and Chambers, *Abortion Politics*, 115.

[168] Gould interviewed by O'Neill.

[169] Marsh and Chambers, *Abortion Politics*, 114.

[170] House of Commons Standing Committee C, *Minutes of Proceedings on the Abortion (Amendment) Bill*, 18 December 1979. TNA, MH 156/569, briefing note by D. Brereton, 'Abortion: Mr Corrie's Amendment Bill', 4 July 1979. See generally Marsh and Chambers, *Abortion Politics*.

[171] *Hansard*, HC, 15 February 1980, vol. 978, cols 1931–2019; 29 February 1980, vol. 979, cols 1715–809. See generally Marsh and Chambers, *Abortion Politics*.

[172] Gould interviewed by O'Neill.

[173] Ibid.

[174] TNA, MH 156/571, Letter from the Private Secretary, 10 Downing Street, to Jeremy Knight, DHSS, 31 January 1980. See further TNA, CAB 128/67/9, Minutes of Cabinet Meeting, 6 March 1980.

When it became clear that the Bill would inevitably fall due to a lack of time, Corrie withdrew it,[175] leaving his supporters to '[wallow] unprofitably in a welter of bitterness and recrimination'.[176] Commentators concluded that the Bill had been badly mishandled,[177] with its sponsors 'foolish', 'greedy',[178] and 'blinded by the frustration caused by their repeated failures to amend the Act in the previous decade'.[179] It seems likely that a more limited measure aiming purely to reduce the upper time limit for abortion would have succeeded.[180] Corrie himself acknowledged that a lesson must be learnt by those who sought reform 'not to ask for too much next time because they simply won't get it through the House of Commons'.[181]

The impact of Corrie's defeat on campaigners was significant. Marge Berer recalls both that 'the steam came out of the anti-abortion movement', and that fractures within the Pro-Choice movement now blew wide open:

> After Corrie was over, we had a national conference and there was a whole discussion of what next, what are we going to do next? And I put a motion on the table, that we should broaden out and become a reproductive rights network. Boom! Explosion! ... [I]t basically brought out this whole disagreement about whether it was politically correct to work only on abortion or not, and if it would get you anywhere.[182]

Angry debate centred on whether attempting to work within the broader Labour Movement was appropriate and effective and whether focusing on abortion as a single issue was alienating to some women, particularly black and working-class women who might face greater pressure to limit their fertility.[183] Berer recalls that, while the broader feminist movement was more diverse, on abortion it was a 'very white movement'.[184] A paper from the conference emphasised, '[w]e are offered – or denied – particular methods of contraception, abortion or sterilization, depending on who we are. And we are encouraged – or prevented – from having children on the same basis.'[185] NAC

---

[175] *Guardian*, 26 March 1980; Marsh and Chambers, *Abortion Politics*, 142.

[176] *Times*, 15 March 1980.

[177] Ibid.

[178] Munday interviewed by O'Neill.

[179] Paintin, *Abortion Law Reform in Britain*, 92.

[180] Marsh and Chambers, chapter 5. See also Paintin, ibid.

[181] Corrie quoted in *Guardian*, 21 March 1980. See further Marsh and Chambers, *Abortion Politics*, 179.

[182] Berer interviewed by O'Neill.

[183] Eileen Cook recalls, 'I suppose, NAC women tend to think, if women don't have the right to abortion, then everything else falls. It's like taking the first card away, and lots of other rights will fall with it. I think the Women's Reproductive Rights people were more inclusive about all the other things, they wanted to see them altogether.' Cook interviewed by O'Neill. See further Berer interviewed by O'Neill. For more on the differential pressures faced by black women, see Chapter 2, p. 42; Bryan, Dadzie and Scafe, *The Heart of the Race*, 103–05.

[184] Berer interviewed by O'Neill.

[185] NAC 'The Case for Change', cited in Thomlinson, *Race, Ethnicity and the Women's Movement in England, 1968–1993*, 168.

split in 1983 as a result: the larger section continued in the same vein as a single-issue campaign, with others leaving to form the short-lived Women's Reproductive Rights Campaign.[186]

In any case, it would be almost another decade before the movement faced another threat on the scale of the Corrie Bill. One seasoned observer proclaimed that 'a truce has now been declared' within Parliament, with two strongly anti-abortion MPs drawing high places in the Private Members' Bills ballot the following year and using them to pursue other concerns.[187]

Corrie's message had been clearly heard: his would be the last Ballot Bill attempting wide-ranging restrictive reform of the Abortion Act. While a number of further attacks on the Abortion Act would be made over the following eight years, all were Presentation Bills and Ten Minute Rule Bills, serving to highlight ongoing disquiet but with little hope of passing into law. The first of these, brought by the young, newly elected Liberal MP David Alton, was a modest, one-clause Ten Minute Rule Bill that envisaged the reduction of the upper time limit for abortion to 24 weeks.[188] The proposal commanded broad support following the repeated, distressing 'living abortus' cases that Life had publicised to such good effect. Now, with almost everybody agreed that 'really 24 weeks was more sensible', David Steel acted as a co-sponsor.[189] While the Bill failed to progress, its exclusive focus on the upper time limit suggested that Alton had learnt the lesson of Corrie's failure. This approach – of chipping away at the Abortion Act through narrowly focused measures calibrated to maximise support from moderates – would now become dominant.

In this light, the two other restrictive Bills proposed during this period – one in the Lords and one in the Commons – now appeared anachronistic: after the 'saga' of the Corrie Bill, Parliament had tired of the issue, with most uncommitted MPs 'wishing it would go away'.[190] The first proposed a tightening of the social clause so as to limit access to abortion to those exceptional cases of 'genuine medical grounds of substance', disallowing it 'for trivial reasons or abortion on request'.[191] The second was proposed by the Tory MP Peter

---

[186] Berer recalls, 'some of us just left NAC as a consequence. We weren't welcome, we didn't want to be there.' Berer interviewed by O'Neill. Cook, on the other hand, 'stayed on the Abortion Campaign side' and was glad that this split coincided with her own move to Scotland: '[T]he whole of the Scottish Abortion Campaign was on the NAC side. So . . . I just moved from the sort of, what at the time was a very divisive situation in London, to what was quite a relief to be in Scotland.' Cook interviewed by O'Neill. See further Thomlinson, *Race, Ethnicity and the Women's Movement in England, 1968–1993*, 168–69.

[187] Lord Houghton, husband of Vera Houghton (former ALRA Chair) in *Hansard*, House of Lords, 6 December 1982, vol. 437, col. 61.

[188] Abortion (Amendment) Bill, *Hansard*, HC, 22 April 1980, vol. 983, cols 221–26.

[189] David Steel interviewed by Jane O'Neill, 5 February 2018, also noting the importance of Alton being 'a fellow Liberal'.

[190] Marsh and Chambers, *Abortion Politics*, 182.

[191] Lord Robertson, Abortion (Amendment) Bill [HL], see *Hansard*, Lords, 6 December 1982, vol. 437, col. 56.

Bruinvels, who is today perhaps mainly remembered for a level of explicit homophobia exceptional even by the standards of the mid-1980s.[192] Bruinvels proposed the reduction of the upper time limit and the addition of a provision requiring that 'the father of the unborn child [be] consulted about the mother's intention to terminate the pregnancy' or – where a couple were married – requiring his consent for the abortion.[193] The Bills failed. The question of the appropriateness of the 'social clause' now appeared closed, with Parliament having no interest in 'putting the clock back'.[194]

This period also saw the first debate of a proposal for liberalising reform since the Abortion Act had been introduced.[195] Criticising the marked variation in access to services, Jo Richardson (Lab) proposed a 'sensible and humane' measure to ensure equality of access to an essential women's health service, without charge, as for other NHS operations.[196] Avoiding the spectacle of a male MP arguing against the measure, Jill Knight made the opposing case: disparity in access to NHS services reflected 'that some doctors operate the law as Parliament intended and will not carry out the operation unless they believe that there are good reasons for doing so, while others abort any woman who asks'; and, far from being a health service like any other, abortion was 'not supposed to be available to all comers'.[197] The Richardson Bill failed its first reading by a solid margin.[198] It nonetheless suggested an emerging confidence amongst Pro-Choice advocates to claim abortion as an essential, mainstream health service like any other.[199] However, first they would be forced back onto the defensive as David Alton won a high place in the Private Members' ballot.

The Alton Bill 1988

David Alton (Lib) had been elected in 1979 at just 24 years old, becoming 'the baby of the House'.[200] The son of a native Irish speaker, Alton was a 'small,

---

[192] He told the BBC, 'I do not agree with homosexuality. I think that Clause 28 [of the Local Government Act 1988] will help outlaw it and the rest will be done by AIDS, with a substantial number of homosexuals dying of AIDS. I think that's probably the best way.' BBC Radio 4, 'The Reunion: Stonewall'.

[193] Infant Life (Preservation) and Paternal Rights Bill 1987.

[194] Lena (by then Lady) Jeger, arguing against the Robertson Bill in *Hansard*, Lords, 6 December 1982, vol. 437, cols 69, 105.

[195] NHS Act 1977 (Amendment) Bill 1981.

[196] Richardson in *Hansard*, HC, 1 July 1981, vol. 7, cols 877–79. On variation in access to services, see Chapter 2, pp. 33–35.

[197] Knight in *Hansard*, HC, 1 July 1981, vol. 7, col. 879.

[198] Ayes 139; Noes 215.

[199] LARC believed such a measure might also 'bring about a change in public attitudes', paving the way for decriminalisation. Modern Records Centre, University of Warwick, Papers of Andrew Whitehead, MSS.21/1528/AB/8, Toni Gorton and Anne Kingsbury, LARC, 'Fight to commit the next Labour Government to legislate for AWRTC', c. 1980.

[200] The unofficial title given to the youngest member of the House of Commons.

fine-featured, soft-spoken, intense and pious' Catholic,[201] who espoused a politics rooted in 'authentic human values' and social justice.[202] Writing in *The Guardian*, Polly Toynbee concluded that, from a pro-choice perspective, he was 'not a very satisfactory villain'.[203] With the notable exception of Norman St John-Stevas in 1970, earlier Bills had been largely brought by MPs who claimed no particular interest in the issue of abortion, who were not distinguished by strong religious belief, and who found the Pro-Life movement too extreme to help with pragmatic, moderate reform. In Alton, for whom principled opposition to abortion would become a career-defining issue, the movement had finally found their parliamentary champion. Jack Scarisbrick describes him as 'very skilful, intelligent, charismatic, [a] very good speaker, and with imagination: a tactician as well'. Moreover, with abortion now accepted as a woman's issue within Parliament, Alton was also able to 'parry the stuff, "what do you know about it? You are a miserable male"' with '"look, I am a father and a husband and I have children, I know what I am talking about"'.[204]

While the fate of previous bills showed that abortion law reform would not be easy, Alton nonetheless enjoyed several advantages. First, while he came from a different political tradition, his natural support was to be found amongst Tories who, by 1987, held a large majority in Parliament, with many frustrated that a meaningful vote on abortion had been repeatedly blocked. Second, as a Liberal, Alton might – like Steel – hope to attract votes from the Labour benches. Third, he had learnt the lesson of Corrie's defeat, accepting that a wide-ranging attempt to restrict the grounds for abortion would be doomed to fail. While outside Parliament Alton would compare the 'human destruction' caused by legal abortion to the atrocities of Nazi Germany and the Black Death,[205] within it, he would make a pragmatic case for narrowly targeted reform designed to speak to moderates. His Bill thus translated his absolute principled moral opposition to abortion into a single proposal: a reduction of the upper time limit for most abortions to 18 weeks.[206] While Life likewise remained 'steadfastly absolutist' in its opposition to abortion, it agreed that 'anything that reduces the amount of killing is to be supported, provided you are making it absolutely clear that you would not be satisfied with that'.[207] However, in order to secure the support of moderates, Alton agreed to an

---

[201] 'With Men and God on his Side', *Guardian*, 1 October 1987.

[202] Alton, *What Kind of Country?*

[203] 'With Men and God on his Side', *Guardian*, 1 October 1987.

[204] Scarisbrick interviewed by O'Neill.

[205] Alton, 'Truth Should Speak to Power'.

[206] Abortion (Amendment) Bill 1988, permitting abortion until 28 weeks where necessary to prevent a woman's death or grave permanent injury, in cases of incest or rape of a minor or where 'the child is likely to be born dead, or with physical abnormalities so serious that its life cannot be independently sustained'.

[207] Scarisbrick interviewed by O'Neill.

exception permitting abortion after 18 weeks in the case of serious fetal anomaly, which would prove unpopular with campaigners.[208]

As ever, campaigning was fierce. 'Back Alton's Bill – Yes' (BABY) was met with 'Fight the Alton Bill' (FAB). Meetings and writing campaigns were organised; posters, leaflets, badges and car stickers proliferated.[209] FAB held a benefit performance at the Hackney Empire and large demonstrations in London and Glasgow, with female MPs taking a prominent role.[210] Ann Henderson, a Scottish Abortion Campaign and trade union activist, recalls of the Glasgow demonstration:

> I remember being proud to take the [National Union of Railwaymen] banner and the men who came – it was important. And it was a huge demonstration . . . there were trade union banners from all over Scotland, and the photographs of the hall being completely full and just . . . it just was the place to be, really.[211]

SPUC responded with public meetings and religious vigils.[212] MPs toured the country, addressing 'increasingly rowdy' meetings, attended by large groups of supporters and protesters: Alton reported that the police had to hold back Pro-Choice demonstrators attempting to storm the church doors at one large rally.[213] With Pro-Life campaigners convinced that minds would change if people could only see for themselves what was involved in abortion, Parliament was 'flooded' with postcards of an 'eighteen-week baby in the womb'.[214] Life made a video documentary: '18 Weeks: Dead or Alive'.[215] SPUC took out a double-page colour advertisement in several national newspapers, with a statement signed by 300 MPs, clergy, peers, doctors, activists and others. Their advertisement featured a large photograph of an 18 week fetus, with the caption: 'We've abolished the death penalty for murderers and terrorists. Shouldn't we abolish it for him, too?'[216] Media interest was intense: in the seven months that the Bill was before Parliament, Diane Munday reports having participated in 83 broadcasts about it.[217]

---

[208] See Dee, *The Anti-Abortion Campaign in England*, 103–04.

[209] Wellcome Library, SA/NAC/B/6/4/2, SPUC, 'Facts on the Abortion (Amendment) Bill, c. 1987; SA/NAC/B/6/1/5, Bulletin of the Fight the Alton Bill Campaign, no. 4, 1988; *Catholic Herald*, 8 January 1988; *Catholic Herald*, 18 March 1988; *Church Times*, 6 May 1988; *Sunday Times*, 17 January 1988.

[210] Including Jo Richardson, Harriet Harman, Diane Abbott (Lab) and Teresa Gorman (Con). *Independent*, 22 January 1988. See Wellcome Library, SA/NAC/B/6/1/5, 'FAB Presents Women's Choice', flyer and event programme.

[211] Henderson interviewed by O'Neill.

[212] *Church Times*, 6 May 1988.

[213] Widdecombe, *Strictly Ann*, 168.

[214] Ibid., 165.

[215] Wellcome Library, SA/NAC/ B/6/4/2, BABY flyer, c. 1988.

[216] *Independent*, 15 January 1988; *Human Concern* no. 25, 1.

[217] Diane Munday Papers (awaiting cataloguing in the Wellcome Library), memo from Diane Munday to Ian Jones, 'What I Do Within my PR Role', 27 November 1988.

Alton enjoyed an uneasy relationship with his supporters on the Tory benches.[218] While some of them continued to criticise irresponsible women and to champion individual responsibility,[219] his framing of the issue shared more with the socialist feminist language of Pro-Choice campaigners. Alton spoke of compassion, social responsibility and women's needs. He emphasised female support for his Bill,[220] enlisting five female co-sponsors and ensuring that the results of the Second Reading vote were read in a woman's voice.[221] He argued:

> Women are frequently pressurised into abortions by men. Men too often leave a woman in the lurch, having used their sexuality without responsibility. Those who maintain that abortion is purely a woman's issue do women no service; it allows men to evade their responsibilities, and without changes in men's attitudes women will not be truly liberated.[222]

Alton also claimed that abortion had significant negative consequences on women's health[223] and emphasised the desperate situation of those travelling for late abortions, who would be 'duly despatched on an aeroplane back to the countries from which they came, without any care or compassion'.[224] Making brief reference to an issue that would gain far greater prominence in subsequent years, he decried sex-selective abortion.[225]

In the 1987 general election, 41 women had been elected to Parliament, 21 of them for Labour, representing a significant expansion of the 'terrifying cabal of ginger perms' that had opposed Corrie.[226] Their importance was now such as to provoke a group of Labour Catholic MPs to organise in support of Alton and against 'strident feminism' within the party.[227] Further, they were now joined by powerful female Conservative allies, reflecting a 'remarkable consensus' that 'stretches from every woman Labour Member right across to the Conservative Women's National Committee'.[228] Their defence of the Abortion Act partly echoed that of earlier debates, framing abortion as 'the lesser of two evils',[229] in view of social deprivation, poor support for pregnant

---

[218] Widdecombe, *Strictly Ann*, 164, recalls he was initially frosty, seeing her as 'one of those right-wing Thatcherites'.

[219] E.g. Dicks in *Hansard*, HC, 22 January 1988, vol. 125, cols 1228–96; Knight in *Hansard*, HC, 22 January 1988, vol. 125, cols 1228–96.

[220] E.g. Alton in *Hansard*, HC, 22 January 1988, vol. 125, col. 1231; Alton, *What Kind of Country?*, 175–80.

[221] Widdecombe, *Strictly Ann*, 165.

[222] Alton in *Hansard*, HC, 22 January 1988, vol. 125, col. 1235.

[223] Alton in *Hansard*, HC, 22 January 1988, vol. 125, col. 1230.

[224] Alton in *Hansard*, HC, 22 January 1988, vol. 125, col. 1232.

[225] *Hansard*, HC, 22 January 1988, vol. 125, col. 1230.

[226] See generally Wellcome Library, SA/NAC/B/6/2, 'Labour Women's Action Committee – Women Fighting for Women: The Fight Against Alton's Bill and the Labour Party', c. 1987.

[227] *Observer*, 17 January 1988.

[228] Wise in *Hansard*, HC, 22 January 1988, vol. 125, col. 1291.

[229] Steel in *Hansard*, HC, 22 January 1988, vol. 125, col. 1240.

women, cuts to family planning budgets and inadequate welfare benefits.[230] Much to Alton's irritation, his opponents continued to emphasise 'hard cases' that he felt bore little resemblance to everyday abortion practice,[231] repeatedly citing the needs of the 'vulnerable, the not very intelligent and the inadequate'.[232] However, they also placed a powerful emphasis on the right of women to control their own bodies and challenged Alton's claim to speak for women: Clare Short (Lab) instructed the 'overwhelmingly male House of Commons' that '[e]very man in this House who has ever used a woman's body and walked away and did not know the consequence has no right to vote on the Bill'.[233] While not yet offering personal accounts of abortion, these MPs nonetheless placed powerful emphasis on the importance of their own experiences as women.[234]

Alongside emphasising social justice and women's rights, Alton also placed a new focus on scientific fact, grounding his case for reform in a morally inflected account of clinical advances:

> In 1967, let alone in 1929, medics could not take an electrocardiogram of the baby, which shows its heartbeat and reaction to painful stimuli as its heartbeat increases. Twenty years ago, it would have been impossible accurately to date the exact time of gestational development or the characteristics of the developing child. Clearly, ultrasound scanning, chorionic villus sampling and amniocentesis have changed all that. Since 1967 we have revolutionised our awareness of the humanity of the developing child.[235]

Alton's concern with later abortion fell on the fertile ground that had been ploughed by almost two decades of sustained publicity surrounding 'living abortus' cases, with details of a new case again emerging at the most politically expedient moment. The 'Carlisle Baby' was said to have lived for three hours following an abortion at 21 weeks, performed in July 1987, following a diagnosis of Ehlers–Danlos syndrome.[236] These events were publicised some six months later, at the time of the Bill's Second Reading.[237] Again, some detected 'distorted reporting' and cynical political expediency in this timing,

---

[230] Richardson in *Hansard*, HC, 22 January 1988, vol. 125, cols 1272–77.

[231] Alton in *Hansard*, HC, 22 January 1988, vol. 125, col. 1234.

[232] MacKay in *Hansard*, HC, 22 January 1988, vol. 125, col. 1238; see further Richardson in *Hansard*, HC, 22 January 1988, vol. 125, col. 1187; Moonie, *Hansard*, HC, 22 January 1988, vol. 125, cols 1247–49.

[233] Short in *Hansard*, HC, 22 January 1988, vol. 125, col. 1260.

[234] E.g. Short in *Hansard*, HC, 22 January 1988, vol. 125, col. 1260.

[235] Alton in *Hansard*, HC, 22 January 1988, vol. 125, col. 1228, see further col. 1230; and Alton, *What Kind of Country?*, 172. On the shift to scientifically grounded arguments, see Franklin, 'Fetal Fascinations', 190–205.

[236] A group of rare inherited conditions affecting connective tissue. Symptoms are relatively mild in some, disabling in others and, in rare cases, life-threatening.

[237] The Alton Bill began its Second Reading in January 1988 and the case was reported in early February. See 'Inquiry Demand after Baby "Left to Die"', *Catholic Herald*, 12 February 1988.

whilst others alleged a cover-up.[238] For his part, Alton argued that the case vindicated his concerns with the upper time limit and the performance of abortion for minor disabilities.[239] However, while his focus on the upper time limit was designed to maximise support for his Bill, Alton nonetheless faced an uphill struggle to convince Parliament that the meaning of 'later' might logically be separated from viability.[240] The RCOG rejected his proposed 18 week limit as having 'no scientific basis', as doing little to reduce the total number of abortions, and as discriminating against women most in need.[241] Alton stood accused of a 'deeply dishonest' translation of principled opposition into whittling away at the Abortion Act,[242] with the 18 week limit 'plucked out of the air'. After all, asked one supporter of the Act, if 'he believes that abortion is murder, surely it is murder at 16 weeks, 14 weeks or 12 weeks?'.[243]

The Bill nonetheless commanded a majority at what Alton claimed to be the best-attended Second Reading debate since World War Two:[244] 296 voted for it and 251 voted against. Whilst the number voting in favour included 55 Labour MPs, it did not escape the notice of contemporary commentators that every one of them was male.[245] While this majority offered Alton the hope of success, when it reached its Report stage, once again the Bill was talked out without reaching a final vote.[246] Pro-Life campaigners were 'angry and scandalised that a measure of such moral importance could be sabotaged by ... the pro-abortion lobby', with 'the tactics of despair' again thwarting the will of Parliament.[247] An Early Day Motion signed by more than 100 MPs and 'representations ... from thousands of people' requested more time 'to decide this important matter'.[248] None was forthcoming. With even those Bills that appear to have enjoyed a substantial parliamentary majority having no real prospect of changing the law, Alton reflected that the Abortion Act was now in the 'unique constitutional position' of being set 'in concrete' as 'a great untouchable'.[249]

---

[238] See discussion in *Hansard*, HC, 6 May 1988, vol. 132, cols 1191–95; and 8 June 1989, vol. 154, cols 460, 462.

[239] See generally Alton, *What Kind of Country?*, 173–75.

[240] E.g. *Hansard*, HC, 22 January 1988, vol. 125, col. 1244; 6 May 1988, vol. 132, col. 1197.

[241] RCOG, *Report on the Advantages and Disadvantages of Imposing an 18 Week Gestational Limit on Legal Abortion*.

[242] Short in *Hansard*, HC, 22 January 1988, vol. 125, col. 1259.

[243] Mackay in *Hansard*, HC, 22 January 1988, vol. 125, col. 1236.

[244] Alton in *Hansard*, HC, 24 April 1990, vol. 171, col. 222.

[245] Wellcome Library, SA/NAC/B/6/2, 'Labour Women's Action Committee – Women Fighting for Women: The Fight Against Alton's Bill and the Labour Party', c. 1988; *Guardian*, 15 February 1988.

[246] *Hansard*, HC, 6 May 1988, vol. 132, cols 1186–215; see *Guardian*, 7 May 1988.

[247] Keith Davies (Life) and Christopher Whitehouse (SPUC), respectively, each cited in *Church Times*, 13 May 1988.

[248] Alton in *Hansard*, HC, 13 May 1988, vol. 133, col. 650.

[249] Alton with Holmes, *Whose Choice Anyway?*, 174.

While it had failed to achieve statutory reform, the Alton Bill nonetheless left its mark, reframing the central issues at the heart of the political debate and laying the foundations from which subsequent attacks on the Abortion Act would be launched. For White, Benyon and Corrie, an overarching concern with the permissibility of abortion had translated into questions of individual responsibility, the appropriate grounds for abortion, and the kind of woman who was 'deserving' of access to it (with a bright line drawn between selfish, promiscuous, feckless single women and over-burdened, poverty-stricken mothers worn down by repeated pregnancies). Now, with the Abortion Act having become embedded in practice, previously pervasive criticisms of those seeking abortion for frivolous reasons faded away to be replaced by competing claims to speak for women, contrasting visions of social justice and contestation regarding the medical consequences of abortion for women's mental and physical health. Importantly, Alton translated his own absolute principled opposition into a very different political question: how late in pregnancy should abortion be allowed? This pragmatic decision from a devout Catholic reflected an understanding that most moderate MPs viewed later abortions as qualitatively different from earlier ones, an assumption that had been notably absent within earlier parliamentary debates.[250] This allowed Alton to frame the need for reform as grounded in a morally infused vision of the science of fetal development that was revealing new truths regarding the 'humanity' of the unborn.[251] However, Colin Harte (SPUC) would later reflect that while the Bill had been supported by those 'with good motives', the strategic choice to focus on later abortion had undermined the anti-abortion position: '[T]he argument became "why are we aborting viable babies?", not babies overall.'[252]

In debates regarding the Alton Bill, the issue of abortion for fetal anomaly had also become more prominent, particularly in relation to later abortion. In 1967, the central concern voiced in Parliament regarding this ground had turned on the number of 'normal' pregnancies that would necessarily be sacrificed to avoid the birth of one disabled child. Now, while not yet led by disability rights advocates within Parliament, the issue was reframed as one of discrimination against disabled people, with Alton rejecting the 'defeatism' of abortion in favour of 'uninhibited, unqualified, unconditional love ... backed up by practical support, care and resources'.[253] The irony that his own Bill had made a pragmatic concession in permitting abortion after 18 weeks in the

---

[250] Chapter 1, pp. 17–18.
[251] See generally Franklin et al., *Off-Centre*. For the subsequent importance of such claims, see this chapter, p. 102; and Chapter 7, pp. 230, 232–33.
[252] Interviews cited in Dee, *The Anti-Abortion Campaign in England*, 108.
[253] *Hansard*, HC, 22 January 1988, vol. 125, cols 1234–35.

presence of very serious fetal anomalies was not lost on disability rights campaigners.[254]

The Alton Bill had one further important practical consequence: it greatly added to pressure on Government, with fury at this further denial of the opportunity for a meaningful vote provoking a flurry of further activity. The following parliamentary session saw no fewer than six Private Members' Bills, two adjournment debates, 112 parliamentary questions on abortion,[255] and the development of a '"lateral arabesque" school of anti-choice activity', whereby amendments relating to abortion were proposed to any Bill where even the remotest connection to abortion might be claimed.[256]

Two of these Bills were introduced by then-Tory MP Ann Widdecombe, a recent convert to Catholicism due to her views on abortion.[257] Having drawn seventh place in the Private Members' ballot, Widdecombe now became the first female MP to introduce a restrictive abortion measure, electing to revive the Alton Bill.[258] In Scarisbrick's view 'a great girl with lots of guts',[259] Widdecombe deployed all available 'ruses and antics' to 'choke off other bills' standing in the path of her own (with only the first six Ballot Bills ensured a Second Reading debate). When she failed due to the adept use of obscure parliamentary procedure by the veteran Labour MP Dennis Skinner, she deployed an equally arcane measure to wreak her revenge,[260] before promptly proposing a further abortion bill.[261] While these efforts enjoyed no real prospect of success, they powerfully illustrated that until MPs were permitted a meaningful vote, they would be 'back, and back and back'.[262] Four other bills were proposed in the same session by male Tory MPs focusing either on conscientious objection rights or the need to restrain alleged profiteering within the 'abortion industry'.[263]

One further measure was presented to the Commons in early 1990. Following in the footsteps of Jo Richardson, Dawn Primarolo (Lab) tabled a Presentation Bill that framed abortion as a normal and essential part of a comprehensive health service for women, which the Government thus had

---

[254] See Dee, *The Anti-Abortion Campaign in England*, 104–05. See further Widdecombe, *Strictly Ann*, 167.

[255] Freeman in *Hansard*, HC, 27 July 1989, vol. 157, cols 1386–87.

[256] Cossey, 'The Politics of the Abortion Pill', 54.

[257] Widdecombe, *Strictly Ann*, 242–50. Widdecombe would much later win a seat in the European Parliament for the United Kingdom Independence Party (UKIP) and then become a parliamentary candidate for the short-lived Brexit Party.

[258] Widdecombe, Abortion (Amendment) Bill 1989.

[259] Scarisbrick interviewed by O'Neill.

[260] See Widdecombe, *Strictly Ann*, 169–72, on her use of the 'I Spy Strangers' rule to disrupt an adjournment debate called by Skinner.

[261] Abortion (Treatment of Non-Resident Women) Bill 1989 (a Ten Minute Rule Bill).

[262] Widdecombe, *Strictly Ann*, 170.

[263] Bennet, Abortion (Financial Benefits) Bill 1989; Hargreaves, Abortion (Rights of Ancillary Workers) Bill 1989; Amess, Abortion (Right of Conscience) (Amendment) Bill 1989; Braine Abortion (Amendment of Grounds) Bill 1989.

a duty to provide.[264] However, Primarolo also went much further, proposing that a new ground be added to the Abortion Act to permit termination in all cases where two doctors formed a good faith view that a fetus had not yet achieved viability, with decision-making power left to women before that point. As a Presentation Bill, this was designed not to achieve immediate reform but rather to signal a new front in MPs' willingness to push for radical liberalising change.

The 1990 Reforms

In the meantime, the House of Lords had also been active. In early 1987, Hugh Montefiore, the Bishop of Birmingham, had introduced a Bill with the 'modest aim' of reducing the upper time limit for abortion to 24 weeks.[265] When he retired, a Select Committee had already begun its scrutiny, and Douglas Houghton – husband of the ALRA campaigner Vera – took up the Bill so that the Committee might complete its work.[266] Having taken evidence from a range of sources, it concluded that an upper time limit had been read into the Abortion Act entirely 'inadvertently' but recommended that a 24 week limit should now be enshrined on the face of the statute for most abortions.[267] Lord Houghton introduced a Bill to implement its recommendations and, in March 1990, this completed all legislative stages in the House of Lords, becoming the first abortion Bill to do so in either House since 1967.[268]

While no time to debate the Houghton Bill was offered in the Commons, another opportunity for reform now presented itself. The Human Fertilisation and Embryology Bill was a long and complex Government Bill designed to address some of the pressing regulatory and ethical questions raised by advances in embryo research and infertility treatment services.[269] Piloting it through Parliament was a sensitive and difficult enough task, and the Health Secretary, Kenneth Clarke, was initially firmly against allowing the Bill to be 'hijacked' by amendments on abortion law.[270] However, he now came under sustained pressure from all sides. Given recent frenzied parliamentary activity, the reported promise that Pro-Life MPs would 'go away for a while' if given a

---

[264] Medical Services for Women Bill 1990; presented at *Hansard*, HC, 27 March 1990, vol. 170, cols 240–42.

[265] Infant Life (Preservation) Bill (HL) 1986; *Hansard*, Lords, 28 January 1987, vol. 483, col. 1406.

[266] Houghton, Infant Life (Preservation) Bill 1987. House of Lords, *Special Report with Evidence of the Select Committee on the Infant Life (Preservation) Bill [H.L.]*, 1986–1987, HL 153.

[267] House of Lords, *Report of the Select Committee on the Infant Life (Preservation) Bill [H.L.]*, 1987–1988, HL 50, paras 17, 59. Contrary to this view, we have seen that the inclusion of an upper time limit was deliberate: Chapter 1, p. 15.

[268] Abortion (Amendment) Bill No. 2 (HL) 1988.

[269] *Report of the Committee of Inquiry into Human Fertilisation and Embryology*, Cmnd 9314, 1984 ('The Warnock Report'); see generally Mulkay, *The Embryo Research Debate*.

[270] Widdecombe, *Strictly Ann*, 189. See further Clarke in *Hansard*, HC, 24 April 1990, vol. 171, col. 265.

meaningful vote must have been attractive,[271] and David Alton and Ann Widdecombe each saw his agreement to accept abortion amendments to be a direct consequence of their own Bills.[272] Moreover, notwithstanding the opposition of the major Pro-Choice groups,[273] pressure also now came from Douglas Houghton, who saw the Bill as the perfect vehicle for an amendment designed to achieve a 'sensible lull in this otherwise interminable controversy', permitting 'the moderates to get abortion out of politics!!'.[274] David Steel concurred, seeing the entrenchment of a 24 week limit as necessary to prevent easy majorities for future attempts to restrict the Abortion Act.[275] Clarke was convinced.

With a meaningful vote in sight, campaigning reached fever pitch. Clarke's office was targeted by 'the Socialist Workers party outside with a tannoy attacking Tory attempts to restrict a woman's right to choose, and the Society for the Protection of Unborn Children inside, presenting ... an embryo and demanding that we reduce the limit to 18 weeks'.[276] Between 2,000 and 3,000 women joined a march called at short notice in defence of the Act,[277] and 10,000 Pro-Life campaigners coalesced in the 'biggest lobby in the life of this Parliament'.[278] The best-publicised intervention, however, was one that demonstrated anti-abortion campaigners' belief in the intuitive persuasive power of the visual: SPUC posted a plastic model of a 20 week fetus to every MP, accompanied by a description of fetal development.[279] While some condemned this as 'a gross act of bad taste',[280] others welcomed the controversy as a sure sign of success.[281] Houghton would later claim that SPUC must have spent 'well over £500,000' on this initiative, its distribution of the film *The Silent Scream* and newspaper advertisements.[282]

It was now widely accepted that the main issue for Parliament to consider was that of a gestational limit and at 'what point, if at all, do the rights of the

---

[271] Widdecombe in *Hansard*, HC, 24 April 1990, vol. 171, col. 199.

[272] Alton in *Hansard*, Lords, 12 December 2007, vol. 697, col. 308; Widdecombe, *Strictly Ann*, 170, 189.

[273] E.g. Wellcome Library, SA/NAC/B/7/7, NAC flyer, 'Stop the Amendment Campaign', 1990; NAC flyer, 'Week of Action', c. 1990.

[274] London School of Economics (LSE) Archives, Papers of David Steel, STEEL/B/2/2, Letters from Douglas Houghton to David Steel, 6 February and 21 March 1990.

[275] LSE Archives, STEEL/B/2/2, Letters from David Steel to M. Tearse (Co-ord), 3 July 1989 and Douglas Houghton, c. March 1990. Clarke in *Hansard*, HC, 24 April 1990, vol. 171, col. 264.

[276] Clarke in *Hansard*, HC, 24 April 1990, vol. 171, col. 265.

[277] Richardson in *Hansard*, HC, 24 April 1990, vol. 171, col. 184.

[278] Alton in *Hansard*, HC, 24 April 1990, vol. 171, col. 221.

[279] *Human Concern* no. 30, summer 1990, 7; *Guardian*, 23 April 1990; *Times*, 24 April 1990.

[280] Mackay in *Hansard*, HC, 24 April 1990, vol. 171, col. 243, describing the impact on a secretary who had opened the package following a recent miscarriage.

[281] Phyllis Bowman (SPUC), cited in *Times*, 24 April 1990.

[282] Houghton in *Hansard*, Lords, 18 October 1990, vol. 522, col. 1068. On the use of fetal imagery in anti-abortion campaigning, see generally Dee, *The Anti-Abortion Campaign in England*, 134–38; and Chapter 4, pp. 143–49.

unborn child prevail over those of the mother?'.[283] A novel mechanism was conceived to test opinion by starting 'down the middle of the strongly held passions',[284] with Houghton reportedly involved in its design.[285] A Government amendment – to be put to the vote only once MPs had been given the opportunity to vote on a series of potential changes to it – foresaw the entrenchment of a 24 week limit on the face of the Abortion Act, with exceptions permitting abortion until 28 weeks for risk of grave permanent injury to a woman's health or substantial risk of serious handicap, or without limit where there was a serious risk to the woman's life. This was accompanied by a list of possible amendments to the amendment, with voting conducted 'pendulum' style beginning with options at the extremes (18 and 28 weeks). With a general upper time limit agreed, MPs would then be invited to vote on setting a different time limit for the exceptional cases. The result was a horribly complex set of votes, with some amendments foreseen for the second round of voting potentially becoming redundant in light of decisions made in the first.[286] Around a dozen 'idiots' guides' on how to vote were said to be in circulation.[287]

While there was strong support within Parliament for reducing the number of later abortions, there was significant disagreement as to whether this would be better achieved through legal reform or improved sex education and family planning.[288] Proponents of a lower legal limit combined assertions of medical advance and the sanctity of life,[289] with Alton explaining that 'quantum leaps in our knowledge' have 'revolutionised our knowledge about the unborn child', making it 'absurd to leave our laws in the dark ages'.[290] Others emphasised that medical advances would continue to push down the age of viability and that Parliament must legislate for the future, with 'a reduction of four weeks in the time limit for abortion [not offering] fair reflection of 23 years of advancement in medical science'.[291] The Carlisle Baby was frequently referenced.[292]

Those leading the case for restrictive reform were again very different from those opposing it. Eight MPs made speeches in support of restrictive reform:

---

[283] Widdecombe in *Hansard*, HC, 24 April 1990, vol. 171, col. 189.

[284] Clarke in *Hansard*, HC, 24 April 1990, vol. 171, col. 265.

[285] According to Madeleine Simms, see Paintin, *Abortion Law Reform in Britain*, 97.

[286] Clarke in *Hansard*, HC, 24 April 1990, vol. 171, col. 264.

[287] Richardson in *Hansard*, HC, 24 April 1990, vol. 171, col. 184. E.g. see LSE Archives, STEEL/B/2/2, *Human Fertilisation and Embryology Bill: Abortion: Guide to new clause 4* (authorship unknown).

[288] E.g. Clarke in *Hansard*, HC, 24 April 1990, vol. 171, col. 263; Barron, col. 258.

[289] E.g. Amess in *Hansard*, HC, 24 April 1990, vol. 171, col. 254; Paisley, col. 235.

[290] *Hansard*, HC, 24 April 1990, vol. 171, col. 223.

[291] Kellett-Bowman in *Hansard*, HC, 24 April 1990, vol. 171, col. 241; Smyth, col. 241, Amess, col. 255.

[292] E.g. *Hansard*, HC, 24 April 1990, vol. 171, cols 174, 193, 219, 226–27. The case had already been the subject of a separate adjournment debate, see HC, 8 June 1989, vol. 154, cols 460–68.

all but Widdecombe were men; all but Alton were Tories o
Unionists; most had been in Parliament for many years; and
were distinguished by their strong religious beliefs, with their number including two church ministers.[293] On the other side, eight women and three men made the case against restrictive reform; most were Labour; and all but three had entered Parliament in the 1980s, suggesting a powerful generational shift.[294] Again, they made their case strongly in terms of women's rights, with Theresa Gorman (Con) finding herself branded an 'Amazon'[295] for her attack on male colleagues 'who do not have to bear the responsibility of an unwanted birth and pregnancy' and should therefore not have 'the temerity, arrogance, inhumanity and insensitivity' to make decisions for women that do.[296] Those who persisted in trying to restrict women's abortion rights were influenced by theology, 'one of the deepest, most misogynous strands in human society':

> For centuries, theologians have equated sex with sin and celibacy with grace. They have regarded women as little more than flower pots in which future generations of children, preferably boy children, are reared. Time and again we hear people pay lip-service to a woman's rights in this, yet when it comes down to it they legislate to give priority to the rights of the foetus that she carries. Whatever time limit they come up with, whether 18 weeks or some other, their motivation is to prevent a woman from controlling her fertility.[297]

After years of thwarted attempts to reach a meaningful vote on the issue of the upper time limit on abortion, the opportunity finally arrived. The limit of 18 weeks proposed by Alton was tested first and overwhelmingly rejected by 355 to 165 votes. Limits of 28, then 20, then 26 and finally 22 weeks were each similarly proposed and failed, leaving the 24 week limit set out in the Government amendment to be written into the Abortion Act.[298] In practice, this served to entrench the status quo, with the RCOG having already advised doctors to respect an upper limit of 24 weeks for most abortions,[299] and 'doctors in the real world' guided more by this advice than the previously 'unsatisfactory state of the law.'[300]

---

[293] Braine, Alton, Duffy, (Rev) Paisley, Cormack, (Rev) Smyth, Duffy and Widdecombe. Braine, Father of the House, was first elected in 1950; others had entered Parliament in the 1960s and 1970s, with just Widdecombe and Smyth having arrived in the 1980s.

[294] Harman, Nicholson, Gorman, Primarolo, Short, Barron, Gordon, Mahon, Steel, Richardson and Mackay: all but the last three had entered Parliament in the 1980s (this count excludes Doran, who spoke specifically about the Scottish legal position).

[295] Smyth in *Hansard*, HC, 24 April 1990, vol. 171, col. 240.

[296] Gorman in *Hansard*, HC, 24 April 1990, vol. 171, cols 232, 229.

[297] Gorman in *Hansard*, HC, 24 April 1990, vol. 171, cols 229–30.

[298] See Table 1 in Chapter 7, p. 236 for a summary of the voting.

[299] RCOG C37/1-29, RCOG, *Report on Fetal Viability and Clinical Practice*, 1985, 9; see Chapter 5, pp. 154–55.

[300] Warden, 'Abortion Minefield for Doctors,' 1076.

The support of professional organisations for a 24 week limit had offered a crucial reference point for MPs seeking to navigate what Widdecombe described as the 'impossible question' of 'when is a child a child?':

> If an arbitrary line is to be set somewhere between conception and birth then reasons for the decision have to be given. Should it be when a child is capable of being born alive, when a child is fully developed in terms of organs, lungs and limbs and has only growth left to achieve, when it quickens in the womb, when it is capable of feeling pain? The undecided peered at pictures in medical textbooks and stayed undecided.[301]

On the contrary, the RCOG had offered the 'undecided' a basis for believing that, while drawing a line at 18, 20 or 28 weeks was indeed 'arbitrary', drawing one at 24 weeks was not. Its view was frequently cited in Parliament and was undoubtedly influential.[302] The alternative that came closest to being accepted was 22 weeks, suggesting that the major point of dispute was less whether 'viability' offered the appropriate moral marker but, rather, precisely when it occurred.[303] The series of heart-wrenching and well-publicised stories of babies born alive following late abortions had also played a vital role in entrenching the significance of viability in the parliamentary consciousness as an important 'moral watershed'.[304]

With an upper time limit agreed, MPs then voted on a second tranche of amendments. These resulted in the removal of the upper time limit for abortion where continuing the pregnancy might cause grave permanent injury to a woman's health and – far more controversially – in the presence of substantial risk of serious fetal anomaly (with this latter amendment tabled by Jo Richardson).[305] Finally, MPs voted to 'uncouple' the Abortion Act from the Infant Life Preservation Act to avoid confusion in cases where two statutes with different time limits might potentially apply in the same case.

A further possibility to introduce amendments came at the Report stage. Jo Richardson now proposed a public register – for David Alton, 'a blacklist' – of doctors who held a conscientious objection to abortion in order to ensure that women did not suffer unnecessary delay due to consulting them.[306] Amendments tabled respectively by Harriet Harman (Lab) and Emma Nicholson with David Price (both Con) sought to permit abortion during

---

[301] Widdecombe, *Strictly Ann*, 167.

[302] E.g. *Hansard*, HC, 24 April 1990, vol. 171, cols 173, 267. The RCOG wrote to all MPs, with replies confirming that its views would 'carry very particular weight', e.g. RCOG B/10/12/4, Letter from Brittain, 3 May 1988, and other correspondence. The Government also distributed an account of the views of the Royal Colleges to MPs: TNA, CAB 128/89/15, Minutes of Cabinet Meeting, 28 April 1988.

[303] Ayes 255; Noes 301. E.g. see Widdecombe in *Hansard*, HC, 24 April 1990, vol. 171, col. 191, arguing that viability meant 22 weeks.

[304] Bishop of York in *Hansard*, Lords, 18 October 1990, vol. 522, col. 1048.

[305] Passed respectively with 337 to 146 and 277 to 201 votes.

[306] Richardson in *Hansard*, HC, 21 June 1990, vol. 174, col. 1158; Alton, col. 1148.

the first 12 weeks of pregnancy either on the woman's request or, alternatively, with just one doctor's signature. It was argued that such changes might cut red tape and thus reduce the numbers of later abortions.[307] While these amendments reflected a widely shared sensibility of a qualitative difference between earlier and later abortions, they were bitterly opposed as introducing 'abortion on demand'[308] and making it easier to have an abortion 'for the most trifling reason'.[309] For the first time, Pro-Life MPs moved into a grudging defence of the Abortion Act for, whatever its failings,

> at least it requires good reasons to be given for abortion. It provides some, albeit paltry, recognition of the fact that the unborn child is special and that abortion is special and cannot be equated with a simple operation, such as having a tooth out. If we remove the medical grounds, we remove that minimum recognition of the difference between such operations.[310]

The amendments were defeated; however, the proposal that only one medical signature be required failed by just 28 votes.

A further liberalising amendment aimed to extend the Abortion Act to Northern Ireland. In line with the convention that abortion is subject to an unwhipped vote, the Government had remained neutral on all other amendments. It nonetheless strongly opposed this one, arguing that it dealt with a devolved matter and would be 'offensive to the overwhelming majority of people in the Province'.[311] It was defeated by a margin of two to one.

A further tranche of amendments included two tabled by a backbench Conservative MP, Robert Key. The first clarified the legality of selective reduction of multiple pregnancies, a procedure that had become more common given the practice of simultaneous implantation of several embryos in assisted reproduction.[312] The second gave the Government the power to 'license a broader class of places' for the use of abortifacients, recognising that the development of RU486 (mifepristone, the 'abortion pill') raised the future possibility of abortions being performed safely without the need for specialised facilities. Clarke advised that the first would avoid leaving law 'shrouded in doubt' and the second ensured that, were RU486 to be licensed, the Government would have the necessary power to regulate its use, avoiding the need 'for a private Member's Bill on every Friday for several years'.[313] In an exchange that would be closely picked over some 30 years later, he denied

---

[307] Harman in *Hansard*, HC, 21 June 1990, vol. 174, col. 1137; Nicholson, cols 1150–51.

[308] Leigh in *Hansard*, HC, 21 June 1990, vol. 174, col. 1158.

[309] Braine in *Hansard*, HC, 21 June 1990, vol. 174, col. 1144.

[310] Widdecombe in *Hansard*, HC, 21 June 1990, vol. 174, col. 1164. See also Duffy, col. 1151.

[311] Bottomley in *Hansard*, HC, 21 June 1990, vol. 174, cols 1161–62. See Chapter 6, p. 203.

[312] It was previously unclear whether such procedures – where a fetus was killed but not immediately expelled from the body – were caught either by the criminal prohibition on 'unlawful procurement of miscarriage' or by the Abortion Act, which applies where 'a pregnancy is terminated'; see generally Kennedy and Grubb, *Medical Law*, 1481–84.

[313] Clarke in *Hansard*, HC, 21 June 1990, vol. 174, col. 1200.

Ann Widdecombe's suggestion that this was 'merely a paving measure ... for self-administered home abortion', explaining that RU486 would be used 'only in closely regulated circumstances' such as a GP's surgery.[314] The two amendments passed with large majorities.

Two final amendments were related to abortion for fetal anomaly. Pro-Life MPs had been horrified at the removal of the upper time limit on this ground, suggesting that it resulted from tiredness and confusion.[315] Two eminent academic lawyers with links to the Pro-Life movement – John Finnis and John Keown[316] – had claimed that the change meant that '[i]f abortion on any of the four grounds results in the delivery of a living and viable foetus, it would be lawful to destroy it during birth for any reason at all, from harelip to hair colour'.[317] Their view was criticised as 'scaremongering' and an unacceptable 'smear on the medical profession',[318] and the attempt to reverse the vote failed by a narrow margin.[319] The second amendment took a different tack, aiming to increase scrutiny through requiring more detailed reporting regarding the anomaly for which an abortion was performed, revealing 'whether doctors are aborting for spina bifida, hydrocephalus and cystic fibrosis or for harelip and club foot'.[320] This resulted in an equal division of the House and fell to be determined on the Speaker's vote, which by convention is cast to leave a Bill as it emerged from Committee. Anti-abortion MPs were again shocked, having been so confident of the success of this amendment that one supporter had already left, reportedly coming close to crashing his car on hearing the news.[321] However, their failure was not absolute: Clarke was convinced of the merits of the proposed measure, pledging to implement it through regulation notwithstanding the outcome of the vote.

The Human Fertilisation and Embryology Bill then moved to the House of Lords. Given that the abortion clause closely replicated the terms of the recently approved Houghton Bill, its success there was largely assured, notwithstanding concerns regarding the new clauses permitting abortion beyond viability.[322] The removal of the upper time limit in these cases would continue as an important focus of dispute, with campaigners maintaining a watchful eye on the additional data generated by the enhanced reporting requirements introduced in line with Clarke's promise.[323]

---

[314] *Hansard*, HC, 21 June 1990, vol. 174, cols 1195, 1201.

[315] Cormack in *Hansard*, HC, 21 June 1990, vol. 174, col. 1181.

[316] Finnis and Keown would each work closely with Pro-Life campaigners in litigation; see Chapter 5, p. 167 and pp. 159–60.

[317] *Hansard*, HC, 21 June 1990, vol. 174, col. 1185.

[318] Doran in *Hansard*, HC, 21 June 1990, vol. 174, col. 1184; Steel, col. 1188.

[319] Ayes 215; Noes 229. The previous vote had been lost by a wider margin: Ayes 201; Noes 277.

[320] Widdecombe in *Hansard*, HC, 21 June 1990, vol. 174, col. 1190.

[321] Widdecombe, *Strictly Ann*, 193.

[322] *Hansard*, Lords, 18 October 1990, vol. 522, cols 1042–119.

[323] See Chapter 5, pp. 173–76.

Conclusion

By 1990, the Abortion Act had been subject to over two decades of sustained campaigning, with many hundreds of hours spent debating it within Parliament. With the possibility of a meaningful vote repeatedly thwarted by the manipulation of parliamentary procedures, anti-abortion campaigners were bitterly disappointed at the 'numbing political defeat' suffered when such an opportunity finally materialised.[324] Jack Scarisbrick recalls:

> [T]he high point [of campaigning] was the first 15, 20 years . . . It was difficult to sustain momentum in the face of continual defeat, and the sense that even MPs, Pro-Life MPs, were still talking about lowering the upper limit and never really going for the jugular. The religious leaders and other people who should be speaking out had gone silent and had given up on it.[325]

The movement had also learnt an important, painful lesson regarding the possibility of achieving reform through a Private Member's Bill, with such measures repeatedly blocked by 'procedures which are firmly rooted in the nineteenth century'.[326] In response, successive generations of MPs have been necessarily creative in their attempts to amend or defend the Act, pushing arcane parliamentary procedures to their limits and sometimes hastening their reform. The Abortion Act's legacy is also written into the parliamentary rule book: Widdecombe's revenge on Dennis Skinner resulted in reform of the 'I Spy Strangers' rule, which she had used to disrupt his debate;[327] later instances of creativity would hasten reform of the allocation of slots for Ten Minute Rule Bills and contribute to the introduction of more robust regulation of the work of All-Party Parliamentary Groups.[328]

The Abortion Act had nonetheless survived largely intact. It was now well embedded in practice and its broad framework commanded widespread support amongst moderate MPs. For the first time, attempts at liberalising reform had achieved equal prominence to restrictive ones and, over the years to follow, they would gain further momentum. Moreover, while attacks on the Act would continue, their framing had now definitively changed. White, Benyon and Corrie had presented what they claimed to be pragmatic, moderate reforms that restricted the Abortion Act to the limits originally intended for it and abortion to truly 'deserving' categories of women. The sponsors of future attempts at restrictive reform would tend to follow not in their footsteps but in those of David Alton: they would be distinguished by the central role of

---

[324] Lord Houghton in *Hansard*, Lords, 18 October 1990, vol. 522, col. 1201.

[325] Scarisbrick interviewed by O'Neill. See generally Dee, *The Anti-Abortion Campaign*, chapter 5.

[326] Widdecombe, *Strictly Ann*, 169–70, citing Bernard Braine. See further Hindell and Simms, *Abortion Law Reformed*, 231–33; Brazier and Fox, 'Enhancing the Backbench MP's Role as a Legislator', 201–11.

[327] Widdecombe, *Strictly Ann*, 171–72, describing how she had cried out 'I spy strangers' during Skinner's debate, leading to the chamber being cleared.

[328] See Chapter 7, pp. 225–26. and 241–42.

religious belief in driving their parliamentary work; they would translate principled opposition to abortion into narrowly framed measures that sought to chip away at the Abortion Act; they would implicitly accept access to abortion in early pregnancy in order to focus on the upper time limit and, increasingly, the fetal anomaly ground of the Act; and they would advance morally infused visions of scientific fact and clinical advance as justifying the need for reform. However, with abortion rights now claimed as a key plank of women's liberation, these attacks would be led by women and often framed in a language of women's rights. They would be met by a powerful opposition, with Labour women MPs continuing to play a leading role.[329]

For now, with anti-abortion MPs having promised to 'go away' for a while if offered a meaningful vote, a rare hiatus of relative calm would follow in Parliament. In 1990, Margaret Thatcher was ousted, leaving the Conservatives to hang onto power for nearly seven more years under John Major; then, in 1997, a Labour Government was elected under Tony Blair, ushering in a large influx of new female Labour MPs and decisively shifting the parliamentary arithmetic around abortion.

[329] See Chapter 7.

4

The Battle for Normalisation

Abortions are safe. Abortions are normal. Abortions are healthcare.[1]

Disputes about abortion are never just about abortion.[2] In the mid-1970s, the eminent journalist, staunch critic of the Sexual Revolution and later Catholic convert Malcolm Muggeridge went so far as to argue that abortion attacked 'the very basis of our mortal existence', with Britain at a crossroads:

> Either we go on with the process of shaping our own destiny without reference to any higher being than Man, deciding ourselves how many children shall be born, when and in what varieties, and which lives are worth continuing and which should be put out ... Or we draw back, seeking to understand and fall in with our Creator's purpose for us rather than to pursue our own, in true humility praying, as the founder of our religion and our civilisation taught us. Thy will be done.[3]

In passing the Abortion Act, Parliament had signalled a clear choice regarding not just the permissibility of abortion but also the changing values of a country in the midst of a demographic revolution.[4] Contestation regarding the Act's implementation would continue to lie on the fault line between the tectonic plates of changing sexual, gender and familial norms and the respective weight placed on religion and science in shaping our understanding of the world.

Parliament had sent a second clear signal in 1990: from that moment it should have been clear to all informed observers that the battle for comprehensive restrictive reform of the Abortion Act had been definitively lost. This would provoke a relative hiatus in Parliamentary activity until the mid-2000s, and when attacks returned they would look very different: narrowly focused measures designed to chip away at the Act would replace the full-scale assaults of White, Benyon and Corrie. In the meantime, however, the question of how the Act should be interpreted and implemented would continue to be fiercely contested. For one side, with the parliamentary battle to defend the Act won,

---

[1] Abortion Rights, tagline in email signature (22 January 2020), on file with the authors.
[2] See Sanger, *About Abortion*, for a compelling exploration of this argument in the US context.
[3] 'What the Abortion Argument is About', *Sunday Times*, 2 February 1975.
[4] Brown, *Religion and the Demographic Revolution*.

abortion should be accepted as an inevitable part of women's experience and made easily accessible on request without judgement or stigma, as part of mainstream healthcare. For the other, if abortion was ever acceptable, this was only as an exceptional measure of last resort to be offered for compelling reasons after careful, painful deliberation and leaving an inevitable legacy of guilt and suffering. While one side thus sought the normalisation of abortion as a safe, effective intervention and an imperative of public health and women's liberation, the other raged against the trivialisation of an immoral and profoundly harmful procedure.

In the next chapter, we will consider those disputes that found focus in questions of the Act's legal meaning, ending in the courts. Here, we explore some other ongoing struggles regarding the implementation of the Act, spanning the five decades of its existence but with a particular focus on the period of the hiatus in Parliamentary activity from 1990 to the mid-2000s. During this period, abortion services would become further embedded and extended, new technologies would be developed that made abortion technically easier and safer, and abortion on request would become more widely accepted. These broad changes offered the context that would shape the attacks on the Abortion Act when they again started to gather momentum in Parliament.

Over the course of this period, while those who sought the normalisation of abortion would appear to be increasingly in the ascendancy, their victories would nonetheless remain contested and ambivalent. NHS-funded abortion services would become far more readily accessible; however, rather than being embedded within mainstream healthcare, they would be increasingly outsourced to non-NHS providers such as BPAS and Marie Stopes International (MSI). With these providers taking a very liberal interpretation of the Act, abortion would become increasingly available on request, yet popular concerns would flare where abortion was believed to be sought without compelling reason and painful prior reflection. Contestation would focus, in particular, on the role of non-NHS abortion providers and their liberal interpretation of the Abortion Act, the safety of abortion in general and any new technical innovation in particular, and the impact of abortion on women. Finally, a silent revolution whereby prenatal testing and screening technologies became routinely embedded as a normal part of antenatal care, underpinned by the possibility of the termination of affected pregnancies, would come into tension with changing attitudes towards disabled people.

A Demographic Revolution

Familial, sexual and gender norms have changed dramatically over the last five decades. In the colourful prose of Ann Widdecombe, in the early years after the Abortion Act came into effect,

[t]he wild decade which was the sixties had fizzled out and taken with it much of its optimism, while its legacy of permissiveness had yet to turn into moral anarchy in what remained largely a socially conservative country. Divorce was easier but still not lightly sought, abortion available but widely frowned upon, homosexual acts legal but in the closet, pre-marital sex widespread but without the wholesale promiscuity which was to come . . .[5]

By the early 1990s, sociologists were proclaiming a demographic revolution, with sexuality freed from an intrinsic and inevitable connection with reproduction and reproduction increasingly freed from a connection with marriage.[6] Our understandings of intimate relationships were becoming more fluid, with bonds between partners understood as less constrained by legal and social expectations and more concerned with personal values, trust and emotional communication. When these intimate bonds cease to exist, it is now widely accepted that relationships may be dissolved, with marriage no longer seen by most as a relationship that must necessarily last for life. Over that period, Britons have tended to become sexually active earlier but to marry much later, to cohabit before – or as an alternative to – marriage, increasingly rarely to have a first sexual experience with a spouse or fiancé(e) and to have fewer children, with almost one in five women today remaining childless.[7] Half of British women will be childless on their thirtieth birthdays compared to around two-fifths of their mothers' and just one-fifth of their grandmothers' generations.[8] The result is a significant extension of the period during which women are simultaneously likely to be sexually active and not intending to become pregnant, with success in achieving this aim dependent on improved sex education, contraception and access to abortion.[9] This has been accompanied by significant shifts in female education and employment. The past 50 years have seen a massive expansion in the numbers continuing into higher

---

[5] Widdecombe, *Strictly Ann*, 96.

[6] See generally Giddens, *Modernity and Self-Identity*; Giddens, *The Transformation of Intimacy*; Beck and Beck-Gernsheim, *The Normal Chaos of Love*; Smart and Neale, *Family Fragments?*; Jamieson, 'Changing Intimacy'; Cook, *The Long Sexual Revolution*.

[7] Office for National Statistics (ONS), *Childbearing for Women Born in Different Years, England and Wales: 2019*; ONS, *Marriages in England and Wales: 2017*; ONS, *Birth Characteristics in England and Wales: 2019*. See generally Wellings et al., 'The prevalence of unplanned pregnancy and associated factors in Britain', 1807–16; Sheldon and Wellings, *Decriminalising Abortion in the UK*, introduction; Jamieson, 'Changing intimacy'; Hall, *Sex, Gender and Social Change in Britain since 1880*; Lewis, *Women in Britain since 1945*.

[8] ONS, *Childbearing for Women Born in Different Years, England and Wales: 2019*, comparing women born in 1989, 1961 and 1934. Those born in 1989 were, on average, 30.7 years old at the birth of their first child compared to 23 years old for those born in 1948.

[9] See ONS, *Birth Characteristics in England and Wales: 2019*. Sheldon and Wellings, *Decriminalising Abortion in the UK*, introduction; Swales and Taylor, 'Moral Issues'; Curtice et al. (eds), *British Social Attitudes: The 36th Report*. See generally Cook, *The Long Sexual Revolution*.

education, where women now study in higher numbers than men,[10] and in participation in the labour market, with many more women now working full time and establishing themselves in careers before starting a family.[11] Women generally now expect (and are expected) to work outside the home: less than one in 10 British adults (8 per cent) now agree that 'a man's job is to earn money, a woman's job is to look after the home and the family', compared to 43 per cent in 1983.[12]

While cause and effect are inextricably intertwined, the increased availability and acceptability of safe legal abortion facilitated by the Abortion Act were fundamental parts of these seismic changes. For ALRA campaigner Dilys Cossey, the Abortion Act freed women to feel more secure and to enjoy sex, with the fear of pregnancy having fundamentally shaped sexual experiences before it, as boyfriends were 'trying to get at you, and you were trying to stop them … because if you got pregnant the price was so *high*'.[13] Fellow campaigner Diane Munday emphasises that access to safe, legal abortion allowed women to 'keep to their plans and achieve their goals':

> Women feel in charge of their lives. It used to be that – what was in charge was the risk of pregnancy. There was always that shadow. And quite often the shadow fell; everything you planned, wanted to do, was stopped, by that. Now women have the confidence to know that they don't necessarily have to go through with an unplanned pregnancy.[14]

Pro-Life commentators tend to agree that easier access to abortion was closely related to shifting gender norms, whilst taking a far less positive view of the meaning of these changes. The co-founder of Life, Jack Scarisbrick, identifies 'abortionism' as cause and effect of the 'relentless debauching of society', contributing to a wide range of harms, including the rise of 'gangs of feral girls' who 'prey on the most forlorn housing estates', 'female drunkenness, drug use and yobbishness', leaving 'no place for poetry and not much for chivalry':

> Today's western society has come closer to publicly sweeping aside a basic code of sexual conduct than probably any previous one in history … [The] Sexual Revolution, of which 'liberalised' abortion is a key element, has not liberated women. On the contrary, it has made them ever more available to the predatory male. Every abortion is a profound affront to a woman's dignity, integrity and

---

[10] Some 57% of students in higher education are female: Higher Education Statistics Agency, *Higher Education Student Statistics: UK, 2019/20.*

[11] The employment rate among women of 'prime working age' (aged 25–54) has risen from 57% in 1975 to a record high of 78% in 2017; full-time employment has risen from 29% in 1985 (when data on hours of work began) to 44% in 2017. See Roantree and Vira, *The Rise and Rise of Women's Employment in the UK.*

[12] Attar Taylor and Scott, 'Gender' in Phillips et al. (eds), *British Social Attitudes: The 35th Report.*

[13] Dilys Cossey interviewed by Jane O'Neill, 4 October 2017.

[14] Diane Munday interviewed by Jane O'Neill, 10 November 2017.

femininity ... Women yearn to be cherished. But modern womanhood has lost much of its dignity and 'mystery' and hence male respect. It is difficult to cherish that which is not respected.[15]

He argues for a 'new feminism' to liberate women from the idea that they must be the same as men and 'equally competitive', allowing them to 'rejoice in their complementarity'.[16] Josephine Quintavalle takes a different tack, but one that is no less critical, asking:

> Why is it that a pregnant student feels they can't carry on with their degree? How about accommodating the pregnancy of the student: isn't that what women's rights are all about? ... If women are going to be pregnant in that sort of spectrum between 20 and 35, it's clearly a time when they are going to be professionally realising themselves and then wanting to get jobs, etc. Are they liberated if the only solution to an unplanned pregnancy is to have an abortion?[17]

These changing gender and familial norms are themselves part of a wider, ongoing secularisation of views.[18] The proportion of British adults who identify as Christian has plummeted over the last 50 years: over half now claim to have no religion, two-thirds only attend religious services for weddings, funerals and baptisms, very low confidence is expressed in religious organisations, and the non-religious have become both more confident in their own beliefs and less tolerant of strong expressions of Christianity in public discourse.[19] The result is a decay in 'discursive Christianity', the process whereby people derive and express their customs from the Christian discourses of their time and place.[20] This, in turn, has been accompanied by a strengthening of confidence in science as an alternative way of interpreting and understanding the world, with trust in secular scientific institutions and the benefits of medical advancement very high.[21]

These changes have profoundly marked British life and public opinion, including on abortion. The authoritative British Social Attitudes Survey has asked a representative sample of British adults about their views on abortion for almost four decades. Over that period, a relatively consistent minority of around one in 10 adults has opposed abortion in all circumstances, with a

---

[15] Scarisbrick, *Let There Be Life*, 57. See also Jack Scarisbrick interviewed by Jane O'Neill, 7 November 2017.

[16] Scarisbrick, *Let There Be Life*, 60. See also Alton, *What Kind of Country?*

[17] Josephine Quintavalle interviewed by Jane O'Neill, 6 October 2017.

[18] See generally Brown, *Religion and the Demographic Revolution*; Wilson, *Religion in Secular Life*; Voas and Crockett, 'Religion in Britain', 11–28; Bruce, *British Gods: Religion in Britain Since 1900*.

[19] Curtice et al. (eds), *British Social Attitudes: The 36th Report*; McAnulla, 'Secular Fundamentalists?', 124–45.

[20] Brown, *The Death of Christian Britain*; see further Wilson, *Religion in Secular Life*.

[21] See Curtice et al. (eds), *British Social Attitudes: The 36th Report*; Wilson, *Religion in Secular Life*; Wellcome Trust, *Wellcome Trust Monitor Survey Report*.

correspondingly large majority having consistently accepted the permissibility of abortion in 'traumatic' cases (where there is a risk to the life of the pregnant woman). The most marked changes have come with regard to the proportion who believe that 'the law should allow an abortion when the woman decides on her own she does not wish to have the child', rising from 29 per cent in 1984 (with over half believing it should not) to 70 per cent in 2016.[22]

Secularisation has had a marked impact on Pro-Life campaigning. As John Deighan (SPUC) explains, religious belief has offered an alternative point of reference for Pro-Life campaigners:

> If you lose that, then your reference point is the culture. You are in a river that's flowing down, your only reference points are the other things going down the river with you. But if you have a religious background – if you are Jewish, Muslim, Christian – you have got something on the bank, so you can see how far down the river's flowing. . . . So they are more likely to think, that's a big issue, 'thou shalt not kill' is a big issue. No matter what the tide is saying in the particular society I am in.[23]

While SPUC and Life have always fiercely defended their formal separation from the churches, they had nonetheless relied heavily on them for grass-roots mobilisation. Over time, this support base would dwindle as membership of the liberal churches fell and some – including the Church of England – took a more permissive view on abortion. Those with strongly anti-abortion views would decline in numbers and become more marginal to mainstream opinion, being concentrated within the smaller Evangelical churches and the Catholic Church. Even here, a growing number of Catholics chose to ignore their Church's official teaching on the issue. Eileen Cook recalls that her Catholic mother believed that the Pope was wrong on contraception and abortion, and 'if the Pope was a woman, the Pope would understand! [laughs]'.[24]

Religious identity would remain the most important determinant of where people stood in the abortion debate. However, with a strengthening of confidence in science and technology not just permeating daily life in practical ways but also providing an alternative way of understanding the world, disagreement would come to play out less through contesting moral values and more

---

[22] See Attar Taylor, 'British Attitudes to Abortion'; Curtice et al. (eds), *British Social Attitudes: The 36th Report*; Gill, *Theology Shaped by Society*, 49–50; Jelen and Wilcox, 'Causes and Consequences of Public Attitudes Toward Abortion', 489–500. See also Clements and Field, 'Abortion and Public Opinion in Great Britain', 429–44; Clements, 'Religion and the Sources of Public Opposition to Abortion in Britain', 369–86; Gray and Wellings, 'Is Public Opinion in Support of Decriminalisation?'.

[23] John Deighan interviewed by Jane O'Neill, 29 January 2018.

[24] Eileen Cook interviewed by Jane O'Neill, 11 November 2017. While support for abortion remains lower among Catholics, their opinions have nonetheless become gradually more closely aligned with that of the general public: Attar Taylor, 'British Attitudes to Abortion'; Curtice et al. (eds), *British Social Attitudes*. On how Catholic women negotiated church teachings in their personal lives, see generally Geiringer, *The Pope and the Pill*.

as a matter of contested scientific claims. Each side would now position itself as relying upon objective fact and defending women's true interests against opponents blinded by ideology and self-interest.[25] However, the long-term trend towards secularisation undoubtedly worked against the Pro-Life movement as religious arguments became increasingly marginal to mainstream beliefs, public trust rose in secular scientific institutions and declined in churches,[26] and scientifically framed claims of the harms caused by abortion were challenged by the major professional medical bodies. Over time, the movement would come to perceive itself as facing 'a battle of biblical proportions, where the institutions and Parliament and big business is all lined up on one side and we [the Pro-Life movement] have got a few tents on the other'.[27] Campaigning would be re-energised by the emergence of smaller anti-abortion groups that drew on the direct support of US religious organisations, explicitly seeking 'the imposition of Christian moral values through legislation'.[28] However, older generations of campaigners would greet them with ambivalence: Jack Scarisbrick reflects that while groups such as 40 Days for Life are 'very enthusiastic', their campaigns risked being perceived as 'threatening', 'militant and aggressive', thus giving 'the wrong impression'.[29]

Expanding Access to Abortion Services: Abortion Charities and Clinic Protests

Over time, Pro-Choice campaigners and service providers became able to move off the defensive and to press for the expansion of abortion services as a normal part of healthcare that should be routinely and freely available on the NHS in the same way as any other health service. Stark regional variation in access to NHS services remained a particular source of frustration: as we have seen, the first proposal for liberalising statutory reform considered by Parliament had focused on this disparity.[30] It is ironic that what Jo Richardson failed to achieve with this proposal would eventually come about as an incidental effect of the policies of a Conservative Government. The form taken by this change, which relied on a dominant role for the abortion charities, has been a highly distinctive and significant aspect of the Abortion Act's biography: it would entrench the long-term sustainability of a permissive model of service provision and give a platform to a powerful voice for further liberalising reform. However, the fact that services continued to be offered

---

[25] See further Chapter 7.

[26] Curtice et al. (eds). *British Social Attitudes*, 32; Wilson, *Religion in Secular Life*.

[27] Peter Saunders interviewed by Jane O'Neill, 9 November 2017.

[28] *Times*, 23 July 2005. See also Soper, *Evangelical Christianity in the United States and Britain*, 104–14; Lowe and Page, 'On the Wet Side of the Womb'; Lowe and Hayes, 'Anti-Abortion Clinic Activism, Civil Inattention and the Problem of Gendered Harassment'.

[29] Scarisbrick interviewed by O'Neill. See further Scarisbrick, *Let There Be Life*, 3.

[30] See Chapter 3, p. 92.

outside the NHS, albeit funded by it, gave them an ambivalent status and offered an important, ongoing focus for Pro-Life campaigning.

The Expansion of the Abortion Charities

As we have seen, the NHS had been given no additional resources to cope with the surge in demand for legal abortion after 1967 and, by the early 1970s, less than half of all abortions were performed within it.[31] A highly lucrative for-profit sector quickly emerged in response to the demand and then dwindled rapidly as its prices were undercut by the charities. Over the 1970s, BPAS had expanded rapidly from its base in Birmingham (home of Hugh McLaren), absorbing LPAS, taking over several private-sector nursing homes and concentrating on the areas where NHS services were least available, first in England, then Wales and then establishing a limited presence in Scotland (with a centre in Glasgow, home of Ian Donald).[32] From 1976, it was joined by Marie Stopes International (MSI), operating mainly in England, which would grow to become the second major charitable service provider.[33] Women refused access to NHS services were thus increasingly likely to be able to access economically priced services within the charitable sector. Marked regional variation in access to NHS services stabilised and became entrenched.[34]

However, this was to change as, hoping to stretch health budgets by relying on market principles, the Thatcher Government encouraged NHS commissioners to purchase health services from outside agencies.[35] This new arrangement had a particularly significant effect with regard to abortion services, permitting health authorities to bypass anti-abortion hospital consultants whilst retaining the possibility of dictating standards of care.[36] Agency arrangements for abortion care had been trialled with BPAS in Birmingham, where senior doctors including Hugh McLaren had radically restricted the number of abortions performed within the NHS.[37] With such services often comparing favourably to those within the NHS in terms of safety as well as

---

[31] See Chapter 2; Figure 1, p. 117.

[32] BPAS Archives, 'First Full Pregnancy Advisory Service Approved in Wales', BPAS Press Release, 6 April 1978; 'BPAS Consolidates Success in Glasgow with Open Evening', BPAS Press Release, 15 May 1978.

[33] On the history of MSI, see MSI Reproductive Choices, 'Our History'. In 2020, the organisation changed its name to distance itself from the eugenic views of Marie Stopes. See 'Abortion Provider Changes Name over Marie Stopes Eugenic Link', BBC News, 17 November 2020.

[34] See Chapter 2.

[35] Ham, *Health Policy in Britain*, chapter 2.

[36] Munday, 'The Development of Abortion Services since 1968', 12.

[37] 'Midlands Move to Increase NHS Abortions', *Guardian*, 16 February 1978; BPAS Archives, Francois Lafitte, 'Provision for Abortion in the West Midlands: Comments on the Regional Health Authority's Working Party Report', June 1978, 4.

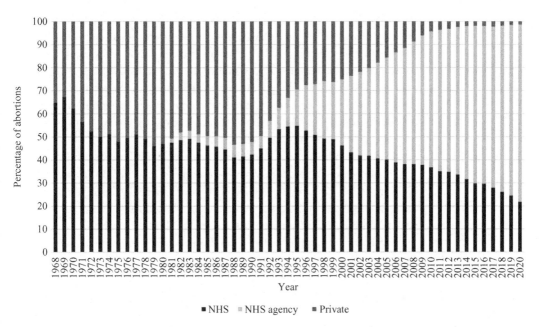

Figure 1 Funding arrangements for abortion for women resident in England and Wales, 1968-2020[38]

cost,[39] these arrangements expanded rapidly: in 1981, 1.8 per cent of abortions for women resident in England and Wales were provided this way, rising to 7.5 per cent in 1992 and 28.7 per cent in 2000.[40] The stark regional variations in NHS funding of abortion services that had previously appeared intractable now gradually disappeared. By 2020, 98.6 per cent of abortions in England and Wales were funded by the NHS, with 77 per cent taking place in the independent sector.[41]

Figure 1 illustrates the dramatic impact of these changes. The proportion of abortions performed within the NHS (shown in black) initially declined sharply, as the number of legal abortions rose and outstripped NHS capacity to perform them; stabilised as numbers began to flatten out and services became established both inside and outside the NHS; and, finally, as services were outsourced to the independent sector under agency arrangements, again

---

[38] Authors' own graph created from data in Department of Health and Social Care, 'Abortion Statistics 2020: Data Tables'.

[39] Fowkes, Catford and Logan, 'Abortion and the NHS: The First Decade', 219, measuring mortality rate, complication rate, concurrent sterilisation rate and proportion of abortions performed after the first trimester. See further Munday, 'The Development of Abortion Services since 1968', 12; Brewer and Huntingford, 'Mortality from Abortion', 562.

[40] Abortion statistics in this chapter have been collated from multiple volumes, published variously as *Registrar General's Statistical Review of England and Wales, Supplement on Abortion* for 1968–1973; Office of Population Censuses and Surveys, *Abortion Statistics* for 1974–2001; and Department of Health, *Abortion Statistics, England and Wales* for 2002–2020. Non-resident women were ordinarily ineligible for NHS funding and are not included in these numbers.

[41] Ibid.

started to decline (a small bulge in NHS provision in the early 1990s may have reflected the recognition that where NHS providers refused to offer abortion services in-house, they would lose budget to the non-NHS sector). At the same time, the proportion of services funded by the NHS (black and light grey combined) increased slowly from the early 1980s and then rapidly from the early 1990s as agency arrangements became more common. As a result, privately funded abortions (shown in dark grey) dwindled from a peak of 54 per cent in 1979 to just 1 per cent in 2020.

BPAS was ambivalent about these developments. It had responded to what it had hoped was a temporary problem, hoping to 'wind up' as soon as the NHS was able to provide all legal abortions. Agency arrangements were welcomed only as an interim solution that allowed the Government to 'systematically employ the charities to undertake all that the NHS is not doing'.[42] However, over time, this 'interim solution' would become firmly embedded, offering a highly distinctive and enormously important feature of service provision in England and Wales (with Scottish services remaining largely within the NHS). The steadily increasing proportion of abortions performed by charities operating with an explicitly pro-choice mandate would be a powerful engine in driving a permissive interpretation of the Abortion Act. The charities would also take on an important role in pushing other service innovations, complaining bitterly when NHS providers were slow to follow suit. Moreover, the commissioning of their services by the NHS – an institution famously described by the Tory politician Nigel Lawson as 'the closest thing the English people have now to a religion'[43] – was an important mark of approval, and a steady income stream from NHS commissioners ensured their financial sustainability, directly supporting their advocacy work.

The 'Abortion Industry' and Clinic Protests

While this change was enormously important in driving a permissive implementation of the Abortion Act, it nonetheless sat in clear tension with attempts to normalise abortion within mainstream NHS services. Within Pro-Life literature, non-NHS providers would be repeatedly singled out for criticism, with little relevance attached to the fact that for-profit providers would now gradually all but disappear. Within such literature, where reference was made to BPAS and MSI as 'charities', the term was invariably enclosed within inverted commas or prefaced with 'so-called', with frequent reference made to the size of operating budgets or the amounts spent on staff salaries. When BPAS and MSI moved to 'normalise' abortion or to remove barriers to services, Pro-Life campaigners discerned attempts to 'trivialise' it, attacking the 'conveyor belt culture' of a profit-motivated 'abortion industry'. Claims

[42] Lafitte, 'How the Charities Fill the Gap', 12; see further Chapter 2, p. 48.
[43] Lawson, The View from No. 11, 613.

that women were actively encouraged to end pregnancies surfaced regularly, including in allegations that MSI had paid staff performance bonuses for reducing the number of women who had decided not to proceed with an abortion following an initial consultation,[44] and they underpinned a profound conviction that providers systematically downplayed or ignored the profound harms caused by abortion to all concerned.[45]

In some instances, Pro-Choice campaigners would join Pro-Life campaigners in raising concerns regarding official policies where the option of having an abortion might appear to have become pressure to do so. For some years, the Ministry of Defence had a policy of forcing women who became pregnant whilst serving in the armed forces to choose between pregnancy and career, with one lawyer involved in the subsequent compensation campaign describing 'a culture of abortion', with the 'military hospital lined up ready to do the operation'.[46] More recently, financial support for children in families claiming child tax credit or universal credit has been restricted to the first two children in a family, with the Conservative Government explaining that those families should 'face the same financial choices about having children as those supporting themselves solely through work'.[47] This policy implicitly relies on women having the means of fertility control, including through abortion.

Pervasive in Pro-Life accounts of an 'abortion industry' is the belief that service providers operate in bad faith, being motivated by money or eugenic beliefs.[48] Jack Scarisbrick offers a rare acknowledgement that this may not always be the case, recognising that many abortion providers act in the – albeit 'profoundly wrong-headed' – belief that they are helping women. He accepts that it is thus 'wrong to portray all doctors and nurses engaged in the abortion trade as brutes'. He continues, however:

> Some may be. Abortion is big business. Some of the private clinics are probably staffed by dregs of the medical profession who are making big bucks out of what they are doing, day after day. Abortion charities like BPAS and Marie Stopes have profitable 'agency agreements' with the NHS by which abortions are done

---

[44] A claim categorically denied by MSI. See 'One of Britain's Largest Abortion Providers "Paid its Staff Bonuses for Encouraging Women to go Through with Procedures" Claims Watchdog in Damning Report', *Daily Mail*, 20 October 2017.

[45] See generally Lowe, '(Re)imagining the "Backstreet"', 203–18.

[46] Cited in 'Didn't Know the Rules were Against the Law. Now they are Paying the Price', *Independent*, 12 July 1994. See further Hadley, *Abortion*, 101–03.

[47] Albeit that many of those affected are not unemployed but in low-paid jobs. See Welfare Reform and Work Act 2016; Kennedy, 'Two Child Limit in Universal Credit and Child Tax Credits'. On the impact of this policy see e.g. Church of England and Child Poverty Action Group, 'No one Knows What the Future Can Hold'; 'Two-Child Benefits Cap Cuts Support for Over 1 million Children During Pandemic', *Guardian*, 15 July 2021; Goretti Horgan interviewed by Jane O'Neill, 30 April 2017.

[48] The most detailed investigation of eugenic motivation is offered by Farmer, *By Their Fruits*.

in the private sector at the taxpayers' expense ... Many women report that their abortion clinic was a callous place and they were treated almost as cattle.[49]

With abortion having rapidly become a technically easier procedure that did not require the facilities of a hospital, the outsourcing of abortion services also resulted in the proliferation of standalone clinics located physically outside of the NHS, which offered convenient sites for protest.

The US campaigner Don Treshman visited Britain in 1993, shortly after the murder of a US abortion doctor at a protest attended by members of his group, Rescue America (an event that Treshman described as 'unfortunate' whilst also noting that many more 'babies' would have died at the doctor's hands had he survived).[50] While US campaigners would go on to bomb, burn and vandalise abortion clinics and kill several further clinic staff, similar violence was not seen in Britain, leaving Treshman to criticise the 'feeble' approach of campaigners and those who 'consider themselves to be Christians but who still believe there is a right to abortion'.[51] Nonetheless, before he was excluded on the basis that his presence was unconducive to the public good, he trained '150 British disciples'.[52]

Treshman's visit inspired Father James Morrow, a Scottish priest and full-time campaigner, to found Rescue UK, representing a marked departure from the approach of SPUC and Life. Depending on one's perspective, Morrow was an 'inspiring crusader' or an 'obstructive zealot'[53] who aimed to 'convert the world to Catholicism'.[54] He argued that the Biblical imperative – '[r]escue those being lead [sic] away to death, Hold back those who are being dragged to the slaughter'[55] – gave campaigners the right to intervene to save the unborn from death in what he called the 'abortuary'.[56] His followers aimed to prevent targeted clinics from 'commit[ing] offences on a daily basis against humanity', declaring their conduct lawful because it aimed to prevent illegal abortions being carried out for 'social rather than legal reasons'.[57] However, they were met in force: at the first clinic protest, Morrow's supporters – reportedly coming mainly from the USA and Ireland – found themselves preceded by Pro-Choice campaigners and 'vastly outnumbered by camera crews and

---

[49] Scarisbrick, *Let There Be Life*, 2

[50] Cohen in *Hansard*, House of Commons (HC), 19 May 1993, vol. 225, col. 241; see further 'Doctor Killed During Abortion Protest', *Washington Post*, 11 March 1993.

[51] 'U.S. Abortion Protesters Shunned by the British', *New York Times*, 13 April 1993.

[52] Ibid.

[53] 'Obituary: Canon James Morrow, Priest and Pro-Life Campaigner', *Scotsman*, 21 September 2010.

[54] *Guardian*, 8 November 1993.

[55] BPAS Archives, 'Rescue' pamphlet, no date, citing Proverbs, 24:11.

[56] Morrow, *A Constitutional Right to Rescue Unborn Children*; 'Obituary: Canon James Morrow, Priest and Pro-Life Campaigner', *Scotsman*, 21 September 2010.

[57] *Morrow and others* v *DPP* (6 July 1993) unreported.

policemen'.[58] Undeterred, on a subsequent occasion, a dozen of them managed to enter a clinic, causing considerable distress to staff and patients. They subsequently faced fines for their 'aggressive demonstration'.[59] Morrow was also arrested on several other occasions, generally for breach of the peace and once for an assault on a pregnant clinic manager.[60] The second liberalising abortion Bill since 1968 was introduced by Harry Cohen (Lab) in 1993 as a response to the group's 'fanaticism' in forcing women who had made 'an often painful and difficult decision ... to run the gauntlet of its abuse and intimidation'.[61]

While Cohen's attempt to introduce new powers to curb their activities would fail, Rescue UK would eventually disappear, leaving Morrow to reflect that he had 'written, typed, printed, published, leafleted, advertised, marched, lobbied, picketed, argued, debated, lectured, phoned, broadcast, counselled, travelled, harassed, begged, borrowed and prayed – and [had] three million dead babies to show for it'.[62] Nonetheless, his work had attracted significant publicity, offering a powerful visible reminder of religiously grounded opposition to abortion and directly challenging any attempt to normalise services. In later years, Rescue UK would be followed by several other small direct-action groups, including 40 Days for Life, the Good Counsel Network, the Helpers of God's Precious Infants and Abort67. These groups, which have small and overlapping memberships, reflect the increasingly international agenda of the US anti-abortion movement, which offers them inspiration and support.[63] They typically formally eschew violence,[64] relying on a wide range of tactics including the display of large images of dismembered fetuses, 'bearing public witness' and conducting prayer vigils, handing out literature, model fetuses or rosary beads, and filming women entering abortion clinics or seeking to engage them in dialogue, with offers of practical support and 'pavement counselling' against abortion and with women sometimes called 'Mum' or warned that they will go to Hell.[65] Members typically deny that they are

---

[58] 'Abortion Clinics under Guard after Clashes: Police Arrest 20 as Violence Flares during Protest by Militant "Pro-Life" Group', *Independent*, 31 March 1993.

[59] Per Watkins LJ, *Morrow*.

[60] According to Cohen in *Hansard*, HC, 19 May 1993, vol. 225, col. 242. See further *R v Morrow and others* (26 March 1993) unreported; 'Obituary: Canon James Morrow, Priest and Pro-Life Campaigner', *Scotsman*, 21 September 2010.

[61] Abortion Clinics (Access) Bill, see *Hansard*, HC, 19 May 1993, vol. 225, cols 241–44.

[62] 'Obituary: Canon James Morrow, Priest and Pro-Life Campaigner', *Scotsman*, 21 September 2010.

[63] Lowe and Hayes, 'Anti-Abortion Clinic Activism, Civil Inattention and the Problem of Gendered Harassment', 330–46.

[64] The Good Counsel Network requires those picketing clinics to sign a 'Statement of Peace', see *Dulgheriu v London Borough of Ealing* [2018] EWHC 1667 (Admin), [8].

[65] Hayes and Lowe, '"A Hard Enough Decision to Make"'; Lowe and Hayes, 'Anti-Abortion Clinic Activism, Civil Inattention and the Problem of Gendered Harassment'; Lowe and Page, 'On the Wet Side of the Womb', 165–80; Jackson and Valentine, 'Performing "Moral Resistance"?', 225–31. Abort67's complaint about a Channel 4 *Dispatches* programme that had shown them

protesters, claiming rather that they are there to help women and that there is no aggression in their 'benign' actions, which are 'axiomatically acts of love and care'.[66] This view reflects strongly held beliefs that abortion harms women[67] and undermines their natural role as mothers.[68]

However, as had been evident to Don Treshman, clinic protests would never gain the same traction in the far more secular British context as in the USA, and more established Pro-Life campaigners would sometimes join those questioning their motivation and impact. Jack Scarisbrick reflects:

> As for picketing of abortion clinics, those taking part have to answer two questions: why am I doing this? and what impact will it have on passers-by, the clinic staff and its clients? The desire to threaten and punish, though subconscious, may be hard at work and it is easy for small handfuls of protestors to look like cranks. It is easy to *seem* to intimidate.[69]

There has nonetheless been a marked increase in Pro-Life activity outside clinics in recent years,[70] causing 'significant emotional and psychological damage' to women accessing services.[71] When residents were invited by one Council to give a view on the presence of the protesters outside an MSI clinic, an overwhelming majority replied that the activities outside the clinic were having a detrimental effect on the locality and supported the imposition of a safe access zone, prohibiting such activities within it.[72] BPAS has responded with a 'Back Off' campaign to call for legislation to impose safe access zones around clinics.[73] While the Government rejected such a measure as disproportionate,[74] some individual councils have moved to establish them on an ad hoc basis,[75] and there have been recent attempts in Parliament to legislate for them.[76]

---

filming women entering a clinic was rejected, Ofcom, 'Ofcom Broadcast and On Demand Bulletin', no. 330, 5 June 2017, 72–94. On protests in Northern Ireland, see Chapter 6, pp. 208–9.

[66] Lowe and Hayes, 'Anti-Abortion Clinic Activism, Civil Inattention and the Problem of Gendered Harassment', 338.

[67] Ibid., 338–39.

[68] Lowe and Page, 'On the Wet Side of the Womb'.

[69] See e.g. Scarisbrick, *Let There Be Life*, 3, emphasis in original; Scarisbrick interviewed by O'Neill: '[Y]ou've got to be very careful. You can so easily give the wrong impression. You can so easily seem to be threatening and to be completely insensitive to what is for many of the women going in and out of the place, a traumatic time.'

[70] Lowe and Hayes, 'Anti-Abortion Clinic Activism, Civil Inattention and the Problem of Gendered Harassment'.

[71] *Dulgheriu* v *London Borough of Ealing* [2018] EWHC 1667 (Admin), [2019] EWCA Civ 1490; Lowe and Hayes, 'Anti-Abortion Clinic Activism, Civil Inattention, and the Problem of Gendered Harassment', 330–46.

[72] *Dulgheriu* (Admin), [10], [48–50].

[73] BPAS, 'Back Off'.

[74] Javid, Abortion Clinic Protest Review in *Hansard*, HC, 13 September 2018, vol. 646, Written Statements.

[75] Under Section 59, Anti-Social Behaviour, Crime and Policing Act 2014, giving local authorities the right to make public spaces protection orders.

[76] See Chapter 7, pp. 256–57.

The contrast with Scotland, where abortion services have been provided largely within the NHS, has been noteworthy. Ann Henderson notes pride amongst Scottish Pro-Choice campaigners that abortion services are delivered within the NHS and, moreover, that

> those delivering the service have not been subjected to the same level of kind of direct abuse and picketing that has happened with Abort67 and other of the kind of more American-type tactics. That's happened partly because down south with so many abortions being delivered, paid for by the NHS, but delivered in private clinics, it's easier to locate the clinic and harass the women who are accessing services than it is where services are provided through major NHS facilities, as is the case in Scotland.[77]

In very recent years, however, clinic protests have also increased north of the border, driven by the arrival of US-inspired anti-abortion groups, resulting in the establishment of a Scottish 'Back Off' campaign and the announcement of plans to introduce buffer zones.[78]

Improving the Technical Ease, Safety and Acceptability of Abortion

The proliferation of standalone abortion clinics has relied partly on the fact that over time abortion has become a technically far easier and much safer procedure that no longer requires hospital facilities. After 1967, with abortions performed openly and in increasing numbers, clinicians quickly developed relevant skills and innovation was rapid. The practice of contemporaneous sterilisation was rejected; first vacuum aspiration and then abortion pills transformed the way that abortion services were offered; and innovations in pregnancy testing contributed to abortions generally taking place earlier in pregnancy.[79] Combined, the impact of these changes has been profound. In the early years of the Abortion Act, abortion was a major operation, typically accompanied by a week's stay in hospital, with a significant risk of complications and, indeed, death.[80] Today, the mortality rate for abortion stands at 0.32 per 100,000 women (compared to 9.7 per 100,000 for those who carry a pregnancy to term),[81] with a very high

---

[77] Ann Henderson interviewed by Jane O'Neill, 25 July 2017.

[78] Back Off Scotland, 'About'; 'Poll: 82 Per Cent of Scots want End to Abortion Clinic Protests', *National*, 25 January 2021. In interview, Eileen Cook also noted the early signs of the spread of clinic protests, with 40 Days for Life spending their most recent annual protest 'camped outside the Royal Infirmary, for probably the whole of the 40 days'. Cook interviewed by O'Neill. 'Nicola Sturgeon: Glasgow and Edinburgh could Introduce Buffer Zones' *The National* 27 June 2022.

[79] Olszynko-Gryn, 'The Feminist Appropriation of Pregnancy Testing in 1970s Britain', 871–73.

[80] Lane recorded a maternal mortality rate of 9 per 100,000 for dilation and curettage procedures, rising to 126 per 100,000 for hysterotomies (with risks increased tenfold for each procedure where accompanied by contemporary sterilisation), and an average length of hospital stay of 7.8 days in 1968, falling to 5.3 days in 1971, *Lane Report*, vol. 2, para 165. See also Sood, 'Some Operative and Postoperative Hazards of Legal Termination of Pregnancy'.

[81] On the risks currently associated with abortion, see RCOG, *The Care of Women Requesting Induced Abortion*; NICE and RCOG, *Abortion Care. NICE Guideline*. On mortality rates associated with maternity, see Knight et al. (eds), *Saving Lives, Improving Mothers' Care*.

proportion of abortions performed as outpatient procedures very early in pregnancy.[82] Armed with these technical innovations and improved safety records, service providers have pushed hard for the removal of regulatory restrictions, which are seen as imposing unwarranted barriers to best clinical practice.

Claims for the safety of abortion would be fiercely contested by Pro-Life campaigners, who increasingly disputed the objectivity of those who made them, with professional medical bodies decried along with 'pro-abortionist' academics.[83] Jack Scarisbrick protests that Pro-Choice campaigners have 'made a creature of' the RCOG, which, 'while professing to be officially neutral … [has] become an engine of abortionism', consistently ignoring the harms that it caused:[84]

> It is, of course, asking much of any professional to admit that he has been actively doing harm to those who he claimed to be helping. It is not easy for the medical profession to admit that they are actively generating mental disease and are the chief reason why a horrible disease like breast cancer is now the commonest form of cancer … [Abortionism] cannot engage in reasoned debate. It is incoherent. It can offer only slogans, assertions and old myths. It evades and fudges. It will break the most basic rules of scientific research and not hesitate to ignore norms of academic discourse.[85]

In response to a perceived closing in the ranks of 'establishment' bodies – including Government, professional medical bodies and major research funders – Pro-Life campaigners would place an increasing emphasis on the production of their own evidence.[86] Plans to establish a research centre to offer an alternative to what 'Governments and the major grant-making foundations fund' never came to fruition.[87] However, the movement would go on to commission its own experts or gather its own research into the mental health consequences of abortion,[88] the correlation between abortion and breast cancer,[89] the existence of fetal sentience,[90] and the operation of the conscientious objection clause and fetal anomaly ground of the Abortion Act.[91] As the disputation of basic facts regarding the safety of abortion and

---

[82] In 1969, over a third of abortions took place at 13 weeks or over, compared to just 6% in 2020. See annual abortion statistics.

[83] Scarisbrick, *Let There Be Life*, 25.

[84] Ibid., 26–28.

[85] Ibid., 29.

[86] See ibid. (emphasis in original), complaining that the RCOG 'simply refused to begin to consider that there was even an *association*' between abortion and breast cancer; and Gardner, 'Abortion and Breast Cancer', alleging 'clear evidence of attempts to cover this up through ignoring, concealing or misclassifying incriminating data'.

[87] Scarisbrick, *Let There Be Life*, 60.

[88] Rawlinson, *The Physical and Psycho-Social Effects of Abortion on Women*, see below.

[89] Carroll, *Abortion and Other Pregnancy-Related Risk Factors in Female Breast Cancer*.

[90] McCullagh, *Fetal Sentience*; Rawlinson, *Human Sentience before Birth*.

[91] See Chapter 7, pp. 241–4., on the work of the Pro-Life All Party Parliamentary Group in gathering evidence; and this chapter, pp. 131–33, on Post-Abortion Syndrome.

women's experience of it became a central feature of the battle for the normalisation of abortion, new alliances would form between Pro-Choice campaigners, service providers and professional medical bodies, who shared a common interest in refuting fallacious claims regarding the dangers of abortion.[92]

Vacuum Aspiration and Outpatient Abortion Services

At the time of the introduction of the Abortion Act, Dorothea Kerslake – the consultant and ALRA member who had overseen the development of NHS abortion services in Newcastle – was also working to introduce vacuum aspiration abortion to the English-speaking world. Following the publication of an important paper in 1967, this technique was quickly accepted as highly effective and very safe in early pregnancy, leading clinicians to abandon more invasive surgical techniques.[93] With many other minor surgical procedures now routinely available on an outpatient basis, BPAS called for day-care abortion services as 'a logical and necessary' move; in 1979, it persuaded the Government to authorise a pilot 'for an initial and experimental period of two years'.[94] Careful to avoid any accusation of profit motivation, BPAS charged the same fee regardless of whether a woman preferred to stay overnight and ensured that treatment was otherwise identical.[95] Its pilot showed that day-care abortion was administratively simple, safe and strongly preferred by women, and that the 'overwhelming majority' were treated uneventfully.[96]

With its new service, BPAS again saw itself as driving service innovation, normalising abortion care and 'reducing the extent to which unwanted pregnancies interfere with the lives of women'.[97] It protested against restrictions on its services, which did not apply to NHS providers, with women required to live within a 50 mile radius of the clinic and to have their GPs' approval.[98] In response, it explored the possibility of offering outpatient services from a mobile clinic 'stationed, for a day or two each week or fortnight, in or near the patient's home area',[99] and complained when the Department of Health and Social Security (DHSS) refused to authorise the scheme for 'political'

---

[92] Ann Furedi interviewed by Jane O'Neill, 23 August 2017.

[93] Kerslake and Casey, 'Abortion Induced by Means of the Uterine Aspirator', 30; Berić and Kupresanin, 'Vacuum Aspiration Using Pericervical Block for Legal Abortion as an Outpatient Procedure up to the 12th Week of Pregnancy', 619–20; Potts et al., *Abortion*, 183.

[94] BPAS Archives, BPAS Press Release, 6 February 1979.

[95] BPAS Archives, BPAS Press Release, 29 January 1976.

[96] Just 500 of 6,900 eligible patients chose to stay overnight and only a small number required post-operative overnight care (e.g. for heavy bleeding or abdominal pain), BPAS Archives, BPAS, *Two Years' Experience with Out-Patient Abortion: A Report on Day Care from the British Pregnancy Advisory Service*, May 1978, 14 and 10.

[97] Ibid., 10.

[98] Ibid., 1–2.

[99] BPAS Archives, BPAS, 'Mobile Day-Care Clinic', 1 March 1976.

reasons.[100] Complaints that restrictions on services were grounded in ideology rather than concerns for patient safety were now common amongst service providers, with particular criticism raised regarding the additional level of regulation for non-NHS providers. It was suggested that a requirement that saw many patients forced to undergo two pelvic examinations was unnecessary in early pregnancy and constituted 'a form of digital rape': it was thus 'time that the DHSS clarifies the clinical grounds on which it bases many of the requirements made of bureaux, knowing that practice will be entirely different and unregulated, in NHS general and hospital services and in private practice'.[101] Madeleine Simms complained that the same GP would be free to follow his clinical judgement if his patients visited him in his surgery but 'compelled to practice what he may regard as inferior medicine' where consulted in a pregnancy advice bureau.[102]

BPAS was also deeply critical of the slow roll-out of outpatient early abortion services within the NHS, complaining that any attempt to reduce barriers to services was 'subjected to an unceasing propaganda barrage from the vociferous diehard minority'.[103] SPUC was pleased to claim a victory when two Area Health Authorities decided 'either to "defer" a decision to open a clinic' or 'categorically dropped the whole idea'.[104] It had campaigned hard on this issue, believing that day-care services had nothing to do with 'women's liberation' and everything to do with eugenics and profit maximisation.[105] In addition to their impact on NHS service providers, these campaigns also had a clear effect on Government: one civil servant reflected that approval for outpatient services was slowed because 'the barrage of propaganda ... about "lunch-time abortions" had made day-care controversial', and it was initially restricted to the charities because the Health Minister, David Owen, favoured them.[106] This distinction angered both for-profit providers, with one

---

[100] BPAS Archives, Nan Smith to Professor Lafitte, 'Mobile Day-Care Clinic' Departmental Memorandum, 18 March 1976, reporting, however, that the DHSS had seen no insurmountable legal or medical difficulties with such a scheme.

[101] Gugenheim and Chandler, Letter to *The Lancet*, 21 August 1982, 436.

[102] Simms, Letter to *The Lancet*, 21 August 1982, 436.

[103] BPAS Archives, Francois Lafitte, 'Provision for Abortion in the West Midlands: Comments on the Regional Health Authority's Working Party Report', June 1978, 1. See generally Simms, 'Day-Care Abortion', 1253, by 1980 estimating that BPAS and PAS together provided 'about three times as many day-care abortions as all N.H.S. hospitals put together'; Rowlands 'Day-Care Abortion in the NHS', 1–4; *The Lancet*, 'Alternative Pathways for Abortion Services', 24 May 1980, 1121.

[104] Wellcome Library, Papers of the Abortion Law Reform Association (ALRA), SA/ALR/G/17, Letter from Phyllis Bowman to members, 16 September 1981.

[105] Wellcome Library, Papers of the National Abortion Campaign (NAC), NAC/E/4/1, SPUC leaflet, *Day-Care Abortion – A Woman's Right to Lose?*, c. 1980.

[106] The National Archives (TNA), MH 156/547, Internal memorandum, J. H. Lutterloch (DHSS), 'Day-Care in the Private Sector', 19 April 1979.

threatening legal action,[107] and anti-abortion campaigners, who saw little difference between the two. SPUC argued:

> [W]hereas abortionists will claim that most private abortions are carried out by 'charities' – one must remember that the incomes of these concerns are enormous. For example, the British Pregnancy Advisory Service, a leading abortion charity, now grosses over £2,000,000 per annum of which over £1,300,000 goes out in fees to the doctors, counsellors and others in their employment . . . In cases of social abortion the main beneficiary can be the doctor (building his nest egg).[108]

Disputes simmered on, erupting again in the mid-1990s when a move to offer early abortions with local anaesthesia meant that the procedure could now take as little as 10 minutes. MSI announced a 'walk-in, walk-out' abortion service, which would help 'remove the stigma' and allow women to fit an abortion into a busy working life.[109] It argued that the one remaining barrier to 'an entirely trouble-free abortion' was now 'the outmoded 1967 legislation, which insists on the prior written consent of two doctors before an abortion can proceed', and challenged legislators 'to provide a new legal framework to match the service, and finally guarantee women's fundamental right to choose for themselves'.[110] For their part, anti-abortion campaigners attacked these 'quickie', 'lunchtime abortions' as 'the ultimate in a fast economy': '[Y]ou have fast food and now you can have a fast abortion.'[111] Once again, moves to introduce similar services within the NHS were slow.[112]

'The Pill That Changes Everything'

Such disputes came into still clearer focus from the early 1990s, with the licensing of the abortion pill, RU486, making possible early medical (as opposed to surgical) abortion. Heralded by *Time* magazine as 'the pill that changes everything',[113] its developers argued that this was an 'unpregnancy pill' or 'contragestive' that blurred the boundaries between contraception and abortion and offered the potential for a private and de-medicalised procedure.[114] With early medical abortion, women could end pregnancies by placing pills in their own bodies, potentially heralding the obsolescence of legal restrictions, for '[h]ow could a state control swallowing?'.[115] The first UK

---

[107] Ibid., acknowledging that such a challenge would not be without merit.

[108] Wellcome Library, NAC/E/4/1, SPUC, 'A Foetus is a Baby – Don't Forget', leaflet c. 1980.

[109] 'Fury over "Lunch-Hour Abortions"', *Independent*, 28 June 1997.

[110] Ibid.

[111] Ibid., also noting that MSI made 'millions of pounds out of these procedures'.

[112] 'Abortion: The Right to Choose an Abortion – In Your Lunch Break', *Independent*, 15 October 1997.

[113] *Time*, 14 June 1993, cover page.

[114] Baulieu, *The Abortion Pill*, 18.

[115] 'Moral Property', *Boston Globe*, 17 July 1989.

trials, conducted in Edinburgh by David Baird, found RU486 to be highly effective in early pregnancy when administered with a low dose of prosta-glandin.[116] In July 1991, the UK became one of the first countries to license it for use.[117]

While the abortion pill was broadly welcomed by pro-choice campaign-ers,[118] anti-abortion campaigners were horrified: RU486 was 'chemical war-fare on the unborn',[119] reflecting a larger philosophy of trivialising and 'making abortions easier and easier'.[120] SPUC commented:

> You take a tablet to get rid of a headache. You take a tablet to stop getting pregnant. And now you take a tablet to get rid of a child ... Terrifyingly, some people now talk of the death and destruction of the tiny unborn human life by a powerful chemical steroid as being more convenient.[121]

Life suggested that the pills would be 'physically and psychologically dam-aging' to women and increase pressure on them to end their pregnancies.[122] The Pro-Life MP Kenneth Hind (Con) secured an emergency debate in the House of Commons to call for the withdrawal of 'one of the first drugs developed purely and simply to kill'. Putting to one side the 'pro-life argu-ments', which were 'perfectly clear', Hind advanced a detailed consideration of the available scientific evidence, concluding that it did not support the deci-sion to license RU486. The result was 'danger to the health of the women who take it', with potentially long-term costs to the NHS given the risk of produ-cing 'deformed and damaged children'.[123] Echoing initiatives that had enjoyed some success on the other side of the Channel,[124] SPUC fought unsuccessfully to generate support for a boycott of RU486's manufacturer and – again reflecting an enhanced focus on scrutinising and contesting scientific evi-dence – called for greater transparency regarding the process for approving new medicines.[125]

---

[116] Cameron, Michie and Baird, 'Therapeutic Abortion in Early Pregnancy with Antiprogestogen RU486 Alone or in Combination with Prostaglandin Analogue (Gemeprost)', 459.

[117] David Baird interviewed by Gayle Davis, 13 November 2017. See Sheldon, *Beyond Control*, chapter 7, for a detailed account of events.

[118] For a notable exception, see Klein, Raymond and Dumble, *RU 486: Misconceptions, Myths and Morals*, 29, attacking this 'non-private, extensively medicalized, and complicated abortion method'.

[119] SPUC, 'A Dose of Lies: False claims about RU486, the Abortion Drug', leaflet c. 1989, on file with authors.

[120] Phyllis Bowman (SPUC) cited in Moorehead, 'Boycott Call for Abortion Pill Firm's Products', 1.

[121] Catherine Francoise, cited in 'Abortion: The New Pill', *Sunday Times Magazine*, 6 January 1991, 41.

[122] Nuala Scarisbrick, Life, cited in 'French Hope to Market Abortion Pill in Britain', *Times*, 23 July 1990.

[123] Hind in *Hansard*, HC, 22 July 1991, vol. 195, col. 884.

[124] 'Une loi providentielle ...', *Le Monde*, 31 October 1988.

[125] 'Boycott Roussel and Hoechst' and 'MPs Demand Change in Drug Licensing Laws', *Human Concern*, no. 32, Autumn 1991.

Use of abortion pills was initially significantly limited due to side effects, burdensome storage requirements and onerous regulatory restrictions.[126] However, the development of a more effective prostaglandin would transform the experience of early medical abortion,[127] with studies reporting a safety record that compared favourably with a shot of penicillin.[128] As pregnancy testing grew in sophistication, accuracy and availability, increasing numbers of women seeking abortion would meet the gestational limit for early medical abortion. Abortion pills would decrease the need for the involvement of an experienced specialist doctor, further allowing gynaecologists to detach themselves from the provision of services.[129] Moreover, abortion pills would open the door to telemedical services, revolutionising the reality of illegal abortion in many countries, as women unable to access local services discovered that they could source abortion pills online. Newspapers began to report the dangers of '[d]eadly abortion pills sold to desperate teenage girls on [the] internet', with Life locating this 'huge danger' within a broader casualisation of attitudes towards abortion.[130] The risks were clear: some online suppliers were known to send sugar pills, inadequate instructions for use or nothing at all.[131] However, abortion pills offered a far safer alternative than other means of ending a pregnancy outside formal health services, and women-led, not-for-profit collectives were established to prescribe and supply authentic pills. They would have a powerful impact in many countries where abortion was illegal, including on the island of Ireland.[132]

Women's Experience of Abortion

Alongside contested clinical evidence regarding its safety would come even fiercer disputes regarding women's experience of abortion. Each side of the debate would present itself as the true advocate of women's interests, criticising their opponents for ignoring inconvenient evidence and propagandising regarding women's experience. In Parliament, Labour women were becoming increasingly confident in rejecting a focus on women in the most desperate circumstances and asserting abortion as a necessary part of reproductive healthcare.[133] This reflected the development of a more nuanced articulation of abortion within the women's movement. A 1979 article by Eileen

---

[126] See Jones, 'Setting up Services'; Mansour and Stacey, 'Abortion Methods'; and Silvestre, 'The French Experiences'; 'Speeding up the Right to Choose', *Times*, 22 July 1991.

[127] For a summary, see Bristow, 'Misoprostol and the Transformation of the "Abortion Pill"'.

[128] Cates, Grimes and Schulz, 'The Public Health Impact of Legal Abortion', 25–28.

[129] Anna Glasier interviewed by Gayle Davis, 13 November 2017, reflecting that this was not necessarily 'a good thing'.

[130] 'Deadly Abortion Pills sold to Desperate Teenage Girls on Internet for 78p', *Mirror*, 25 January 2014; 'Concern over Abortion Pills Bought Online', *BBC Newsbeat*, 11 February 2013.

[131] Leading Women on Waves to publish details of some bogus suppliers: Women on Waves, 'Warning, Fake Abortion Pills for Sale Online!!'.

[132] See Chapter 6; Sheldon, 'Empowerment and Privacy?'.

[133] See Chapter 3.

Fairweather in the magazine *Spare Rib* had called for feminists to move 'beyond the slogans' and to recognise 'the complexity of abortion and its emotional significance'.[134] Fairweather acknowledged ambivalence about abortion, echoing some of the arguments made by anti-abortion advocates: that abortion might 'simply be another weapon men use against us', that 'choice' was illusory in a context of insufficient support for parenting, and that women – particularly black women – sometimes faced compulsory abortion and sterilisation. Moreover, she argued, many women who had abortions faced an unacknowledged 'legacy of shame, secrecy, and often pain which goes so deep you can't even bear to think about it – much less fight *back*'.[135]

Importantly, however, these experiences were not marshalled into arguments for the restriction of abortion services. While Fairweather's article touched a nerve, prompting other women to write and speak about their own ambivalent experiences of abortion, they repeatedly emphasised that these had not altered their pro-choice beliefs.[136] Indeed, Fairweather emphasised that acknowledging these experiences was vital to campaigning because '[t]he only way abortion will cease to be each woman's guilty secret, and becomes something she is prepared to fight for publicly, is through our saying, without apology – yes, if necessary, we put women first'.[137] NAC and *Spare Rib* organised a poignant public meeting where women stood and shared their personal experiences, often for the first time. This had a profound effect both on those present and the Pro-Choice Movement in general. Marge Berer recalls it as a 'defining moment':

> [T]here were hundreds of women in the room, probably 400, I don't think I'm exaggerating ... [and they were invited] to stand up and talk about their experience of abortion. ... It brought out all the stresses and tensions, and issues around relationships, and disagreements about contraception, and failure to use contraception or to use it well enough, or having to deal with the fact that you used it and it failed on you anyway. ... It showed that the anti-abortion accusation that women just went off to have an abortion because they wanted to go skiing next weekend was just rubbish. In effect, it discredited the anti-abortion position. ... People were crying, it was very emotional. All of a sudden it was more than just, 'safe abortion on demand, a woman's right to choose', you know, marching down the street. It was: this is women's lives we are talking about. And this is women's experience that we are talking about. And here it is in all its complexity. I think it changed the way everybody saw abortion, forever, from then on.[138]

---

[134] Fairweather, 'The Feelings behind the Slogans', 26–30.

[135] Emphasis in original, ibid., 28.

[136] See various letters, *Spare Rib*, no. 90, January 1980, 22; and generally Jolly, 'The Feelings behind the Slogans', 112.

[137] Fairweather, 'The Feelings behind the Slogans', 28.

[138] Marge Berer interviewed by Jane O'Neill, 6 October 2017. See further Jan McKenley (NAC) in Thynne, 'The Feelings Behind the Slogans Part 2'; Jolly, 'The Feelings behind the Slogans', 105.

These discussions also contributed to the creation of the Women's Reproductive Rights Campaign, with its broader focus on reproductive justice, encompassing women's right to have children (resisting pressured sterilisation, abortion, and long-acting reversible contraceptives) alongside the right to choose abortion.[139]

Several collections of testimonies with a broadly pro-choice sensibility followed, aiming to break the silence and stigma associated with abortion,[140] and rejecting the urge to propagandise through reliance on artificial tropes of women who have 'emerged' from abortion either 'strengthened' or 'traumatized for life'.[141] Pro-Choice activism would henceforth place a sustained emphasis on sharing diverse experiences of abortion, challenging stigma and rejecting stereotypes: a powerful common thread that runs through a series of NAC's 'Speak Outs' organised in the 1990s,[142] to much more recent social media campaigns, such as #ShoutYourAbortion, more than two decades later.[143]

Pro-Life groups would also claim to reflect women's experience and represent their interests, with a powerful woman-protective turn in their campaigning.[144] In 1987, inspired by the US organisation Victims of Abortion, SPUC established a group to offer counselling and educational programmes for women suffering from 'abortion trauma'.[145] British Victims of Abortion was run by Bernadette Thompson, who had described her ongoing regret regarding an abortion some 16 years earlier in a women's magazine and subsequently found herself 'inundated' with calls, including many from women 'aborted through so-called charities' who did not want to return to them for support in grieving.[146]

Thompson's testimony was the first in a collection published by SPUC, *And Still They Weep: Personal Stories of Abortion*. While aiming to counter the 'conspiracy of silence' and the 'myths and distortions' in popular discourses

---

[139] Wellcome Library, SA/NAC/D/1/1, AAC Newsletter, June/July 1982; Wellcome Library, Papers of Wendy Savage, PPWDS/2/3, Co-ord Inform, no. 18, June 1980, p. 7. See Chapter 3, pp. 130–31.

[140] Published accounts include Pipes, *Understanding Abortion*; Neustatter and Newson, *Mixed Feelings*; Winn, *Experiences of Abortion*. These volumes – which collected accounts of women's experiences extending back over many years – are drawn on extensively in Chapter 2, pp. 39–46.

[141] Neustatter and Newson, *Mixed Feelings*, 3.

[142] Glasgow Women's Library, Papers of the Scottish Abortion Campaign (SAC), SAC 5.6, 'Speaking Out for Choice', in *Women's Choice: A Magazine of Reproductive Rights*, vol. 2 no. 1, spring 1994, 10–12; see e.g. 'Abortion: How do Women Feel Now? It is Not the Same Experience for Everybody', *Independent*, 28 August 1993.

[143] See Millar, *Happy Abortions*, 2; Pollitt, *Pro*, 15.

[144] Lee, *Abortion, Motherhood and Mental Health*, locates the beginnings of this shift in the mid-1980s, with claims of Post-Abortion Syndrome becoming a prominent concern from the late 1980s and early 1990s. For the development of woman-protective arguments in the USA, see generally Siegel, 'The Right's Reasons', 1641–92; Siegel, 'Dignity and the Politics of Protection'.

[145] See Symonds, *And Still They Weep*, xv; Amess in *Hansard*, HC, 27 July 1989, vol. 157, col. 1377; *Human Concern*, no. 47, spring 1998, 11; no. 49, summer 1999, 9.

[146] Amess in *Hansard*, HC, 27 July 1989, vol. 157, col. 1377.

surrounding abortion (which were believed to reflect 'hidden agendas'),[147] the book nonetheless shared significant common ground with the collections of women's accounts published in the 1980s and the NAC Speak Outs. It likewise criticised as thin and unconvincing the rhetoric of 'a woman's right to choose': over 90 per cent of women counselled by Thompson were said to have ended their pregnancies to please their husband, boyfriend, parents or peer group.[148] It also emphasised the importance of acknowledging women's experiences, albeit here with a strong emphasis on feelings of regret, ambivalence and guilt: one contributor believed her cancer to be punishment for an earlier abortion.[149]

However, any common ground extended only so far. Rather than an acceptable option for any woman facing unwanted pregnancy, abortion was presented as profoundly harmful to all concerned. Women's guilt did not reflect the stigmatising effect of wider societal judgements but was rather a natural reaction to its intrinsic wrongness. Abortion was not emancipatory, as '[f]or all our liberation, women are still weeping'.[150] Far from reflecting a woman's agency, 'if a woman's role as mother is so devalued, it's difficult for her to value what's in her womb'.[151] Abortion services were criticised not for erecting undue obstacles to abortion but rather for making it too easy. At best, they allowed insufficient time and professional support for women to explore ambivalence; at worst, eugenicist or profit-motivated service providers with 'a vested interest in seeing the unborn baby die' would pressurise or cajole women into unnecessary abortions.[152] True informed consent to abortion was believed impossible: even 'with the best information and wise counsel, it would take approximately six months for a woman to unravel and resolve all the dimensions of a choice to abort or not. By that time, of course, she will have become well attached to the growing baby within her.'[153]

And Still They Weep differed in a further crucial respect, which illustrates the growing importance of scientific evidence in Pro-Life campaigning. While the NAC Speak Outs and earlier collections had allowed women's stories to speak for themselves, here it was left to a heavily credentialed psychiatrist and pioneer of intensive 'post-abortion healing courses' to explain their meaning.[154] With regard to Thompson's own story, Professor Philip Ney 'MD, MA, FRCP(C), FRANZCP' explained that she had 'struggled to become fully human' as 'there are parts of the person that God intended her to be that

---

[147] Symonds, *And Still They Weep*, xv–xvi.

[148] Bernadette Thompson in Symonds, *And Still They Weep*, 9.

[149] 'Tessa' in Symonds, *And Still They Weep*, 24–25.

[150] Symonds, *And Still They Weep*, back cover.

[151] Bernadette Thompson in Symonds, *And Still They Weep*, 9.

[152] See e.g. 'Tessa' in Symonds, *And Still They Weep*, 22.

[153] Symonds, *And Still They Weep*, 92.

[154] Philip Ney in Symonds, *And Still They Weep*, 3. See further Hopkins, Reicher and Saleem, 'Constructing Women's Psychological Health in Anti-Abortion Rhetoric'.

never developed or that died when she had an abortion'.[155] Women could 'never be the same person they were before an abortion', for when 'we dehumanise a baby, we become less human ourselves'.[156] With such little sense of their own intrinsic worth, women saw little value in others and became 'wantonly destructive and murderous'.[157] Their wider families also suffered: there were many post-abortion relationship breakdowns;[158] children were damaged, for if 'the mother who tells you she loves you has killed your little brother or sister, what is a mother and what is love?';[159] and fathers with no legal right to prevent an abortion were less likely to feel responsibility for any child.[160]

This seamless weaving together of religious, moral, clinical and experiential understandings into a powerful condemnation of the 'physical, mental and spiritual wounds and scars' caused by abortion would become pervasive in Pro-Life campaigning,[161] finding its most powerful focus in assertions of the existence of a new psychiatric disorder: Post-Abortion Syndrome.[162] Professional medical bodies have refused to recognise a causal link between abortion and mental health problems, with an authoritative review of the evidence concluding that the rates of mental health problems for women with an unwanted pregnancy were the same whether they had an abortion or gave birth.[163] In response, Pro-Life campaigners have gathered their own evidence, concluding that certifying abortions on mental health grounds was legally questionable, that abortion does nothing to alleviate any psychiatric problems that already exist and, indeed, that it risks causing a psychiatric disturbance in women.[164] They found some parts of the media to be less sceptical regarding the existence of Post-Abortion Syndrome than were the professional bodies: in particular, the *Daily Mail* has reported that abortion could result in 'violence towards children, sleeplessness, eating disorders and alcoholism'.[165]

---

[155] Philip Ney in Symonds, *And Still They Weep*, 3.

[156] Ibid.

[157] Ibid., 120.

[158] Ibid., 138, quoting a figure of 80%.

[159] Ibid., 26, 120.

[160] A parallel, predominantly US literature emerged to describe the negative psychological consequences of abortion for men. See Cochrane, *Healing a Father's Heart*; Condon and Hazard, *Fatherhood Aborted*.

[161] Ney in Symonds, *And Still They Weep*, xix.

[162] See Lee, *Abortion, Motherhood and Mental Health*, for a detailed account explaining the emergence of Post-Abortion Syndrome as a response to the failure of explicitly moralised claims regarding the wrongness of abortion and broader trends to medicalise human experience within the 'Syndrome Society'.

[163] Academy of Medical Royal Colleges, *Induced Abortion and Mental Health*.

[164] Rawlinson, *The Physical and Psycho-Social Effects of Abortion on Women*. Members included David Alton and members of Feminists Against Eugenics, Life and SPUC.

[165] *Daily Mail*, 10 January 1997, 33. See also *Sunday Express*, 25 November 2001, 1–2; 'Tyranny of Freedom of Choice', *Evening Standard*, 28 June 1994; and generally Lee, *Abortion, Motherhood and Mental Health*.

The Acceptability of Abortion

The battle to normalise abortion has relied not just on claims regarding its safety but also on the acceptance of its morality. A more secular, liberal individualist population has become increasingly accepting of abortion in 'social' as well as 'traumatic' cases. Pro-Life commentators complain that the Abortion Act has led to a 'slightly numbed conscience across the country',[166] with 'the drip, drip, drip' over time ensuring 'what was abnormal becomes normal'.[167] Nonetheless, public opinion has remained equivocal, at times contradictory, and sensitive to the circumstances leading to an abortion.[168] Pro-Choice interventions that argue for the celebration of abortion as a happy event for many women[169] and 'the most powerful expression of human agency there can be'[170] have gained only limited traction. The sociologist Erica Millar describes the existence of a dominant emotional script that

> depicts abortion as an incredibly difficult choice made in response to extraneous circumstances that are beyond the woman's immediate control; it requires women to justify their abortions, preferably by citing the best interests of their potential children, to grieve their lost children after abortion, and to keep their abortions secret out of a sense of shame or guilt.[171]

Reflecting on the fiftieth anniversary of the 1967 Act, the former chair of the Voice for Choice coalition Lisa Hallgarten likewise explains that studies of women who have had abortions describe largely positive emotions, but story-lines in dramas have tended to follow a familiar narrative arc of 'secrecy, shame, relationship conflict, and regret', with the 'metaphorical ghost of previous abortions haunt[ing] protagonists through psychiatric morbidity, infertility, and an impressive range of improbable abortion complications'.[172] These stories make remarkably frequent reference to the possibility of the woman's death, a vanishingly rare occurrence in real life.[173]

While public acceptance of abortion has grown steadily over the past decades and representations in popular culture appear gradually to be

---

[166] Quintavalle interviewed by O'Neill.

[167] Scarisbrick interviewed by O'Neill.

[168] Clements and Field, 'Abortion and Public Opinion in Great Britain', 429–44; Curtice et al. (eds), *British Social Attitudes: The 36th Report*.

[169] Millar, *Happy Abortions*.

[170] Furedi, *The Moral Case for Abortion*, 8. See further Pollitt, *Pro*.

[171] Millar, *Happy Abortions*, 1. See further Hadley, 'The "Awfulisation" of Abortion', 7–9; Ellie Lee's discussion of 'abortion negativity' in Lee, 'Young Women, Pregnancy, and Abortion in Britain' and Kilday and Nash, 'The Silent Scream of Shame?'.

[172] Hallgarten, 'Abortion Narratives', 1989.

[173] See also Sisson and Kimport, 'Telling Stories about Abortion', 413–18, noting that 13.5% of stories about a woman considering abortion ended with her death, whether or not she obtained the abortion (compared to an actual incidence of mortality from abortion in the UK of 0.00032%, see this chapter, p. 123.).

changing,[174] an ongoing, profound cultural ambivalence about abortion runs like a leitmotif through discussions of the Abortion Act in Parliament and broader public debate. Two broad themes dominate the media consideration of abortion from the early 1990s. First, while abortion is increasingly broadly accepted, there is an ongoing concern with its 'trivialisation' where cases fall outside the script described by Millar. This has resulted in an important focus on motivation and the quality of decision-making. Second, where women seeking abortion once risked being cast as feckless, promiscuous or selfish, such criticisms were becoming increasingly rare, almost entirely disappearing after the 1990s. With each side of the debate presenting itself as advocates for women, criticism has come to focus ever more exclusively on those providing services or, occasionally, those pressurising women to access them. In these accounts, women feature as victims rather than villains.[175]

Concerns with decision-making around abortion came to the fore in the late 1980s with the development of therapies that used fetal neural tissue in the treatment of Parkinson's disease.[176] What appears to have been a purely hypothetical concern that a woman might deliberately conceive and abort for instrumental reasons (to produce fetal tissue for therapeutic use) was deemed sufficiently serious to warrant the establishment of a committee to consider whether revision of the Peel Code was necessary. With far greater weight now attached to women's agency in making abortion decisions, the resulting Polkinghorne Code put more emphasis on women's wishes regarding the disposal of fetal tissue than had Peel. However, this was balanced against the new concern regarding abortion for purely instrumental reasons. The result was Polkinghorne's 'separation principle': a woman should consent only in general terms to the use of fetal tissue, being offered no information about specific future use; such consent should be sought only after she had consented to an abortion; the research team should be different from her clinical team; and no form of inducement for donation should be offered.[177]

Similar concerns also inspired a rare legislative success for Pro-Life parliamentarians. In 1994, with a shortage in available human eggs said to be hampering infertility treatment services and research, the recently formed Human Fertilisation and Embryology Authority initiated a consultation regarding the acceptability of using eggs extracted from human cadavers and

---

[174] Haynes, 'How a Crop of New Movies Is Changing the Narrative About Abortion', *Time*, 13 March 2020.

[175] See Bigman, 'Abortion in American Film since 2001', discussing a similar shift in film portrayals.

[176] See generally Gillon, 'Ethics of Fetal Brain Cell Transplants', 1212; Fine, 'The Ethics of Fetal Tissue Transplants', 5.

[177] *Review of the Guidance on the Research Use of Fetuses and Fetal Material* (*Polkinghorne Report*). A further degree of separation was later built in with the subsequent establishment of the Human Developmental Biology Resource (an embryonic and fetal tissue bank funded by the Medical Research Council and the Wellcome Trust), limiting further controversy on this issue. See Human Developmental Biology Resource, 'General Information'.

aborted fetuses.[178] Horrified at the prospect of getting 'rid of an unwanted baby to make a wanted one' and the 'start of a lucrative market in aborted foetuses', the veteran anti-abortion parliamentarian Jill Knight (Con) successfully attached an amendment to ban the practice to a Government Bill.[179] While many MPs shared Knight's intuitive revulsion, her success in pre-empting the outcome of an active public consultation also owed much to her skill as a parliamentary tactician. She would later claim to have succeeded in securing more private members' legislation than any other MP, having relied on the same tactic to secure the passage of the notorious clause 28 prohibiting the 'promotion of homosexuality'.[180]

A further story linking abortion and assisted reproductive technology followed shortly concerning the practice of 'selective reduction' following the implantation of multiple embryos during in vitro fertilisation. It has been suggested that selective abortion is troubling because, unlike those cases where abortion represents a rejection of pregnancy altogether, here 'the element of choice enters directly into the maternal role', involving 'a denial of the myth of the all-giving, all-accepting mother' and permitting women 'to decide just what kind of child they choose to mother'.[181] By extension, selective reduction allows a choice to be made regarding how many and which future children should result from a pregnancy. While the legality of this practice was put beyond doubt in 1990, it continued to provoke unease, reflecting a wider concern with the trivialisation of reproductive decision-making. In explaining why, Ann Widdecombe MP (Con) implicitly evokes the spectre of 'designer babies':

> When a woman discovers in the early stages that she is having a multiple birth – quite often these days, as a result of being overimplanted through IVF techniques; the doctor creates the situation which he solves by selective reduction – how does she choose? If there is nothing wrong with them but there are simply too many, how does she choose? On the grounds of sex, hair colour, colour of eyes?[182]

In 1996, these concerns crystallised in reports of a woman who had asked her doctor to reduce her twin pregnancy to a singleton.[183] With the woman initially described as a single mother of limited means, SPUC applied for an

---

[178] HFEA, *Donated Ovarian Tissue in Embryo Research and Assisted Conception*. See generally Mulkay, *The Embryo Research Debate*, 143–48.

[179] See *Hansard*, HC, 12 April 1994, vol. 241, col. 158; Criminal Justice and Public Order Act 1994, Section 156 Prohibition on use of cells from embryos or fetuses.

[180] Baroness Knight of Collingtree interviewed by Mike Greenwood, 9 May 2012. See Local Government Act 1988, Section 28, repealed in 2000 (in Scotland) and 2003 (in the rest of the UK).

[181] Katz Rothman, *The Tentative Pregnancy*, 242–43.

[182] Widdecombe in *Hansard*, HC, 21 June 1990, vol. 174, col. 1195; Alton in *Hansard*, HC, 21 June 1990, vol. 174, col. 1206.

[183] *Sunday Express*, 4 August 1996.

injunction to prevent an abortion until she had been informed that they could offer her financial support to allow her to continue the twin pregnancy. It then transpired that the abortion had already taken place and, later, that the woman was married and wealthy. A discernible shift of tone occurred in the media coverage, which had previously been largely sympathetic towards her.[184]

This story was shortly followed by another of a woman who had conceived a multiple pregnancy while being treated with super-ovulation drugs.[185] Notwithstanding medical advice regarding the likely outcome of her decision, Mandy Allwood explained that she refused to 'choose which ones should live and which ones should die' and intended to keep '*all* my 8 babies'.[186] In the subsequent media frenzy Allwood was initially reified as selflessly maternal, then – as details emerged of a previous abortion and relationship problems – savagely attacked and even suspected of having deliberately conceived to sell her story.[187] She went on to give birth prematurely, losing all eight babies within hours of their birth. After a funeral marked by a painful and intrusive 'media pantomime', the circus moved on, leaving Allwood feeling like 'a piece of meat'.[188]

These two stories reflect a broader cultural ambivalence regarding abortion, with each woman momentarily caught in the headlights of a fascinated press and variously portrayed as victim or villain as details of her private life were picked over. In the case of sex-selective abortion, such ambivalence is also powerfully refracted through wider cultural anxieties regarding race and ethnicity.[189] From the early 1980s, reports that women in India were terminating pregnancies to avoid the birth of female children fuelled concerns that this might also be occurring in Britain,[190] prompting proposals for legal reform.[191] In 1994, Sarbjit Lall, a 29 year-old woman with three daughters, died from massive internal bleeding and a cardiac arrest following an abortion performed at 18 weeks. While secretly intending to avoid the birth of a fourth girl, Lall had told staff at her clinic that she was depressed and could not cope financially with another child. The coroner found no evidence of wrongdoing by the clinic and strongly condemned Lall as 'devious and dishonest'.[192] While a concern with sex selection would take firmer hold over the following

---

[184] See generally Sheldon, 'Multiple Pregnancy and Re(pro)ductive Choice', 100.

[185] 'When the Story's Over', *Observer*, 27 January 2002.

[186] 'I'm Going to Have All My 8 babies', *News of the World*, 11 August 1996 (emphasis in original).

[187] E.g. 'How to Sell your Babies in 8 Easy Steps', *Independent on Sunday*, 11 August 1996, noting how the '"Fairy tale" became a scramble for cash' and reporting that Allwood had sold her story to a Sunday newspaper for £350,000 and hoped to make £1 million in sponsorship deals and television commercials. See generally Sheldon, *Beyond Control*.

[188] 'When the Story's Over', *Observer*, 27 January 2002.

[189] Unnithan and Dubuc, 'Re-visioning Evidence', 742–53; Kasstan and Unnithan, 'Arbitrating Abortion', 491–505.

[190] E.g. *Times*, 24 December 1980; 16 July 1982; 4 January 1988; 5 January 1988; *Lancet*, 8 November 1986, 1090; 8 April 1989, 774; *British Medical Journal*, vol. 296, 7 May 1988, 1312.

[191] See Chapter 7, pp. 225, 239–41.

[192] '"Devious" Woman Died after Abortion', *Independent*, 5 March 1994.

decades, this framing would be firmly reversed: far from being condemned, women requesting sex-selective abortion would be understood as victims of coercive partners or families and a patriarchal culture, who were failed both by individual doctors[193] and by clinics' inadequate enforcement of the safeguards contained in the Abortion Act.[194]

Concerns with the trivialisation of abortion have also repeatedly played out in discussions of 'repeat abortion' (a term criticised for its connotation of 'repeat offenders').[195] Media reports of the numbers of women who end more than one pregnancy often cite concerns that the Abortion Act is being abused to allow abortion as 'just another form of contraception', and that women should have 'learned their lesson' after a first abortion.[196] Josephine Quintavalle told the *Daily Mail*:

> Abortion is an unpleasant and harrowing experience for women and to hear it is happening repeatedly makes your hair stand on end. These figures show that sadly, abortion is being seen by many as a form of contraception. But is this surprising when we live in a society which says it's all right to have an abortion once. [sic] If it's fine once, why not two, three or four times. [sic][197]

A Life spokesperson concurred, seeing 'repeat abortions' as the result of '"no questions asked" abortion on demand [that] trivialises the process so much that it is no longer seen as the last resort'.[198] In these more recent reports, the focus of blame has again shifted away from the women concerned towards the service providers who are criticised for providing treatment without question rather than recommending counselling, raising safeguarding concerns or signposting other kinds of support.[199]

Finally, with public support for abortion declining steadily as a pregnancy advances, later abortion has been seen as a more morally serious matter, particularly once viability has been reached.[200] In 2004, *The Telegraph* claimed to expose 'a horrific underground industry' in which women wishing to end their pregnancies beyond the 24 week limit for 'social' reasons were travelling to a Spanish abortion clinic on the recommendation of BPAS.[201] The paper's

---

[193] Lee, 'Constructing Abortion as a Social Problem', 15–33.

[194] See Chapter 7, pp. 239–41.

[195] Hoggart, Newton and Bury, 'Repeat Abortion', 26–30.

[196] See e.g. 'NHS Spends £1m a Week on Repeat Abortions: Single Women using Terminations "as Another Form of Contraceptive"', *Daily Mail*, 13 May 2012, citing Nadine Dorries MP as suggesting that abortion is permitted 'over and over again for purely social reasons. Girls now get pregnant and think, "it doesn't matter, I'll just get an abortion"'; '1,300 Women Have had at Least FIVE Abortions', *Daily Mail*, 20 March 2008.

[197] Quoted in 'NHS Spends £1m a Week on Repeat Abortions: Single Women using Terminations "as Another Form of Contraceptive"', *Daily Mail*, 13 May 2012.

[198] Stuart Cowie (Life) cited in ibid.

[199] See e.g. 'Abortions: Five Teenagers Among Women who had at Least their 6th Termination in UK Last Year', *Sky News*, 19 November 2019.

[200] See Gallup, 'Abortion'. For the same pattern in parliamentary voting patterns, see Chapter 7, Table 1, p. 236.

[201] 'British Pregnancy Advisory Service Helps Women get Illegal Abortions', *Telegraph*, 10 October 2004; 'British Doctor Admits Arranging Abortions in Eighth Month', *Telegraph*, 21 November 2004; 'Abortion Scandal: Transcripts', *Telegraph*, 10 October 2004.

criticism focused firmly on the actions of BPAS rather than the women said to be seeking abortion in such cases. While not claiming that it had broken the law in its own clinics or benefitted financially from a referral, an accompanying editorial was entitled 'Making a Killing', implicitly referencing concerns with profit motivation.[202] Anti-abortion commentators responded with calls for a withdrawal of all NHS funding to BPAS,[203] a full and vigorous investigation and criminal proceedings,[204] claiming that its practice of referring women to Spain illustrated 'the horror of the abortion industry and the banality of [its] bureaucracy of death'.[205] While an investigation by the Chief Medical Office found no evidence of illegal conduct, BPAS was criticised for giving out the Spanish clinic's number too readily and without appropriate advice to women.[206] It responded that it had already revised its practice, and the Department of Health drew a line under the matter.[207]

Mainstreaming Prenatal Screening and Testing and Abortion for Fetal Anomaly

Underpinning these media reports regarding the therapeutic use of fetal tissue, selective reduction, sex selection and 'repeat' and later abortion lies an important cultural ambivalence regarding cases where abortion is believed to take place for non-serious reasons or without careful consideration. This same tension has been apparent in discussions of abortion for fetal anomaly. In 1967, this was seen as the most respectable reason for seeking abortion. Indeed, controversy had centred primarily on the number of healthy pregnancies that might be 'sacrificed' to weed out one 'defective' one.[208] However, over the following years, as prenatal screening and testing became more accurate and sophisticated, a 'silent revolution' transformed it from an exceptional process of relevance only to women at high risk of giving birth to a child with an impairment into a routine part of antenatal care, underpinned by the possibility of the lawful abortion of affected pregnancies.[209]

The impact was profound. For the first time, prenatal testing gave women the possibility of rejecting a pregnancy because of the specific traits of the future child.[210] As testing became more routine, Katz Rothman has suggested

---

[202] *Telegraph*, 10 October 2004.

[203] *Third Sector*, 'Opinion: Hot Issue – Should the Government Withdraw the Annual £12m Funding to BPAS?'.

[204] See 'Charity Defends Abortion Advice', *BBC News*, 10 October 2004, citing Life; *Third Sector*, 'Opinion: Hot Issue – Should the Government Withdraw the Annual £12m Funding to BPAS?'.

[205] Mohler, 'Carnage in the Womb'.

[206] Department of Health, Letter from the Chief Medical Officer to Primary Care Trust and Strategic Health Authority Chief Executives, 21 September 2005; and Department of Health, 'An Investigation into the BPAS Response into the Requests for Late Abortions – A Report from the CMO', September 2005.

[207] Dyer, 'Charity Did Not Break Law in Giving Information About Late Abortions', 716.

[208] See Chapter 1, p. 10.

[209] Löwy, 'Prenatal Diagnosis, Surveillance and Risk', 567.

[210] Ibid.

that every pregnancy became a 'tentative' one, fully accepted only once the health of the fetus was established.[211] Moreover, the most important of these new technologies – ultrasound – opened a window on the womb, coming to enjoy a cultural significance that went far beyond its diagnostic use.[212] More recent critics of prenatal screening and testing have argued that abortion for fetal anomaly is eugenicist, discriminatory, and reflects a troubling casualisation of attitudes towards life. Its proponents initially advanced it as an important contribution to addressing a public health problem and, later, as a means of empowering women through the provision of important additional information about their pregnancies. Again, the quality of women's decision-making would become a central focus of such disputes.

New Technologies and Changing Attitudes towards Disability

Pro-Life commentators have long criticised the availability of abortion for reason of fetal anomaly.[213] However, the issue would gain greater prominence from the early 1980s. In 1981, Life called for a law to prohibit deliberately ending the life of a disabled neonate or performing abortion on the basis of fetal sex or fetal anomaly.[214] As we will see, the charity would also repeatedly seek to raise these issues in the courts, with some measure of success.[215] In the same year, SPUC launched its Handicap Division with a half-page advertisement in *The Times*, aiming to 'affirm the right of all handicapped people to live', to oppose prenatal testing and abortion for disability, to safeguard disabled neonates; and to challenge claims that disabled people were unhappy or a burden on families or taxpayers.[216] These campaigns would increasingly be fronted by disabled people: the SPUC Handicap Division was led by Alison Davis, who had spina bifida, with its *Times* advertisement featuring a foot-written message by Marilyn Carr, who had been born without arms.[217]

Over time, concerns with abortion for fetal anomaly would also move more into the mainstream of disability rights campaigning, whilst taking time to gain significant broader traction. Whilst the initial impulses for the legalisation

---

[211] Katz Rothman, *The Tentative Pregnancy*; see further Gammeltoft and Wahlberg, 'Selective Reproductive Technologies', 201.

[212] Löwy, 'Prenatal Diagnosis', 290; Petchesky, 'Fetal Images'.

[213] For an erudite early discussion, see St John-Stevas, *The Right to Life*, with the first of several questions posed on the book's cover being 'Have mothers the right to kill their babies if they are hopelessly deformed?'.

[214] Wellcome Library, SA/NAC/E/4/2, Draft of Protection of Disabled Children Bill 1981; *Times*, 20 November 1981. For the Pro-Choice response, see Wellcome Library, SA/ALR/G/16, Co-ord, 'Screening for Foetal Abnormality', memo, c. 1981; 'Screening', NAC Newsletter, July/August 1984, 23; NAC Newsletter, April–June 1985; *Breaking Chains*, no. 47, November/December 1987.

[215] See Chapter 5, pp. 170–76.

[216] Wellcome Library, SA/NAC/E/4/1/3, SPUC Handicap Division, flyer c. 1980s; *Human Concern*, no. 7, spring 1981, 1. See further *Human Concern*, no. 9, spring 1981, 4–5, 8; no. 14, autumn 1983, 8; no. 22, summer 1986, 2; no. 27, summer 1989, 6; no. 28, autumn 1989, 8.

[217] *Times*, 23 November 1981.

of abortion on this ground had been thalidomide and rubella, the diffusion of prenatal screening and testing was driven in the 1970s and 1980s by a desire to reduce the incidence of Down's syndrome, a condition that was widely perceived as a public health problem.[218] Studies conducted in the 1990s suggested that accepting testing and terminating an affected pregnancy continued to be seen as the responsible course of conduct: mothers of Down's children who declined screening were widely believed to be at fault,[219] with one in 10 obstetricians believing that this rendered their children undeserving of state support.[220] When, in 1993, the RCOG announced that the development of maternal serum testing 'could Halve Down's Syndrome Births', it thus had grounds for its apparent confidence that the technology would be embraced by patients, that affected pregnancies would be terminated, and that these facts were to be celebrated.[221] As the technology became more sophisticated and screening was routinely embedded in antenatal care, terminations for Down's syndrome increased rapidly: 28 abortions were reported as a result of this diagnosis in 1968, rising to 283 in 1995 and 693 in 2020 (with 14 of them after 24 weeks).[222] While obstetricians and gynaecologists claimed – with some justification with regard to hereditary disorders – that increased testing responded to demand from women, the move to recognise maternal age as a risk factor for Down's syndrome appears rather to have been driven by doctors and the media.[223] Concerns would also start to emerge that accepting prenatal testing might be an expression of conformity rather than of choice, with ultrasound sometimes embraced as a chance to 'meet' the baby without consideration of its diagnostic purpose or because it was expected by health professionals.[224] Illana Löwy notes the powerful effects of the deceptively simple question that may accompany the offer of prenatal testing: 'Madam, would you like to know if your baby is all right?'[225] These concerns with the normalisation of prenatal screening and testing dovetailed into more general Pro-Life concerns with the trivialisation of abortion and the alleged 'conveyor belt culture' within abortion services.

The understanding of disability as a public health problem would be subject to increasing challenge as people with disabilities became more visible within

---

[218] Löwy, 'Prenatal Diagnosis, Surveillance and Risk', 568; Wright, *Downs*.

[219] Marteau and Drake, 'Attributions for Disability', 1127–32.

[220] Green, 'Obstetricians' Views on Prenatal Diagnosis and Termination of Pregnancy', 228–32, found one in 10 obstetricians surveyed in 1993 held this view.

[221] Archives of the Royal College of Obstetricians and Gynaecologists, RCOG/N4/1993, 'New Test could Halve Down's Syndrome Births', Press Release, July 1993. See Löwy, 'Prenatal Diagnosis', 290–99, on the pervasiveness of such assumptions in the early history of prenatal testing.

[222] See annual abortion statistics. Note that there is evidence of under-reporting: Department of Health, *Matching Department of Health Abortion Notifications and Data from the National Down's Syndrome Cytogenetic Register, 2013*.

[223] Löwy, 'Prenatal Diagnosis, Surveillance and Risk', 572.

[224] Thomas, *Down's Syndrome Screening and Reproductive Politics*, offers a useful summary of the research on this issue at 3–5.

[225] Löwy, 'Prenatal Diagnosis', 299.

mainstream education and communities and more vocal in public debate, with a particular focus on changing attitudes towards people with Down's syndrome.[226] In 1996, Lord Brentford – a hereditary peer and president of the leading Anglican evangelical organisation, the Church Society – proposed a Bill to prohibit abortion on the basis of a diagnosis of Down's.[227] In 2001, in a sign of how this issue had become a focus for disability rights campaigns as well as anti-abortion ones, the newly founded Disability Rights Commission (DRC) proclaimed the fetal anomaly ground of the Abortion Act to be incompatible with valuing disability and non-disability equally.[228] In 2004, a BBC Radio 4 documentary seized upon the mistaken premise that a small increase in the number of babies born annually with Down's syndrome resulted from more women choosing to continue with affected pregnancies. Its key message – that this reflected a more 'caring Britain', which was increasingly accepting of disability – reflected a very different sensibility from the condemnatory attitudes towards women who refused prenatal testing seen just a decade earlier.[229] This would combine powerfully with concerns regarding post-viability terminations, particularly when the anomaly in question was believed to be a non-serious one: two significant legal cases on this issue are considered in the following chapter.[230]

Concerns with the mainstreaming and normalisation of prenatal testing have also found recent focus with regard to non-invasive prenatal testing (NIPT), which relies on the study of fetal DNA in maternal blood to give a highly accurate indication of the likely presence of Down's, Edwards' and Patau's syndromes.[231] While a positive result needs to be confirmed through amniocentesis, NIPT can significantly reduce the number of women who run the risk of miscarriage associated with this procedure.[232] It is thus said to offer a technical improvement rather than a conceptual revolution.[233] However, its efficiency has itself been criticised by Pro-Life commentators as reflecting a

---

[226] On the movement away from the segregation of those with disabilities within geographically isolated institutions towards greater care in the community, see Thomas, *Down's Syndrome Screening and Reproductive Politics*; Wright, *Downs*.

[227] Termination of Pregnancy (Restriction) Bill [HL] in *Hansard*, House of Lords, 14 May 1996, vol. 572, col. 393.

[228] 'Disabled Group in Abortion Law Attack', *Telegraph*, 22 August 2001. The DRC was replaced by the Equality and Human Rights Commission in 2007.

[229] BBC Radio 4, 'Born with Down's', 24 February 2008. For criticism of both the flawed statistical analysis (the BBC was apparently ignorant of the important role played by increasing maternal age at birth in driving this trend) and what Ben Goldacre saw as the programme's 'crass moral judgment', see 'Scientific Proof that we Live in a Warmer and More Caring Universe', *Guardian*, 29 November 2008.

[230] Chapter 5, pp. 173–76.

[231] Go, van Vugt and Oudejans, 'Non-invasive Aneuploidy Detection using Free Fetal DNA and RNA in Maternal Plasma', 372–82; 'NHS to Offer Safer Down's Syndrome Test to Pregnant Women', *Guardian*, 29 October 2016.

[232] 'Down's Syndrome Test could see Condition Disappear, C of E warns', *Guardian*, 19 January 2018.

[233] Bianchi, Oepkes and Ghidini, 'Current Controversies in Prenatal Diagnosis 1', 6–11. See generally Löwy, 'Prenatal Diagnosis, Surveillance and Risk', 577.

'search and destroy' approach to fetal anomaly, driven by a 'eugenicist' Government concerned with saving money.[234] Given, first, that it is likely to lead to greater uptake in testing and, second, that a large majority of women are known to choose to terminate affected pregnancies, some fear that NIPT risks creating 'a world without Down syndrome' and the loss of a special group of people who make a unique contribution to society.[235]

The clear tension between changing attitudes towards disabled people and the development of increasingly sophisticated prenatal screening and testing has been partly mediated by a growing acceptance of a woman's right to make decisions about her pregnancy. In his foreword to the Nuffield Council for Bioethics report on NIPT, Professor Tom Shakespeare, a respected sociologist and commentator on disability issues who has achondroplasia, notes that society is 'built on the liberal ethos of autonomy', with prospective parents thus allowed to make 'free and fully informed decisions about their future families' and having a right to information regarding chromosomal abnormalities and inherited genetic conditions. However,

> [t]his requires health professionals who are supportive, and information provision that is balanced and accurate. This also means learning about the rich and varied lives of disabled people, not just knowing about genetic spelling mistakes. Finally, it means being confident that our society will welcome disabled children, and support them and their families appropriately.[236]

The Church of England took a similar view.[237] However, this uneasy accommodation between respecting the rights of women and avoiding discriminatory attitudes towards disabled people places considerable weight on the issue of exactly what information should be offered to those considering prenatal testing and abortion, who should contribute to it, and how it should be conveyed. This would remain an important site of dispute.[238]

Ultrasound and Visualisation

A particularly significant role in both clinical practice and popular culture has been played by one specific prenatal diagnostic tool: ultrasound.[239] Pioneered by the eminent gynaecologist and SPUC founding member Ian Donald, ultrasound was initially dismissed as the 'dream of a mad, red-headed Scotsman' by doctors who had spent years in 'training their hands to see'.[240]

---

[234] Farmer, 'Abortion'. See further Chapter 7, pp. 242–43.
[235] This was the key message of a documentary presented by Sally Phillips, a popular comedic actor and mother of Ollie, a child with Down's syndrome. Richards, *A World Without Down Syndrome?*, screened on BBC2, 8 November 2016.
[236] Shakespeare in Nuffield Council on Bioethics, *Non-Invasive Prenatal Testing*, vii.
[237] General Synod of the Church of England, *Valuing People with Down's Syndrome*.
[238] See Chapter 7, pp. 236–7, 242.
[239] See generally contributions to Tansey and Christie (eds), *Looking at the Unborn*; McNay and Fleming, 'Forty Years of Obstetric Ultrasound 1957–97', 3–56.
[240] See Tansey and Christie (eds), *Looking at the Unborn*, 62 and 34, respectively.

Professor Charles Whitfield, who succeeded Donald as the Regius Professor of Midwifery at The Queen Mother's Hospital in Glasgow, explains that while ultrasound was intended to improve the care of both of 'our two patients', 'the fetus was, of course, the subject that was really exercising most of us':

> ... [At] a time when astronauts were beginning to go up in the sky and round the world and it seemed odd to a lot of us, who thought that we were experts on the fetus, that there had been no mortality among the astronauts but there was still much among our fetuses ... all we could do was listen to its heartbeat and try to feel its outline.[241]

This would now change radically. It is perhaps ironic that a technology developed by a leading Pro-Life advocate and intended also to improve the care of the second of 'our two patients' would contribute to the more accurate identification of fetal anomalies, resulting in the termination of larger numbers of affected pregnancies.[242] Ultrasound was first used for the prenatal diagnosis of anencephaly in the early 1970s, then spina bifida in 1975, Down's syndrome from the late 1980s and then – particularly with the removal of the upper time limit for abortions for fetal anomaly in 1990 – a range of other conditions.[243]

Ultrasound would also gain a significance beyond its diagnostic use, playing an important role in political campaigns around abortion. Pro-Life campaigners had long believed that if people could only see what was involved in abortion opinion would inevitably turn against it. Josephine Quintavalle explains:

> People are not going to sit and read pages and pages of descriptions ... of abortion or whatever, but a picture is different, the image is what counts ... [We] realised how you can write 20 pages that nobody will read, but you show one image and you've got the story across.[244]

Frequent use was made of imagery designed to shock, with distress 'an appropriate response ... [as] the life of an unborn person is considerably more important than hurt feelings'.[245] Lenart Nilsson's beautiful photographs of free-floating fetuses (photographed as if in the womb but actually following abortion) were also often used and were believed 'really [to have] awoken the conscience of many more people'.[246] An advertisement published in

---

[241] Professor Charles Whitfield in Tansey and Christie (eds), *Looking at the Unborn*, 62. Ultrasound might also be used to guide amniocentesis, rendering it safer: Löwy, 'Prenatal Diagnosis, Surveillance and Risk', 572.

[242] Willocks in Tansey and Christie (eds), *Looking at the Unborn*, 46.

[243] McNay and Fleming, 'Forty Years of Obstetric Ultrasound 1957–97', 3–56; Tansey and Christie (eds), *Looking at the Unborn*; see Chapter 3, p. 104, on the removal of the upper time limit for abortion on this ground.

[244] Quintavalle interviewed by O'Neill.

[245] Abort67, 'Why We Show Images'. See also Wellcome Library, SA/NAC/E/4/1/3, SPUC flyer, 'A Foetus is a Baby – Don't Forget', no date, featuring a picture captioned as a rubbish bag full of 'dead babies [that] had reached foetal ages of 18 to 24 weeks before being killed by abortion'.

[246] Phyllis Bowman in *Human Concern*, no. 25, spring 1988, 1, discussing Nilsson's photographs of the 'Drama of Life Before Birth', first published in *LIFE* magazine in 1965. See generally Jülich, 'Lennart Nilsson's Child Is Born', 627–48.

If women had glass tummies would they ever have abortions?

Over 172,000 unborn babies are aborted in Britain every year.

That's more than the entire population of Swansea, and one, on average, every three minutes.

From figures like this you can see how easy it is to get an abortion.

Yet, as the law stands, no woman can have one unless two doctors testify that her 'mental or physical health are at risk.'

Of course, some doctors are openly in favour of 'easier' abortion.

And they can be very generous in their interpretation of 'risk to mental or physical health.'

But should it cover a woman who is upset at the prospect of interrupting her job?

Or a woman who can't face the thought of dirty nappies and teething again?

Or an unmarried woman who is ashamed of being pregnant. And doesn't know how she would cope with a baby, anyway?

(She wouldn't have to. For every unwanted baby, there are 30 childless couples who would love to adopt it).

But one thing is certain.

However inconvenient a pregnancy might be, many women would think twice about an abortion if they could see how quickly the baby develops inside them.

After 23 days from conception – even before most women are sure they're pregnant – the baby's heart is beating.

As early as one month the baby has a head, with eyes, nose, mouth and brain.

As early as two months the baby will grab an instrument placed in its palm, and after nine weeks it can suck its thumb.

As early as three months the baby can kick legs and feet, it has its own fingerprints, and starts to 'breathe' through the umbilical cord.

It is already perfectly formed.

It already has its own personality.

By the time a baby is born it has been living for nine months.

And an abortion takes that life away.

We are not using such emotive phrases to accuse or upset women who have had or are thinking of having an abortion.

But because we believe that a great many people – men as much as women – are concerned at the casual acceptance of abortion.

And would like to see this trend reversed.

If you are one of them there is something you can do to help.

Send a little of your money so that we can continue our campaign to protect the unborn child.

To continue to educate the public, to rally support in Parliament, and eventually to get the law on abortion changed.

We hope you will consider this an important cause.

We think it's a matter of life and death.

THE SOCIETY FOR THE PROTECTION OF UNBORN CHILDREN.

I would like to support your campaign to protect the unborn child.
'I enclose a cheque/postal order payable to SPUC for £_____ or please debit my Access/Barclaycard/American Express.   *DELETE AS APPLICABLE

Card no._____Signature_____

Name_____
(BLOCK CAPITALS PLEASE)
Address_____

Please send your donation to: The Society for the Protection of Unborn Children, 7 Tufton Street, Westminster, London SW1P 3QN. For further information telephone 01-222 5845.

1983 featured a sketch of a pregnant woman gazing down at her miraculously transparent belly, asking the question, '[i]f women had glass tummies would they ever have abortions?', and giving the response, 'many women would think twice about an abortion if they could see how quickly the baby develops inside them'.[247] Ultrasound was an important step beyond these static images, appearing precisely to give women 'glass tummies' and offering moving images of life in utero for the first time to make 'a case against abortion that reason hardly need supplement'.[248] As the routine use of ultrasound in clinical practice increased, these images would become an important cultural reference point, offering the 'social birth' of a new human before the moment of its physical separation from the woman's body.[249]

Campaigners made full use of this potential. Donald himself regularly showed a film of a real-time ultrasound scan at political meetings in the late 1970s, apparently so infuriating the women who attended an event in Milan that he had to be 'hurried out by the back door in case of trouble'.[250] He then travelled to Rome, where he had an audience with a 'delighted' Pope and a Cardinal who carried reprints of his work on a small tray.[251] However, it was the 1984 US film *The Silent Scream* that most fully exploited the campaigning potential of ultrasound, using it to show abortion from 'the viewpoint' of its 'victim'. Viewers were helped to decipher grainy ultrasound images by the narration offered by Dr Bernard Nathanson, an obstetrician and former Pro-Choice campaigner turned Pro-Life advocate. Dr Nathanson explained how, 'sensing aggression in its sanctuary', the 'child ... screams' as it tries to escape 'being torn apart'.[252]

While *The Silent Scream* was credited with winning 'many converts to the pro-life cause',[253] the plausibility of claiming awareness and motivation in a fetus of 12 weeks was fiercely disputed by medical experts, who described how the film had been altered for dramatic effect.[254] Ian Donald testified to the accuracy of the 'fetal activities' shown in the film whilst remaining silent regarding Nathanson's interpretation of them.[255] Professor Stuart Campbell, who had worked as Donald's research registrar in the late 1960s, was less

---

[247] *Daily Mirror*, 25 June 1983; *Private Eye*, 15 July 1983; Wellcome Library, SA/ALR/G/17, Letter from Phyllis Bowman to SPUC members, 30 August 1983. Image reproduced on p. 145, with kind permission of SPUC.

[248] Stith, 'Facing the Unborn'.

[249] Lupton, *The Social Worlds of the Unborn*. See further Dubow, *Ourselves Unborn*; Petchesky, 'Fetal Images'; Roberts, *The Visualised Foetus*.

[250] Alix Donald in Tansey and Christie (eds), *Looking at the Unborn*, 80, explaining that his film made 'unthinkable' the more permissive Italian abortion law they sought.

[251] Ibid.

[252] Dabner, *The Silent Scream*, 1984.

[253] 'The Pro-Life Legacy of Dr. Bernard Nathanson', *National Review*, 22 February 2011.

[254] Wallis and Banta, 'Medicine: Silent Scream', *Time*, 25 March 1985.

[255] Affidavit signed by Donald (23 February 1985) submitted to US Senate, Subcommittee on the Constitution, Committee on the Judiciary, *The Medical Evidence Concerning Fetal Pain*, First Session, 21 May 1985 (S. Hrg. 99-429, Serial No. J-99-28), 5–6.

circumspect, criticising the narration and arguing that the film had been manipulated.[256] Screenings arranged for the House of Commons were cancelled, with ALRA explaining that 'no one in the country of medical eminence [was] prepared to accept that the film formed the basis for a proper discussion of the moral, psychological and medical issues of abortion'.[257] The episode suggested that British politicians would place considerable weight on expert medical advice in their interpretation of such images and that the confrontational tone of the film was less palatable to a British audience. Some British Pro-Life campaigners also had concerns: whilst recognising that the 'desire to hit people hard and shock' was natural, Jack Scarisbrick worried that use of *The Silent Scream* was potentially damaging, risking 'confirm[ing] the convenient belief that pro-lifers are misogynistic fanatics'.[258]

British campaigners nonetheless made important use of the medium of film. The ProLife Alliance was founded as a political party in 1996 by Josephine Quintavalle's son, Bruno. It aimed to field election candidates against MPs seen as being pro-abortion, arguing that 'the mass destruction and trivialisation of human life – and its corrupting effect on society as a whole – is the supreme challenge of our time'.[259] Specifically, the Alliance intended to field sufficient candidates to win the right to air a party political broadcast, which it would use to show a film of an abortion that might 'wak[en] the nation's conscience'.[260] The film – which lasted a little under five minutes – explained the processes involved in different forms of abortion, using 'prolonged and graphic images of the product of suction abortion: aborted foetuses in a mangled and mutilated state, tiny limbs, a separated head, and the like'.[261] While not suggesting that the images were manipulated or objecting to the commentary, the BBC refused to screen the film, citing restrictions on the broadcasting of 'offensive' material. It likewise rejected two further versions of the film, with the images of the fetuses progressively more blurred, before a fourth – which replaced the offending pictures with a blank screen bearing the word 'censored' and a commentary describing the concealed images – was approved and shown five days before the general election.[262] In a subsequent

---

[256] See interview in 'The Truth Behind a Moving Piece of Propaganda', *Guardian*, 9 January 1985. Nathanson later accepted that the film involved occasional use of slow motion, explaining that it was necessary for 'clarifying or understanding' what was happening. US Senate, 'The Medical Evidence Concerning Fetal Pain', 8.

[257] ALRA, *Breaking Chains*, January/February 1985. See further 'The Silent Scream', NAC Newsletter, April–June 1985, 22; 'The Silent Scream', *Breaking Chains*, no. 38, 1985, 7; 'Anti-Abortionists: The Silent Scream', *NAC News*, spring 1986, 20.

[258] Scarisbrick, *Let There Be Life*, 3.

[259] Quoted in Read, 'The Pro-Life Movement', 454.

[260] See interview in 'I want to Wake up this Nation's Conscience', *Observer*, 27 February 2005; see further *Daily Mail*, 20 March 1997, 22; *Times*, 20 March 1997, 12; *Guardian*, 15 March 2002, 8. See also 'Partywatch: ProLife Alliance', *Guardian*, 24 May 2001; Read, 'The Pro-Life Movement'. See further Quintavalle interviewed by O'Neill; Deighan interviewed by O'Neill.

[261] *R v BBC ex parte ProLife Alliance* [2003] UKHL 23, [3].

[262] Ibid., [4].

judicial review of the BBC's refusal to show earlier versions of its film, the Alliance argued that 'the more terrible the abuses authorised by parliament the less right one has to depict the reality'.[263] Having succeeded in the Court of Appeal,[264] it lost the case in the House of Lords, which found that the BBC had acted lawfully, with the film particularly likely to have been offensive to women who had terminated pregnancies.[265] Lord Hoffman took particular aim at any suggestion that abortion was a decision made 'lightly', suggesting that it was 'often a traumatic emotional experience'.[266] Josephine Quintavalle concluded that 'the United Kingdom would not look abortion in the face'.[267]

Eventually, an abortion was shown for the first time on British television in 2004 as part of a documentary, *My Foetus*, which followed its heavily pregnant presenter as she reviewed the evidence and considered her own pro-choice views.[268] It was now Life that contested the value of the footage (of a vacuum aspiration procedure at seven weeks), complaining that '[t]he baby's remains were unrecognisable and only served to reinforce the commonly-held notion that early pregnancies are nothing but a "bunch of cells". It was hard to realise that we were looking at the killing of a real human being.'[269] However, *My Foetus* also considered a second form of visual evidence, which the presenter found to offer the greatest challenge to her pro-choice beliefs: beautiful, detailed 3D and 4D ultrasound images (with the fourth dimension being real-time movement) produced using techniques developed by Ian Donald's former registrar, Professor Stuart Campbell. If early ultrasound had offered a window into the womb, 3D imaging cleaned the glass: it was heralded by anti-abortion campaigners as exposing the 'delightful reality of the humanity of the unborn baby'.[270] Images were widely reproduced in the media, often linked explicitly to the question of the upper time limit for abortion. The *Daily Mail* published 'amazing pictures from inside the womb that shine new light on the abortion debate', featuring an image of an apparently upright fetus with the caption '[a]t week 12 this foetus is walking. At 15, it's yawning.'[271] The claim that fetuses could smile was also widely reported.[272] Campbell, an eminent clinician and researcher, was most frequently quoted in media reports not to

[263] Bruno Quintavalle quoted in 'Judge blocks ProLife broadcast', *Guardian*, 24 May 2001.

[264] *R v BBC ex parte ProLife Alliance* [2002] EWCA Civ 297.

[265] Per Lord Hoffman, *R v BBC ex parte ProLife Alliance* [2003] UKHL 23, [80].

[266] Ibid.

[267] Quintavalle interviewed by O'Neill.

[268] Black, *My Foetus*, screened on Channel 4, 20 April 2004. See also Roberts, *The Visualised Foetus*.

[269] Nuala Scarisbrick, cited in Roberts, *The Visualised Foetus*, 61.

[270] Josephine Quintavalle for the ProLife Alliance, quoted in 'Scanner Pioneer Urges Curb on Abortion', *Guardian*, 29 June 2004. See further Roberts, *The Visualised Foetus*; Savell, 'Life and Death before Birth'.

[271] For discussion of this and other media reports, see Roberts, *The Visualised Foetus*, chapter 3; Kirklin, 'The Role of Medical Imaging in the Abortion Debate', 426.

[272] 'Proof Babies Smile in Womb', *Evening Standard*, 12 September 2003; 'Scanner Shows Unborn Babies Smile', *BBC News*, 13 September 2003; 'The Foetus who Broke into a Big Smile. . . Aged

explain the technology's diagnostic value but rather to offer an intuitive, common-sense explanation of how the technology revealed the humanity of the unborn. His article in *The Telegraph* was entitled 'Don't Tear a Smiling Foetus from the Womb'.[273] In the *Guardian*, he explained:

> The more I study foetuses the more I find it quite distressing to terminate babies who are so advanced in terms of human behaviour ... For normal babies being terminated for social reasons it's probably unacceptable nowadays to be terminating them much after 14 weeks. They can suck their thumbs, they can open their eyes, they can perform complex movements. I think it's time we got our act together.[274]

While 3D and 4D imaging were widely heralded as an important advance in clinical terms, the question of their significance to calls to reform the Abortion Act would remain fiercely contested.[275]

Conclusion

While 1990 had brought emphatic defeat for those seeking wide-ranging restrictive reform of the Abortion Act, contestation would continue regarding the Act's interpretation ˙and implementation, coming to turn on the 'normalisation' of abortion. Two starkly conflicting visions underpinned these disputes. The first – reflected in the slogan: 'Abortions are safe. Abortions are normal. Abortions are healthcare'[276] – holds that abortion should be accepted as a necessary and inevitable part of everyday life and made routinely available and easily accessible within mainstream health services. The second fiercely resists 'normalisation' as equating to the trivialisation of a procedure that – if ever acceptable – should remain an exceptional measure of last resort, available only in the most serious and compelling of circumstances. Over time, the first of these visions has undoubtedly been in the ascendancy: access to abortion on request has expanded, with a growing proportion of services funded by the NHS; abortion has become a far safer and less technically demanding procedure; and prenatal screening and testing have been mainstreamed in antenatal care, underpinned by the availability of abortion where a fetal anomaly is detected. Yet each new technical innovation or service development – from outpatient services to the abortion pill to NIPT – has offered a lightning rod for a new storm of protest, often ostensibly narrowly

Only 17 weeks', *Daily Mail*, 11 October 2010; 'Baby Captured Smiling in the Womb by Ultrasound', *Telegraph*, 14 November 2014; Lee, 'The Trouble with "Smiling" Fetuses'.

[273] 'Don't Tear a Smiling Fetus from the Womb', *Telegraph*, 4 October 2006.

[274] 'Scanner Pioneer Urges Curb on Abortion', *Guardian*, 29 June 2004. See further Campbell, '4D and Prenatal Bonding', 243.

[275] See Chapter 7.

[276] Abortion Rights, tagline in email signature (22 January 2020), on file with the authors.

focused on issues of technical efficiency or safety but always also reflecting conflicting visions of gender, family, religion, science and the public good.

In many instances these broader disputes would also find focus in disputes regarding the legal meaning of particular words or phrases of the Abortion Act. We turn to consider some of these in the next chapter.

5

The Battle for Legal Meaning

> We believe most of the abortions that are taking place are not actually complying with the law ... about 98% of abortions are probably illegal if we could depend on the judges to uphold the law.[1]

An instructive exchange occurred as the Bill that would become the Abortion Act was passing through the House of Commons. Norman St John-Stevas asked Alice Bacon, a Home Office minister, for advice on the impact of a suggested change in its wording. She replied that it would be impossible to know until the Act was tested in the courts and that 'might not be for a very long time.' A frustrated St John-Stevas pointed out that the Bill purported to 'amend and clarify the law', but even the Home Office could not explain what it would mean in practice.[2] Yet Bacon was doing no more than describing an inherent feature of any law well known to lawyers: in holding the final authority to explain the meaning of the words used by Parliament, courts also make law.[3]

Similar advice was given to an audience of doctors following the Abortion Act's introduction by an experienced lawyer, Geoffrey Howe QC, then on the cusp of the parliamentary career that would later see him enter Government and, ultimately, play a prominent role in the downfall of Margaret Thatcher. Like Bacon, Howe explained that the Abortion Act would be given meaning only once it reached the courts. He went on to describe some of the influences that would play out in that process, advising that judges should not be regarded as 'desiccated legal automata, quite uninfluenced by public opinion and considerations of public policy', and noting that a significant role might also be played by juries who would themselves be 'influenced by their experience of the 1967 Act, as reported in the press'.[4] Howe can perhaps be forgiven for failing also to predict the enormous importance of the role that would be

---

[1] John Deighan interviewed by Jane O'Neill, 29 January 2018.
[2] See Hindell and Simms, *Abortion Law Reformed*, 183–84.
[3] Diplock, *The Court as Legislators*, 6. See further Duxbury, *Elements of Legislation*; Nelken, *The Limits of the Legal Process*; Cotterell, *The Sociology of Law*.
[4] Howe in Medical Protection Society, *The Abortion Act 1967 Proceedings of a Symposium* (hereafter MPS, *Symposium*), 72.

played by campaigners: opposing factions would pick over statutory language, stretching it to its limits to extend access to abortion services or carefully selecting the right case to force a more restrictive interpretation of its terms, with both sides equally well aware of the value of a well-targeted legal action in shaping opinion. Over the five decades to follow, dozens of legal challenges concerning the interpretation and implementation of the Act would be brought, with many more threatened: campaigners would have a hand in almost all of them.

Through this process, the meaning of the Abortion Act would be given. The judges called to arbitrate on these disputes would frequently pause to acknowledge that abortion excites strong passions before emphasising that this was none of their concern: their task was purely to apply the law, 'free of emotion or predilection'.[5] Nonetheless, they would venture onto terrain where narrowly drawn, sometimes apparently esoteric issues of interpretation sat firmly on broader moral, social and political fault lines. Each judge necessarily brought their own moral sensibilities to bear, albeit – as we will see – with some taking more care to conceal them than others. Each would necessarily consider statutory language that was already heavily saturated with the meaning given to it in practice, with clinical views weighing heavily in their determinations. Each would operate within a morally and politically charged environment, with many of the cases before them generating significant media interest. And each would work with a collection of interpretative principles and presumptions that offered significant flexibility in negotiating ageing statutory language, which they would read in ways inevitably coloured by changing social norms and clinical realities.[6]

It is unsurprising that the 'social clause', which had so exercised parliamentarians, would feature heavily in the cases before them. Yet potential issues that had passed largely unremarked in 1967 would also become heavily disputed, as evolving technologies and clinical practices rendered otiose statutory language that had once appeared clear and as public opinion grew more liberal. Courts would thus determine not just in what circumstances two doctors might certify that grounds for an abortion had been met and what processes must be followed in reaching such a decision, but also how late in pregnancy an abortion might be performed and how early in pregnancy the requirements of the Abortion Act applied, what it means to say that treatment for the termination of pregnancy had been performed by a doctor or taken place on approved premises, and exactly which workers and activities were covered by the conscientious objection provision. Taking these cases together, it is striking how little of the modern meaning of the Abortion Act would have been apparent even to the best informed and most farsighted commentator in

---

[5] *Paton v BPAS* [1978] 2 All ER 987, 989.
[6] Duxbury, *Elements of Legislation*.

1967. Indeed, like Bacon and Howe, the best informed and most farsighted would themselves have been well aware of this fact.

How Late, How Early, How Legal?

A case in point was the important issue of the Abortion Act's temporal reach. As we have seen, the question of an upper time limit for abortion had been almost entirely ignored by Parliament in 1967, to the extent that it had been later suggested that one had been read into the Act only inadvertently.[7] The issue of how early in pregnancy it was necessary to comply with the Abortion Act was equally unclear. These important questions – 'how early, how late, and how legal?'[8] – would be answered by the courts only following complex and lengthy processes whereby meaning was first disputed and shaped outside them, with campaigners, the media, doctors and professional bodies each playing an important role.

How Late?

A time limit was not originally specified on the face of the Abortion Act but was rather read into it by the Infant Life (Preservation) Act 1929, with the Abortion Act offering no protection against prosecution for its offence of 'destruction of a child' who was 'capable of being born alive'.[9] The ambiguous and poorly understood 1929 Act had been designed not with abortion in mind but rather to address a legal lacuna whereby no offence was committed if a child was killed during the process of spontaneous birth but before becoming fully separated from the body of the woman.[10] Reflecting the state of medical science in the 1920s, it contained a rebuttable presumption that capacity to be born alive was acquired at 28 weeks' gestation. Following the passage of the Abortion Act, the 1929 Act gained enormous new significance, and its inadequacies became swiftly apparent. First, the concept of a rebuttable presumption was poorly understood, with some apparently believing that there was rather a bright line rule: the investigation into the Wanstead baby (which was said to have 'cried out' following a termination at 20 weeks) concluded that no offence had been committed as the procedure had occurred 'well within the Abortion Act upper limit of 28 weeks'.[11] Second, capacity for life depends heavily on the quality of antenatal investigation, delivery and available

---

[7] See Chapter 3, p. 100.

[8] Tunkel, 'Abortion', 253–56.

[9] The 1929 Act applies in England and Wales; the Criminal Justice Act (NI) (1945) makes the same provision for Northern Ireland; in Scotland, the relevant offences are at common law.

[10] There would be no 'procurement' of 'unlawful miscarriage' under the 1861 Act and no murder, which requires the killing of a child fully born and separate from the body of the mother.

[11] See Tunkel, 'Abortion', 255. See further Chapter 3, p. 80.

neonatal care, and advances in these fields had rendered the presumption that it was achieved only at 28 weeks an anachronism.

As we have seen, the upper time limit for abortion quickly became a major focus of contestation and campaigning. Life relied on its whistle-blower network to uncover potential abuses of the law, which were then reported to the police and media, with newspapers in the late 1970s regularly carrying stories of aborted babies left gasping for air on hospital sluice boards.[12] While subsequent investigations typically found no evidence of illegality and resulted in no further action, in 1983, a consultant gynaecologist was charged with attempted murder. At a time when gestational age was still often determined by palpitation rather than ultrasound, Anthony Hamilton had misdiagnosed a 33 week pregnancy as one of 23 weeks. Following a prostaglandin induction, a baby was delivered 'alive and crying', survived and was subsequently adopted. Hamilton accepted his 'undoubtedly remarkable' error but denied that the baby had been left to die. Charges against him were subsequently dismissed due to insufficient evidence, an outcome that Life found 'astonishing'. Nonetheless, the case had succeeded in focusing minds on 'the horrible state of the abortion law and the confusion into which it has thrown the public and the doctors'.[13]

The RCOG responded with an expert working group, which made a number of recommendations that tended to confirm existing best practice.[14] The group offered a clinical definition of the term 'capable of being born alive': this required 'good evidence that survival is a reasonable possibility, given the availability of what is currently regarded as the best neonatal care'.[15] A 24 week upper limit was recommended as offering an appropriate balance between protecting most fetuses capable of surviving extrauterine life and ensuring sufficient time for access to legal abortion for most women.[16] Further, gestational age should be established by the best means available, including routine use of ultrasound above 20 weeks.[17] These recommendations were initially respected on a voluntary basis and subsequently incorporated into licensing requirements for non-NHS service providers, with all abortions after 24 weeks to be performed within NHS facilities.[18] The effect

---

[12] See Chapter 3, pp. 79–80, 96–97.

[13] 'A Moral Dilemma for the Doctors', *Times*, 29 September 1983; 'Abortion Doctor Cleared by JPs', *Times*, 16 September 1983.

[14] Archives of the Royal College of Obstetricians and Gynaecologists (RCOG Archives), RCOG C37, RCOG, *Report on Fetal Viability and Clinical Practice by a Representative Committee Comprising RCOG, BPA, RCGP, RCM, BMA, DHSS*, 1985, citing a 1980 Letter from E. A. J. Alment, RCOG President, noting that 24 weeks marked the point in pregnancy at which 'at present and in the future . . . an expelled fetus might have a prospect of survival', 14.

[15] Ibid., 9.

[16] Ibid., 15.

[17] Ibid., 17.

[18] *Hansard*, House of Lords (HL), 18 October 1990, vol. 522, cols 1038–39.

was marked: 142 abortions had been reported at 25 weeks or over in 1981; there were 24 in 1987.[19]

However, the existence of a clear clinical definition did not resolve the issue of the legal meaning of 'capable of being born alive', with academic commentators noting at least three possible distinct interpretations of the phrase.[20] Anti-abortion campaigners thus turned to the courts, relying on an argument set out by Gerard Wright QC, an 'unconditionally Pro-Life' lawyer.[21] Wright claimed that the law was 'by no means as permissive as it is treated as being': to be 'capable of being born alive', a child did not – as the RCOG had it – require some prospect of survival but, rather, must merely show some primitive signs of life. If so, then other than where performed to preserve a woman's life, abortion was illegal at – or even before – 20 weeks of pregnancy.[22]

Wright's opportunity to test this argument came in the late 1980s, when he was invited to represent Robert Carver, an Oxford University student and member of SPUC, which supported his legal action. Carver had been horrified to learn that his ex-girlfriend was intending to terminate a pregnancy of 20 weeks and argued that an abortion would be illegal at that gestation.[23] However, the court rejected his claim, preferring the RCOG's understanding of the term 'viability', with Wright's interpretation not accepted by 'a wide body of eminent medical opinion'.[24] Carver was nonetheless more successful outside the courts: following the media furore, his former girlfriend felt unable to go through with the termination, leaving him to raise their child.[25] The Tory MP Peter Bruinvels responded with a Presentation Bill highlighting men's lack of legal rights in abortion decisions.[26]

Another case followed shortly, brought by a woman who claimed that her doctors' negligent failure to confirm the existence of a suspected fetal anomaly had denied her the option of terminating her pregnancy. Despite being a rare case in which anti-abortion campaigners had no apparent hand, the judgement offered considerably more support to Wright's reading of the law: 'capable of being born alive' was found to require only existence of 'a live child . . . living by reason of its breathing through its own lungs alone', with no mention of a reasonable prospect of survival.[27] While heralded by some as implying a much lower time limit for most abortions,[28] this developing line of case law was then cut short. In 1990, Parliament voted by a large majority to amend the Abortion

---

[19] Office of Population Censuses and Surveys, *Abortion Statistics* for 1981 and 1987.

[20] Pearl and Grubb, 'Protecting the Life of the Unborn Child', 340.

[21] Wright, 'The Culture of Death'.

[22] Wright, 'The Legality of Abortion by Prostaglandin'; Wright, 'Capable of Being Born Alive?'.

[23] *C v S* [1987] 1 All ER 1230.

[24] Ibid., 1241.

[25] 'Anti-Abortion Man Raises Baby Alone', *Sunday Times*, 17 January 1988. See also *Guardian*, 28 February 1987; *Daily Mail*, 30 October 1987, 16 December 1987; *Times*, 11 August 1989.

[26] See Chapter 3, p. 92.

[27] *Rance v Mid-Downs AHA* [1991] 1 All ER 801, 817.

[28] E.g. Widdecombe in *Hansard*, House of Commons (HC), 24 April 1990, vol. 171, col. 191.

Act to provide that most abortions would be lawful only where a pregnancy had 'not exceeded its twenty-fourth week'.[29] Viability was now accepted as offering a 'moral watershed' in the regulation of abortion, and existing clinical practice was followed in taking 24 weeks as the appropriate threshold.[30]

It had been hoped that this amendment would enshrine a bright line test that commanded widespread support, permitting 'the moderates to get abortion out of politics!!' by addressing the issue that had commanded the easiest parliamentary majorities for restrictive reform.[31] However, the new wording of the Act, providing that a pregnancy must not have 'exceeded its twenty-fourth week', would also be revealed to be ambiguous: was a week 'exceeded' at the same moment that it was completed or only on the following day? In other words, would an abortion performed at 24+0 weeks be lawful or was the legal cut off 23+6 weeks? For many years, this narrow and seemingly esoteric question passed unnoticed. While most service providers worked to a gestational limit of 23+6 weeks, in 2007, BPAS sought and obtained advice from the Department of Health that confirmed that it would be lawful to change its practice to offer abortions until 24+0 weeks.[32] However, in 2014, the Department became concerned that this previous interpretation of the Abortion Act (and thus the advice given to BPAS) was incorrect. Having consulted with a select group of medical stakeholders, it revised its previous interpretation of the law: henceforth, it deemed abortions lawful only when performed until 23+6 weeks.[33]

Aware that it was likely to be subject to 'criticism led by BPAS' for 'changing its mind', the Department of Health now took the extraordinary decision not to publicise its revised understanding of the law.[34] Unaware, doctors continued to rely on the previous guidance and carried out a small number of abortions that, under this new interpretation, fell outside the protection offered by the Abortion Act and were thus criminal offences carrying a potential sentence of life imprisonment.[35] Four years later, any move to inform service providers was again 'put on hold (at No. 10's request)' in light of renewed media interest in abortion following the outcome of the Irish abortion referendum.[36] The Government finally published its revised

---

[29] Section 1(1)(a).

[30] See Chapter 3, p. 104.

[31] As Douglas Houghton had suggested to David Steel, see Chapter 3, p. 101.

[32] Email from the Department of Health to BPAS, 29 October 2007, cited in Ann Furedi, Witness Statement, *BPAS v SS Health and Social Care* [2019] EWHC 1397 (Admin) (*BPAS 2019*), on file with the authors.

[33] *BPAS 2019*, [14–22].

[34] Furedi, Second Witness Statement, [30], *BPAS 2019*, citing a note from Andrea Duncan, a senior civil servant, to the Minister (December 2014), on file with the authors.

[35] Furedi, Witness Statement, [36], *BPAS 2019*, noting 13 terminations reported at 24+0 weeks in 2017–2018, on file with the authors.

[36] Andrea Duncan submission to the Minister (16 July 2018), cited in *BPAS 2019*, [26]. See further Furedi, Second Witness Statement, [35], *BPAS 2019*, on file with the authors.

interpretation of the law only in 2018, prompted by BPAS's licence renewal application, which specified that some clinics would carry out abortions up to 24+0 weeks.[37] As it had predicted, BPAS was outraged, not least by the Department's 'almost cavalier attitude' in having failed to communicate such an important change.[38] BPAS also struggled to understand how, 'if two sets of legal advice had drawn two different conclusions, the Department could now maintain the position to be clear-cut'.[39] When the Department stood firm, BPAS went to court. While critical of the Government's handling of the matter, both the High Court and the Court of Appeal found against BPAS: each read the Abortion Act to permit abortion only until 23+6 weeks, with expert medical testimony regarding accepted clinical practice in dating pregnancies playing a determinative role in shaping their view.[40]

The 23+6 weeks case illustrates the challenge of drafting unambiguous statutory language. It also showed that pro-choice advocates would be no less pugnacious than their opponents in fighting for a preferred interpretation of the Abortion Act. For Ann Furedi, BPAS had demonstrated that 'we will not let even one-day be shaved off the time limit without a fight', ensuring that the Department of Health would be unlikely to treat abortion services 'in this casual way' in the future:

> No one thought we would be prepared to risk the possible clamour from 'the antis' if we were 'out and proud' about our abortion provision at the edge of the legal limit. We were warned we risked headlines denouncing late abortion in the *Mail* . . . [and] that our action would likely lead to a successful parliamentary action to reduce the time limit much more substantially. We demonstrated that the main problem we face is not the antis – who have been silent and invisible – but Department officials and the professionals they co-opted to make their case.[41]

The entrenchment of a 24 week limit on the face of the Abortion Act was thus the result of a lengthy process. It followed sustained media attention, fostered by Life, which helped to provoke the introduction of professional guidelines that reflected procedures and protocols that had already developed and become embedded as clinical best practice. Initially accepted by doctors on a voluntary basis, these guidelines were then reflected in licensing requirements, subsequently confirmed by the courts and only much later enshrined in statute. The meaning of the 24 week limit would then itself be contested within medical practice, with the courts confirming the interpretation of the term offered by the Government's authoritative medical experts.

[37] *BPAS 2019*, [26–27].
[38] Furedi, Witness Statement, [30], *BPAS 2019*, on file with the authors.
[39] Furedi, Second Witness Statement, [38], *BPAS 2019*, on file with the authors.
[40] *BPAS 2019*; *BPAS v Secretary of State for Health and Social Care* [2020] EWCA Civ 355.
[41] Email from Ann Furedi to Sally Sheldon and others, 15 May 2019, on file with the authors.

Moreover, the 24 week limit has become significant even where it has no formal legal relevance, colouring the interpretation and implementation of other legal provisions. While there is no longer a legal upper time limit for abortions on the grounds of a 'substantial risk' of 'serious handicap', it appears that this test is subject to more restrictively interpretation after 24 weeks.[42] Further, while a woman who procures her own abortion outside the requirements of the Abortion Act formally commits a criminal offence at any stage of pregnancy, the 24 week limit seems to have become informally embedded in prosecution policy, with all reported prosecutions in Britain in recent years concerning women who had acted after 24 weeks, with frequent reference to this limit in sentencing remarks.[43] The best known of these cases is that of Sarah Catt, who had the misfortune to be tried before a member of the Lawyers' Christian Fellowship, an organisation committed to applying 'God's justice on the ground'.[44] The 'manifestly disproportionate' sentence of eight years awarded to her by Mr Justice Cooke was later reduced significantly on appeal,[45] and his *obiter* criticism that the Abortion Act was 'wrongly, liberally construed in practice so as to make abortion available essentially on demand prior to 24 weeks' attracted widespread coverage and criticism in the liberal press: *The Guardian* criticised his 'judicial machismo' and lack of empathy with 'a woman badly in need of care and treatment'.[46]

How Early?

If the question of the upper time limit was for many years unclear, so too was the issue of how early in pregnancy it was possible to commit the offence of 'unlawful procurement of miscarriage' and, thus, at what point it became necessary to comply with the Abortion Act in order to avoid potential prosecution.[47] Glanville Williams, leading criminal lawyer and architect of the Abortion Act, moved from an early view that the relevant moment was that of fertilisation[48] to believing that the legislation was unspecific and offered scope for a different interpretation.[49] While Keown suggests that this change showed Williams permitting 'his fervent personal views in favour of relaxed abortion laws to corrupt his legal analysis', it was this latter view that would prevail.[50]

[42] This chapter, p. 174.
[43] *R v Catt* (Leeds Crown Court, 17 September 2012); *R v Towers*, discussed in 'Shildon Woman Jailed over Poison Termination', *BBC News*, 17 December 2015; *R v Mohamed*, discussed in 'Jury Convicts Mother who Destroyed Foetus', *Telegraph*, 26 May 2007.
[44] See Lawyers' Christian Fellowship, 'Mission & Vision'.
[45] *R v Catt* [2013] EWCA Crim 1187.
[46] 'It's Judicial Machismo that Jails Women like Sarah Catt', *Guardian*, 18 September 2012.
[47] Tunkel, 'Abortion', 254. See also St John-Stevas, *The Agonising Choice*, 37–39.
[48] Williams, *The Sanctity of Life and the Criminal Law*, 141.
[49] Williams, *Textbook of Criminal Law*, 294.
[50] Keown, '"Morning After" Pills, "Miscarriage" and Muddle', 296, 309.

The question of 'how early' had first received serious attention in 1977, when a Manchester consultant writing in the *British Medical Journal* described his practice of 'menstrual regulation': the evacuation of the uterus 10–18 days after a missed period.[51] On being advised that his actions were probably illegal, he promptly ceased them, thus ending – in the view of one academic lawyer, Victor Tunkel – the 'open and ethical performance, with skill and success, of routine procedures at just the time when they are medically most desirable'.[52] Tunkel's call for a short, non-controversial reform 'to put beyond prosecution' these methods of 'the new contraception' was considered by campaigners but ultimately went unanswered.[53] The issue arose again shortly after, when MSI advertised that they would insert intrauterine devices up to 10 days after intercourse. When warned that this might be illegal, the charity stopped advertising (though possibly not offering) the service.[54]

The importance of the boundary between contraception and abortion gained far greater importance regarding the 'morning after pill', which had been available on prescription from the early 1980s. In 2000, following the decision to remove the requirement for a prescription, SPUC brought a legal challenge, resulting in what John Keown describes as 'one of the most important decisions ever handed down by a High Court judge'.[55] Relying on Keown's detailed historical research, SPUC argued that the offence of 'unlawful procurement of miscarriage' must be understood as it would have been at the time it was passed, which meant prohibiting all attempts to procure a miscarriage from fertilisation. Given that the morning after pill could prevent the implantation of a fertilised egg, it was thus not a contraceptive but an abortifacient and, unless the provisions of the 1967 Act were met, its supply and use were potentially unlawful (as, by extrapolation, were other forms of oral contraception).[56]

The case was heard by Sir James Munby, an eminent and sometimes outspoken judge who would serve a five year term as President of the Family Division of the High Court.[57] While *The Guardian* had criticised Mr Justice Cooke for 'judicial machismo' and 'medieval' views, Mr Justice Munby provoked the wrath of the *Daily Mail* for his excessive liberalism.[58] In a

---

[51] Goldthorp, 'Ten Minute Abortions', 562.

[52] Tunkel, 'Abortion', 253.

[53] Tunkel, 'Abortion', 254; Wellcome Library, Papers of Wendy Savage, PPWDS/C/1/10, Letter from Judy Cottam (Abortion Law Reform Association) to Jo Chambers and Gill Kent (Birth Control Campaign), 20 October 1980.

[54] Tunkel, 'Abortion', 254.

[55] Keown, '"Morning After" Pills, "Miscarriage" and Muddle', 319. *R (Smeaton) v Secretary of State for Health* [2002] EWHC 610 (Admin), [27].

[56] *Smeaton*, [72]. See generally Keown, '"Morning After" Pills, "Miscarriage" and Muddle'; Tunkel, 'Modern Anti-Pregnancy Techniques and the Criminal Law'.

[57] See *Guardian*, 3 August 2017, describing him as 'one of the most outspoken judges of his generation'.

[58] 'Fury at Top Family Court Judge who Said we Should Applaud the End of the Nuclear Family and Welcome the New Reality of Single and Same-Sex Households', *Daily Mail*, 4 June 2018; *Guardian*, 'It's Judicial Machismo that Jails Women like Sarah Catt', 18 September 2012.

lengthy and erudite judgement, he pored over the same mass of historical and contemporary medical authorities as had Keown, reaching very different conclusions. Mr Justice Munby accepted that he was obliged to work 'strictly and faithfully' with the statutory language that Parliament had chosen, which could not simply be rewritten in light of the enormous medical, social and cultural changes since 1861.[59] However, medical understandings at the time were 'complex and contradictory',[60] the Act predated the development of oral contraceptives by almost a century,[61] and it was 'always speaking', with 'miscarriage' an ordinary word of flexible meaning that must be interpreted in light of current medical knowledge.[62] As such, 'unlawful procurement of miscarriage' should be understood as involving the termination of an established pregnancy, which exists only following implantation.[63]

Mr Justice Munby noted his relief at avoiding the 'unattractive' possibility that 'a judge in 2002 were to be compelled by a statute 141 years old to hold that what thousands, hundreds of thousands, indeed millions, of ordinary honest, decent, law abiding citizens have been doing day in day out for so many years is and always has been criminal'.[64] While the judgement was not appealed, Keown continued the argument in the law journals.[65] Well over a century after the relevant law had been passed, the legal boundary between contraception and abortion was clarified, and the question of how early in pregnancy it was necessary to comply with the Abortion Act appears – for the time being at least – settled.[66]

The Doctors' Gatekeeper Role

The 'Social' Ground

While questions of 'how late, how early' had received scant attention in Parliament, extensive care had been given to the framing of the grounds for abortion, with multiple formulations of the so-called social clause debated before agreement was reached regarding its inclusion and precise wording. Abortion would be lawful where two doctors believed in good faith that 'continuance of pregnancy would involve risk to the life of the pregnant woman, or of injury to the physical or mental health of the pregnant woman or any existing children of her family, greater than if the pregnancy were terminated', with the doctors permitted to take account of her 'actual or

---

[59] *Smeaton*, [333].

[60] *Smeaton*, [165].

[61] For a brief history, see *Smeaton*, [192].

[62] *Smeaton*, [349].

[63] *Smeaton*, [353].

[64] *Smeaton*, [51], [394].

[65] Keown, '"Morning After" Pills, "Miscarriage" and Muddle', 296–319.

[66] See Sheldon, 'The Regulatory Cliff Edge between Contraception and Abortion', 762–65, for a discussion of ongoing problems with the boundary thus drawn.

reasonably foreseeable environment'.[67] Behind this deliberately open-textured provision hovered the image of the economically disadvantaged, downtrodden, multiparous mothers who had consulted Dugald Baird during the depression: social factors were to be treated as part of a holistic medical assessment, with broad scope allowed for clinical discretion. Nonetheless, Parliament had been clear that there was no intention to permit 'abortion on demand'.[68]

As we have seen, the social clause immediately became the most common ground for certifying abortion, with its interpretation – and the processes to be followed before forming a view – fiercely disputed between clinicians. Some eminent doctors maintained that it required a specific threat to the individual woman's health beyond the general risks posed by childbirth[69] or – where abortion was to be authorised on mental health grounds – the presence of a recognised psychiatric disorder.[70] Others maintained that the desire for an abortion was sufficient indication of threat to a woman's mental health to certify the need for one or relied on the 'statistical argument' in defence of a liberal interpretation.[71] For C. B. Goodhart,[72] a Cambridge expert in the ecological genetics of snails and, perhaps more pertinently, a founding member of SPUC:

> Since the almost nonexistent risk to the life of a healthy woman in an abortion properly performed early on in pregnancy is indeed likely to be less than the present very low, but not wholly negligible, risk in normal childbirth, it is hard to see how any doctor could justify a refusal to give such a certificate. Whatever Parliament may have intended, this is in effect abortion on demand, subject only to a doctor's right to refuse to participate if he can prove a genuine conscientious objection.[73]

With Sir John Peel, past president of the RCOG, summarising that the Act had introduced a 'chaotic muddle',[74] legal challenges were inevitable, with their eventual outcome far from self-evident to contemporary commentators. Three cases brought in the 1970s on different facts and raising different legal issues offered early insights into how the courts would respond.

First, in 1974, a rare prosecution was reported of a doctor who claimed to have complied with the terms of the Abortion Act.[75] Dr Smith, a GP with a specialist abortion practice, exemplified Ingram's 'Cash Before Delivery' model of medical practice. During an appointment of around 15 minutes,

---

[67] Sections 1(1)(a) and (2). See generally Hindell and Simms, *Abortion Law Reformed*, and Chapter 1.

[68] Ibid.

[69] Peel in MPS, *Symposium*, 32.

[70] This latter was 'Sim's position': see Chapter 2, p. 36.

[71] See Chapter 2.

[72] Friday, 'Charles Goodhart: A Twentieth Century Life'.

[73] Letter in *British Medical Journal*, vol. 2, no. 5600, 4 May 1968, 298.

[74] Peel in MPS, *Symposium*, 31–32.

[75] *R v Smith* [1974] 1 All ER 376.

Dr Smith did not perform an internal examination on the young woman who had consulted him regarding an abortion, nor did he take a medical history, nor consult a colleague. Without advising her of the need for a second opinion, he explained that he could terminate her pregnancy as soon as she was able to find a fee of £150 (more than double the amount then charged by BPAS). Dr Smith argued in court that if any woman wanted a termination then that was itself a powerful indication of the risk to her mental health of continuing a pregnancy. However, the court found that he had acted unlawfully in allowing himself no opportunity to form a good faith opinion, which would have required 'careful enquiries on a number of matters'.[76] His large fee, the request that it be paid in cash in advance, and his lack of transparency likewise indicated his bad faith.

Two years later, the interpretation of the provision was contested in a second case: Bill Paton sought an injunction to prevent his wife from ending a pregnancy and thereby 'destroy[ing] a child which is half mine'.[77] This offered the first of several occasions in which SPUC, who supported Mr Paton, and BPAS, who had agreed to perform Mrs Paton's abortion, would square up on opposite sides of a courtroom, while campaigners chanted slogans at each other outside it.[78] Mr Paton's case preceded Carver's and, while seeking the same outcome, was argued on a very different basis: that Mrs Paton did not meet the grounds for an abortion under the 'social clause'. Mr Paton had some grounds for confidence: at the time, the Medical Defence Union (MDU) advised that doctors should generally seek a husband's consent before operating on a married woman,[79] and two contemporary legal commentators reasoned that, 'in the case of an abortion apparently "on demand" [sympathy might] guide the court towards a decision in favour of the father'.[80] Mr Paton argued that the case highlighted a legal 'grey area' where a woman could 'hoodwink' doctors into believing that an abortion was necessary, that Mrs Paton had no proper grounds for seeking a termination and, 'not to mince words, that she was being spiteful, vindictive and utterly unreasonable'.[81] However, the High Court was unconvinced, finding no indication that the certifying doctors had acted in bad faith and holding that it was not for the court to scrutinise the substance of clinical decisions. The 'great social responsibility' of implementing the Abortion Act had rather been 'firmly placed by the law on the shoulders of the medical profession', and it would not just be 'a

---

[76] *Smith*, 382.

[77] *Daily Express* (Glasgow), 18 May 1978; *Paton v BPAS* [1978] 2 All ER 987 (*Paton 1978*).

[78] SPUC contributed £1,500 to his costs. See *Liverpool Echo*, 23 May 1978; *Liverpool Daily Post*, 25 May 1978.

[79] MDU, *Consent to Treatment*, cited in O'Neill and Watson, 'The Father and the Unborn Child'.

[80] O'Neill and Watson, 'The Father and the Unborn Child', 174, 180.

[81] *Paton 1978*, 992; 'Husband has no Power to Stop Abortion', *Telegraph*, 25 May 1978.

bold and brave judge' but also a 'foolish' one who would seek to interfere.[82] An attempt to appeal to the European Court of Human Rights also failed.[83]

The third case in the 1970s was not included in any legal reports and is thus less well remembered today but nonetheless casts significant light on the operation of the 'social clause' at the time. It involved a libel action brought by Dr Philip Bloom, a specialist in psychosexual problems, who had certified that Sue Kentish qualified for an abortion and was horrified to find himself denounced in the *Babies for Burning* investigation.[84] Like Dr Smith, he explained to the court that 'one must respect a woman's right to choose' whether or not to have a baby.[85] However, Bloom was unlike Smith in multiple other respects: he worked openly at the heart of the medical establishment in Harley Street; his fee was modest; his record-keeping was meticulous; Kentish was referred by a gynaecologist who had questioned her and performed a physical examination; Bloom conducted his own detailed interview, exploring Kentish's early childhood, relationships and motivation; and he offered a detailed justification of his recommendation in favour of abortion, explaining that Kentish had no maternal feelings and might react neurotically to an unwanted pregnancy.

The Bloom interview is reproduced largely verbatim in *Babies for Burning*,[86] with Litchfield and Kentish clearly convinced that it needed none of the elaborate embellishment or invention included elsewhere, and its adequacy was subject to detailed exploration in the subsequent legal action. While Bloom claimed to have conducted a 'perfectly normal interview',[87] Litchfield and Kentish argued that all participants were 'going through the motions, knowing, in advance, the outcome and the conclusions' of this 'horrible, shameful sham', and that the Abortion Act was being 'abused and treated with contempt', for if Kentish qualified for an abortion 'then *no* woman is fit to bear a child'.[88] For Litchfield and Kentish, the meaning of the Abortion Act was clear: '[D]octors are supposed to establish, regardless of the wishes of the mother, whether or not it will be *harmful* for her to have a child. The distinction is not *that* subtle', and Bloom was evidently 'wanting in good

---

[82] *Paton 1978*, 992, citing Scarman LJ, in *Smith*, at 378, regarding the 'great social responsibility'.

[83] *Paton v UK* [1980] ECHR 408. For collected media reports, see Wellcome Library, PPWDS/C/ 5/1, BPAS, 'The Paton Case', Newsletter Supplement, September 1978.

[84] See Chapter 2. Various papers submitted in the court case, including the transcript of the interview with Kentish, are available in the BPAS Archives.

[85] BPAS Archives, Statement of Claim, *Bloom v Litchfield, Kentish and others*, QBD (7–8 March 1977).

[86] Litchfield and Kentish, *Babies for Burning*, 79–89.

[87] House of Commons, *Special Reports and Minutes of Evidence of the Select Committee on the Abortion (Amendment) Bill*, 1974–1975, HC 692-II, para. 1348. A footnote offers Litchfield and Kentish's response: that it was not the interview that was abnormal but rather the conclusions drawn from it.

[88] Litchfield and Kentish, *Babies for Burning*, 79, 89, emphasis in original.

faith'.[89] The libel action thus turned on the extent to which medical reasoning under the Act was amenable to external scrutiny and whether Dr Bloom's opinion was 'a reckless, casual, incompetent opinion' or 'a conclusion correctly formed on adequate material'.[90]

The case was heard by Sir Aubrey Steed Melford Stevenson – variously described as 'the worst judge since the war' or, more charitably, the 'last of the grand eccentrics'[91] – who made no effort to conceal his distaste for all concerned. Investigatory journalism was 'not a very attractive occupation', particularly 'when you find it initiated and pursued by two people, one of whom is falsely pretending to be pregnant, and both of whom are pretending to be man and wife'.[92] As for 'that relatively new section of the community called psychiatrists', a rambling passage compared them to those 'ladies one sometimes saw on racecourses in a tent who wanted their hands crossed with a bit of silver for a prophecy as to the winner of the next race'. The jury were thus directed to use their common sense, being 'just as well qualified' to form a view as 'gentlemen who have a long list of distinguished letters after their name'.[93] Taking his own advice, Mr Justice Melford Stevenson offered a line-by-line dissection of Dr Bloom's justification for certifying the need for an abortion, inviting the jury to consider whether 'anybody could reasonably and fairly … come to the conclusions expressed':

> 'There are symptoms of early disturbance. She was a bed-wetter. In her teens she was shy, uncertain and a loner'. Members of the Jury, how many people have we met like that? You have to consider whether that fact, taken in conjunction with all the other facts, justifies the view that she was going to suffer injury to mental health …. 'She withdraws into stress and feels all tight inside'. That was in answer to a leading question from the doctor, and is none the worse for that. But how many of us from time to time have felt tight inside …?[94]

The jury found in Dr Bloom's favour but, followed the judge's strong advice to be moderate in any compensation payment, awarding him one halfpenny (and leaving him liable for an estimated £20,000 in costs).[95] While his barrister

---

[89] BPAS Archives, *Bloom* v *Litchfield, Kentish and others*, QBD (7–8 March 1977), unreported, court transcript, 28, all emphasis in original.

[90] BPAS Archives, *Bloom*, Judge's summing up, 11.

[91] Sir Robin Dunn cited in 'Retired Judges Rally to the Defence of Melford Stevenson', *Times*, 1 November 1994; and Devlin, *Easing the Passing*. Melford Stevenson held the dubious distinction of the record for having his sentences taken to appeal, though also for 'getting away with it', 'Goodbye to the Garden House Judge', *Guardian*, 10 April 1979.

[92] BPAS Archives, *Bloom*, Judge's summing up, 6.

[93] Ibid., 7–8.

[94] Ibid., 17–18.

[95] 'Sex Expert Wins 1/2p Damages over Abortion Libel', *Guardian*, 11 March 1977.

believed that he had a good case for appeal, Bloom could not face a further trial given his age and the 'considerable strain' of the first.[96]

If an appeal had been made it would have been likely to have relied, in part, on the judge's willingness to scrutinise the substance of Dr Bloom's decision. Coming from a judge considered a maverick, this stands as a clear anomaly in an otherwise unbroken judicial consensus – already visible in *Smith* and *Paton* – that has drawn the line between lawful and unlawful practice on the basis of good faith adherence to accepted norms of clinical practice, reflecting a broader judicial deference to doctors' professional morality as well as their technical skill.[97] Abortion was now available 'subject only to the attitude of the surgeon concerned',[98] 'governed by medical ethics [rather] than by legal requirement',[99] with judicial scrutiny extending only to ensuring that proper processes had been followed and an 'authentic clinical evaluation' made.[100] This was 'not yet quite [abortion] on demand': the powers given to doctors under the Abortion Act were permissive and the courts would police compliance with professional standards.[101] However, it was 'abortion on request' from at least some doctors. Moreover, as public and medical opinion became more liberal and increasing numbers of women in England and Wales were treated in the charitable sector, this would gradually become the dominant practice in early pregnancy.

Challenges to the meaning of the 'social clause', underpinned by wider concerns regarding the number of abortions and the legitimacy of specific reasons for accessing them, would nonetheless be an ongoing feature of the Abortion Act's biography. The next of these was noteworthy for coming not in the courts but as a result of administrative action: following the failure of the Corrie Bill, in the early 1980s the Conservative Government attempted to enforce a more restrictive interpretation of the clause in England and Wales by changing the wording of abortion notification forms.[102] While previously a question had requested details of any 'non-medical' reasons for a termination, the new forms required information only regarding the 'main medical

---

[96] BPAS Archives, *Lafitte and ors* v *Serpentine Press and ors*, Memorandum Regarding other Relevant Actions 1974-L-4183. On the strain on the doctors named in *Babies for Burning*, see Chapter 2, p. 60.

[97] See generally Montgomery, 'Conscientious Objection'; Montgomery, 'Law and the Demoralisation of Medicine'.

[98] Ormrod, 'A Lawyer Looks at Medical Ethics', 18, 21–22.

[99] Hoggett, 'The Abortion Act 1967', 257.

[100] Harrington, 'Of Paradox and Plausibility', 317.

[101] Ormrod, 'A Lawyer Looks at Medical Ethics', 18; Hart, 'Abortion Law Reform', 393–94.

[102] Abortion Law Reform Association (ALRA), *Breaking Chains*, no. 22, May/June 1981, 2. See generally correspondence in Wellcome Library, Papers of the National Abortion Campaign (NAC), SA/NAC/B/7/2/6/5.

condition(s)' justifying abortion.[103] In Scotland, forms continued to ask for the 'main indication(s)' for abortion.[104]

Pro-Choice campaigners furiously condemned this move by a 'reactionary Government' to restrict access to abortion, which they dubbed 'backdoor Corrie'.[105] Dr Peter Huntingford, a former member of SPUC turned staunch advocate of liberal abortion laws, protested that, more than a decade after the Abortion Act's introduction, 'doctors are now being asked to find reasons to satisfy what I regard as an interpretation of the law'.[106] He responded to the form's request for the 'main medical condition(s)' for abortion by writing 'NONE', explaining that he was 'unable to certify that disease exists when none is present'.[107] The Chief Medical Officer wrote to remind him that 'non-medical factors alone do not provide legal justification for termination', that 'statistical factors must have a medical basis which also must be notified', and that the Abortion Act required 'a current medical condition which puts at risk the life, or, physical or mental health of the patient' or that such a condition was a foreseeable consequence of the pregnancy.[108] When Huntingford refused to back down, the Government referred the matter to the police.[109] While ultimately no prosecution was brought, The Lancet warned that a future Director of Public Prosecutions might take 'the opposite attitude',[110] and Marge Berer reported that 'even the threat of prosecution' was making some doctors 'much more cautious'.[111] A previous year-on-year increase in the number of abortions reported for resident women in England and Wales now faltered and declined for the first time. As the storm passed, however, the numbers resumed their previous steady upward trajectory.[112]

Attempts to argue that doctors were interpreting the social clause too liberally also continued in the courts, but now with no real chance of success,

[103] Abortion Regulations 1968 and Abortion (Amendment) Regulations 1980, each including the notification form.
[104] Abortion (Scotland) Amendment Regulations 1980 No. 1866 (S.169), including the notification form.
[105] Berer, 'Abortion Notification Forms', 857; Wellcome Library, Papers ALRA, SA/ALR/G/16, LARC Bulletin, 'Backdoor Corrie', January 1982 and ALRA, Breaking Chains, no. 25, January/February 1982, 1; Wellcome Library, SA/NAC/B/7/2/2, NAC, ALRA and LARC, 'Stop DHSS! Demonstration', flyer, 9 February 1982.
[106] Wellcome Library, SA/NAC/B/7/2/6/1, Letter from Peter Huntingford to Sir Henry Yellowlees, 7 October 1981.
[107] Wellcome Library, SA/NAC/B/7/2/6/1, Letter from Peter Huntingford to Marge Berer, 16 November 1981.
[108] Wellcome Library, SA/NAC/B/7/2/2, Letter from Henry Yellowlees, July 1981.
[109] Deitch, 'Challenge Deferred over Abortion Notification Forms', 575; South Wales Argus, 6 February 1982; Times, 22 January 1982.
[110] Deitch, 'Challenge Deferred over Abortion Notification Forms', 575.
[111] Wellcome Library, SA/NAC/B/7/2/2, Marge Berer (NAC), Open Letter to BMA and RCOG, 11 February 1982.
[112] For resident women in England and Wales, numbers rose from 1968 until 1980 and plateaued between 1981 and 1983, with a small decline from 1982 (163,045) to 1983 (162,161), before resuming a steady increase.

other than where there were clear signs of negligence or dishonesty. In 1993, the eminent Catholic jurist and philosopher John Finnis defended Father James Morrow against a charge of disorderly conduct following Rescue UK's occupation of an abortion clinic. The court made short shrift of Finnis' argument that Morrow's actions were justified in aiming to prevent abortions being performed for 'social rather than legal reasons'.[113] With it now clear that courts would focus only on ensuring that proper processes had been followed and a genuine clinical evaluation made, future litigants would tend rather to focus on procedural inadequacies. Moreover, they would increasingly frame their challenges within the broader woman-protective concerns that had become dominant in anti-abortion campaigns. Henceforth, a robust role for medical gatekeepers would be presented not as a mechanism for checking abusive practice and filtering out unmeritorious cases but rather as an essential mechanism for safeguarding vulnerable women and ensuring fully informed consent. The previous criticism of women's motivations, as seen in *Paton*, now largely evaporated, with women rather figuring as victims failed by inadequate procedures.[114]

This shift was powerfully exemplified in a series of actions from the late 1990s, supported by Life and brought by women alleging that they suffered from 'Post-Abortion Syndrome'.[115] In a first case, a woman complained that she had not been informed of the 'recognised risk' of post-traumatic stress disorder after abortion.[116] In a second, a 'mother of six who believes abortion is murder' complained of inadequate counselling, explaining that she was left so 'mentally traumatised after abortion that she felt compelled to have another baby'.[117] A third, much later case reflected a growing emphasis in the political debate on the question of fetal sentience: a woman claimed that her informed consent was undermined by her clinic's failure to tell her that her fetus might feel pain at 23 weeks' gestation. She sought a court declaration that newly published National Institute for Health and Care Excellence (NICE) guidelines were unlawful in failing to require the provision of this information, for '[w]omen should be able to decide what they want to do, but they must be told the truth of what is involved'.[118]

A third fathers' rights case likewise turned not on the substance of the doctors' decision but rather on allegedly 'gravely deficient' procedures at the clinic involved, with only one doctor consulted before an abortion was

---

[113] *Morrow and ors v DPP* QBD CO/215/93 (6 July 1993). See further Chapter 4, pp. 120–21, on the activities of Rescue UK.

[114] See Chapter 4, pp. 131–33, on the woman-protective turn in campaigning, also detailing how these trajectories are visible in debates regarding selective abortion.

[115] See generally Lee, *Abortion, Motherhood and Mental Health*.

[116] 'Woman to Sue NHS over Abortion', *Daily Mail*, 13 June 1999.

[117] 'Mother of Six Sues Doctors for Abortion Trauma', *Daily Telegraph*, 14 Dec 2001.

[118] 'Why Wasn't I Told the Baby I Aborted at 23 Weeks Might be Able to Feel Pain?', *Mail on Sunday*, 3 May 2020; NICE and RCOG, *Abortion Care Guideline [NG140]*.

approved. Stephen Hone explained that he would 'never have been in court' without the ProLife Alliance.[119] Josephine Quintavalle explained why they had deemed it important to support his case:

> Nobody ever expected the abortion could be stopped, because legally it can't, but it's important that there's been a focus on the fact that it's a complete travesty of the law the way abortion is provided in this country. You just sign up for it, no questions are asked. In the early stages you just sign on the dotted line, and even later in pregnancy [abortion clinics] are not taking on board their duties towards women.[120]

Concerns with procedural laxity would come to a head in 2012. First, in January, a Care Quality Commission inspection found that a doctor had 'pre-signed' abortion certification forms, leaving the woman's details to be completed afterwards.[121] Second, in February, *The Telegraph* published its investigation into sex-selective abortion, citing a doctor who had told a woman, 'I don't ask questions. If you want a termination, you want a termination'; it claimed to have demonstrated that 'abortion on demand, often dismissed as a myth, is in fact routine'.[122] Andrew Lansley, the Conservative Secretary of State for Health, responded promptly. Lambasting those engaged 'in a culture of . . . ignoring the law', he argued that many women were denied necessary support as a result.[123] He referred the doctors identified in the *Telegraph* sting to the General Medical Council (GMC) and the police and ordered a mass, unannounced inspection of all abortion clinics. The latter identified pre-signing of forms at six further sites. Those sites promptly changed their practice,[124] and one doctor involved in the sex selection investigation was temporarily suspended by the GMC for having falsified paperwork.[125] With no further action envisaged, a rare private prosecution was brought against some of the doctors involved in the *Telegraph* investigation by Abort67, backed by the Christian Legal Centre.[126] The prosecution was taken over in order that it might be dropped by the Crown Prosecution Service (then led by Keir Starmer, the subsequent leader of the Labour Party), which

---

[119] 'Sad Tale of an Affair that Ended and an Abortion Row that Goes On and On', *Guardian*, 31 March 2001.

[120] 'UK Man Goes To Court To Try Prevent Abortion', *CNS News*, 7 July 2008.

[121] Care Quality Commission, 'Findings of Termination of Pregnancy Inspections Published'.

[122] 'Abortion Anxieties', *Telegraph*, 23 February 2012.

[123] 'One in Five Abortion Clinics Breaks Law', *Telegraph*, 22 March 2012.

[124] See Care Quality Commission, 'Findings of Termination of Pregnancy Inspections Published'.

[125] 'Ban Lifted on Abortion Doctor who Agreed to Gender-Based Termination', *Telegraph*, 24 February 2016.

[126] US anti-abortion groups have been far more willing to pursue this strategy: see generally Harlow and Rawlings, *Pressure through Law*.

concluded that charges were not in the public interest.[127] Pro-Life advocates were again bitterly disappointed: Dr Peter Saunders (Christian Medical Fellowship; CMF) reflected that 'we have a law which is not being upheld'.[128]

The Department of Health and BPAS each responded to these events by publishing advice on how the Abortion Act should be interpreted, with noteworthy differences between the two sets of guidance.[129] The Department's more restrictive reading of the Act suggested that treating certification as a 'rubber stamp' exercise was 'contrary to the spirit' and 'incompatible with the requirements of the Abortion Act'.[130] However, in contrast to the 'backdoor Corrie' moves of the early 1980s, there was no apparent aim to impose a reading that sought to reduce the number of abortions; indeed, its guidance rather emphasised the need for 'a high quality, legal service that meets the needs of women', who are entitled to impartial information before reaching their decisions.[131]

These events left some doctors 'nervous about their everyday practice', with some anecdotal evidence of a chilling effect.[132] However, a liberal interpretation of the social clause has remained dominant. The distance travelled over previous decades was illustrated by a further newspaper 'sting' in 2017. As in *Babies for Burning* many years earlier, a *Daily Mail* reporter posed as a woman seeking an abortion. She was told by a call centre worker that there was no need to meet the doctors who would certify that she met the legal grounds for abortion: they would fill out the necessary forms based on the reasons given by telephone.[133] Having told the call centre 'I just don't want to have the baby', she found that her medical notes recorded that the 'client is unable emotionally to continue with pregnancy' (a reason that fits with the requirements of the 'social clause').[134] The resulting *Daily Mail* report made no criticism of women who choose to terminate pregnancies for social reasons, rather expressing concerns that inadequate certification reflected flawed consent and safeguarding procedures. It was published alongside an interview with a former patient under the damning banner 'I Expected Sympathy. . . but Marie

---

[127] 'Gender Abortion: Criminal Charges not in "Public Interest" Says CPS', *Telegraph*, 4 September 2013; 'Abortion Investigation: Group Launches Private Prosecution', *Telegraph*, 14 October 2014.

[128] Peter Saunders interviewed by Jane O'Neill, 9 November 2017.

[129] Department of Health, *Guidance in Relation to Requirements of the Abortion Act 1967*; BPAS, *Britain's Abortion Law*; for discussion, see generally Sheldon, 'British Abortion Law'.

[130] Department of Health, *Guidance in Relation to Requirements of the Abortion Act 1967*, para. 20.

[131] Ibid., paras 32, 3.

[132] See Bristow, 'Introduction' and Lee, 'Recent Myths and Misunderstandings about the Abortion Law', both in BPAS, *Britain's Abortion Law*; and Chapter 8, p. 271.

[133] 'Abortions Signed Off after Just a Phonecall: How Marie Stopes Doctors Approve Abortions for Women They've Never Met', *Mail Online*, 5 March 2017.

[134] Ibid.

Stopes Abortion Clinic was like Being on a Conveyor Belt, Says Mother Accused of "Wasting their Time" when she Backed Out'.[135]

In sum, while the text of the 'social clause' has remained unaltered for five decades, it has been increasingly liberally interpreted to result in a general situation of abortion on request, at least in early pregnancy. Clinical discretion is subject to the important limitation that it be exercised in 'good faith', reading in a requirement to adhere to relevant norms of best practice. However, such norms have also evolved over time in line with changing social mores and clinical realities. There can be little doubt that it would have been unlawful for a doctor in the 1970s to certify the need for an abortion based on notes taken by a call centre worker: the BPAS Chair, Francois Lafitte, reflected at the time that 'no doctor acting in good faith could, in my view, sign an abortion certificate without further questioning the patient'.[136] Likewise, many practices prevalent in the 1970s would be considered unethical and potentially unlawful today. A contemporary consultant psychiatrist would be unlikely to give evidence – as did an expert witness in *Bloom* – that a woman would 'want a child if she is a normal person', with her request for termination thus necessarily prompting any responsible doctor to undertake extensive further investigation into her motivation and mental health.[137] Professional and potentially legal sanction would likely face a contemporary doctor who adopted the practices described in Chapter 2 of dissuasion, cajolement or prevarication in order deliberately to block or delay access to lawful abortion services and, *a fortiori*, one who refused a woman's request on the basis that their hospital worked 'to preserve the lives of our babies and not deliberately destroy them' or made simultaneous sterilisation a precondition of access to abortion.[138]

The 'Serious Handicap' Ground

The fetal anomaly ground of the Abortion Act – allowing two doctors to authorise an abortion on the basis of a good faith opinion that there is a 'substantial risk of serious handicap'[139] – also leaves wide scope for the exercise of clinical discretion, with the good faith requirement again reading in evolving norms of professional practice. As with the social clause, this

---

[135] 'I Expected Sympathy... but Marie Stopes Abortion Clinic was like Being on a Conveyor Belt, Says Mother Accused of "Wasting their Time" when she Backed Out', *Daily Mail*, 22 December 2016.

[136] BPAS Archives, Witness Statement, *Lafitte and ors* v *Serpentine and ors* (1978) QBD, 16.

[137] Dr Benaim, a consultant psychiatrist, see BPAS Archives, *Bloom*, Judge's summing up, 14–15.

[138] See Chapter 2, pp. 33, 35–36. In interview, Anna Glasier reflected that she had not heard of any doctor requiring simultaneous sterilisation anywhere she had worked and that there would be 'almost nobody that would even mention sterilisation to a woman who was coming for an abortion'. Anna Glasier interviewed by Gayle Davis, 13 November 2017.

[139] Section 1(1)(d).

ground would come to be interpreted through the lens of an increasing emphasis on the need to respect patient autonomy; however, it would also be read in light of changing understandings of disability. In 1967, concerns regarding this ground had focused on the inherent vagueness of the phrase 'substantial risk', which, combined with the far less accurate prenatal testing available at the time, was feared likely to lead to 'the slaughter of thousands of potentially healthy children to avoid the birth of a few deformed ones'.[140] Over subsequent years, more sophisticated screening and testing became routine parts of antenatal care, the risk of misdiagnosis radically diminished, a wider range of anomalies became identifiable, and an increasingly vocal disability rights movement foregrounded concerns with discrimination and civil rights.[141] Controversy would thus come to centre less on the possibility of misdiagnosis and more on the normalisation of abortion as a response to fetal anomaly, focusing on a question of little apparent concern to Parliament in 1967: the meaning of 'serious handicap'.

Pro-Life groups have campaigned long and hard on the issues of abortion for fetal anomaly and the treatment of disabled neonates, seeing the two as inextricably linked. Jack Scarisbrick explains that as 'prenatal "search and destroy" techniques became ever more efficient, i.e. ruthless, and doctors faced the possibility of litigation if a disabled child slipped through the net, it was becoming almost a duty to dispose of any special-needs child who had the good fortune to be born'.[142] Moreover, with people more readily 'shocked by neo-natal than by pre-natal killing', a focus on the former might 'help people to perceive the enormity of abortionism'.[143] Again, Life relied on its whistle-blower network for information, reporting to local police at least eight 'very clear-cut' cases where 'a child with a very modest little handicap' was 'not given the normal kind of warmth and milk and love a normal baby would have'.[144] When no action resulted, Life alleged cover-ups, explaining that the police would find 'either that the corpse and often the records of the case had disappeared or that, by a coincidence, their arrival coincided with the discovery that the child, after all, loved milk and was gulping it down'.[145]

Life did, however, succeed in persuading the authorities to prosecute in one case, resulting in a three week trial conducted in a 'blaze of publicity'.[146] Having first confirmed that his parents did not wish him to survive,

---

[140] *Hansard*, HC, 29 June 1967, vol. 749, col. 1050; Chapter 1, p. 10.

[141] Chapter 4, pp. 139–46.

[142] Scarisbrick, *Let There Be Life*, 36.

[143] *LIFE and Neo-Natal Killing: What the Issues Are*, 6, cited in Harlow and Rawlings, *Pressure through Law*, 219.

[144] Scarisbrick, *Let There Be Life*, 36. See further Wellcome Library, SA/ALR/G/17, 'Police Probe Baby's Death', *Life News*, no. 7, autumn/winter 1980; Diane Munday Papers, 'A Slice of Life', *Life News*, no. 24, April 1991.

[145] Scarisbrick, *Let There Be Life*, 36. See further Diane Munday Papers, 'A Slice of Life', *Life News*, no. 24, April 1991.

[146] See Harlow and Rawlings, *Pressure through Law*, 219; *R v Arthur* (1981) 12 BMLR 1.

Dr Leonard Arthur had prescribed nursing care only and an opiate-based painkiller for John Pearson, a baby with Down's syndrome, who died three days later with untreated bronchopneumonia.[147] Dr Arthur was acquitted of attempted murder on the basis that he had not undertaken positive acts to end John's life but had rather instituted a 'holding operation' that allowed nature to take its course. This legal reasoning has been strongly criticised,[148] and Dr Arthur's acquittal is probably best understood as reflecting the difficulties of persuading juries to convict where a doctor has acted in accordance with a mainstream medical practice, particularly in cases that involve strongly emotive issues.[149] Indeed, Arthur was reported to be the first doctor since Aleck Bourne (in 1938) to be charged with a criminal offence for having offered treatment that many of his colleagues would not censure.[150] Such support played an important role in his trial, with Sir Douglas Black, President of the Royal College of Physicians, giving evidence that his actions were ethical in light of John's parents' wishes.[151]

The decision to acquit Dr Arthur appears to have been widely welcomed, and women in the courtroom reportedly cried 'Thank God!' when it was announced.[152] It was followed by a period of soul-searching, with some suggesting that these 'very delicate and difficult cases' were better trusted 'to the discretion of the medical profession',[153] and the Director of Public Prosecutions conceding that it may have been a mistake to press charges.[154] When Dr Arthur died shortly after, his MP noted the stress caused by the trial and criticised the hounding of a fine, 'humane, tenacious and principled' Christian man, who had been much loved by his patients.[155]

There could not have been a starker contrast with Jack Scarisbrick's view that Dr Arthur was rather a 'sinister' 'Angel of Death', the trial was 'a travesty of justice' with the judge excessively deferential to the medical profession and clearly prejudiced against children with Down's syndrome, and the legal and medical professions and general public had been 'poisoned ... by the elitist eugenics of abortionism'.[156] However, Scarisbrick nonetheless had some justification for concluding that 'an apparent defeat had become a modest pro-life

---

[147] Wellcome Library, SA/ALR/G/17, 'Police Probe Baby's Death', *Life News*, no. 7, autumn/ winter 1980. This was apparently the 11th such case reported, see *Times*, 6 November 1981; *Daily Mirror*, 6 November 1981.

[148] Kennedy and Grubb, *Medical Law*, 2165; Gunn and Smith, 'Arthur's Case and the Right to Life of a Down Syndrome Child', 705–15.

[149] Rozenberg, *The Case for the Crown*, 73.

[150] *Times*, 6 November 1981; *Daily Mirror*, 6 November 1981.

[151] *Arthur*, 21; *Times*, 6 November 1981; *Daily Mirror*, 6 November 1981.

[152] 'Women Cry "Thank God" as Dr Arthur is Cleared', *Times*, 6 November 1981.

[153] Lord Vernon in *Hansard*, HL, 10 December 1981, vol. 425, cols 1435–36.

[154] Sir Thomas Hetherington DPP, cited in Edwards, *The Attorney General, Politics and the Public Interest*, 421–22.

[155] 'Why I Grieve for Leonard Arthur', *Times*, 5 January 1984.

[156] Scarisbrick, *Let There Be Life*, 36–38.

victory': *Arthur* proved 'a big shock to the medical profession', exposing divisions within it and prompting new guidelines from the British Paediatrics Society.[157] With Scarisbrick far from alone in hoping that the case would stimulate further debate,[158] it offered an important legal landmark in shifting attitudes towards the care of disabled children: in Scarisbrick's view, halting, if only temporarily, the 'moral disintegration' of paediatrics.[159]

While they took longer to come, it was inevitable that challenges to the fetal anomaly ground of the Abortion Act would also follow, with concerns reflecting changing attitudes to disability and given a powerful new focus by the removal of the upper time limit on this ground and the introduction of more detailed reporting requirements.[160] In 2003, reflecting the increased visibility of people with disabilities in leading campaigns, an action was brought by the Reverend Joanna Jepson, a young, mediagenic Church of England curate, who had herself been born with a cleft palate.[161] Jepson was not an experienced anti-abortion campaigner, a fact neatly illustrated by her later, apparently unselfconscious adoption of a wire coat hanger logo for a project on 'design, fashion and faith'.[162] The suggestion that she should front the case was made by the veteran campaigner Josephine Quintavalle, who astutely predicted that Jepson 'would go down well in the papers'.[163]

Jepson followed the publication of annual abortion statistics in 2001, which recorded a termination after 24 weeks for reason of cleft palate (where cells making up the structures of the palate, lips and face fail to fuse together). Reverend Jepson requested a police investigation, then launched a judicial review of the decision not to charge the doctors involved.[164] She framed her challenge within a 'move towards a less discriminatory society' where it was wrong 'that babies lose their lives for trivial reasons',[165] and she posed a powerful rhetorical question, which would be echoed in subsequent campaigns: '[I]s society saying I should have died?'[166] A 'media frenzy' followed,[167] revealing the identity of the hospital and doctor involved, with the latter's

---

[157] Ibid., 39.

[158] *Guardian*, 7 November 1981.

[159] Diane Munday Papers, 'A Slice of Life', *Life News*, no. 24, April 1991.

[160] See Chapter 3, pp. 103–4, on the removal of the upper time limit; Abortion Regulations 1991, schedule 2; Chapter 4, pp. 140–43, on changing attitudes to disability.

[161] 'I Want to Wake Up This Nation's Conscience', *Observer*, 27 February 2005.

[162] Jepson, 'The Empty Hanger'.

[163] Interview in 'I Want to Wake Up This Nation's Conscience', *Observer*, 27 February 2005.

[164] *R (Jepson)* v *Chief Constable of the West Mercia Police Constabulary* [2003] EWHC 3318. 'Curate Wins Abortion Challenge', *BBC News*, 1 December 2003; Hewson, 'Clinical Negligence'.

[165] 'Curate Wins Abortion Challenge', *BBC News*, 1 December 2003.

[166] 'Police Examine "Cleft Palate" Abortion', *BBC News*, 28 October 2002.

[167] *In the Matter of an Appeal to the Information Tribunal under Section 57 of the Freedom of Information Act (FOIA)* 2000 No EA 2008/0074, [62]. See further 'I Want to Wake Up This Nation's Conscience', *Observer*, 27 February 2005.

address subsequently posted online and those concerned by the abortion encouraged to write to him.[168]

While Rev. Jepson was found to have legal standing, the case did not proceed to trial. This may have reflected a legal assessment of the difficulty of challenging a doctor's good faith belief regarding the meaning of 'serious handicap' or an understanding of the inherent uncertainty of the likely level of disability involved in a diagnosis of cleft palate.[169] Possibly, campaigners had already gained the publicity that they had sought.[170] Indeed, there was some evidence of a chilling effect on clinical practice: some hospitals now began to convene ethics panels to consider terminations after 24 weeks,[171] and Antenatal Results and Choices, a charity that offers non-directive information and support to those undergoing antenatal screening, recorded a 'Jepson effect' whereby some women reported having been refused abortion due to 'worries since that cleft lip and palate case'.[172] A subsequent move by the Department of Health to reduce the level of granular detail included in published abortion statistics to avoid the risk of identification of the women or doctors involved was also successfully challenged, with the ProLife Alliance arguing that greater transparency improved accountability, prevented a 'cavalier attitude' where doctors might 'make mistakes or lose their sense of proportion', and allayed fears that abortions were being performed for 'trivial reasons'.[173]

With powerful claims regarding disability discrimination coming into ever greater tension with claims for patient autonomy and clinical discretion, it was inevitable that the fetal anomaly ground would be subject to further legal challenge, and, in 2021, a crowd-funded legal action reached the courts. It was brought by Heidi Crowter, an experienced disability rights campaigner who has Down's syndrome,[174] Aidan Lea-Wilson, a child with Down's syndrome, and Máire Lea-Wilson, his mother. They sought a declaration that the fetal anomaly ground was incompatible with their human rights and those of the unborn (paving the way to its repeal or restriction to the same 24 week limit as most other abortions), a declaration that the Abortion Act should be interpreted in a way compatible with human rights norms such that a diagnosis of Down's syndrome should not be understood to meet the test of 'seriously

---

[168] *FOIA*, [19]. 'Doctor May be Charged over Late Abortion', *Daily Mail*, 23 September 2004.

[169] Ranging from a relatively minor impairment to a potentially life-threatening deformity, Ann Furedi interview in 'Curate Wins Abortion Challenge', *BBC News*, 1 December 2003.

[170] 'No Charges in Late Abortion Case', *BBC News*, 16 March 2005.

[171] *FOIA*, [80].

[172] Fisher, 'Post-24 Week Termination for Fetal Anomaly', 29.

[173] *FOIA*, [77–79, 82 and 91]. See further 'Abortion: The Lives that Should not Have Been Lost', *Telegraph*, 9 July 2011.

[174] See '"My Life is Just as Important as Everybody Else's": Meet the Disability Leaders', *Guardian*, 3 December 2018. Don't Screen Us Out, 'Press Release'; Crowter, 'Downright Discrimination'.

handicapped', and an end to the continued public funding of abortions authorised under this ground.[175] Crowter explained:

> At the moment in the UK, babies can be aborted right up to birth if they are considered to be 'seriously handicapped'. They include me in that definition of being seriously handicapped – just because I have an extra chromosome! Can you believe that? What it says to me is that my life just isn't as valuable as others, and I don't think that's right.[176]

For her part, Máire Lea-Wilson described the anguish of being repeatedly offered a termination following a diagnosis of Down's syndrome at 35 weeks, arguing that the Abortion Act contributed to a negative view of disability and that such 'biased and discriminatory' 'poor communication' would end if the 'discriminatory law did not exist'.[177] Her evidence cast a spotlight on the challenges faced by doctors in ensuring that women are fully aware of all options open to them whilst avoiding displaying their own moral judgement of any choice that might be made and explaining the likely nature of a future child's disability in a way that neither denies nor exaggerates the challenges and accompanying joys of raising a child diagnosed with a genetic anomaly, which in some cases may translate into a wide spectrum of abilities and disabilities.[178]

In considering the arguments, the High Court was required to give modern meaning to the text of an Act shaped by understandings of disability grounded in the beliefs of the 1960s. The claimants emphasised that developments over the past five decades meant that a new interpretation was now needed: first, society's attitudes towards people with disabilities had changed dramatically; and, second, improvements in screening and testing meant that Down's syndrome can now be detected long before 24 weeks, leaving no need for a higher upper time limit for abortions performed on this basis.[179] However, the High Court noted that a very difficult balance had to be struck by Parliament between recognising the special moral status of the fetus and protecting the rights of women, emphasised the consequences for 'women whose choices would be curtailed (and potentially made criminal)' were the action to succeed, and concluded that the case raised 'intensely difficult issues which are better debated in Parliament'.[180] The claimants responded by renewing their crowdfunding campaign, raising over £125,000, and requesting permission to

---

[175] *R (Crowter and ors) v Secretary of State for Health* [2021] EWHC 2536 (Admin).

[176] Don't Screen Us Out, 'Press Release'.

[177] Witness Statement of Máire Lea-Wilson, *Crowter*, on file with the authors, [2], [27].

[178] Thomas, *Down's Syndrome Screening and Reproductive Politics*; Williams, 'Framing the Fetus in Medical Work', 2085–95; Staham, Solomou and Green, 'Late Termination of Pregnancy', 1402–11.

[179] *Crowter*, [118–19].

[180] *Crowter*, [144], [130].

appeal, which was granted. The decision of the Court of Appeal is pending as this book goes to press.[181]

Treatment for the Termination of Pregnancy

While 'substantial' and 'serious' are open-textured norms that deliberately leave scope for clinical discretion, the same is less obviously true of provisions that an abortion would be lawful only where 'a pregnancy is terminated by a registered medical practitioner' or that 'any treatment for the termination of pregnancy' must be carried out in an NHS hospital or place approved by the Government. In 1967, these requirements were agreed with little debate as necessary to avoid unsafe backstreet abortions performed illicitly by unskilled providers. With legal abortions then 'done by surgical methods', it was accepted that the 'knife with the cutting edge' should be 'operated by a registered medical practitioner',[182] acting openly in a properly equipped facility. However, as safer, technically easier means of performing an abortion developed, these provisions would also be strongly contested. Some would argue that taking a restrictive interpretation of them was increasingly liable to hinder clinical innovation and undermine best practice, cutting against the goal of ensuring the safety of abortion services.[183] For their part, anti-abortion campaigners discerned moves to ignore or subvert necessary safeguards to smooth the 'conveyor belt' services offered by a profit-motivated industry. While they would increasingly focus on woman-protective arguments in resisting service innovations, the first major challenge to them was framed around concerns regarding the rights and interests of nursing staff.

'Terminated by a Registered Medical Practitioner'

From the early days of the implementation of the Abortion Act, there had been important tensions regarding the role of nurses in the provision of services under it. Nursing staff had no voice in the authorisation of abortions yet were deeply involved in the care of women undergoing them, with some feeling obliged to act in a way that was contrary to their own convictions.[184] The issue came to a head in the early 1970s regarding second-trimester medical inductions, where a miscarriage is provoked using an infusion of prostaglandins. This procedure carried lower risks and required a less lengthy

---

[181] Don't Screen Us Out, 'Press Release – Woman with Down's Syndrome's Landmark Case against UK Govt over Discriminatory Abortion Law to be Heard by Court of Appeal'.

[182] *RCN v DHSS* [1981] 1 All ER 545, 554.

[183] See generally Sheldon, 'British Abortion Law', 283.

[184] E.g. Wellcome Library, SA/ALR/C/27, Submission to the Lane Committee by A. Smith, Scottish Association of Executive Councils, 20 December 1971.

period of recuperation than surgical techniques.[185] However, it also entailed a new dimension for nurses on the hospital ward: while a doctor would initiate the procedure with the insertion of a catheter, nurses began the infusion of prostaglandins, kept it topped up, and provided ongoing care and support to women during a process that might last anything from 18 to 30 hours.[186] Nurses were thus performing acts directly causative of abortion.

In 1976, the Life Nurses Group complained that this procedure was illegal as the Abortion Act offered protection only where 'a pregnancy is terminated by a registered medical practitioner'. Having taken legal advice, the Royal College of Nursing (RCN) agreed, advising nurses that they should no longer administer prostaglandins for abortion.[187] The RCOG declared itself appalled at a situation that had 'no parallel in the normally accepted relationship between medical and nursing staff'.[188] It pressed for 'an urgent clarification' and, if necessary, amendment of the Abortion Act.[189] The Government now intervened, publishing guidance on interpretation of the Act that confirmed the legality of previous practice.[190] For the furious Life Nurses Group, nurses were being treated as 'the meat in this sandwich between the "overworked" doctors and the abortionist politicians who wish to keep the production of abortions running smoothly'.[191]

The RCN now took to the courts, complaining that nurses who refused to administer prostaglandins risked breaching employment contracts, while those who complied might break the law.[192] It lost in the High Court, which confirmed the Government's reading of the Abortion Act, and appealed to the Court of Appeal, led by Lord Denning MR. Probably the most influential judge of his generation, Lord Denning was famous for his common-sense approach, protection of the underdog and – as a patron of the Lawyers' Christian Fellowship – strongly religious, morally conservative views.[193] Departing from the unabashed willingness to make policy that characterises

---

[185] The National Archives (TNA), MH156/579, J. S. Metters to Mr Knorpel, Medical Induction Terminations: *RCN v DHSS*; Medical Background, Agreed Statement, 10 November 1980; Department of Health, 'Medical Induction Methods of Termination of Pregnancy (1980–)'.

[186] RCOG Archives, RCOG/A/16/19, RCN, 'Nurses and Abortion', December 1979; see also RCN, 'The RCN and Abortions', 29 August 1979, 2–3; Hordern, *Legal Abortion*, 120–21; Williams, 'Successful Appeal by Royal College of Nursing on Medical Termination of Pregnancy', 1091.

[187] RCOG Archives, RCOG/A/16/19, RCN, 'Nurses and Abortion', December 1979; 'Nurses' Role in Abortion', *British Medical Journal*, 13 September 1980.

[188] RCOG Archives, RCOG/A/16/19, Letter from E. A. J. Alment to members, '1967 Abortion Act – Legal Interpretation Concerning Nurses', 17 December 1979.

[189] Ibid.

[190] RCOG Archives, RCOG/A/16/19, DHSS Letter to Medical and Nursing Officers, 21 February 1980.

[191] Wellcome Library, SA/ALR/G/17, 'Nurses Challenge Ruling on Prostaglandin Abortions', *Life News*, no. 7, autumn/winter 1980, 7.

[192] *RCN v DHSS*, High Court of Justice Affidavit, 2 July 1980. See further RCOG Archives, RCOG/A/16/19, Letter from Catherine M. Hall, RCN, to E. A. J. Alment, 1 July 1980.

[193] Freeman, *Lord Denning*; 'Lord Denning, 'The Century's Greatest Judge, Dies at 100', *Independent*, 6 March 1999.

many of his judgements, he reasoned that the negative practical consequences of offering a restrictive reading of its terms could not justify ignoring the words of the Abortion Act. Treatment for termination of pregnancy meant the 'continuous act of administering the prostaglandin from the moment it was started until the fetus was expelled from the mother's body', with such actions therefore lawful only if undertaken by a doctor. If the Government 'wanted nurses to terminate pregnancies', reasoned Lord Denning, a change to the statute would be required. In the meantime, if the doctor advises abortion, he should do it himself, and 'young women who are dedicated by their profession and training to do all they can to preserve life' should be protected from the 'heart-rending' and 'soul-destroying' work of destroying it.[194] He also expressed a more general criticism of the Abortion Act, which he opined, *obiter dicta*, was interpreted 'so loosely that abortion has become obtainable virtually on demand'.[195] His two colleagues in the Court of Appeal concurred.

Complaints now erupted from the other side. Lord Denning's tone was 'objectionable', his *obiter* comments went far 'beyond the legal ruling that it was in his jurisdiction to make',[196] and the practical consequences of his decision were severe: with it impractical for a doctor to visit a patient every 15–30 minutes during a procedure lasting up to 30 hours, around 8,500 women each year would now need either to undergo a riskier surgical procedure or be denied access to abortion altogether.[197] The RCOG pleaded for 'the intention of the 1967 Act' to be 'restored by an alteration in the statute as a matter of urgency'.[198] In the event, this proved unnecessary. On appeal, the House of Lords overturned the Court of Appeal's judgement and reinstated that of the High Court: for it to be lawful, a doctor must 'accept responsibility' for all stages of an abortion, without necessarily carrying out specific tasks in person.[199] Previous practice resumed.

The outcome of this case had been finely balanced: five of the nine judges who considered it ruled in favour of the RCN; however, as three of the four who found for the Government sat in the House of Lords, their view prevailed.[200] While it concerned a narrow legal issue, broader influences on the courts' reasoning are visible both in Lord Denning's evident antipathy towards

---

[194] *RCN v DHSS* [1981] 1 All ER 545, 555–57.

[195] *RCN*, 554.

[196] 'Spotlight: What Happens Now?', *Nursing Mirror*, 27 November 1980; Neustatter, 'Participation of Nurses in Abortions', 1199; Savage, 'Nurses and the Medical Termination of Pregnancy', 1491.

[197] TNA, MH 156/579, J. S. Metters to Mr Knorpel, Medical Induction Terminations: *RCN v DHSS*; Medical Background, Agreed Statement, 10 November 1980; J. S. Metters to Chief Medical Officer, 'Medical Induction Terminations', 12 November 1980; see further 'Abortion: The Doctor's Responsibility', *British Medical Journal*, 22 November 1980, 1432.

[198] 'Nursing and the Medical Termination of Pregnancy', *British Medical Journal*, 15 November 1980.

[199] *RCN*, Lord Diplock, 569–70; Lord Keith, 575; Lord Roskill, 577.

[200] Smith, 'Abortion', 323.

liberal abortion laws and in the House of Lords' concern to avoid the disruption of established medical practice.[201] The decision also reflects a contemporary, strongly hierarchical understanding of the relationship between doctors and nurses, who feature in the judgements either as vulnerable young women in need of protection or as 'handmaidens' whose actions might be legally understood as those of the responsible doctor.[202] There is a clear contrast with the less hierarchical sensibility that Lady Hale would bring to bear in reflecting on *RCN* some 30 years later: in this more recent view, nurses were professionals with discrete qualifications and competencies, with 'the doctor performing those tasks that are reserved to a doctor and the nurses and others carrying out those tasks which they are qualified to perform'.[203]

RCN is also remembered by lawyers as offering an authoritative statement of Parliament's intention in passing the Abortion Act. Parliamentary intention offers an important guide to statutory interpretation but is a post hoc legal construct, requiring judges to peer back through history to distil clarity and meaning from the confusion and noise surrounding a law's creation, and it offers only broad concepts that can be fleshed out with changing conceptions that reflect contemporary social and clinical realities.[204] In 1981, with the Abortion Act now well embedded into clinical practice, the House of Lords found that it had been intended that 'socially acceptable abortions should be carried out under the safest conditions attainable'.[205] In 2014, with the overwhelming majority of terminations funded by the NHS and performed within the abortion charities, Lady Hale would discern a further strand to Parliament's intention: to provide for an abortion service within the NHS, as well as in approved clinics in the private or voluntary sectors.[206] Over the years, the 'safest conditions attainable' and the 'socially acceptable abortion' would both come to acquire very different meanings in light of shifting social norms and clinical realities.

The expansive reading of statutory language offered in *RCN* would later become enormously significant in the context of early medical abortion, where it would be accepted that an abortion was 'performed by a registered medical practitioner' where a nurse acting under a doctor's supervision handed abortion pills to a woman, and, indeed, where the woman self-administered them (again, a finding not seen as inevitable by authoritative contemporary commentators).[207] Moreover, when it was decided that women should be permitted to take the second course of abortion pills at home, later courts would rely on *RCN* to reject challenges brought first by SPUC and then the Christian

---

[201] E.g. Lord Keith, *RCN*, 575.
[202] Montgomery, 'Doctors' Handmaidens'.
[203] *Greater Glasgow Health Board* v *Doogan* [2014] UKSC 68 (*Doogan 2014*), [9].
[204] Dworkin, *Law's Empire*; see further Duxbury, *Elements of Legislation*.
[205] *RCN*, 575.
[206] *Doogan 2014*, [27].
[207] Kennedy and Grubb, *Medical Law*, 1478–79.

Legal Centre to confirm that this requirement was met where a doctor had prescribed the pills and remained available by telephone.[208] While untested in the courts, it has also been argued that it would be lawful for nurses operating as part of a multidisciplinary team to perform vacuum aspiration abortions provided that the treatment is prescribed by a doctor who remains available if needed.[209] Interpretation of the provision that an abortion must be 'performed by a registered medical practitioner' as requiring supervision and responsibility rather than hands-on involvement would thus again demonstrate the elasticity of statutory language to accommodate evolving technologies, institutional contexts and professional dynamics.

Place of Provision

The requirement that any treatment for the termination of pregnancy should be carried out in an NHS hospital or other approved place would also be heavily disputed. The meaning of this provision had appeared clear in the context of a discrete surgical event taking place in an operating theatre. It was far less so with regard to early medical abortion, which involves a series of events occurring over time and potentially in different locations. One common protocol involves a consultation, followed by the prescription then sequential administration of mifepristone then misoprostol separated by a delay of two to three days, provoking a miscarriage that typically occurs several hours after taking the misoprostol, followed later by a medical examination to confirm that the abortion is complete. The Government initially advised that 'treatment for the termination of pregnancy' included all stages of that process from administration of medicines to subsequent miscarriage, which must therefore take place within approved premises.[210] However, as early medical abortion became safer and side effects were reduced, this advice was revised so that only the administration of pills was considered 'treatment': a woman would still need to make multiple visits to the clinic, but she might thus legally return home to miscarry.

Over time, BPAS began to push to be allowed to give women misoprostol to take at home, removing what it saw as an unnecessary additional clinic visit that left women at risk of miscarrying on the journey home. Since 1990, the Government had had the power to licence a broader 'class of places' for the use

---

[208] *SPUC Pro-Life Scotland* v *Scottish Ministers* [2019] CSIH 31; *R (Christian Concern)* v *Secretary of State for Health and Social Care* [2020] EWCA Civ 1239.

[209] Argent and Pavey, 'Can Nurses Legally Perform Surgical Induced Abortion?', 79; Sheldon and Fletcher, 'Vacuum Aspiration for Induced Abortion Could Be Safely and Legally Performed by Nurses and Midwives'.

[210] Chief Medical Officer and Chief Nursing Officer, 'Abortion Act 1967: Medical Termination of Early Pregnancy', Professional Letter PL/CMO (91)/9, PL/CNO (91)/4, 5 July 1991, on file with the authors; Colvin, 'The Legal Situation', 19. See Chapter 4, p. 129.

of abortion pills.[211] However, while accepting the clinical safety of the home use of misoprostol, it had not used its statutory powers, preferring to move 'very cautiously' in light of 'very strongly held views'.[212] Frustrated by the delay, in 2011, BPAS went to the courts. After repeated attempts by anti-abortion campaigners to use litigation to force a more restrictive interpretation of the Abortion Act, this was the first legal challenge to attempt to achieve a more liberal one. BPAS argued that the current, restrictive reading of the 'place of provision' requirement undermined the delivery of safe, evidence-based abortion services and cut against Parliament's intention in passing the Abortion Act, with no 'sensible reason' to prevent those eligible for legal abortion from taking misoprostol safely at home.[213] The Abortion Act should thus be interpreted in light of significant changes in medical practice,[214] with 'treatment' understood to include the prescription and supply of abortion pills but not their administration, which should therefore not need to take place on approved premises.[215]

This was BPAS's first appearance before Mr Justice Supperstone, the judge who would later find against it in the 23+6 weeks case. It was opposed by the Government, which conceded that the international data suggested that home use would probably be safe but argued that BPAS's interpretation of the law represented, 'in a highly controversial area, a very significant shift of responsibility from the democratically elected and accountable Secretary of State to the medical profession'.[216] SPUC also intervened, taking a different tack. While beginning with a clear statement of its moral position on abortion, it concentrated on a detailed rebuttal of the evidence advanced by BPAS regarding the safety of home use.[217] This may have influenced Mr Justice Supperstone: according to Ann Furedi's recollection of the trial, at one point he compared home use of abortion pills 'to women drinking gin in a hot bath'.[218] He also accepted SPUC's second argument: that a narrow reading of 'treatment' (excluding the administration of pills) risked restricting the scope of conscientious objection rights.[219] Further, he agreed with the Government's central claim: that this power had been deliberately left in its hands, and 'treatment for the termination of pregnancy' includes the administration of abortion pills,

---

[211] See Chapter 3, p. 105.

[212] Evidence of Dawn Primarolo, Minister for Public Health, in House of Commons Science and Technology Committee (STC), *Scientific Developments Relating to the Abortion Act 1967: Twelfth Report of Session 2006–7*, vol. 2., Ev 48, Q361.

[213] Supplementary Skeleton Argument on Behalf of the Claimant, *BPAS v Secretary of State for Health* [2011] EWHC 235 (Admin), (*BPAS 2011*) [8], on file with the authors; Ann Furedi, 'A Shocking Betrayal of Women's Rights', *Spiked*, 28 October 2008.

[214] See generally Bristow, 'Misoprostol and the Transformation of the "Abortion Pill"'.

[215] Skeleton Argument on Behalf of the Claimant, *BPAS 2011*, [35], on file with the authors.

[216] Skeleton Argument for the Secretary of State, *BPAS 2011*, [20], [39], on file with the authors.

[217] First Witness Statement of Paul Tully (SPUC), *BPAS 2011*, on file with the authors.

[218] Email from Ann Furedi to Sally Sheldon and others, 15 May 2019, on file with the authors.

[219] *BPAS 2011*, [35].

which must, therefore, take place on approved premises. The Government immediately confirmed that it had no plans to use its powers to license a broader class of places for their use: with its reluctance explicitly attributed to political caution rather than clinical need and SPUC's intervention on the issue of conscientious objection having been accepted, this was a clear victory for anti-abortion campaigners.

Watching from north of the border, David Baird – a pioneer of early medical abortion – was dismayed, believing tentative discussions with the Scottish law officers to have been curtailed by BPAS's defeat. He criticised the charity's decision to go to court, explaining 'you didn't have to change the law, you had to say that this was a change in the management of the process, which had already been decided'.[220] Earlier statutory interpretations laid down in *RCN* and *C v S* had done precisely this, confirming an expansive reading of the law that was already accepted in clinical practice, whereas here BPAS had invited a court to approve an interpretation of the Abortion Act that was not already thus embedded. BPAS nonetheless found crumbs of victory within its defeat. First, both the Government and Court had accepted the argument that women's homes might also be deemed to constitute 'a class of places' within the terms of the Act, paving the way for home use to be permitted under existing statutory powers.[221] Moreover, Ann Furedi detected an important shift in the public mood:

> Throughout the decade of discussions, officials have repeatedly iterated their fears about how proposals for home-use of abortion drugs will be reported by the press and received by the public. They do not seem to appreciate that times have changed to the point where abortion is accepted and acceptable – especially in the earliest weeks of pregnancy. The media coverage of our court case is an accurate reflection of the general opinion – overwhelmingly balanced and accurate, and implicitly supportive.[222]

It would nonetheless be another six years before change would follow, and, when it came, it would result from the quiet medical diplomacy espoused by Baird. With the statutory power to license a 'broader class of places' devolved to Scottish and Welsh ministers, on the eve of the fiftieth anniversary of the Abortion Act, the Scottish Government licensed women's homes for the use of misoprostol within the first nine weeks of pregnancy.[223] The timing was not lost on John Deighan (SPUC), who saw it as a 'gift' to the 'pro-abortion world', with the move driven by 'ideology . . . rather than reason or even medicine'.[224] It was now SPUC's turn to mount a legal challenge. The charity argued that

---

[220] David Baird interviewed by Gayle Davis, 13 November 2017.
[221] *BPAS 2011*, [32].
[222] Furedi, 'Our 10-Year Struggle to Improve Abortion Care', 1.
[223] The Abortion Act 1967 (Approval of Place for Treatment for the Termination of Pregnancy) (Scotland) 2017, issued 26 October 2017.
[224] Deighan interviewed by O'Neill.

the designation of women's homes as a 'class of places' was too broad and that home use of pills was contrary to the requirement that abortion be carried out by a medical practitioner, which – even on the broad interpretation offered in *RCN* – required a greater level of supervision than availability by telephone.[225] SPUC lost on both counts. Wales now followed Scotland,[226] and a range of medical bodies and women's organisations lined up alongside BPAS to attack Westminster's refusal to undertake this 'simple measure' to 'improve the wellbeing of women' in England.[227]

Almost 30 years after acquiring the power to do so, the UK Government quietly slipped out its approval of home use of misoprostol in England between Christmas and New Year 2018.[228] While their campaigns had succeeded in delaying this move for over a decade beyond the point when the Government had acknowledged its safety,[229] this was a clear defeat for anti-abortion campaigners. SPUC attacked the decision as 'authorising backstreet abortions' and creating 'dreadful threats to women's health'.[230] Moreover, while the terms of this approval were cautious and applied only to misoprostol, more radical change would soon be forced by the COVID-19 pandemic.[231]

Conscientious Objection

Finally, the scope of the conscientious objection clause would come under sustained challenge, offering a particularly significant focus for Pro-Life advocates, who raised repeated allegations of discrimination against conscientious objectors in appointments processes, with nurses describing particularly acute difficulties in seeking to rely on its protection.[232]

It is unclear whether the first major case to reach the courts on conscientious objection was supported by an anti-abortion group, with the plaintiff's

---

[225] *SPUC Pro-Life Scotland* v *Scottish Ministers* [2019] CSIH 31.

[226] The Abortion Act 1967 (Approval of Place for Treatment for the Termination of Pregnancy) (Wales) 2018, issued 20 June 2018.

[227] 'Let Women take Abortion Pill at Home, Hunt Told', *Times*, 27 April 2018, discussing a *Times* letter signed by representatives from 20 groups; Lord et al., 'Early Medical Abortion', 155.

[228] Department of Health and Social Care, 'The Abortion Act 1967 – Approval of a Class of Places' (2018).

[229] Evidence of Dawn Primarolo, Minister for Public Health, in STC, *Scientific Developments*, Ev 48, Q361.

[230] John Deighan in 'New Campaign Promotes Killing Their Babies in DIY Abortions', *LifeNews. com*, 3 April 2018.

[231] See Chapter 7, pp. 257–60.

[232] National Records of Scotland, HH102/1232, E. McGirr, University of Glasgow Department of Medicine, to M. Macdonald, Scottish Home and Health Department, 30 July 1974; Sclare and Geraghty, 'Termination of Pregnancy', 60; and see generally *Report of the Committee on the Working of the Abortion Act* (*Lane Report*), vol. 1, paras 371–73; House of Commons Social Services Committee, *Abortion Act 1967 'Conscience Clause'*, Tenth Report, 17 October 1990, HC 123; All-Party Parliamentary Pro-Life Group, *A Report into Freedom of Conscience in Abortion Provision*.

solicitor refusing to confirm or deny this fact.[233] However, it is very unlikely that Barbara Janaway would have had the financial means to take a case to the House of Lords without such assistance, and she was represented by Gerard Wright, the 'unconditionally Pro-Life' barrister who had earlier acted for Robert Carver and would later represent Victoria Gillick.[234] A Catholic, Mrs Janaway had worked as a medical secretary but was sacked following her refusal to type a letter of referral for an abortion. To SPUC's bitter disappointment, her claim to be protected by the conscientious objection provision was unanimously rejected by the High Court, Court of Appeal and House of Lords, each of which agreed that typing such a letter necessarily occurred before 'treatment for the termination of pregnancy' took place and was therefore not covered by the protection offered to those who 'participate in any treatment authorised by [the Abortion] Act'.[235] Indeed, neither did protection extend to GPs asked to certify the need for an abortion, as the relevant form must be signed before treatment could be offered.[236] While in practice GPs were able to opt out of providing such certification,[237] the category of those offered statutory protected under the Abortion Act was thus relatively narrowly drawn.

Following *Janaway*, Sir Bernard Braine MP (Chair of the Pro-Life All Party Parliamentary Group) succeeded in persuading the House of Commons Social Services Committee to investigate this issue, and it was 'inundated' with evidence. While much of it was anonymous and anecdotal and specific cases were hard to prove, the Committee accepted that there was evidence of discrimination against conscientious objectors.[238] However, it saw no easy way to reconcile the conflicting interests of individual health professionals and pregnant women needing appropriate treatment.[239] It recommended that consideration be given to extending the conscientious objection provision to cover some ancillary staff, such as Mrs Janaway.[240] No action followed.

In the meantime, SPUC publicised its willingness to support those affected, intervening in a number of cases where the exact parameters of what was included in 'treatment authorised by this Act' were deemed unclear.[241] In one instance, it was reported that managers at a hospital with limited overnight staffing had repeatedly asked a young African nurse to insert vaginal pessaries to soften the cervix the day before a surgical abortion or, alternatively, to put

---

[233] Dyer, 'Receptionists May Not Invoke Conscience Clause', 1493–94.
[234] Mrs Gillick famously sought to establish that parental consent should be required before contraception could be prescribed for a minor, *Gillick v Wisbech AHA* [1986] AC 112.
[235] *R v Salford Health Authority ex parte Janaway* [1988] 3 All ER 3 1079; 'Dismissal Stands on Abortion Typist', *Times*, 13 February 1987.
[236] *Janaway*, per Lord Keith, 1083.
[237] *Doogan 2014*, [36].
[238] House of Commons Social Services Committee, *Abortion Act 1967 'Conscience Clause'*, Tenth Report, 17 October 1990, HC 123.
[239] Ibid., para. 43.
[240] Ibid., para. 46.
[241] Wellcome Library, NAC/E/4/1, SPUC, 'Nurses and the Abortion Law', no date.

them on the patient's bedside table and instruct her how to insert them, claiming that this would not involve her in an abortion. She was said to be 'left in peace' only after her church put her in touch with SPUC, which provided a solicitor's letter and guaranteed her legal fees if necessary.[242] In another case, SPUC paid legal costs for a nurse threatened with dismissal for refusal to complete documentation relating to an amniocentesis test 'where the only solution offered to mothers is abortion'.[243]

However, it would take almost five decades before the precise meaning of 'participation in treatment' for health professionals would be established in the courts.[244] Two Catholic midwives, Mary Doogan and Connie Wood, had worked for many years at Glasgow's Southern General Hospital, with Doogan having reportedly delivered more than 5,000 babies.[245] In 2010, a reorganisation of services resulted in a small but increased number of late medical abortions taking place in the labour ward where they worked. As conscientious objectors, Doogan and Wood were not expected to offer direct care to these patients. However, as labour ward coordinators, they were asked to supervise and support other midwives who did so, to book patients in and to delegate tasks. Supported by SPUC, who paid over £500,000 in legal expenses,[246] Doogan and Wood argued that these general duties amounted to 'participation in treatment'. On the other side, BPAS and the Royal College of Midwives (RCM) jointly intervened in support of the Greater Glasgow Health Board, arguing that 'participation in treatment' meant direct, hands-on care.

Doogan and Wood lost at first instance but succeeded on appeal, with the Edinburgh Court of Session finding that a right of conscientious objection was given out of respect for 'strong moral and religious convictions', given that 'the process of abortion is felt by many people to be morally repugnant' and that the provision should thus be interpreted widely.[247] However, that decision was overturned by the Supreme Court, which found that to 'participate' meant to take part in a 'hands-on' capacity, broadly accepting the interpretation that was entrenched in existing practice and reflected in RCM guidelines.[248] The ruling was welcomed by the RCM and BPAS, which argued that Lady Dorian's 'broad and unprecedented interpretation of conscientious objection' risked allowing a tiny number of conscientious objectors to make care undeliverable in many NHS settings.[249] For their part, Doogan and Wood complained that

---

[242] Hargreaves in *Hansard*, HC, 27 July 1989, vol. 157, col. 1373.

[243] Wellcome Library, NAC/E/4/1, SPUC, 'Nurses and the Abortion Law', no date.

[244] *Greater Glasgow Health Board (Appellant)* v *Doogan and another (Respondents) (Scotland)* [2013] CSIH 36 (*Doogan 2013*); *Doogan 2014*.

[245] Alton in *Hansard*, HL, 23 March 2018, vol. 790, cols 588–89.

[246] SPUC, 'Fundraise'.

[247] *Doogan 2013*, [38].

[248] *Doogan 2014*, [30].

[249] 'Catholic Midwives Must Supervise Abortions, Supreme Court Decides', *Telegraph*, 17 December 2017.

the Supreme Court's narrower reading rendered the provision effectively meaningless for senior midwives on a labour ward, and each took early retirement.[250]

SPUC was again bitterly disappointed, believing the judgement to confirm 'second-class status in midwifery for those who only deliver babies and don't kill them'.[251] John Deighan later reflected:

> [I]t will sound extreme me saying this, but it's when you know you live in a tyranny, where you can have the black letter of the law say one thing, and the agencies of the government do the exact opposite. So, judges judging that nurses should have to participate in ending lives ... Lady Hale said, you need to follow orders even if you think you are killing someone.[252]

These disputes regarding the interpretation of the conscientious objection exemption have been so fiercely contested because they lie on the broader moral fault line outlined in the last chapter regarding the appropriate place for religious faith within society and the normalisation of abortion. For the Court of Session, a view of abortion as an exceptional procedure, 'felt by many people to be morally repugnant', justified an expansive meaning of the provision as the taint of complicity might potentially attach to any form of 'participation' broadly construed. For those who accept abortion as a normal part of women's healthcare, 'conscientious objection' is more readily understood as involving a right of 'religious refusal', which permits the unethical abandonment of professional obligations to patients for reason of non-verifiable personal beliefs, undermining best practices grounded in scientific evidence and secular medical ethics. If not removed altogether, the provision should thus be narrowly interpreted so as to avoid disruption of essential health services.[253] While scrupulously avoiding explicit comment on the morality of abortion, this latter understanding can be glimpsed in Lady Hale's judgement, which notes that, as a 'necessary corollary' of the duty of care owed to patients, any conscientious objector is under an obligation to refer the case to another professional who does not share it.[254] This *obiter* comment, made without the qualification that such a duty only applies when the statutory grounds for a legal abortion are met, was immediately criticised by SPUC for appearing implicitly to accept the routine availability of abortion on request.[255]

---

[250] Ibid.; 'Midwife Relates how she was Forced out over Refusal to Supervise Abortions', *Catholicireland.net*, 24 April 2018.

[251] Paul Tully (SPUC) cited in 'Supreme Court Rules against Glasgow Midwives', *Catholic Herald*, 17 December 2014.

[252] Deighan interviewed by O'Neill.

[253] Fiala and Arthur, 'There Is No Defence for "Conscientious Objection" in Reproductive Health Care', 254–58; see generally Montgomery, 'Conscientious Objection'.

[254] *Doogan 2014*, [40].

[255] For Paul Tully's criticism on this point, see 'Supreme Court Rules against Glasgow Midwives', *Catholic Herald*, 17 December 2014.

As abortion has become increasingly normalised and public opinion has become less tolerant of strong expressions of Christianity, those opposing abortion and wishing to opt out of services have become gradually more marginal. Peter Saunders explains that, just as people used to talk about the Church of England being 'the Tory Party at prayer', CMF was once seen as 'the British Medical Association at prayer'. Yet over the past five decades, as the general population gradually became less religious, the views of CMF members have become less aligned with those of secular doctors, with the introduction of the Abortion Act accelerating the shift. CMF members became more conservative as the wider medical profession became increasingly liberal and, in the view of Saunders, went 'off the rails' on abortion. Today,

> the medical profession is almost rabidly liberal, fanatically liberal, far more liberal than most people in society are. And I think that is because the medical profession is just so deeply involved and committed to the whole process, and there are so many doctors who are involved, and I think it's very difficult when all your colleagues are committed to a particular course, to take an opposing view. Or it makes you very unpopular [laughs] ... It's hard to stand up against the mainstream and [if] you do, there are consequences of you doing it. But once they have, then they become more fortified in that position.[256]

Ann Widdecombe likewise describes a shifting culture concerning the implementation of the conscientious objection clause, recalling that one consultant had told the Social Services Select Committee that 'when she had left England to work in Australia the culture was that you had to justify carrying out an abortion but that by the time she returned you had to justify being unwilling to do so. Yet the law had not changed.'[257] Rather, any such change has been in the implementation and interpretation of the clause through the lens of an increasing acceptance of abortion as a necessary part of women's healthcare and a growing marginalisation of religious belief within health professions that have gradually grown more secular and liberal.[258]

Conclusion

Abortion is governed by the oldest statutory framework regulating any area of medical practice in the UK.[259] However, while the text of the Abortion Act 'speaks from the past', having remained largely unchanged for more than five decades, it necessarily takes effect only through interpretation, a

---

[256] Saunders interviewed by O'Neill.

[257] Widdecombe, *Strictly Ann*, 192.

[258] Chapter 4.

[259] Morris and Jones, *Blackstone's Statutes on Medical Law*, begins with the Offences Against the Person Act (1861), moves onto the Infant Life Preservation Act (1929), and extracts just two other statutes before reaching the Abortion Act (1967) on p. 3 of 278 pages of chronologically ordered extracts of English statutes.

contemporaneous activity shaped by changing clinical realities, social norms, cultural anxieties and moral sensibilities.[260] The Act has been given meaning through the daily acts of interpretation of individual doctors, which have been refined through discussion in medical symposia and learned journals, settled into norms of received practice and professional guidelines, and ultimately been subject to confirmation – or, far more rarely, revision – in the courts. The abortion charities, with their specifically pro-choice mission, have played an important part in driving service innovation, often pushing at the limits of the statutory language to achieve the most permissive interpretation available. BPAS has been particularly pugnacious in these fights, refusing to allow 'even a day to be shaved off' the upper time limit for abortion without a sustained struggle.[261]

Pro-Life groups have also played an enormously important part in this process, having had a hand in almost all of the cases discussed in this chapter. Whilst generally not pursuing private prosecutions, they have reported alleged abuses to the police, encouraged and supported claimants in civil cases and sometimes intervened directly. While often unsuccessful in formal legal terms, they have used litigation strategically to publicise specific concerns with the implementation of the Abortion Act and maintained a spotlight on prosecution decisions: one senior prosecutor in the late 1980s singled out Life as the 'most troublesome' and persistent of all lobby groups.[262] While impossible to quantify, the resulting fear of public exposure has had an undoubted chilling effect on clinical practice (as was seen in the 'Jepson effect' and changing practice after *Arthur*), and their actions have sometimes helped to provoke the introduction of clinical guidelines. Finally, they have had a powerful influence on successive governments of both political hues, inspiring marked caution regarding any relaxation of regulatory controls. In these ways, Pro-Life groups have had undoubted success in slowing, if not preventing, the boundaries of the law being 'pushed further out'.[263]

While contestation regarding its meaning has been a consistent feature of the Abortion Act's long life, the focus and framing of these disputes has changed over time in line with the shifting focus of the moral debate, with legal argumentation reflecting rhetorical strategies most likely to prove persuasive to concrete audiences within specific historical, cultural and political contexts.[264] Early interventions – such as *Paton* or 'backdoor Corrie' – sought a restrictive interpretation of the Act in order to limit access to services, with the aim that women who did not meet the Act's criteria would be required to

---

[260] On this dual nature of statutory norms, see Black, 'Regulatory Conversations'; Sheldon, 'British Abortion Law'.

[261] This chapter, p. 157.

[262] Anonymous senior Crown Prosecutor, cited in Harlow and Rawlings, *Pressure through Law*, 220.

[263] Nuala Scarisbrick cited in ibid., 219.

[264] See generally Harrington, *Towards a Rhetoric of Medical Law*.

continue their pregnancies. More recently, claims that undeserving women might 'hoodwink' unwary doctors into wrongly certifying the need for abortion or that nurses must be protected from emotionally upsetting work have largely evaporated. The need for a more restrictive interpretation of the Act has rather been claimed necessary to safeguard vulnerable patients and to ensure fully informed consent, reflecting the wider woman-protective focus in Pro-Life campaigning. These disputes have increasingly focused on the safety of abortion, invoking a bitterly disputed scientific evidence base. Finally, Pro-Choice advocates have now moved off the defensive. BPAS has twice come proactively to the courts to attempt to force a liberal interpretation of the Abortion Act. Like Pro-Life groups before it, it has struggled in seeking to challenge mainstream clinical practice whilst also appreciating the wider strategic value of such litigation.

With such struggles ongoing, the legal meaning of the Abortion Act continues to evolve.

6

The Battle for Northern Ireland

I mean I don't know how many interviews or meetings I would have with Westminster MPs ... I had a meeting with the Shadow Labour Spokesperson for ... either Health or Women's Rights, I can't remember which. From Liverpool, so you would think she would be pretty sussed in. And she didn't know ... [that] women in Northern Ireland had to pay to have an abortion in England. Now that was not unique. I would have newspaper reporters coming over to interview me from England, and they would be saying things like, 'do I need my passport?'. Because they didn't realise that Northern Ireland was a part of the UK. And I don't know how many newspapers, media people – like I thought we were pretty open, gave it a lot of publicity – but still didn't realise that women had to pay for an abortion, they couldn't get it in Northern Ireland. And that is quite recently ... I always likened it to the Berlin Wall. I called it the Abortion Wall. It was never going to come down overnight like the Berlin Wall, it was going to be chip, chipping away, and a brick was going to come away every now and again, and that is exactly what has happened.[1]

The final line of the Abortion Act, reading almost as an afterthought, is that '[t]his Act does not extend to Northern Ireland'.[2] Over the years following the Act's introduction, the numbers of legal abortions rapidly rose across Britain; however, the situation was starkly different over the Irish Sea. In Northern Ireland, access to legal services remained dependent on the therapeutic exception carved out by *Bourne*, providing that no offence was committed when an abortion was performed to 'preserve the life of the mother', including to prevent her from becoming a 'mental or physical wreck'.[3] Moreover, this vaguely worded test was subject to a narrow reading within the region and, indeed, one that became more restrictive over time.[4] While tens of thousands

---

[1] Audrey Simpson interviewed by Jane O'Neill, 27 September 2017.
[2] Section 7(3).
[3] *R v Bourne* [1938] 3 All ER 615.
[4] To require that any adverse effects on a woman's health must be 'real and serious' and 'permanent or long term': see *Western Health and Social Services Board v CMB and the Official Solicitor* (unreported 1995); *Down Lisburn Health and Social Services Board v CH and LAH* (unreported 1995); *In the Matter of an Application by the Family Planning Association of Northern Ireland for Judicial Review* [2003] NIQB 48.

of abortions were performed in 1960s England on the basis of *Bourne*, just 12 were performed in Northern Ireland from 2017 to 2018.[5]

The Abortion Act would nonetheless be of profound significance to Northern Ireland, making its story that of a UK statute rather than purely a British one. First, tens of thousands of Northern Irish women would access abortion services provided under it elsewhere in the UK, with 'taking the boat' becoming a well-understood euphemism. This operated as a safety valve, minimising the maternal mortality and morbidity that has accompanied restrictive laws elsewhere and almost certainly slowing the introduction of formal legal change within the region. Second, as a campaign for legal reform began to emerge, hopes and fears would for many years be focused firmly on the Abortion Act. Third, while the Abortion Act has shaped the recent history of Northern Ireland, so too has Northern Ireland shaped the biography of the Abortion Act. Northern Irish politicians and campaigners have played a distinctive and influential role in debates regarding the Abortion Act, and, in very recent years, legal reform in Northern Ireland has served to increase pressure for repeal, or radical amendment, of abortion law in other parts of the UK.

This chapter tells that story. We begin by exploring in more detail the consequences of the decision not to extend the Abortion Act to Northern Ireland and charting the emergence of campaigns for and against liberalising abortion law reform, which focused heavily on the possibility of such an extension. We then consider events at Westminster (which retained legislative responsibility for criminal justice in Northern Ireland until 2010), before moving to Stormont (which debated abortion on multiple occasions both before and after that point), and ending with the collapse of the Northern Ireland Assembly in 2017. This sets the scene for a return to Westminster in the next chapter, where debate concerning Northern Ireland's abortion law would explode in 2018, with implications that continue to ripple outwards at the time of writing and may yet contribute to a fundamental reshaping of abortion laws for the rest of the UK.

Abortion in Northern Ireland

In 1980, a small group of women came together to work on issues related to women's lives in Northern Ireland, calling themselves 'Women in Media'. Their first publication was a short booklet about abortion, which featured an 'Abortion Game' set out to resemble a Monopoly board, offering a stark picture of the options open to women in Northern Ireland.[6] Players might be lucky enough to land on a square marked 'period comes relax' or to 'have

---

[5] House of Commons (HC) Women and Equalities Committee, *Abortion Law in Northern Ireland*, Eighth Report of Session 2017–2019, HC 1584, 2019.

[6] Women in Media, *A Woman's Choice*, 17 reproduced on p. 193.

money and sympathetic GP', encountering one of those doctors prepared to refer women for an abortion on medical grounds.[7] Others would be less fortunate. Reflecting the dangerous self-abortion methods in use in these earlier years,[8] other squares featured 'friend uses knitting needles', 'take gin and hot baths', 'sterilization', 'commit suicide', 'puncture uterus go to hospital', and 'die from septicaemia'.[9] Some women did indeed die in the process.[10] Others resorted to concealing pregnancies and abandoning their newborn babies: three such were reportedly found in just one month in 1980, two of whom were dead.[11] Audrey Simpson was the Northern Ireland Director of the Family Planning Association (FPANI) from 1988 until her retirement from the organisation in 2015. Her mother had told her about backstreet abortion:

> [S]he remembered a woman doing it for somebody. It was an area called Sandy Row, very working-class, Protestant area. People were queueing up in the back alleyway. So, it was done. And there were some deaths, there were four known deaths too. . . . And we often find stories about . . . babies being found in black plastic bin liner bags. That happened on more than one occasion. And there's also what I would call middle-class neglect. We had a young mum, she was doing her A Levels . . . by the time she got to us she was over 24 weeks pregnant. And her parents didn't realise she was pregnant, didn't notice . . . and she had the baby, and her parents never knew. She gave the baby for adoption.[12]

Other women were coerced or persuaded to continue unwanted pregnancies, with some sequestered in mother and baby institutions or the notorious Magdalene laundries, which operated across the island of Ireland.[13] The then Northern Irish Health Minister, Edwin Poots (Democratic Unionist Party; DUP), claimed many years later that the region's restrictive abortion laws ('not having the ability to pop into a facility that can basically give you an abortion on demand') had had the 'happy result of many tens of thousands of births' in

---

[7] Public Record Office of Northern Ireland (PRONI), HSS/13/40/36, Northern Ireland Abortion Campaign (NIAC), 'Abortion in Northern Ireland: The Results of a Survey Carried Out by the Northern Ireland Abortion Campaign among General Practitioners in Northern Ireland', 1982.

[8] McCormick, 'No Sense of Wrongdoing', 125.

[9] Women in Media, A Woman's Choice, 17. On sterilisation as a precondition of abortion, see Chapter 2, p. 42.

[10] A handwritten file note recording information provided by the Registrar General's Office notes four deaths from 1967 to 1978 and one from 1979 to 1983: PRONI, HSS/13/40/36, A. Kennedy, 'Illegal Abortion Deaths', 4 March 1983.

[11] McGivern, Abortion in Northern Ireland, reprinted in Bourke et al. (eds), Field Day Anthology of Irish Writing Volume V, 390–91. For a case involving concealment of birth, see R v Hopkins [2005] NICC 1 Crown Court (21 January 2005).

[12] Simpson interviewed by O'Neill.

[13] McCormick and O'Connell, Mother and Baby Homes and Magdalene Laundries in Northern Ireland, 1922–1990.

The Abortion Game

GAOL

TAKE GIN AND HOT BATHS

PERIOD COMES RELAX

FRIEND USES KNITTING NEEDLES

PUNCTURE UTERUS GO TO HOSPITAL

STERILIZATION

TAKE A CHANCE

12 weeks Don't tell anyone

Go HOME AND RELAX

Have D and C on N.H.S.

Appointment at Clinic

See Psychiatrist

Have money and sympathetic G.P.

Missed your Period Go To PANIC!

Appointment with O.P.A.A. lose one days Pay

Find £100

Go To ENGLAND

Over 16 weeks Hysterotomy

Too LATE Lose Your TURN

COMMIT SUICIDE

Friend tells you of someone she knows

GO

Die from Septicaemia

Admit to HOSPITAL

Haemorrhage

Have Backstreet Abortion.

PANIC!!

Northern Ireland.[14] In 2019, Jim Shannon MP (DUP) estimated this number to be 100,000.[15]

The 'Abortion Game' also featured a 'Go to England' square, accompanied by a small sketch of a ferry, representing the journey to seek services under the Abortion Act. This reality was also reflected in the name of the London-based Irish Pro-Choice group, Imelda (Ireland Making England the Legal Destination for Abortion).[16] The idea of 'taking the boat' would become entrenched as an important part of the history of abortion on the island of Ireland, eventually becoming supplemented by the arrival of cheap flights.[17] While the numbers are likely to represent an underestimate, given the incentive for women to claim an English address in order to access NHS-funded services, by the 1980s over 1,500 Northern Irish residents were taking the boat each year; numbers declined only in the early years of this century, as the 'morning after pill' became available over the counter and home use of abortion pills sourced on the Internet became widespread.[18] While abortion travel was thus common, it was often challenging. Information about services was often difficult to find, with leaflets containing details of British abortion clinics deemed to fall within an early prohibition on the advertising of services 'abroad'.[19] Women might struggle to explain their absence from home, with difficulties sometimes further compounded by the Troubles.[20] Costs could be prohibitive,[21] even as support groups were established on both sides of the Irish Sea and the abortion charities offered fee waivers.[22]

While Northern Irish women's accounts of accessing abortion services share much with those of women elsewhere in the UK, they are also painfully marked by the difficulties encountered in travelling, a heightened fear of discovery, and feelings of guilt and stigma.[23] Non-marital sex itself was

---

[14] *Official Report of the Northern Ireland Assembly* (hereafter NIA, *Official Report*), 19 March 2013, response to oral questions AQO 3693/11-15.

[15] *Hansard*, HC, 9 July 2019, vol. 663, col. 213.

[16] See Speaking of Imelda, 'Why Imelda?'.

[17] This euphemism was reflected in the title of the 2015 documentary 'Take the Boat' by Hamet and Robin.

[18] Abortion statistics have been collated from multiple volumes, published as Office of Population Censuses and Surveys, *Abortion Statistics* for 1974–2001 and Department of Health, *Abortion Statistics, England and Wales* for 2002–2020.

[19] Northern Ireland Abortion Law Reform Association (NIALRA), *Abortion in Northern Ireland: The Report of an International Tribunal* (hereafter *Tribunal*), 39.

[20] Fairweather, McDonough and McFadyean, *Only the Rivers Run Free*, 45–48.

[21] Boyle and McEvoy, 'Putting Abortion in Its Social Context', 283, 289; Rossiter, *Ireland's Hidden Diaspora*; Women in Media, *A Woman's Choice*, 24.

[22] The Irish Women's Abortion Support Group was founded in the early 1980s, followed by the Irish Abortion Solidarity Campaign in 1990. See Rossiter, *Ireland's Hidden Diaspora*, 24. BPAS reported treating 279 women from Northern Ireland in 1986 on a free or reduced fee basis, at a total cost of £29,009. See NIALRA, *Tribunal*, 41–43.

[23] Boyle and McEvoy, 'Putting Abortion in Its Social Context'.

strongly condemned, with women supposed to 'go up the aisle as a virgin'.[24] Some related feelings of 'walking in to a murder house' and worries of 'never be[ing] able to go to church again' for doing a 'wrong thing'; those who experienced no guilt sometimes worried that this was 'inappropriate'.[25] One woman reported the perceived difference of Irish women from English women, hinting at the process of normalisation described in Chapter 4:

> You see in here yesterday . . . every Irish girl who was in here was crying, upset, nervous, shaking. You see them English girls . . . it didn't take that out of them, they were so cool about it all . . . must be because it's so acceptable here. I might as well go home and say that I'd murdered somebody last night cause that's how bad they would look on it.[26]

Many women described the 'terrible desolation of being on your own' and needing to travel to what they perceived as 'a foreign country'.[27] There was a profound sense of the need for secrecy, with one woman reporting how she had pretended to her family to have been on holiday: '[S]he'll call tomorrow night and I'll have to say "Mum, I had a great weekend" and get the make-up on and the hair done and put on a good show.'[28] Women who had been 'found out' would suffer, with the result that 'to this day people don't speak to them and say ". . . that bitch had an abortion"'.[29] Medical check-ups might be feared on the basis that women's bodies would somehow 'reveal' the abortion.[30]

Secrecy and stigma limited early attempts to build a political campaign: abortion was an 'unmanageable and unmentionable subject' and mainstream women's groups tended to be 'familist' rather than feminist in their approach.[31] Bill Rolston, who worked with the Northern Ireland Abortion Law Reform Association (NIALRA) in the 1980s, described doing his 'darnedest' not to get photographed at public debates on abortion 'in case my mother would see the photograph', leaving this work to an English colleague whose mother did not live on the next street.[32] As NIALRA's major letter writer, he used the 'nom de guerre, C. Daly' as 'an homage to the Catholic Bishop of the time', Cahal Daly.[33] Goretti Horgan would go on to co-found Alliance for

---

[24] Ibid., 295. See further McCormick, *Regulating Sexuality*, 8, on the importance of 'female purity' across the religious divide in Northern Ireland and a 'wider view' of 'higher moral standards of behaviour than its more secular English neighbour'.

[25] Boyle and McEvoy, 'Putting Abortion in Its Social Context', 296.

[26] Ibid., 300.

[27] Ibid., 300.

[28] Ibid., 297.

[29] Ibid., 297–98. However, see this chapter, p. 198, for accounts that suggest far greater levels of empathy and solidarity between women.

[30] Ibid., 298.

[31] Hill, *Women in Ireland*; Galligan, 'Women in Northern Ireland's Politics', 205–06; Evason, *Against the Grain*, 27.

[32] Bill Rolston interviewed by Jane O'Neill, 29 April 2017.

[33] Ibid.

Choice (AFC) in the mid-1990s. She reported being 'really shocked' by the women's groups meetings that she attended in these earlier years:

[E]very time I raised the question of abortion it was as if I, I don't know, said something really rude and people didn't want to talk about it. I mean they just didn't want to talk about it, and literally would actually deny it when I would say, 'there is probably a woman in this room who has had an abortion'. They would go, 'don't be ridiculous!' [laughs] It was really, really difficult.[34]

Audrey Simpson likewise reported that while FPANI would gradually become known as 'the agency working for abortion rights', 'the feminist movement were saying nothing'.[35]

The shoots of a recognisable reform movement thus emerged only slowly outside of the women's movement, and with an initial emphasis on support rather than political campaigning. In 1970, following the attempted suicide of a 19 year-old woman who had been unable to access an abortion, the Ulster Pregnancy Advisory Association (UPAA) was established.[36] As its charitable status made it difficult for it to publicise its services, NIALRA was founded alongside it to take on this role and also to work for a limited relaxation of the law.[37] In 1980, Charlotte Hutton, a 21 year-old working-class woman from Belfast, died in a backstreet abortion.[38] This provoked the establishment of a more radical group: the Northern Ireland Abortion Campaign (NIAC). In the first major activist intervention to publicise the situation of women in Northern Ireland, NIAC delivered a copy of a British Airways ticket attached to a coat hanger to every MP, explaining that these were the only two ways for Northern Irish women to get abortions.[39] While its 'minimum demand' was for the extension of the Abortion Act, NIAC also campaigned for a 'woman's right to choose'.[40] However, it eventually came to the conclusion that it was limited by being a women-only group. In 1984, it 'ran out of steam' and was gradually superseded by a second iteration of NIALRA.[41]

The new NIALRA sought to position itself as a moderate group, hoping to represent men and women who might not 'wholeheartedly' support 'a woman's right to decide'[42] and to avoid being dismissed as a group of 'raving

[34] Goretti Horgan interviewed by Jane O'Neill, 30 April 2017.
[35] Simpson interviewed by O'Neill.
[36] NIALRA, *Tribunal*, 31; PRONI, HSS/13/37/48, 'A Woman's Right to Choose?', *Scope*, June 1981; Women in Media, *A Woman's Choice*, 23.
[37] NIALRA, *Tribunal*, 14; London School of Economics (LSE) Archives, Papers of Merlyn Rees, Merlyn-Rees/7/4, NIALRA Factsheet attached to Letter from Jim Reid (NIALRA Chairman) to Harold Wilson MP, 15 May 1972.
[38] NIALRA, *Tribunal*, 15–16.
[39] NIALRA, *Tribunal*, 16.
[40] PRONI, HSS/13/40/36, NIAC, 'Abortion in Northern Ireland', 1982; NIALRA, *Tribunal*, 15–16.
[41] Evason, *Against the Grain*, 27; Rolston interviewed by O'Neill.
[42] Wellcome Library, SA/NAC/B/7/6, Letter from NIALRA (Anne and Bill) to NAC (Leonora Lloyd), 13 March 1986.

feminists'.[43] It focused exclusively on the goal of extending the Abortion Act to the region. This was seen as 'simple, and understandable [and] in the abstract, doable', in that it didn't require the support of local politicians,[44] but nonetheless it represented 'a change for the better, especially in relation to eliminating backstreet abortions'.[45] On this basis, it hoped to counter widespread opposition to abortion 'on the part of religious leaders, doctors, politicians, and "respectable" public opinion in Northern Ireland'.[46]

NIALRA would also struggle to break through a climate of secrecy, ignorance and implacable opposition to abortion.[47] At a time when abortion rallies in London were attracting many thousands, in Belfast a picket outside a party conference would attract 'a dozen people, if you were lucky'.[48] Rather, NIALRA focused on rational argument and evidence, believing there to be such a logic to its position that if it was possible to start a debate, 'it would be like a snowball going downhill and you would get somewhere'.[49] In 1987, it staged an event to mark the twentieth anniversary of the Abortion Act. Overseen by an 'international panel of lawyers, civil libertarians, doctors and academics', a 'tribunal' heard evidence from professionals, campaigners and women who had experience of abortion within Northern Ireland or had accessed services in England, concluding by strongly recommending the extension of the Abortion Act.[50] To the evident frustration of its organisers, it failed to break through what they saw as a 'conspiracy of silence', with limited publicity given to its findings.[51] NIALRA was also aware that it had an important 'Achilles heel': the making of demands for legal change to the 'British imperial state'.[52] It took an essentially pragmatic position on this issue, accepting the Abortion Act 'warts and all', for '[w]hether we like it or not – and some of us do, while others do not – legislation for us is determined in Westminster'.[53]

NIALRA would, in turn, eventually be superseded by the Women's Right to Choose Group (WRCG), which was explicitly set up to be 'more feminist'. It

---

[43] Anna Eggert, in NIALRA, *Tribunal*, 18. See further, Wellcome Library, Papers of the National Abortion Campaign (NAC), SA/NAC/B/7/6, Letter from NIALRA to NAC, 13 March 1986.

[44] Rolston interviewed by O'Neill, repeating '[i]n the abstract – let me underline that many, many times!'. See further NIALRA, *Tribunal*, 17–20.

[45] Glasgow Women's Library (GWL), Papers of the Scottish Abortion Campaign, SAC 5/4, NIALRA paper on Abortion Law, Northern Ireland and rationale, c. 1986.

[46] Ibid.

[47] NIALRA, *Tribunal*. This was also reflected in a meeting entitled 'Breaking the Silence' organised by NIAC in Belfast in February 1984, see NIALRA, *Tribunal*, iv.

[48] Rolston interviewed by O'Neill.

[49] Ibid.

[50] NIALRA, *Tribunal*.

[51] Organisers' Letter to participants, cited in NIALRA, *Tribunal*, 7.

[52] Ward, 'The Woman's Movement in the North of Ireland', 155; Rolston interviewed by O'Neill.

[53] Wellcome Library, SA/NAC/B/7/6, Letter from NIALRA (Anne and Bill) to NAC (Leonora Lloyd), 13 March 1986. See generally Ward, 'The Woman's Movement in the North of Ireland', 155; NIALRA, *Tribunal*, 4.

took a similarly pragmatic position on the issue of campaigning for the extension of British legislation. Horgan, a co-founder, explains:

> Derry was a very Catholic city, a very national city, and we found ourselves making arguments that really don't fit politically at all with what most people here think. We found ourselves kind of saying 'are we not citizens of the UK? Do we not have a right to equal citizenship?' even though most of us didn't want to be part of the UK [laughs] ... We got some slagging for it, actually. We got people, you know, saying that we were selling out ... [but] you have to be pragmatic, and women have no choice but to be pragmatic if they are facing unwanted pregnancy.[54]

With the Abortion Act having made it much easier for Northern Irish women to access safe, legal services elsewhere in the UK, WRCG also raised money to support their travel.[55] Notwithstanding the experiences of shame and stigma described above, Horgan recalled that some donations came from wealthy women but also 'amazing' amounts came from communities in the 'poorest part of the city, where people were living on benefits and they don't have the money to keep their lights on'. In one case, the husband of a woman facing an unwanted pregnancy had gambled their savings and run off 'with whatever change was left in the house'.

> [Her] next door neighbour had gone around this council housing estate, she lives on a crescent, had gone around every house in the crescent saying, you know, '[this woman] has been in a really bad way since her man ran off. She had a bit of a fling and now she's pregnant and she really needs to go to England and I am collecting to try to help her get there.' And out of 13 houses in a crescent in a Catholic, working-class, like poor working-class area, that woman collected £180. Yep. The level of solidarity that there was was just amazing.[56]

WRCG would eventually be replaced by AFC, which remains very active today, and other groups that supported women's travel.[57]

As the work of groups that supported access to abortion became more widely known, opposition to them emerged. With increasing awareness of women travelling to England for abortions, in 1977 'the Irish Roman Catholic hierarchy' had set up an organisation to support those experiencing 'crisis pregnancies'.[58] Life NI was established in response to the creation of NIAC in 1980,[59] also offering practical support to enable women to continue pregnancies, as well as counselling, education and advocacy work. SPUC likewise established a Northern Ireland branch. Both groups were careful to avoid

---

[54] Horgan interviewed by O'Neill.

[55] Ibid.

[56] Ibid.

[57] Rossiter, *Ireland's Hidden Diaspora*.

[58] PRONI, HSS/13/37/48, 'A Woman's Right to Choose?', *Scope*, June 1981.

[59] PRONI, HSS/13/37/48, note on Mr Patten's 23 April 1981 meeting with Life representatives on abortion law reform, 27 April 1981.

being perceived as too closely associated with any religious organisation, with Life giving contact names that were 'studiously non-identifiable as Catholic', for '[n]o matter how anti-abortion the Northern Protestant might be, an anti-abortion organisation with overwhelmingly Catholic overtones would still not have a large appeal'.[60]

With early pro-reform campaigns in the region heavily focused on fighting for the Abortion Act to be extended to Northern Ireland, the campaigning of SPUC and Life naturally centred on making the case against any such extension, with the Act attacked as fundamentally 'other' to the unique history and character of Northern Ireland. While debate was 'relatively civilised', it was robust.[61] Life member, Old Testament scholar and evangelical commentator Dr Gordon Wenham argued that the Abortion Act was 'bad law', with 'the death toll of Ulster babies in abortion clinics in a single year exceed[ing] the total dead in eleven years of the troubles'.[62] He offered a powerful cautionary tale regarding the impact of the Abortion Act elsewhere in the UK, drawing heavily on the stories then circulating in the British media and explaining that the Act had allowed abortion on demand for frivolous reasons, including where 'a girl could not fit into a dress for her sister's wedding!'. He claimed that its extension to Northern Ireland would mean that 'mothers need no longer care for their children'.[63] At meetings with UK Government ministers in the early 1980s, Life explained that the Abortion Act had resulted in the 'death of 1.5 million children',[64] 'the choking of hospital waiting lists in gynaecology, the growth of an undesirable commercial sector, the influx of women from abroad for whom the Act was never designed, and discrimination against those wishing to practice gynaecology who had a conscientious objection to abortion'.[65]

Westminster: 'The Government Has No Plans for Amending the Law'

'Much Better to Leave It for the Time Being'

With their central demand being the extension of the Abortion Act to Northern Ireland, the attention of pro-reform campaigners was initially

---

[60] *Irish Times*, 8 October 1980.

[61] Horgan interviewed by O'Neill, comparing these older groups to the different style of Precious Life. Simpson likewise notes a 'respectful' relationship, with FPANI occasionally referring women to Life for practical support, Simpson interviewed by O'Neill.

[62] PRONI, HSS/13/37/48, G.J. Wenham (Department of Semitic Studies, Queen's University Belfast), 'Abortion in Northern Ireland', c. 1980. See further PRONI HSS/13/40/ 36, correspondence.

[63] Wenham, ibid.

[64] PRONI, HSS/13/37/48, note on Mr Patten's 23 April 1981 meeting with Life representatives on abortion law reform, 27 April 1981.

[65] PRONI, HSS/13/40/36, Life papers sent in preparation for meeting with Minister of State for Health Northern Ireland, c. April 1984.

directed firmly towards Westminster. However, while the reestablishment of direct rule in 1972 appeared to offer new possibilities, campaigners would find the UK Government implacably opposed to action. Moral issues were seen as matters for local resolution, Northern Irish people and politicians were believed to be uniformly and unequivocally opposed to any reform, and the region's distinctive position on moral issues was conceived as a kind of 'glue' that bound it together, protecting against social and political disintegration.[66] Moreover, in a period when the region suffered from marked deprivation and acute social problems,[67] Northern Ireland received very little time or attention,[68] with many MPs – including Northern Ireland Secretaries of State – deeply ignorant regarding its affairs.[69]

Further, with Charlotte Hutton in 1981 being the last woman reported to have died from a backstreet abortion in Northern Ireland, the 'safety valve' offered by the Abortion Act had made it easier for politicians to 'ignore the whole thing'.[70] Bill Rolston reflected,

> if we were an island a thousand miles from the nearest land, who knows what might have worked out differently. But certainly the build-up, the sheer demand of all these thousands of women year in year out, would have led to something different. I am not sure what … And so, although that is the safety valve for a woman who is in desperation, it is also politically a problem in terms of changing the law. It's both at once.[71]

On the rare occasions that Westminster could be persuaded to turn its attention to the issue, the first priority of successive governments would be to avoid destabilising progress towards a lasting political settlement. In 1972, NIALRA's attempt to persuade Westminster to take an interest in the subject was firmly rebuffed, with the Conservative Secretary of State noting that it was not 'an opportune time' to raise the subject,[72] and his Labour opposite number agreeing that the issue must 'take second place at the moment to the major problem of bringing peace to Ulster'.[73] In 1978, Roy Mason, the Labour Northern Ireland Secretary of State, was asked to comment on whether further study should be given to a range of potential law reform projects for the region. His brief response in the margin notes:

---

[66] Whitaker and Horgan, 'Abortion Governance in the New Northern Ireland'; Smyth, 'The Cultural Politics of Sexuality and Reproduction in Northern Ireland', 663.

[67] Evason, *Against the Grain*.

[68] Coulter, 'Direct Rule and the Unionist Middle Classes', 169–70; Prior, *A Balance of Power*, 191.

[69] E.g. 'Karen Bradley Admits Ignorance of Northern Ireland Politics', *Guardian*, 7 September 2018; 'Obituary: James Prior, Former Northern Ireland Secretary of State', *Irish Times*, 7 January 2017, citing Prior's description of Northern Ireland as a 'foreign country' to him. See also Horgan's comments, this chapter, p. 210.

[70] Simpson interviewed by O'Neill.

[71] Rolston interviewed by O'Neill.

[72] LSE Archives, Papers of Merlyn Rees, Merlyn-Rees/7/4, Letter from William Whitelaw to Merlyn Rees, 7 July 1972.

[73] LSE Archives, Papers of Merlyn Rees, Merlyn-Rees/7/4, Letter from Merlyn Rees to Jim Reid, 26 May 1972.

Divorce law reform – fine

Homosexual law reform – fine

Abortion law reform!!! – this is too much, too indigestible, the pace is too fast – politicians in Northern Ireland and the people too would revolt if we tried to bring in this almost on top of the others, which are quite controversial enough – therefore, much better to leave it for the time being.[74]

The view that it was 'much better to leave it for the time being' would remain firmly entrenched across successive governments, albeit becoming more difficult to defend in light of human rights obligations and an increased acceptance of abortion elsewhere in the UK. In 1981, a civil servant wrote:

Ministers know well that abortion is an active and emotional issue with 'rights', women's and foetuses', on both sides; offering no simple choice between happiness and misery. They may wish to bear in mind –

(a) that such a distinction as there is now between the law in GB [Great Britain] and Northern Ireland may be difficult to sustain always, especially when one main result is that Northern Ireland simply exports its problems;

(b) that law enforcement is not always easy in an area which may be seen by many responsible people as one for legitimate personal decision; and

(c) that it is not impossible that the issue will be taken up in a European context and that we find ourselves confronted, as on homosexuality, with a human rights decision.[75]

It would become increasingly difficult to justify replying to calls for reform with nothing more than 'the Government has no plans for amending the law': in 1982, a civil servant from the Northern Ireland Office reported 'a feeling over here' that this 'curt answer' was 'not enough and that we should give a brief reason for not intending to legislate'.[76] This would nonetheless remain the official, uneasy mantra of successive administrations.

Where a reason was given for the refusal to legislate, it would be the strong and consistent opposition of Northern Irish parliamentarians. One NIALRA campaigner cites the example of an MP elected to Westminster on an abstentionist ticket as an Independent Nationalist, who went to the House of Commons on just two occasions, 'one of which was to vote for a tightening of abortion laws which did not apply in Northern Ireland anyway'.[77] Goretti Horgan would later comment that Northern Irish MPs were focused on

[74] PRONI, HSS/13/37/48, Letter from A. R. Brown (Northern Ireland Office; NIO) to the Northern Ireland Standing Advisory Commission on Human Rights, 18 January 1978, advising against a study of abortion law.

[75] PRONI, HSS/13/33/24, Memo, R. G. Smartt (NIO), 4 March 1981, referring to the case of *Dudgeon* v *UK* [1981] 4 EHRR 149, which was then before the courts. See further PRONI, HSS/13/37/48, Note for the Record, 'Mr Patten's Meeting on Abortion Law Reform', 27 April 1981, recording that a minister in the Northern Ireland Office had told a deputation from Life NI that the Government might be forced to act by a finding that the law breached human rights norms.

[76] PRONI, HSS/13/37/48, 'Restricted' note from Alexander NIO to Dugdale DHSS, c. April 1982; Mills DHSS to Alexander NIO, 7 April 1982.

[77] Marilyn Hyndman, describing the history of NIAC, NIALRA, *Tribunal*, 16.

proving to people in Northern Ireland that they are really anti-abortion, complaining that they had kept 'the most backward version of this place alive in Westminster', allowing people there to believe that all Northern Irish people 'think the way that those bloody dinosaurs do'.[78] Bill Rolston notes that Westminster was 'not going to step over local MPs', wryly adding even though 'it was direct rule and they were stepping over them and on them in every other way, every day of the week'.[79]

Pressure for reform built across the 1980s. Life NI became sufficiently concerned to send delegations to Westminster,[80] and NIALRA forged links with British campaign groups.[81] In 1984, the British Medical Association (BMA) passed a resolution in support of the extension of the Abortion Act to Northern Ireland, with their letter to inform the Government being just 'one of several pro-Abortion Act 1967 letters which Ministers have received in recent months'.[82] The involvement of groups from outside the region nonetheless remained controversial: civil servants questioned why campaign groups outside Northern Ireland felt 'obliged to speak on behalf' of women within it and suggested that the apparent overwhelming balance of opinion in Northern Ireland is 'perhaps why groups like NIALRA are looking outside the Province to obtain support'.[83] The BMA resolution was likewise attacked by one Northern Irish doctor as a measure whereby 'a small number of local doctors are able to gain support from those on the mainland and thrust upon the rest of us, policy which may be disagreeable'.[84] Moreover, the Abortion Act itself was unpopular, with critical accounts of its operation elsewhere in the UK widely reported. The *Irish News* concluded that Northern Ireland had been fortunate in avoiding its evils and that 'any attempt to foist English abortion legislation on the North would be met by a remarkable alliance of nationalist and unionist opposition ... There is enough death and destruction in Northern Ireland without ... yet another form of attack on the sanctity of human life.'[85]

---

[78] Horgan interviewed by O'Neill. See further Horgan, 'A Holy Alliance?'.

[79] Rolston interviewed by O'Neill.

[80] See correspondence in PRONI, HSS/13/37/48 and HSS/13/40/36.

[81] Including the National Union of Students Women's Committee, NAC, SAC and ALRA, which joined them in urging the UK Government to extend to Northern Irish women 'the same rights which their sisters in Britain enjoy'. See e.g. PRONI, HSS/13/37/48, Letters to James Prior, NIO, 21 January 1982 and 8 March 1982; GWL, SAC 9/3, *Socialist Organiser* article, 9 November 1984; Letter from SAC to NIALRA, 18 December 1984.

[82] PRONI, HSS/13/40/36, *Belfast Telegraph*, 'Patten Urged by BMA to Legalise Abortion in Ulster', 29 May 1985.

[83] PRONI, HSS/13/40/36, Internal Letter discussing SAC inquiry, 20 December 1984; draft reply attached to an internal letter dated 13 March 1985.

[84] PRONI, HSS/13/40/36, J. A. Beirne, Hon. Secretary of Western Division BMA, cited in 'Abortion – Doctor Replies', *Derry Journal*, 5 April 1985; Life NI, cited in 'Abortion Proposal Rejected by Group', *Belfast Telegraph*, 24 July 1984. The motion was proposed by Belfast doctor Gabriel Scally at the 1984 Annual Representative Meeting. PRONI, HSS/13/40/36, 'Patten Urged by BMA to Legalise Abortion in Ulster', *Belfast Telegraph*, 29 May 1985.

[85] *Irish News*, 9 July 1984, discussing the BMA resolution.

Nonetheless, in 1990, it appeared that the Westminster Government's path of studied inaction might be blown off course when a proposal to extend the Abortion Act to Northern Ireland was tabled as an amendment to the Human Fertilisation and Embryology Act.[86] In support, David Steel argued that, with no government in Stormont and women forced to travel, it was time to extend the rights given to all other female citizens of the UK.[87] David Alton condemned the amendment as 'extraordinarily arrogant', 'neo-colonialist', and in direct contradiction to the wishes of Stormont.[88] The Reverend Ian Paisley, founder and leader of the DUP, likewise proclaimed that the issue of abortion ran 'to the very gut and heart of the Ulster people', citing 'overwhelming opposition' to the Abortion Act.[89] Moreover, he claimed, abortion was already available where needed in the region because of '[f]oetal abnormality, rape, risk to the physical health of a mother and severe psychological trauma'.[90]

By convention, abortion is treated as an issue of conscience and subject to a free vote at Westminster. While this was respected for all other abortion law amendments tabled to the 1990 Act, the Government opposed just this one, noting that the proposed reform concerned a devolved matter and would be 'offensive to the overwhelming majority of people in the Province'.[91] It was defeated by a margin of two to one.[92]

Abortion in the Twilight Zone

Nonetheless, the campaign for reform continued to grow louder during the 1990s, bolstered by surveys revealing growing support for some liberalising reform amongst both doctors and the general population in Northern Ireland.[93] In 1993, the campaign also received a significant boost from the publication of an influential report written by an eminent Belfast law professor, Simon Lee, for the Northern Ireland Standing Advisory Commission on

[86] See Chapter 3.

[87] Steel in *Hansard*, HC, 21 June 1990, vol. 174, cols 1142–43.

[88] *Hansard*, HC, 21 June 1990, vol. 174, cols 1148–49. See further SPUC, *Human Concern*, no. 30, summer 1990, 8.

[89] Paisley in *Hansard*, HC, 21 June 1990, vol. 174, col. 1153.

[90] Paisley in *Hansard*, HC, 21 June 1990, vol. 174, col. 1154. See this chapter, p. 204, on the inconsistent provision of abortion in such cases in Northern Ireland at the time.

[91] Bottomley in *Hansard*, HC, 21 June 1990, vol. 174, cols 1161–62.

[92] Ayes 131; Noes 267.

[93] FPANI, Northern Ireland Women's European Platform and Alliance for Choice, *Submission of Evidence to the CEDAW Committee Optional Protocol: Inquiry Procedure*, Transitional Justice Institute Research Paper No. 15-01, 2015, 60–61; PRONI, HPA/3/3, Birth Control Trust (BCT), 'New Opinion Poll Shows Increased Support in Northern Ireland for Legal Abortion on Social Grounds', 11 November 1994; PRONI, HSS/13/52/46, correspondence between N. Lunn (DHSS) and M. Simms (BCT), 10 February 1995, 30 May 1995; Francome, 'Gynaecologists and Abortion in Northern Ireland', 389–94.

Human Rights.[94] Lee argued that abortion law had been left to operate in a 'twilight zone', being so uncertain as to violate the standards of international human rights law. As a result, some women were wrongly forced to travel to end their pregnancies despite being legally eligible to do so within Northern Ireland, with decisions resting on the 'moral views and legal boldness of doctors'.[95] While uncertainty was compounded by the 'astonishing' fact that no official abortion statistics were collected in Northern Ireland,[96] the 'best informed guess' was that most abortions in Northern Ireland were performed for reason of fetal anomaly on the basis of a widely shared but mistaken assumption that such abortions were lawful under *Bourne*.[97]

Lee was clearly correct in suggesting that the law was unclear and poorly understood.[98] One senior gynaecologist explained that '[e]very time you carry out an abortion, you are left wondering if you are going to get arrested for it. It's an appalling situation. People are very frightened.'[99] And arrest was not the only concern: Audrey Simpson recalls that 'there were still a lot of guns around in Northern Ireland, and there were still doctors being murdered in Canada and America'.[100] While abortion was available 'under the counter' in some parts of the local NHS,[101] there was significant geographical and class inequality in access to services. Simpson remembers being contacted by a hospital in a rural area:

> [I]t was the Director of Clinical Services and he said 'I've got a woman here who has – she'd had her 20 week scan, foetal abnormality has been detected, what do we do with her? She doesn't want to continue with the pregnancy.' And the bottom line was, the only hospital who were doing any were the Royal. You know, quietly doing them, would be the Royal. So I said, 'well, you could refer her to the Royal, or you could pay for her to go to England'. ... And he said 'we'll send her to the Royal for advanced diagnostic testing'. So if they did that, then the woman would go, and then the Royal would be able to do it. Quietly. Then the Royal said, 'wait a minute here, why are we becoming the, in inverted commas, abortion centre for Northern Ireland? If you have a woman in the same circumstances, you deal with that woman.' And therefore they stopped taking women from other hospitals. Quite rightly so.[102]

---

[94] PRONI, HPA/3/3, S. Lee, *Abortion Law in Northern Ireland: The Twilight Zone*, Standing Advisory Commission on Human Rights for Northern Ireland, May 1993; S. Lee, *An A to K to Z of Abortion Law in Northern Ireland: Abortion on Remand*, Standing Advisory Commission on Human Rights, February 1994.

[95] PRONI, HPA/3/3, Lee, *Abortion Law in Northern Ireland*, para. 10.

[96] PRONI, HPA/3/3, Lee, *An A to K to Z of Abortion Law in Northern Ireland*, para. 4.2.

[97] PRONI, HPA/3/3, Lee, *Abortion Law in Northern Ireland*, para. 15.

[98] See e.g. Francome, 'Gynaecologists and Abortion in Northern Ireland', 389–94; Simpson, 'The Victorian Law of Northern Ireland', 7.

[99] W. Thompson, Professor of Gynaecology at Queens, cited in PRONI, HSS/13/52/46, 'Abortion Row Brews', *Ulster News Letter*, 7 February 1994.

[100] Simpson interviewed by O'Neill.

[101] Horgan interviewed by O'Neill.

[102] Simpson interviewed by O'Neill.

Lee's findings were widely reported,[103] with one newspaper proclaiming that '[r]adical changes to Northern Ireland's abortion law could be just around the corner'.[104] They were also fiercely contested: Life warned the Northern Ireland Standing Advisory Commission on Human Rights to keep out of the 'right to life' debate,[105] and SPUC entitled its annual conference 'Forcing Abortion on Northern Ireland'.[106] While Lee had emphasised that reform of Northern Ireland's abortion laws should be attentive to the region's own needs rather than 'simply mimicking the law in England',[107] this message did not appear to have been well heard. Northern Irish MPs issued a press release opposing reform:

> We do not want the abortion culture which has so undermined the family in this country tainting our people and our standards of medicine ... In Northern Ireland we have never lost our respect for women, for children and for the family and we have no intention of allowing English-based organisations to impose laws, eroding our quality of family life, against the wishes of our people.[108]

Meanwhile, FPANI began planning what would turn out to be a very long campaign for clarification of the law.[109]

The UK Government felt obliged to respond to the Lee Report but walked a painfully fine line in doing so. It could not deny that statistics were inadequate: its own unpublished figures revealed that in 1992/1993 there had been 44 primary diagnoses of 'therapeutic abortion', 1,129 of 'spontaneous abortion', and 627 of 'unspecified abortion', with the substantial number in the last category reflecting 'either an incomplete description of the diagnosis or a reluctance to be specific in what is a sensitive area'.[110] Officials were aware, however, that any attempt to improve coding practice risked exerting a chilling effect on practice, with 'even more reluctance to use the "therapeutic abortion" code (even where appropriate) if the subject is known to be under scrutiny'.[111]

Nor could the Government easily refute the claim that the law was unclear, with internal discussions amply illustrating the confusion. A doctor within the Department of Health was invited to comment. He explained that most

---

[103] The *Belfast Telegraph* ran an extended special feature on 'Abortion, the Dilemma, the Debate' on 29 March 1995 and 12 April 1995: see PRONI, HPA/3/3.

[104] PRONI, HSS/13/52/46, 'Abortion Law Changes Firmly on Agenda', *South Belfast Herald and Post*, 25 May 1995.

[105] PRONI, HSS/13/52/46, 'Stay Out of Abortion Row, Rights Body Told', *Belfast Telegraph*, 3 August 1993.

[106] PRONI, HSS/13/52/46, 'Forcing Abortion on Northern Ireland', *Newtownards Chronicle*, 18 November 1993.

[107] PRONI, HPA/3/3, Lee, *Abortion Law in Northern Ireland*, para. 20.

[108] PRONI, HSS/13/52/46, issued by Martin Smyth MP (Ulster Unionist Party), 23 March 1995.

[109] PRONI, HPA/3/3, 'Dear Colleague' Letter from Audrey Simpson, 3 April 1995.

[110] PRONI, HSS/13/52/46, R. Beckett (DHSS) Memo, 'Restricted Policy. Abortion Statistics', 12 October 1994, citing figures for 1992/1993.

[111] Ibid.

doctors within Northern Ireland probably believed abortion to be legal in the case of severe fetal anomaly, that such abortions were not legal and that most doctors would welcome clarification of the law. He concluded, however, by denying that there was 'any doubt in the minds of the medical profession as to the circumstances where abortion is legal in Northern Ireland' and advising against the publication of official guidance on the matter.[112] The inconsistencies in this view did not go unremarked upon by the colleague who had solicited it.[113]

To agree an official response, the Conservative Secretary of State, Patrick Mayhew, convened a meeting of ministers and senior civil servants in the Northern Ireland Office. Those present acknowledged that the law was unclear and 'difficult to defend' given that the middle classes could travel to access abortion services whilst the working classes could not.[114] However, while a proposal from FPANI for a Commission of Inquiry was considered, it was firmly rejected.[115] First, there was no need for any further confirmation that the law was unclear. Second, there was a danger that a Commission would make recommendations to which the Government would then need to react.[116] Rather, there was benefit in 'keeping the overall political temperature in Northern Ireland as low as possible', with a decision better deferred for six months when it might be 'somewhat cooler'.[117] The one female minister present – Baroness Denton – wondered, with some prescience, if 'in following this analysis, the time would ever be right to make a change'.[118]

A senior official in the Department of Health concluded:

> In the light of the opinions expressed by Simon Lee, Professor of Juresprudence [sic], Queen's University and High Court judges, it would be difficult, it [sic] not impossible, to argue against the contention that the Northern Ireland abortion law is unclear. Equally, if the Government publicly accepted that the law is unclear, it would be difficult to defend a 'do nothing' stance. **It is therefore recommended that the Secretary of State's response does not express any view on the state of the law.**[119]

The chosen course was thus one of studied inaction and carefully choreographed ignorance.[120] A one-sentence response to a parliamentary question

---

[112] PRONI, HSS/13/52/46, Dr C. Hall to A. Sharp, 1 March 1995.

[113] PRONI, HSS/13/52/46, A. Sharp to N. Lunn, 14 March 1995.

[114] PRONI, HSS/13/52/46, Confidential Minutes of Meeting of Ministers, 19 April 1995.

[115] PRONI, HSS/13/52/46, J. P. Bill (DHSS), 'Abortion Law in NI', 14 February 1995.

[116] PRONI, HSS/13/52/46, Comments of Mayhew and Ancram, Confidential Minutes of Meeting of Ministers, 19 April 1995.

[117] Ibid.

[118] Ibid.

[119] PRONI, HSS/13/52/46, J. J. M. Harbison, 'Restricted – Policy: Abortion Law in Northern Ireland', DHSS, memo sent to civil servants in a range of departments including the NIO and DHSS, 4 May 1995, [14], emphasis in original.

[120] On the idea of choreographed ignorance see Proctor and Schiebinger (eds), *Agnotology*; Sheldon, 'Empowerment and Privacy?', 823.

reiterated that the Government did not propose any changes to the law at present.[121] While privately aware that the law was unclear, publicly the Government maintained that 'medical colleagues in the Department do not consider that there is any doubt in the minds of the medical profession about the circumstances in which abortions are legal in Northern Ireland' (a claim that apparently relies on the confused opinion of the single doctor cited above).[122] While privately briefed on 'a surprising degree of support among both sections of the community in Northern Ireland for the liberalisation of the existing law',[123] publicly the Government noted that the overwhelming majority of the representations it had received expressed opposition to change and that abortion was properly a matter for Northern Irish MPs.[124] It did, however, commit to improving the quality of abortion statistics.[125]

In 1997, there appeared to be a second chance that this long-established status quo might be disrupted. 'New Labour' came to power, bringing with it a substantial injection of the female Labour MPs who had been the traditional defenders of liberal abortion laws. For the first time, women numbered more than 10 per cent of MPs and, moreover, 101 of the 120 women elected represented Labour.[126] Further, whilst in opposition, the incoming Prime Minister, Tony Blair, and Northern Ireland Secretary, Mo Mowlam, had each voted in support of the extension of the Abortion Act to Northern Ireland. Pro-Choice campaigners grew optimistic, noting that Mowlam was 'radical' and '100% committed' to reform.[127] With a Labour Government in power, Pro-Choice campaigners were for the first time 'welcomed to Westminster', finding 'people were willing to have a dialogue'.[128] In anticipation, they wound up WRCG, realising that collecting money to help women travel to England for abortions was 'running to stay still', and established AFC.[129] Horgan recalls:

> [W]e thought, 'happy days, Labour are coming!' and what we needed to do now was . . . to set something up to be able to cheerlead Labour when they extend the

[121] *Hansard*, HC, 24 May 1995, vol. 260, col. 267.

[122] PRONI, HSS/13/52/46, Letter from N. Lunn (DHSS) to M. Simms (BCT), 30 May 1995.

[123] PRONI, HSS/13/52/46, 'Restricted – Policy. Background Note: Abortion Law in Northern Ireland', c. spring 1995, discussing polls suggesting significant support for some liberalisation amongst both the public and consultant gynaecologists.

[124] See PRONI, HSS/13/52/46, Letter from Patrick Mayhew to Charles Hill (Chairman, Standing Advisory Committee on Human Rights), 10 May 1995, and letter from Patrick Mayhew to Harry Barnes MP, 3 July 1995.

[125] PRONI, HSS/13/52/46, Letter from Patrick Mayhew to Charles Hill, 10 May 1995.

[126] See House of Commons Library, *Women in Parliament and Government, Briefing Paper Number 01250*, 4 March 2019. No women were elected by Northern Irish constituencies.

[127] Simpson interviewed by O'Neill. See PRONI, HPA/3/3, Letter from M. Mowlam, Shadow Northern Ireland Secretary, to K. Fearon and A. Ahern (Alliance for Choice NI), 15 November 1995, noting that '*I am not the MP who needs to be convinced of the right to choose for the women of Northern Ireland*' (emphasis in original).

[128] Simpson interviewed by O'Neill.

[129] Horgan interviewed by O'Neill.

Abortion Act and defend the doctors and the clinics who would be providing abortion. I mean we *genuinely* thought that that was what was going to happen, and so we set up Alliance for Choice ... I realise now that that was incredibly naïve of us but, at the time, we just were stupid enough to believe politicians' promises.[130]

The anticipated change in tack was not forthcoming. When the Good Friday Agreement was signed in 1998, the Labour Government fell into line behind the long-standing position that the Abortion Act would be extended only with the broad support of the people of Northern Ireland. Indeed, it was rumoured that, in order to encourage all parties to sign, Mowlam had privately committed that there would be no subsequent move to extend the Act.[131] She would later cite the failure to achieve such reform as one of her greatest regrets.[132]

Abortion politics would now take a more radical turn. Rather than 'cheerleading' the extension of the Abortion Act, AFC would direct its energies towards becoming a very visible, highly creative campaign group, and a new, home-grown anti-abortion group would emerge to challenge it. Having enjoyed a 'respectful' relationship with SPUC and Life, Audrey Simpson recalls that Precious Life, directed by Bernie Smyth, was a different proposition, taking actions that included 'following people into taxis, throwing leaflets into the taxis [and] verbally abusing staff':

> We worked with a young woman Social Services had referred to us, who wasn't even pregnant but we were helping her through other stuff, contraception and relationships, and they saw her coming out of our service one night – because we used to work late on a Thursday night – and they followed her down the streets, and two weeks later they saw her walking up the street, and they were shouting at her, 'you murdered your baby, you murdered your baby'. She wasn't even pregnant. That's just the tip of it.[133]

With its offices firebombed and counsellors' homes picketed, UPAA would now, after 30 years, close its doors. While claiming responsibility for the picketing but not the firebombing, Smyth nonetheless welcomed this closure as a 'moral victory' for Precious Life.[134] Whilst 'horribly upsetting' for those targeted, Horgan notes that this more radical turn in Northern Irish abortion politics was in some ways 'very good' for the reformers:

> [I]n terms of actually making Pro-Choice be seen as the rational, sensible, caring [side, ... Precious Life] have been excellent. Because they are just so extreme and so nasty and so religious ... we've now adopted a kind of a thing where when we are debating [Bernie Smyth], we just let her talk, and say, 'I don't think

---

[130] Ibid.

[131] Horgan and O'Connor, 'Abortion and Citizenship Rights in a Devolved Region of the UK', 39.

[132] 'Mo: My Regrets', *Belfast Telegraph*, 5 July 2008.

[133] Simpson interviewed by O'Neill.

[134] 'UK Campaigners Force Pregnancy Centre Closure', *BBC News*, 5 August 1999; 'Abortion and the Reality of Life in the Modern Ireland', *Belfast Telegraph*, 5 July 2008.

that most people would agree with this kind of extremism. I don't think most people are this uncar'ing.'[135]

Westminster during Power-Sharing

With public and parliamentary awareness of the issue growing on both sides of the Irish Sea,[136] there would be one further significant opportunity for Westminster to debate the extension of the Abortion Act to the region before control over criminal justice was devolved to Stormont. The Human Fertilisation and Embryology Act 1990, which had earlier been used as a vehicle for abortion law reform, would eventually require updating. As we will see in the following chapter, this further opportunity to table abortion law amendments would be firmly grasped by MPs on both sides of the debate. However, while a raft of restrictive reform measures was put to a vote, a second group of amendments proposing liberalising changes would be blocked without debate, prompting furious accusations that the Labour Government had acted 'in an asymmetrical way, so that those who sought at an earlier stage to curtail abortion rights were heard, but those who seek at this stage to extend them are to be silenced'.[137]

Given that it was officially neutral on the issue of abortion law, the Government's action – coordinated by Harriett Harman, then Minister for Women and Leader of the House – was unusual. The move was defended as necessary to protect the available parliamentary time for matters that went 'to the very heart' of the Bill,[138] with Harman herself expressing concerns that liberalising abortion reform in the Commons might provoke further restriction in the Lords.[139] However, with restrictive amendments given time for debate and Parliament awarded a Christmas recess of 'unprecedented length', each explanation rang hollow.[140] Kenneth Clarke (Con), who as Health Secretary had created time for abortion law reform to be debated in 1990, described the Government's action as a 'particularly cynical' piece of political expediency designed to prevent a vote.[141] While flatly denied by the parties said to be involved, it was widely rumoured that the Government had blocked the entire raft of liberalising reforms in order to prevent just one amendment from coming to a vote: the extension of the Abortion Act to Northern Ireland.

---

[135] Horgan interviewed by O'Neill.

[136] From the late 1990s, Horgan notes that it was 'being raised all the time really at Westminster – at least a couple of times a year, in questions and EDMs [Early Day Motions] and things like that'. Horgan interviewed by O'Neill.

[137] Mactaggart in *Hansard*, HC, 22 October 2008, vol. 481, col. 331. See further Chapter 7, p. 237.

[138] Primarolo in *Hansard*, HC, 22 October 2008, vol. 481, col. 323.

[139] 'Harman to Block Commons Votes on Liberalising Abortion Laws', *Guardian*, 21 October 2008.

[140] Clarke in *Hansard*, HC, 22 October 2008, vol. 481, col. 331.

[141] Clarke in *Hansard*, HC, 22 October 2008, vol. 481, cols 329–30.

It was further reported that this reflected a secret deal with the DUP, which had offered its support for a controversial anti-terrorist measure as the quid pro quo for the blocking of the Northern Ireland amendment.[142] While impossible to verify, the available evidence offers some support for at least the first of these claims. Horgan reported that campaigners were on the point of travelling to Westminster when they received a call from Emily Thornberry (Lab), who was due to table it:

> [Thornberry had] been called to No. 10 and she had been told that she couldn't put down the amendment, that if she did she would destroy the peace process and she would make life very difficult for the prime minister, who was Gordon Brown. . . . And I was like, 'do you not think we are the ones [who] know? Both sides are both against it and for it, and it would make no difference to the peace process. This is just a load of nonsense.' . . . And then it became obvious that it wasn't going to happen actually, because although Diane Abbott took it over, and she put down the amendment in October, it became clear then that, okay, the apparatus is against it, so it's not going to go through.[143]

Marge Berer, by then the Chair of the UK Voice for Choice coalition, likewise reports having been told that 'if we would drop Northern Ireland, we would get the other six amendments [that we were supporting]. It was outrageous and we said no.'[144]

With legislative responsibility for criminal justice due shortly to be transferred to the Northern Ireland Assembly, Diane Abbott argued that women in Northern Ireland would thus be denied for another generation the rights that had been enjoyed elsewhere in the UK for 40 years.[145] Goretti Horgan put it more forcefully, suggesting that women's abortion rights were now 'in the hands of an evangelical Taliban'.[146] Attacking the 'misguided political opportunism' and 'shocking act of betrayal' of Labour ministers 'who have built their careers claiming support for women's rights',[147] Horgan recalls events as 'a horrible slap in the face'.[148] Again, she complained bitterly regarding the apparent assumption that Northern Irish MPs spoke for the public, with the fact that a majority of births in both Derry and Belfast were outside of marriage rendering untenable any suggestion that Northern Ireland was 'some

---

[142] For reports of this deal, see 'Harman to Block Commons Votes on Liberalising Abortion Laws', *Guardian*, 21 October 2008; Editorial, *Guardian*, 22 October 2008; '42 Day Detention: Bribes and Concessions that Got DUP on Side', *Times*, 12 June 2008. For a denial, see Donaldson in *Hansard*, HC, 22 October 2008, vol. 481, col. 331.

[143] Horgan interviewed by O'Neill; Audrey Simpson gave the same account, interviewed by O'Neill.

[144] Marge Berer interviewed by Jane O'Neill, 6 October 2017.

[145] *Hansard*, HC, 22 October 2008, vol. 481, col. 328.

[146] Horgan, 'Foreword' in Rossiter, *Ireland's Hidden Diaspora*, 20.

[147] Horgan cited in Rossiter, *Ireland's Hidden Diaspora*, 163.

[148] Horgan interviewed by O'Neill.

great Christian ... conservative nation'.[149] She further notes that around half of the DUP MPs at the time were creationists:

> They literally think that we lived at the same time as dinosaurs ... I don't believe for a moment that anybody in Westminster thinks that the whole of the population in Northern Ireland thinks that the earth is only 6,500 years old. I am sure that they know that that is not the case. So why do they think that we agree with these cretins over abortion but not over all their other weird notions? ... They call themselves the Caliban, like they are followers of Caleb who is this biblical character. They want the law to reflect an Old Testament reading of the Bible. I mean, they are the equivalent of people who want sharia law ... they are a disgrace. That is the long and the short of it. They go in there to Westminster and they just disgrace the lot of us.[150]

With AFC having campaigned heavily for the extension of the Abortion Act and having 'honestly thought that it would happen', she relates that

> after all the manoeuvring there was in 2008, I think we kind of gave up a little bit [laughs] on any political party in Westminster actually choosing to do the right thing by women in Northern Ireland. It just seems as if, as if Northern Ireland isn't really seen as part of the United Kingdom. And because it isn't really seen as part of the United Kingdom then they are never going to do anything for the women here.[151]

Stormont: *'Bleak House'*

The Long Battle for Legal Clarification

While it would require the transfer of legislative responsibility for criminal justice in 2010 before campaigners might look to it for legal reform, Stormont had gained responsibility for health in 1998. When Westminster ignored calls for a Commission of Inquiry following the publication of the Lee Report, FPANI had thus turned to the Northern Irish courts to request the clarification of existing law.[152] Simpson relates:

> We took nine months to build up a case and we kept it completely in-house, and nobody in Northern Ireland knew that we were doing it ... as soon as we lodged it, the story broke ...and all hell did break loose. It took 15 months to get it to court, and ... there were something like 12 barristers and an equal number of solicitors on this case. There wasn't enough room for them all. Because we had interveners: Precious Life, Life, SPUC, the Catholic Church [laughs], everybody! ... And then it took 18 months for judgement, it was in the law journals as the longest judgement ever awaited. And then when it came out, he

---

[149] Ibid.
[150] Ibid.
[151] Ibid.
[152] *FPANI v Minister for Health, Social Services and Public Safety* [2004] NICA 37.

ruled against us. . . . [But] the three appeal judges ruled in our favour. So by initiating that process, the amount of publicity that attracted, it just really, really blew the lid off the situation in Northern Ireland.[153]

The Northern Irish Court of Appeal confirmed the need for the law to be clarified, noting that any uncertainty might 'easily be removed' by official guidance for health professionals.[154] In fact, the subsequent process of establishing the precise legal meaning of the notoriously ambiguously worded *Bourne* judgement – which had 'left plenty of loose ends and ample scope for clarification'[155] – was tortuous, highly politicised and painfully slow. Six drafts of the guidance were produced and fiercely disputed – with SPUC successfully bringing a legal action to challenge one iteration and threatening it against another[156] – before a final version was published in 2016. This process would thus take more than 20 years following the publication of the Lee Report and FPANI's first calls for clarification of the law and over a decade from the Court of Appeal judgement requiring its production.[157] Simpson recalls that

once [John Larkin, the strongly anti-abortion Attorney General] became involved, each draft became more and more strict, until one of the drafts actually said to give women counselling would probably be illegal, which was obviously to get back at FPA [the Family Planning Association], even though that was settled in Europe, by *Open Door* in Dublin, that was well settled then. So the drafts that came out, before the ones that are in circulation now, were so draconian. It was dreadful. But there was such a backlash from everybody. There never would have been before.[158]

The penultimate draft of the guidance, produced under Health Minister Edwin Poots (DUP), offered the most restrictive interpretation of the law yet.[159] While abortion had not hitherto been prominent within the work of human rights organisations in Northern Ireland, this draft was 'a game changer',

[153] Simpson interviewed by O'Neill.

[154] *FPANI*, per Sheil LJ, [4].

[155] *Royal College of Nursing* v *Department of Health and Social Security* [1981] AC 800 (per Lord Diplock).

[156] *In the Matter of an Application by SPUC for Judicial Review* [2009] NIQB 92; for a chronology of events, see Northern Ireland Assembly, AQW 23793/11-15, 12 June 2013.

[157] Department of Health, *Guidance for Health and Social Care Professionals on Termination of Pregnancy in Northern Ireland*. For a more detailed account of this process, see Sheldon et al., 'Too Much, Too Indigestible, Too Fast', 761–96.

[158] Simpson interviewed by O'Neill, citing *Open Door Counselling and Dublin Well Woman* v *Ireland* [1992] ECHR 68 (29 October 1992), which confirmed the right of counselling services to offer pregnant women information about abortion facilities abroad. On Larkin, see 'Law Officer likens Abortion to "Shooting a Baby in Head"', *Independent.ie*, 21 October 2012.

[159] Department of Health, *The Limited Circumstances for a Lawful Termination of Pregnancy in NI*. For a blistering response, see RCN, *Response of the Royal College of Nursing to a DHSSPS Consultation on the Limited Circumstances for a Lawful Termination of Pregnancy in Northern Ireland*.

achieving what several decades of pro-choice advocacy had not: prompting mainstream human rights organisations to raise human rights concerns regarding restrictions on access to abortion.[160] Amnesty International, the Committee on the Administration of Justice, the Northern Ireland Human Rights Commission (NIHRC) and the Equality Commission each now intervened for the first time,[161] with 'some of the men … dragged screaming and kicking to agree'.[162] A small number of Northern Irish women politicians also became involved.[163]

The 2016 guidance represented an important victory for pro-reform campaigners: it was notably more liberal than the previous version, and the legacy of a focus on human rights would prove crucial over the following years. However, the process of clarifying the law had also cast a powerful spotlight on an area of long-standing legal ambiguity. Crucially, there was no longer any space for lingering confusion concerning the lawfulness of abortion for fetal anomaly, with a more restrictive understanding of the law now vehemently defended even by those who had earlier accepted the legality of abortion in a wider range of circumstances. In 1990, the Reverend Ian Paisley had been one of many to accept that abortion was already available 'where needed' for serious fetal anomaly or where a pregnancy resulted from rape.[164] Now he would join other Northern Irish politicians in vigorously defending an interpretation of the law that excluded termination in these cases and in opposing moves to relax the law to permit them, even in cases of fetal anomalies so severe as to be incompatible with life.

Combined with earlier Government work to improve the clinical coding used by gynaecologists, this had a marked chilling effect on practice. In 1978, it was estimated that around 400 terminations were performed within Northern Ireland's health services.[165] By 2005, this number had dwindled to 82,[166] by 2011/2012 it was 35,[167] and in 2017/2018 just 12 abortions were reported.[168] Simpson remembers that campaigners were fully aware that this was a likely consequence of their campaign to clarify the law but believed it a price worth paying:

---

[160] O'Rourke, 'Advocating Abortion Rights in Northern Ireland', 716.

[161] Ibid., 730.

[162] Simpson interviewed by O'Neill, describing the experiences of herself and other women on the Equality Commission in gaining agreement from male colleagues.

[163] Including Baroness May Blood (Labour peer) and Anna Lo (Alliance Member of the Legislative Assembly): Simpson interviewed by O'Neill; Rolston interviewed by O'Neill.

[164] Paisley, this chapter, p. 203.

[165] PRONI, HSS/13/33/24, N. Dugdale, 'Abortion and Contraception (note for the Minister)' (DHSS), 26 July 1976, further noting that 'medical practice under the law in NI does not seem widely divergent from the explicit criteria written into the "reformed" law in Gt. Britain'.

[166] NIA, *Official Report*, 2 December 2008, answer to written question of Simon Hamilton (DUP), QWA 2577 (09).

[167] House of Commons Women and Equalities Committee, *Abortion Law in Northern Ireland*.

[168] Ibid.

[I]f you knew the right people, you could get an abortion here. Particularly around fetal abnormality. There were a lot of D&Cs [dilation and curettage procedures] done in the private clinic. ... [I] had some senior civil servants saying, 'Audrey, you know, you are going to make it so things will have to be tightened up now'. And my response to that was 'you can't make an omelette without breaking eggs'. And why was it right for some woman who was incredibly articulate and middle class, and knew the right people and went to the right parties, could get an abortion here, when somebody who was the complete reverse couldn't? So for me, it was a rights issue. And yes, it did make things more restrictive, and it started a whole legal process that went on ... But look what it achieved. It blew the lid off the whole thing and brought it out into the open. People started talking about it.[169]

While the Abortion Act retained a powerful role in framing the political debate, campaigners now also began to question whether its extension remained the appropriate goal. Simpson reflects that

obviously we were supportive of the '67 Act being extended to Northern Ireland, but that's not what the focus of our campaign was ... it's a flawed piece of legislation anyway, and everybody wants to amend it, so why would we want to take a piece of flawed legislation? Because we also knew that, as it's an English piece of legislation, we would never get Sinn Féin on board to take on a piece of English legislation, to apply it to Northern Ireland. ... If we were going to effect change, it was going to be for one, fetal abnormality, then 12 weeks – just gradually, the way we did everything else. ... We wouldn't have gained anything by getting the '67 Act unless we had brave doctors to interpret it more loosely. So we wouldn't really have gained a lot by getting it, to be honest.[170]

Horgan likewise notes that AFC now began to work hard 'to take the criminal law out of this altogether and just make it about a woman's health'.[171] Working closely with activists in the Republic of Ireland as well as a range of civil society organisations, AFC campaigned creatively, with an emphasis on disrupting the silence around abortion and raising awareness of the individual stories behind the statistics of women forced to travel to access services or to self-induce abortions.[172] When asked what the group was doing to force change, one activist replied, 'what are we not doing?'.[173]

One further factor was crucial to these campaigns. The use of abortion pills had radically redrawn the squares of the 'Abortion Game' discussed earlier, placing the possibility of safe early medical abortion in women's own

---

[169] Simpson interviewed by O'Neill.
[170] Ibid.
[171] Horgan interviewed by O'Neill.
[172] Ibid.
[173] Kellie O'Dowd (AFC) cited in Enright, McNeilly and de Londras, 'Abortion Activism, Legal Change, and Taking Feminist Law Work Seriously', 359. See further Campbell and Clancy, 'From Grassroots to Government'.

hands.[174] The pills' online availability was an open secret amongst a generally Internet-savvy population and their use was widely reported, with the influential BBC current affairs programme *Spotlight* increasing public awareness of Women on Web as 'a feminist organisation with a doctor at the other end'.[175] Campaigners also took every opportunity to inform women about such groups, sometimes openly courting prosecution in order to do so.[176] In 2013, a mass-signature open letter was published including the names of many – mainly women – who had either used abortion pills to end pregnancies or helped others to do so.[177] The impact of the growing use of abortion pills was apparent in the reported abortion statistics: while the number of Northern Ireland residents travelling to access services in England had initially gradually risen across the 1970s and then stabilised during the 1980s and 1990s, numbers would now halve in the space of 15 years from 1,391 in 2002 to 724 in 2016.[178]

While concerns were expressed in the media regarding the public health risks of buying medicines online,[179] the authorities at first appeared to be turning a blind eye.[180] However, this came to a sudden end in 2016, with the conviction of a 19 year-old who had ended an early pregnancy using pills. Imposing a suspended sentence, the judge noted his discomfort at being asked to enforce a 150 year-old statute.[181] In a second case, a young man and woman were released with a caution in light of evidence of the impact of legal proceedings on the woman's fragile mental health.[182] A further prosecution was brought against a mother charged with procuring abortion pills to allow her teenage daughter to end a pregnancy conceived during an abusive relationship,[183] with the mother going on to seek judicial review of the decision to prosecute.[184]

These cases played a powerful role in increasing public awareness of and empathy with Northern Irish women experiencing unwanted pregnancies.

---

[174] See generally Hervey and Sheldon, 'Abortion by Telemedicine in Northern Ireland'; Sheldon, 'Empowerment and Privacy?'. For the 'Abortion Game', see this chapter, p. 193.

[175] Horgan interviewed by O'Neill.

[176] 'Northern Irish Women Ask to be Prosecuted for Taking Abortion Pills', *Guardian*, 23 May 2016; see generally Campbell and Clancy, 'From Grassroots to Government', 220.

[177] 'Over 100 Women Sign Abortion Change Protest Letter', *BBC News*, 11 March 2013.

[178] Collated from annual statistical volumes.

[179] E.g. 'Concern over Abortion Pills Bought Online', *BBC Newsbeat*, 11 February 2013.

[180] A freedom of information request submitted by Dr Goretti Horgan found that no woman had been convicted under Section 58 between 1 April 2007 and 31 March 2015 (on file with the authors).

[181] 'Northern Irish Woman Given Suspended Sentence over Self-Induced Abortion', *Guardian*, 4 April 2016.

[182] 'Man and Woman Cautioned over "Abortion Pills" in Northern Ireland', *Belfast Telegraph*, 19 January 2017.

[183] 'Pro-Choice Activists Picket Derry Police Station over Mother's Abortion Trial', *Guardian*, 15 July 2015.

[184] BPAS, *JR76 Case Report*.

The story of Sarah Ewart, a young woman given a diagnosis of anencephaly following her 20 week scan, would also have a very significant impact. Advised that there was no prospect of her child surviving and that she faced the likelihood of a 'very traumatic' birth, Ewart was also told that she could not have a legal termination within Northern Ireland until 'the baby has passed away'. She thus travelled to England to end her pregnancy, away from the support of family and friends but accompanied by Stephen Nolan, a well-known broadcaster, who reported her story.[185] Ewart emerged as a powerful advocate for legal reform,[186] and increasing numbers of other women also wrote to newspapers or called phone-ins to tell their own stories.[187]

Public opinion within Northern Ireland was now moving firmly in favour of treating abortion as a matter for medical regulation and not criminal law.[188] Simpson notes:

> [T]he sea shift has been incredible. You've even got a supportive press, as well. The big thing is that you've got more politicians speaking out, more doctors speaking out, importantly more women speaking out. We've got human rights organisations finally involved. And when I think about it, that's all happened in a relatively short space of time … Women sum up the situation perfectly. Women's voices, to me, are the strongest lobbyists and campaigners.[189]

With mainstream human rights organisations now actively engaged on the issue, the NIHRC would now bring a legal action arguing that the failure to permit abortion in cases of fatal fetal anomaly or pregnancies resulting from rape or incest was incompatible with human rights law. The case was won in the High Court, lost in the Court of Appeal, and then proceeded to the Supreme Court.[190]

'Bleak House'

While public opinion in Northern Ireland was changing, this was not reflected within Stormont. Religion has played a prominent role in political debates in the region, with a 'holy alliance' of evangelical Protestantism and fundamentalist Catholicism finding common ground in opposition to abortion,[191] and privately sympathetic Members of the Legislative Assembly (MLAs) tending to keep their heads down.[192] Moreover, the Good Friday Agreement had

---

[185] BBC Radio Five Live, 'Sarah Ewart's Abortion Journey from Northern Ireland'.
[186] 'Woman's Abortion "Ordeal" Considered by NI Health Officials', *BBC News*, 9 October 2013.
[187] Simpson interviewed by O'Neill.
[188] ARK, *Northern Ireland Life and Times Survey*, 2016; Gray, *Attitudes to Abortion in Northern Ireland*.
[189] Simpson interviewed by O'Neill.
[190] *In the Matter of an Application by the Northern Ireland Human Rights Commission for Judicial Review* [2015] NIQB 96; [2017] NICA 42; [2018] UKSC 27. See further this chapter, p. 220.
[191] Horgan, 'A Holy Alliance?'.
[192] Simpson interviewed by O'Neill; Horgan interviewed by O'Neill.

hardened lines between nationalist and republican parties, even as they softened in the wider public.[193] This left little space for the emergence of other types of politics, including feminism, and resulted in a 'policy impasse' even on less controversial issues.[194] Moreover, the Assembly was for many years a virtual male monopoly. While the proportion of female representatives would gradually grow, reaching almost one third by 2018,[195] the framing of the debate in terms of women's rights would struggle to gain the same traction as in Westminster.[196] Meanwhile, Precious Life appeared to have gained a significant influence, with Horgan recalling that Bernie Smyth

> had a pass to go in and out of the Assembly, as if she was a special advisor or something. Precious Life provided the secretariat of the All-Party Pro-Life Group. If you go onto the Precious Life Facebook page, you would see photographs of Bernie Smyth with every single political party, with members of every single party . . . they are genuflected to practically.[197]

Stormont has voted on abortion a number of times, on each occasion using the opportunity to send a strong signal to Westminster that the Abortion Act was not wanted. In 1984, a short-lived Assembly established to scrutinise decisions made by the Northern Ireland Office passed a first motion opposing the extension of the 'failed [Abortion] Act' by 74 votes to one.[198] The Reverend Ivan Foster MLA (DUP), the Presbyterian Minister who had proposed the motion, noted that he was 'much more at ease with the Bible in my hand and my finger waving in the air than perhaps I am with an Order Paper'.[199] Others explained that women sought abortion for 'facile reasons, for convenience or any other excuse',[200] with many girls who 'have been committing fornication' having abortions to get rid of the children 'conceived in lust'.[201]

The same message was repeated on further occasions. In 2000, claiming that the Abortion Act had introduced 'legalised carnage', Jim Wells (DUP) commended a similar motion as a means of sending 'a very clear, cross-

[193] ARK, *Northern Ireland Life and Times Survey 2018*; Hayward and McManus, 'Neither/Nor'; Gray, Horgan and Devine, 'Do Social Attitudes to Abortion Suggest Political Parties in Northern Ireland are Out of Step with their Supporters?'.

[194] Goretti Horgan notes: '[T]here is no anti-poverty strategy, there is no childcare strategy . . . [and] if they can't agree on things like that then what hope is there that they would agree on abortion?'. Horgan interviewed by O'Neill.

[195] House of Commons Library, *Women in Parliament*.

[196] See Chapter 3, pp. 87–88, 95–96, 103, on the growing dominance of the 'women's rights' frame at Westminster; Pierson and Bloomer, 'Anti-Abortion Myths in Political Discourse', on the conservative ideas of gender underpinning abortion debates in Stormont; and Chapter 7, p. 261, for signs of change.

[197] Horgan interviewed by O'Neill.

[198] NIA, *Official Report*, 29 February 1984, 81. The Assembly ran from 1982 to 1986 but was boycotted by nationalist parties, rendering it impossible to devolve any functions to it. See Bogdanor, *Devolution in the United Kingdom*, 104–05.

[199] NIA, *Official Report*, 29 February 1984, 78.

[200] Close in NIA, *Official Report*, 29 February 1984, 96.

[201] Thompson in NIA, *Official Report*, 29 February 1984, 89.

community message ... that the people of Northern Ireland totally resist any extension of the 1967 Abortion Act to this community'.[202] In 2007, Stormont passed a motion opposing an early draft of the guidelines introduced following the FPANI court case,[203] again taking the opportunity to send a 'clear message to Westminster' against extending the 1967 Act.[204] In 2013, it debated a measure designed to end the work of a Marie Stopes clinic, which had recently opened in Belfast in order to provide a small number of legal abortions and offer referrals to its British clinics, with speakers frequently prefacing their remarks by firmly stating their opposition to the Abortion Act.[205]

Nonetheless, with public opinion changing and women increasingly prepared to speak out about their experiences, the issue of legal reform was becoming increasingly difficult to ignore. With official guidance published in 2013 finally clarifying that abortion was not lawful for reason of fetal anomaly or where a pregnancy resulted from sexual assault, the Justice Minister, David Ford (Alliance), wrote to the Health Minister, Edwin Poots (DUP), to suggest that their two Departments work together on the issue. With no response forthcoming, the Justice Department proceeded alone to consult on whether abortion should be permitted in cases of fatal fetal anomaly and pregnancy resulting from sexual assault,[206] eventually recommending a narrowly drawn reform in just the former case.[207] Ford then twice asked the Executive to agree to the introduction of such a measure in the Assembly.[208] When this failed, backbench Alliance MLAs responded by tabling two amendments to a criminal justice Bill: the first was worded 'extremely cautiously and strictly' to permit abortion only in the presence of a fatal fetal anomaly where 'medical intervention cannot change the outcome',[209] and the second sought to permit abortion where pregnancy resulted from rape, incest or serious sexual assault.[210]

Notwithstanding the narrow framing of the proposed amendments, the ensuing debate was again haunted by the spectre of the Abortion Act. MLAs from all major parties prefaced their comments by noting their own personal

[202] NIA, *Official Report*, 20 June 2000, 103.
[203] Motion proposed by Mrs Iris Robinson (DUP) in NIA, *Official Report*, 22 October 2007.
[204] Wells in NIA, *Official Report*, 22 October 2007.
[205] Amendment 1, Criminal Justice Bill in NIA, *Official Report*, 12 March 2013; 'NI Assembly Fails in Bid to Change Abortion Law', *BBC News*, 12 March 2013.
[206] Department of Justice, *The Criminal Law on Abortion. Lethal Foetal Abnormality and Sexual Crime. A Consultation on Amending the Law by the Department of Justice*.
[207] Department of Justice, *The Criminal Law on Abortion. Lethal Foetal Abnormality and Sexual Crime. Response to the Consultation and Policy Proposals*.
[208] This summary of events is taken from Ford in NIA, *Official Report*, 10 February 2016, 111–13.
[209] Dickson in NIA, *Official Report*, 10 February 2016, 78(2)–79(1).
[210] The amendments to the Justice Bill (No 2) 2016 (NI) were tabled by Stewart Dickson and Trevor Lunn (fetal anomaly) and Anna Lo (sexual assault). NIA, *Official Report*, 10 February 2016.

opposition, and that of their party, to the 'obnoxious' Act.[211] Trevor Lunn, one of two MLAs to propose the fatal fetal anomaly amendment, agreed that no Member would want to see the Act extended to Northern Ireland.[212] Others complained that the amendments risked creating a 'further creeping' of the Act into Northern Ireland,[213] or indeed 'worse'.[214] David Ford was just one of many MLAs who felt obliged to refute 'the serious misrepresentation' that 'a modest amendment dealing solely with fatal foetal abnormality … [is] the 1967 Act by the back door'.[215]

While the Department of Justice had already consulted extensively on the proposed changes, each amendment was nonetheless rejected in favour of a further Commission of Inquiry. With 'a collective inability to agree legislation',[216] Mike Nesbitt (Ulster Unionist Party) argued that MLAs found themselves in a kind of *Bleak House* … in the Chancery Courts, waiting day after day after day after day for a decision that never comes'.[217] While the Commission went on to recommend the introduction of a tightly worded statutory exception to permit abortion in the presence of a fatal fetal anomaly,[218] any chance of further deliberation was lost with the collapse of power-sharing and suspension of the devolved institutions in January 2017.

Outside Stormont

As the period without functioning government in Stormont gradually extended, several significant events would shape the public debate. First, the Supreme Court handed down two important judgements. In June 2017, it ruled on the case of a 15 year-old Northern Irish girl, supported by her mother, who had terminated her pregnancy at a private clinic in Manchester at a total cost of around £900. She claimed that the failure to allow a UK citizen and resident of Northern Ireland access to abortion free of charge

---

[211]   McCarthy in NIA, *Official Report*, 10 February 2016, 94(1)–(2); see also Pengelly (DUP), 81(2); Ruane (Sinn Féin), 82(2); McKinney (Social Democratic and Labour Party), 89(1); Lyttle (Alliance), 107(2).

[212]   Lunn in NIA, *Official Report*, 10 February 2016, 119(2).

[213]   McCarthy in NIA, *Official Report*, 10 February 2016, 80(2); see also Kelly, 84(1).

[214]   McKinney in NIA, *Official Report*, 10 February 2016, 89(1); see further Kelly, 85(2).

[215]   Ford in NIA, *Official Report*, 10 February 2016, 115(2). For others who likewise felt obliged to deny that this is 'some sort of thin end of the wedge or back door to something worse, like the 1967 Act', see NIA, *Official Report*, 10 February 2016: Nesbitt, 92(1); B. McCrea, 105(1); Ruane 84(1); Lunn, 119(2).

[216]   McCallister in NIA, *Official Report*, 10 February 2016, 109(2). John McCallister was a member of the Ulster Unionist Party until early 2013, when he resigned and co-founded the short-lived NI21 party.

[217]   Nesbitt in NIA, *Official Report*, 10 February 2016, 91(2).

[218]   Department of Justice and Department of Health, *Report of the Working Group on Fatal Fetal Abnormality Healthcare and the Law on Termination of Pregnancy for Fatal Fetal Abnormality: Proposals to the Minister of Health and the Minister of Justice*, published in April 2018, following delay caused by the continuing absence of devolved institutions.

under the NHS in England was unlawful. A majority of a sharply divided Court dismissed the action, citing the general scheme that saw separate authorities in each of the four countries of the UK provide free health services to those usually resident there.[219] Nonetheless, widespread media coverage was given to the Court's *obiter* comments on the 'deeply unenviable position' of women in Northern Ireland and the 'embarrassment, difficulty, and uncertainty' faced in their 'urgent need to raise the necessary funds' to access abortion services.[220] The following year, judgement was handed down in the case begun some years earlier by the NIHRC. In formal legal terms, the Commission lost: it was found to lack the legal standing to bring the case in its own right and thus failed to obtain the declaration of incompatibility that it had sought.[221] However, a majority of the seven judges who heard the case accepted that Northern Irish abortion law breached human rights norms in failing to permit abortion in the presence of a fatal fetal anomaly or where a pregnancy resulted from rape or incest. These findings also gained widespread attention in the media and at Westminster. Given that the case had been lost on the issue of standing, Sarah Ewart then began – and eventually won – an action in her own name.[222]

Second, in early 2018, the monitoring committee of the Convention on the Elimination of All Forms of Discrimination Against Women (CEDAW) published a damning report finding that women in Northern Ireland were subject to grave and systematic rights violations when compelled either to carry a pregnancy to term or to travel outside the jurisdiction for a legal abortion. It made wide-ranging recommendations including, *inter alia*, the repeal of Sections 58 and 59 of the 1861 Act, the adoption of legislation permitting abortion on expanded grounds, and a moratorium on the application of current criminal laws concerning abortion.[223] Its intervention resulted from a joint request for an inquiry under CEDAW's Optional Protocol made by FPANI, the Northern Ireland Women's European Platform and AFC, supported by a detailed volume of evidence.[224]

Third, in April 2019, the House of Commons Women and Equalities Committee published a damning report on Northern Ireland's abortion law.[225] Evidence had been taken in Belfast, Derry and London, with

---

[219] *R (on the application of A and B)* v *Secretary of State for Health* [2017] UKSC 41.
[220] Per Lord Wilson, ibid. [6–7].
[221] *In the matter of an application by the Northern Ireland Human Rights Commission for Judicial Review* [2018] UKSC 27. See further Chapter 7, p. 251.
[222] *Ewart's Application* [2019] NIQB 88.
[223] CEDAW, *Inquiry Concerning the United Kingdom of Great Britain and Northern Ireland under Article 8 of the Optional Protocol to the Convention on the Elimination of All Forms of Discrimination against Women*, CEDAW/C/OP.8/GBR/1, 2018.
[224] The submission took over a year to prepare and ran to over 100 pages. See O'Rourke, 'Advocating Abortion Rights in Northern Ireland', 716, 725; O'Rourke, 'Bridging the Enforcement Gap?', 1.
[225] House of Commons Women and Equalities Committee, *Abortion Law in Northern Ireland*.

Committee members later to report that hearing women's testimonies had offered the most 'harrowing' experience of their time in Parliament.[226] The Committee made a number of recommendations, including the need for better information and guidance for women and healthcare professionals on certain aspects of the law; the need to introduce measures to improve access to services in the UK for marginalised women and girls, and that the UK Government should legislate as a matter of urgency to allow access to abortion within Northern Ireland in cases of fatal fetal anomaly.[227]

Finally, the campaign for reform in Northern Ireland was given a powerful boost by events south of the border. In May 2018, following a bitterly contested campaign, the Republic of Ireland voted by a large majority to repeal the Eighth Amendment of the Irish Constitution and to permit abortion on request within the first 12 weeks of pregnancy and, thereafter, in tightly limited circumstances.[228] In the British and Irish media, this move was generally lauded as humane and long overdue, with reports even in the conservative press often accompanied by images of smiling young people travelling home to vote, emphasising its modernising and progressive nature.[229] A rare critical commentary was offered in *The Spectator*, where Melanie McDonagh decried what she saw as partisan media coverage, concluding:

> The result of this vote is, of course, that the pressure is now on Northern Irish politicians to follow the Republic, an interesting inversion of the old unionist trope that Home Rule is Rome Rule; indeed Mary Lou McDonald, Sinn Fein leader, cheerfully suggested that women may be travelling from north to south to procure abortions. Rarely have I been so grateful for the robust and intransigent character of the DUP; hang on in there Arlene.[230]

Not only had the referendum result cast a powerful spotlight on the equally restrictive law in the North, it also had the important result of prompting Sinn Féin to radically revise its earlier policy and now to join calls for liberalisation of the law within 'a limited gestational period'. McDonald was now pictured with Sinn Féin's leader in Stormont, Michelle O'Neill, holding a sign proclaiming that the 'north is next'.[231] While the 'robust and intransigent character' of the DUP had hitherto indeed been of sustained importance to blocking even the most modest reform of the law, the party would now find itself increasingly politically isolated.

---

[226] See e.g. Ford in *Hansard*, HC, 9 July 2019, vol. 663, col. 201.

[227] House of Commons Women and Equalities Committee, *Abortion Law in Northern Ireland*, chapter 10.

[228] Health (Regulation of Termination of Pregnancy) Act 2018. See generally de Londras, '"A Hope Raised and then Defeated"?', 33–50, for a critical discussion.

[229] E.g. 'Is Ireland Heading for a Yes Vote?', *Daily Mail*, 25 May 2018.

[230] Referring to Arlene Foster, DUP leader. 'What Really Happened in Ireland's Abortion Referendum', *Spectator Blogs*, 26 May 2018.

[231] 'Sinn Féin Votes to Change Abortion Policy', *BBC News NI*, 16 June 2018.

The resounding victory of the 'Yes' side in the Irish referendum also had one further important effect: it highlighted the possibility of achieving reform that went far beyond the restrictive regulatory framework of the Abortion Act. With the human rights frame now dominant and campaigners elsewhere in the UK fighting for decriminalisation of abortion, any call for the extension of the Act appeared long forgotten. Campaigners coalesced powerfully behind the demand for decriminalisation of abortion in Northern Ireland, adopting the hashtags #NowforNI, #theNorthIsNow and #theNorthIsNext. As we will see in the next chapter, with no end in sight to the suspension of the Northern Ireland Assembly, the chorus of condemnation of human rights abuses becoming louder, and online access to abortion pills having let the 'genie ... out of the bottle',[232] it would become ever harder for the Westminster Government to continue its long-standing strategy of studied inaction.

Conclusion

The story of the Abortion Act is inextricably intertwined with that of Northern Ireland. The Act has offered a legal basis for over 60,000 women from the region to end unwanted pregnancies safely, operating as an important 'safety valve' that reduced maternal mortality and morbidity and thereby decreased pressure for reform. The Act was also the major focus of decades of campaigning within Northern Ireland, with repeated calls for its extension countered by its use as a cautionary tale against even the most limited legal reforms. So too has Northern Ireland had an important impact on the Abortion Act. While bitterly complaining about any attempts on the part of Westminster to interfere in Northern Ireland's abortion law, the region's MPs have been an ongoing, vocal presence in parliamentary debates regarding the Abortion Act and a consistent bloc in votes in favour of restrictive amendments to it and against liberalising reform. Moreover, while officially denied, it appears that the inclusion of an amendment seeking to extend the Act to Northern Ireland in 2008 was the reason for the failure of a wider raft of liberalising amendments to reach a vote. However, after decades of struggle, during which Westminster had managed to avoid addressing the issue, the stage was now set for a new and decisive battle, and the changes now demanded of Northern Ireland's abortion law would be far more radical than a simple extension of the Abortion Act.

[232] Ann Furedi interviewed by Jane O'Neill, 23 August 2017.

7

The Parliamentary Battle for Modernising Reform

> My aim is simple ... an Act of Parliament that is fit for now, not for 51 years ago, and certainly not for 157 years ago.[1]

> Time and medical technology have moved on, and so has the mood of the nation.[2]

The year 1990 had offered a tipping point in the biography of the Abortion Act. With a liberal interpretation of its terms widespread in practice, a definitive vote had now demonstrated Parliament's broad support for it. The period to follow would be marked by a significant hiatus in Parliamentary activity, ending only in the mid-2000s as the Human Fertilisation and Embryology Act returned to Parliament, again offering a vehicle for abortion law amendments. However, when the battle for restrictive reform began to regain some traction, it would look very different. Further, over time, Pro-Life campaigners would gradually be forced into a grudging defence of the Abortion Act, as the most powerful calls for root-and-branch reform increasingly came from Pro-Choice advocates. A striking amount of common ground would now be shared in the framing of the arguments made by the two sides of the debate: indeed, denuded of broader context, it is impossible to know whether the two short epigraphs at the beginning of this chapter form part of a wider argument for restrictive or liberalising reform. Each side would now argue that the ageing Abortion Act was not fit for purpose, requiring updating in light of changing political, medical and social norms. Each would speak a language of civil liberties and the empowerment of women, and each would claim to be backed by scientific fact and medical authority. Where the two sides divided was in their factual beliefs: more than ever, the gulf between them would be presented not as a moral but rather an empirical one, with the battle for modernisation reflecting competing versions of reality.

---

[1] Diana Johnson in *Hansard*, House of Commons (HC), 23 October 2018, vol. 648, col. 142.
[2] Nadine Dorries in *Hansard*, HC, 31 October 2006, vol. 451, col. 156.

A Hiatus in Parliament

For many years, Pro-Life MPs had dominated the parliamentary agenda, confident of achieving significant restrictive reform of the Abortion Act if only they were allowed a meaningful vote. However, in 1990, when finally given such an opportunity, Parliament had used it largely to confirm the status quo. Anti-abortion MPs now retreated to lick their wounds. From 1987 to 1989, 13 proposals for restrictive reform measures had been made; from 1990 to 1993, there were none. Moreover, no future MP was now likely to squander the once-in-a-lifetime opportunity to bring a Ballot Bill on attempting restrictive abortion law reform. When a trickle of restrictive reform proposals began again, they were Presentation or Ten Minute Rule Bills, which might test parliamentary opinion and highlight issues of concern but enjoyed no real prospect of passing into law.[3]

This hiatus period would also mark a clear break between the old and new styles of reform strategy, with sponsors of further restrictive measures tending largely to follow in the footsteps of David Alton rather than those of John Corrie. Like Alton, they would be distinguished by a strong role for their Christian faith in driving their parliamentary work but would carefully make the case for reform in secular terms. Like Alton, they would eschew a language of personal responsibility and family values in favour of one of social justice, discrimination, civil liberties, and the protection and empowerment of women. Like Alton, they would speak a language of modernisation and scientific progress, offering a vision of science that melded clinical facts with moral concepts and common-sense intuition.[4] They would, however, generally be distinguished from Alton in both gender and party. In the early 1970s, Jo Richardson had been derided for suggesting that the issue of abortion was one on which women might claim special authority; now female voices would dominate both sides of the parliamentary debate, with Tory women taking up leadership of the case for restrictive reform.[5]

Future sponsors of restrictive reform measures would also tend to follow Alton in avoiding comprehensive assaults on the Abortion Act in favour of narrowly targeted measures that worked within its broad framework. Just two restrictive reform measures tabled during this hiatus period – proposed by the staunch anti-abortion advocate and Catholic MP David Amess and the Anglican Laurence Robertson (both Con) – proposed radical change to the grounds for abortion. Parliament's response illustrated how much it had tired

---

[3] See Appendix 2. One liberalising reform proposal was also discussed in this period: Harry Cohen's Clinic Access Bill, see Chapter 4, p. 121.

[4] See Lowe and Page, 'Rights-Based Claims Made by UK Anti-abortion Activists', 133–44, for similar observations regarding the arguments made by anti-abortion activists.

[5] See further Chapter 3.

of the issue and this approach to it.[6] A list of up to 11 supporters can be supplied with a Bill, with names typically selected carefully to demonstrate breadth of support. The Robertson Bill, which sought to restrict abortion to cases where a woman's life was at risk or where conception resulted from rape, was co-sponsored by four late middle-aged, white, male, socially conservative, Christian, Tory MPs representing English constituencies.[7] Parliament had moved on.

The other Bills introduced over this period adopted what would now become the dominant approach, focusing on a narrow issue that might hope to command mainstream support. David Amess also tabled a Bill that aimed to prohibit sex selection through either abortion or pre-implantation genetic diagnosis, arguing that 'Mother Nature' was best left 'to take her own course'.[8] The Bill was opposed by the Labour MP Glenda Jackson on the basis that abortion for reason of sex alone was already illegal and that the recently formed Human Fertilisation and Embryology Authority should be allowed to complete an ongoing consultation on pre-implantation genetic diagnosis.[9] The Bill was narrowly defeated at its first reading.[10] In the House of Lords, Lord Brentford (a hereditary peer and president of the leading Anglican evangelical organisation, the Church Society) proposed the prohibition of abortion on the basis of a diagnosis of Down's syndrome,[11] and Bernard Braine put forward a Bill to ban 'partial-birth abortion', a practice not used in the UK but that had attracted particular controversy in the USA.[12] Each passed its first reading without division, as is the convention in the House of Lords, then progressed no further.

Braine's Bill was then taken up by the Catholic Conservative MP and joint secretary of the Pro-Life APPG, Elizabeth Peacock. With the issue of abortion law reform frequently provoking initiatives that tested the parliamentary rule book, Peacock discovered a creative way to win time for her Bill.[13] Slots for Ten Minute Rule Bills were allocated to those MPs who arrived first at the Public Bill Office on a given morning. However, Peacock felt it unreasonable to have to 'spend the night with three bearded Labour MPs' camping outside the Office overnight. Instead, she left a teddy bear, garlanded with the message

---

[6] Abortion (Amendment) Bill in *Hansard*, HC, 31 January 1997, vol. 289, col. 647; Prohibition of Abortion (England and Wales) Bill in *Hansard*, HC, 21 October 2005, vol. 437, col. 1161.

[7] Laurence Robertson, David Amess, Julian Brazier and Sir Nicholas Winterton (the husband of Ann Winterton MP, on whom see further this chapter, pp. 232–34).

[8] Children (Prohibition of Sex Selection) Bill in *Hansard*, HC, 23 February 1993, vol. 219, cols 769–70.

[9] *Hansard*, HC, 23 February 1993, vol. 219, col. 770.

[10] Ayes 87; Noes 106.

[11] Termination of Pregnancy (Restriction) Bill [H.L.] in *Hansard*, House of Lords (HL), 14 May 1996, vol. 572, col. 393.

[12] Partial-Birth Abortion (Prohibition) Bill [H.L.] in *Hansard*, HL, 13 December 1995, vol. 567, col. 1279. See generally Dubow, *Ourselves Unborn*, 169–83.

[13] Peacock Partial-Birth Abortion Bill 1996.

'I am Elizabeth Peacock's research assistant queueing for a bill for LIFE'.[14] According to one MP who magnanimously ceded a place in the queue to the bear, the incident accelerated reform to a 'less open but more civilised allocation of slots'.[15] In presenting her Bill, Peacock quoted Dr Bernard Nathanson, narrator of *The Silent Scream*, to attack this 'obsolete' and 'destructive operation', which she described in graphic detail.[16] She was opposed by Ann Clwyd (Lab), who cited the BMA and the RCOG to argue that methods of abortion must remain a matter of clinical judgement, noted that the procedure was not used in the UK, with the debate thus a waste of parliamentary time, and criticised Peacock's use of '[e]motive, grisly descriptions of abortion procedures' as a 'tactic' designed to 'shock and repulse' and thus to attract support for further legislation to limit the availability of legal abortion.[17]

This would now become the dominant pattern: a female Tory MP would propose a narrowly focused reform measure that it was hoped would gain widespread support, justify it with reference to medical fact, citing the support of named or unnamed individual doctors, and either not mention her Christian faith or note it merely to explain its irrelevance to her stance. Opposition would be led by a female Labour MP who would rail against the measure, identifying it as a prelude to a broader attack on women's abortion rights, locate the proposal within a general, religiously grounded opposition to abortion, and cite the opposition of professional medical bodies. Each side would claim to represent the interests of women and each would claim to be supported by science. Dispute regarding values and principles would be increasingly superseded by contested claims regarding empirical reality, with accusations flying that the other side was ignoring or concealing facts that did not support its ideological position.

With the professional medical bodies now having swung firmly in support of the Abortion Act, the two sides were not evenly situated in these disputes. In opposing the authoritative pronouncements of the professional medical bodies, Pro-Life advocates would find themselves either reliant on dissident medical voices or needing to gather their own evidence.[18] The Catholic Co-chair of the Pro-Life APPG, Claire Curtis-Thomas (Lab), marked the 35th anniversary of the Abortion Act with an Early Day Motion noting an association between abortion and breast cancer and calling for further research, as 'women who have the right to choose also have the right to know what they

---

[14] Flynn, *How to Be an MP*, 201.

[15] Ibid.

[16] Peacock in *Hansard*, HC, 4 December 1996, vol. 286, cols 1042–43. See Chapter 4, pp. 146–47, on *The Silent Scream*.

[17] Clwyd in *Hansard*, HC, 4 December 1996, vol. 286, cols 1043–44. The Bill passed its first reading without a vote but failed at its second reading.

[18] See further Chapter 4, pp. 123–33.

are choosing'.[19] She sent a survey to doctors to gather her own evidence of the association, a move condemned by the charity Breast Cancer Care as implying that women's 'life choices and behaviours could be to blame for their illness', and by scientists concerned with her 'haphazard' approach to research.[20] This was a precursor to the far more significant dispute shortly to follow in the first general parliamentary review of abortion law since the early 1970s. Disagreement over scientific fact would now be at the centre of disputes, and it would be powerfully amplified by the differences in the style, approach and personality of the two major protagonists in the debate.

The Human Fertilisation and Embryology Act Returns

As the announcement of plans to update the Human Fertilisation and Embryology Act 1990 ended the hiatus in parliamentary disputes over the Abortion Act, two MPs were poised to take a significant role in the ensuing fight. The first was Evan Harris, a doctor, Liberal Party spokesperson on science, a member of the BMA's National Council, a Humanist, author of a 'secularist manifesto', and secretary of the Pro-Choice and Sexual Health APPG.[21] Harris's vocal advocacy for the liberalisation of laws regarding abortion, embryo research and assisted dying would earn him death threats and the soubriquet 'Dr Death' from the *Daily Mail*.[22] Above all, for leading scientists, Harris was Parliament's most 'passionate advocate of evidence-based policy' and 'voice for rationality and evidence', standing 'head and shoulders above all other MPs for wit and intellectual fluency on all science issues'.[23]

The contrast with his opponent could scarcely have been more marked. The flamboyant MP Nadine Dorries (Con) would now become the public face of the Pro-Life movement within Parliament.[24] While the *Daily Mail* dismissed Harris as a 'nerd',[25] *The Guardian* derided Dorries as a 'highly energetic advocate of bad science', with a casual relationship to the truth and a predilection for conspiracy theories.[26] Like Harris, Dorries had trained as a health-care professional, dating her passionate commitment to abortion law reform

---

[19] Early Day Motion (EDM) 1826, '35th Anniversary of the Abortion Act 1967', 28 October 2002, signed by 11 other MPs.

[20] 'MPs Launch Abortion Cancer Probe', *BBC News*, 22 January 2004.

[21] 'A Secularist Manifesto', *Guardian*, 18 September 2018.

[22] 'Anti-Abortionists Bombard MP with Hate Mail and Death Threats', *Independent*, 20 May 2006; 'Meet Dr Death, the Lib Dem MP Evan Harris Who Backs Embryo Experiments, Euthanasia and Freer Abortions', *Daily Mail*, 31 October 2007.

[23] See Dr Chris Tyler, Professor David Nutt, Dr Robin Lovell-Badge and Dr Ben Goldacre quoted in Science Media Centre, 'Reaction to Evan Harris Losing His Parliamentary Seat'.

[24] 'The End of Choice?', *Guardian*, 19 May 2008.

[25] 'Meet Dr Death', *Daily Mail*, 31 October 2007.

[26] 'Nadine Dorries vs. Science', *Guardian*, 10 November 2010, citing her own admission that her blog was '70% fiction'.

to an experience of a 'botched abortion' whilst working as a nurse and knowing 'when I stood with that little boy in my arms that one day I would have the opportunity to defend babies such as him'.[27] The similarities ended there. While Dorries gained ministerial roles in Boris Johnson's Government, launching a 'war on Woke' as Culture Secretary,[28] she had previously enjoyed a rocky relationship with her party. She famously described a previous Prime Minister and his Chancellor as 'two arrogant posh boys ... who don't know the price of milk',[29] and her appearance on a celebrity TV show – which she claimed would allow her to engage directly with voters on issues such as abortion – gained her a high public profile and the popular soubriquet 'Mad Nad' and temporarily lost her the Tory whip.[30] Dorries is a member of the Cornerstone Group of Tory MPs dedicated to 'traditional values' of 'faith, flag and family'.[31] Whilst describing herself as 'pro-choice' and no 'religious fundamentalist',[32] she has focused heavily on Christian concerns in her parliamentary work, telling *The War Cry* that

> [m]y faith constantly gives me my reference point. It keeps me grounded. I am not an MP for any reason other than because God wants me to be. There is nothing I did that got me here; it is what God did. There is nothing amazing or special about me, I am just a conduit for God to use.[33]

The Science and Technology Committee Report

With disagreement over abortion now focusing increasingly on disputed empirical facts, a robust account of the science had become key to influencing voting on further reform of the Abortion Act. Having failed to persuade Parliament to establish a joint committee of the Houses of Commons and Lords to investigate,[34] the House of Commons Science and Technology Committee (STC) thus launched its own review of the 'scientific, medical and social changes' regarding abortion since 1967.[35]

---

[27] *Hansard*, HC, 20 May 2008, vol. 476, col. 259.

[28] '"Crackpot" Crackdown: New Culture Secretary Nadine Dorries Will Stop Woke Art Projects Being Funded by Taxpayers', *Sun*, 16 September 2001.

[29] 'MP Dorries Calls PM and Chancellor "Arrogant Posh Boys"', *BBC News*, 23 April 2012. The 'posh boys' were David Cameron and George Osborne.

[30] MacLeod, '82% Aware of Mad Nad'; 'Nadine Dorries Suspended by Conservative Party in Row over I'm a Celebrity Appearance', *Independent*, 6 November 2012.

[31] Cornerstone Group, 'About Us'. See further Chapter 8, pp. 274–75.

[32] Dorries in *Hansard*, HC, 20 May 2008, vol. 476, col. 259; HC, 7 September 2011, vol. 532, col. 364.

[33] Bovey, 'MP Calls for Lower Abortion Time Limit', 4–5.

[34] House of Commons Science and Technology Committee (STC), *Human Reproductive Technologies and the Law: Fifth Report of Session 2004–5*, para. 308.

[35] House of Commons STC, *Scientific Developments Relating to the Abortion Act 1967: Twelfth Report of Session 2006–7*, vol. 1, para. 1.

The membership of a Select Committee is selected to be representative of the House of Commons. The STC included Harris (whose general enthusiasm for all matters scientific was evidenced by a lengthy membership during which he rarely missed a meeting, regardless of the specific issue considered) and Dorries (who joined in the parliamentary session that the STC was due to investigate abortion and attended virtually no meetings on any of the other issues considered during her membership).[36] Nonetheless, having agreed a remit that explicitly excluded moral issues and focused on establishing scientific fact, there must have been hopes that the STC might reach unanimous conclusions. Evidence was taken from a 'balanced panel of campaign groups' merely to establish what bodies of scientific evidence were important to the moral debate.[37] While accusations of bias were nonetheless made regarding the resulting selection of issues for further consideration, these at least came from both sides.[38] The STC adopted rigorous scientific conventions regarding the evaluation of evidence and was advised by two of the UK's most senior doctors.[39] Most importantly, its eventual report refrained from recommending how MPs should vote, recognising that the science was only one of the factors to be considered.[40]

However, while the STC remained carefully within this remit, its findings had undeniable implications for the moral and political debate. 4D fetal imaging technology was found to be useful for identifying anatomical abnormalities but to provide no new scientific insights of relevance to abortion.[41] No grounds were identified for believing that fetal viability occurred at an earlier gestational age than in 1990, to suggest that a fetus might consciously feel pain or to contradict the RCOG guidance that abortion was a very safe procedure.[42] The requirement for two doctors' signatures was found to have no apparent benefit with regard to first trimester abortions, and indeed was determined potentially to have the negative impact of contributing to delay.[43] It was also concluded that nurses could safely certify abortions, prescribe the medicines used in an early medical abortion and carry out early surgical procedures,[44]

---

[36] See minutes of meetings at Commons Select Committee, 'Formal Minutes – Science and Technology Committee (Commons)'.

[37] STC, *Scientific Developments*, vol. 1, paras 2–4.

[38] House of Commons STC, *Scientific Developments Relating to the Abortion Act 1967: Twelfth Report of Session 2006–7*, vol. 2. Abortion Rights, Ev 212, suggested that the selection of issues was initiated in a climate dominated by 'the misleading narrative of an increasingly vocal anti-abortion lobby'; Comment on Reproductive Ethics (CORE), Ev 76, para. 1.3, argued that it followed the agenda of 'the Abortion Law Reform lobby'.

[39] Professor Allan Templeton FMedSci, former President of the RCOG, and Professor Malcolm Chiswick FRCP, former President of the British Association of Perinatal Medicine.

[40] STC, *Scientific Developments*, vol. 1, para. 3.

[41] Ibid., paras 61–63.

[42] Ibid., paras 35, 59, 140, 150, 154.

[43] Ibid., para. 99.

[44] Ibid., para. 108.

and, subject to proper arrangements being made for follow-up, that permitting home use of misoprostol would be safe.[45]

The Catholic Labour MP and Pro-Life APPG and long-standing STC member Robert Flello nonetheless joined the majority in agreeing on the text of the final STC report, suggesting the possibility of separating moral belief from findings of scientific fact. Just one STC member voted against: Bob Spink, another Conservative MP with a colourful history and turbulent relationship with his party.[46] While Nadine Dorries did not vote on the report, she joined Spink in tabling an alternative to it. Their minority report professed to work within the STC's agreed remit, generally avoiding explicit normative claims. However, in offering a detailed critique of the STC's rigour and objectivity and a systematic rebuttal of its findings, it necessarily worked against the grain of established scientific method and dominant medical orthodoxy. *The Guardian*'s science writer and evidence-based medicine expert Ben Goldacre damned it as 'a rollercoaster ride of pseudoscience and dubious data', offering a stark contrast with the approved report, which was a 'rigorous' and 'transparent' 'masterclass in spotting fallacious science'. He concluded that the two differed not in moral values but 'in something much more simple: the quality of the science, the selectivity of the quoting, and the quality of the referencing'.[47]

The two reports also differed in a range of more subtle ways that would set the tone for subsequent debate of the Abortion Act. First, the minority report relies upon a morally inflected understanding of medical advance, echoing the submissions of several anti-abortion organisations who had claimed that it was 'unsustainable' to divorce consideration of medical facts from ethics, with abortion always a matter of 'serious moral concern'.[48] It offers a vision of science infused with common-sense intuition and necessarily intertwined with ethical norms and concepts: for example, it recommends that modern medicine 'must acknowledge and respect an emerging personhood in the womb'.[49]

Second, the minority report is pervaded by suspicion of medical hierarchies, suggesting the need for more democratic, populist modes of knowledge production. The STC's two medical advisers – one of them a former President of the RCOG – were deemed 'not neutral', having 'vested interests

---

[45] Ibid., para. 123.

[46] Spink would later defect, first to the UK Independence Party (UKIP) and then to sit as an Independent, before being convicted of electoral fraud: 'Bob Spink Guilty: Former Tory and UKIP MP Handed Six-Months Suspended Jail Sentence for Tricking Elderly People', *Independent*, 5 January 2018.

[47] 'Oooooh I'm in the Minority Report!', *Guardian*, 31 October 2007; 'Minority Out of Control', *Guardian*, 3 November 2007.

[48] STC, *Scientific Developments*, vol. 2: CORE, Ev 76, para. 1.4; CMF, Ev 172, para. 3; LCF, Ev 177; Maranatha Community, Ev 193; Life, Ev 220; ProLife Alliance, Ev 72, para. 1.2. Cf the submission from SPUC, welcoming the evidence-based approach, Ev 201, paras 1–2.

[49] STC, *Scientific Developments*, vol. 1, 75. The text of the minority report was read into the STC's minutes for 29 October 2007, see 71–83 in the same volume.

and minds made up on some of the key issues'.[50] The decision to request declarations of conflicts of interest was deemed an 'unprecedented' and disreputable attempt to undermine witnesses.[51] It nonetheless acknowledged that the written evidence submitted by 'specific organisations and individuals' was shaped by 'ideological and financial interests', with particular criticism reserved for the RCOG, which was 'in bed together' with Pro-Choice groups and had systematically ignored studies that did not support 'a pro-choice agenda'. The RCOG and the RCN were criticised as out of touch with their 'grassroots members', who should have been consulted on the empirical evidence to be presented, implying that clinical facts are to be determined democratically.[52] Likewise, it suggested that the RCOG clinical guidelines for abortion care should be reviewed following consultation that included 'both sides of the argument' and evidence from a 'more even balance of pro-choice and pro-life advisors'.[53]

The STC's selection of oral witnesses was also attacked as flawed and partial. The minority report offered its own categorisation of those who had given written evidence into two camps – 'pro-restriction' or 'pro-liberalisation' – suggesting that as submissions of written evidence were essentially evenly divided between the two, the STC should thus have chosen an equal number of oral witnesses from each. The result of this highly unorthodox approach – whereby a Select Committee's oral witness list would be determined by counting and categorising submissions of written evidence – would have been the inclusion of more 'pro-restriction' witnesses to counterbalance the inclusion of major abortion service providers and professional medical bodies, all of whom were categorised as 'pro-liberalisation'.[54]

Finally, the minority report cited individual medical researchers to raise multiple points of substantive disagreement with the evidence base set out in professional medical bodies' guidelines.[55] Where there was disagreement between experts regarding fetal sentience and viability, it was argued that the fetus should be given 'the benefit of the doubt'. Moreover, where dissident medical voices raised concerns, women had a 'right to know' conflicting expert views about fetal development and the health risks associated with abortion, and they should be empowered through the provision of more information and greater time to make a fully informed choice.[56]

---

[50] Ibid., 71–73.

[51] Ibid., 73. This request followed the receipt of written submissions from doctors who did not practise in relevant areas of medicine but were associated with organisations with 'strong views on abortion': see paras 5–10 in the same volume.

[52] Ibid., 73–78.

[53] Ibid., 73–78.

[54] Ibid., 72, including MSI, the Family Planning Association, Antenatal Results and Choices, the Faculty of Sexual and Reproductive Health, the British Association of Perinatal Medicine, the BMA and the RCN.

[55] In particular Anand on fetal sentience, Coleman on mental health, and Brind on the link with breast cancer; see STC, *Scientific Developments*, vol. 1, 81–82.

[56] Ibid., 80–81.

The Parliamentary Debates

These disputes in the STC would set the tone for parliamentary debate in the decade to follow. Most immediately, two Ten Minute Rule Bills were tabled during the session in which the Committee was taking evidence.[57] The Bills were proposed by Dorries and Ann Winterton (Conservative Vice-Chair of the Pro-Life APPG and also an MP who had enjoyed a turbulent relationship with her party, being twice sacked from party roles for telling racist jokes).[58] Each Bill focused on women's 'right to know',[59] proposing the mandatory provision of counselling and information to women contemplating abortion and an obligatory 'cooling-off' period between the request for an abortion and its performance (7 days for Winterton, 10 for Dorries). These measures reflected a deep suspicion of an 'abortion industry', where women were rushed into decisions by 'a hardcore group of doctors who have built their careers on the acceptance of abortion'.[60] The two MPs explained that they aimed to empower a woman to make 'calm and well-thought-through decisions',[61] avoiding the situation where she might have 'a pregnancy test on Monday, a scan on Tuesday and the abortion on Wednesday, all with no one asking her if she is sure'.[62]

Each Bill also included an additional measure. For Winterton, this was the separation of physical and mental health indications on abortion certification forms, with the 'catch-all ground of risk of injury to the physical or mental health' serving to obscure the reasons for abortion, as the eugenicist 'abortion lobby' deliberately set out to 'destroy any evidence that does not fit its aims'.[63] Dorries proposed the reduction of the upper time limit for most abortions to 21 weeks, rejecting viability as the key reference point in favour of an intuitive, morally infused understanding of scientific advance: she explained that 'some doctors' believed a fetus to be sentient from 18 weeks and, with images reproduced in newspapers 'showing the smiles, the thumb-sucking and the kicking', it was 'hard to disagree'.[64] When issues of viability, fetal sentience and the use of feticide (which the RCOG recommended from 20 weeks) were considered together, the evidence for a modernisation of the law was said to be

---

[57] Dorries, Termination of Pregnancy Bill 2006; Winterton, Termination of Pregnancy (Counselling and Miscellaneous Provisions) Bill 2007.

[58] 'How a Racist Joke Became no Laughing Matter for Ann Winterton', *Guardian*, 2 May 2002; 'Howard Sacks MP for her Cockle-Picker Joke', *Telegraph*, 26 February 2004; and 'MP Ann in "White Country" Storm', *Manchester Evening News*, 27 September 2005, reporting outrage after a third comment that Britain is 'thankfully a predominantly white, Christian country'.

[59] Dorries in *Hansard*, HC, 31 October 2006, vol. 451, cols 157; Winterton, HC, 5 June 2007, vol. 461, col. 139.

[60] Winterton in *Hansard*, HC, 5 June 2007, vol. 461, col. 139.

[61] Dorries in *Hansard*, HC, 31 October 2006, vol. 451, cols 155, 157.

[62] Winterton in *Hansard*, HC, 5 June 2007, vol. 461, col. 138.

[63] Winterton in *Hansard*, HC, 5 June 2007, vol. 461, cols 138–39: '[T]he abortion-on-demand lobby was established by people like Margaret Sanger – an elitist who quite openly called for abortion for the poor, for people who had been in prison, and for any of those she regarded as second-class citizens.'

[64] Dorries in *Hansard*, HC, 31 October 2006, vol. 451, cols 155–57.

'overwhelming and compelling': it was '2006 – not 1967 and not 1990. Time and medical technology have moved on, and so has the mood of the nation.'[65]

Opposition was again led by female Labour MPs, who argued that the Bills were opposed by professional medical bodies and formed part of a wider campaign 'fuelled and funded by religious conservatives from Washington to Rome' to allow some individuals the right to impose 'their morality on others, risking the physical and mental health of thousands of women'.[66] The Bills would erect barriers and create delay, prolonging anguish in a context where most women have already reached a decision before reaching an abortion clinic.[67] While counselling was important for those who wanted it, it should be non-directed and non-compulsory.[68] Each Bill failed by a solid margin. However, Dorries was undeterred, going on to table a Presentation Bill that proposed an upper time limit of 20 weeks.[69]

With these measures, Winterton and Dorries no doubt hoped to build momentum for restrictive measures when the Human Fertilisation and Embryology Act returned to Parliament. Campaigners now sensed the possibility of 'huge changes in the law',[70] with *The Guardian* predicting 'the greatest challenge to women's abortion rights in nearly 20 years'.[71] On one side, armed with the findings of the STC, Evan Harris drew up a wide-ranging raft of liberalising amendments. These were framed as evidence-driven measures to modernise an outdated law: abortion would be made lawful on request, subject only to the certification of one doctor that a pregnancy had not exceeded 24 weeks; it might be lawfully performed by nurses and midwives and in primary care facilities; and the Abortion Act would be extended to Northern Ireland.[72] Outside Parliament, Harris was strongly supported by professional medical bodies and the Voice for Choice coalition, which included a range of service providers, civil society organisations and Abortion Rights (which had formed in 2003 through the merger of NAC and ALRA, continuing the former's close relationship with the trade unions).

On the other side, the Alive and Kicking coalition of anti-abortion and Christian organisations was established.[73] Its members were painfully aware that the odds were now stacked against them. Peter Saunders (Christian

---

[65] Dorries in *Hansard*, HC, 31 October 2006, vol. 451, col. 156.

[66] Moffatt in *Hansard*, HC, 5 June 2007, vol. 461, col. 140; McCafferty, 31 October 2006, vol. 451, cols 157–59.

[67] Moffatt in *Hansard*, HC, 5 June 2007, vol. 461, col. 140.

[68] McCafferty in *Hansard*, HC, 31 October 2006, vol. 451, col. 159.

[69] Winterton: Ayes 107; Noes 182. Dorries: Ayes 108; Noes 187. Termination of Pregnancy Bill in *Hansard*, HC, 18 December 2006, vol. 454, col. 1172.

[70] Peter Saunders interviewed by Jane O'Neill, 9 November 2017.

[71] 'The End of Choice?', *Guardian*, 19 May 2008.

[72] For a summary, see Sheldon, 'A Missed Opportunity to Reform an Outdated Piece of Legislation'.

[73] Including CARE, the Christian Medical Fellowship, CORE, Evangelical Alliance, Guild of Catholic Doctors, Lawyers' Christian Fellowship, Life, Maranatha, ProLife Alliance, Real Choice and Student Life Net; see Christian Concern, 'Targeted Abortion Campaign Launched'.

Medical Fellowship) reflects that early abortion is largely accepted with only a 'very small minority' of British people believing that 'life begins at conception' and with most taking a gradualist moral view, which apportions different value to the unborn at different gestations.[74] At the same time, he saw grounds for cautious optimism regarding the possibility of restricting abortion at later gestations given that newspapers were full of '4D ultrasounds showing babies moving in the womb', stories of late abortion for disability, 'babies surviving after botched abortions', and neonates surviving at 23 and 24 weeks' gestation.[75] The coalition was thus necessarily strategic: 'If you are fighting a war you have got to think in terms of this valley, this mountain, this ridge, this coast, this country', being realistic about what policy changes are 'achievable in a multi-faith society'.[76] It called for a substantial reduction in the upper time limit, an end to 'discriminatory abortion up until birth for disabled babies', and fully informed consent for women contemplating abortion.[77] Whilst modest compared to the aims of earlier campaigns, even these proposals were now deemed too risky by some. Both SPUC and Right to Life (a group led by Phyllis Bowman, which had splintered from SPUC in 1999) were notable absences within the Coalition's membership. Jack Scarisbrick (Life) recalls that SPUC had opposed the attempt to 'try and negotiate some reform that is worth having' on the basis that this might bring even greater deregulation of early abortions.[78]

In 2007, the long and complex Bill designed to update the Human Fertilisation and Embryology Act 1990 finally arrived in Parliament. Harris's group decided to delay tabling liberalising amendments to it so as to focus first on defeating restrictive ones, which were to be considered at its Committee stage. In particular, Pro-Choice MPs were concerned about the 'classic tactic' whereby 'a range of proposals are put forward, some extreme, others apparently less so, and suddenly a vote for a reduction to 20 weeks looks like a brilliant, liberal solution'.[79] Moreover, the range of proposals was potentially confusing for MPs unused to voting without whips and often unwilling to engage with a highly emotive issue, which can generate some very 'nasty letters'.[80] When Emily Thornberry MP (Lab) was given a list of 'generally pro-choice, but soft pro-choice' people to speak with, she reported being 'very alarmed by how soft' they turned out to be.[81]

The most significant restrictive amendment was tabled by Nadine Dorries, who sought a reduction of the upper time limit for abortion to 20 weeks, with

[74] Saunders interviewed by O'Neill.
[75] Ibid.
[76] Ibid.
[77] Christian Concern, 'Targeted Abortion Campaign Launched'.
[78] Cited in 'I Am a Rather Unsubtle Sort of Chap', *Catholic Herald*, 21 December 2007.
[79] Anne Quesney (MSI) in 'The End of Choice?', *Guardian*, 19 May 2008.
[80] Emily Thornberry in ibid.
[81] Ibid.

a supporting campaign – 20 Reasons for 20 Weeks – ⟨
Evangelical group Christian Concern.[82] The day before the
reported to be 'in triumphal mood ... blue eyes intense
anticipating a win.[83] She argued that the measure would modernise the law
in line with scientific advance, emphasising the importance of 4D imaging
technologies in permitting us to see a fetus 'walk in the womb' and 'suck its
thumb'.[84] Now in the House of Lords, David Alton likewise explained that
these technologies had opened 'a vivid window into the womb' and that new
evidence had emerged regarding the capacity of the fetus to feel pain, completely changing the terms of the debate.[85] Ann Widdecombe came closest to a
religiously framed argument in noting that the images allowed us to see 'what
we are so wantonly – and I would say wickedly – destroying'.[86]

However, while newspapers had frequently linked 3D and 4D images to
calls for a lower time limit, the STC had found that these new technologies had
no relevance to the issue of abortion, and they had no clear impact on voting,
with most MPs rather remaining convinced that viability was 'the nub of the
argument'.[87] Notwithstanding marked changes to the composition of
Parliament in the intervening years, the pattern of voting on the upper time
limit closely resembled that seen in 1990. As can be seen in Table 1, all
amendments seeking to lower the upper time limit were rejected and the
existing 24 week upper time limit survived intact. Again, a proposed restriction to 22 weeks came closest to success, suggesting disagreement regarding
the exact timing of viability rather than a serious challenge to its status as the
key reference point.[88] Here, Parliament again followed medical opinion: Evan
Harris explained that 'viability' had been set on the guidance of paediatricians
and neonatologists at 24 weeks in 1990, and their advice remained
unchanged.[89]

In line with the strategic priorities set out by the Alive and Kicking
coalition, Pro-Life MPs also tabled several further narrowly framed amendments that sought to tighten the fetal anomaly ground and make specific
provision regarding informed consent. The Catholic Vice-Chairs of the Pro-
Life APPG, Claire Curtis-Thomas (Lab) and Baroness Masham (Crossbench),
took leading roles, framing their case in a language of civil liberties. Curtis-
Thomas proposed the prohibition of abortion for reason of disability, gender,

[82] 'Christian Fundamentalists Fighting Spiritual Battle in Parliament', *Telegraph*, 17 May 2008.
[83] Ibid.
[84] Dorries in *Hansard*, HC, 20 May 2008, vol. 476, col. 263; see also Leigh, 20 May 2008, vol. 476, col. 227.
[85] Alton in *Hansard*, HL, 12 December 2007, vol. 697, col. 312.
[86] Widdecombe in *Hansard*, HC, 20 May 2008, vol. 476, col. 271.
[87] Francois in *Hansard*, HC, 20 May 2008, vol. 476, col. 268. See further on same day of debate: Penning, cols 244–45. For contrary views, see Widdecombe, col. 270; Dorries, col. 260.
[88] E.g. *Hansard*, HC, 12 May 2008, vol. 475, col. 1129; 20 May 2008, vol. 476, cols 231, 267.
[89] *Hansard*, HC, 20 May 2008, vol. 476, col 250; 12 May 2008, vol. 475, col. 1140.

Table 1 House of Commons voting on the upper time limit for abortion under the 'social clause'.

	1990			2008		
Weeks of gestation	Ayes	Noes	Majority against reduction	Ayes	Noes	Majority against reduction
12				71	393	322
16				84	387	303
18	165	355	190			
20	189	358	169	190	332	142
22	255	301	46	233	304	71

race or sexual orientation of the future child.[90] Masham, who had been disabled in a riding accident, focused exclusively on abortion for fetal anomaly, aiming to 'right a tragic discrimination concerning babies in the womb' and 'curb abuses of the present law, involving abortion on the basis of such minor disabilities as cleft palate or club foot'.[91] While campaigns to repeal or restrict the fetal anomaly grounds were now often led by disabled people outside Parliament, Masham was the first to do so within it, and this undoubtedly enhanced her credibility: the veteran pro-choice parliamentarian Joyce Gould complained that many failed to realise that this 'wasn't an equality argument' but 'an anti-abortion' one.[92]

Exceptionally, a further restrictive amendment was tabled by a male, self-declared atheist with no apparent link to anti-abortion campaigning.[93] Having been born with a cleft palate, Nick Palmer (Lab) explained to laughter that his mother had been advised that he could have a 'decent quality of life so long as [he] did not make the mistake of choosing a career that involved public speaking'. He proposed a measure to ensure that women were provided with 'strictly neutral information' about fetal anomaly in a briefing pack covering life expectancy, quality of life, availability of treatment and support groups.[94] His proposal was criticised as 'patronising, onerous and unnecessary'.[95] A further amendment, tabled by Curtis-Thomas, proposed the mandatory offer of counselling and provision of information to support and empower women considering abortion. The information would include details of embryonic and fetal development at two-weekly intervals, a description of abortion methods and any risks associated with each, information about any disability of a future child, and the possibility of adoption, with it argued that it would bolster informed consent in a context where '[c]onsultations at the

---

[90] Curtis-Thomas in *Hansard*, HC, 12 May 2008, vol. 475, col. 1133.

[91] *Hansard*, HL, 12 December 2007, vol. 697, col. 302.

[92] Joyce Gould interviewed by Jane O'Neill, 4 October 2017.

[93] 'Amendment Could Cut Number of Late Abortions', *Guardian*, 19 May 2008.

[94] *Hansard*, HC, 20 May 2008, vol. 476, col. 266.

[95] Blunt in *Hansard*, HC, 20 May 2008, vol. 476, col. 265.

hairdresser's have taken longer than the time it took to make a decision to have an abortion'.[96] The proposal was criticised for 'prolonging the agony' of women who have 'already made a difficult and ... traumatic decision'.[97]

With all restrictive amendments defeated, the MPs led by Harris now prepared to table liberalising amendments. While these were far more radical than anything considered in Parliament before, their chances of success appeared strong: there was a Labour majority in the Commons with a significant number of female Labour MPs; they were supported by the robust evidence base set out in the STC report; they commanded substantial support from medical bodies; and the earlier votes on restrictive reform suggested a willingness within Parliament to be guided by the clinical evidence. Peter Saunders (CMF) recalls that Pro-Choice MPs 'should have absolutely walked it'.[98] However, as we have seen, this was not to be. To avoid a vote on the extension of the Abortion Act to Northern Ireland, the Labour Government blocked further debate of abortion through a whipped procedural motion.[99] Saunders concludes that, in deciding to hold back their amendments, Pro-Choice campaigners 'basically shot themselves in the foot, blew it, and made a huge tactical blunder'; then came the 2010 election, 'the Tories got in and the chance was gone'.[100]

The Ongoing Battle for Restrictive Reform

When the Conservatives returned to power, it would be in coalition with the Liberal Democrats but without Evan Harris.[101] While the new Government emphasised that there were no plans to change abortion law, there was nonetheless a notable change of atmosphere: senior Tory ministers were reported to support lower time limits for abortion,[102] and Life was appointed to the Government's Sex and Relationships Education Council and short-lived Sexual Health Forum, with BPAS conspicuously 'uninvited' from the latter.[103]

The election also saw Fiona Bruce join Nadine Dorries on the Conservative benches and as a member of the Cornerstone Group of Tory MPs. Claiming that her priority in Parliament was 'defending and fighting for the sanctity of

---

[96] *Hansard*, HC, 20 May 2008, vol. 476, col. 228.

[97] McCafferty in *Hansard*, HC, 20 May 2008, vol. 476, cols 237, 239.

[98] Saunders interviewed by O'Neill.

[99] *Hansard*, HC, 22 October 2008, vol. 481, cols 324–35.

[100] Saunders interviewed by O'Neill.

[101] 'Lib Dem MP Evan Harris Loses Oxford West and Abingdon', *BBC News*, 7 May 2010.

[102] 'Abortion Law: David Cameron Has "No Plans" for New Rules', *BBC News*, 6 October 2012; 'Theresa May Backs Abortion Limit Cut after Jeremy Hunt 12 Week Call', *Times*, 6 October 2012.

[103] 'Anti-Abortionists on Sex Education Panel... to Fury of the Left', *Daily Mail*, 29 May 2011; 'Anti-Abortion Group Drafted in as Sexual Health Adviser to Government', *Guardian*, 24 May 2011.

human life',[104] Bruce would gradually take over as the parliamentary face of the Pro-Life movement. A member of the Council of the Evangelical Alliance, Bruce chose to focus on parliamentary issues 'that would matter to Christ',[105] including the encouragement of adult prayer[106] and the promotion of daily worship in schools to teach children the importance of acknowledging God.[107] A solicitor by training, she would also place a strong focus on human rights and civil liberties in her parliamentary work, chairing the Conservative Party Human Rights Commission and serving as the UK's global envoy on the human right to freedom of religion or belief. Bruce was also a far more sober politician than Dorries, bringing a lawyer's concern for evidence to her work. With debate framed less in terms of disputed values and more in terms of competing empirical claims, during her time as co-chair the Pro-Life APPG would engage in extensive knowledge production, establishing a series of inquiries into specific aspects of the Abortion Act that might hope to shape the parliamentary agenda and feed into proposals for restrictive reform. Along with measures proposed as necessary to protect and empower women, these issues would form the basis for restrictive reform efforts over the following decade. Following what was now a well-established pattern, Pro-Life MPs would avoid comprehensive assaults on the Abortion Act in favour of narrowly framed measures that aimed to chip away at it. These measures would generally be led by Tory women and justified in Parliament not with reference to their Christian faith but rather as offering necessary modernisation of an ageing law in line with scientific advance and civil liberties.

'Independent' Counselling and Informed Consent

With the parliamentary arithmetic having swung back in favour of Pro-Life advocates, further proposals for restrictive reform were inevitable. First, Nadine Dorries took advantage of Andrew Lansley's wide-ranging NHS reform bill to renew calls to protect women from an 'abortion industry ... paid £60 million to carry out terminations'. She proposed a statutory duty to offer 'independent' counselling to all women seeking to access abortion services.[108] The desire for independent counselling was not in itself controversial. However, the rub was that the criterion of 'independence' proposed by Dorries would not be met by any private body that offered abortion services, thus excluding charitable abortion providers from counselling the women they went on to treat – but not organisations with 'a specific political and religious

---

[104] Evangelical Alliance, 'Question Time'.
[105] Christians in Parliament, 'Fiona Bruce MP'; see further Evangelical Alliance, 'Question Time'.
[106] EDM 854, 'Importance of Prayer', 24 January 2018.
[107] EDM 219, 'School Worship', 30 June 2015.
[108] *Hansard*, HC, 7 September 2011, vol. 532, col. 362, amendments tabled to the Health and Social Care Act 2011.

anti-abortion agenda'.[109] While accepting the need for impartial counselling, opponents argued that statutory reform was not necessary to achieve it, rejected the significant smear on health professionals accused of 'wilfully ignoring' both law and professional guidance, and decried the suggestion that 'thousands of women do not actually know what they are doing'.[110] The amendment failed by a wide margin.[111]

Reflecting her suspicion of the RCOG, Dorries also tabled a second amendment that sought to require NICE, the body that publishes evidence-based national guidance on health services, to issue compulsory requirements for the care of women seeking abortion.[112] She dismissed existing clinical guidelines, produced by the RCOG, as 'probably written by men',[113] arguing that the involvement of NICE would ensure impartiality. Paradoxically, however, she sought also to specify some aspects of the contents of the guidelines, leading the Government to warn that such interference would risk damaging NICE's reputation for independence.[114] Dorries withdrew the amendment following assurances that the need for independent counselling would be specified in regulation, albeit with a definition of 'independent' that would not exclude service providers from offering counselling to the women they might treat.[115]

Sex Selection

While Fiona Bruce avoided Dorries' overt displays of hostility towards the professional bodies, she shared her emphasis on the need to protect and empower women. In 2013, she took up the concern with sex-selective abortion that had been earlier highlighted in *The Telegraph*, recasting it within a woman-protective frame to argue that British Asian women were sometimes forced to end wanted pregnancies in order to avoid the birth of female children.[116] This was 'gender discrimination in its worst form' and a form of violence against women 'even before they have a chance to live'.[117] A first Bill aimed to require the compilation of statistics on the gender of aborted fetuses. A second was more ambitious: co-sponsored by female MPs drawn from 'all parts of the House',[118] it aimed to amend the Abortion Act to 'clarify' that

---

[109] See British Humanist Association, 'Health and Social Care Bill, 2010–2011 Report Stage'.

[110] Abbott in *Hansard*, HC, 7 September 2011, vol. 532, cols 380–81 and Umunna, cols 371–72.

[111] Ayes 118; Noes 368.

[112] *Hansard*, HC, 7 September 2011, vol. 532, col. 362. Currently, the National Institute for Health and Care Excellence (the organisation's title but not the acronym has changed over time).

[113] *Hansard*, HC, 7 September 2011, vol. 532, col. 366.

[114] Milton in *Hansard*, HC, 7 September 2011, vol. 532, col. 384.

[115] Ibid., col. 383. NICE guidelines were eventually developed eight years later, in collaboration with the RCOG: NICE and RCOG, *Abortion Care Guideline [NG140]*.

[116] See Chapter 5, pp. 168–69, on the *Telegraph* investigation.

[117] *Hansard*, HC, 16 April 2013, vol. 561, cols 169–70; 'Gender Abortion: It's Time for Urgent Action – With or Without the Government', *Telegraph*, 22 January 2015.

[118] *Hansard*, HC, 4 November 2014, vol. 587, col. 679.

abortion on the grounds of fetal sex was not permitted.[119] Some 20 years earlier, David Amess' plea to leave 'Mother Nature' alone had been defeated at its first reading. Now, no MP took the opportunity to make the customary speech opposing either Bill. The first passed its first reading without a division and just one MP – Glenda Jackson (Lab), who had earlier spoken against Amess – voted against the second.

While each Bill suffered the typical fate of a Ten Minute Rule Bill and fell without a second reading, Bruce had been the first MP to win a vote on a restrictive abortion law measure in over two decades, and, indeed, she could claim 'one of the most overwhelming majorities ever seen' on any issue.[120] She thus had strong grounds for hoping to secure a majority for a further, similarly framed measure tabled as an amendment to the Government's Serious Crime Bill (2015).[121] If accepted, this would almost certainly pass into law. Opposition now mobilised, with her amendment attacked as a wedge measure designed to build support for more radical restrictive reform. Fiona Mactaggart (Lab) had previously supported Bruce but now had a change of heart:

> I have since read something from an organisation in America that is closely linked to the all-party pro-life group that she chairs. The head of that group stated:
>
> 'I propose that we – the pro-life movement – adopt as our next goal the banning of sex ... selective abortion. By formally protecting all female fetuses from abortion on the ground of their sex, we would plant in the law the proposition that the developing child is a being whose claims on us should not depend on their sex ... This sense of contradiction will be further heightened among radical feminists' –
>
> I think he means people like me –
>
> 'the shock troops of the abortion movement. They may believe that the right to abortion is fundamental to women's emancipation, but many will recoil at the thought of aborting their unborn sisters.'[122]

Bruce's hopes for securing a majority now crumbled, leaving the Pro-Life MP John Pugh (Lib Dem) to reflect on the impossibility of achieving consensus on any proposed change to abortion law, with debate becoming 'polarised horribly and quickly', and the earlier 'total agreement throughout the Chamber' on this issue having nonetheless ended in 'total stalemate at the end of the

---

[119] Abortion Statistics Bill 2013, Abortion (Sex Selection) Bill 2014.

[120] Ayes 181; Noes 1. See 'MPs' Move Could Outlaw Gender Abortion within Months', *Telegraph*, 22 January 2015.

[121] *Hansard*, HC, 23 February 2015, vol. 593, cols 113–17.

[122] *Hansard*, HC, 23 February 2015, vol. 593, cols 129–30. On such 'wedge' tactics, see generally McGuinness, 'A Guerrilla Strategy for a Pro-Life England'.

day'.[123] Arguing that Bruce's proposal was unnecessary as fetal sex was not a legal ground for abortion, Ann Coffey (Lab) tabled an alternative amendment to commit the Government to investigate the incidence of sex-selective abortion and, where necessary, to act 'to change prejudices, customs, traditions' that created pressure towards it.[124] With the Bruce amendment defeated, this second measure passed almost unanimously.[125] By its nature, the analysis of demographic data that was subsequently published could neither prove nor disprove the existence of individual cases of sex-selective abortion. However, it showed that the practice was not occurring in sufficiently large numbers to result in imbalances in sex ratios at birth within any British ethnic community.[126]

Fetal Anomaly

With Bruce installed as Co-chair, the Pro-Life APPG would place a significant emphasis on developing its own evidence base, with this work informing a series of restrictive reform initiatives. In 2013, it established a 'parliamentary inquiry' into abortion for fetal anomaly, citing equality concerns, human rights arguments, and a lack of transparency regarding abortion decisions.[127] This Commission found that allowing abortion until birth on grounds of fetal anomaly was discriminatory. It recommended repealing the relevant subsection of the Abortion Act or reducing the time limit foreseen within it in line with that for 'able bodied babies', adopting a range of measures to enhance scrutiny and monitoring, strengthening women's decision-making through the provision of 'practical and balanced information' and promoting adoption as a positive option for those considering abortion.[128] The Commission modelled itself on a Select Committee in the presentation of its call for evidence and its final report, claiming to include 'differing opinions and views', emphasising its crossbench membership and omitting mention of the Pro-Life APPG.[129] For Pro-Choice advocates, this gave 'a wholly unmerited and unjustified veneer of officialdom' to an 'unofficial inquiry' by 'anti-choice MPs'.[130] One of those who gave evidence, Professor Nicolette Priaulx, complained that she had participated in ignorance of its bias. She fed her concerns

---

[123] *Hansard*, HC, 6 July 2015, vol. 598, col. 109.

[124] Section 84, Serious Crime Act 2015.

[125] Ayes 491; Noes 2. The Bruce amendment failed: Ayes 201; Noes 292.

[126] Department of Health and Social Care, *Sex Ratios at Birth in Great Britain, 2013–17*.

[127] Bruce et al., *Parliamentary Inquiry into Abortion on the Grounds of Disability*. Unusually, the authorship of the report is not specified within it. Our attribution relies on the fact that Bruce chaired the Commission and is listed as the contact point for any inquiries.

[128] Ibid.

[129] Ibid., 7. Members included Fiona Bruce, Robert Flello, Jill Knight, John Pugh and Baroness Masham.

[130] Education for Choice, 'The "Parliamentary Inquiry" on Abortion and Disability'; Ministry of Truth, 'The Anti-Abortion Lobby's Sham Parliamentary Inquiry'.

into an investigation into the conduct of APPGs, which went on to recommend the introduction of rules to avoid further confusion between the unofficial work of APPGs and the official work of Select Committees.[131]

Two Bills followed in the House of Lords, with the findings of the Bruce Commission – described as an 'independent parliamentary inquiry' – cited in the debates regarding them.[132] The Bills were introduced by Kevin Shinkwin, a peer 'devout in his Christian faith' and 'tireless in the application of his theology to the cause of conservative philosophy'.[133] Lord Shinkwin had been born with a brittle bone disease and entered Parliament following a distinguished career of working to tackle disability discrimination, which saw him briefly appointed to the Equality and Human Rights Commission (EHRC).[134] He introduced his first Bill by thanking the surgeon who had 'rebuilt' him as a child, his family and friends for their support, the House of Lords for its 'tireless work to advance disabled people's rights', and 'our Holy Mother for her non-discriminatory, sustaining love'.[135] The Bill adopted the Bruce Commission's proposal for repeal of the fetal anomaly ground of the Abortion Act, a 'corrosive, unjust and deeply discriminatory anomaly' that offered 'a licence to kill disabled people'.[136] Voice for Choice complained that, in seeking to prohibit abortions even in the case of fatal fetal anomaly, the Bill was 'simply incompatible with the very human rights the EHRC is tasked with championing', triggering a formal investigation and Lord Shinkwin's resignation from the EHRC.[137]

The second Shinkwin Bill offered an important change of tack whilst again drawing on the recommendations of the Bruce Commission. First, it proposed amending the fetal anomaly ground to include the same upper time limit of 24 weeks as for most other abortions. Second, firing a further salvo in the war over objective information, it proposed that prior to an abortion 'the parents of that child must be given full and accurate information regarding all options following a prenatal diagnosis of disability, including the keeping of that child', with information provided to them to 'include material written by groups representing people with experience of the anomaly in question'.[138] While

[131] House of Commons Committee on Standards, *All-Party Parliamentary Groups: Sixth Report of Session 2013–14*, HC 357, Ev w2; Parliamentary Commissioner for Standards, *Guide to the Rules on All-Party Parliamentary Groups*.

[132] Alton in *Hansard*, HL, 21 October 2016, vol. 774, cols 2547–50; see further Stroud, col. 2555.

[133] Archbishop Cranmer, 'Kevin (Lord) Shinkwin Appointed to Equality and Human Rights Commission'.

[134] Government Equalities Office, 'New Commissioner for the Equality and Human Rights Commission'.

[135] *Hansard*, HL, 21 October 2016, vol. 774, col. 2545.

[136] *Hansard*, HL, 21 October 2016, vol. 774, col. 2547; 'Tory Peer Lord Shinkwin Warns Britain's Abortion laws are a "Licence to Kill Disabled People"', *Telegraph*, 10 March 2017; Abortion (Disability Equality) Bill [HL] 2016/17.

[137] Humanists UK, 'Anti-Abortion Activist Resigns as Equality and Human Rights Commissioner'.

[138] Abortion (Disability Equality) Bill 2017.

each Bill failed to progress, they maintained a focus on the issue of abortion for fetal anomaly as an important ongoing area for contestation. Three years later, Fiona Bruce would table a Presentation Bill that revived concerns regarding late abortions for minor disabilities, proposing an amendment of the Abortion Act to exclude cleft lip, cleft palate and clubfoot as grounds for abortion.[139]

Conscientious Objection

The Pro-Life APPG's next inquiry investigated conscientious objection, which had gained prominence following the *Doogan* case, finding evidence of increasing pressure to participate in abortions and recommending strengthening the protection offered to objectors.[140] However, it again attracted criticism for presenting its work as official parliamentary business on its website. Armed with the rules introduced following her experience of giving evidence to the previous inquiry, Priaulx now complained to the Parliamentary Standards Commissioner, who found that the Pro-Life APPG had breached transparency rules. Bruce was forced to apologise, and the report was published with its link to the Pro-Life APPG prominently acknow-ledged.[141] It would nonetheless subsequently be referenced frequently as a cross-party 'parliamentary inquiry' or 'the inquiry that was conducted here in Parliament', with no mention of its connection with the Pro-Life APPG.[142]

The inquiry's recommendations would be cited in support of two further Bills introduced in the House of Lords by Baroness Nuala O'Loan (Crossbench), a lawyer, former police ombudsman and leading Catholic commentator.[143] Arguing that *Doogan* had narrowed the protection offered to conscientious objectors, O'Loan sought to extend it to include the kinds of duties that had been asked of Doogan and Wood, as well as to doctors asked to certify that the grounds for abortion were met and to those involved in the withdrawal of life-sustaining treatment.[144] The Bills were presented, first, as offering necessary clarification and modernisation and, second, as ensuring

---

[139] Abortion (Cleft Lip, Cleft Palate and Clubfoot) Bill. *Hansard*, HC, 3 June 2020, vol. 676, col. 887.

[140] All-Party Parliamentary Pro-Life Group, *A Report into Freedom of Conscience in Abortion Provision*. See discussion of *Doogan* in Chapter 5, pp. 185–86.

[141] See Parliamentary Commissioner for Standards, 'Rectification'. See further Priaulx, 'Pro-Life Inquiries'.

[142] EDM 861, 'Conscientious Objection (Medical Professionals) Bill', 24 January 2018, citing the inquiry in support of the second Bill; O'Loan in *Hansard*, HL, 26 January 2018, vol. 788, col. 1197; 23 March 2018, vol. 790, col. 607.

[143] See 'Nuala O'Loan: Christians Have a Duty and Right to Bring Their Beliefs into the Public Square', *Irish News*, 13 February 2020, arguing for the importance of religious faith in guiding public service. O'Loan regularly writes for *The Irish Catholic* newspaper, see *Irish Catholic*, 'Nuala O'Loan'.

[144] Conscientious Objection (Medical Activities) Bill [HL] 2015; Conscientious Objection (Medical Activities) Bill 2017.

liberty, equality and social inclusion in a context where British society was growing more secular and less tolerant of religiosity. They were attacked as 'unnecessary and potentially dangerous' to the effective delivery of an abortion service and as elevating 'a healthcare professional's important personal beliefs above their duty to the patient'.[145]

Protection of the Unborn

While claims regarding civil liberties have become increasingly prominent in attacks on the Abortion Act, claims foregrounding fetal rights have become less so, with the Abortion (Foetus Protection) Bill 2017 offering a rare exception. It was introduced by the Conservative peer Baroness Emma Nicholson, described in one pen portrait as an 'accomplished missionary' who was prone to 'repeated proclamation[s] of faith' and 'the setting of any experience in a spiritual context'.[146] While not proceeding beyond its first reading, Nicholson's apparent motivation for seeking an upper time limit of 12 weeks on most abortions appears clear from the Bill's title, the reasons given for tabling a similar amendment in 1990 and her earlier praise for German law, which she understood as providing that 'a pregnant lady, can have an abortion at any time up to 12 weeks, with nothing except a consultation with a medical professional and three days' waiting time – but after 12 weeks nothing is allowed, unless the health of the mother is severely compromised'.[147]

More commonly, reform proposals focusing on protection of the unborn have come to be presented either in terms of discrimination (as in the case of proposed reform of the fetal anomaly ground) or in terms of advances in scientific understanding of fetal development (as with proposals focusing on viability and the upper time limit). The issue of fetal sentience has offered an increasingly significant focus, with the Pro-Life APPG's most recent inquiry focusing on this issue. Given earlier complaints, the resulting report was formatted differently from that of a Select Committee, with prominent acknowledgement that it expressed the views of the Pro-Life APPG.[148] The report acknowledges uncertainty regarding the time at which a fetus can first feel pain and 'growing recognition that foetal sentience should be reappraised and taken more seriously'. On this basis, it calls upon the RCOG to update its guidance on the issue and recommends that the precautionary principle

[145] Young in *Hansard*, HL, 26 January 2018, vol. 788, cols 1197–99.
[146] 'Profile: Backbencher with Real Backbone: Emma Nicholson MP, Accomplished Missionary', *Independent*, 23 October 2011.
[147] *Hansard*, HL, 21 October 2016, vol. 774, col. 2550. See Chapter 3, pp. 104–5, on the amendment that she tabled in 1990, and Taylor and Wilson, 'UK Abortion Law', criticising this characterisation of the German law.
[148] All-Party Parliamentary Pro-Life Group, *Foetal Sentience & Pain*.

should be followed, with analgesia for the fetus offered to women from the start of the second trimester and required from 18 weeks' gestation.[149]

Devolution

Pro-Life MPs also took a keen interest in one final important issue debated in this period. In 2014, a fiercely contested referendum campaign resulted in a vote against Scottish independence, with this result influenced by the promise of extensive further devolution of powers to Holyrood. Abortion would emerge as an important point of tension in the resulting negotiations as, indeed, it had been during the earlier devolution of powers in the late 1990s.[150] At that time, while some ministerial powers under the Abortion Act had been devolved to Scotland and Wales, the power to legislate on abortion had been reserved to Westminster.[151] For Wales, this was consistent with a general policy of devolving only executive powers;[152] for Scotland, it had appeared to many to be a patronising and anomalous exception.[153]

The devolution of ministerial powers over abortion had not resulted in Holyrood devoting any significant attention to the issue.[154] Nonetheless, the prospect of also transferring legislative powers over abortion emerged as an important focal point for the expression of sharply conflicting hopes and fears regarding devolution, the relationship between Westminster and Holyrood, Scottish national identity and the role of religion within it.[155] In 1998, the Labour Government had asserted the need to retain legislative control over abortion in Westminster to ensure a consistent statutory framework that would avoid cross-border abortion travel, which – as Northern Ireland had shown – would impact most significantly on the most vulnerable.[156] Beyond

[149] Ibid.; RCOG, *Fetal Awareness*.

[150] See generally Bogdanor, *Devolution in the United Kingdom*; Chapter 6 on Northern Ireland.

[151] Including the power to approve a class of places for the performance of abortions, which would achieve huge significance in debates regarding the home use of misoprostol, see this chapter, pp. 257–60. See Scotland Act 1998 (Transfer of Functions to the Scottish Ministers etc.) Order 1999/1750, art. 2, Sched. 1; National Assembly for Wales (Transfer of Functions) Order 1999/672, art. 2(b), Sched. 1.

[152] See generally Bogdanor, *Devolution in the United Kingdom*. Legislative powers were acquired later, see Government of Wales Act 2006, Sched. 7A.

[153] Steel in *Hansard*, HL, 27 July 1998, vol. 592, col. 1285.

[154] A petition proposed by British Victims of Abortion had been discussed but had not resulted in the action sought: for women considering abortion to be given 'impartial and factual information' on fetal development and the risks associated with abortion, with the proposal itself accused of bias. Abortion (Information on Procedures and Risks) Petition PE608 discussed in Scottish Parliament, Minutes of the Public Petitions Committee, 18 March 2003 and 1 October 2003. See Chapter 4, pp. 131–33, on British Victims of Abortion.

[155] See generally Moon, Thompson and Whiting, 'Lost in the Process?'; Thomson, 'Abortion Law and Scotland'.

[156] Dewar in *Hansard*, HC, 31 March 1998, vol. 309, cols 1107–08; see further Fyfe, cols 1099–100; Osborne, col. 1102; McKenna, col. 1106; Gould in *Hansard*, HL, 27 July 1998, vol. 592, col. 1288; and Young, col. 1294.

this official explanation lay fears regarding the power of the Catholic Church within Scotland,[157] and familiar concerns that any change would be a precursor to 'a further assault' on the Abortion Act, with some discerning a cynical ploy to strike at 'the weakest link', concentrate 'the forces of reaction' on Scotland and undermine the ability to galvanise women 'to stand shoulder to shoulder north and south of the Border'.[158]

Those who sought devolution of control over abortion – with Scots prominent amongst them – protested that the reservation smacked 'of political manipulation, cynicism and cowardice',[159] arguing that the Scottish Parliament could be trusted to treat the issue with the seriousness that it deserved.[160] Many asserted a vision of a more progressive Scottish Parliament, which might debate abortion in a 'better fashion', with women likely to be better represented than at Westminster.[161] Moreover, with Scotland having achieved more consistent NHS funding for abortion and the performance of a higher proportion of terminations in early pregnancy,[162] it was argued that it could offer a 'beacon of good practice to which the rest of the country can turn for examples'.[163] With uneasy alliances between Pro-Life and Scottish MPs emerging, three amendments aiming to devolve legislative competence over abortion were put to a vote in 1998, including one proposed by David Steel (a Scot) and vocally supported by David Alton. However, given the solid Labour majority in the Commons, all amendments had been defeated, with abortion law remaining a reserved matter.[164]

When the issue of further devolution of powers was considered again in 2016, Labour's position remained unaltered; however, it now lacked a majority in Parliament. It managed to ensure that devolution of competence for abortion was not initially provided for within the Bill that would become the Scotland Act 2016.[165] However, amendments to include it were now tabled by Pro-Life MPs, reportedly in the hope that Scotland might 'lead the way' on

---

[157] Eileen Cook interviewed by Jane O'Neill, 11 September 2017, notes the fear amongst Westminster MPs that the Scottish Parliament would be more influenced by religion and therefore more likely to restrict abortion laws.

[158] Mackie in *Hansard*, HL, 27 July 1998, vol. 592, cols 1295–96 and Kennedy, col. 1292.

[159] Fox in *Hansard*, HC, 31 March 1998, vol. 309, cols 1093–95.

[160] Salmond (Scottish National Party) in *Hansard*, HC, 31 March 1998, vol. 309, col. 1100 and Wallace, col. 1097; see also Mackay in *Hansard*, HL, 17 June 1998, vol. 590, col. 1579 and 27 July 1998, vol. 592, col. 1298; Fox in *Hansard*, HC, 31 March 1998, vol. 309, col. 1094. The Scottish Abortion Campaign likewise supported devolution of legislative control of abortion: Cook interviewed by O'Neill; Liz Armstrong and Anne McChlery (SAC) in 'No More Reservations About Abortion Rights: The Scottish Abortion Campaign comments', Engender, no. 16, November 1997, 7.

[161] Salmond in *Hansard*, HC, 31 March 1998, vol. 309, col. 1101–03.

[162] Steel in *Hansard*, HL, 27 July 1998, vol. 592, col. 1287.

[163] Linklater in *Hansard*, HL, 27 July 1998, vol. 592, col. 1297.

[164] Fox amendment: Ayes 160; Noes 278. Steel amendment: Contents 45; Not Contents 88. Mackay amendment: Contents 70; Not Contents 127.

[165] The Smith Commission, *Report of the Smith Commission for Further Devolution of Powers to the Scottish Parliament*, nonetheless noting that this was an 'anomalous health reservation' and

changing the Abortion Act.[166] Labour MPs repeated the argument that 'a woman's right to choose should be determined by robust medical evidence and not by where they live',[167] and they attacked the proposal as 'the thin end of the wedge', which would lead 'to a new round of intensive, targeted pressure for restrictions both north and south of the border, and the fragmentation of important healthcare rights'.[168] Reflecting old divisions, the amendments were initially strongly opposed by a range of civil society organisations, women's groups and trade unions, and supported by SPUC.[169] However, they also attracted strong support from Scottish National Party (SNP) MPs who denied the 'false choice' between 'nationalism and feminism'.[170] Noting that, as a gay man, he had considerable sympathy with the significance of abortion as a tough and important issue for women, Stewart McDonald (SNP) argued strongly that Scotland was 'not a nation of social conservatives'. Powers should come to Scotland in order 'to improve and protect a woman's right to choose and to access quality healthcare'.[171] Others criticised Labour for an apparent lack of confidence in Holyrood, with Deidre Brock (SNP) finding it

> extraordinary that, despite all three main parties in Scotland being led by women and the Scottish Parliament having brought in some of the most progressive legislation on equal marriage in the world, the Labour party apparently still feels that Scotland's people need male-dominated Westminster to protect women's rights.[172]

The Conservative Government opposed the amendments tabled by Pro-Life MPs. However, following further consultation and indications that Holyrood was unlikely to act to restrict the Abortion Act,[173] it announced support for the devolution of competence over abortion, which duly passed into

---

recommending further consideration, para. 61. On Labour's influence on this point, see 'Labour Forced Smith Commission to Drop Abortion Law', *Scotsman*, 30 November 2014.

[166] Amendments tabled by Edward Leigh (Con) and John Pugh (Lib Dem), see *Hansard*, HC, 6 July 2015, vol. 598, col. 74; 'Pro-Life MPs to Devolve Abortion Issue to Holyrood', *Scotsman*, 29 June 2015.

[167] Murray in *Hansard*, HC, 9 November 2015, vol. 602, cols 102–03, citing the Engender statement.

[168] 'This Threat to Abortion Law Must Be Fought by MPs of All Hues', *Guardian*, 8 November 2015.

[169] Engender, 'Joint Statement on Scotland Bill, Amendment EC56, "Abortion"'; Lynn Murray (Chair of SPUC, Edinburgh) cited in 'Pro-Life MPs to Devolve Abortion Issue to Holyrood', *Scotsman*, 29 June 2015.

[170] McDonald in *Hansard*, HC, 9 November 2015, vol. 602, col. 110.

[171] *Hansard*, HC, 9 November 2015, vol. 602, col. 110.

[172] *Hansard*, HC, 9 November 2015, vol. 602, col. 137; see also Crawley in *Hansard*, HC, 6 July 2015, vol. 598, cols 110–11.

[173] Sturgeon in Scottish Parliament, *Official Report*, 10 September 2015, col. 21, confirming that there was 'no intention of legislating to change the current time limits for abortion'; see further the much greater support given to a motion committing to oppose 'any attempt to undermine women's access to safe and legal abortion in Scotland' (Scottish Parliament, Motion ref. S4M-14524, 'Commitment to Women's Reproductive Rights', 15 October 2015, 22 signatories) compared to another noting the 'fundamental rights of babies to be protected both before and

law.[174] While Joyce Gould reports being 'terribly worried' by the move, Labour had lacked the numbers to block it.[175]

Opposing the move, Yvette Cooper (Lab) had argued that those who believed current British abortion laws 'are broadly right ... are stronger if we stand together to defend them against those who want to turn back the clock, rather than leaving each other to face the heat of the campaign alone'.[176] However, following devolution, the Scottish First Minister again publicly confirmed her support for women's 'right to choose, within the limits that are currently set down in law',[177] and the first related issues subsequently discussed within Holyrood concerned how Scotland might make better provision for women needing to travel from Northern Ireland for abortion services,[178] and how to address the needs of Scottish women seeking access to later abortion.[179] Contrary to Cooper's fears, it seems likely that the greater existential threat to the Abortion Act would come not from Pro-Life but from Pro-Choice campaigns and, indeed, as the tide turned in their favour, that devolution might tend towards creating opportunities for liberalising reform.[180]

The Battle for Liberalising Reform

Decriminalisation

In 2015, BPAS published a booklet that aimed to begin a conversation about decriminalisation of abortion:

> The 1967 Abortion Act was a tremendous achievement for its time, and has served women well. But as we approach the fiftieth anniversary of this legislation, it is time to move on. We need to bring the law into line with clinical developments, women's needs and the social reality of 2015 – where abortion is accepted as a fact of life.
>
> It is time to push away from the idea enshrined in the Abortion Act of women as victims of their circumstances, and instead promote the view that we trust

after birth' (Scottish Parliament, Motion ref. S4M-14542, 'Devolution of Abortion Law', 19 October 2015, no other signatories).

[174] Mundell, Secretary of State for Scotland, in *Hansard*, HC, 9 November 2015, vol. 602, col. 137; Section 53 Scotland Act 2016.

[175] Gould interviewed by O'Neill; Cook interviewed by O'Neill; Ann Henderson interviewed by Jane O'Neill, 25 July 2017.

[176] 'This Threat to Abortion Law Must Be Fought by MPs of All Hues', *Guardian*, 8 November 2015.

[177] Scottish Parliament, *Official Report*, 17 November 2016, col. 18.

[178] Ibid. See further Kezia Dugdale commenting on Northern Ireland's abortion law as breaching human rights: Scottish Parliament, *Official Report*, 7 June 2018, cols 22–23.

[179] Scottish Parliament, *Official Report*, 30 November 2016, cols 13–14; 16 March 2016, cols 32–33.

[180] For example, see discussion regarding the authorisation of home use of misoprostol, pp. 257–60.

women to make rational decisions, and that we trust doctors' professional judgment in providing the best standard of care.[181]

In 2016, it launched its 'We Trust Women' campaign, offering a decisive break from the defensive campaigning of earlier years and riding the wave of a growing momentum for women's rights encapsulated in the #MeToo movement. The campaign video 'Standing on the Shoulders of Giants' traces a direct line back to the suffragettes, detailing victories and setbacks overcome by earlier generations of women in the fight for equality, and concluding that overturning the 'outdated, patriarchal law' criminalising abortion remained important unfinished business.[182] These were the opening salvoes in the battle for decriminalisation.

The campaign quickly acquired the support of a range of advocacy groups and, more gradually, medical bodies: first the RCM, followed by the RCOG, RCN, BMA, and Royal College of General Practitioners (RCGP).[183] While Pro-Choice campaigners would frequently reference clinical evidence in support of the need for reform, these professional bodies were increasingly speaking a language of civil liberties, gender equality and 'standing up for the rights of women and girls'.[184] SPUC responded to 'We Trust Women' with its own campaign, 'We Care About Women', which challenged what it saw as plans for a dangerous deregulation of services. Its work, and that of other Pro-Life groups, would become ever more reactive to Pro-Choice demands for liberalising reform.[185] Moreover, in making the case against deregulation, it would now be Pro-Life groups who would seek to defend the Abortion Act as offering essential safeguards, invoking the spectre of 'DIY' or 'backstreet abortions'.[186]

Calls for a liberalisation of abortion laws also grew within Parliament. *Hansard* records over 60 occasions on which attempts have been made to reform abortion law since the Abortion Act came into effect, around three-quarters of them proposals for restrictive measures.[187] Just one attempt at liberalising reform is recorded between 1968 and 1990. The veteran Pro-Choice MP Jo Richardson, who had tabled it, recalled that in those early decades 'the anti-abortionists ... made the running' and pro-choice

---

[181] BPAS, *Abortion*.

[182] BPAS, 'We Trust Women'.

[183] 'Midwives Revolt over Abortion', *Daily Mail*, 16 May 2016; RCOG, 'RCOG Backs Decriminalisation of Abortion'; RCN, *Decriminalisation of Termination of Pregnancy: A Position Statement*; BMA, *The Removal of Criminal Sanctions for Abortion: BMA Position Paper*; RCGP, 'RCGP to Support Decriminalisation of Abortion'.

[184] E.g. Lesley Regan, RCOG President, in RCOG, 'RCOG Backs Decriminalisation of Abortion'.

[185] The list of campaigns for 2019 has been removed, but current campaigns, which at the time of writing also enjoy a largely defensive focus, can be seen at SPUC, 'Campaigns'.

[186] Lowe, '(Re)imagining the "Backstreet"'.

[187] See Appendix 2, listing 61 occasions when abortion law reform measures were proposed between April 1968 and November 2021. Twelve of the 16 occasions when attempts were made to liberalise the law came from 2017 onwards.

amendments were never selected for debate.[188] Now the boot was apparently on the other foot: two-thirds of the liberalising reform proposals since 1968 have been recorded since 2017, and it is SPUC who complains of bias, attacking the former Speaker John Bercow as 'in thrall to abortion activists'.[189]

Moreover, the liberalising proposals made in Parliament would become increasingly ambitious. In 2014, Baroness Jenny Tonge, an independent peer and former doctor, argued that the termination of pregnancy should be contingent on the good faith opinion of just one doctor rather than two.[190] Just three years later, Diana Johnson MP (Lab) proposed the decriminalisation of abortion before 24 weeks in England and Wales. Johnson was Co-chair of the Sexual and Reproductive Health APPG, a barrister and a long-standing campaigner on the contaminated blood scandal.[191] Like Harris and Tonge, she emphasised the law's poor fit with modern clinical practice and social norms. However, while Harris and Tonge had spoken as doctors, Johnson attacked the criminal prohibitions as part of a 'Victorian criminal law passed before women even had the right to vote', and argued that women must be recognised 'as the authors of our own lives'.[192] In targeting the underlying criminal prohibitions against abortion, her Bill sought not to amend the Abortion Act – as Harris and Tonge had proposed – but rather to render it largely redundant before 24 weeks. Marge Berer, then Chair of the Voice for Choice coalition, reflected that Harris's proposals had been 'the best we could get at that point', but now 'even those are too restrictive'.[193]

The Johnson Bill was opposed by Maria Caulfield (Con), a former nurse and member of the Conservative Christian Fellowship, who reports regularly incurring the wrath of party whips for going head to head with fellow Tories.[194] While elsewhere 'unabashed' regarding her Catholicism,[195] Caulfield's 10 minute speech eschewed faith-based claims in favour of a rapid-fire list of the alleged dangers of decriminalisation and advanced a grudging defence of the Abortion Act as containing 'some of the few protections and regulations' necessary for 'a major and often risky procedure'.[196] The Bill passed its first reading by 30 votes, offering an important gauge of

---

[188] NAC (ed.), *A Celebration of 25 Years of Safe, Legal Abortion 1967–1992*, 27.

[189] SPUC, 'Pro-abortion House of Commons Speaker Stands Down Leaving "Untold Damage to Unborn Babies and their Mothers"'. Bercow was Speaker from 2009 to 2019. See Appendix 2.

[190] Abortion Act 1967 (Amendment) Bill [HL] 2014. See 'A Chance to Create an Abortion Law that's Fit for Purpose – Let's Take it', *Huffington Post*, 11 June 2014.

[191] In which people with haemophilia and other bleeding disorders had contracted HIV and hepatitis as a result of being treated with contaminated blood-clotting products during the 1970s and 1980s.

[192] *Hansard*, HC, 13 March 2017, vol. 623, cols 26–28.

[193] Marge Berer interviewed by Jane O'Neill, 6 October 2017.

[194] 'Maria Caulfield: I Will Risk the Wrath of My Party to Stand Up for the People of Lewes', *Argus*, 30 May 2017.

[195] 'Christian Candidates in the Spotlight: Maria Caulfield and the Battle for Lewes', *Christian Today*, 31 May 2017.

[196] *Hansard*, HC, 13 March 2017, vol. 623, cols 26–28.

Parliamentary opinion.[197] The RCOG President, Lesley Regan, noted that it 'lit a touch paper among like-minded MPs', offering the 'first sign' of a 'significant shift' towards seeing abortion care as an integral part of women's healthcare that should be treated and regulated accordingly.[198]

The changing political climate was also visible in a further noteworthy development. Jess Phillips (Lab) now became the first parliamentarian publicly to acknowledge having had an abortion. While noting that abortion is a 'pedestrian' and 'common' procedure, she recognised that nonetheless her revelation would be 'newsworthy in a way Jeremy Hunt's prostate exam wouldn't be' because the 'battle to make women's health a mundane reality is far from won'.[199] Seeking to normalise abortion, she also made a point of '[sticking] up for the women who are not the difficult cases, as well as those who are'.[200] The 'difficult cases' were also powerfully addressed: Heidi Allen, a Conservative (and later Independent Group) MP, likewise now shared her own experience of abortion, explaining that when she 'made the incredibly hard decision', she was having seizures every day and 'not able to control my own body, let alone care for a new life'. She went on to criticise the Northern Irish law:

> Are people seriously telling me that, in a civilised world, rape, incest or a foetus that is so sadly deformed it could never live are not sufficient grounds for a woman to have the power to decide for herself – that she should not make that decision? No. Enough.[201]

Northern Ireland

With legislative competence for abortion devolved to Stormont and Holyrood, Diana Johnson's first Ten Minute Rule Bill had applied only to England and Wales. In October 2018, she brought a second Bill that also included Northern Ireland. Within the months between the two, the Northern Ireland Assembly had collapsed leaving the region without a functioning devolved Government, the Irish referendum had seen a landslide in favour of liberalising abortion law reform, and both CEDAW and the Supreme Court had found Northern Irish law to breach human rights standards.[202] It was now not just politically possible to include Northern Ireland within an abortion bill but impossible to exclude it. Johnson framed the case for reform in terms of the need for modernisation, attacking 'one of the harshest abortion regimes in the world'. While health and criminal justice were devolved matters, Westminster

---

[197] Ayes 172; Noes 142.
[198] Regan, 'Abortion', 133.
[199] 'I Had an Abortion and I will Keep Fighting for This Right for All', *Guardian*, 27 May 2018. At the time, Hunt was Secretary of State for Health and Social Care.
[200] *Hansard*, HC, 5 June 2018, vol. 642, col. 244.
[201] Ibid., col. 240.
[202] See Chapter 6, pp. 219–21.

retained legislative competence for human rights: Johnson argued that it was thus obliged to address the ongoing breach of Northern Irish women's human rights by decriminalising abortion; devolution might be respected by leaving it to a reconstituted Northern Ireland Assembly to determine how to provide for abortion services. With the campaign for decriminalisation having gained momentum, Johnson was able to cite the support of professional medical bodies, human rights groups, service providers, women's organisations and unions.[203] She was also supported by a cross-party group that included a number of prominent female Conservative MPs, including Sarah Wollaston, Chair of the Health Select Committee.[204]

Johnson was strongly opposed by Fiona Bruce, who argued that the Bill would remove protections from vulnerable women and potentially lead to sex-selective abortion; its proposed 24 week upper time limit was 'out of step with scientific progress and public opinion', and the human rights case for reform was built on 'a report by a minor UN sub-committee [CEDAW], which does not have any standing to rule on the UK's legal obligations in this respect', and a 'non-binding judgment of the Supreme Court'. Most importantly, abortion was a devolved matter, with the Bill an 'ignoble' attempt to take advantage of the collapse of the Northern Ireland Assembly 'to foist legislation unconstitutionally on to the people of Northern Ireland'.[205] While the devolution argument appeared to weigh with SNP MPs, who largely abstained, the second Johnson Bill nonetheless succeeded by a larger margin than the first.[206]

This second Bill was debated during the turbulent parliamentary context that followed the Brexit referendum, which had already been exploited to significant effect by Stella Creasy (Labour and Cooperative Party). An award-winning campaigner with a strong track record on maternity rights and pay-day loans,[207] Creasy was powerfully supported by a parliamentary researcher, Cara Sanquest, who had co-founded the London–Irish Abortion Rights Campaign.[208] With Parliament bitterly divided over Brexit, the Conservative Government had lost its majority in a snap general election in June 2017. It was now dependent on a 'confidence and supply' agreement with that most hard line of anti-abortion political parties, the DUP, which was at pains to emphasise that 'the rights of the unborn child trump any political

[203] *Hansard*, HC, 23 October 2018, vol. 648, cols 141–43.
[204] Wollaston and Heidi Allen would subsequently defect to the short-lived Independent Group of MPs.
[205] *Hansard*, HC, 23 October 2018, vol. 648, cols 143–46.
[206] Ayes 208; Noes 123, with just two SNP MPs voting, one on each side. The same Bill would later be introduced in the House of Lords by Baroness Barker, failing to progress beyond its first reading: *Hansard*, HL, 15 January 2020, vol. 801, col. 710.
[207] Her work for more robust regulation of payday lenders won her *The Spectator*'s Campaigner of the Year prize (2011), see 'Stella Creasy: Labour's Rising Star Who's Taking on Wonga', *Observer*, 25 November 2012.
[208] Sanquest later won an award for her work on this issue: 'The Parliamentary Staff Awards 2019: The Winners', *Prospect Magazine*, 5 February 2020.

agreement'.[209] Nonetheless, this volatile context would offer unusual opportunities.

Describing an unusually fraught parliamentary session in the late 1980s, the veteran abortion law reform campaigner Dilys Cossey had complained of the '"lateral arabesque" school of anti-choice activity', whereby amendments relating to abortion were proposed to any Bill where there could be the remotest connection.[210] Now the same strategy would be fully exploited by Stella Creasy. She achieved an early success with a proposal to secure access to NHS-funded services for Northern Irish residents who travelled to end pregnancies in England. The Government had vigorously and successfully opposed such a demand in the courts.[211] However, it capitulated in the face of Creasy's plan to table an amendment to this effect to the Queen's Speech. With significant support from 'dozens of Conservative MPs', including several former ministers, it was possible that Creasy's amendment would be accepted.[212] If so, DUP MPs would have been forced either to support a legislative programme that improved abortion access for Northern Irish residents or, alternatively, to vote down the entire programme.[213] With its wafer-thin majority threatened, the Government now swiftly agreed to provide the funding demanded.[214] The number of Northern Irish residents accessing abortion services in England and Wales, which had gradually dwindled over the previous decades as women began to access abortion pills online, now rose by half over the two following years.[215]

Creasy faced death threats.[216] Undeterred, she secured an emergency debate on Northern Ireland[217] and then took advantage of the vehicle offered by a series of Bills designed to address the absence of a functioning Executive in Stormont. A first amendment required the Government to publish guidance to officials regarding the provision and management of public services within Northern Ireland in light of the incompatibility of the region's abortion law with human rights norms.[218] A second sought to prevent taxpayers' money

---

[209] Ian Paisley, cited in 'Free NHS Abortions Offered to Northern Irish Women in Scotland and Wales', *Independent*, 5 July 2017.

[210] Cossey, 'The Politics of the Abortion Pill', 54.

[211] *R (A and B) v Secretary of State for Health* [2017] UKSC 41. See Chapter 6, pp. 219–20.

[212] 'Northern Irish Women Win Access to Free Abortions as May Averts Rebellion', *Guardian*, 29 June 2017.

[213] 'Move on Free NHS Abortions for Northern Ireland Women Is Hailed and Criticised in Equal Measure', *Belfast Telegraph*, 30 June 2017.

[214] *Hansard*, HC, 23 October 2017, vol. 630, Written Statement HCWS192.

[215] From 724 in 2016 to 1,053 in 2018, see Department of Health, *Abortion Statistics, England and Wales*, volumes for 2016 and 2018.

[216] 'Anti-Abortion Activist Tells Labour MP "Hopefully She Will Die Like Jo Cox"', *Independent*, 5 July 2017. 'Court Upholds Ban on Anti-Abortion Poster Targeting Stella Creasy', *Guardian*, 6 May 2020.

[217] *Hansard*, HC, 5 June 2018, vol. 642, cols 205–57.

[218] Section 4, Northern Ireland (Executive Formation and Exercise of Functions) Act 2018; Ayes 207; Noes 117. For the resulting guidance, see *Hansard*, HC, 30 January 2019, vol. 653,

being used to perpetuate 'human rights abuses' by defending the abortion law or prosecuting women under it.[219]

Creasy's definitive victory followed shortly, with an enormously ambitious amendment that required the UK Government to implement the wide-ranging recommendations of the CEDAW report into abortion in Northern Ireland.[220] Recognising that health and criminal justice fell within the legislative competence of Stormont, Creasy argued that her amendment respected devolution: first, it dealt with human rights, a matter of reserved responsibility; and second, it would come into effect only if the Northern Ireland Assembly remained suspended and unable to legislate on the matter on 21 October 2019. In the meantime, Westminster had a duty to act as 'human rights delayed are human rights denied'.[221] The tabling of amendments dealing with important substantive issues to a narrowly focused process Bill was nonetheless hugely controversial.[222] The proposal was said to drive 'a coach and horses through the principle of devolution'[223] and to jeopardise fragile talks regarding the restoration of the Northern Ireland Government.[224] Fiona Bruce repeated that too much authority was being given to CEDAW.[225] Others noted that the amendment went far beyond the Supreme Court's *obiter* findings of human rights breaches and the recommendations of the Women and Equalities Committee,[226] argued that the Bill was not the best vehicle for these changes,[227] and complained at being asked to legislate in a 'hop, skip, jump and a prayer manner'.[228] The drafting of the amendment was also criticised:[229] it was unclear whether it would decriminalise abortion just in Northern Ireland or also in England and Wales;[230] whether it would apply only to consensual abortions or also those provoked as a result of assault or the surreptitious administration of pills;[231] and whether it would create an upper time limit for abortion of 24 or 28 weeks.[232]

---

col. 40WS; 'Northern Ireland Secretary Accused of Misleading MPs after Refusing to Act on Abortion and Same-Sex Marriage Bans', *Independent*, 30 January 2019.

[219] Northern Ireland Budget (Anticipation and Adjustments) (No. 2) Bill 2019; *Hansard*, HC, 5 March 2019, vol. 655, cols 911, 926, amendment withdrawn.

[220] See Chapter 6, p. 220.

[221] *Hansard*, HC, 9 July 2019, vol. 663, col. 180.

[222] Further substantive amendments tabled to the Bill included one designed to bring Northern Ireland into line with the rest of the UK in recognising same-sex marriage.

[223] Campbell in *Hansard*, HC, 9 July 2019, vol. 663, col. 167; see further Paisley, col. 167; Dodds, cols 173–74; and Wilson, col. 190.

[224] E.g. Hoare in ibid., col. 190.

[225] Ibid., col. 185.

[226] Miller in ibid., col. 172, citing House of Commons Women and Equalities Committee, *Abortion Law in Northern Ireland*, Eighth Report of Session 2017–2019, HC 1584, 2019.

[227] Merriman in *Hansard*, HC, 9 July 2019, vol. 663, cols 199, 208.

[228] Paisley in ibid., col. 205.

[229] Penrose, Northern Ireland Office Minister in ibid., col. 222.

[230] Ford in ibid., col. 202.

[231] Ford in ibid., vol. 663, col. 202.

[232] Paisley in ibid., col. 204.

However, technical concerns were swept aside in an emphatic show of support for the amendment, which passed by 332 to 99 votes. All MPs who had taken up seats representing Northern Irish constituencies opposed it.[233] The UK Government maintained to the end that abortion law reform was a matter for Stormont. Many Tories joined the Prime Minister and Northern Ireland Secretary in abstaining, and those who did vote were relatively evenly split.[234] However, the support of other parties was overwhelming: all 10 Liberal Democrat MPs who voted were in favour, as were 220 of 225 from Labour and 20 of 22 from the SNP. The amendment, lightly revised to address technical problems, was accepted by a still larger majority in the House of Lords.[235]

With the Northern Ireland Assembly still suspended in October 2019, the Creasy amendment passed into law. Sections 58 and 59 of the Offences Against the Person Act were repealed for Northern Ireland, with all ongoing prosecutions under them dismissed.[236] Close to the deadline, it was rumoured that the Conservative Government was attempting to buy DUP support for its Brexit withdrawal deal with the promise of returning responsibility for the legal change to Stormont, prompting Creasy to criticise the use of 'women as "bargaining chips"'.[237] If true, this attempt – with its powerful echoes of 2008[238] – was unsuccessful. In a final 'high stakes move', the DUP attempted to recall the Assembly to facilitate the repeal of the measure.[239] It failed. Abortion was now largely decriminalised in Northern Ireland.

For decades, debate regarding the reform of Northern Irish abortion law had focused on the possibility of extending the Abortion Act. The regulations published by the UK Government, following a period of consultation, went much further. Henceforth, a woman could no longer be prosecuted for anything done in relation to her own pregnancy. Offences by others would result in a fine rather than onerous criminal sanctions. Abortion would be available on request within the first 12 weeks of pregnancy. Nurses and midwives, as well as doctors, would be permitted to perform abortions. Services might be offered in primary care settings. The second course of medication used in an early medical abortion could be taken in the woman's own home.[240] Nonetheless, it was with some justification that the UK

---

[233] Ten DUP MPs and one independent MP. Sinn Féin MPs do not take up their seats.

[234] Ayes 72; Noes 84.

[235] Contents 182; Not Contents 37.

[236] Including that of the mother who had sourced abortion pills for her teenage daughter, 'Prosecution of Woman Who Bought Abortion Pills for Daughter Dropped', *Irish Legal Times*, 23 October 2019.

[237] 'Abortion Rights Used to Get DUP to Back Brexit Deal, Says Stella Creasy', *Guardian*, 16 October 2019.

[238] See Chapter 6, pp. 210–11.

[239] 'High Drama another Possible Blow to Stormont's Battered Image' and 'Sinn Féin Calls for "Intensive Talks"', *BBC News*, 21 October 2019.

[240] Northern Ireland Office, *A New Legal Framework for Abortion Services in Northern Ireland; The Abortion (Northern Ireland) Regulations 2020* (SI 2020 No. 345).

Government claimed that the regulations brought Northern Ireland into line with the rest of the UK.[241] As was the case in practice elsewhere in the UK, if not reflected in the formal letter of the Abortion Act, abortion should now be freely available on request in early pregnancy; thereafter, it would be permitted on grounds closely modelled on those laid down in the Act. A right of conscientious objection was provided, framed in the same terms as in the Act.[242] While the long-standing campaign for the Abortion Act to be extended to Northern Ireland had been superseded by the fight for decriminalisation, important aspects of the regulations were the Abortion Act by another name. After decades of defending the existence of a different law in Northern Ireland, the UK Government had moved seamlessly to proclaiming the merits of consistency.

Moreover, while it had long been asked when Northern Ireland would follow the rest of the UK in liberalising its abortion laws, now questions were raised regarding when the rest of the UK might follow Northern Ireland.[243] Proposing that women should be excluded from criminal liability for inducing their own abortions, Maria Miller (Con) recently asserted the need to treat women in England and Wales in the same way as those in Northern Ireland, on the basis that 'our values and our rights are what unite our four nations. To treat women differently in those nations weakens those ties.'[244]

The reform of the Northern Irish law was an emphatic victory for Pro-Choice campaigners in Northern Ireland and their champions in Westminster. Moreover, it entrenched an understanding of abortion access as an issue of civil liberties and public health: the Royal Society for Public Health would subsequently include decriminalisation of abortion in Northern Ireland within its top 10 public health achievements of the 21st century.[245] Ann Furedi detected an important change of mood in Westminster: politicians were now 'picking up on the idea that abortion is no longer this kind of controversial vote-losing thing' and that 'to *not* support it' is to 'be seen to be discriminating against women'.[246] Most immediately, this sentiment was visible in support for buffer zones around abortion clinics, with Bills proposed by Sarah Olney (Lib Dem) and Rupa Huq (Lab).[247] The Huq Bill was strongly opposed by Fiona Bruce as disproportionate, unnecessary in light of existing regulatory powers, and threatening a wide range of 'fundamental liberties,

---

[241] Explanatory Memorandum to The Abortion (Northern Ireland) Regulations 2020 (SI 2020 No. 345), paras 7.12, 7.16; 'Abortion: Northern Ireland Opens New Chapter but Questions Remain', *BBC News*, 31 March 2020.

[242] Regulation 12.

[243] See Hodgson, Creasy and Allen in *Hansard*, HC, 23 July 2019, vol. 663, cols 1225, 1226 and 1227, respectively.

[244] *Hansard*, HC, 23 November 2021, vol. 704, col. 290.

[245] Royal Society of Public Health, 'Top 20 Public Health Achievements of the 21st Century'.

[246] Ann Furedi interviewed by Jane O'Neill, 23 August 2017.

[247] Olney Presentation Bill, *Hansard*, HC, 11 March 2020, vol. 673, col. 276; Huq Ten Minute Rule Bill, Demonstrations (Abortion Clinics) Bill 2020.

many hard-won, underpinning our democracy', including freedoms of speech, assembly, conscience, religion and expression and rights to peaceable protest and to receive information.[248] It nonetheless passed its first reading by a majority of more than four to one.[249]

Pandemic

The new Northern Ireland abortion regulations were deeply contested and much would remain to be determined by the manner of their implementation. One aspect of the ensuing controversy could not have been anticipated. Two days before the regulations were published, the UK went into its first period of 'lockdown' in response to the COVID-19 pandemic; Nadine Dorries was the first MP to receive a positive diagnosis of the disease. With people exhorted to 'stay home, protect the NHS, save lives', a hasty and radical re-evaluation of the appropriate conduct of many aspects of everyday life ensued. This included the recommendation of greater use of telemedicine for early medical abortion, thereby avoiding the need for women to attend clinics.[250] The Department of Health was initially persuaded but quickly withdrew the necessary approval when it transpired that Matt Hancock, Secretary of State for Health, had not been consulted. To the fury of Pro-Choice campaigners, the Government now confirmed that it would not permit telemedical services and opposed an amendment to the Coronavirus Bill that sought to allow them,[251] with its confusion caught in hastily drafted explanatory text on its website.[252] However, within days, it was persuaded to perform a second hasty U-turn, ordering that both sets of pills used in a medical abortion might be taken at home for a two year period.[253] It also took the opportunity to confirm that it was 'crystal clear' that there was no statutory requirement for either doctor to have seen or examined the woman, that assessment could take place via webcam or telephone, and that doctors could rely on information gathered from other multidisciplinary team members in reaching a good faith opinion.[254]

---

[248] *Hansard*, HC, 24 June 2020, vol. 677, col. 1317.

[249] Ayes 213; Noes 47.

[250] RCOG, *Coronavirus (Covid-19) Infection and Abortion Care: Information for Healthcare Professionals*.

[251] *Hansard*, HC, 24 March 2020, vol. 674, col. 248; amendment tabled by Baronesses Bennett and Barker, see *Hansard*, HL, 25 March 2020, vol. 802, cols 1759–63. See *R (Christian Concern)* v *Secretary of State for Health and Social Care* [2020] EWHC 1546, [16–29] for a summary of events.

[252] Stating '[t]he information on this page has been removed because it was published in error. This was published in error. There will be no changes to abortion regulations.' Government of the UK, 'Temporary Approval of Home Use for Both Stages of Early Medical Abortion'.

[253] Department of Health and Social Care, 'The Abortion Act 1967 – Approval of a Class of Places' (2020), paras 2–3.

[254] Bethell in *Hansard*, HL, 25 March 2020, vol. 802, col. 1762.

It was now Pro-Life campaigners who complained, citing an 'unprecedented assault from the abortion lobby' under the cover of the pandemic.[255] Right to Life launched an emergency fundraising appeal, emphasising the risks of 'DIY abortions'.[256] SPUC threatened legal action, alleging opportunism and 'trivialising the taking of human life'.[257] In the event, it was Christian Concern that went to the courts, arguing that the case concerned not just abortion but the very nature of democracy: 'abortion tycoons' and 'activist civil servants' acting 'as lobbyists for the abortion industry' had 'become a monster which the democratic government has no real power to stop'.[258] While the case was swiftly and robustly dismissed, controversy would rumble on.[259]

With governments in Westminster, Cardiff and Holyrood having moved rapidly to approve fully telemedical abortion services, Stormont came under pressure to exercise its newly acquired powers to do likewise. It refused, stating that the pandemic would rather force reconsideration of how abortion services could be rolled out and, in the meantime, women could continue to travel to England.[260] BPAS responded with the offer of free telemedical services to women in the region, *Informing Choices NI* launched a Central Access Point to provide a pathway into local abortion services[261] and, notwithstanding the Northern Ireland Executive's resolute refusal to consider commissioning abortion services, some Northern Ireland Health Trusts began to offer them.[262] Almost 3,000 women within Northern Ireland would legally terminate pregnancies within the region over the next two years (compared to just 30 in the two years before).[263] However, services remained piecemeal and precarious, with some women forced either to travel to Britain to access services or to source abortion pills online.[264]

With no signs of progress towards the commissioning of abortion services, the Northern Ireland Human Rights Commission turned to the courts and

---

[255] Right to Life, 'Emergency'.

[256] Ibid.

[257] SPUC, 'SPUC Seeks Legal Recourse as Government Extends DIY at Home Abortion due to Coronavirus Crisis'.

[258] Christian Concern, 'Why We're Taking "DIY" Abortion Case to Court of Appeal'.

[259] See *R (Christian Concern)* v *Secretary of State for Health and Social Care* [2020] EWHC 1546, [2020] EWCA Civ 1239. See further 'Pills by Post', *Sun*, 22 May 2020; Christian Concern, 'DIY Abortion Policy Led to Home Abortion at 28 Weeks'.

[260] 'Coronavirus: Home Abortions Approved during Outbreak', *BBC News*, 31 March 2020.

[261] Informing Choices NI was established following the closure of FPANI in May 2019 to take forward its work. See Informing Choices NI, *Strategic Plan 2020–2023*.

[262] BPAS, 'BPAS Launches Emergency Abortion Pills by Post for Women in Northern Ireland amid Shameful Political Gameplay with Women's Health during the Covid-19 Pandemic'. The service was suspended in July, possibly as a result of a warning letter sent by the Northern Irish Department of Health. See *In the Matter of an Application by the Northern Ireland Human Rights Commission For Judicial Review.* [2021] NIQB 91 (*NIHRC 2021*), [24], for a chronology of events.

[263] 1,373 in 2019/2020 and 1,514 from April 2020 to May 2021, *NIHRC 2021*, [69].

[264] NIHRC, *2021 Fact Sheet*; Rough, *Abortion in Northern Ireland*.

won a judgement that Brandon Lewis, Secretary of State for Northern Ireland, had failed in his legal duty to act 'expeditiously' to ensure the provision of services.[265] While some delay was inevitable given the unforeseen pressures of responding to the pandemic, the court found that it was not sustainable to leave medical professionals to develop services without any formal commissioning, support, medical guidance or funding.[266] Moreover, it was 'dispiriting' but nonetheless clear that court action was necessary to convince the Northern Ireland Executive to move on these matters,[267] and that Lewis had likewise determined only to escalate action if there were 'external pressure' to do so: his previously 'negligible' engagement on the issue had only 'stepped up' when the NIHRC took to the courts.[268] Issuing a clear rebuke to governments in both Westminster and Stormont, Mr Justice Colton reminded them that those in public office 'must obey and apply the law' even where they did not agree with its terms.[269]

Lewis's failure to intervene echoes decades of earlier studied government inaction on abortion law in Northern Ireland.[270] However, when finally forced to act, the language in which he did so offered a stark contrast to that of his predecessors. Taking further powers that would enable him to compel action from Stormont, Lewis emphasised that 'the devolution settlement does not absolve us of our responsibility to uphold the rights of women and girls', who have 'a human right to be able to access quality healthcare' and are 'legally and morally entitled' to abortion services.[271] When no action was forthcoming, Lewis laid further regulations to allow the Northern Irish Department of Health to commission and fund abortion services without the prior approval of the Stormont Executive, warning that if the Department did not now act he would intervene further,[272] and that he expected to see movement in 'days to weeks'.[273]

Debate has also continued in Westminster regarding the making permanent of the fully telemedical abortion services that were initially approved for just two years during the pandemic. When the UK Government thwarted plans to table an amendment to decriminalise abortion to its flagship Domestic Abuse

[265] Under Section 9 of the Northern Ireland (Executive Formation etc) Act 2019; see *NIHRC 2021*; NIHRC, *2021 Fact Sheet*.

[266] The Abortion (Northern Ireland) Regulations 2021 (SI 365); *NIHRC 2021*, [7.5].

[267] *NIHRC 2021*, [103–04].

[268] Ibid., [92–98], noting no evidence of action from April to September 2020 beyond a single attempt to arrange a call with the Department of Health, which took three months to arrange.

[269] Ibid., [104].

[270] See Chapter 6.

[271] The Abortion (Northern Ireland) Regulations 2021; Lewis in *Hansard*, HC, 23 March 2021, vol. 691, Written Statement HCWS875. 'DUP will "Vigorously Oppose" UK Intervention to Speed Up NI Abortion Services', *Guardian*, 18 March 2021.

[272] Brandon Lewis, 'Northern Ireland Update'. *Hansard,* HC, 19 May 2022 (Statement UIN HCWS39).

[273] Jayne McCormack, 'Abortion in NI: Health Officials Told to Set Up Services', *BBC News*, 19 May 2022.

Bill,[274] Diana Johnson instead proposed amendments to make the measure permanent for England.[275] With Pro-Life MPs raising concerns regarding the safety of telemedical services and the possibility of effective safeguarding,[276] Johnson withdrew her amendment, having first extracted a promise of a review to consider these issues.[277] The safety of telemedical services remained fiercely disputed by Pro-Life groups,[278] and, following the promised public consultation, the Government announced an end to telemedical services, claiming that its priority was 'women being able to access health services in a safe, secure way'.[279] However, it was overruled by Parliament, which voted in favour of an amendment to the Health and Social Care Act 2022 tabled by the Conservative peer Liz Sugg to make telemedicine for early abortion care permanent in England,[280] a move already undertaken in Wales.[281] The intervention was warmly welcomed by the RCOG as a 'vital decision that protects women's rights to access the healthcare they deserve and gives them the choice of accessing early abortion care at home'.[282]

Further attempts to amend abortion law continue on both sides of the Irish Sea. In Stormont, a Bill to prevent terminations on the grounds of non-fatal fetal anomalies failed by a narrow margin.[283] Meanwhile, in Westminster, the Health and Social Care Act had earlier been used as a vehicle for a number of other abortion amendments. Diana Johnson (Lab) and Maria Miller (Con) proposed the exclusion of women's criminal liability for inducing or participating in their own abortions.[284] Pro-Life MPs again argued for a reduction in the upper time limit to 22 weeks, denouncing the 'outdated' science

---

[274] See Wollaston in *Hansard*, HC, 5 June 2018, vol. 642, col. 226. This possibility was avoided by creatively drafting a clause providing for the extraterritorial enforceability of enforced abortion without mentioning Section 58 of the Offences Against the Person Act, thus rendering an amendment seeking to amend or repeal it to decriminalise abortion inadmissible.

[275] *Hansard*, HC, 6 July 2020, vol. 678, cols 720–21, amendment to the Domestic Abuse Bill 2020.

[276] Ibid., see Robinson, col. 724; Leigh, col. 732; Bruce, col. 735; Lockhart, col. 750.

[277] Atkins in ibid., cols 716, 769.

[278] Compare Aiken et al., 'Effectiveness, Safety and Acceptability of No-Test Medical Abortion Provided via Telemedicine' and Edward Morris, RCOG President, in RCOG, 'New Study Finds Telemedicine for Abortion Care Is Safe and More Accessible' with SPUC, *At-Home Abortions*, Right to Life, 'Medical Professionals Open Letter Regarding "Home" Abortion Schemes' and Christian Concern, *Abortion at Home: A Mystery Client Investigation*.

[279] Department of Health and Social Care, 'Press Release. England to Return to Pre-pandemic System for Early Abortions' (24 February 2022).

[280] Section 178 of the Health and Care Act 2022. This represents only the second occasion in more than fifty years that substantive amendment has been made to the text of the Abortion Act.

[281] Eluned Morgan, Minister for Health and Social Services, 'Arrangements for Early Medical Abortion at Home' (Welsh Government, Written Statement, 22 February 2022).

[282] Edward Morris, President of the RCOG, cited in RCOG, 'Press Release: Parliament votes to make telemedicine for early medical abortion permanent in England' (31 March 2022).

[283] Severe Fetal Impairment Abortion (Amendment) Bill (2021), defeated by 43 Ayes to 45 Noes, Northern Ireland Assembly Official Report (14 December 2021).

[284] Miller in *Hansard*, HC, 23 November 2021, vol. 704, col. 290.

underpinning the current limit,[285] for a prohibition on sex-selective abortion, and to make abortion on grounds of fetal anomaly subject to the same time limit as that for most other abortions.[286]

These ongoing points of contestations are the most recent skirmishes in a war that has now lasted for more than five decades, with the opposing sides and government actors increasingly coming to share a common vernacular.[287] When Pro-Choice groups and professional medical bodies square up to Pro-Life and Christian organisations, the dispute between them is no longer framed primarily in terms of moral disagreement over the rightness or wrongness of abortion. Rather, each argues that it cares for women and desires their empowerment, each advocates for civil liberties and human rights, each claims strongly to be supported by the science and criticises the other for ignoring inconvenient truths that challenge its ideological position, and each purports to desire a law that is fit for purpose in the 21st century. Where they differ markedly is in their understanding of basic facts regarding the safety of abortion services, their acceptability to women, and the bona fides of those who offer them.

Conclusion

An unbroken thread of contestation can be traced across the more than half a century since the Abortion Act was enacted. However, much has changed in the framing of this dispute. John Corrie launched a comprehensive assault on the Abortion Act, framing his case in terms of personal responsibility and family values. More recent attacks have been framed in a language of modernisation, scientific advance and civil rights, proposing narrowly focused measures designed to chip away at specific aspects of the Act whilst implicitly accepting its broad framework. Moreover, while Corrie claimed to speak for a moral majority, more recent attacks have typically been led from the margins by MPs guided by their Christian faith and often at odds with mainstream views even within their own party. Jack Scarisbrick concludes that while the movement's intellectual case is 'as coherent as ever', the Pro-Life presence in the House of Commons is now 'pretty feeble', with 'no great hero or heroine' and with the APPG lacking its former bite.[288]

---

[285] Bruce in *Hansard*, HC, 23 November 2021, vol. 704, col. 287, and Leigh, col. 287.

[286] Ibid., see Bruce, col. 288; Lockhart, col. 292.

[287] This is increasingly visible in Stormont as well as Westminster, where recent debates regarding the fetal anomaly ground for abortion display an increased foregrounding of concerns for modernisation and civil liberties. See 'Abortion Legislation: Non-fatal Disabilities' Motion, 20 June 2020; Abortion (Amendment) Bill 2021 proposed by Paul Givan (DUP), 15 March 2021; and Severe Fetal Impairment Abortion (Amendment) Bill 2021 (14 December 2021), all in *Official Report of the Northern Ireland Assembly*.

[288] Jack Scarisbrick interviewed by Jane O'Neill, 7 November 2017.

With so much now shared in the normative framing of the debate, contestation has increasingly centred on profoundly disputed visions of empirical reality. Reflecting on future priorities for the Pro-Life movement, Josephine Quintavalle notes a need to 'up our professional input ... [and] to move into that intellectual high ground and start to get evidence and concerns across at a proper professional level'.[289] With Pro-Choice advocates relying on the authoritative pronouncements of professional medical bodies in asserting the safety of abortion, Pro-Life campaigners have a steep hill to climb. Suggestions that these medical bodies are themselves 'in bed with' Pro-Choice campaigners appear to have fallen on largely deaf ears within Parliament, and Pro-Life groups have struggled to avoid accusations of bias in their own attempts at knowledge production. Peter Saunders reflects that the movement now faces 'a battle of biblical proportions, where the institutions and parliament and big business is all lined up on one side and we have got a few tents on the other'.[290]

---

[289] Josephine Quintavalle interviewed by Jane O'Neill, 6 October 2017.
[290] Saunders interviewed by O'Neill.

8

A Biography of the 'Great Untouchable'

> If abortion is mentioned, up go the barricades to defend the right to life or the right to choose. On no other issue is there such a dialogue of the deaf in this Chamber, with the slightest concession to one side being seen as enabling the wholesale destruction of the other ... The House is normally left defending the Abortion Act 1967 – with all its weakness [sic], which are acknowledged even by some of its major proponents – as though it were holy writ.[1]

Five decades on, the Abortion Act remains, apparently set in concrete as a 'great untouchable'.[2] The disputes that it inspires no longer bring out protesters counted in the hundreds of thousands and, were petitions still signed and delivered in hard copy, they would no longer require transportation by shopping trolley.[3] Nonetheless, David Steel reports that he continues to receive hate mail and letters of thanks in equal measure, and the parliamentary debates regarding the Act still become 'polarised horribly and quickly',[4] remaining 'undoubtedly the nastiest' that take place on any subject.[5]

The Abortion Act's impressive longevity does not then result from any lack of desire to change it. In the preceding pages, we have described some of the struggles that have shaped its biography. We have noted more than 60 occasions since 1968 when proposals for reform of abortion law have been recorded in *Hansard*:[6] on this idiosyncratic and unsatisfactory measure, we believe that the Abortion Act may be the most contested piece of legislation in British parliamentary history.[7] The Act has survived these repeated assaults with its text barely altered, lying at the heart of the oldest statutory framework

---

[1] Pugh in *Hansard*, House of Commons (HC), 6 July 2015, vol. 598, col. 109.

[2] David Alton in 'Saving the Alton Bill', *Times*, 21 May 1988.

[3] Chapter 1, p. 13.

[4] Pugh in *Hansard*, HC, 6 July 2015, vol. 598, col. 109.

[5] Alton, *What Kind of Country?*, 170.

[6] See Appendix 2, listing reform proposals between April 1968, when the Abortion Act came into effect, and May 2022, when this book went to press. Multiple abortion law reform amendments tabled to a single bill are counted as one occasion.

[7] This is a difficult claim to test, with the parliamentary library not storing records in a way that permits easy comparisons. We acknowledge that, on other measures, other laws might claim this dubious honour.

to govern any medical procedure,[8] and offering the paradigm case for the difficulties of achieving reform by Private Members' legislation.[9] Its extraordinary resilience has inspired great creativity in those who have battled to reform it, with its story offering a case study in the manipulation and exploitation of the parliamentary rule book and, indeed, on several occasions prompting its rewriting.[10]

In the preceding pages, we have taken seriously the insight that written norms are both rooted in the past, enshrining a set of historically contingent values and practices, but also that, as linguistic structures that can take effect only through acts of interpretation, they are simultaneously constantly evolving.[11] While the meaning of any law reflects elements of continuity and change as it strains and flexes between these twin pressures, the resulting tensions have inevitably been particularly visible in a law characterised by such sustained controversy and remarkable longevity. The Abortion Act was passed by a specific Parliament to address a particular set of problems at a given moment in UK history. However, its meaning – as a landmark measure of public health and humanity or a monstrous denial of God's will; as a key moment in the path towards female equality and social justice or a eugenicist, profit-driven betrayal of women and their unborn children; as a set of inadequate but necessary safeguards or an anachronistic artefact of misogyny and medical paternalism – has been furiously debated and frequently recast over the years. Further, while the Act's text reflects the social norms and clinical practices of the 1960s, its interpretation and implementation have been shaped through complex, dynamic and ongoing processes of dispute, negotiation, consolidation, rupture and revision by an evolving cast of actors rooted in social, demographic, professional and institutional contexts that have changed dramatically over the past five decades. This book has aimed to tell that story.

In this concluding chapter, we first briefly recall the influence of some of the groups of actors who have given meaning to the Abortion Act over the past five decades. We then turn briefly to consider the shifting social and cultural landscapes that informed their work and were themselves profoundly shaped by the Abortion Act.

Shaping the Abortion Act

In 1967, a young Liberal MP was lucky enough to draw a high place in the Private Members' Ballot. With the encouragement and support of the Abortion Law Reform Association, he elected to use this rare opportunity to address one of the great social reform issues of his time. David Steel explained

---

[8] Chapter 5, p. 187.
[9] Chapter 3, pp. 97, 107.
[10] Chapter 3, p. 107; Chapter 7, pp. 225–26, 241–42.
[11] Chapter 1, pp. 18–19.

that he did not intend to introduce abortion on demand; rather, he hoped to eradicate dangerous backstreet abortions and to address the suffering of desperate women overwhelmed by the demands of repeated maternity.[12] Women would be permitted to terminate their pregnancies only in deserving cases and under conditions of strict medical control. Over the decades to follow, whilst unsafe, illegal abortion would remain one of the leading causes of maternal death worldwide, it would be close to eradicated in the UK.[13]

Medical gatekeepers were key to Steel's vision and most took their role very seriously. When the Abortion Act first entered into force, a woman might expect to undergo searching medical interviews and physical examinations before two doctors approved her request to terminate a pregnancy. If her reasons were not considered serious enough or her doctor was ideologically opposed to abortion, she might be refused or come under sustained pressure to continue her pregnancy or obstacles might be deliberately placed in her way; indeed, she might be offered an abortion only on condition of agreeing to a simultaneous sterilisation.[14]

Fifty years on, while a lawyer might quibble that no medical procedure is available 'on demand', abortion is now widely available on request within early pregnancy: professional codes of practice emphasise the importance of respecting women's own decisions and services are largely funded by the NHS. Assessment can take place via webcam or telephone, certifying doctors may choose to rely on information gathered from nurses or counsellors in forming an opinion, and legal formalities are likely to be completed quickly behind the scenes. An insistence that a woman agree to be sterilised as a precondition for access to abortion would be both unlawful and grounds for disciplinary sanction.[15] In sum, the changes to women's experiences of accessing abortion services have been seismic, yet they have occurred without amendment of the text of the Abortion Act.

For some, this means that most abortions today are simply illegal.[16] This is to misunderstand the operation of law. Even the very earliest commentators were aware that the Abortion Act would acquire meaning over time and that the judges who would give it were not 'desiccated legal automata' impervious to public policy and other concerns.[17] While these judges would frequently preface their rulings by emphasising that they could speak only to issues of law and not ethics, their own moral views would inevitably shape their rulings and

---

[12] Chapter 1, p. 9.
[13] Ganatra et al., 'Global, Regional, and Subregional Classification of Abortions by Safety, 2010–14'; Sedgh et al., 'Induced Abortion'.
[14] Chapter 2, pp. 29–46.
[15] Chapter 2, pp. 35, 42.
[16] Chapter 5, pp. 152, 167, 169.
[17] Howe in Medical Protection Society, *The Abortion Act 1967 Proceedings of a Symposium* (hereafter MPS, *Symposium*), 72.

would sometimes be clearly visible within them.[18] They would also be influenced by a powerful and pervasive concern with public policy factors, foremost amongst them a marked reluctance to disrupt medical practice conducted in good faith. The Abortion Act's use of open-textured norms (such as 'serious' and 'substantial') and its requirement that doctors reach an 'honest' (rather than a 'reasonable') opinion that an abortion is justified deliberately left broad scope for the exercise of clinical discretion, subject to professional norms of good practice. Judges would work hard to protect this, relying heavily on established clinical understandings to give legal meaning to the provisions of the Act and confirming the legality of accepted medical practices even where it was necessary to stretch the meaning of less open-textured statutory language to do so.[19]

In determining the meaning of the Abortion Act, the courts have frequently looked back to Parliament's intention in passing it as offering one important guide to its interpretation. However, the exercise of peering back through history to distil clarity and meaning from the confusion and noise surrounding the Act's passage would necessarily be conducted through the lens of contemporary views. Moreover, it would yield only broad concepts to be fleshed out with conceptions that had evolved in line with changing social and clinical realities.[20] In the authoritative statement of the parliamentary intention behind the Abortion Act, the House of Lords found that the Act was intended to ensure that 'socially acceptable abortions should be carried out under the safest conditions attainable'.[21] Yet the 'safest conditions attainable' imply very different requirements for a treatment whereby a woman places pills in her own body than for a technically demanding surgical procedure performed under general anaesthetic, and a 'socially acceptable abortion' has taken on a different meaning as a growing majority of the British public have come to believe that abortion is permissible when a woman decides on her own that she does not wish to have a child.[22]

In holding the final authority to give meaning to statutory text, courts also make law.[23] However, they are far from the only actors to play a role here. By the time that the first disputes arrived before them, the Abortion Act was already heavily saturated with the meanings given to it in clinical practice. These reflected the daily acts of interpretation of individual doctors, which were reinforced or revised through discussion and debate at colloquia and in the pages of learned journals before settling gradually into received practices and influential professional codes.[24] Indeed, doctors were sometimes well

---

[18] E.g. Chapter 5, pp. 160, 178, 181.

[19] E.g. Chapter 5, p. 178.

[20] Chapter 5, p. 179.

[21] *Royal College of Nursing* v *Department of Health and Social Security* [1981] 1 All ER 545, 575.

[22] Chapter 4, pp. 113–14.

[23] Chapter 5, pp. 151–52.

[24] Chapter 2, pp. 29–39.

aware of the merits of quietly adopting a practice and allowing it to become embedded ahead of any potential court challenge rather than seeking prior judicial permission for it.[25] Senior doctors played a particularly important role in entrenching liberal or restrictive interpretations of the Abortion Act within their hospitals, training future generations of doctors in their image and radically affecting a woman's prospects of accessing NHS abortion services in different regions in a 'postcode lottery' that endured for decades.[26]

While doctors thus also played an important role in giving meaning to the Abortion Act, neither did they operate in a vacuum. In the early years, the nurses with whom they worked are likely to have exerted an influence that tended towards a more conservative interpretation of its terms.[27] Further, women seeking the safe, legal abortions that they had heard were now available were not passive in the processes by which the Act acquired meaning. Following its introduction, they arrived in their GPs' surgeries in rapidly growing numbers, sometimes showing considerable resilience and ingenuity in overcoming any hurdles placed in their path. Doctors' interpretations of the Act were not abstract exercises: they were developed in meetings with real women who described concrete problems, anxieties and aspirations. In some instances, doctors came to suspect and resent attempts to manipulate them through concocted stories, potentially hardening their opposition to abortion.[28] However, the more marked effect is likely to have been that seen in the young David Paintin, whose encounters with patients provoked a significant liberalisation in his views.[29]

Whilst formally proclaiming their neutrality on an issue deemed a matter for the conscience of individual MPs, successive governments have also played an important role in shaping the Abortion Act. Indeed, the Act's longevity owes much to government action and studied inaction: the conditions within which attempts to reform it might (or, more frequently, might not) reach a meaningful vote have been carefully managed over the decades and apparently used on occasion as a bargaining chip to buy support for some unrelated political end.[30] Successive governments have also relied on statutory powers to shape the Act's implementation, sometimes effecting changes that had been proposed, and defeated, in Parliament.[31] Most significantly, the current regime for licensing non-NHS abortion service providers is rooted in concerns regarding the taxi touts and 'Cash Before Delivery' doctors of the late 1960s and early 1970s, having been designed to protect the Act from restrictive statutory reform through implementing administrative curbs on the worst

---

[25] E.g. Chapter 5, p. 182.
[26] Chapter 2, pp. 32–34.
[27] Chapter 2, pp. 29–30, 61–62.
[28] Chapter 2, p. 43.
[29] Chapter 2, p. 33.
[30] Chapter 6, p. 210. Chapter 7, p. 255.
[31] E.g. Chapter 3, 106; Chapter 5, pp. 165–66.

abuses.[32] While many abortion service providers initially welcomed this additional layer of regulation, over time they came to resent it as singling out abortion care in a medically unnecessary and politically motivated way.[33] The UK Government has also sometimes attempted to dictate a specific understanding of statutory text through official guidance. In the early 1980s, 'backdoor Corrie' measures appear to have had some limited success in imposing a more restrictive reading of the Abortion Act.[34] Northern Irish ministers would likewise stand accused of attempting to use official guidance to rewrite abortion law: it would take 15 years and six bitterly contested drafts before such guidance would finally be agreed.[35]

The meaning of any law is carved out through the interpretative labour of those who work within it, those who are subject to it and those responsible for its enforcement. Less usual is the significant and sustained role that has been played in the Abortion Act's biography by one further important group of actors: campaigners. US scholars have tended to cite the Act's longevity as evidence that, unlike their US counterparts, British anti-abortion campaigners 'failed miserably' as politicians 'ran away from the abortion issue': one authoritative account notes that they were not just thwarted in attempts 'to reduce the quality and availability of abortion services but [they] also saw them expand through increased public funding and the loosening or elimination of medical gatekeeping requirements'.[36] This captures an important comparative truth. However, campaigners on both sides of the fence have nonetheless played an enormously significant role in shaping the Abortion Act through their impacts on lawmakers and policymakers, the courts and doctors and their own moves into service provision.

First, campaigners exerted an important and sustained influence on Parliament and successive governments. While many politicians indeed 'ran away' from the abortion issue, influence on law reform must be measured not just in whether it was achieved but also in how successfully it was blocked. Campaigners' skills in mobilising protesters, generating negative headlines, sowing division within and between political parties and snarling up legislative agendas have been a powerful factor in successive governments' reluctance to give parliamentary time to the issue. This cemented the Abortion Act as a 'great untouchable' even in the face of widespread recognition of its flaws. In the early years, the inherent difficulties of achieving reform by Private Members' legislation were skilfully exploited by a small cohort of pro-choice MPs and their supporters outside Parliament. With the tide now turning in favour of liberalising reform, the same is likely to be true for anti-abortion

---

[32] Chapter 3, pp. 74–75.
[33] Chapter 4, pp. 125–27.
[34] Chapter 5, pp. 165–66.
[35] Chapter 6, pp. 212–13.
[36] Halfmann, *Doctors and Demonstrators*, 2–3; see also Soper, *Evangelical Christianity in the United States and Britain*.

advocates, imbuing them with a potential strength that far exceeds their dwindling numbers.[37]

Further, while instances of statutory reform of abortion law have been rare over the last 50 years, those that have occurred have been profoundly shaped by the ongoing work of campaigners. Most obviously, radical reform of Northern Ireland's abortion law came about only as a result of bitterly fought, highly visible Pro-Choice campaigns, and it was shaped by the findings of a CEDAW report secured by their work. On the other side of the Irish Sea, Pro-Life campaigners' work marked the most significant reform to be introduced to the Abortion Act in its five decade history: the enshrining of a 24 week upper limit for most abortions. It is surprising now to recall that the Parliament that passed the Abortion Act gave no attention to the question of an appropriate upper time limit. Only later did this emerge as a significant point of concern and dispute, and only later again did it become entrenched as the major point of contestation regarding the Act, gradually displacing an earlier emphasis on the legitimacy of specific kinds of reasons for seeking abortion. This focus on later abortion was fostered by the stories of babies left gasping for breath on hospital sluice boards that Life worked hard to uncover and publicise from the 1970s: this helped to provoke the development of professional guidelines, to fuel a desire for reform within Parliament, and to entrench viability as an important moral watershed.[38]

Campaigners have also had a marked influence on the Government's use of its statutory powers under the Abortion Act, thereby profoundly shaping its implementation. In the late 1970s, Dr Malcolm Potts complained that the approval of every possible simplification of abortion treatment protocols was 'unreasonably retarded', as governments 'look[ed] over their shoulders at the banners, broadcasts and broadsheets of the right-to-life movement'.[39] More recently, successive governments delayed for almost three decades before authorising a broader class of places for the use of abortion pills, latterly explicitly attributing their caution to political sensitivities rather than any doubts regarding the safety of such an expansion.[40] Today, the Government appears to fear Pro-Choice campaigners as much as anti-abortion ones: the Department of Health recently chose to leave unwitting doctors to carry out potentially illegal terminations rather than risk the wrath of BPAS by updating its guidance on the interpretation of the Abortion Act.[41] The painful contortions of a Government now apparently trying to look over both shoulders simultaneously were visible in the two rapid U-turns taken before the introduction of fully telemedical abortion services during the COVID-19

---

[37] Chapters 3 and 7.

[38] Chapter 2, pp. 50–55; Chapter 3, pp. 79–80, 96–97.

[39] BPAS Archives, Malcolm Potts, 'Medical and Social Experience in Legal Abortion' in Birth Control Trust, *Abortion: Ten Years On*, May 1978, 19–21.

[40] Chapter 5, pp. 180–83.

[41] Chapter 5, pp. 156–57.

pandemic[42] and in later contestation regarding whether those services should be made permanent.[43]

Second, campaigners and sympathetic journalists have exerted an important influence on clinical practice, including through their use of whistle-blowers, 'sting' investigations and 'mystery shopper' exercises. One local MP in the late 1970s complained:

> In the West Midlands even an unavoidable mistake by the BPAS is used by the strong anti-abortion lobby in the region to create the impression that BPAS is medically incompetent, financially grasping and morally bankrupt. As an example, one case was related to me at great length, and with great glee, by one of the leaders of the anti-cause concerning a mistaken diagnosis of a woman who had a double uterus – hardly an everyday condition.[44]

The effect on those working under this harsh, sustained spotlight is impossible to quantify but easy to imagine. Some insight is given by Diane Munday's speaking notes for a talk given to BPAS staff in the 1980s. With Life's whistle-blower network highly active at the time and *Babies for Burning* still fresh in minds, Munday warned of the need to avoid doing anything 'that could be used against us by those who would destroy us'. Her use of capitals indicates the urgency of her message:

> So my message to you is to be constantly aware. Is difficult . . . Repeat – MUST NOT [JEOPARDISE] PATIENT CARE OR COMPASSIONATE APPROACH BECAUSE OF PARANOIA ABOUT SPIES. ON OTHER HAND MUST BE ALERT TO FACT THAT NOT ALL WHO APPROACH US (PERSONALLY OR ON PHONE) ARE FRIENDLY AND GENUINE.[45]

Far less frequently, the boot has been on the other foot. As anti-abortion groups moved into offering counselling services, Pro-Choice advocates have also sometimes been prompted to conduct 'mystery shopper' exercises, using them to publicise instances of poor counselling practice or the provision of biased and misleading information.[46]

Third, campaigners have worked to shape the meaning of the Abortion Act through court actions, hoping not just for formal legal success but also to provoke media interest, to shape public opinion, and to influence clinical practice. While two legal challenges have been brought by BPAS and one by FPANI, it has largely been Pro-Life groups that have made use of this strategy. Over the last five decades, they have offered financial, practical, and moral

---

[42] Chapter 7, pp. 257–8.

[43] Chapter 7, pp. 259–60.

[44] BPAS Archives, Hodgson, 'A View of Abortion from the W Midlands' in Birth Control Trust, *Abortion: Ten Years On*, May 1978, 27–28.

[45] BPAS Papers, 'Speaking Notes' (c. 1980s), speaking notes written by Diane Munday, capitals and underlining in original. Awaiting cataloguing in the Wellcome Collection.

[46] See Lee, *Abortion, Motherhood and Mental Health*, 145–47; Brook, *Crisis Pregnancy Centres*.

support to dozens of litigants, threatened or brought legal actions in their own names, and effectively lobbied prosecutors to pursue cases.[47] While only very rarely succeeding in formal terms, these cases have nonetheless had an important impact. While Jack Scarisbrick was shocked and disappointed not to see Dr Leonard Arthur convicted of murder, he claimed victory in provoking debate and hastening changes in paediatric practice.[48] Robert Carver failed to obtain an injunction to prevent his former girlfriend from terminating her pregnancy, but the ensuing media attention accomplished the same goal.[49] Joanna Jepson's court action provoked significant public debate regarding the fetal anomaly ground of the Abortion Act, leading to procedural changes in some hospitals.[50] Heidi Crowter has attracted significant sympathetic media coverage and popular support, notwithstanding her defeat in the High Court.[51] Finally, controversy regarding sex-selective abortion has undoubtedly influenced practice: one 'mystery shopper' recently reported that she had 'offered a trivial reason for having an abortion' but had been reassured by BPAS that 'any reason other than the sex of the baby is a valid reason to us'.[52] Pro-Life groups have also frequently used legal cases to publicise alleged procedural failings in informed consent, counselling or safeguarding, thereby challenging the 'normalisation' or 'trivialisation' of a medical intervention that they believe to be profoundly harmful.[53]

Last but by no means least, campaigners have had a powerful impact on the implementation of the Abortion Act through their own moves into service provision. Believing that abortion was too readily available to women before other solutions had been fully explored, Pro-Life groups set up Life Houses and established their own counselling services to encourage women to continue their pregnancies.[54] However, the most influential move into service provision came from the ALRA campaigners who founded LPAS and BPAS, later joined by MSI. The abortion charities undercut and helped to force out of operation the profiteering 'Cash Before Delivery' doctors who were a marked feature of the Abortion Act's early years, thereby removing a compelling reason for restrictive statutory reform.[55] They also played an important role in making services available to those women who could not access them locally within the NHS: this transformed a disparity in access to legal abortion into a disparity in access to NHS funding, which would itself be eliminated as

[47] Chapter 5.
[48] Chapter 5, pp. 172–73.
[49] Chapter 5, p. 155.
[50] Chapter 5, p. 174.
[51] Chapter 5, pp. 174–76.
[52] Christian Concern, 'Abortion for "Any Reason" Other than Sex-Selection, Says BPAS'.
[53] Chapter 5, pp. 169–70.
[54] Chapter 4, pp. 49–50.
[55] Chapter 2, pp. 46–49.

NHS commissioners acquired powers to purchase their services and thus to bypass senior NHS doctors who were ideologically opposed to abortion.[56]

The abortion charities have also played an important role in consistently, and sometimes very vocally, pushing for the most liberal interpretation of the Abortion Act. The contrast with Scotland, where almost all services are provided within the NHS, is instructive. Scottish doctors have occasionally been exasperated by the pugnacious approach of BPAS, believing quiet medical diplomacy more effective in securing liberalising change.[57] However, whilst BPAS was prepared to go to court to defend its practice of offering terminations up to and including 24+0 weeks of pregnancy, a range of informal lower gestational limits for abortion have persisted within Scottish NHS boards, reflecting the attitudes of individual doctors, midwives and health service managers and resulting in a steady stream of Scots travelling south to access later abortion services.[58] David Baird reflects, '[a]s long as you can export the problem, it won't be solved'.[59]

The growing dominance of the abortion charities has also had other important, unintended effects. The founders of BPAS hoped that the organisation might wither away as abortion services became mainstreamed within the NHS.[60] In the event, in England and Wales, over three-quarters of abortions are currently commissioned from an independent sector dominated by BPAS and MSI.[61] With most abortions provided in this way, capacity within NHS facilities has declined: medical students may complete their training with no opportunity to gain practical experience of the most common gynaecological procedure sought by women, and the ability to offer high-quality abortion care to those with complex comorbidities who need treatment within an NHS hospital is reduced.[62] This development also sits in significant tension with attempts to normalise abortion services as part of mainstream NHS women's healthcare, sustaining Pro-Life attacks on a profit-motivated 'abortion industry' and leaving standalone abortion clinics as visible focal points for protests and prayer vigils.[63]

---

[56] Chapter 4, pp. 116–18.

[57] E.g. Chapter 5, p. 182.

[58] Chapter 5, pp. 156–57, on the BPAS case; Cochrane and Cameron, 'Attitudes of Scottish Abortion Care Providers towards Provision of Abortion after 16 Weeks' Gestation within Scotland', 215–20; Purcell et al., 'Access to and Experience of Later Abortion', 101–08; Anna Glasier interviewed by Gayle Davis, 13 November 2017, noted that 'to our shame, we are not doing very well with providing late abortion', locating the historical reason in midwives' reluctance to be involved with later terminations.

[59] David Baird interviewed by Gayle Davis, 13 November 2017.

[60] Chapter 4, p. 118.

[61] Department of Health and Social Care, *Abortion Statistics for England and Wales: 2020*. See Chapter 4, pp. 116–18.

[62] BPAS, *Medically Complex Women and Abortion Care*.

[63] Chapter 4, pp. 118–23.

Finally, the move into service provision gave the abortion charities an important dual role, guaranteeing the financial sustainability of their advocacy work and bridging divides between medical organisations and Pro-Choice campaign groups to facilitate strategically important alliances. From this basis, BPAS has played a key role in pioneering and driving clinical change across the whole sector, from the development of outpatient services to streamlined treatment protocols for abortion pills.[64] Its wider influence has been a source of particular anger and frustration for anti-abortion campaigners, who see the charity as lying at the 'epicentre' of Pro-Choice campaigns, with a significant influence on professional medical bodies and its 'fingerprints on stacks of things'.[65] BPAS was surely one of those contemplated by Christian Concern when it warned that 'abortion tycoons' and 'activist civil servants' acting 'as lobbyists for the abortion industry' have now become 'a monster which the democratic government has no real power to stop'.[66]

In sum, it is true that campaigners have had little success in achieving statutory reform of the 'great untouchable'. However, along with doctors and other health professionals, women seeking treatment, the courts and government, they have played a very significant role in giving meaning to a living law. We turn next briefly to recall some salient features of the rapidly changing social and cultural landscape in which the Abortion Act was rooted and how it shaped and was shaped by that landscape.

Shaping the UK

In the mid-1970s, the eminent journalist and later Catholic convert Malcolm Muggeridge claimed that the Abortion Act was of existential significance:

> Either we go on with the process of shaping our own destiny without reference to any higher being than Man, deciding ourselves how many children shall be born, when and in what varieties, and which lives are worth continuing and which should be put out . . . Or we draw back, seeking to understand and fall in with our Creator's purpose for us rather than to pursue our own, in true humility praying, as the founder of our religion and our civilisation taught us. Thy will be done.[67]

In passing the Abortion Act, Parliament had signalled a clear choice. However, with the Act resting on a fault line between the shifting tectonic plates of a society undergoing a demographic revolution, ongoing contestation was inevitable. The Abortion Act was both artefact and driver of an increasing rejection of religious norms in favour of an emphasis on science in ordering

---

[64] Chapter 4, pp. 125–27; Lohr et al., 'Simultaneous Compared with Interval Medical Abortion Regimens Where Home Use Is Restricted', 635–41.

[65] John Deighan interviewed by Jane O'Neill, 29 January 2018.

[66] Christian Concern, 'Why We're Taking "DIY" Abortion Case to Court of Appeal'.

[67] 'What the Abortion Argument Is About', *Sunday Times*, 2 February 1975.

understandings of the world, of rapidly changing familial, gender and other social norms, and of significant changes within the medical relationship, clinical practice and abortion technologies.

Secularisation was central to this story. Over the course of the Act's life, the UK has witnessed steady declines in religious faith, church attendance, and a wider discursive Christianity whereby people derive and express their customs and values with reference to Christian traditions.[68] This has inevitably contributed to a fall in the influence of the Pro-Life movement, with Christian belief having been a powerful motivation for many (though not all) within it and with churches having offered it important infrastructure for mass mobilisation.[69] In recent years, a proliferation of smaller, more radical Pro-Life groups has re-energised campaigning. However, with these newer groups unapologetic about their religious motivation and adopting a more confrontational tone, this has cut against the efforts of the longer-established groups to appeal to mainstream, secular public opinion, pushing anti-abortion campaigns to the margins of public opinion.[70]

These broad trends are also visible within Parliament, where the first MP to speak against the Bill that would become the Abortion Act was William Wells MP (Lab), a Catholic who began – as would many to follow him – by dismissing the relevance of his faith to the issue at hand. Nonetheless, Wells emphasised that he was 'not only upholding the common tradition of Christianity, but ... protecting principles which stand at the very root of an ordered society'.[71] In those early days, with the Church of England sometimes described as 'the Tory party at prayer', most of his fellow-travellers would likewise stand firmly and proudly on a ground of mainstream family-values Conservativism built on the bedrock of an unspoken Christian heritage.[72] More recently, many of the most prominent parliamentary advocates of restrictive abortion law reform have been members of the Tory Cornerstone Group, which likewise emphasises 'the spiritual values which have informed British institutions, her culture and her nation's sense of identity for centuries, underpinned by the belief in a strong nation state'.[73] However, while Wells plausibly claimed to represent widely shared beliefs in common traditions, the Cornerstone Group was founded in explicit recognition that this centre ground had shifted and needed to be 'pull[ed back] kicking and screaming' towards it.[74] Calls for restrictive abortion law reform today come increasingly

---

[68] Chapter 4, pp. 113–15.

[69] Chapter 3, pp. 70–71; Chapter 4, p. 114.

[70] Chapter 4, pp. 121–22.

[71] *Hansard*, HC, 22 July 1966, vol. 732, col. 1081.

[72] See generally Chapter 3.

[73] Cornerstone Group, 'About Us'.

[74] Edward Leigh, the Group's leader, cited in 'Conservative MPs call for "Moral Values" Agenda', *ePolitix.com*, 25 July 2005. Other members include Nadine Dorries, Fiona Bruce, the late David Amess and Laurence Robertson: see Cornerstone Group, 'About Us'; see further Chapter 7, p. 228.

from the margins of a Conservative party that has grown more socially liberal and within a Parliament where other major parties have formally committed to decriminalising abortion.[75] Leading anti-abortion MPs now work not just with the longer-established Pro-Life organisations that John Corrie considered too extreme for his purposes but also, on occasion, with the newer, more radical groups.[76] These MPs are distinguished from the parliamentary mainstream in the emphasis that they place on religious faith in driving their parliamentary work.[77] And many of their political biographies are marked by the visible trappings of outspoken outsiders who refuse to toe party lines: sacking, defections, loss of the party whip, regular 'ticking off' by the Whips' office and being conspicuously passed over for elevation.[78]

Secularisation has been accompanied by a growing confidence in science as an alternative way to interpret and understand the world, with contestation regarding the Abortion Act increasingly focused on disputed facts rather than competing values.[79] For many Pro-Choice campaigners, the shift in Pro-Life argumentation has been wholly disingenuous, with opposition to abortion remaining fundamentally rooted in religion and 'grey-haired male dominance'.[80] For their part, Pro-Life campaigners claim that the science is on their side and that their opponents are blinded by self-interest, emotion and dogma,[81] with their views 'certainly not objective' but rather 'very emotive', 'very partial' and 'driven by satisfying their will rather than their intellect'.[82]

In making scientific claims regarding the safety of abortion, Pro-Choice campaigners have come to rely increasingly on the authoritative pronouncements and evidence base laid out by professional medical and scientific bodies.[83] In seeking to challenge them, Pro-Life advocates have made use of a wide range of strategies, many of which were powerfully illustrated in the minority report tabled by Nadine Dorries and Bob Spink MPs to the House of Commons Science and Technology Committee report on abortion.[84] First, professional bodies are dismissed as biased and dominated by members who have built careers within an 'abortion industry'. The need for more democratic means of scientific knowledge production is asserted, with calls for a seat at the

---

[75] Labour Party, *It's Time for Real Change: The Labour Party Manifesto 2019*, 48; Liberal Democrats, *Stop Brexit Build a Brighter Future: Manifesto 2019*, 61.

[76] Chapter 7, pp. 234–35.

[77] Chapter 7, pp. 228, 237–8, 242, 243, 244, 250.

[78] See Chapter 7 for instances of these events in the political careers of, respectively, Ann Winterton (Con), Bob Spink (Con then UKIP then Independent), Nadine Dorries (Con), Maria Caulfield (Con) and Ann Widdecombe (Con then UKIP then Brexit Party).

[79] See generally Chapters 4 and 7.

[80] Marge Berer interviewed by Jane O'Neill, 6 October 2017. See also Joyce Gould interviewed by Jane O'Neill, 4 October 2017; Diane Munday interviewed by Jane O'Neill, 10 November 2017; Lee, *Abortion, Motherhood and Mental Health*.

[81] Chapter 4, pp. 124–25.

[82] Deighan interviewed by O'Neill.

[83] Chapter 4.

[84] Chapter 4, pp. 230–31.

table for those with anti-abortion views.[85] Second, campaigners have worked hard to build an alternative evidence base through their own investigations and inquiries or by commissioning reports from sympathetic experts.[86] Third, they have denied the possibility of separating science from ethics.[87] Fourth, they have presented themselves as the true advocates for women, arguing that those considering abortion have a right to all information, including the findings of outlier clinical studies that disrupt claims for consensus regarding its safety.[88] Finally, they have placed significant faith in the intuitive power of visual imagery as offering access to a moral and biological truth unmediated by experts, believing that people would surely rise up against abortion if only they could see what it involved and that 'if women had glass tummies, they wouldn't have abortions'.[89]

The decline in discursive Christianity has been accompanied by a rise in liberal individualism, with campaigners on both sides reflecting this shift in the framing of their arguments through an increased emphasis on civil liberties and women's rights. While the Abortion Act is often claimed as a product of the second-wave women's liberation movement, in fact the Act not only predated the movement but also helped to drive and to shape it. Safe, effective fertility control allowed women to be more actively involved in the public sphere, including in political campaigning. Moreover, the need to defend the Act was a powerful force both in galvanising the movement and in channelling it in a reformist and more moderate direction, helping to 'make feminism respectable in British politics'.[90] These early campaigns also grounded important, if sometimes uneasy, coalitions with male-dominated trade unions and the Labour Party that persist today.[91]

Again, the effect of these changes can also be seen within Parliament. It was repeated attacks upon the Abortion Act – led mainly by Tories and, initially, almost entirely by men – that offered the first impetus for female Labour MPs to bond together as such, underpinning the articulation of a new self-confidence that would subsequently be mobilised in other contexts.[92] While David Steel had presented the Abortion Act as a humane and necessary public health measure, Labour women defended it as a fundamental prerequisite for female liberty and equality. Initially, the understanding of abortion as an issue of women's rights was the preserve of a small and marginal – if undeniably formidable – group of female Labour MPs, memorably described by one

---

[85] Chapter 4, p. 230.
[86] Chapter 4, pp. 124–5; Chapter 7, pp. 238, 241–42, 243, 244–5.
[87] Chapter 7, p. 230.
[88] E.g. Chapter 7, pp. 232–3; 236–7; 238–9.
[89] Chapter 4, pp. 143-49.
[90] Marshall, *Real Freedom*, 113.
[91] Chapter 3, pp. 71–72, 85–7.
[92] Chapter 3, pp. 87–88.

sketch writer as a 'terrifying cabal of ginger perms vitriolically united'.[93] However, this understanding would gradually become dominant, laying the basis for broadening coalitions. While in the early 1970s Lena Jeger MP was derided for claiming abortion to be an issue on which women had a particular authority to speak,[94] over time it would come to be understood as the paradigmatic 'women's concern'. This would render possible cross-party alliances between female MPs regardless of their divisions on 'political issues',[95] with an important early role played by the group Tories for Choice and a growing number of Conservative women later emerging as vocal advocates for liberalising reform by the 1990s.[96]

The women's rights frame would relatively quickly also be adopted by anti-abortion campaigners, then by their supporters within Parliament and later by professional medical bodies and governments in Westminster and Holyrood, and, finally, it would also take root within Stormont.[97] The understanding of abortion as an issue of women's human rights resulted in an overwhelming majority voting in favour of reform of Northern Ireland's abortion law. At the time of writing, this new law remains only partially implemented and, if the biography of the Abortion Act teaches anything, it is that its meaning will continue to evolve over time. However, after decades of calls for Northern Ireland's abortion law to be brought into line with that in force in the rest of the UK, the new law – and the understanding of abortion as an issue of women's human rights that it helped to entrench in Westminster – is now adding to pressure for liberalising reform in England, Wales and Scotland.[98]

This growing dominance of an understanding of abortion as a women's rights issue is itself rooted in seismic shifts in gender and familial norms, which are again intertwined with processes of secularisation. Sexuality has been gradually freed from an intrinsic and inevitable connection with reproduction, which itself has been untethered from a necessary connection with marriage.[99] Along with improved sex education and contraception, access to safe, legal abortion has been central to these changes, becoming a normal – if often unspoken – part of British women's lives: today, up to one in three of us will terminate a pregnancy at some point in our lives. Safe, effective fertility control has supported women's increased participation in higher education and the labour market; it has enabled women to establish themselves in careers before starting a family; and, once they have done so, it has allowed them to limit their family size: most abortions are carried out on women who are already mothers.[100]

---

[93] 'The Abortion Debate – Or Is It Debacle?', *Sunday Times*, 10 February 1980.

[94] Chapter 3, p. 73.

[95] Childs, *New Labour's Women MPs*, 100–02; Chapter 3, p. 103.

[96] E.g. Chapter 3, p. 103 and Chapter 7, p. 60.

[97] Chapter 4, pp. 131–33; Chapter 3, pp. 72–73; Chapter 7, pp. 232, 247, 249, 259 and 261.

[98] Chapter 7, p. 256.

[99] Chapter 4, pp. 110–14.

[100] Department of Health and Social Care, *Abortion Statistics for England and Wales: 2020*.

For Pro-Choice campaigners, access to safe, legal abortion has been an essential stepping stone in the battle for female equality and liberty, allowing women to 'keep to their plans and achieve their goals', with 'the confidence to know that they don't necessarily have to go through with an unplanned pregnancy'.[101] Pro-Life campaigners have likewise recognised the enormous significance of these changes but dispute their meaning, regretting that women are encouraged to believe that they must be 'equally competitive' with men rather than 'rejoic[ing] in their complementarity'[102] or questioning why women must fit their families around education and employment structures rather than vice versa.[103] Without questioning the need for safe, legal abortion, Pro-Choice campaigners have likewise queried the meaning of 'choice' in these debates: a more recent turn towards a politics grounded in 'reproductive justice' has reflected an understanding that women's decisions are often constrained in ways shaped *inter alia* by class, race, and disability, as well as by gender, and an awareness of the risk that sometimes choice may blur into expectation.[104]

Class has intersected with gender in important ways in these debates. The Abortion Act's architects were driven by concerns that rich women were able to access 'Harley Street legal' abortions while poor women sought help in the backstreets: ALRA campaigners understood themselves as fighting above all for the 'worn out mother of many children with an ill or illiterate or feckless or brutal or drunken or otherwise inadequate husband'.[105] Within this motivation, their opponents have identified an 'abiding interest in poor women centred on a desire to stop them from breeding,' repeatedly attacking Pro-Choice campaigners, abortion service providers and sympathetic government officers as eugenicists.[106] Over time, class inequalities in access to abortion have been greatly mitigated by the gradual assumption of responsibility for services within the NHS. However, concerns persist regarding the impact of socioeconomic inequalities on women's ability to continue and motivation for ending pregnancies and the possible thinness of a language of 'choice' in contexts where women's actions are heavily constrained by external pressures, not least financial ones.[107]

Whilst Pro-Life campaigners have also sometimes discerned a desire to ensure racial purity within the eugenic motivation attributed to those who supported liberal abortion laws,[108] race has been a far less evident focus of attention in the UK than in parallel debates in the USA.[109] Nonetheless, it has

---

[101] Munday interviewed by O'Neill.
[102] Scarisbrick, *Let There Be Life*, 60.
[103] Josephine Quintavalle interviewed by Jane O'Neill, 6 October 2017.
[104] Chapter 4, pp. 129–31.
[105] Simms, 'Legal Abortion in Great Britain', 81.
[106] Alton, 'Foreword', in Farmer, *By Their Fruits*, vii–ix, viii.
[107] Chapter 4, pp. 119 and 129–31.
[108] E.g. Farmer, *By Their Fruits*, 231–40.
[109] E.g. Solinger, *Pregnancy and Power*; Roberts, *Killing the Black Body*.

undoubtedly marked some women's experience of seeking access to abortion services, influencing doctors' determinations of whether an abortion was justified or whether simultaneous sterilisation should be required as a condition of access to it.[110] These experiences contributed to the establishment of a break-away Pro-Choice campaign group in the early 1980s.[111] Race has been a still less prominent feature of the battles fought within what has until very recently been an almost entirely white UK Parliament,[112] with explicit reference to it made in only one of the hundreds of amendments proposed to the Abortion Act over the past five decades.[113] However, race was also an important implicit feature of Fiona Bruce's attempts to enshrine a statutory prohibition on sex-selective abortion, a reform presented as essential to addressing discriminatory and coercive cultural practices within British South Asian communities. Whilst failing to achieve statutory reform, these efforts contributed not just to focusing attention on sex-selective abortion, but also to framing concerns regarding it in a racialised way.[114]

Ideas of nationhood have also sometimes been important within abortion debates, with the Conservative Cornerstone Group's philosophy reflecting how, for some, opposition to abortion sits comfortably within a broader political ideology of 'faith, flag and family'. The place of abortion as a cipher for broader concerns was particularly clear in the debate of Northern Ireland's abortion law, where colonial legacies have left religious and national identities deeply intertwined. Westminster's response reflected its broader relationship with, and fears and ignorance of, the region; Stormont's rejection of the Abortion Act relied on claims of a strong, distinctive, Northern Irish national identity.[115] Understandings of nationhood have also been important in debates concerning the devolution of legislative competence over abortion to Scotland, with advocates relying upon very different political visions of the union and Scotland's role within it. Early calls for the devolution of these powers were sometimes made in the hope of seeing Holyrood act to restrict access to abortion, opponents arguing that abortion laws were stronger if 'we stand together to defend them'[116] and, more recently, the SNP offered a vision of a more progressive, socially liberal Scotland that was better able to promote and protect women's rights.[117]

Changing attitudes towards disability have also played an important role in the Abortion Act's biography. The Act was passed in a period marked by

---

[110] Chapter 2, p. 42; Chapter 4, p. 130.
[111] Chapter 3, pp. 90–91; Chapter 4, pp. 130–31.
[112] Uberoi and Lees, *Ethnic Diversity in Politics and Public Life*.
[113] Chapter 7, pp. 235–36.
[114] Chapter 7, pp. 239–41.
[115] Chapter 6.
[116] 'This Threat to Abortion Law Must Be Fought by MPs of All Hues', *Guardian*, 8 November 2015.
[117] Chapter 7, p. 247.

eugenic beliefs, with popular anxieties and sympathies shaped by knowledge of the effects of thalidomide and rubella exposure. Legal abortion was widely seen both as the best available solution to a significant public health problem and a means of protecting the family, with the woman who gave birth to a disabled child believed less able to care for her other children and unlikely to conceive again.[118] While the inclusion of a fetal anomaly ground was contested, controversy thus initially focused mainly on those 'perfectly normal unmaimed human lives' that might be 'sacrificed for the sake of one who would be born with some physical deformity' given the rudimentary nature of screening and testing at the time.[119] In facilitating legal abortion in cases of suspected anomaly, the Abortion Act underpinned a silent revolution whereby increasingly sophisticated screening and testing has been integrated into mainstream antenatal care, profoundly shaping women's experiences of maternity.[120] Over time, as these technologies became increasingly accurate and more widely adopted, earlier concerns were replaced by new ones framed in a language of civil liberties: that their use may be discriminatory; that what was presented as a choice might sometimes be experienced as expectation; and that, given their prevalence, uptake and accuracy, the collective result of individual choices could be the complete disappearance of some groups of disabled people.[121] Down's syndrome has been a particular focus for these concerns, with the changing nature of debate regarding the Abortion Act offering a window onto shifting attitudes, as people with Down's syndrome moved out of institutions into communities to become a more accepted, visible and active part of British life and a vocal force in campaigning.[122]

The resulting tensions between competing claims for the civil liberties of disabled people and women considering abortion have been only partly mediated through a focus on improving the quality and impartiality of the information, support and counselling given to those offered screening or testing or receiving a diagnosis of fetal anomaly.[123] The intractability of these disputes reflects in part their framing with reference to the text of an Act grounded in the beliefs of the 1960s, with formal control over abortion decisions entrusted to doctors charged to consult a list of state-sanctioned grounds for when abortion is justifiable against an implicit assumption that other reasons are not. Today, doctors are expected to walk a line so thin as to be near invisible between ensuring that women offered prenatal screening and testing or given a diagnosis of fetal anomaly are fully aware of all options open to them, whilst avoiding displaying moral judgement of any choice that might be made and explaining the likely nature of a future child's disability in a way

---

[118] Chapter 1; Sheldon, *Beyond Control*, 42–44.
[119] Mahon in *Hansard*, HC, 13 July 1967, vol. 750, col. 1358; Chapter 1, p. 10.
[120] Chapter 4, pp. 139–43.
[121] Chapter 4, pp. 142–43.
[122] Chapter 4, pp. 141–42.; Chapter 5, pp. 170–76.
[123] Chapter 4, p. 143.; Chapter 7, pp. 241–43.

that neither denies nor exaggerates the challenges and accompanying joys of raising a child with a genetic anomaly that may translate into a wide spectrum of abilities and disabilities.[124]

Debates regarding the Abortion Act also open a window onto shifting understandings of clinical practice and medical authority, exposing a marked decline in medical paternalism. In 1969, a medical symposium was convened to consider the implications of the then freshly printed Abortion Act. It was addressed by the eminent gynaecologist Aleck Bourne, who, 30 years earlier, had played such an influential role in shaping UK abortion law.[125] Then in his 83rd year, Bourne predicted that 'in this room in a hundred years' there would likely still be 'another collection just like us' discussing abortion and 'the legitimate indications for it'.[126] Just past the halfway point, Bourne has been only partly vindicated: while abortion is still discussed at medical colloquia, subsequent generations of doctors have tended to reject his belief that the 'legitimate indications' for it are properly a matter for clinical determination, preferring rather to respect the decisions of their patients.

In the late 1960s and early 1970s, doctors defended the exercise of a clinical discretion so broad as to encompass an enormous diversity in views, with some of their number prejudging all requests for abortion favourably or unfavourably, and 'covert ethical, religious, and personal motives' often to be inferred behind the ostensible medical rationale given for their decisions.[127] A marked shift in practice has reflected general trends towards doctors becoming more liberal, with abortion decisions increasingly viewed through the lens of respect for patient autonomy;[128] women generally 'appearing more sure about what they want', with doctors thus considering it not their 'duty to persuade them, or to try and persuade them, or to try and make them think hard about the alternatives';[129] and doctors gradually conceding personal authority over controversial decisions, with an emphasis on evidence-based medicine, clinical guidelines and acceptance of greater external scrutiny over medical practice.[130] Ann Furedi also notes an important change in those health professionals who apply to work at BPAS, who are increasingly those who see abortion as 'a cause in our life that is worthwhile, and that's value-based, that we are kind of fighting for'. She reflects that the doctors who applied to work at BPAS were once those approaching retirement who 'settled into' abortion care as unchallenging work that offered regular hours; however, more recent recruits have tended to be younger and 'absolutely driven' to work in abortion care, with BPAS nurses and midwives likewise describing their

---

[124] Thomas, *Down's Syndrome Screening and Reproductive Politics.*
[125] Chapter 1, p. 7.
[126] MPS, *Symposium*, 83.
[127] Ingram, 'Abortion Games', 969; Chapter 2, pp. 29–39.
[128] Chapter 4, p. 187.
[129] Glasier interviewed by Davis.
[130] See generally Sheldon, 'British Abortion Law'.

motivation as wanting to 'be with women and to help women ... to get the result out of that pregnancy that they want'.[131]

Finally, the implementation of the Abortion Act both facilitated and was profoundly shaped by clinical innovations that have changed abortion care almost beyond recognition over the past five decades. In the late 1960s, abortion was a technically demanding, risky surgical procedure performed under general anaesthesia and requiring an average of one week's recuperation in a nursing home.[132] Following the introduction of the Abortion Act, abortions were increasingly performed openly in hospitals, data were gathered and published and best practice was shared. The practice of simultaneous sterilisation was shown to increase the risk of mortality dramatically and was swiftly abandoned, with an immediate impact on death rates.[133] Dilatation and curettage procedures were largely replaced by vacuum aspirations under local anaesthesia, dramatically improving clinical outcomes and paving the way for outpatient services.[134] In turn, vacuum aspiration is now being rapidly superseded by abortion pills, making possible the telemedical services that became widespread during the COVID-19 pandemic.[135] Moreover, the use of abortion pills has accelerated trends for abortions to take place earlier in pregnancy when abortion is at its safest: almost nine out of 10 abortions are now performed before 10 weeks, with a safety record that compares favourably to an injection of penicillin.[136]

These technological innovations have also had a profound impact on political campaigns around the Abortion Act. To anti-abortion advocates, they have been promoted through exaggerated safety claims and have exacerbated trends in making abortion too readily accessible, trivialising a morally serious and profoundly harmful procedure that should only ever be available as a last resort.[137] To Pro-Choice campaigners and service providers, they have facilitated the normalisation of a safe and necessary health service, rendering ever more anachronistic the restrictive controls enshrined at a time when safe abortion depended upon a skilled surgical team and a well-equipped operating theatre.[138] Ann Furedi notes that, in earlier years, people repeatedly asked her: '[I]f women can get safe abortions and they can get them fairly easily, why are we even bothering about what the law says?' However, this changed with abortion pills:

---

[131] Ann Furedi interviewed by Jane O'Neill, 23 August 2017.
[132] Chapter 2, p. 29; Chapter 4, p. 123.
[133] Chapter 2, p. 36.
[134] Chapter 4, pp. 125–27.
[135] Chapter 4, pp. 127–29; Chapter 7, pp. 257–60.
[136] Department of Health and Social Care, *Abortion Statistics for England and Wales: 2020*; Cates, Grimes and Schulz, 'The Public Health Impact of Legal Abortion', 25–28.
[137] Chapter 4.
[138] Chapter 4.

[T]he barriers that the law creates, that we never even really thought about back in the early nineties, are the ones that are actually the problem ... [The] reason now why it's an issue about who can carry out an abortion is because the procedures that we are using at the moment for very early abortions, which are now the overwhelming majority, could just as easily be done by nurses or even healthcare assistants ... The reason why premises is an issue is because with early medical abortion, the obvious place for a woman to take tablets is in her own home, and not to make repeated visits to a clinic.[139]

The Future

While the Abortion Act's biography has unfolded, most people have gone about their daily lives generally not thinking too much about it. Even during the furious campaigns of earlier years, David Steel believed that his sponsorship of the Act did less to dent his popularity with constituents than had his opposition to the visit of the South African rugby team during apartheid.[140] Today, while the Abortion Act has profoundly shaped their lives, few modern Britons can describe its provisions even in the broadest terms.[141] Pro-Choice advocates complain that the fight for decriminalisation faces the initial hurdle of needing to convince people that abortion remains a criminal offence: neatly illustrating the point, then Labour leader Jeremy Corbyn celebrated the anniversary of the Abortion Act by tweeting '50 years ago today abortion was decriminalised under Labour'.[142]

However, those active in disputes regarding the Abortion Act care very much indeed, appearing to agree on just one thing: that there will never 'be a middle ground, not in any way, shape or form'.[143] The divide between them is so wide and so intractable because it follows a fault line between the tectonic plates of a changing UK, reflecting not just deep conflicts over values but also starkly divergent beliefs regarding the most basic empirical facts. Over time, these plates have shifted gradually in favour of Pro-Choice campaigners. The Pro-Life movement is painfully aware that it now faces 'a battle of biblical proportions',[144] believing the medical profession, trade unions and academia to be pitted against it,[145] and that it is 'almost impossible for a Pro-Lifer, even an established journalist, to write anything that challenge[s] abortionism'.[146] The movement nonetheless awaits 'another Wilberforce' who will end abortion[147] and 'an objective assessment' that will look back and ask:

---

[139] Furedi interviewed by O'Neill, speaking before the approval of fully telemedical abortion services.
[140] Steel, *Against Goliath*, 80.
[141] ICM Unlimited, *Abortion Documentary Survey*; Gray and Wellings, 'Is Public Opinion in Support of Decriminalisation?'.
[142] Corbyn, '50 years ago today ...'.
[143] Berer interviewed by O'Neill.
[144] Peter Saunders interviewed by Jane O'Neill, 9 November 2017.
[145] Deighan interviewed by O'Neill.
[146] Jack Scarisbrick interviewed by Jane O'Neill, 7 November 2017.
[147] Alton, *What Kind of Country?*, 170.

[H]ow could these guys have had the Universal Declaration of Human Rights; how could [they] have had the European Convention on Human Rights; how could they have had the International Covenant on Civil and Political Rights; how could they have had the UN Convention on the Rights of the Child? All of them stating that every human being – some of them say person . . . – has the right to life. How could that all have been happening when we had those laws in place?[148]

For their part, Pro-Choice campaigners believe that the moral argument was won long ago and are deeply frustrated with a popular media that persists in discussing abortion as if it were an issue with two equally situated sides. Now a formidable and articulate octogenarian, Diane Munday contrasts the tone of BBC programming regarding the fiftieth anniversaries of the Sexual Offences Act (which was celebrated as a landmark of social justice) and the Abortion Act: she condemns the inclusion of Pro-Life contributors in every programme on the latter as akin to including a homophobe in all programmes on the former to explain why 'gays or queers should go to prison for homosexual acts'.[149]

Sensing that they are now in the ascendancy, Pro-Choice advocates have nonetheless become more ambitious. It is now their campaigns that pose the greater existential threat to the Abortion Act, with the Pro-Life movement pushed into its grudging defence.[150] Ann Furedi is characteristically optimistic:

> What I've found is that it is far easier trying to explain to people why abortion should not be a criminal offence than it is to explain all of the nuances of the 1967 Act as it stands at the moment and why that should be reformed. You know, to say to someone: 'Do you think that someone should, that a woman should be able to make a decision about whether she stays pregnant or whether she ends it? Do you think that politicians should decide that, or should it be a decision that she takes with her doctor? Do you think a woman should be sent to prison for carrying out a procedure that makes her unpregnant? Should doctors be sent to prison for carrying out a procedure that a woman wants?'[151]

Diane Munday reports having joined David Steel and other campaigners in the House of Commons bar to celebrate the successful passage of the Abortion Act in 1967. She accepted only half a glass of champagne, explaining that she would take the second half-glass when the law was changed to allow women to decide for themselves whether to continue or to end a pregnancy.[152] In one important sense, the remainder of her drink is long overdue: this change has already largely been achieved in practice through the interpretation given to the Act. However, with the 'great untouchable' still on the statute books, 50 years on, Munday is still waiting, and the Abortion Act's biography continues to unfold.

---

148 Deighan interviewed by O'Neill.
149 Munday interviewed by O'Neill. See further Chapter 1, p. 1.
150 E.g. Chapter 7, p. 250.
151 Furedi interviewed by O'Neill.
152 Munday, presentation at *Abortion Act 1967 Conference: A Promise Fulfilled?* Royal College of Obstetricians and Gynaecologists, London, 24–25 October 2017.

Appendix 1

The Abortion Act 1967 (original text)

1967 Chapter 87. An Act to amend and clarify the law relating to termination of pregnancy by registered medical practitioners. [27 October 1967]

BE IT ENACTED by the Queen's most Excellent Majesty, by and with the advice and consent of the Lords Spiritual and Temporal, and Commons, in this present Parliament assembled, and by the authority of the same, as follows: –

Medical Termination of Pregnancy

1. (1) Subject to the provisions of this section, a person shall not be guilty of an offence under the law relating to abortion when a pregnancy is terminated by a registered medical practitioner if two registered medical practitioners are of the opinion, formed in good faith –
     (a) that the continuance of the pregnancy would involve risk to the life of the pregnant woman, or of injury to the physical or mental health of the pregnant woman or any existing children of her family, greater than if the pregnancy were terminated; or
     (b) that there is a substantial risk that if the child were born it would suffer from such physical or mental abnormalities as to be seriously handicapped.
   (2) In determining whether the continuance of a pregnancy would involve such risk of injury to health as is mentioned in paragraph (a) of subsection (1) of this section, account may be taken of the pregnant woman's actual or reasonably foreseeable environment.
   (3) Except as provided by subsection (4) of this section, any treatment for the termination of pregnancy must be carried out in a hospital vested in the Minister of Health or the Secretary of State under the National Health Service Acts, or in a place for the time being approved for the purposes of this section by the said Minister or Secretary of State.
   (4) Subsection (3) of this section, and so much of subsection (1) as relates to the opinion of two registered medical practitioners, shall not apply to the termination of a pregnancy by a registered medical practitioner in a case where he is of the opinion, formed in good faith, that the termination is

immediately necessary to save the life or to prevent grave permanent injury to the physical or mental health of the pregnant woman.

Notification

2. (1) The Minister of Health in respect of England and Wales, and the Secretary of State in respect of Scotland, shall by statutory instrument make regulations to provide –

   (a) for requiring any such opinion as is referred to in section 1 of this Act to be certified by the practitioners or practitioner concerned in such form and at such time as may be prescribed by the regulations, and for requiring the preservation and disposal of certificates made for the purposes of the regulations;

   (b) for requiring any registered medical practitioner who terminates a pregnancy to give notice of the termination and such other information relating to the termination as may be so prescribed;

   (c) for prohibiting the disclosure, except to such persons or for such purposes as may be so prescribed, of notices given or information furnished pursuant to the regulations.

   (2) The information furnished in pursuance of regulations made by virtue of paragraph (b) of subsection (1) of this section shall be notified solely to the Chief Medical Officers of the Ministry of Health and the Scottish Home and Health Department respectively.

   (3) Any person who wilfully contravenes or wilfully fails to comply with the requirements of regulations under subsection (1) of this section shall be liable on summary conviction to a fine not exceeding one hundred pounds.

   (4) Any statutory instrument made by virtue of this section shall be subject to annulment in pursuance of either House of Parliament.

Application of Act to visiting forces etc.

3. omitted

Conscientious objection to participation in treatment.

4. (1) Subject to subsection (2) of this section, no person shall be under any duty, whether by contract or by any statutory or other legal requirement, to participate in any treatment authorised by this Act to which he has a conscientious objection:

   Provided that in any legal proceedings the burden of proof of conscientious objection shall rest on the person claiming to rely on it.

   (2) Nothing in subsection (1) of this section shall affect any duty to participate in treatment which is necessary to save the life or to prevent grave permanent injury to the physical or mental health of a pregnant woman.

   (3) In any proceedings before a court in Scotland, a statement on oath by any person to the effect that he has a conscientious objection to participating in any treatment authorised by this Act shall be sufficient

evidence for the purpose of discharging the burden of proof imposed upon him by subsection (1) of this section.

Supplementary provisions.

5. (1) Nothing in this Act shall affect the provisions of the Infant Life (Preservation) Act 1929 (protecting the life of the viable foetus).

   (2) For the purposes of the law relating to abortion, anything done with intent to procure the miscarriage of a woman is unlawfully done unless authorised by section 1 of this Act.

Interpretation

6. In this Act, the following expressions have meanings hereby assigned to them: –

   'the law relating to abortion' means sections 58 and 59 of the Offences Against the Person Act 1861, and any rule of law relating to the procurement of abortion;
   'the National Health Service Acts' means the National Health Service Acts 1946 to 1966 or the National Health Service (Scotland) Acts 1947 to 1966.

Short title, commencement and extent

7. (1) This Act may be cited as the Abortion Act 1967.

   (2) This Act shall come into force on the expiration of the period of six months beginning with the date on which it is passed.

   (3) This Act does not extend to Northern Ireland.

THE ABORTION ACT (As Amended 1990, Changes in Bold)

Medical Termination of Pregnancy

1. (1) Subject to the provisions of this section, a person shall not be guilty of an offence under the law relating to abortion when a pregnancy is terminated by a registered medical practitioner if two registered medical practitioners are of the opinion, formed in good faith –

   (a) **that the pregnancy has not exceeded its twenty-fourth week and that the continuance of the pregnancy would involve risk, greater than if the pregnancy were terminated, or of injury to the physical or mental health of the pregnant woman or any existing children of her family; or**

   (b) **that the termination is necessary to prevent grave permanent injury to the physical or mental health of the pregnant woman; or**

   (c) **that the continuance of the pregnancy would involve risk to the life of the pregnant woman, greater than if the pregnancy were terminated; or**

   (d) **that there is a substantial risk that if the child were born it would suffer from such physical or mental abnormalities as to be seriously handicapped.**

(2) In determining whether the continuance of a pregnancy would involve such risk of injury to health as is mentioned in paragraph (a) **or (b)** of subsection (1) of this section, account may be taken of the pregnant woman's actual or reasonably foreseeable environment.

(3) Except as provided by subsection (4) of this section, any treatment for the termination of pregnancy must be carried out in a hospital vested in the Secretary of State for the purposes of his functions under the National Health Service Acts, or in a place for the time being approved for the purposes of this section by the Secretary of State.

(3A) **The power under subsection (3) of this section to approve a place includes power, in relation to treatment consisting primarily in the use of such medicines as may be specified in the approval and carried out in such manner as may be so specified, to approve a class of places.**

(4) Subsection (3) of this section, and so much of subsection (1) as relates to the opinion of two registered medical practitioners, shall not apply to the termination of a pregnancy by a registered medical practitioner in a case where he is of the opinion, formed in good faith, that the termination is immediately necessary to save the life or to prevent grave permanent injury to the physical or mental health of the pregnant woman.

Notification

2. omitted (provisions unaltered)

Application of Act to visiting forces etc.

3. omitted (provisions unaltered)

Conscientious objection to participation in treatment

4. omitted (provisions unaltered)

Supplementary provisions

5. (1) **No offence under the Infant Life (Preservation) Act 1929 shall be committed by a registered medical practitioner who terminates a pregnancy in accordance with the provisions of this Act.**

(2) **For the purposes of the law relating to abortion, anything done with intent to procure a woman's miscarriage (or in the case of a woman carrying more than one foetus, her miscarriage of any foetus) is unlawfully done unless authorised by section 1 of this Act and, in the case of a woman carrying more than one foetus, anything done with intent to procure her miscarriage of any one foetus is authorised by that section if –**

(a) **the ground for termination of the pregnancy specified in subsection (1)(d) of that section applies in relation to any foetus and** the thing is done for the purpose of procuring the miscarriage of the foetus, or

(b) any of the other grounds for termination of the pregnancy specified in that section applies.

Interpretation

6. omitted (provisions unaltered)

Short title, commencement and extent

7. omitted (provisions unaltered)

Appendix 2

Legislative Proposals Aiming to Restrict or Liberalise Access to Abortion, as Recorded in *Hansard* 1968–2022

	Sponsor (political party): short title	Means of introduction and year	Select summary of major measures proposed. NB measures that passed into law are listed in bold. Measures likely to have restricted access to abortion services are given in normal typeface; those likely to have had a liberalising effect are italicised	Discussion at pages:
1	Norman St. John-Stevas (Con): A Bill to Improve the Law Governing Abortion and the Status and Rights of the Medical Profession in Relation thereto	Ten Minute Rule Bill (TMRB) 1969	One certifying doctor to be an NHS consultant gynaecologist (or approved equivalent); abortion to be performed or supervised by that doctor	pp. 37–38
2	Sir Bryant Godman Irvine (Con): Abortion Law (Reform) Bill	Ballot 1970	One certifying doctor to be an NHS consultant gynaecologist (or approved equivalent); abortion to be performed or supervised by that doctor	pp. 37–38
3	John Hunt (Con): Medical Services (Referral) Bill	Presentation 1972	Only a doctor, accredited official or charity to be permitted to charge a fee for referring someone for medical services	pp. 37–38
4	Michael Grylls (Con): Abortion (Amendment) Bill	Presentation 1973	To restrict payment of a fee for referral or recommendation regarding abortion services	p. 38
5	Michael Grylls (Con): Abortion (Amendment) Bill	Ballot 1974	Only a doctor or other approved person to be permitted to receive payment for giving advice or information about abortion services	p. 38
6	James White (Lab): Abortion (Amendment) Bill	Ballot 1975	The grounds for abortion to be restricted to cases of risk of 'serious' injury to health or 'grave' risk to life. Most abortions after 20 weeks (or 24 in case of 'major disability') to be prohibited. Further restrictions to be introduced regarding the doctors able to certify abortion; the making of payments for abortion referrals or advice about services; the approval for premises to be used for abortion services; the licensing of premises offering advice or referrals regarding abortion services; the provision of information about abortion to minors; and the research use of fetal tissue. With her consent, to require a woman's GP to be informed of her abortion. Access to abortion services to be restricted to UK residents	pp. 68–76
7	William Benyon (Con): Abortion (Amendment) Bill	Ballot 1976	Most abortions after 20 weeks (24 weeks where substantial risk of serious handicap) to be prohibited. Further restrictions to be introduced regarding the doctors able to certify abortion. Pregnancy testing and advisory bureaux and abortion referral agencies that charge fees to be licenced and regulated. With her consent, to require a woman's GP to be informed of her abortion. Conscientious objection rights to be strengthened. Enforcement mechanisms to be strengthened	pp. 76–78

Sponsor (political party): short title	Means of introduction and year	Select summary of major measures proposed. NB measures that passed into law are listed in bold. Measures likely to have restricted access to abortion services are given in normal typeface; those likely to have had a liberalising effect are italicised	Discussion at pages:
8 Bernard Braine (Con): Abortion (Amendment) Bill	TMRB 1978	Most abortions after 20 weeks (excluding cases of substantial risk of serious handicap, risk to a woman's life, or risk of grave permanent injury to her health) to be prohibited. Conscientious objection rights to be strengthened. Pregnancy testing and advisory bureaux and abortion referral agencies that charge fees to be licenced and regulated. Criminal prosecution of individual officers of organisations offering abortion services to be made easier	p. 77
9 John Corrie (Con): Abortion (Amendment) Bill	Ballot 1979	The grounds for abortion to be restricted to cases involving: (1) substantial risk of serious handicap; (2) the need to preserve the woman's life (with a new requirement to avoid abortion methods that result in the destruction of a fetus unless medically necessary); and (3) risk to life or 'serious' injury to health 'substantially' greater than if the pregnancy were terminated, subject to a 20 week limit (with a new statutory power for Government to introduce a lower time limit subject to the approval of Parliament). Connections between pregnancy counselling and abortion services to be regulated. Criminal prosecution of individual officers of organisations offering abortion services to be made easier. Conscientious objection rights to be strengthened	pp. 78–92
10 David Alton (Lib): Abortion Amendment Bill	TMRB 1980	Most abortions after 'less than 24 weeks' to be prohibited	p. 91
11 Jo Richardson (Lab): National Health Service Act 1977 (Amendment) Bill	TMRB 1981	*Health authorities to have a duty to provide NHS abortion facilities within their area.*	p. 92
12 Lord Robertson (Crossbench): Abortion (Amendment) Bill [HL]	HL 1982	The grounds for abortion to be restricted to require 'serious' risk of 'substantially' greater injury to the woman's health than if the pregnancy were terminated	p. 91
13 Bishop of Birmingham: Infant Life (Preservation) Bill [HL]	HL 1986	To provide an upper time limit of 24 weeks for most abortions	p. 100

(cont.)

Sponsor (political party): short title	Means of introduction and year	Select summary of major measures proposed. NB measures that passed into law are listed in bold. Measures likely to have restricted access to abortion services are given in normal typeface; those likely to have had a liberalising effect are italicised	Discussion at pages:
14	Peter Bruinvels (Con): Infant Life (Preservation) and Paternal Rights Bill	Presentation 1987	Most abortions to be prohibited after 22 weeks; 'the father of the unborn child' to be consulted where a termination is intended, and his consent to be required where he is the 'mother's husband'	pp. 91–92, 155
15	Lord Houghton (Lab): Infant Life (Preservation) Bill [HL]	HL 1987	To provide an upper time limit of 24 weeks for most abortions	p. 100
16	Nicholas Winterton (Con): Abortion (Financial Benefit) Bill	Presentation 1987	Doctors who refer a woman for abortion to be required to make a declaration that they will obtain no financial or other benefits as a result	
17	Edward Leigh (Con): Abortion (Treatment of Non-Resident Women) Bill	Presentation 1987	Doctor offering abortion to a non-resident woman to be required to notify a doctor in her country of ordinary residence regarding her abortion	
18	David Alton (Lib Dem): Abortion (Amendment) Bill	Ballot 1987	Most abortions to be prohibited after the 'beginning of 18th week' ('the end of the 28th week' where abortion is necessary to save the life of the woman or the child is likely to be born dead or with physical abnormalities incompatible with independently sustained life)	pp. 92–100
19	Lord Houghton (Lab): Abortion (Amendment) Bill (No.2) [HL]	HL 1988	To provide an upper time limit of 24 weeks for most abortions (no time limit where there is risk to the woman's life or of 'serious damage' to her health or in case of substantial risk that the child would be seriously handicapped)	p. 100
20	Ann Widdecombe (Con): Abortion (Amendment) Bill	Ballot 1989	Most abortions to be prohibited after the 'beginning of 18th week' ('the end of the 28th week' where necessary to save the woman's life or where a child would suffer from a specified severe physical or mental disability; or where pregnancy results from rape or incest committed when the woman was under 18; without specified limit, where abortion is immediately necessary to save the woman's life or prevent grave permanent injury to her health)	p. 99
21	David Amess (Con): Abortion (Right of Conscience) (Amendment) Bill	Presentation 1989	All doctors and nurses to be required to give a positive indication that they have no conscientious objection to abortion before they can be required to participate in performing one	p. 99

	Sponsor (political party): short title	Means of introduction and year	Select summary of major measures proposed. NB measures that are listed in bold. Measures likely to have restricted access to abortion services are given in normal typeface; those likely to have had a liberalising effect are italicised	Discussion at pages:
22	Nicholas Bennett (Con): Abortion (Financial Benefit) Bill	Presentation 1989	Doctors who refer a woman for abortion to be required to make a declaration that they will obtain no financial or other benefits as a result	p. 99
23	Ken Hargreaves (Con): Abortion (Rights of Ancillary Workers) Bill	Presentation 1989	Any workers other than doctors engaged in abortion treatment to be required to give a positive indication that they have no conscientious objection to abortion before they can be required to perform or assist in one	p. 99
24	Ann Widdecombe (Con): Abortion (Treatment of Non-Resident Women) Bill	Presentation 1989	Doctors offering abortion to a non-resident woman to be required to notify a doctor in her country of ordinary residence regarding her abortion	p. 99
25	Bernard Braine (Con): Abortion (Amendment of Grounds) Bill	Presentation 1989	The grounds for abortion to require 'serious' risk of 'substantially' greater injury to the woman's health than if the pregnancy were terminated	p. 99
26	Dawn Primarolo (Lab): Medical Services for Women Bill	Presentation 1990	*Abortion to be permitted on request until viability in England and Wales. The Health Secretary to be under a duty to provide a comprehensive health service for women in England and Wales, including abortion services*	pp. 99–100
27	Various (Government and Private Members in both House of Commons (HC) and House of Lords (HL))	Amendment of Human Fertilisation and Embryology Act 1990	(HC Committee): **Most abortions to be subject to an upper time limit of 24** (or 18, 28, 20, 26 or 22) **weeks; and 28 weeks** (or 24 weeks or ***without an upper time limit***) ***where there is a substantial risk of serious handicap.*** *Abortion to be permitted before 12 weeks with the consent of one doctor.* **The Abortion Act to be 'uncoupled' from the Infant Life Preservation Act** (*no offence committed under the latter where an abortion is performed in accordance with the former*) (HC Report): *Abortion to be permitted before 12 weeks on request, or alternatively with the authorisation of just one doctor. A register to be created of all those exercising a right of conscientious objection. The Abortion Act to be extended to Northern Ireland.* **The Government to gain the power to approve a 'class of places' for the performance of medical abortion. The legality of selective reduction of multiple pregnancies to be clarified.** *Abortion for fetal anomaly to be prohibited after 28 weeks* (i.e. reversing the amendment agreed at HC Committee). More detailed information required regarding fetal anomaly	pp. 100–106

	Sponsor (political party): short title	Means of introduction and year	Select summary of major measures proposed. NB measures that passed into law are listed in bold. Measures likely to have restricted access to abortion services are given in normal typeface; those likely to have had a liberalising effect are italicised	Discussion at pages:
28	David Ames (Con): Children (Prohibition of Sex Selection) Bill	TMRB 1993	(HL): Where a child is capable of being born alive, to require a doctor to take all reasonable steps to preserve life. Abortion for fetal anomaly to be prohibited after 28 weeks (i.e. reversing the amendment approved at HC Committee)	p. 225
29	Harry Cohen (Lab): Abortion Clinics (Access) Bill	TMRB 1993	*To prohibit obstruction of access, intimidation or harassment of women or staff using an abortion clinic and to require GPs to give information on counselling services to women seeking an abortion*	p. 121
30	Lord Braine (Con): Partial-Birth Abortion (Prohibition) Bill [HL]	HL 1995	To prohibit 'partial-birth' abortions (except where a doctor believes it immediately necessary as the only means to save the woman's life)	p. 225
31	Viscount Brentford (Con): Termination of Pregnancy (Restriction) Bill [HL]	HL 1996	To prohibit abortions being certified on the grounds that the future child would have Down's syndrome	p. 142. 225
32	Elizabeth Peacock (Con): Partial-Birth Abortion Bill	TMRB 1996	To prohibit 'partial-birth' abortions (except where a doctor believes it immediately necessary as the only means to save the woman's life)	pp. 225–26
33	David Ames (Con): Abortion (Amendment) Bill	TMRB 1996	The grounds for abortion to require 'serious' risk of 'substantially' greater injury to the woman's health than if the pregnancy were terminated	pp. 224–25
34	Laurence Robertson (Con): Prohibition of Abortion (England and Wales) Bill	Presentation 2005	To prohibit abortion in England and Wales, other than where the pregnancy causes a risk to the woman's life or conception had resulted from rape	pp. 224–225
35	Nadine Dorries (Con): Termination of Pregnancy Bill	TMRB 2006	To reduce the upper time limit for most abortions to 21 weeks and to introduce a seven day 'cooling-off' period between first contact with a doctor and access to abortion, during which a woman should be counselled regarding the respective medical risks of termination and carrying a pregnancy to term as a condition of informed consent	pp. 232–33

(cont.)

Sponsor (political party): short title	Means of introduction and year	Select summary of major measures proposed. NB measures that passed into law are listed in bold. Measures likely to have restricted access to abortion services are given in normal typeface; those likely to have had a liberalising effect are italicised	Discussion at pages:
36 Nadine Dorries (Con): Termination of Pregnancy Bill	Presentation 2006	To reduce the upper time limit for most abortions to 20 weeks; to introduce a seven day 'cooling-off' period between first contact with a doctor and access to abortion, during which a woman should be counselled regarding the respective medical risks of termination and carrying a pregnancy to term as a condition of informed consent to abortion	p. 233
37 Ann Winterton (Con): Termination of Pregnancy (Counselling and Miscellaneous Provisions) Bill	TMRB 2007	To separate description of physical and mental health risks on abortion certification and notification forms and to require counselling followed by a seven day 'cooling-off' period as a condition of informed consent to abortion	pp. 232–33
38 Various (Private Members in both HC and HL) (A raft of liberalising amendments was blocked by a Government programme motion at Report and therefore not debated)	Amendment of Human Fertilisation and Embryology Act 2008	(HL): To repeal the fetal anomaly ground for abortion (HC Committee): To reduce the upper time limit for abortion to 12, 14, 16, 18, 20, 22 or 23+6 weeks. To repeal the fetal anomaly ground for abortion and prohibit abortion on the grounds of disability, gender, race or sexual orientation. At least five days prior to abortion, doctors to be required to offer women counselling and information regarding embryonic and fetal development at two week intervals, the 'physical, psychological and psychiatric' risks associated with abortion including a description of abortion methods used at different gestations and the risks associated with each, and provide contact details of adoption services and other sources of health and advice (including information on any disability or abnormality). Where a woman is warned of a substantial risk of serious handicap in her future child, no termination to take place until a doctor has provided information regarding life expectancy, expected intellectual and functional development and treatment options, contact details for supportive service providers and the offer of counselling	pp. 234–37

	Sponsor (political party): short title	Means of introduction and year	Select summary of major measures proposed. NB measures that passed into law are listed in bold. Measures likely to have restricted access to abortion services are given in normal typeface; those likely to have had a liberalising effect are italicised	Discussion at pages:
39	Nadine Dorries (Con)	Amendment of Health and Social Care Act 2012	'Independent' information, advice and counselling services to be available to women requesting an abortion (defined as that provided by either a statutory body or 'a private body that does not itself provide for the termination of pregnancies'). All organisations offering advice regarding unplanned pregnancy to follow evidence-based guidance produced by a professional medical organisation specified by the Government. NICE to be required to make recommendations regarding the care of women seeking abortion, including the option of receiving independent information, advice and counselling about the procedure, its potential health implications and alternatives, including adoption	pp. 238–39
40	Fiona Bruce (Con): Abortion Statistics Bill	TMRB 2013	The Government to be required to compile statistics on the gender ratios of fetuses aborted in the UK and, where available, overseas	p. 239
41	Fiona Bruce (Con): Abortion (Sex-Selection) Bill	TMRB 2014	To 'clarify' the Abortion Act by adding an explicit prohibition of abortion on the grounds of sex	pp. 239–40
42	Baroness Jenny Tonge (Independent Lib Dem): Abortion Act 1967 (Amendment) Bill [HL]	HL 2014	*Abortion to be permitted following certification by one doctor (rather than two)*	p. 250
43	Fiona Bruce (Con) and Ann Coffey (Lab)	Amendment of Serious Crime Act 2015	(Bruce): To provide that the Abortion Act 1967 should not be interpreted as allowing a pregnancy to be terminated on the grounds of fetal sex (Coffey): To assess the evidence regarding the incidence of abortion on the grounds of fetal sex and to determine a plan to tackle any concerns thereby substantiated	pp. 240–41
44	Baroness Nuala O'Loan (Crossbench): Conscientious Objection (Medical Activities) Bill [HL]	HL 2015	No health professional with a conscientious objection to be under a duty to participate in the withdrawal of life-sustaining treatment, activities under the Human Fertilisation and Embryology Act 1990, or any activity relating to abortion (including 'supervision, delegation, planning or supporting of staff involved in such activity). Employers must not discriminate against or victimise those with such an objection	pp. 243–44

(*cont.*)

	Sponsor (political party): short title	Means of introduction and year	Select summary of major measures proposed. NB measures that passed into law are listed in bold. Measures likely to have restricted access to abortion services are given in normal typeface; those likely to have had a liberalising effect are italicised	Discussion at pages:
45	Lord Kevin Shinkwin (Con): Abortion (Disability Equality) Bill [HL]	HL 2016	To repeal the fetal anomaly ground of the Abortion Act	p. 242
46	Diana Johnson (Lab): Reproductive Health (Access to Terminations) Bill	TMRB 2017	*Abortion to be decriminalised before 24 weeks in England and Wales*	pp. 250–51
47	Baroness Nuala O'Loan (Crossbench): Conscientious Objection (Medical Activities) Bill [HL]	HL 2017	No health professional with a conscientious objection to be under a duty to participate in withdrawal of life-sustaining treatment, activities under the Human Fertilisation and Embryology Act 1990 or any activity relating to abortion (including 'supervision, delegation, planning or supporting of staff' involved in such activity). Employers must not discriminate against or victimise those with such an objection	pp. 243–44
48	Baroness Emma Nicholson (Con): Abortion (Foetus Protection) Bill [HL]	HL 2017	Most abortions to be prohibited after 12 weeks	p. 244
49	Lord Kevin Shinkwin (Con): Abortion (Disability Equality) Bill [HL]	HL 2017	To impose a 24 week upper time limit on abortions certified under the fetal anomaly ground. Before an abortion can be performed on this ground, full and accurate information must be provided regarding all available options ('including the keeping of that child'), and this must include information provided by disability family support groups and organizations 'led and controlled by disabled people'	pp. 242–43
50	Diana Johnson (Lab): Abortion Bill	TMRB 2018	*To decriminalise abortion performed with the woman's consent until 24 weeks and repeal the offence of 'concealment of birth' (England, Wales and Northern Ireland), and to ensure that timely access to abortion is not impeded by the exercise of conscientious objection rights (England and Wales)*	pp. 251–52

(cont.)

	Sponsor (political party): short title	Means of introduction and year	Select summary of major measures proposed. NB measures that passed into law are listed in bold. Measures likely to have restricted access to abortion services are given in normal typeface; those likely to have had a liberalising effect are italicised	Discussion at pages:
51	Stella Creasy (Lab & Co-op)	Amendment of Northern Ireland (Executive Formation and Exercise of Functions) Act 2018	**To require the UK Government to issue guidance on how Northern Ireland departments should operate in relation to the incompatibility of continued enforcement of abortion offences and the human rights of Northern Irish people, and to report to Parliament on the guidance and plans to address the impact of the suspension of Stormont on human rights obligations**	p. 253
52	Stella Creasy (Lab & Co-op)	Amendment of Northern Ireland Budget (Anticipation and Adjustments) (No. 2) Act 2019	*To prevent spending within Northern Ireland on prosecuting abortion offences*	pp. 253–254
53	Stella Creasy (Lab & Co-op)	Amendment of Northern Ireland (Executive Formation) Act 2019	**To require the UK Government to act expeditiously to implement CEDAW recommendations regarding abortion law in Northern Ireland; to decriminalise abortion before viability; to end prosecutions for abortion; and to regulate for the provision of abortion within Northern Ireland. This section should come into effect only if the Northern Ireland Executive is not re-established by 21 October 2019**	pp. 254–55
54	Baroness Barker (Lib Dem): Abortion Bill [HL]	HL 2020	*To decriminalise abortion performed with the woman's consent until 24 weeks, repeal the offence of 'concealment of birth', and ensure that timely access to abortion is not impeded by the exercise of conscientious objection rights in England and Wales*	pp. 252
55	Sarah Olney (Lib Dem): Protest (Abortion Clinics) Bill	Presentation 2020	*To prohibit anti-abortion protests within 150 metres of abortion clinics*	p. 256
56	Baroness Bennett (Green)	Amendment of Coronavirus Act 2020	*To make temporary changes to abortion law, allowing for fully telemedical abortion services and permitting nurses and midwives to certify the need for an abortion*	p. 257

(cont.)

	Sponsor (political party): short title	Means of introduction and year	Select summary of major measures proposed. NB measures that passed into law are listed in bold. Measures likely to have restricted access to abortion services are given in normal typeface; those likely to have had a liberalising effect are italicised	Discussion at pages:
57	Fiona Bruce (Con): Abortion (Cleft Lip, Cleft Palate and Clubfoot) Bill	Presentation 2020	To provide that cleft lip, cleft palate and clubfoot are not to be counted as 'substantial handicaps' for the purpose of the fetal anomaly ground	p. 243
58	Rupa Huq (Lab): Demonstrations (Abortion Clinics) Bill	TMRB 2020	*To prohibit abortion demonstrations within a 150 metre 'buffer zone' around abortion clinics*	pp. 256–257
59	Diana Johnson (Lab)	Amendment of Domestic Abuse Act 2021	*To remove the requirement for a woman to attend a hospital or licensed premises for abortion in cases where she is believed to be subject to coercive control*	pp. 259–260
60	Rupa Huq (Lab) and Diana Johnson (Lab)	Amendment of Police, Crimes, Sentencing and Courts Bill 2021	*(Huq): To prohibit anti-abortion protests within 150 metres of abortion clinics* *(Johnson): To decriminalise abortion before viability and to introduce a new offence of non-consensual abortion*	
61	Maria Miller (Con)/Diana Johnson (Lab), Fiona Bruce (Con) and Carla Lockhart (DUP), Baroness Liz Sugg (Con)	Amendment of Health and Social Care Bill 2021	(HC): (Miller/Johnson): *To exclude a woman's criminal liability for procuring her own abortion pre-viability* (Bruce): To reduce the upper time limit for most abortions to 22 weeks (Lockhart): To make abortion on the grounds of fetal anomaly subject to the same upper time limit as most other abortions. To provide that abortion on the grounds of fetal sex is illegal (HL): (Sugg): **To maintain provision of telemedical early medical abortion services**	p. 260

Explanatory Note

The small number of reform proposals that passed into law are indicated in bold. Those that would have tended to liberalise the law are italicised; those that would have tended to restrict it are not italicised. We have relied here on our own classification of measures as 'restrictive' or 'liberalising' relative to the law in place at that time. Where a measure would have represented a formal restriction of the law we have classified it as such, even where it was motivated by a desire to protect against more wide-ranging restriction (e.g. Lord Houghton's proposed enshrinement of a 24 week upper time limit on the face of the Abortion Act; see Chapter 3, p. 100).

This table includes only Bills and amendments recorded in *Hansard* between 1968 and May 2022 that were intended to have a direct impact on provision of or access to abortion services. It excludes any draft Bills that were never formally presented to Parliament or amendments that were not selected for debate or were otherwise blocked without discussion (e.g. the raft of liberalising proposals co-ordinated by Evan Harris MP in 2008; see Chapter 7, pp. 233–34, 237). Occasions when abortion law was discussed other than on the basis of a specific reform measure are likewise excluded, as is debate of measures that would have had only an indirect effect on the provision of abortion services (even where this appears to have been a motivating factor for the proposed reform, e.g. devolution of legislative competence over abortion; see Chapter 7, pp. 245–48). Multiple amendments tabled to a single Bill are grouped together and recorded as one instance of attempted reform.

The measures recorded above were proposed either as amendments to Government legislation or as Private Members' Bills. In the House of Commons, Bills can be tabled as Ballot Bills, Ten Minute Rule Bills or Presentation Bills. Priority is given to Ballot Bills, which thus have the best chance of being debated and becoming law. Ten Minute Rule Bills are given a 'prime time' ten minute speaking slot in the House of Commons, allowing MPs to make their case, generate debate and test the opinion of the House on an issue. Any MP can introduce a Presentation Bill: these are not debated but can sometimes serve to publicise an issue. Members of the House of Lords have an unrestricted right to introduce Private Members' Bills, with a ballot used to determine the order in which they receive their first reading.

Where a published Bill or amendment was available to us, we have used that as the basis for our summary of its major provisions. Where Bills have been subject to amendment as they passed through Parliament, we have relied on the most recent iteration of it available to us. Where the text of a draft Bill was never published (as is the case for some Ten Minute Rule Bills) or was otherwise unavailable to us, we have relied on its title and/or the description of its planned content offered to Parliament by its sponsor. Parliamentarians' party affiliations are given as at the date that the Bills or amendments were tabled.

Appendix 3

List of Interviewees

David Baird was an honorary consultant gynaecologist, Royal Infirmary of Edinburgh, and Emeritus Professor of the Medical Research Council Centre for Reproductive Health. While Professor and Chairman of Obstetrics and Gynaecology at the University of Edinburgh, Baird's team pioneered the development of a medical 'abortion pill'.

Marge Berer has worked in the UK and internationally since 1976 as an advocate for sexual and reproductive health rights. She worked with the National Abortion Campaign before chairing the Voice for Choice coalition of Pro-Choice organisations from 2007 until 2010, and she co-founded and chaired the International Consortium for Medical Abortion from 2002 until 2011. She helped found and has coordinated the International Campaign for Women's Right to Safe Abortion since 2015.

Eileen Cook was consistently involved in Pro-Choice campaigning since the first meeting of the National Abortion Campaign in London in 1975 and as part of its Trades Union Liaison Committee. After moving to Scotland in 1983, Cook continued her involvement in the Dundee National Abortion Campaign, the Scottish Abortion Campaign and Abortion Rights.

Dilys Cossey is a long-term campaigner for abortion and contraceptive rights, having been Secretary of the Abortion Law Reform Association during the passing of the Abortion Act. She went on to work with the Birth Control Campaign, the Family Planning Association (which she chaired from 1987 to 1993) and Brook (which she chaired from 1995 to 2001), campaigning for free contraception on the NHS and in defence of the Abortion Act.

John Deighan has been the Chief Executive Officer of the Society for the Protection of the Unborn Child Scotland since 2015, having been involved in Pro-Life campaigning since the 1990s. Deighan chaired the East Kilbride Society for the Protection of Unborn Children group and the Paisley Pro-Life Group, and he stood as a ProLife Alliance parliamentary candidate in two Westminster elections. He was Parliamentary Officer with the Scottish Bishops' Conference from 1999 until 2015.

Ann Furedi was the Chief Executive Officer of the British Pregnancy Advisory Service from 2003 until 2020, a charity that provides non-profit abortion and sexual health services and also advocates to protect and extend access to these services. With a background in journalism, which introduced her to the issue of abortion provision, Furedi previously worked with the Family Planning Association and the Birth Control Trust.

Anna Glasier is an honorary professor at the University of Edinburgh and the London School of Hygiene and Tropical Medicine. Glasier trained in obstetrics and gynaecology, practicing and researching in reproductive health, particularly contraception and abortion. She was Director of Family Planning and Well Woman Services for Lothian until 2010, and she chaired the Guideline Development Group for both the Royal College of Obstetricians and Gynaecologists and World Health Organization guidance on induced abortion.

Joyce Gould was a Labour Party official and, from 1993 until her retirement in 2019, a Labour peer. She has a long-standing interest in sexual health and has been involved in campaigns to defend the Abortion Act. She was an executive member of the Women's National Commission (1970–1975) and Chief Women's Officer of the Labour Party (1975–1985). Gould chaired the All-Party Parliamentary Group for Sexual and Reproductive Health for over twenty years and has been President of the Family Planning Association since 2000.

Ann Henderson is a long-standing campaigner in the Labour Movement and for women's rights, having been involved in the Scottish Abortion Campaign and subsequently Abortion Rights as a member of their Executive Committee and in the Abortion Rights Committee Scotland. She is a former Scottish Trades Union Congress assistant secretary and Scotland commissioner to the Women's National Commission.

Goretti Horgan has been involved in Pro-Choice campaigning in the UK and Republic of Ireland since 1979. Having been national organiser of the 1983 campaign against the Eighth Amendment, Horgan moved to Northern Ireland and set up a Women's Right to Choose group in Derry, before becoming a founder-member of Alliance for Choice in Northern Ireland in 1997. She has conducted extensive social policy research including into the effects of criminalising abortion.

Diane Munday was a key member of the Abortion Law Reform Association from 1962, acting as Vice-Chair and main spokesperson, and then General Secretary from 1968. She began working for the British Pregnancy Advisory Service in 1974 and remained there for 16 years as its parliamentary, public and press relations officer, remaining active in campaigns to defend the Abortion Act and pursuing a number of libel actions regarding claims made about the work of the British Pregnancy Advisory Service.

Josephine Quintavalle is a long-standing campaigner in the Pro-Life movement. Quintavalle was a crisis pregnancy counsellor for Life for 20 years after moving to London in the 1970s. She founded Comment on Reproductive Ethics in 1994, a Pro-Life public interest group focused on issues surrounding human reproduction, and stood as an election candidate for the ProLife Alliance.

Bill Rolston worked as part of the Northern Ireland Abortion Law Reform Association in the 1980s, which aimed to stimulate debate of abortion law reform and achieve the extension of the Abortion Act to Northern Ireland. He has been involved in an advisory capacity with both the Family Planning Association and Marie Stopes International (now MSI Reproductive Choices) in Northern Ireland and, more recently, Informing Choices Northern Ireland.

Peter Saunders is a former general surgeon who has been involved in the Pro-Life movement internationally and domestically since moving to the UK in 1989. He was Chief Executive of the Christian Medical Fellowship until December 2018, participating in advocacy work with a focus on the medical evidence associated with abortion.

Jack Scarisbrick has been a key figure in the Pro-Life movement over many decades. Scarisbrick founded Life in 1970 with his wife, Nuala, as a charity that was absolutely opposed to abortion. Life was primarily focused on providing pregnancy testing and counselling and facilitating alternatives to abortion. He was its National Chairman for 47 years before stepping down in 2017.

Audrey Simpson is Chair of the Board of Trustees for Informing Choices Northern Ireland. She joined the Family Planning Association (FPA) as Northern Ireland Director in 1988, acting as Chief Executive of the FPA UK from 2012 to 2015. She introduced a non-advisory counselling service for women facing unplanned pregnancy and increased the visibility of the FPA's advocacy work concerning abortion rights in Northern Ireland. During this time, FPANI won an important judicial review action requiring the publication of official guidance regarding Northern Ireland's abortion law and was one of the organisations that requested a Convention on the Elimination of All Forms of Discrimination Against Women inquiry into abortion in the region.

David Steel was a Liberal then Liberal Democrat MP (1965–1997) and leader of the party (1976–1988). He was subsequently made a life peer as Baron Steel of Aikwood (serving 1997–2020). Steel introduced the Private Member's Bill that was to become the Abortion Act 1967. He continued to play a major role in the defence of the Abortion Act in Parliament over the following decades, and in recent years he has argued for further liberalisation of the law.

Caroline Woodroffe is an epidemiologist, public health specialist and contraception campaigner. She was Director of the Brook Advisory Centres between 1970 and 1986, when Brook began to incorporate pregnancy testing and abortion referral into their services. She was called as a witness before the Lane Committee into the Working of the Abortion Act (1971–1974). She is a former Chair of the Birth Control Trust.

Bibliography

ARCHIVES AND COLLECTIONS

Cadbury Research Library, University of Birmingham
Papers of Francois Lafitte

Glasgow Caledonian University Archive Centre
Papers of One Parent Families Scotland
Scotland Trades Union Congress Archives

Glasgow Women's Library
Edinburgh Women's Centre Archive
Papers of the Scottish Abortion Campaign

London School of Economics Archives
Papers of David Steel
Papers of Merlyn Rees

Modern Records Centre, University of Warwick
Papers of Andrew Whitehead
Trades Union Congress Archives

National Records of Scotland
Papers of the Lord Advocate's Department
Papers of the Scottish Home and Health Department

Public Record Office of Northern Ireland
Papers of the Department of Health and Social Services
Papers of the Health Promotion Agency

Royal College of Obstetricians and Gynaecologists Archive

The National Archives

Cabinet Papers
Papers of the Department of Health and Social Security
Papers of the Director of Public Prosecutions
Papers of the Minister of State's Office

Wellcome Library

Ephemera Collection
Papers of the Abortion Law Reform Association
Papers of the Birth Control Campaign
Papers of the British Pregnancy Advisory Service (material referenced in the book was
    consulted prior to this material being donated to the Wellcome Library, where it
    was subsequently reordered and catalogued)
Papers of the National Abortion Campaign
Papers of Wendy Savage

SERIAL GOVERNMENT PUBLICATIONS

Legislature Proceedings

Hansard, Debates of the Parliament of the United Kingdom
Official Report of the Northern Ireland Assembly
Official Report of the Scottish Parliament

Statistical Volumes

Common Services Agency, *Scottish Health Statistics* (1966–1999)
Department of Health, *Abortion Statistics, England and Wales* (2002–2014)
Department of Health and Social Care, *Abortion Statistics for England and Wales*
    (2015–2020)
Information Services Division (NHS Scotland), *Abortion Statistics* (2009–2019)
Office of Population Censuses and Surveys, *Abortion Statistics* (1974–2001)
Public Health Scotland, Termination of Pregnancy Statistics (2020–2021)
Registrar General's Statistical Review of England and Wales, Supplement on Abortion
    (1968–1973)
Scottish Home and Health Department, *Health Bulletin* (1968–2002)

ORAL HISTORY INTERVIEWS

Baird, David, interviewed by Gayle Davis, 13 November 2017
Berer, Marge, interviewed by Jane O'Neill, 6 October and 8 November 2017
Cook, Eileen, interviewed by Jane O'Neill, 11 September 2017
Cossey, Dilys, interviewed by Jane O'Neill, 4 October 2017
Deighan, John, interviewed by Jane O'Neill, 30 January 2018
Furedi, Ann, interviewed by Jane O'Neill, 23 August 2017

Glasier, Anna, interviewed by Gayle Davis, 13 November 2017

Gould, Joyce, interviewed by Jane O'Neill, 4 October 2017

Henderson, Ann, interviewed by Jane O'Neill, 25 July 2017

Horgan, Goretti, interviewed by Jane O'Neill, 30 April 2017

Knight, Jill, interviewed by Mike Greenwood, 9 May 2012, https://sounds.bl.uk/Oral-history/The-History-of-Parliament-Oral-History-Project/021M-C1503X0014XX-0001V0

Munday, Diane, interviewed by Jane O'Neill, 10 November 2017

Quintavalle, Josephine, interviewed by Jane O'Neill, 6 October 2017

Rolston, Bill, interviewed by Jane O'Neill, 29 April 2017

Saunders, Peter, interviewed by Jane O'Neill, 9 November 2017

Scarisbrick, Jack, interviewed by Jane O'Neill, 7 November 2017

Simpson, Audrey, interviewed by Jane O'Neill, 27 September 2017

Steel, David, interviewed by Jane O'Neill, 5 February 2018

Woodroffe, Caroline, interviewed by Jane O'Neill, 26 October 2017

Published Works

Abort67, 'Why We Show Images' (2014), http://abort67.co.uk/why_we_show_images [no longer available].

Abortion Law Reform Association, *A Report on NHS Abortion Services* (London: Abortion Law Reform Association, 1997).

Abse, Leo, *Private Member* (London: Macdonald, 1973).

Academy of Medical Royal Colleges, *Induced Abortion and Mental Health: A Systematic Review of the Mental Health Outcomes of Induced Abortion, Including Their Prevalence and Associated Factors* (London: Academy of Medical Royal Colleges, 2011).

Ackroyd, Peter, *London: The Biography* (London: Chatto & Windus, 2000).

Aiken, Abigail, Patricia A. Lohr, Jonathan Lord, Nabanita Ghosh, and Jennifer Starling, 'Effectiveness, Safety and Acceptability of No-Test Medical Abortion Provided via Telemedicine: A National Cohort Study', *BJOG: An International Journal of Obstetrics and Gynaecology*, vol. 128 no. 9 (2021), 1464–74.

All Party Parliamentary Pro-Life Group, 'A Report into Freedom of Conscience in Abortion Provision' (2016), www.conscienceinquiry.uk/wp-content/uploads/2016/12/Pro-Life-APPG-Freedom-of-Conscience-in-Abortion-Provision.pdf

All Party Parliamentary Pro-Life Group, 'Foetal Sentience & Pain: An Evidence Review' (2020), https://lordalton.files.wordpress.com/2020/03/2020-pro-life-appg-report-on-foetal-pain.pdf

Allen, Isobel, *Counselling Services for Sterilisation, Vasectomy and Termination of Pregnancy* (London: Policy Studies Institute, 1985).

Allen, Isobel, *Family Planning, Sterilisation and Abortion Services* (London: Policy Studies Institute, 1981).

Alton, David, 'Truth Should Speak to Power – The 50th Anniversary of the Abortion Act' (2017), https://davidalton.net/2017/10/27/truth-should-speak-to-power-the-50th-anniversary-of-the-abortion-act-text-of-a-speech-delivered-outside-of-the-british-parliament-on-the-50th-anniversary-of-legislation-that-has-claimed-more-than/

Alton, David, *What Kind of Country?* (Basingstoke: Marshall Pickering, 1988).

Alton, David with Alison Holmes, *Whose Choice Anyway? The Right to Life* (Basingstoke: Marshall Pickering, 1988).

Amery, Fran, *Beyond Pro-Life and Pro-Choice: The Changing Politics of Abortion in Britain* (Bristol: Bristol University Press, 2020).

Amery, Fran, 'Social Questions, Medical Answers: Contesting British Abortion Law', *Social Politics*, vol. 21 no. 1 (2013), 26–49.

Anitha, Sundari and Aisha K. Gill, 'Making Politics Visible: Discourses on Gender and Race in the Problematisation of Sex-Selective Abortion', *Feminist Review*, vol. 120 no. 1 (2018), 1–19.

Archbishop Cranmer, 'Kevin (Lord) Shinkwin Appointed to Equality and Human Rights Commission' (2017), https://archbishopcranmer.com/kevin-lord-shink win-equality-human-rights-commission/

Argent, Vincent and Lin Pavey, 'Can Nurses Legally Perform Surgical Induced Abortion?', *Journal of Family Planning and Reproductive Health Care*, vol. 33 no. 2 (2007), 79–82.

ARK, 'Northern Ireland Life and Times Survey' (2016), www.ark.ac.uk/nilt/2016/index .html

ARK, 'Northern Ireland Life and Times Survey, 2018' (2019), www.ark.ac.uk/nilt/2018/

Armstrong, Liz and Anne McChlery, 'No More Reservations About Abortion Rights: The Scottish Abortion Campaign Comments', *Engender*, no. 16 (1997), 7.

Ashton, J. R., A. Chamberlain, K. J. Dennis, R. G. Rowe, W. E. Waters, and M. J. Wheeler, 'The Wessex Abortion Studies: II. Attitudes of Consultant Gynaecologists to Provision of Abortion Services', *Lancet*, vol. 315 no. 8160 (1980), 140–42.

Attar Taylor, Eleanor, 'British Attitudes to Abortion' (2017), www.natcen.ac.uk/blog/ british-attitudes-to-abortion

Attar Taylor, Eleanor and Jacqueline Scott, 'Gender: New Consensus or Continuing Battleground?' in Daniel Phillips, John Curtice, Miranda Phillips and Jane Perry (eds), *British Social Attitudes: The 35th Report* (London: The National Centre for Social Research, 2018), pp. 56–85.

Back Off Scotland, 'About' (2021), www.backoffscotland.com

Baird, Dugald, 'A Fifth Freedom?', *British Medical Journal*, vol. 2 no. 5471 (1965), 1141–48.

Baird, Dugald, 'Abortion Games', *Lancet*, vol. 298 no. 7734 (1971), 1145.

Baird, Dugald, 'The Abortion Act 1967: The Advantages and Disadvantages', *Royal Society of Health Journal*, vol. 90 no. 6 (1970), 291–95.

Barker, Anthony and Michael Rush, *The Member of Parliament and His Information* (London: Allen & Unwin, 1970).

Baulieu, Etienne-Emile, *The Abortion Pill* (London: Century, 1992).

Bazlinton, Chris and Anne Cowen, *The Guardian Directory of Pressure Groups and Representative Organisations* (London: Wilton House Publications, 1976).

BBC, 'Gay Britannia' (2017), www.bbc.co.uk/programmes/p05bbtf2

BBC, 'Abortion on Trial' (2017), www.bbc.co.uk/programmes/b09b1z7n

BBC Radio 5, 'Sarah Ewart's Abortion Journey from Northern Ireland' (2013), www .bbc.co.uk/programmes/p01jmx4x

BBC Radio 4, 'Born with Down's' (2008), www.bbc.co.uk/programmes/b00fkx0m

BBC Radio 4, 'The Moral Maze: 50 Years of the Abortion Act' (2017), www.bbc.co.uk/programmes/b097c1g3

BBC Radio 4, 'The Reunion: Stonewall' (2009), www.bbc.co.uk/programmes/b00mpmm4

Beck, Ulrich and Elisabeth Beck-Gernsheim, *The Normal Chaos of Love* (Cambridge: Polity Press, 1995).

Berer, Marge, 'Abortion Notification Forms', *Lancet*, vol. 319 no. 8276 (1982), 857.

Berić, Berislav M. and Milan Kupresanin, 'Vacuum Aspiration Using Pericervical Block for Legal Abortion as an Outpatient Procedure up to the 12th Week of Pregnancy', *Lancet*, vol. 298 no. 7725 (1971), 619–21.

Berne, Eric, *Games People Play: The Psychology of Human Relationships* (London: Penguin, 1964).

Bianchi, Diana W., Dick Oepkes, and Alessandro Ghidini, 'Current Controversies in Prenatal Diagnosis 1: Should Noninvasive DNA Testing Be the Standard Screening Test for Down Syndrome in All Pregnant Women?', *Prenatal Diagnosis*, vol. 34 no. 1 (2014), 6–11.

Bigman, Fran, 'Abortion in American Film since 2001', *Oxford Research Encyclopedia of Criminology* (2017), https://oxfordre.com/criminology/view/10.1093/acrefore/9780190264079.001.0001/acrefore-9780190264079-e-16

Black, Julia, *My Foetus* (Channel 4, 2004).

Black, Julia, 'Regulatory Conversations', *Journal of Law and Society*, vol. 29 no. 1 (2002), 163–96.

BMA, 'Agenda of Annual Representative Meeting', *British Medical Journal* (17 June 1978) 1633.

BMA, *The Removal of Criminal Sanctions for Abortion: BMA Position Paper* (London: British Medical Association, 2019).

Bogdanor, Vernon, *Devolution in the United Kingdom* (Oxford: Oxford University Press, 2001).

Boothroyd, Betty, *Betty Boothroyd: The Autobiography* (London: Arrow, 2001).

Bourne, Aleck, *A Doctor's Creed: Memoirs of a Gynaecologist* (London: Gollancz, 1962).

Boutwood, Anne, 'The Effect of the Act on Gynaecological Practice' in Medical Protection Society, *The Abortion Act 1967: Proceedings of a Symposium Held by the Medical Protection Society, in Collaboration with the RCGP at the RCOG* (London: Pitman, 1969), pp. 49–56.

Bovey, Nigel, 'MP Calls for Lower Abortion Time Limit', *The War Cry: Fighting for Hearts and Souls*, no. 6812 (2007), 4–5.

Boyle, Mary and Jane McEvoy, 'Putting Abortion in Its Social Context: Northern Irish Women's Experiences of Abortion in England', *Health*, vol. 2 no. 3 (1998), 283–304.

BPAS, *Abortion: Trusting Women to Decide and Doctors to Practice* (Stratford-upon-Avon: BPAS, 2015).

BPAS, 'Back Off' (2014), https://back-off.org/

BPAS, 'BPAS Launches Emergency Abortion Pills by Post for Women in Northern Ireland amid Shameful Political Gameplay with Women's Health during the Covid-19 Pandemic' (2020), www.bpas.org/about-our-charity/press-office/press-releases/bpas-launches-emergency-abortion-pills-by-post-for-women-in-northern-ireland-amid-shameful-political-gameplay-with-women-s-health-during-the-covid-19-pandemic/

BPAS, *Britain's Abortion Law: What It Says and Why* (Stratford-upon-Avon: BPAS, 2013), www.reproductivereview.org/images/uploads/Britains_abortion_law.pdf

BPAS, 'JR76 Case Report' (c. 2018), www.bpas.org/media/3060/jr76-case-report.pdf

BPAS, 'Medically Complex Women and Abortion Care' (2018), www.bpas.org/media/2074/briefing-medically-complex-women-and-abortion-care.pdf

BPAS, 'We Trust Women: About the Campaign' (2019), https://wetrustwomen.org.uk/about-the-campaign/

Brazier, Alex and Ruth Fox, 'Enhancing the Backbench MP's Role As a Legislator: The Case for Urgent Reform of Private Members Bills', *Parliamentary Affairs*, vol. 63 no. 1 (2010), 201–11.

Brewer, Colin and Peter J. Huntingford, 'Mortality from Abortion: The NHS Record', *British Medical Journal*, vol. 2 no. 6136 (1978), 562.

Briggs, Eleanor M. and Alison E. Mack, 'Termination of Pregnancy in the Unmarried', *Scottish Medical Journal*, vol. 17 no. 12 (1972), 398–400.

Bristow, Jennie, 'Misoprostol and the Transformation of the "Abortion Pill"', *Abortion Review* (2011), www.abortionreview.org/index.php/site/article/908/ [no longer available].

British Humanist Association, 'Health and Social Care Bill, 2010–2011 Report Stage: Nadine Dorries' "Informed Consent" Amendments' (2011), https://humanism.org.uk/wp-content/uploads/bha-briefing-2011-health-social-care-bill.pdf

British Museum, 'Desire, Love, Identity: Exploring LGBTQ Histories' (2018), https://blog.britishmuseum.org/desire-love-identity-exploring-lgbtq-histories/

Brook, 'Crisis Pregnancy Centres' (2014), https://legacy.brook.org.uk/attachments/crisis_preg_centres_rept_10.2.14-2hiFINAL.pdf

Brooke, Stephen, *Sexual Politics: Sexuality, Family Planning and the British Left from the 1880s to the Present Day* (Oxford: Oxford University Press, 2011).

Brookes, Barbara, *Abortion in England, 1900–1967* (London: Croom Helm, 1988).

Brown, Callum G., *Religion and the Demographic Revolution: Women and Secularisation in Canada, Ireland, UK and USA since the 1960s* (Woodbridge: Boydell Press, 2012).

Brown, Callum G., *The Death of Christian Britain: Understanding Secularisation 1800–2000* (London and New York: Routledge, 2nd edition, 2009).

Bruce, Fiona (Chair), 'Parliamentary Inquiry into Abortion on the Grounds of Disability' (2013), https://dontscreenusout.org/wp-content/uploads/2016/02/Abortion-and-Disability-Report-17-7-13.pdf

Bruce, Steve, *British Gods: Religion in Britain since 1900* (Oxford: Oxford University Press, 2019).

Brudenell, Michael, 'Foreword' in Anthony Hordern, *Legal Abortion: The English Experience* (Oxford: Pergamon Press, 1971), pp. ix–xi.

Bryan, Beverly, Stella Dadzie, and Suzanne Scafe, *The Heart of the Race: Black Women's Lives in Britain* (London: Virago, 1985).

Cameron, I. T., A. F. Michie, and D. T. Baird, 'Therapeutic Abortion in Early Pregnancy with Antiprogestogen RU486 Alone or in Combination with Prostaglandin Analogue (Gemeprost)', *Contraception*, vol. 34 no. 5 (1986), 459–68.

Campbell, Emma and Siobhan Clancy, 'From Grassroots to Government: Arts Engagement Strategies in Abortion Access Activism in Ireland' in Colleen

MacQuarrie, Fiona Bloomer, Claire Pierson, and Shannon Stettner (eds), *Crossing Troubled Waters: Abortion in Ireland, Northern Ireland, and Prince Edward Island* (Prince Edward Island: Island Studies Press, 2018), pp. 204–34.

Campbell, Stuart, '4D and Prenatal Bonding: Still More Questions than Answers', *Ultrasound in Obstetrics and Gynecology*, vol. 27 no. 3 (2006), 243–44.

Care Quality Commission, 'Findings of Termination of Pregnancy Inspections Published' (2012), www.cqc.org.uk/content/findings-termination-pregnancy-inspections-published

Carroll, Patrick, *Abortion and Other Pregnancy-Related Risk Factors in Female Breast Cancer* (London: Pension and Population Research Institute, 2001).

Carson, W. G., 'Symbolic and Instrumental Dimensions of Early Factory Legislation: A Case Study in the Social Origins of Criminal Law' in Roger Hood (ed.), *Crime, Criminology and Public Policy* (London: Heinemann, 1974), pp. 107–38.

Cates, Willard, David A. Grimes, and Kenneth F. Schulz, 'The Public Health Impact of Legal Abortion: 30 Years Later', *Perspectives on Sexual and Reproductive Health*, vol. 35 no. 1 (2003), 25–28.

CEDAW, *Inquiry Concerning the United Kingdom of Great Britain and Northern Ireland Under Article 8 of the Optional Protocol to the Convention on the Elimination of All Forms of Discrimination Against Women*, CEDAW/C/OP.8/GBR/1 (New York: Convention on the Elimination of all Forms of Discrimination Against Women, 2018).

Chalmers, Iain and Anne Anderson, 'Factors Affecting Gestational Age at Therapeutic Abortion', *Lancet*, vol. 299 no. 7764 (1972), 1324–26.

Charnock, Hannah, '"This Haunting Sadness": Press Coverage of John Corrie's Abortion (Amendment) Bill, 1979–1980', *Women's History*, vol. 2 no. 5 (2016), 16–22.

Cheetham, Juliet, 'The Lane Committee', comments made at Abortion Act 1967 Conference: A Promise Fulfilled?, Royal College of Obstetricians and Gynaecologists, London, 24–25 October 2017.

Childs, Sarah, *New Labour's Women MPs: Women Representing Women* (London: Routledge, 2005).

Christian Concern, 'Abortion at Home: A Mystery Client Investigation' (2021), https://christianconcern.com/wp-content/uploads/2018/10/CC-Resource-Abortion-At-Home-A-Mystery-Client-Investigation-201210.pdf

Christian Concern, 'Abortion for "Any Reason" Other than Sex-Selection, Says BPAS' (2020), https://christianconcern.com/news/abortion-for-any-reason-other-than-sex-selection-says-bpas/

Christian Concern, 'DIY Abortion Policy Led to Home Abortion at 28 Weeks' (2020), https://christianconcern.com/comment/diy-abortion-policy-led-to-home-abortion-at-28-weeks/

Christian Concern, 'Targeted Abortion Campaign Launched' (2008), https://archive.christianconcern.com/our-concerns/abortion/targeted-abortion-campaign-launched

Christian Concern, 'Why We're Taking "DIY" Abortion Case to Court of Appeal' (2020), https://christianconcern.com/comment/why-were-taking-diy-abortion-case-to-court-of-appeal/

Christians in Parliament, 'Fiona Bruce MP' (2021), www.christiansinparliament.org
.uk/about/members-stories/fiona-bruce-mp/

Church of England Board for Social Responsibility, *Abortion: An Ethical Discussion*
(London: Church Information Office, 1965).

Church of England and Child Poverty Action Group, '"No one Knows What the Future
Can Hold": The Impact of the Two-Child Limit after Three Years' (2020), https://
cpag.org.uk/sites/default/files/files/policypost/No-one-knows-what-the-future-can-
hold-FINAL.pdf

Clark, M., I. Forstner, D. A. Pond, and R. F. Tredgold, 'Sequels of Unwanted
Pregnancy: A Follow-up of Patients Referred for Psychiatric Opinion', *Lancet*,
vol. 292 no. 7566 (1968), 501–03.

Clements, Ben, 'Religion and the Sources of Public Opposition to Abortion in Britain:
The Role of "Belonging", "Behaving" and "Believing"', *Sociology*, vol. 48 no. 2
(2014), 369–86.

Clements, Ben and Clive D. Field, 'Abortion and Public Opinion in Great Britain: A 50-
Year Retrospective', *Journal of Beliefs & Values*, vol. 39 no. 4 (2018), 429–44.

Cochrane, Linda, *Healing a Father's Heart: A Post-Abortion Bible Study for Men*
(Grand Rapids, MI: Baker, 1996).

Cochrane, Rosemary A. and Sharon T. Cameron, 'Attitudes of Scottish Abortion Care
Providers towards Provision of Abortion after 16 Weeks' Gestation within
Scotland', *European Journal of Contraception & Reproductive Health Care*, vol.
18 no. 3 (2013), 215–20.

Colvin, Madeleine, 'The Legal Situation' in Cerys Williams (ed.), *The Abortion Pill
(Mifepristone/RU486): Widening the Choice for Women*, Proceedings of a conference
organised by the Birth Control Trust on 26 October 1989 at the Royal College of
Obstetricians and Gynaecologists (London: Birth Control Trust, 1990), pp. 18–21.

Commons Select Committee, 'Formal Minutes – Science and Technology Committee
(Commons)' (c. 2019), https://old.parliament.uk/business/committees/commit
tees-a-z/commons-select/science-and-technology-committee/formal-minutes/

Condon, Guy and Dave Hazard, *Fatherhood Aborted: The Profound Effects of Abortion
on Men* (Carol Stream, IL: Tyndale House, 2001).

Cook, Hera, *The Long Sexual Revolution: English Women, Sex and Contraception,
1800–1975* (Oxford: Oxford University Press, 2004).

Corbyn, Jeremy, '50 Years Ago Today . . .' (2017), https://twitter.com/jeremycorbyn/
status/923869622193008641

Cornerstone Group, 'About Us' (n.d.), https://cornerstonegroup.wordpress.com/about/

Cossey, Dilys, 'The Politics of the Abortion Pill: Breaking Down Barriers' in Cerys
Williams (ed.), *The Abortion Pill (Mifepristone/RU486): Widening the Choice for
Women*, Proceedings of a conference organised by the Birth Control Trust on
26 October 1989 at the Royal College of Obstetricians and Gynaecologists
(London: Birth Control Trust, 1990), pp. 52–57.

Cotterell, Roger, *The Sociology of Law: An Introduction* (London: Butterworths, 2nd
edition, 1992).

Coulter, Colin, 'Direct Rule and the Unionist Middle Classes' in Richard English and
Graham S. Walker (eds), *Unionism in Modern Ireland* (Basingstoke: Macmillan,
1996), pp. 169–91.

Cowan, David and Daniel Wincott, 'Exploring the Legal' in David Cowan and Daniel Wincott (eds), *Exploring the 'Legal' in Socio-Legal Studies* (London: Palgrave, 2015), pp. 1–31.

Crowter, Heidi, 'Downright Discrimination: Stop the Govt Singling Out Disabled Babies', CrowdJustice.com (2021), www.crowdjustice.com/case/downrightdiscrimination/

Curtice, John, Elizabeth Clery, Jane Perry, Miranda Phillips, and Nilufer Rahim (eds), *British Social Attitudes: The 36th Report* (London: The National Centre for Social Research, 2019).

Dabner, Jack Duane, The Silent Scream (American Portrait Films, 1984).

Davidson, Roger and Gayle Davis, *The Sexual State: Sexuality and Scottish Governance, 1950–80* (Edinburgh: Edinburgh University Press, 2012).

Davis, Gayle and Roger Davidson, '"The Fifth Freedom" or "Hideous Atheistic Expediency": The Medical Community and Abortion Law Reform in Scotland, c.1960–75', *Medical History*, vol. 50 no. 1 (2006), 29–48.

Davis, Gayle, Jane O'Neill, Clare Parker, and Sally Sheldon, 'All Aboard the "Abortion Express": Geographic Variability, Domestic Travel and the 1967 British Abortion Act' in Christabelle Sethna and Gayle Davis (eds), *Abortion across Borders: Transnational Travel and Access to Abortion Services* (Baltimore, MD: Johns Hopkins University Press, 2019), pp. 101–22.

de Londras, Fiona, '"A Hope Raised and then Defeated"? The Continuing Harms of Irish Abortion Law', *Feminist Review*, vol. 124 no. 1 (2020), 33–50.

Dee, Olivia, *The Anti-Abortion Campaign in England, 1966–1989* (New York: Routledge, 2020).

Deitch, Rodney, 'Challenge Deferred over Abortion Notification Forms', *Lancet*, vol. 319 no. 8271 (1982), 575–76.

Department of Health, 'An Investigation into the BPAS Response into the Requests for Late Abortions – A Report from the CMO' (2005), https://webarchive.nationalarchives.gov.uk/20080728104226/http:/www.dh.gov.uk/en/Publicationsandstatistics/Publications/PublicationsPolicyAndGuidance/DH_4119591

Department of Health, *Guidance for Health and Social Care Professionals on Termination of Pregnancy in Northern Ireland* (Belfast: DHSSPS, 2016).

Department of Health, *Guidance in Relation to Requirements of the Abortion Act 1967* (London: Department of Health, 2014).

Department of Health, Letter from the CMO to PCT and SHA Chief Executives (21 September 2005), https://webarchive.nationalarchives.gov.uk/20080728104226/http:/www.dh.gov.uk/en/Publicationsandstatistics/Publications/PublicationsPolicyAndGuidance/DH_4119591

Department of Health, 'Matching Department of Health Abortion Notifications and Data from the National Down's Syndrome Cytogenetic Register, 2013' (2015), https://assets.publishing.service.gov.uk/government/uploads/system/uploads/attachment_data/file/433397/DH_NDSCR_matching_report_2013.pdf

Department of Health, *The Limited Circumstances for a Lawful Termination of Pregnancy in NI: A Guidance Document for Health and Social Care Professionals on Law and Clinical Practice*, draft version (Belfast: DHSSPS, 2013).

Department of Health and Social Care, 'Abortion Statistics 2020: Data Tables' (2021), https://assets.publishing.service.gov.uk/government/uploads/system/uploads/attachment_data/file/992250/abortion-statistics-2020-data-tables_Final.ods

Department of Health and Social Care, 'Sex Ratios at Birth in Great Britain, 2013-17' (2019), https://assets.publishing.service.gov.uk/government/uploads/system/uploads/attachment_data/file/837965/Sex_ratios_at_birth_in_GB__2013-17.pdf

Department of Health and Social Care, 'The Abortion Act 1967 – Approval of a Class of Places' (2018), https://assets.publishing.service.gov.uk/government/uploads/system/uploads/attachment_data/file/768059/Approval_of_home_use_for_the_second_stage_of_early_medical_abortion.pdf

Department of Health and Social Care, 'The Abortion Act 1967 – Approval of a Class of Places' (2020), https://assets.publishing.service.gov.uk/government/uploads/system/uploads/attachment_data/file/876740/30032020_The_Abortion_Act_1967_-_Approval_of_a_Class_of_Places.pdf

Department of Health and Social Security, *Report of the Committee of Inquiry into Human Fertilisation and Embryology*, Cmnd 9314 (London: Her Majesty's Stationery Office, 1984).

Department of Health and Social Security, *The Use of Fetuses and Fetal Material for Research: Report of the Advisory Group (Peel Report)* (London: Her Majesty's Stationery Office, 1972).

Department of Justice, *The Criminal Law on Abortion. Lethal Foetal Abnormality and Sexual Crime. A Consultation on Amending the Law by the Department of Justice* (Belfast: Department of Justice, 2014).

Department of Justice, *The Criminal Law on Abortion. Lethal Foetal Abnormality and Sexual Crime. Response to the Consultation and Policy Proposals* (Belfast: Department of Justice, 2015).

Department of Justice and Department of Health, *Report of the Working Group on Fatal Fetal Abnormality Healthcare and the Law on Termination of Pregnancy for Fatal Fetal Abnormality: Proposals to the Minister of Health and the Minister of Justice* (2018), www.health-ni.gov.uk/sites/default/files/publications/health/report-fatal-fetal-abnormality-April-2018.pdf

Devlin, David, 'Book for Burning?', *The General Practitioner* (20 January 1978).

Devlin, Patrick, *Easing the Passing: The Trial of Doctor John Bodkin Adams* (London: Faber and Faber, 1986).

Dickens, Bernard, *Abortion and the Law* (London: MacGibbon & Key, 1966).

Diggory, P. L. C., 'Some Experiences of Therapeutic Abortion', *Lancet*, vol. 293 no. 7600 (1969), 873–75.

Diplock, Kenneth, *The Court as Legislators* (Birmingham: Holdsworth Club, 1965).

Donald, Ian, 'Naught for Your Comfort', *Journal of the Irish Medical Association*, vol. 65 (1972), 279–89.

Don't Screen Us Out, 'Press Release: Woman with Down's Syndrome Launches Landmark Case against UK Govt over Discriminatory Abortion Law' (2020), https://dontscreenusout.org/press-release-woman-with-downs-syndrome-launches-landmark-case-against-uk-govt-over-discriminatory-abortion-law/

Don't Screen Us Out, 'Press Release: Woman with Down's Syndrome's Landmark Case against UK Govt over Discriminatory Abortion Law Plans to Go onto Court of Appeal' (2021), https://dontscreenusout.org/press-release-court-of-appeal/

Don't Screen Us Out, 'Press Release – Woman with Down's Syndrome's Landmark Case against UK Govt over Discriminatory Abortion Law to Be Heard by Court of Appeal' (2022), https://dontscreenusout.org/press-release-woman-with-downs-syn

dromes-landmark-case-against-uk-govt-over-discriminatory-abortion-law-to-be-heard-by-court-of-appeal/

Dubow, Sara, *Ourselves Unborn: A History of the Fetus in Modern America* (Oxford: Oxford University Press, 2017).

Dubuc, Sylvie and David Coleman, 'An Increase in the Sex Ratio of Births to India-Born Mothers in England and Wales: Evidence for Sex Selective Abortion', *Population and Development Review*, vol. 33 no. 2 (2007), 383–400.

Dudley-Brown, Margaret, 'The Duties of the GP under the Abortion Act', in Medical Protection Society, *The Abortion Act 1967: Proceedings of a Symposium Held by the Medical Protection Society, in Collaboration with the RCGP at the RCOG* (London: Pitman, 1969), pp. 1–8.

Duxbury, Neil, *Elements of Legislation* (Cambridge: Cambridge University Press, 2013).

Dworkin, Ronald, *Law's Empire* (Oxford: Hart Publishing, 1998).

Dyer, Clare, 'Charity Did Not Break Law in Giving Information about Late Abortions', *British Medical Journal*, vol. 331 no. 7519 (2005), 716.

Dyer, Clare, 'Receptionists May Not Invoke Conscience Clause', *British Medical Journal*, vol. 297 no. 6662 (1988), 1493–94.

Education for Choice, 'The "Parliamentary Inquiry" on Abortion and Disability' (2013), https://educationforchoice.blogspot.com/2013/07/the-parliamentary-inquiry-on-abortion.html

Edwards, John, *The Attorney General, Politics and the Public Interest* (London: Sweet & Maxwell, 1984).

Ehrlich, Paul R., *The Population Bomb* (New York: Sierra Club/Ballantine Books, 1968).

Engender, 'Joint Statement on Scotland Bill, Amendment EC56, "Abortion"' (c. 2015), www.engender.org.uk/content/publications/Joint-statement-on-Scotland-Bill—NC56—Abortion.pdf [no longer available].

Enright, Máiréad, Kathryn McNeilly, and Fiona de Londras, 'Abortion Activism, Legal Change, and Taking Feminist Law Work Seriously', *Northern Ireland Legal Quarterly*, vol. 71 no. 3 (2020), 359–85.

Evangelical Alliance, 'Question Time' (2015), www.eauk.org/idea/question-time.cfm

Evason, Eileen, *Against the Grain: The Contemporary Women's Movement in Northern Ireland* (Dublin: Attic, 1991).

Fairweather, Eileen, 'The Feelings behind the Slogans', *Spare Rib*, no. 87 (1979), 26–30.

Fairweather, Eileen, Roisín McDonough, and Melanie McFadyean, *Only the Rivers Run Free: Northern Ireland: The Women's War* (London: Pluto, 1984).

Farmer, Ann, 'Abortion: Woman's Right or Body Parts Industry?', *Catholic Medical Quarterly*, vol. 64 no. 1 (2014), www.cmq.org.uk/CMQ/2014/Feb/abortion_body_parts.html

Farmer, Ann, *By Their Fruits: Eugenics, Population Control and the Abortion Campaign* (Washington, DC: Catholic University of America Press, 2008).

Ferris, Paul, *The Nameless: Abortion in Britain Today* (London: Penguin, 1966).

Fiala, Christian and Joyce H. Arthur, 'There Is No Defence for "Conscientious Objection" in Reproductive Health Care', *European Journal of Obstetrics & Gynecology and Reproductive Biology*, vol. 216 (2017), 254–58.

Fine, Alan, 'The Ethics of Fetal Tissue Transplants', *The Hastings Center Report*, vol. 18 no. 3 (1988), 5–8.

Fisher, Jane, 'Post-24 Week Termination for Fetal Anomaly – The Chilling Effect of the Jepson Campaign' in BPAS, *Britain's Abortion Law: What It Says, and Why* (Stratford-upon-Avon: BPAS, 2013), pp. 28–29.

Flynn, Paul, *How to Be an MP* (London: Biteback Publishing, 2012).

Fowkes, F. G. R., J. C. Catford, and R. F. L. Logan, 'Abortion and the NHS: The First Decade', *British Medical Journal*, vol. 1 no. 6158 (1979), 217–19.

FPANI, Northern Ireland Women's European Platform, and Alliance for Choice, *Submission of Evidence to the CEDAW Committee Optional Protocol: Inquiry Procedure*, Transitional Justice Institute Research Paper No. 15-01 (Jordanstown: Ulster University, 2015).

Francome, Colin, 'Gynaecologists and Abortion in Northern Ireland', *Journal of Biosocial Sciences*, vol. 26 (1994), 389–94.

Franklin, Sarah, 'Fetal Fascinations: New Dimensions to the Medical–Scientific Construction of Fetal Personhood' in Sarah Franklin, Celia Lury, and Jackie Stacey (eds), *Off Centre: Feminism and Cultural Studies* (London: Harper Collins, 1991), pp. 190–205.

Franklin, Sarah, Celia Lury, and Jackie Stacey (eds), *Off Centre: Feminism and Cultural Studies* (London: Harper Collins, 1991).

Freeman, Iris, *Lord Denning: A Life* (London: Hutchinson, 1993).

Friday, Adrian, 'Charles Goodhart: A Twentieth Century Life' (n.d.), www.zoo.cam.ac.uk/alumni/biographies-of-zoologists/charles-goodhart-a-twentieth-century-life

Furedi, Ann, 'Our 10-Year Struggle to Improve Abortion Care', *Abortion Review*, vol. 34 (2011), 1.

Furedi, Ann, *The Moral Case for Abortion* (London: Palgrave Macmillan, 2016).

Galligan, Yvonne, 'Women in Northern Ireland's Politics: Feminising an "Armed Patriarchy"' in Marian Sawer, Manon Tremblay, and Linda Trimble (eds), *Representing Women in Parliament: A Comparative Study* (London: Routledge, 2006), pp. 204–20.

Gallup, 'Abortion' (2019), https://news.gallup.com/poll/1576/abortion.aspx

Gammeltoft, Tine M. and Ayo Wahlberg, 'Selective Reproductive Technologies', *Annual Review of Anthropology*, vol. 43 (2014), 201–16.

Ganatra, Bela, Caitlin Gerdts, Clémentine Rossier, Brooke Ronald Johnson Jr, Özge Tuncalp, Anisa Assifi, Gilda Sedgh, Susheela Singh, Akinrinola Bankole, Anna Popinchalk, Jonathan Bearak, Zhenning Kang, and Leontine Alkema, 'Global, Regional, and Subregional Classification of Abortions by Safety, 2010–14: Estimates from a Bayesian Hierarchical Model', *Lancet*, vol. 390 no. 10110 (2017), 2372–81.

Gardner, Greg, 'Abortion and Breast Cancer – Is There a Link?' *Triple Helix* (2003), www.cmf.org.uk/resources/publications/content/?context=article&id=1088

Geiringer, David, *The Pope and the Pill: Sex, Catholicism and Women in Post-War England* (Manchester: Manchester University Press, 2020).

General Synod of the Church of England, 'Valuing People with Down's Syndrome', GS 2088 (2018), www.churchofengland.org/sites/default/files/2018-01/GS%202088%20-%20Valuing%20People%20with%20Down%27s%20Syndrome.pdf

Giddens, Anthony, *Modernity and Self-Identity: Self and Society in the Late Modern Age* (Cambridge: Polity Press, 1991).

Giddens, Anthony, *The Transformation of Intimacy* (Cambridge: Polity Press, 1992).

Gill, Robin, *Theology Shaped by Society* (Farnham: Ashgate, 2012).

Gillings, Mark and Joshua Pollard, 'Non-portable Stone Artifacts and Contexts of Meaning', *World Archaeology*, vol. 31 no. 2 (1999), 179–93.

Gillon, Raanon, 'Ethics of Fetal Brain Cell Transplants', *British Medical Journal*, vol. 296 no. 6631 (1988), 1212–13.

Glazebrook, P. R., 'Glanville Llewelyn Williams 1911–1997', *Proceedings of the British Academy*, vol. 115 (2002), 411–35.

Go, Attie T. J. I., John M. G. van Vugt, and Cees B. M. Oudejans, 'Non-invasive Aneuploidy Detection Using Free Fetal DNA and RNA in Maternal Plasma: Recent Progress and Future Possibilities', *Human Reproduction Update* vol. 17 no. 3 (2011), 372–82.

Goldthorp, W. O., 'Ten Minute Abortions', *British Medical Journal*, vol. 2 no. 6086 (1977), 562–64.

Gordon, Gerald, *The Criminal Law of Scotland* (Edinburgh: W. Green & Son, 1967).

Gosden, Chris and Yvonne Marshall, 'The Cultural Biography of Objects', *World Archaeology*, vol. 31 no. 2 (1999), 169–78.

Government Equalities Office, 'New Commissioner for the Equality and Human Rights Commission' (2017), www.gov.uk/government/news/new-commissioner-for-the-equality-and-human-rights-commission

Government of the UK, 'Temporary Approval of Home Use for Both Stages of Early Medical Abortion' (2020), www.gov.uk/government/publications/temporary-approval-of-home-use-for-both-stages-of-early-medical-abortion [no longer available].

Gray, Ann-Marie, 'Attitudes to Abortion in Northern Ireland' (2017), www.ark.ac.uk/publications/updates/update115.pdf [no longer available].

Gray, Ann-Marie, Goretti Horgan, and Paula Devine, 'Do Social Attitudes to Abortion Suggest Political Parties in Northern Ireland Are Out of Step with Their Supporters?' (2018), www.ark.ac.uk/pdfs/Features/feature7.pdf

Gray, Ann-Marie and Kaye Wellings, 'Is Public Opinion in Support of Decriminalisation?' in Sally Sheldon and Kaye Wellings (eds), *Decriminalising Abortion in the UK: What Would It Mean?* (Bristol: Policy Press, 2020), pp. 17–36.

Green, Josephine M., 'Obstetricians' Views on Prenatal Diagnosis and Termination of Pregnancy: 1980 Compared with 1993', *British Journal Obstetrics and Gynaecology*, vol. 102 no. 3 (1995), 228–32.

Greenwood, Victoria and Jock Young, *Abortion in Demand* (London: Pluto, 1976).

Gugenheim, Peter S. and Barbara M. Chandler, 'Medical Examination of Patients Attending Registered Pregnancy Advice Bureaux', *Lancet*, vol. 320 no. 8295 (1982), 436.

Gunn, M. J. and J. C. Smith, 'Arthur's Case and the Right to Life of a Down Syndrome Child', *Criminal Law Review*, vol. 1985 (1985), 705–15.

Hadley, Janet, *Abortion: Between Freedom and Necessity* (London: Virago, 1997).

Hadley, Janet, 'The "Awfulisation" of Abortion', *Choices*, vol. 26 no. 1 (1997), 7–8.

Halfmann, Drew, *Doctors and Demonstrators: How Political Institutions Shape Abortion Law in the United States* (Chicago, IL: University of Chicago Press, 2011).

Hall, Lesley, *Sex, Gender and Social Change in Britain since 1880* (London: Macmillan, 2000).

Hallgarten, Lisa, 'Abortion Narratives: Moving from Statistics to Stories', *Lancet*, vol. 391 no. 10134 (2018), 1988–89.

Ham, Christopher, *Health Policy in Britain: The Politics and Organisation of the National Health Service* (Basingstoke: Palgrave, 4th edition, 1999).

Hamet, Camille and Serena Robin, 'Take the Boat' (2015), https://m.imdb.com/title/tt4948196/

Hamill, Evelyn and I. M. Ingram, 'Psychiatric and Social Factors in the Abortion Decision', *British Medical Journal*, vol. 1 no. 5901 (1974), 229–32.

Han, Sallie, 'Pregnant with Ideas: Concepts of the Fetus in the Twenty-First-Century United States' in Sallie Han, Tracy K. Betsinger, and Amy B. Scott (eds), *The Anthropology of the Fetus: Biology, Culture and Society* (New York and Oxford: Berghahn, 2018), pp. 59–82.

Harlow, Carol and Richard Rawlings, *Pressure through Law* (London: Routledge, 2016).

Harrington, John, 'Of Paradox and Plausibility: The Dynamic of Change in Medical Law', *Medical Law Review*, vol. 22 no. 3 (2014), 305–24.

Harrington, John, *Towards a Rhetoric of Medical Law* (London: Routledge, 2017).

Harrington, John, Lucy Series, and Alexander Ruck-Keene, 'Law and Rhetoric: Critical Possibilities', *Journal of Law and Society*, vol. 42 no. 2 (2019), 302–27.

Hart, H. L. A., 'Abortion Law Reform: The English Experience', *Melbourne University Law Review*, vol. 8 no. 3 (1972), 388–411.

Hayes, Graeme and Pam Lowe, '"A Hard Enough Decision to Make": Anti-Abortion Activism outside Clinics in the Eyes of Clinic Users, A Report on the Comments Made by BPAS Services Users' (2015), www.aston.ac.uk/EasySiteWeb/GatewayLink.aspx?alId=256682

Hayward, Katy and Cathal McManus, 'Neither/Nor: The Rejection of Unionist and Nationalist Identities in Post-Agreement Northern Ireland', *Class and Capital*, vol. 43 no. 1 (2019), 139–55.

Hervey, Tamara and Sally Sheldon, 'Abortion by Telemedicine in Northern Ireland: Patient and Professional Rights to Free Movement across Borders', *Northern Ireland Legal Quarterly*, vol. 68 no. 1 (2017), 1–33.

HESA, 'Higher Education Student Statistics: UK, 2019/20' (2021), www.hesa.ac.uk/news/27-01-2021/sb258-higher-education-student-statistics

Hewson, Barbara, 'Clinical Negligence: Denied Access', *Legal Week* (7 December 2005).

HFEA, *Donated Ovarian Tissue in Embryo Research and Assisted Conception: Public Consultation Document* (London: HFEA, 1994).

Hill, Myrtle, *Women in Ireland: A Century of Change* (Belfast: Blackstaff Press, 2003).

Hindell, Keith, *A Gilded Vagabond* (Brighton: Book Guild Publishing, 2012).

Hindell, Keith and Madeleine Simms, *Abortion Law Reformed* (London: Peter Owen, 1971).

Hodges, Mark, 'UK Is Paying an Abortion Activist $600K+ to Write a Book about Abortion for Children' (2017), www.lifesitenews.com/news/uk-oks-600k-for-womens-activist-to-write-abortion-textbook-for-schoolkids

Hoggart, Lesley, 'Socialist Feminism, Reproductive Rights and Political Action', *Capital & Class*, vol. 24 no. 1 (2000), 95–125.

Hoggart, Lesley, Victoria Louise Newton, and Louise Bury, '"Repeat Abortion": A Phrase to be Avoided? Qualitative Insights into Labelling and Stigma', *Journal of Family Planning and Reproductive Health Care*, vol. 43 no. 1 (2017), 26–30.

Hoggett, A. J. C., 'The Abortion Act 1967', *Criminal Law Review*, vol. 1968 (1968), 247–58.

Hopkins, Nick, Steve Reicher, and Jannat Saleem, 'Constructing Women's Psychological Health in Anti-Abortion Rhetoric', *The Sociological Review*, vol. 44 no. 3 (1996), 539–64.

Hordern, Anthony, *Legal Abortion: The English Experience* (Oxford: Pergamon Press, 1971).

Horgan, Goretti, 'A Holy Alliance? Obstacles to Abortion Rights in Ireland North and South' in Aideen Quilty, Sinead Kennedy, and Catherine Conlon (eds), *The Abortion Papers Ireland Vol. II* (Dublin: Attic Press, 2015), pp. 244–55.

Horgan, Goretti and Julia S. O'Connor, 'Abortion and Citizenship Rights in a Devolved Region of the UK', *Social Policy and Society*, vol. 13 no. 1 (2014), 39–49.

Horobin, Gordon, *Experience with Abortion: A Case Study of North-East Scotland* (Cambridge: Cambridge University Press, 1974).

House of Commons, *First Report from the Select Committee on Abortion, 1975–1976*, Vol. 1: Report, HC 573-I (1976).

House of Commons, *Special Reports and Minutes of Evidence of the Select Committee on the Abortion (Amendment) Bill, 1974–1975*, HC 692-II (1975).

House of Commons Committee on Standards, *All-Party Parliamentary Groups Sixth Report of Session 2013–14*, HC 357 (2013).

House of Commons Library, *Women in Parliament and Government, Briefing Paper Number 01250* (2019).

House of Commons Science and Technology Committee, *Human Reproductive Technologies and the Law: Fifth Report of Session 2004-5*, HC7-I (2005).

House of Commons Science and Technology Committee, *Scientific Developments Relating to the Abortion Act 1967: Twelfth Report of Session 2006–7*, Vol. 1, HC 1045-I (2007).

House of Commons Science and Technology Committee, *Scientific Developments Relating to the Abortion Act 1967: Twelfth Report of Session 2006–7*, Vol. 2, HC 1045-II (2007).

House of Commons Social Services Committee, *Abortion Act 1967 'Conscience Clause'*, Tenth Report, HC 123 (1990).

House of Commons Standing Committee C, *Minutes of Proceedings on the Abortion (Amendment) Bill*, HC 494 (1977).

House of Commons Standing Committee C, *Minutes of Proceedings on the Abortion (Amendment) Bill* (1979).

House of Commons Women and Equalities Committee, *Abortion Law in Northern Ireland, Eighth Report of Session 2017–19*, HC 1584 (2019).

House of Lords, *Report of the Select Committee on the Infant Life (Preservation) Bill [H.L.]*, HL 50 (1987–1988).

House of Lords, *Special Report with Evidence of the Select Committee on the Infant Life (Preservation) Bill [HL]*, HL 153 (1986–1987).

Human Developmental Biology Resource, 'General Information' (n.d.), www.hdbr.org/general-information

Humanists UK, 'Anti-Abortion Activist Resigns as Equality and Human Rights Commissioner' (2017), https://humanism.org.uk/2017/12/13/anti-abortion-activist-resigns-as-equality-and-human-rights-commissioner/

Huntingford, Peter, 'The Failure of the NHS: Why the Public & the NHS Need the Charities' in Birth Control Trust (ed.), *Abortion: The NHS and the Charities, A Symposium* (London: Birth Control Trust, 1977), pp. 3–8.

ICM Unlimited, *Abortion Documentary Survey* (2017), www.icmunlimited.com/wp-content/uploads/2017/10/OlOm-Abortion-Documentary-v2.pdf

Informing Choices NI, *Strategic Plan 2020–2023* (Belfast: Informing Choices NI, 2020), https://informingchoicesni.org/wp-content/uploads/2020/07/ICNI-STRATEGIC-PLAN-20-23.pdf

Ingram, I. M., 'Abortion Games: An Inquiry into the Working of the Act', *Lancet*, vol. 298 no. 7731 (1971), 969–70.

Irish Catholic, 'Nuala O'Loan' (2021), www.irishcatholic.com/author/nualaoloan/

Jackson, Lucy and Gill Valentine, 'Performing "Moral Resistance"? Pro-Life and Pro-Choice Activism in Public Space', *Space and Culture*, vol. 20 no. 2 (2017), 225–31.

Jamieson, Lynn, 'Changing Intimacy: Seeking and Forming Couple Relationships' in Lynn Abrams and Callum G. Brown (eds), *A History of Everyday Life in Twentieth-Century Scotland* (Edinburgh: Edinburgh University Press, 2010), pp. 76–102.

Jelen, Ted G. and Clyde Wilcox, 'Causes and Consequences of Public Attitudes toward Abortion: A Review and Research Agenda', *Political Research Quarterly*, vol. 56 no. 4 (2003), 489–500.

Jenkins, Alice, *Law for the Rich: A Plea for the Reform of the Abortion Law* (London: Victor Gollancz, 1960).

Jepson, Joanna, 'The Empty Hanger', www.emptyhanger.co.uk/ [no longer available].

Jolly, Margaretta, '"The Feelings behind the Slogans": Abortion Campaigning and Feminist Mood-Work Circa 1979', *New Formations*, vol. 82 no.1 (2014), 100–13.

Jones, Cecily, '"Human Weeds, Not Fit to Breed?": African Caribbean Women and Reproductive Disparities in Britain', *Critical Public Health*, vol. 23 no. 1 (2013), 49–61.

Jones, Ian, 'Setting Up Services' in Ann Furedi (ed.), *Mifepristone in Practice. Running an Early Medical Abortion Service*, Proceedings of a conference organised by the Birth Control Trust on 22 April 1993 at the Royal Society of Medicine (London: Birth Control Trust, 1990), pp. 19–23.

Jülich, Solveig, 'Lennart Nilsson's Child Is Born: The Many Lives of a Best-Selling Pregnancy Advice Book', *Culture Unbound, Journal of Current Cultural Research*, vol. 7 no. 4 (2015), 627–48.

Kasstan, Ben and Maya Unnithan, 'Arbitrating Abortion: Sex-Selection and Care Work among Abortion Providers in England', *Medical Anthropology*, vol. 39 no. 6 (2020), 491–505.

Katz Rothman, Barbara, *The Tentative Pregnancy: Prenatal Diagnosis and the Future of Motherhood* (London: Pandora, 2nd edition, 1993).

Kelly, Richard, 'Women Members of Parliament', House of Commons Research Briefing (2019), https://commonslibrary.parliament.uk/research-briefings/sn066520/

Kennedy, Ian and Andrew Grubb, *Medical Law* (London: Butterworths, 3rd edition, 2000).

Kennedy, Steven, 'Two Child Limit in Universal Credit and Child Tax Credits', House of Commons Research Briefing (2018), https://commonslibrary.parliament.uk/research-briefings/cdp-2018-0263/

Keown, John, '"Miscarriage": A Medico-Legal Analysis', *Criminal Law Review*, vol. 1984 (1984), 604–14.

Keown, John, *Abortion, Doctors and the Law: Some Aspects of the Legal Regulation of Abortion in England from 1803 to 1982* (Cambridge: Cambridge University Press, 1988).

Keown, John, '"Morning After" Pills, "Miscarriage" and Muddle', *Legal Studies*, vol. 25 no. 2 (2005), 296–319.

Kerslake, D. and D. Casey, 'Abortion Induced by Means of the Uterine Aspirator', *Obstetrics and Gynecology*, vol. 30 no. 1 (1967), 35–45.

Kilday, Anne-Marie and David Nash, 'The Silent Scream of Shame? Abortion in Modern Britain' in Anne-Marie Kilday and David Nash (eds), *Shame and Modernity in Britain: 1890 to the Present* (London: Palgrave Macmillan, 2017), pp. 115–67.

Kind to Women, 'How the 1967 Abortion Act Changes Our Lives' (2018), www .kindtowomen.com/

Kirklin, Deborah, 'The Role of Medical Imaging in the Abortion Debate', *Journal of Medical Ethics*, vol. 30 no. 5 (2004), 426.

Klein, Renate, Janice G. Raymond, and Lynette Dumble, *RU 486: Misconceptions, Myths and Morals* (Melbourne: Spinifex, 1991).

Knight, Marian, Kathryn Bunch, Derek Tuffnell, Judy Shakespeare, Rohit Kotnis, Sara Kenyon, and Jennifer J. Kurinczuk (eds), *Saving Lives, Improving Mothers' Care: Lessons Learned to Inform Maternity Care from the UK and Ireland Confidential Enquiries into Maternal Deaths and Morbidity 2016–18* (Oxford: National Perinatal Epidemiology Unit, University of Oxford, 2020).

Kopytoff, Igor, 'The Cultural Biography of Things: Commoditization as Process' in Arjun Appadurai (ed.), *The Social Life of Things: Commodities in Cultural Perspective* (Cambridge: Cambridge University Press, 1988), pp. 64–92.

Labour Party, 'It's Time for Real Change: The Labour Party Manifesto 2019' (2019), https://labour.org.uk/wp-content/uploads/2019/11/Real-Change-Labour-Manifesto-2019.pdf

Labour Party, *Report of the 74th Annual Conference of the Labour Party* (Blackpool: Labour Party, 1975).

Lafitte, Francois, 'How the Charities Fill the Gap' in Birth Control Trust, *Abortion: The NHS and the Charities, A Symposium* (London: Birth Control Trust, 1977), pp. 9–12.

Lafitte, Francois, *The Abortion Hurdle Race: The Role of the Doctor as a Taker of Abortion Decisions* (Solihull: BPAS, 1975).

Lane, Elizabeth, *Hear the Other Side* (London: Butterworths, 1985).

Lane, Elizabeth (Chair), *Report of the Committee on the Working of the Abortion Act (Lane Report)*, Cmnd. 5579 (London: Her Majesty's Stationery Office, 1974).

Lawson, J. B., D. Yare, S. L. Barron, A. M. E. Querido, and P. R. Phillips, 'Management of the Abortion Problem in an English City', *Lancet*, vol. 308 no. 7998 (1976), 1288–91.

Lawson, Nigel, *The View from No. 11: Memoirs of a Tory Radical* (London: Bantam, 1992).

Lawyers' Christian Fellowship, 'Mission & Vision' (2021), https://lawcf.org/about/mis sion-vision

Lee, Ellie, *Abortion, Motherhood and Mental Health: Medicalizing Reproduction in the United States and Great Britain* (New York: Aldine de Gruyter, 2003).

Lee, Ellie, 'Constructing Abortion as a Social Problem: "Sex Selection" and the British Abortion Debate', *Feminism & Psychology*, vol. 27 no. 1 (2017), 15–33.

Lee, Ellie, 'The Trouble with "Smiling" Fetuses' (2003), www.prochoiceforum.org.uk/ocr_ethical_iss_1.php

Lee, Ellie, 'Young Women, Pregnancy, and Abortion in Britain: A Discussion of "Law in Practice"', *International Journal of Law, Policy and the Family*, vol. 18 no. 3 (2004), 283–304.

Lewis, Jane, *Women in Britain since 1945* (London: Wiley-Blackwell, 1992).

Lewis, T. R. T., 'The Abortion Act', *British Medical Journal*, vol. 1 no. 5638 (1969), 241–42.

Lewis, T. R. T., 'The Abortion Act (1967): Findings of an Inquiry into the First Year's Working of the Act Conducted by the Royal College of Obstetricians and Gynaecologists', *British Medical Journal*, vol. 2 no. 5708 (1970), 529–35.

Liberal Democrats, 'Stop Brexit, Build a Brighter Future: Manifesto 2019' (2019), https://d3n8a8pro7vhmx.cloudfront.net/libdems/pages/57333/attachments/original/1574258742/Lib_Dem_Manifesto_2019.pdf?1574258742

Litchfield, Michael and Susan Kentish, *Babies for Burning* (London: Serpentine, 1974).

Liverpool Museums, 'Coming Out' (2017), www.liverpoolmuseums.org.uk/walker/exhibitions/arts-council-collection/coming-out/index.aspx [no longer available].

Lohr, Patricia A., Jennifer E. Starling, James G. Scott, and Abigail R. A. Aiken, 'Simultaneous Compared with Interval Medical Abortion Regimens Where Home Use Is Restricted', *Obstetrics & Gynecology*, vol. 131 no. 4 (2018), 635–41.

Lord, Jonathan M., Lesley Regan, Asha Kasliwal, Louise Massey, and Sharon Cameron, 'Early Medical Abortion', *BMJ Sexual and Reproductive Health*, vol. 44 no. 3 (2018), 155–58.

Lovenduski, Joni, 'Parliament, Pressure Groups, Networks and the Women's Movement: The Politics of Abortion Law Reform in Britain (1967–83)' in Joni Lovenduski and Joyce Outshoorn (eds), *The New Politics of Abortion* (London: Sage, 1986), pp. 231–56.

Lowe, Pam, '(Re)imagining the "Backstreet": Anti-Abortion Campaigning Against Decriminalisation in the UK', *Sociological Research Online*, vol. 24 no. 2 (2019), 203–18.

Lowe, Pam and Graeme Hayes, 'Anti-Abortion Clinic Activism, Civil Inattention and the Problem of Gendered Harassment', *Sociology*, vol. 53 no. 2 (2019), 330–46.

Lowe, Pam and Sarah-Jane Page, '"On the Wet Side of the Womb": The Construction of "Mothers" in Anti-Abortion Activism in England and Wales', *European Journal of Women's Studies*, vol. 26 no. 2 (2019), 165–80.

Lowe, Pam and Sarah-Jane Page, 'Rights-Based Claims Made by UK Anti-Abortion Activists', *Health and Human Rights*, vol. 21 no. 2 (2019), 133–44.

Löwy, Ilana, 'Prenatal Diagnosis, Surveillance and Risk' in Nick Hopwood, Rebecca Flemming, and Lauren Kassell (eds), *Reproduction: Antiquity to the Present Day* (Cambridge: Cambridge University Press, 2018), pp. 567–80.

Löwy, Ilana, 'Prenatal Diagnosis: The Irresistible Rise of the "Visible Foetus"', *Studies in History and Philosophy of Biological and Biomedical Sciences*, vol. 47 part B (2014), 290–99.

Lupton, Deborah, *The Social Worlds of the Unborn* (Basingstoke: Palgrave, 2013).

Macintyre, Sally, *Single and Pregnant* (London: Croom Helm, 1977).

MacLeod, Harris, '82% Aware of Mad Nad' (2012), https://yougov.co.uk/topics/polit ics/articles-reports/2012/11/23/82-aware-mad-nad

Mansour, Diana and Linda Stacey, 'Abortion Methods' in David Paintin (ed.), *Abortion Services in England and Wales* (London: BCT and PAS, 1990), pp. 29–38.

Marsh, David and Joanna Chambers, *Abortion Politics* (London: Junction Books, 1981).

Marshall, Kate, *Real Freedom* (London: Junius, 1982).

Marteau, Theresa M. and Harriet Drake, 'Attributions for Disability: The Influence of Genetic Screening', *Social Science and Medicine*, vol. 40 no. 8 (1995), 1127–32.

McAnulla, Stuart, 'Secular Fundamentalists? Characterising the New Atheist Approach to Secularism, Religion and Politics', *British Politics*, vol. 9 no. 2 (2014), 124–45.

McCormick, Leanne, '"No Sense of Wrongdoing": Abortion in Belfast 1917–1967', *Journal of Social History*, vol. 49 no. 1 (2015), 125–48.

McCormick, Leanne, *Regulating Sexuality: Women in Twentieth-Century Northern Ireland* (Manchester: Manchester University Press, 2009).

McCormick, Leanne, '"The Scarlet Woman in Person": The Establishment of a Family Planning Service in Northern Ireland, 1950–1974', *Social History of Medicine*, vol. 21 no. 2 (2008), 345–60.

McCormick, Leanne and Sean O'Connell with Olivia Dee and John Privilege, *Mother and Baby Homes and Magdalene Laundries in Northern Ireland, 1922–1990* (Belfast: Northern Ireland Department of Health, 2021).

McCullagh, Peter, *Fetal Sentience* (London: All-Party Parliamentary Pro-Life Group, 1996).

McGivern, Marie-Thérèse, *Abortion in Northern Ireland* (1980) reprinted in Angela Bourke, Siobhán Kilfeather, Maria Luddy, Margaret Mac Curtain, Gerardine Meaney, Máirín Ni Dhonnchadha, Mary O'Dowd, and Clair Wills (eds), *The Field Day Anthology of Irish Writing Volume V: Irish Women's Writing and Traditions* (Cork: Cork University Press and Field Day, 2002), pp. 390–91.

McGrane, F. and J. Nicholls, 'Tribunal on Abortion Rights', *Spare Rib*, no. 56 (1977), 26–27.

McGuinness, Sheelagh, 'A Guerrilla Strategy for a Pro-Life England', *Law, Innovation and Technology*, vol. 7 no. 2 (2015), 283–314.

McGuinness, Sheelagh and Michael Thomson, 'Medicine and Abortion Law: Complicating the Reforming Profession', *Medical Law Review*, vol. 23 no. 2 (2015), 177–99.

McLaren, Hugh, 'The Abortion Bill', *Lancet*, vol. 289 no. 7489 (1967), 565–66.

McNay, M. B. and J. E. Fleming, 'Forty Years of Obstetric Ultrasound 1957–97', *Ultrasound in Medicine and Biology*, vol. 25 no. 1 (1999), 3–56.

Medical Protection Society, *The Abortion Act 1967: Proceedings of a Symposium Held by the Medical Protection Society, in Collaboration with the RCGP at the RCOG* (London: Pitman, 1969).

Millar, Erica, *Happy Abortions: Our Bodies in the Era of Choice* (London: Zed Books, 2017).

Ministry of Truth, 'The Anti-Abortion Lobby's Sham Parliamentary Inquiry' (2013), www.ministryoftruth.me.uk/2013/03/06/the-anti-abortion-lobbys-sham-parliamen tary-inquiry/

Mohler, Albert, 'Carnage in the Womb: An Abortion Scandal Rocks Britain' (2004), https://albertmohler.com/2004/10/18/carnage-in-the-womb-an-abortion-scandal-rocks-britain/

Montgomery, Jonathan, 'Conscientious Objection: Personal and Professional Ethics in the Public Square', *Medical Law Review*, vol. 23 no. 2 (2015), 200–20.

Montgomery, Jonathan, 'Doctors' Handmaidens: The Legal Contribution' in Shaun McVeigh and Sally Wheeler (eds), *Law, Health and Medical Regulation* (Aldershot: Dartmouth, 1992).

Montgomery, Jonathan, 'Law and the Demoralisation of Medicine', *Legal Studies*, vol. 26 no. 2 (2006), 185–210.

Moon, David S., Jennifer Thompson, and Sophie Whiting, 'Lost in the Process? The Impact of Devolution on Abortion Law in the United Kingdom', *British Journal of Politics and International Relations*, vol. 21 no. 4 (2019), 728–45.

Moorehead, J., 'Boycott Call for Abortion Pill Firm's Products' in National Abortion Campaign (ed.), *RU486: A Collection of Articles and Press Cuttings on the 'Abortion Pill'* (London: National Abortion Campaign, n.d.).

Morgan, Lynn M., 'Properly Disposed of: A History of Embryo Disposal and the Changing Claims on Fetal Remains', *Medical Anthropology*, vol. 21 no. 3–4 (2002), 247–74.

Morris, Anne E. and M. A. Jones, *Blackstone's Statutes on Medical Law* (Oxford: Oxford University Press, 10th edition, 2019).

Morrow, James, 'A Constitutional Right to Rescue Unborn Children' (1994), www.humanae-vitae.org/leaflets/constitutional.html

MSI Reproductive Choices, 'Our History' (2020), www.msichoices.org/about-us/our-history/

Mukherjee, Siddhartha, *The Emperor of All Maladies: A Biography of Cancer* (London: Fourth Estate, 2011).

Mulcahy, Linda and David Sugarman, 'Introduction: Legal Life Writing and Marginalized Subjects and Sources', *Journal of Law and Society*, vol. 42 no. 1 (2015), 1–6.

Mulkay, Michael, *The Embryo Research Debate: Science and the Politics of Reproduction* (Cambridge: Cambridge University Press, 1997).

Munday, Diane, 'The Development of Abortion Services since 1968' in Birth Control Trust and Pregnancy Advisory Service (eds), *Abortion Services in England and Wales* (London: Birth Control Trust, 1994), 7–16.

Munday, Diane, untitled presentation at Abortion Act 1967 Conference: A Promise Fulfilled? Royal College of Obstetricians and Gynaecologists, London, 24–25 October 2017.

NAC (ed.), *A Celebration of 25 Years of Safe, Legal Abortion 1967–1992* (London: NAC, 1992).

National Archives, '1967 Sexual Offences Act: 50 Years On' (2017), https://blog.nationalarchives.gov.uk/blog/1967-sexual-offences-act-50-years-lgbt-history/

National Centre for Social Research, *British Social Attitudes*, no. 34 (2017), www.bsa.natcen.ac.uk/latest-report/british-social-attitudes-34/key-findings/context.aspx

Nelken, David, *The Limits of the Legal Process: A Study of Landlords, Law and Crime* (London: Academic Press, 1983).

Neustatter, Andrew and Gina Newson, *Mixed Feelings: The Experience of Abortion* (London: Pluto, 1986).

Neustatter, P. L., 'Participation of Nurses in Abortions', *Lancet*, vol. 316 no. 8205 (1980) 1199–200.

NIALRA, *Abortion in Northern Ireland: The Report of an International Tribunal* (Belfast: Beyond the Pale Publications, 1989).

NICE and RCOG, 'Abortion Care. NICE Guideline [NG140]' (2019) www.nice.org.uk/guidance/ng140

NIHRC, '2021 Fact Sheet: Human Rights Commission Legal Action on Lack of Abortion Services in NI' (2021), www.nihrc.org/uploads/publications/11.01.21_Fact_Sheet_Human_Rights_Commission_Legal_Action_on_Lack_of_Abortion_Services_in_NI_.pdf

Northern Ireland Office, *A New Legal Framework for Abortion Services in Northern Ireland* (London: Northern Ireland Office, 2019).

Nuffield Council on Bioethics, 'Non-Invasive Prenatal Testing: Ethical Issues' (2017), www.nuffieldbioethics.org/wp-content/uploads/NIPT-ethical-issues-full-report.pdf

Ofcom, 'Ofcom Broadcast and on Demand Bulletin', no. 330 (2017), www.ofcom.org.uk/__data/assets/pdf_file/0021/102567/issue-330-broadcast-on-demand-bulletin.pdf

Office for National Statistics, 'Birth Characteristics in England and Wales: 2019' (2020), www.ons.gov.uk/peoplepopulationandcommunity/birthsdeathsandmarriages/livebirths/bulletins/birthcharacteristicsinenglandandwales/2019

Office for National Statistics, 'Childbearing for Women Born in Different Years, England and Wales: 2019' (2020), www.ons.gov.uk/peoplepopulationandcommunity/birthsdeathsandmarriages/conceptionandfertilityrates/bulletins/childbearingforwomenbornindifferentyearsenglandandwales/2019

Office for National Statistics, 'Marriages in England and Wales: 2017' (2020), www.ons.gov.uk/peoplepopulationandcommunity/birthsdeathsandmarriages/marriagecohabitationandcivilpartnerships/bulletins/marriagesinenglandandwalesprovisional/2017

Olszynko-Gryn, Jesse, 'The Feminist Appropriation of Pregnancy Testing in 1970s Britain', *Women's History Review*, vol. 28 no. 6 (2019), 869–94.

O'Neill, Jane, '"Abortion Games": The Negotiation of Termination Decisions in Post-1967 Britain', *History*, vol. 104 no. 359 (2019), 169–88.

O'Neill, P. T. and Isobel Watson, 'The Father and the Unborn Child', *Modern Law Review*, vol. 38 no. 2 (1975), 174–85.

Ormrod, Roger, 'A Lawyer Looks at Medical Ethics', *Medico-Legal Journal*, vol. 46 no. 1 (1978), 18–32.

O'Rourke, Catherine, 'Advocating Abortion Rights in Northern Ireland: Local and Global Tensions', *Social and Legal Studies*, vol. 25 no. 6 (2016), 716–40.

O'Rourke, Catherine, 'Bridging the Enforcement Gap? Evaluating the Inquiry Procedure of the CEDAW Optional Protocol', *American University Journal of Gender, Social Policy & the Law*, vol. 27 no. 1 (2019), 1–30.

Orr, Judith, *Abortion Wars: The Fight for Reproductive Rights* (Bristol: Policy Press, 2017).

Owen, David, *Personally Speaking to Kenneth Harris* (London: Weidenfeld & Nicolson, 1987).

Owen, David, *Time to Declare* (London: Michael Joseph, 1991).

Paintin, David, *Abortion Law Reform in Britain 1964–2003: A Personal Account* (Stratford-upon-Avon: BPAS, 2015).

Parliamentary Commissioner for Standards, 'Guide to the Rules on All-Party Parliamentary Groups' (2015), www.parliament.uk/documents/pcfs/all-party-groups/guide-to-the-rules-on-appgs.pdf

Parliamentary Commissioner for Standards, 'Rectification' (2016), www.parliament.uk/globalassets/documents/pcfs/rectifications/ms-fiona-bruce-rectification.pdf

Pattie, Charles, Ron Johnston, and Mark Stuart, 'Voting without Party?' in Philip Cowley (ed.), *Conscience and Parliament* (London: Frank Cass 1998), pp. 146–76.

Pearl, David and Andrew Grubb, 'Protecting the Life of the Unborn Child', *Law Quarterly Review*, vol. 103 (1987), 340–46.

Peel, Sir John, *Unplanned Pregnancy: Report of a Working Party of the RCOG* (London: Royal College of Obstetricians and Gynaecologists, 1972).

Pereira Gray, Sir Denis, 'The Lane Committee', presentation at Abortion Act 1967 Conference: A Promise Fulfilled? Royal College of Obstetricians and Gynaecologists, London, 24–25 October 2017.

Petchesky, Rosalind Pollack, 'Fetal Images: The Power of Visual Culture in the Politics of Reproduction', *Feminist Studies*, vol. 13 no. 2 (1987), 263–92.

Pierson, Claire and Fiona Bloomer, 'Anti-Abortion Myths in Political Discourse' in Colleen MacQuarrie, Fiona Bloomer, Claire Pierson, and Shannon Stettner (eds), *Crossing Troubled Waters: Abortion in Ireland, Northern Ireland, and Prince Edward Island* (Prince Edward Island: Island Studies Press, 2018), pp. 184–203.

Pipes, Mary, *Understanding Abortion* (London: The Women's Press, 1986).

Polkinghorne, John (Chair), *Review of the Guidance on the Research Use of Fetuses and Fetal Material (Polkinghorne Report)*, CM 762 (London: Her Majesty's Stationery Office, 1989).

Pollitt, Katha, *Pro: Reclaiming Abortion Rights* (New York: Picador, 2015).

Pope Paul VI, 'Humane Vitae' (1968), www.vatican.va/content/paul-vi/en/encyclicals/documents/hf_p-vi_enc_25071968_humanae-vitae.html

Potts, Malcolm, Peter Diggory, and John Peel, *Abortion* (Cambridge: Cambridge University Press, 1977).

Priaulx, Nicky, 'Pro-Life Inquiries: When Is a Parliamentary Inquiry Really a Parliamentary Inquiry?' (2016), https://lawyersforchoice.wordpress.com/page/2/

Priest, R. G., 'The Impact of the Abortion Act: A Psychiatrist's Observations', *British Journal of Psychiatry*, vol. 121 no. 562 (1972), 293–99.

Prior, James, *A Balance of Power* (London: Hamish Hamilton, 1986).

Proctor, Robert N. and Londa L. Schiebinger (eds), *Agnotology: The Making and Unmaking of Ignorance* (Stanford, CA: Stanford University Press, 2008).

Purcell, Carrie, Sharon Cameron, Lucy Caird, Gillian Flett, George Laird, Catriona Melville, and Lisa M. McDaid, 'Access to and Experience of Later Abortion: Accounts from Women in Scotland', *Perspectives on Sexual and Reproductive Health*, vol. 46 no. 2 (2014), 101–08.

Rawlinson, Peter, *Human Sentience Before Birth: Rawlinson Report* (London: CARE, 1996).

Rawlinson, Peter, *The Physical and Psycho-Social Effects of Abortion on Women: A Report by the Commission on Inquiry into the Operation and Consequences of the Abortion Act* (London: CARE, 1994).

RCGP, 'RCGP to Support Decriminalisation of Abortion' (2019), www.rcgp.org.uk/about-us/news/2019/february/rcgp-to-support-decriminalisation-of-abortion.aspx

RCN, 'Decriminalisation of Termination of Pregnancy: A Position Statement' (2018), www.rcn.org.uk/professional-development/publications/pub-007401

RCN, *Response of the Royal College of Nursing to a DHSSPS Consultation on the Limited Circumstances for a Lawful Termination of Pregnancy in Northern Ireland* (Belfast: Royal College of Nursing, 2013).

RCOG, 'Coronavirus (Covid-19) Infection and Abortion Care: Information for Healthcare Professionals' (2020), www.rcog.org.uk/globalassets/documents/guidelines/2020-03-21-abortion-guidance.pdf

RCOG, 'Fetal Awareness: Review of Research and Recommendations for Practice – Report of a Working Party' (2010), www.rcog.org.uk/globalassets/documents/guidelines/rcogfetalawarenesswpr0610.pdf

RCOG, 'New Study Finds Telemedicine for Abortion Care is Safe and More Accessible' (2021), www.rcog.org.uk/en/news/telemedicine-cohort-study-released/

RCOG, 'RCOG Backs Decriminalisation of Abortion' (2017), www.rcog.org.uk/en/news/rcog-backs-decriminalisation-of-abortion/

RCOG, *Report on the Advantages and Disadvantages of Imposing an 18 Week Gestational Limit on Legal Abortion* (London: Royal College of Obstetricians and Gynaecologists, 1987).

RCOG, *The Care of Women Requesting Induced Abortion (Evidence-Based Clinical Guideline No. 7)* (London: Royal College of Obstetricians and Gynaecologists, 2011).

Read, Melvyn D., 'The Pro-Life Movement', *Parliamentary Affairs*, vol. 51 no. 3 (1998), 445–57.

Reagan, Leslie, *Dangerous Pregnancies: Mothers, Disabilities and Abortion in Modern America* (Berkeley: University of California Press, 2010).

Regan, Lesley, 'Abortion: View from Westminster', *International Journal of Gynecology & Obstetrics*, vol. 143 no. 2 (2018), 133-36.

Richards, Clare, *A World without Down Syndrome?* (BBC2, 2016), www.bbc.co.uk/programmes/b07ycbj5

Right to Life, 'Emergency' (n.d.), https://righttolife.org.uk/emergency/ [no longer available].

Right to Life, 'Medical Professionals Open Letter Regarding "Home" Abortion Schemes' (2021), https://righttolife.org.uk/medicalletter

Roantree, Barra and Kartik Vira, 'The Rise and Rise of Women's Employment in the UK', Institute for Fiscal Studies Briefing Note BN234 (2018), https://ifs.org.uk/uploads/BN234.pdf

Roberts, Dorothy, *Killing the Black Body: Race, Reproduction and the Meaning of Liberty* (New York: Vintage Books, 1999).

Roberts, Julie, *The Visualised Foetus: A Cultural and Political Analysis of Ultrasound Imagery* (Oxford: Routledge, 2016).

Rossiter, Ann, *Ireland's Hidden Diaspora: The "Abortion Trail" and the Making of a London–Irish Underground 1980–2000* (London: IASC Publishing, 2009).

Rough, Elizabeth, 'Abortion in Northern Ireland: Recent Changes to the Legal Framework', House of Commons Library Research Briefing (2021), https://commonslibrary.parliament.uk/research-briefings/cbp-8909/

Rowlands, Sam, 'Day-Care Abortion in the NHS: A Survey of 12 Centres', *British Journal of Family Planning*, vol. 5 (1979), 1–4.

Royal Society of Public Health, 'Top 20 Public Health Achievements of the 21st Century' (2019), www.rsph.org.uk/about-us/news/top-20-public-health-achievements-of-the-21st-century.html

Rozenberg, Joshua, *The Case for the Crown: The Inside Story of the Director of Public Prosecutions* (Wellingborough: Equation, 1987).

Sackar, Justice John, *Lord Devlin* (Oxford: Hart, 2020).

Sanger, Carol, *About Abortion: Terminating Pregnancy in Twenty-First Century America* (Cambridge, MA: Belknap Press, 2017).

Savage, Wendy, 'Nurses and the Medical Termination of Pregnancy', *British Medical Journal*, vol. 281 no. 6253 (1980), 1491.

Savell, Kristin L., 'Life and Death before Birth: 4D Ultrasound and the Shifting Frontiers of the Abortion Debate', *Journal of Law and Medicine*, vol. 15 no. 1 (2007), 103–16.

Scarisbrick, J. J., *Let There Be Life* (Leamington Spa: Life, 2007).

Science Media Centre, 'Reaction to Evan Harris Losing His Parliamentary Seat' (2010), www.sciencemediacentre.org/reaction-to-evan-harris-losing-his-parliamentary-seat-2/

Sclare, A. B. and B. P. Geraghty, 'Termination of Pregnancy: The Nurse's Attitude', *Nursing Mirror*, vol. 140 no. 3 (1975), 59–60.

Scottish Trades Union Congress, *Annual Report 1980* (Perth, TUC: 1980).

Sedgh, Gilda, Susheela Singh, Iqbal H. Shah, Elizabeth Åhman, Stanley K. Henshaw, and Akinrinola Bankole, 'Induced Abortions: Incidence and Trends Worldwide from 1995 to 2008', *Lancet*, vol. 379 no. 9816 (2012), 625–32.

Sethna, Christabelle, 'From Heathrow Airport to Harley Street: The ALRA and the Travel of Nonresident Women for Abortion Services in Britain' in Christabelle Sethna and Gayle Davis (eds), *Abortion across Borders: Transnational Travel and Access to Abortion Services* (Baltimore, MD: Johns Hopkins University Press, 2019), pp. 46–71.

Shakespeare, Tom, *Disability Rights and Wrongs Revisited* (New York: Routledge, 2013).

Sheldon, Sally, 'A Missed Opportunity to Reform an Outdated Piece of Legislation', *Clinical Ethics*, vol. 4 no. 1 (2009), 3–5.

Sheldon, Sally, *Beyond Control: Medical Power and Abortion Law* (London: Pluto, 1997).

Sheldon, Sally, 'British Abortion Law: Speaking from the Past to Govern the Future', *Modern Law Review*, vol. 79 no. 2 (2016), 283–316.

Sheldon, Sally, 'Empowerment and Privacy? Home Use of Abortion Pills in the Republic of Ireland', *Signs*, vol. 43 no. 4 (2018), 823–49.

Sheldon, Sally, 'Multiple Pregnancy and Re(pro)ductive Choice', *Feminist Legal Studies*, vol. 5 (1997), 99–106.

Sheldon, Sally, 'The Decriminalisation of Abortion: An Argument for Modernisation', *Oxford Journal of Legal Studies*, vol. 36 no. 2 (2016), 334–65.

Sheldon, Sally, 'The Regulatory Cliff Edge between Contraception and Abortion: The Legal and Moral Significance of Implantation', *Journal of Medical Ethics*, vol. 41 no. 9 (2015), 762–65.

Sheldon, Sally, '"Who Is the Mother to Make the Judgment?": Constructions of Woman in UK Abortion Law', *Feminist Legal Studies*, vol. 1 no. 1 (1993), 3–22.

Sheldon, Sally, Gayle Davis, Jane O'Neill, and Clare Parker, 'Sources' (2021), https://research.kent.ac.uk/abortion-act/sources/

Sheldon, Sally and Joanne Fletcher, 'Vacuum Aspiration for Induced Abortion Could be Safely and Legally Performed by Nurses and Midwives', *Journal of Family Planning and Reproductive Health Care*, vol. 43 (2017), 260–64.

Sheldon, Sally, Jane O'Neill, Clare Parker, and Gayle Davis, '"Too Much, Too Indigestible, Too Fast"? The Decades of Struggle for Abortion Law Reform in Northern Ireland', *Modern Law Review*, vol. 83 no. 4 (2020), 761–96.

Sheldon, Sally and Kaye Wellings, *Decriminalising Abortion in the UK* (Bristol: Policy Press, 2020).

Sheldon, Sally and Kaye Wellings, 'Introduction' in Decriminalising Abortion in the UK (Bristol: Policy Press, 2020), pp. 1–16.

Siegel, Reva B., 'Dignity and the Politics of Protection: Abortion Restrictions under *Casey/Carhart*', *Yale Law Journal*, vol. 117 no. 8 (2008), 1694–800.

Siegel, Reva B., 'The Right's Reasons: Constitutional Conflict and the Spread of Women-Protective Anti-abortion Argument', *Duke Law Journal*, vol. 57 no. 6 (2008), 1641–92.

Silvestre, Louise, 'The French Experiences' in Cerys Williams (ed.), *The Abortion Pill (Mifepristone/RU486): Widening the Choice for Women*, Proceedings of a conference organised by the Birth Control Trust on 26 October 1989 at the Royal College of Obstetricians and Gynaecologists (London: Birth Control Trust, 1990), pp. 16–17.

Sim, Myre, 'Abortion and the Psychiatrist', *British Medical Journal*, vol. 2 no. 5350 (1963), 145–48.

Simms, Madeleine, 'Britain' in Bill Rolston and Anna Eggert (eds), *Abortion in the New Europe: A Comparative Handbook* (Westport, CT: Greenwood Press, 1990), pp. 31–42.

Simms, Madeleine, 'Day-Care Abortion', *Lancet*, vol. 315 no. 8180 (1980), 1253.

Simms, Madeleine, 'Legal Abortion in Great Britain' in Hilary Homans (ed.), *The Sexual Politics of Reproduction* (Aldershot: Gower, 1985), pp. 78–95.

Simms, Madeleine, 'The Great Foetus Mystery', *New Scientist* (1970), 592.

Simpson, A., 'The Victorian Law of Northern Ireland', *Planned Parenthood in Europe*, vol. 22 no. 3 (1993), 7.

Sisson, Gretchen and Katrina Kimport, 'Telling Stories about Abortion: Abortion-Related Plots in American Film and Television, 1916–2013', *Contraception*, vol. 89 no. 5 (2014), 413–18.

Smart, Carol and Bren Neale, *Family Fragments?* (Cambridge: Polity Press, 1999).

Smith Commission, *Report of the Smith Commission for Further Devolution of Powers to the Scottish Parliament* (Edinburgh: Smith Commission, 2014).

Smith, J. C., 'Abortion', *Criminal Law Review*, vol. 1981 (1981), 322–23.

Smyth, Lisa, 'The Cultural Politics of Sexuality and Reproduction in Northern Ireland', *Sociology*, vol. 40 no. 4 (2006), 663–80.

Solinger, Rickie, *Pregnancy and Power: A Short History of Reproductive Politics in America* (New York: New York University Press, 2005).

Sood, Satya V., 'Some Operative and Postoperative Hazards of Legal Termination of Pregnancy', *British Medical Journal*, vol. 4 no. 5782 (1971), 270–73.

Soper, J. Christopher, *Evangelical Christianity in the United States and Britain: Religious Beliefs, Political Choices* (London: Macmillan, 1994).

Southall Black Sisters, 'SBS Urges a No Vote to the Amendment on Sex Selective Abortion on the Serious Crime Bill' (2015, republished 2019), https://southallblacksisters.org.uk/news/sbs-urges-a-no-vote-to-the-amendment-on-sex-selective-abortion-on-the-serious-crime-bill/

Speaking of Imelda, 'Why Imelda?' (2018), www.speakingofimelda.org/why-imelda

Spivak, G. C., 'Can the Subaltern Speak?' in Cary Nelson and Lawrence Grossberg (eds), *Marxism and the Interpretation of Culture* (Chicago: University of Illinois Press, 1988), pp. 271–314.

SPUC, 'At-Home Abortions: The Case against a Permanent Policy' (2021), www.spuc.org.uk/Portals/0/ThemePluginPro/uploads/2021/3/23/SPUC%20%E2%80%93%20At-home%20abortions%20%E2%80%93%20the%20case%20against%20a%20permanent%20policy_12pp_A4_3_web.pdf

SPUC, 'Campaigns' (2021), www.spuc.org.uk/Get-Involved/Campaigns

SPUC, 'Fundraise' (2018), www.spuc.org.uk/ArticleHandler/articleType/ArticleView/articleId/383469/Fundraise

SPUC, 'Pro-abortion House of Commons Speaker Stands Down Leaving "Untold Damage to Unborn Babies and their Mothers"' (2019), www.spuc.org.uk/News/News-Articles/ArticleType/ArticleView/ArticleID/384203

SPUC, 'SPUC Seeks Legal Recourse as Government Extends DIY at Home Abortion due to Coronavirus Crisis' (2020), www.spuc.org.uk/News/ID/384353/SPUC-seeks-legal-recourse-as-government-extends-DIY-at-home-abortion-due-to-Coronavirus-crisis

Staham, H., W. Solomou, and J. Green, 'Late Termination of Pregnancy: Law, Policy and Decision Making in Four English Fetal Medicine Units', *BJOG: An International Journal of Obstetrics and Gynaecology*, vol. 113 no. 12 (2006), 1402–11.

Steel, David, *Against Goliath: David Steel's Story* (London: Pan Books, 1991).

St John-Stevas, Norman, 'Little Enlightenment from Lane', *The Tablet*, vol. 228 (1974), 362.

St John-Stevas, Norman, *The Agonising Choice* (London: Eyre & Spottiswoode, 1971).

St John-Stevas, Norman, *The Right to Life* (London: Hodder, 1963).

St John-Stevas, Norman, *The Two Cities* (London: Faber & Faber, 1984).

Stith, Richard, 'Facing the Unborn', *First Things* (2015), www.firstthings.com/article/2015/08/facing-the-unborn

Sugarman, David, 'From Legal Biography to Legal Life Writing: Broadening Conceptions of Legal History and Socio-legal Scholarship', *Journal of Law and Society*, vol. 42 no. 1 (2015), 7–33.

Swales, Kirby and Eleanor Attar Taylor, 'Moral Issues: Sex, Gender Identity and Euthanasia' in National Centre for Social Research, *British Social Attitudes*, no. 34 (2017), www.bsa.natcen.ac.uk/latest-report/british-social-attitudes-34/key-findings/context.aspx

Symonds, Melanie, *And Still They Weep: Personal Stories of Abortion* (London: Society for the Protection of Unborn Children, 1996).

Tansey, E. M. and D. A. Christie (eds), *Looking at the Unborn: Historical Aspects of Obstetric Ultrasound*, Wellcome Witnesses to Twentieth Century Medicine Seminar Transcript (London: Wellcome, 2000).

Tate Britain, 'Queer British Art 1861–1967' (2017), www.tate.org.uk/whats-on/tate-britain/exhibition/queer-british-art-1861-1967

Taylor, Robert Brett and Adelyn Wilson, 'UK Abortion Law: Reform Proposals, Private Members' Bills, Devolution and the Role of the Courts', *Modern Law Review*, vol. 82 no. 1 (2019), 71–128.

Temkin, Jennifer, 'The Lane Committee Report on the Abortion Act', *Modern Law Review*, vol. 37 no. 6 (1974), 657–63.

'The Royal College of Psychiatrists' Memorandum on the Abortion Act in Practice', *British Journal of Psychiatry*, vol. 120 no. 557 (1972), 449–51.

Third Sector, 'Opinion: Hot Issue – Should the Government Withdraw the Annual £12m Funding to BPAS?' (2004), www.thirdsector.co.uk/opinion-hot-issue-government-withdraw-annual-12m-funding-bpas/article/614146

Thomas, Gareth M., *Down's Syndrome Screening and Reproductive Politics: Care, Choice, and Disability in the Prenatal Clinic* (London: Routledge, 2017).

Thomlinson, Natalie, *Race, Ethnicity and the Women's Movement in England, 1968–1993* (Basingstoke: Palgrave Macmillan, 2016).

Thomson, Jennifer, 'Abortion Law and Scotland: An Issue of What?', *Political Quarterly*, vol. 89 no. 1 (2017), 100–07.

Thynne, Lizzie (dir.), 'The Feelings behind the Slogans Part 2', commissioned for Sisterhood and After: The Women's Liberation Oral History Project (2011), www.bl.uk/collection-items/the-feelings-behind-the-slogans-part-2

Todd, N. A., 'Psychiatric Experience of the Abortion Act (1967)', *British Journal of Psychiatry*, vol. 119 no. 552 (1971), 489–95.

Trades Union Congress, *Annual Report 1975* (Blackpool, TUC: 1975).

Tunkel, Victor, 'Abortion: How Early, How Late, and How Legal?', *British Medical Journal*, vol. 2 no. 6184 (1979), 253–56.

Tunkel, Victor, 'Modern Anti-Pregnancy Techniques and the Criminal Law', *Criminal Law Review*, vol. 1974 (1974), 461–71.

Tunnadine, David and Roger Green, *Unwanted Pregnancy – Accident or Illness?* (Oxford: Oxford University Press, 1978).

Uberoi, Elise and Rebecca Lees, 'Ethnic Diversity in Politics and Public Life', House of Commons Library Research Briefing (2020), https://commonslibrary.parliament.uk/research-briefings/sn01156/

Underwood, Betty, 'The Lane Abortion Report – A Feminist View', *Spare Rib*, no. 24 (1974), 22.

Unnithan, Maya and Sylvie Dubuc, 'Re-visioning Evidence: Reflections on the Recent Controversy around Gender Selective Abortion in the UK', *Global Public Health*, vol. 13 no. 6 (2018), 742–53.

US Senate, Subcommittee on the Constitution, Committee on the Judiciary, 'The Medical Evidence Concerning Fetal Pain', First Session, 21 May 1985 (S. Hrg. 99-429, Serial No. J-99-28) http://njlaw.rutgers.edu/collections/gdoc/hearings/8/86601288/86601288_1.pdf

Vallance, Elizabeth, *Women in the House: A Study of Women Members of Parliament* (London: Athlone Press, 1979).

Voas, David and Alasdair Crockett, 'Religion in Britain: Neither Believing nor Belonging', *Sociology*, vol. 39 no. 1 (2005), 11–28.

Waite, Marjorie, 'Consultant Psychiatrists and Abortion', *Psychological Medicine*, vol. 4 no. 1 (1974), 76–88.

Ward, Margaret, 'The Woman's Movement in the North of Ireland' in Sean Hutton and Paul Stewart (eds), *Ireland's Histories: Aspects of State, Society and Ideology* (London: Routledge 1991), pp. 149–63.

Warden, John, 'Abortion Minefield for Doctors', *British Medical Journal*, vol. 295 no. 6605 (1987), 1076.

Wellcome Trust, 'Wellcome Trust Monitor Survey Report: Tracking Public Views on Medical Research' (2009), https://wellcome.ac.uk/sites/default/files/monitor-wave1-wellcome-sep09.pdf

Wellings, Kaye, Kyle G. Jones, Catherine H. Mercer, Clare Tanton, Soazig Clifton, Jessica Datta, Andrew J. Copas, Bob Erens, Lorna J. Gibson, Wendy Macdowall, Pam Sonnenberg, Andrew Phelps, and Anne M. Johnson, 'The Prevalence of Unplanned Pregnancy and Associated Factors in Britain: Findings from the Third National Survey of Sexual Attitudes and Lifestyles (Natsal-3)', *Lancet*, vol. 382 no. 9907 (2013), 1807–16.

Whitaker, Robin and Goretti Horgan, 'Abortion Governance in the New Northern Ireland' in Lorena Anton, Silvia De Zordo, and Joanna Mishtal (eds), *A Fragmented Landscape. Abortion Governance and Associated Protest Logics in Postwar Europe* (New York: Berghahn, 2016), pp. 245–65.

Who's Who, 'Corrie, John Alexander' (2007), www.ukwhoswho.com/search?q=john+corrie&searchBtn=Search&isQuickSearch=true

Widdecombe, Ann, *Strictly Ann: The Autobiography* (London: Pheonix, 2014).

Wilkes, Eric, 'Working of the Abortion Act', *British Medical Journal*, vol. 2 no. 5966 (1975), 337.

Williams, Clare, 'Framing the Fetus in Medical Work: Rituals and Practices', *Social Science and Medicine*, vol. 60 no. 9 (2005), 2085–95.

Williams, Glanville, *The Sanctity of Life and the Criminal Law* (London: Faber & Faber, 1958).

Williams, Glanville, *Textbook of Criminal Law* (London: Stevens, 2nd edition, 1983).

Williams, Jean Morton and Keith Hindell, *Abortion and Contraception: A Study of Patients' Attitudes* (London: Political and Economic Planning, 1972).

Williams, Robert, 'Successful Appeal by Royal College of Nursing on Medical Termination of Pregnancy', *Lancet*, vol. 316 no. 8203 (1980), 1091.

Wilson, Bryan, *Religion in Secular Life, 50 Years On* (Oxford: Oxford University Press, 2016).

Winn, Denise, *Experiences of Abortion* (London: Macdonald, 1988).

Wivel, Ashley, 'Abortion Policy and Politics on the Lane Committee of Enquiry, 1971–1974', *Social History of Medicine*, vol. 11 no. 1 (1998), 109–35.

Women in Media, *A Woman's Choice* (Belfast: Women in Media, 1980).

Women on Waves, 'Warning, Fake Abortion Pills for Sale Online!!' (2021), www.womenonwaves.org/en/page/974/warning-fake-abortion-pills-for-sale-online

Woods, Simon and Kenneth Taylor, 'Ethical and Governance Challenges in Human Fetal Tissue Research', *Clinical Ethics*, vol. 3 no. 1 (2008), 14–19.

Woolf, Virginia, 'Sketch of the Past' in Jeanne Schulkind (ed.), *Moments of Being* (London: Pimlico, 2002).

Wright, David, *Downs: The History of a Disability* (Oxford: Oxford University Press, 2011).

Wright, Gerard, 'Capable of Being Born Alive?', *New Law Journal*, vol. 131 no. 5989 (1981), 188–89.

Wright, Gerard, 'The Culture of Death: Talk Given at the Symposium of the Guild of Catholic Doctors', *Catholic Medical Quarterly* (1999), www.cmq.org.uk/CMQ/1999/culture_of_death_g_wright.htm

Wright, Gerard, 'The Legality of Abortion by Prostaglandin', *Criminal Law Review*, vol. 1984 (1984), 347–49.

NEWS MEDIA AND PERIODICALS

Argus (Brighton and Hove)
BBC News (online)
BBC Newsbeat
Belfast Telegraph
Birmingham Mail
Boston Globe
British Medical Journal
Camden New Journal
Catholic Herald
CatholicIreland.net
Christian Concern
Christian Today
Church Times
CNS News
Daily Express
Daily Express (Glasgow)
Daily Mail
Daily Mirror
epolitix.com
Evening Standard
Glasgow Daily Record
Glasgow Evening Times
Glasgow Herald
Guardian
Harpies and Quines
Huffington Post
Human Concern
Independent
Independent.ie
Independent on Sunday
Irish Legal Times
Irish News
Irish Times
Lancet
Le Monde

LifeNews.com
Liverpool Daily Post
Liverpool Echo
Mail Online
Mail on Sunday
Manchester Evening News
Medical News Tribune
National
National Review
New York Times
News of the World
Nursing Mirror
Observer
Private Eye
Prospect Magazine
Scotsman
Scottish Daily Record
Sky News (online)
South Wales Argus
Spare Rib
Spectator
Spiked
Sun
Sunday Express
Sunday Telegraph
Sunday Times
Telegraph
Time Magazine
Times
Washington Post

Index

Printed in Great Britain
by Amazon

27881009R00203